Street by Street

HERTFORDSHIRE

Enlarged areas HARLOW, HEMEL HEMPSTEAD, LUTON, ST ALBANS, STEVENAGE, WATFORD

Plus Amersham, Barnet, Bishop's Stortford, Chalfont St Peter, Chesham, Dunstable, Enfield, Hertford, Hitchin, Stansted Airport, Waltham Abbey

G000292354

3rd edition September 2008
© Automobile Association Developments Limited 2008

Original edition printed May 2001

Enabled by OS Ordnance Survey This product includes map data licensed from Ordnance Survey® with the permission of the Controller of Her Majesty's Stationery Office. © Crown copyright 2008. All rights reserved. Licence number 100021153.

The copyright in all PAF is owned by Royal Mail Group plc.

RoadPilot® DRIVING TECHNOLOGY Information on fixed speed camera locations provided by RoadPilot © 2008 RoadPilot® Driving Technology.

Published by AA Publishing (a trading name of Automobile Association Developments Limited, whose registered office is Fanum House, Basing View, Basingstoke, Hampshire RG21 4EA. Registered number 1878835).

Produced by the Mapping Services Department of The Automobile Association. (A03730)

A CIP Catalogue record for this book is available from the British Library.

Printed by Oriental Press in Dubai

Ref: MX116y

Key to map pages	ii–iii
Key to map symbols	iv–1
Map pages - 1:10,000	2–13
Map pages - 1:17,500	14–143
Map pages - 1:25,000	144–185
Index - towns & villages	186–187
Index - streets	188–219
Index - featured places	219–225
Acknowledgements	225

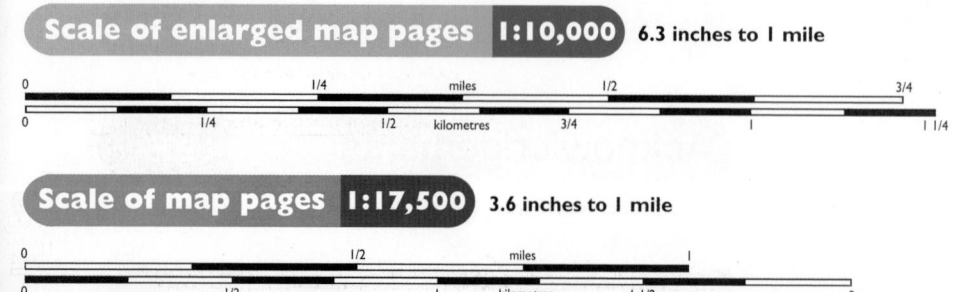

TOWCESTER NORTHAMPTON SP TL Bedford ST NEOT

Biggleswade

M1

Newport Pagnell

Cranfield

A422 A509 14 A421 A507 Shefford

Milton Keynes A421 A4012 Flitwick 146 14
Lower
Stondon
Buckingham A421 Bletchley A5 Ampthill Shillington A600

A413 A4146 154 155 156 Pirton 15
Sharpenhoe Barton-
le-Clay B655 Hitchin
Winslow B4032 Leighton
Buzzard Bramingham Lilley Great Offley

BICESTER A413 24 25 26 27 28 29 30 3
Tilsworth Houghton
Regis Limbury Stopsley Preston

A41 36 37 40 174 175
Northall Dunstable LUTON Luton
Edlesborough B4541 Slip Kimpton
38 39 End

168 169 170 171 172 173
Ivinghoe Dagnall Markyate 46 47 48
Long
Marston A4146 Flamstead Harpenden
Aston Aldbury Little Redbourn Wheathampstea
Clinton Gaddesden

Tring 58 59 60 61 62 63 64 65 66
Wigginton Potten Cupid Marshalswi
56 57 End Berkhamsted Green
Northchurch M1 ST ALBANS

OXFORD 78 79 80 81 84 86
Bellingdon Leverstock
Thame HEMEL 82 Green 83 London
HEMPSTEAD M10 85 Coln

SP 96 97 100 101 102 103 10
SU Chesham Botley Bovingdon Kings
Chinnor Chipperfield 98 99 Langley Bricket Shen
Wood

112 113 114 115 116 117 118 Radlett 120
Amersham WATFORD Borehamwoo
Chorleywood 119

128 129 133 13
Chalfont Rickmansworth Bushey
Common 130 131 132 Stanmore

138 139 140 142 143
Chalfont Northwood Wealdstone
St Peter 141 Pinner Harrow

SU TQ

Marlow MAIDENHEAD

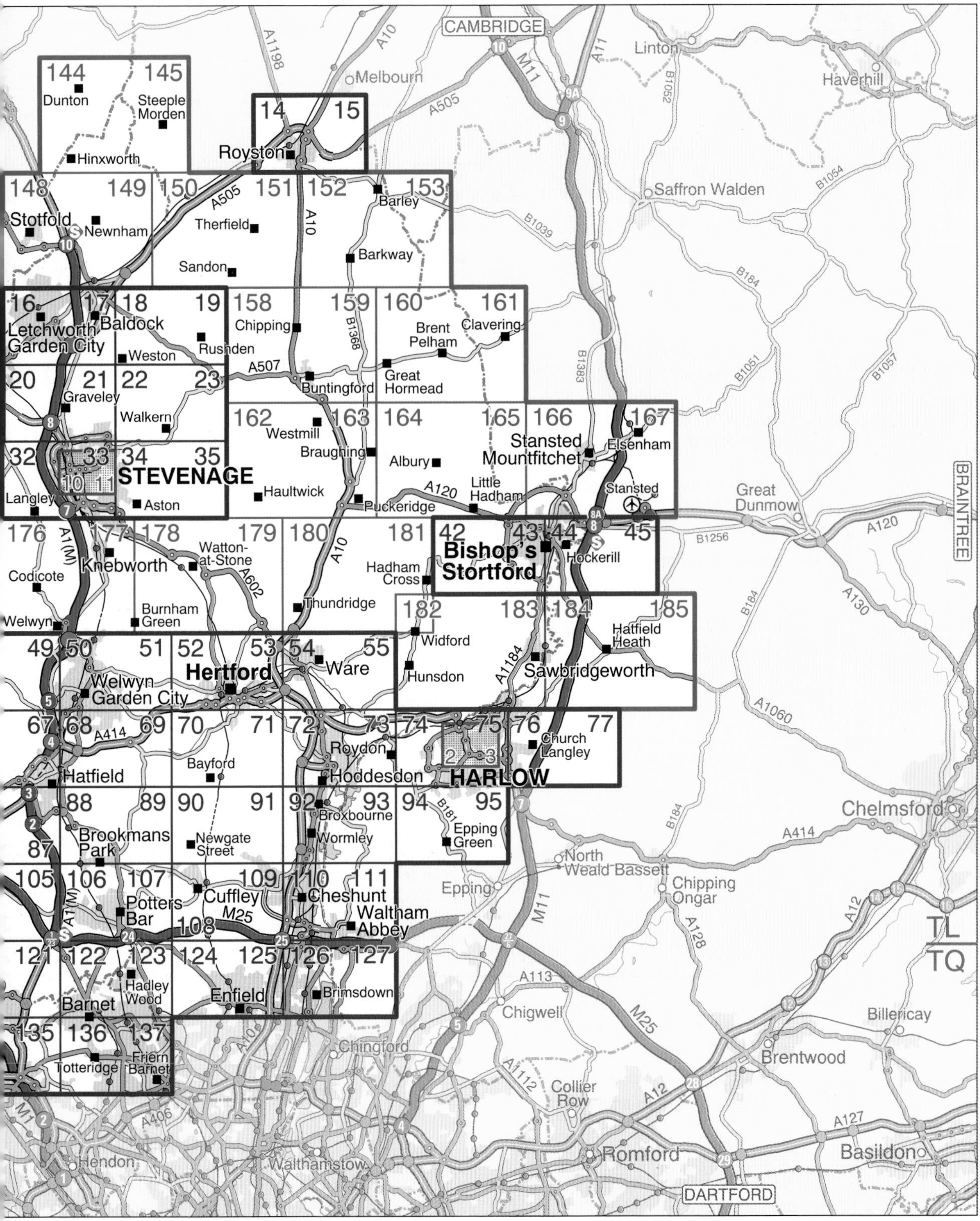

CAMBRIDGE
Linton
Haverhill
Melbourn
144
145
Dunton
Steeple Morden
Hinxworth
14
15
Royston
148
149
150
151
152
153
Stotfold
Newnham
Therfield
Barley
Sandon
Barkway
Saffron Walden
16
17
18
19
158
159
160
161
Letchworth Garden City
Baldock
Weston
Rushden
Chipping
Brent Pelham
Clavering
Buntingford
Great Hormead
20
21
22
23
Graveley
Walkern
162
163
164
165
166
167
Westmill
Braughing
Albury
Stansted Mountfitchet
Elsenham
32
33
34
35
10
11
STEVENAGE
Langley
Aston
Haultwick
Puckeridge
Little Hadham
Stansted
Great Dunmow
BRAINTREE
176
177
178
179
180
181
42
43
44
45
Codicote
Knebworth
Watton-at-Stone
Hadham Cross
Bishop's Stortford
Hockerill
Welwyn
Burnham Green
Thundridge
182
183
184
185
Widford
Hatfield Heath
Hunsdon
Sawbridgeworth
49
50
51
52
53
54
55
Welwyn Garden City
Hertford
Ware
67
68
69
70
71
72
73
74
75
76
77
Hatfield
Bayford
Roydon
Hoddesdon
2
3
HARLOW
Church Langley
88
89
90
91
92
93
94
95
87
Brookmans Park
Newgate Street
Broxbourne
Wormley
Epping Green
Chelmsford
North Weald Bassett
105
106
107
108
109
110
111
Potters Bar
Cuffley
Cheshunt
Waltham Abbey
Epping
Chipping Ongar
121
122
123
124
125
126
127
Barnet
Hadley Wood
Enfield
Brimsdown
Chigwell
Billericay
TL
TQ
135
136
137
Totteridge
Friern Barnet
Chingford
Collier Row
Brentwood
Hendon
Walthamstow
Romford
Basildon
DARTFORD
A1198
A10
A505
M11
A11
B1052
B1054
B1039
B184
B1368
B1383
B1051
B1057
A507
A120
A1(M)
A602
B1256
A130
A1184
A414
A1060
B181
M25
A128
A12
A113
A1112
A406
A127
M1

National Grid references are shown on the map frame of Each Page.
Red figures denote the 100 km square and the blue figures the 1km square.

Example, page 117 : Nascot Wood Infant School 510 198

The reference can also be written using the National Grid two-letter prefix shown on this page, where 5 and 1 are replaced by TQ to give TQ1098

2.5 inches to 1 mile **Scale of map pages 1:25,000**

0 | 1/2 | miles | 1 | 1 1/2

0 | 1/2 | 1 | kilometres | 1 1/2 | 2

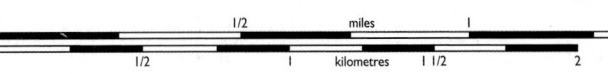

Junction 9	Motorway & junction	⊖	Underground station
Services	Motorway service area	⊖	Light railway & station
	Primary road single/dual carriageway	+++++++++++++	Preserved private railway
Services	Primary road service area	LC	Level crossing
	A road single/dual carriageway	● ● ● ●	Tramway
	B road single/dual carriageway	- - - - - - -	Ferry route
	Other road single/dual carriageway	....	Airport runway
	Minor/private road, access may be restricted	- · - · - · -	County, administrative boundary
← ←	One-way street	▼▼▼▼▼▼▼	Mounds
	Pedestrian area	151	Page continuation 1:25,000
- - - - - - -	Track or footpath	93	Page continuation 1:17,500
	Road under construction	7	Page continuation to enlarged scale 1:10,000
⌐ - - - - ⌐	Road tunnel		River/canal, lake
30	Speed camera site (fixed location) with speed limit in mph		Aqueduct, lock, weir
V	Speed camera site (fixed location) with variable speed limit	465 ▲ Winter Hill	Peak (with height in metres)
40	Section of road with two or more fixed camera sites; speed limit in mph or variable		Beach
50→ ←50	Average speed (SPECS™) camera system with speed limit in mph		Woodland
P P+🚌	Parking, Park & Ride		Park
🚌	Bus/coach station		Cemetery
	Railway & main railway station		Built-up area
	Railway & minor railway station		

Symbol	Description	Symbol	Description
	Industrial/business building		Abbey, cathedral or priory
	Leisure building		Castle
	Retail building		Historic house or building
	Other building	Wakehurst Place NT	National Trust property
	City wall		Museum or art gallery
A&E	Hospital with 24-hour A&E department		Roman antiquity
PO	Post Office		Ancient site, battlefield or monument
	Public library		Industrial interest
i	Tourist Information Centre		Garden
i	Seasonal Tourist Information Centre		Garden Centre Garden Centre Association Member
	Petrol station, 24 hour Major suppliers only		Garden Centre Wyevale Garden Centre
†	Church/chapel		Arboretum
	Public toilet, with facilities for the less able		Farm or animal centre
PH	Public house AA recommended		Zoological or wildlife collection
	Restaurant AA inspected		Bird collection
Madeira Hotel	Hotel AA inspected		Nature reserve
	Theatre or performing arts centre		Aquarium
	Cinema	V	Visitor or heritage centre
	Golf course		Country park
▲	Camping AA inspected		Cave
	Caravan site AA inspected		Windmill
	Camping & caravan site AA inspected		Distillery, brewery or vineyard
	Theme park	•	Other place of interest

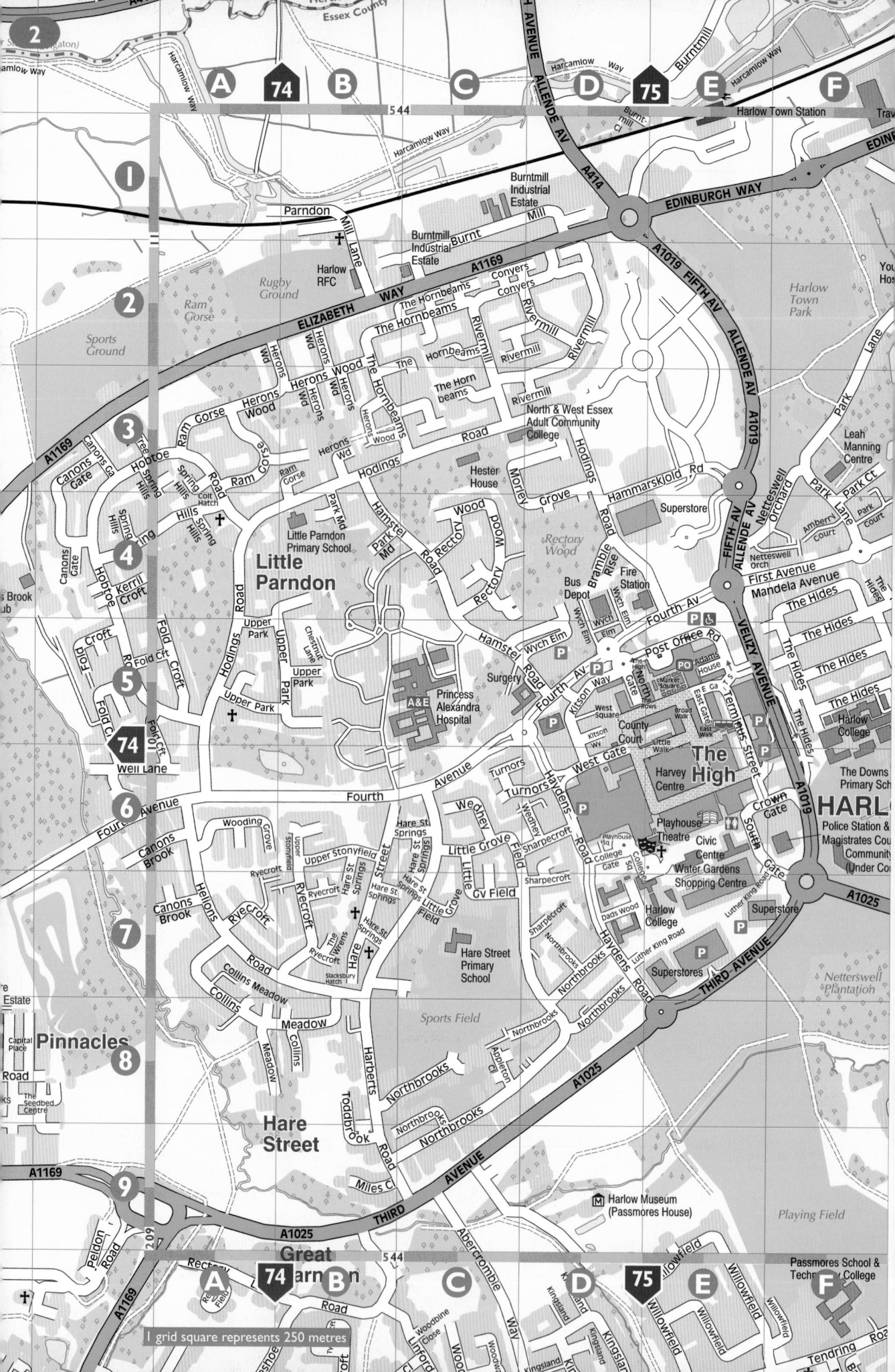

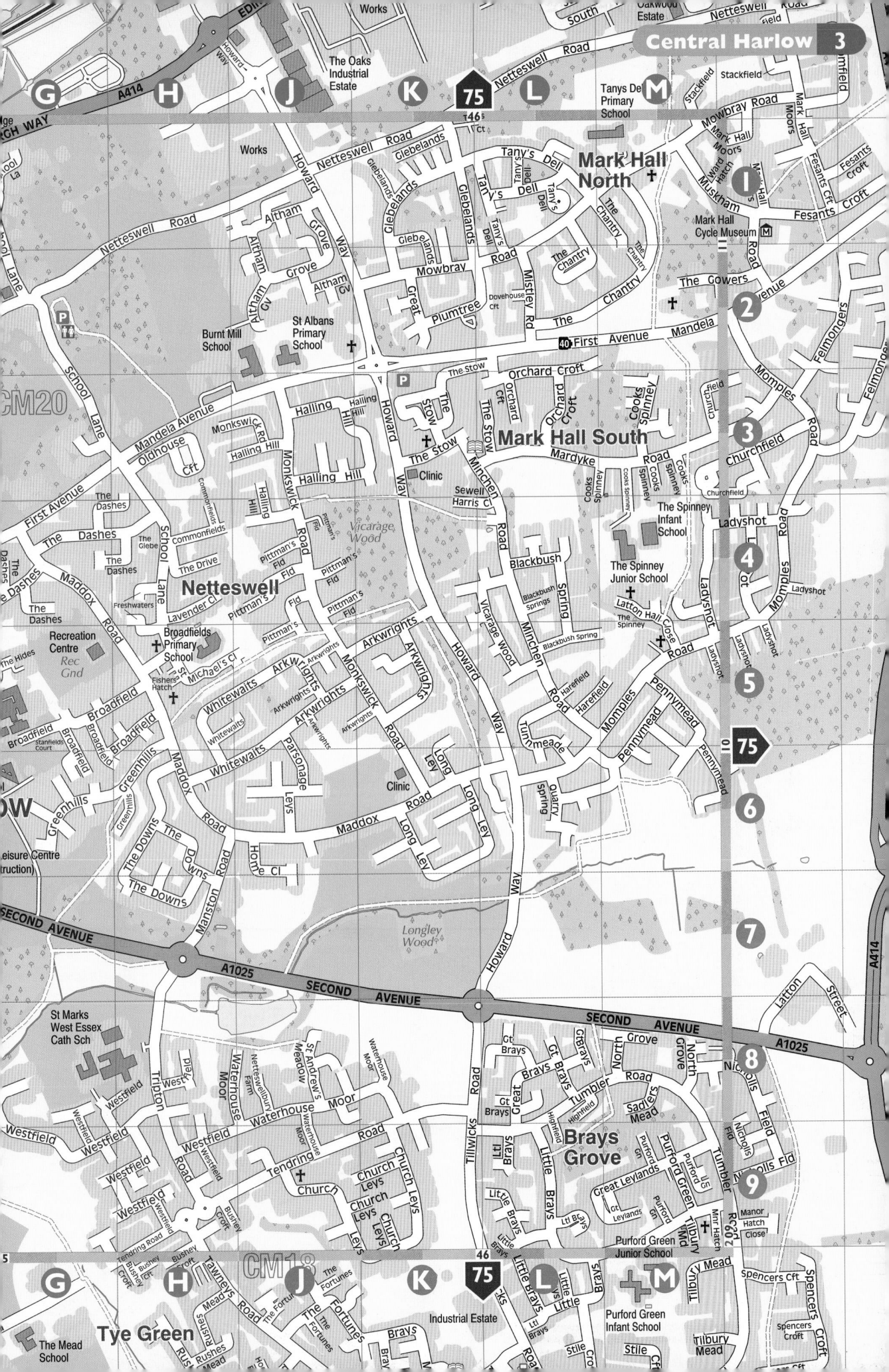

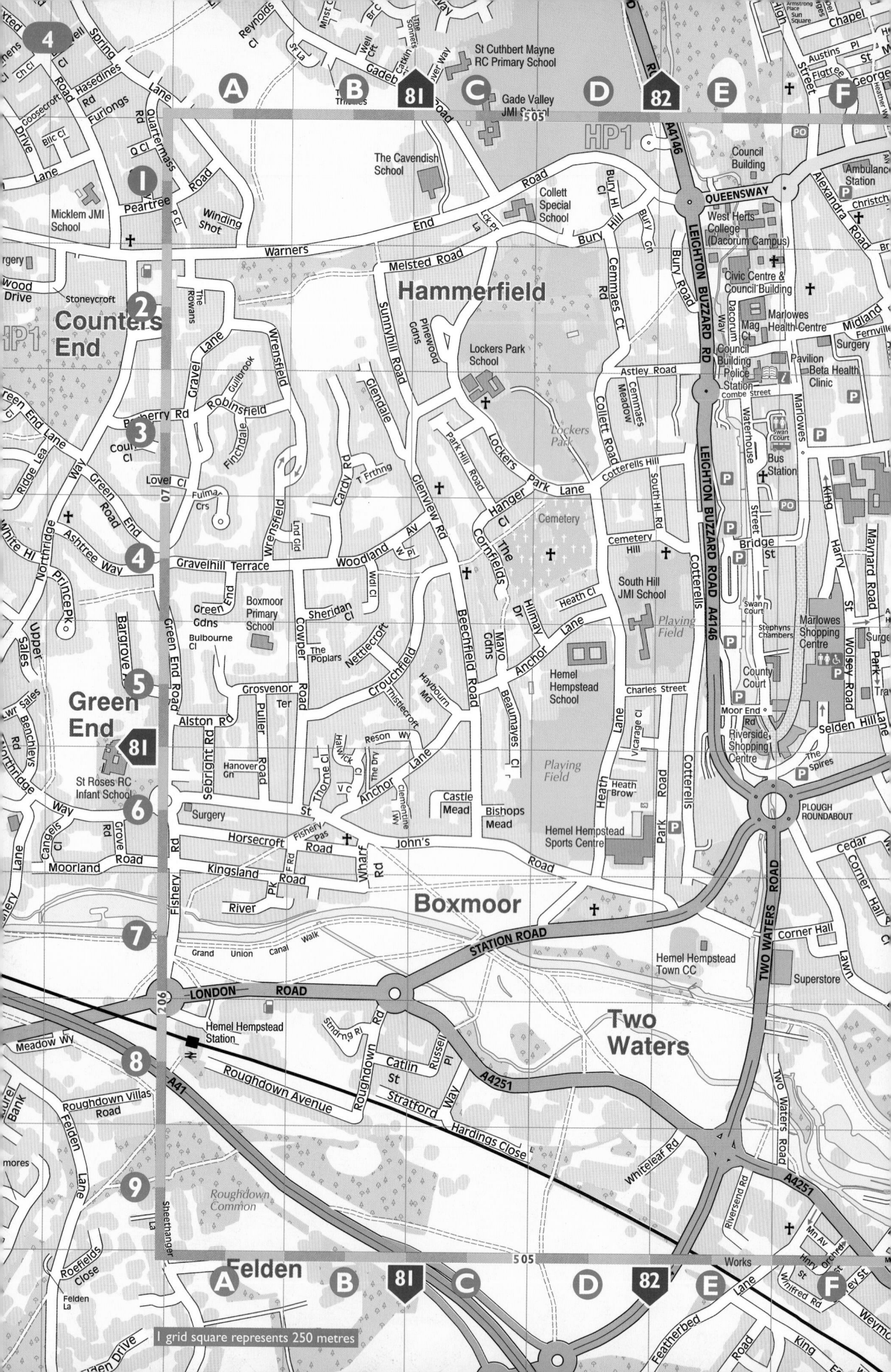

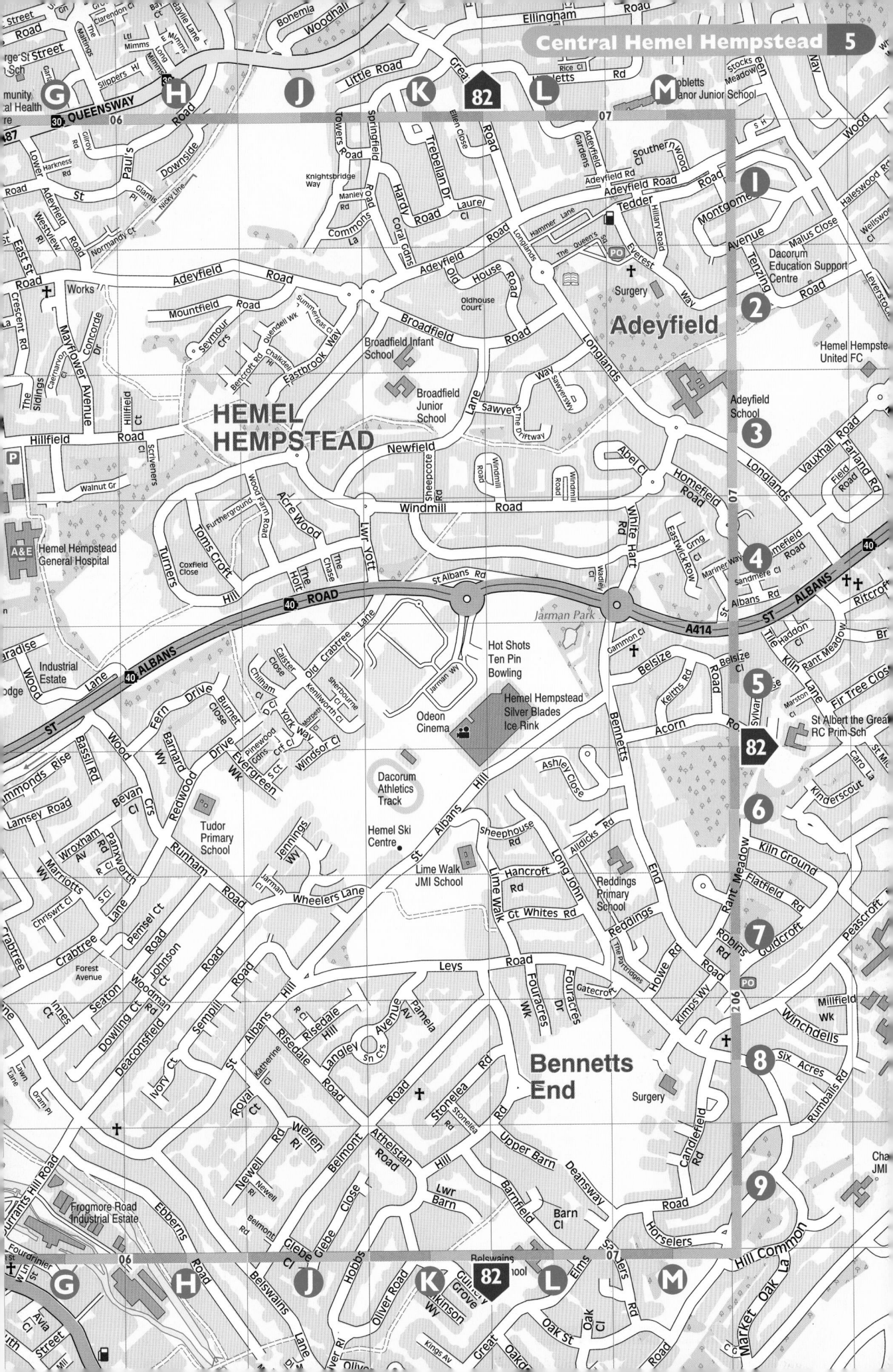

G 30 QUEENSWAY 06 H Road J K 82 L M

I

Adeyfield

2

3

4

5

82

6

7

8

9

HEMEL
HEMPSTEAD

Hemel Hempstead
General Hospital

A&E

Industrial
Estate

Broadfield Infant
School

Broadfield
Junior
School

Oldhouse
Court

The Queen's

Surgery

Dacorum
Education Support
Centre

Hemel Hempstead
United FC

Adeyfield
School

Jarman Park

Hot Shots
Ten Pin
Bowling

Odeon
Cinema

Hemel Hempstead
Silver Blades
Ice Rink

Dacorum
Athletics
Track

Hemel Ski
Centre

Lime Walk
JMI School

Tudor
Primary
School

St Albert the Great
RC Prim Sch

Reddings
Primary
School

Surgery

Bennetts
End

Frogmore Road
Industrial Estate

G H J K 82 L M

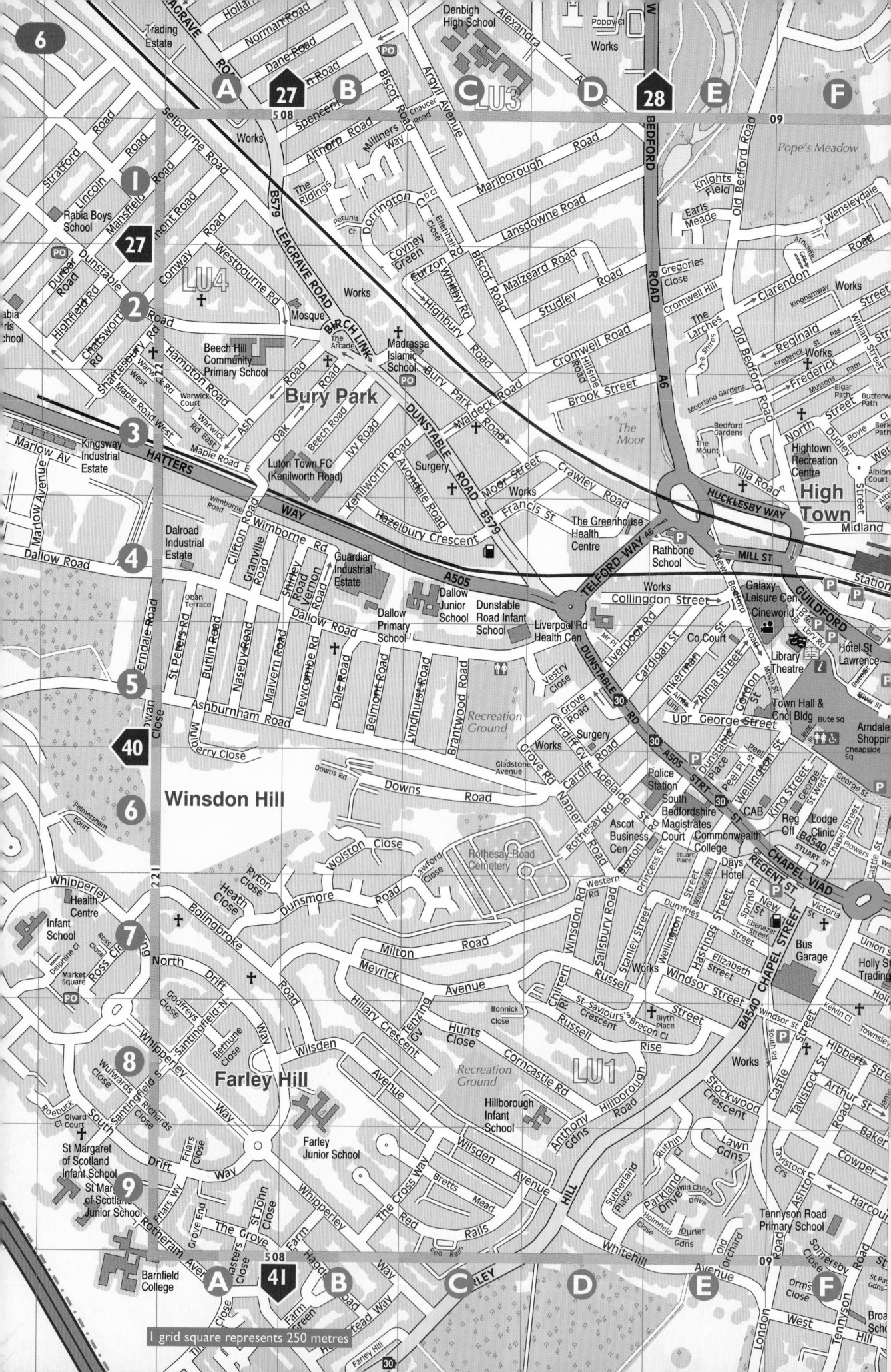

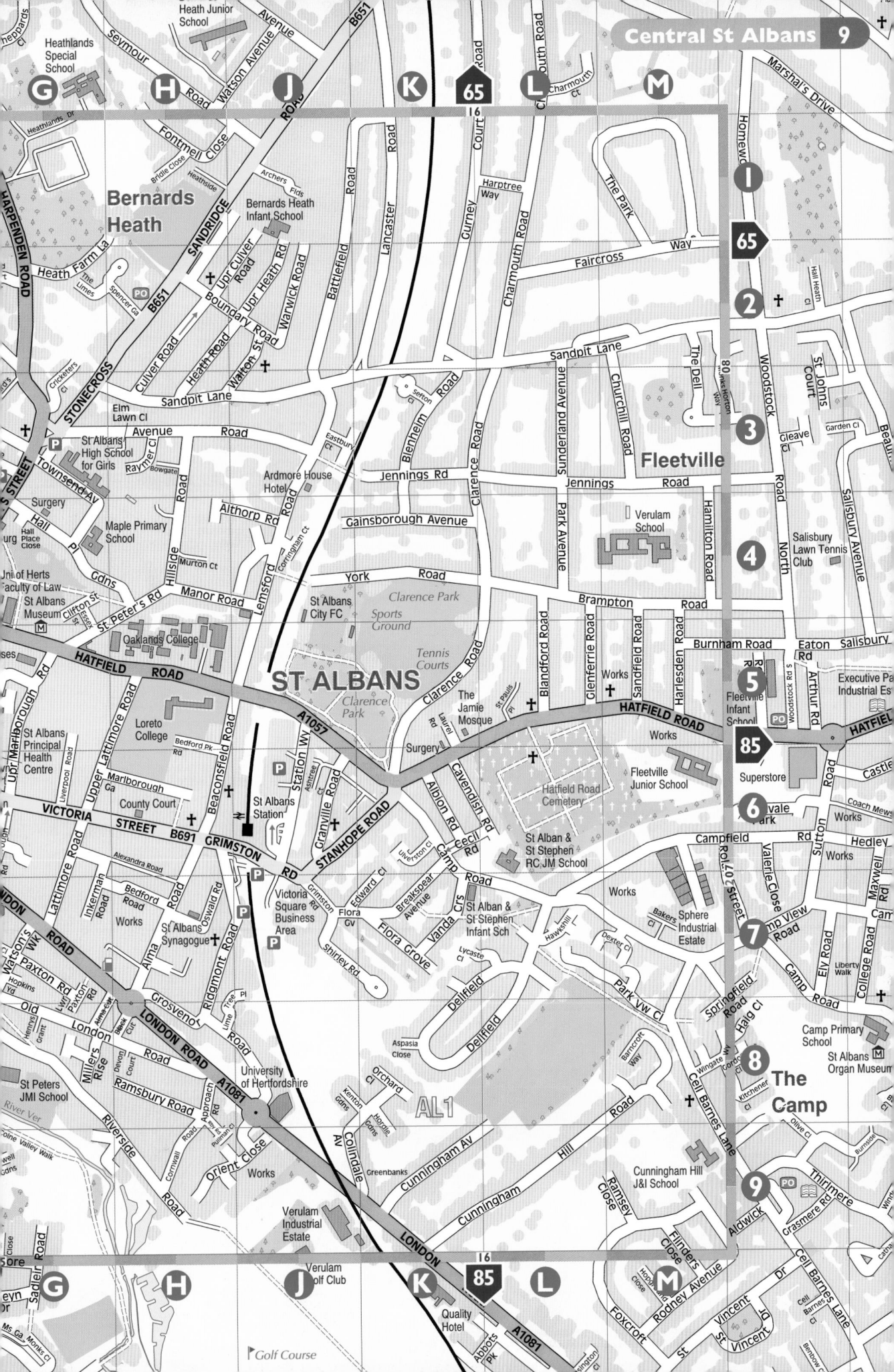

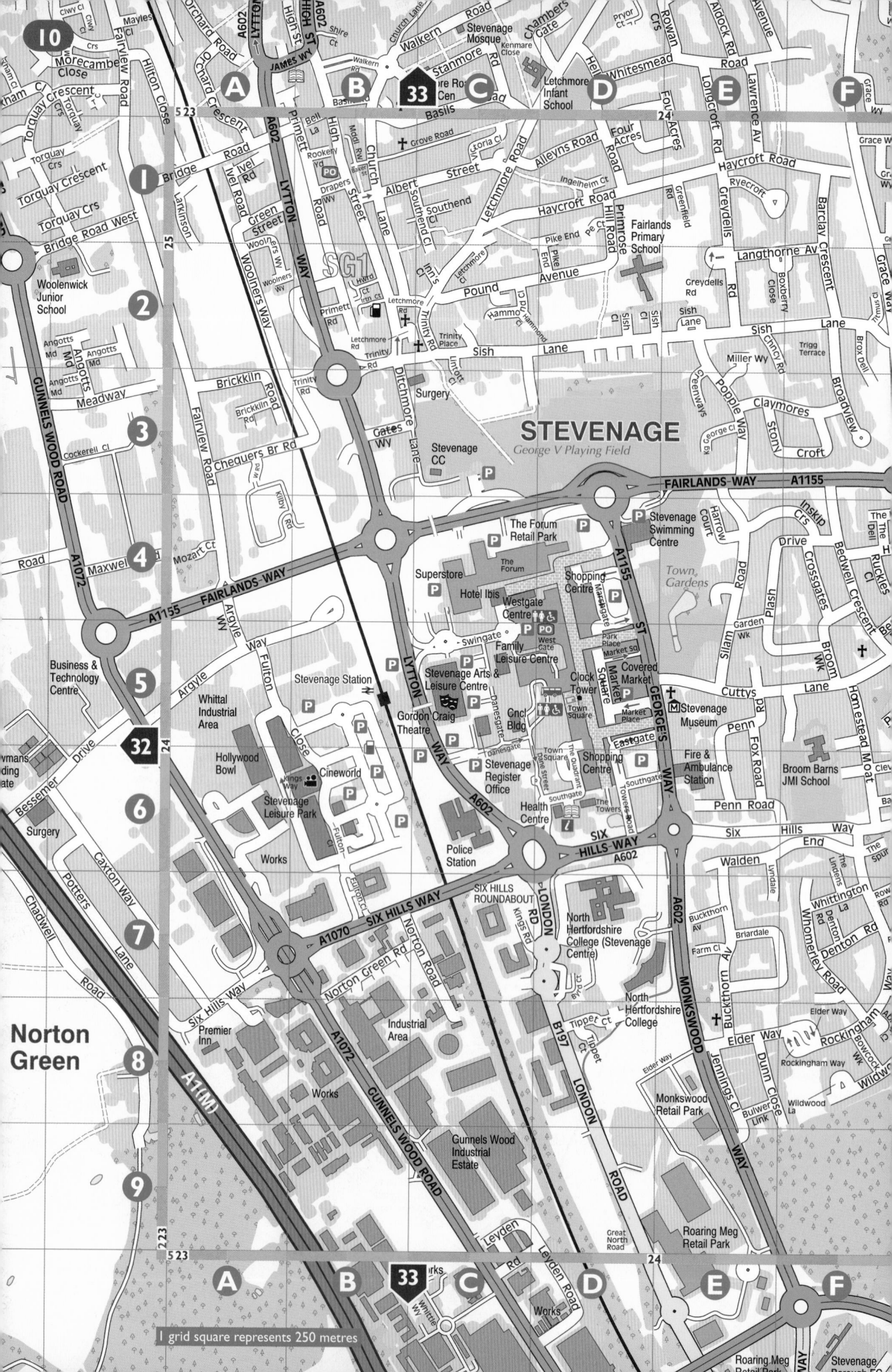

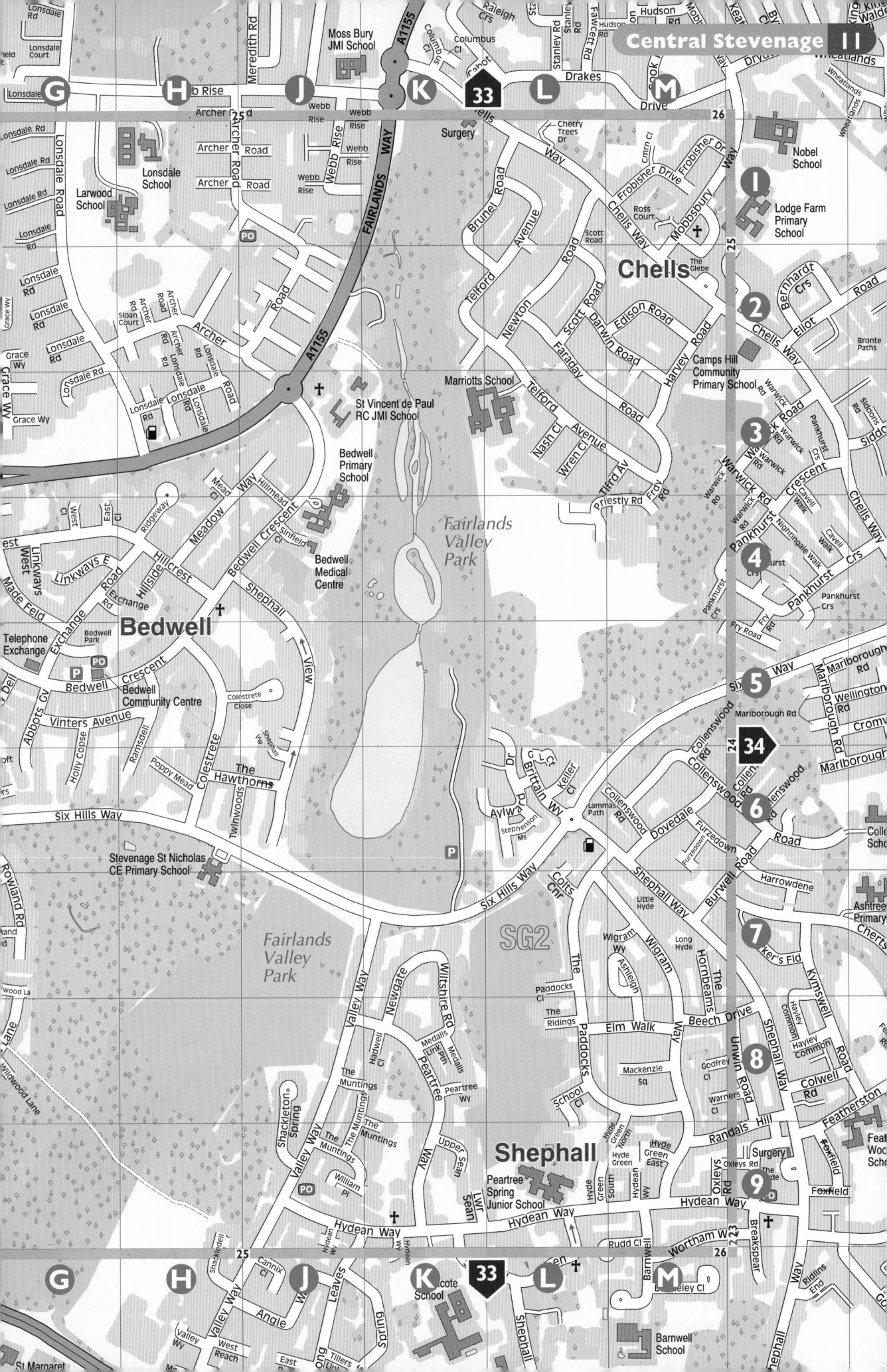

Lonsdale Rd
Lonsdale Court
Lonsdale
G
H
b Rise
J
Webb Rise
K
33
L
Drakes
M
Drive

Raleigh
Columbus Cl
Columbus
Cl
Canot
Cherry Trees Dr
Stanley Rd
Fawcett Cl
Hudson
Cook
Dryden
Wheatlands
By
King
Wal

Moss Bury JMI School
Meredith Rd
A1155
Columbus Way
Surgery

Archer 25 d
26

Archer Road
Archer Road
Archer Road
Webb Rise
Webb Rise
Webb Rise
FAIRLANDS WAY
PO

Lonsdale Rd
Lonsdale School
Larwood School

Way
Brunel Road
Telford Road
Chells
Way
Frobisher Drive
Frobisher Dr
Mobbsury Way
Ross Court
Scott Road
The Glebe
Cmn Cl
Nobel School
1 Lodge Farm Primary School
Bernhardt Crs
Eliot Road
Bronte Paths

Lonsdale Rd
Lonsdale Rd
Lonsdale Rd
Grace Wy
Grace Wy
Grace Wy

Archer Road
Sloan Court
Archer Rd
Lonsdale Rd
Lonsdale Road
Archer Road
Lonsdale Rd
Lonsdale Road

St Vincent de Paul RC JMI School

Newton Road
Scott Road
Darwin Road
Edison Road
Harvey Road
Chells
Camps Hill Community Primary School
Warwick Crs
Warwick Rd
Chells Way
2
Nightingale Walk
Pankhurst Crs
Cavell Walk
Cavell Crs
Chells Way
Siddons
Siddons

Bedwell Primary School
Faraday
Telford Avenue
Nasn Cl
Wren Cl
Priestly Rd
Tlfrd Av
Fry Rd
Warwick Rd
3
Warwick Rd
Warwick Rd
Pankhurst
4
Pankhurst Crs
Pankhurst Crs

West Cl
East Cl
Ridgeway
Mead Cl
MEADOW Way
Hillmead
Bedwell Crescent
Sinfield Cl
Bedwell Medical Centre
Fairlands Valley Park
Fry Road
Fry Road

Linkways West
West Cl
Linkways E
Hillside
Road
Exchange
Shephall
Bedwell
Collenswood Rd
5 Six Hills Way
Marlborough Rd
Marlborough Rd
Marlborough Rd
Wellington Rd
Crom
Marlborough

Telephone Exchange
Abbots Gv
Holly Copse
Vinters Avenue
Ramsdell
Bedwell Park
P PO
Bedwell Crescent
Bedwell Community Centre
Colestrete Close
View
Colestrete
Shephal Vw
34
Collenswood Rd
Collenswood Rd
Dovedale
Furzedown
Collenswood Road
Colle School

Dell
The Hawthorns
Thumwoods
Poppy Mead
Six Hills Way
G L Ct
Keller Cl
Brittain Wy
Aylw's
Dr
Stephenson Ms
Lammas Path
Collenswood Rd
Burwell Road
6
Harrowdene
Ashtree Primary Cherr

Stevenage St Nicholas CE Primary School
P
Six Hills Way
Colts Cnr
Shephall Way
Little Hyde
7
ker's Fld
Kimswell Road

Fairlands Valley Park
SG2
Wigram Wy
Ashleigh
The Hornbeams
Wigram Way
Long Hyde
Beech Drive
Hayley Common
Hayley Common

Valley Way
Newgate
Wiltshire Rd
Paddocks Cl
The Ridings
Paddocks Cl
Elm Walk
Unwin Way
Godfrey Cl
8
Colwell Rd
Featherston
Feat Woo Scho

Hadwell Cl
Link Pth
Medalls Cl
Medalls
Peartree Wy
School Cl
Mackenzie Sq
Warners Cl
Randals Hill
Foxfield
Foxfield

Shackleton Spring
Valley Way
The Muntings
The Muntings
The Muntings
The Muntings
Upper Sean
Peartree Spring Junior School
Shephall
Hyde Green North
Hyde Green
Hyde Green East
Hyde Green South
Hydean Wy
Oxleys Rd
Surgery
9
Oxleys Rd
The Glade

PO
Valley Way
William Pl
LWR Sean
Hydean Way
Hydean Way
Hydean Way
Rudd Cl
en
Barnwell
Wortham W
25 23
26
Breakspear
Ridlins End

G
H
Shacklediell
Cannix Cl
J
Leaves
K
cote School
33
L
M
Berkeley Cl
Barnwell School
Wortham
 Length
Foxfield
Wy
Shephall

Angle
Valley Way
West End
Valley Wy
East Reach
Leaves Spring
Shephall
Tillers
St Margaret

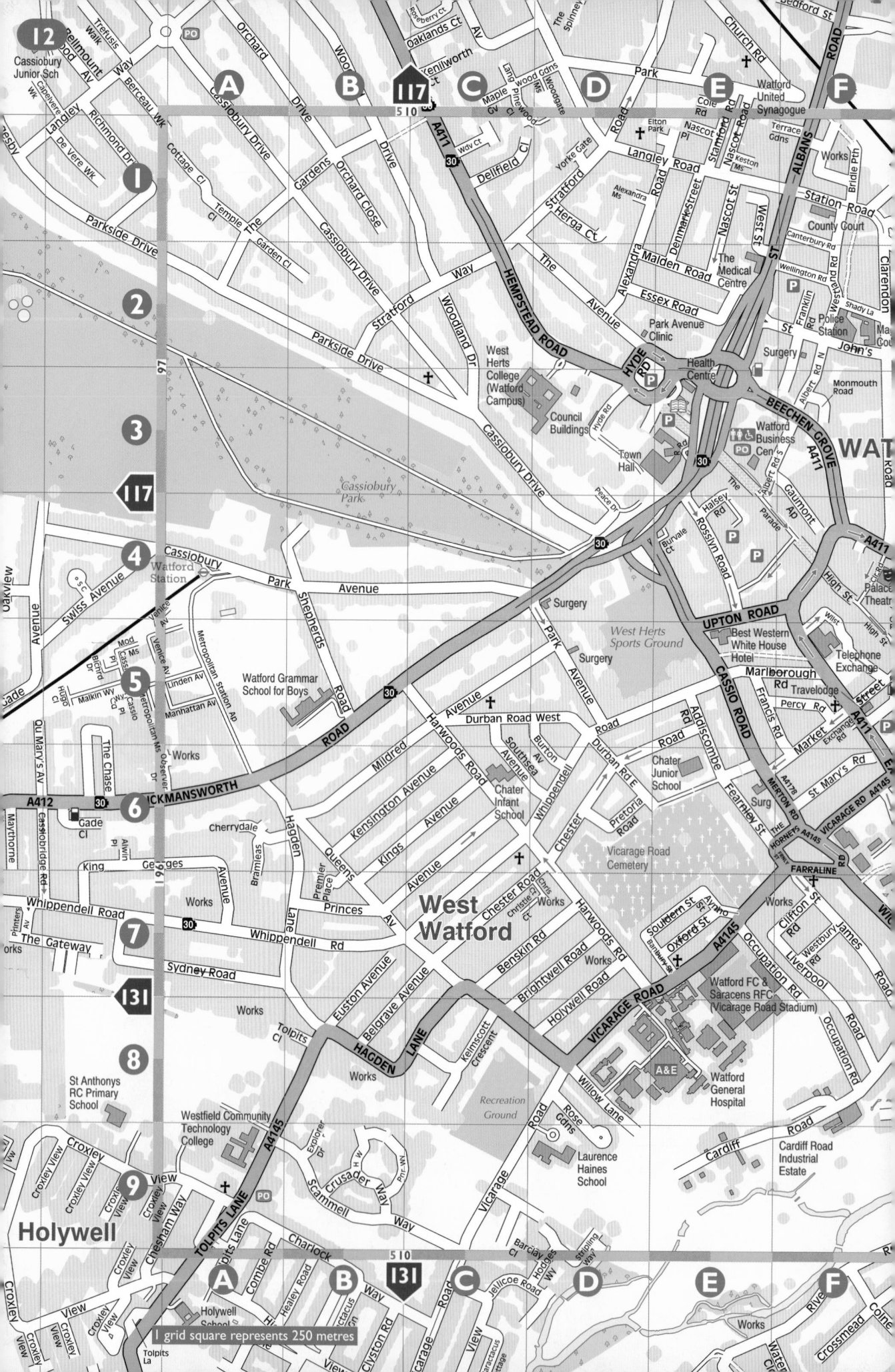

G 37 H J High K L 39 M

Bury Lane
Back
Works
Greenlow
Saxon Way

Holland
Hall

New
Farm

Muncey's
Farm

Goffers
Knoll

Summer
House
Farm

New Road

Health
Farm

A505

The
Meridian
School

Hawthorn Way
Hthn Cl
Elm Walk
The Close
Field Crescent
Newman
Avenue

Hyde Hill
Farm

Icknield Way Path

Cambridgeshire County
Hertfordshire County

Noon's
Folly
Farm

Newmarket Road

Aintree Road
Windsor
Brampton
Road

Burloes
Hall

Burloes
Farm

Lowerfield

B1039 37 H J 152 K L 39 M

B1039

Works

B1039

1
2
3
4
5
6
7
8

44
43
42
41
240

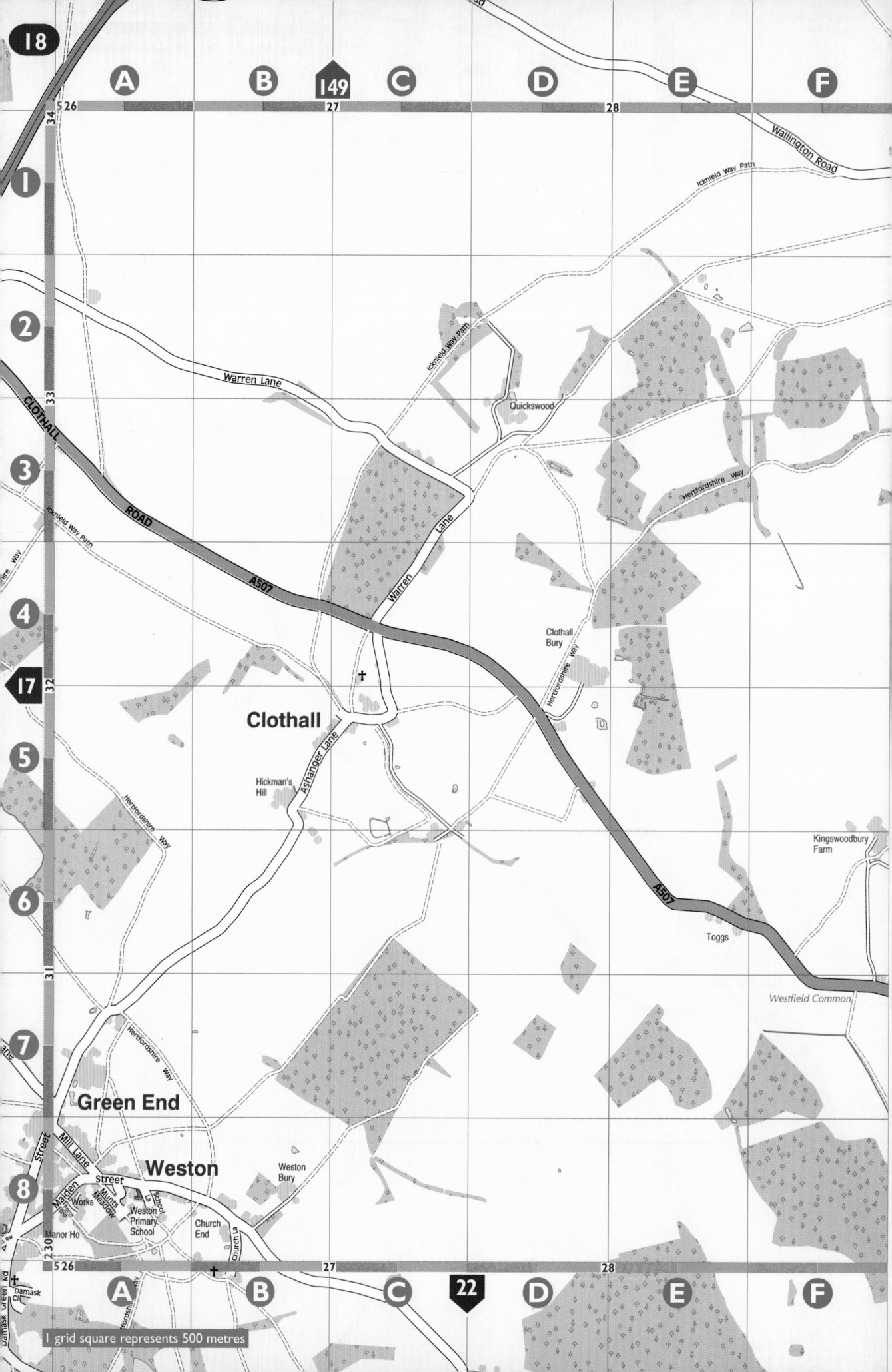

A   B   C   D   E   F

149

5 26
27
28

34
33
CLOTHALL ROAD A507
32
31

Wallington Road

Icknield Way Path

1

2

Warren Lane

Icknield Way Path

Quickswood

Hertfordshire Way

3

Icknield Way Path

Warren Lane

4

17

Clothall Bury

Hertfordshire Way

Clothall

Ashanger Lane

Kingswoodbury Farm

5

Hickman's Hill

Hertfordshire Way

6

A507

Toggs

Westfield Common

7

Hertfordshire Way

Green End

Weston

Weston Bury

8

Street
Mill Lane
Maiden
Works
Street
Munts Meadow
School La
Weston Primary School
Church La
Church End
Manor Ho
2 30

5 26
27
28

Damask Green Rd
Damask Cl

A   B   C   D   E   F

22

1 grid square represents 500 metres

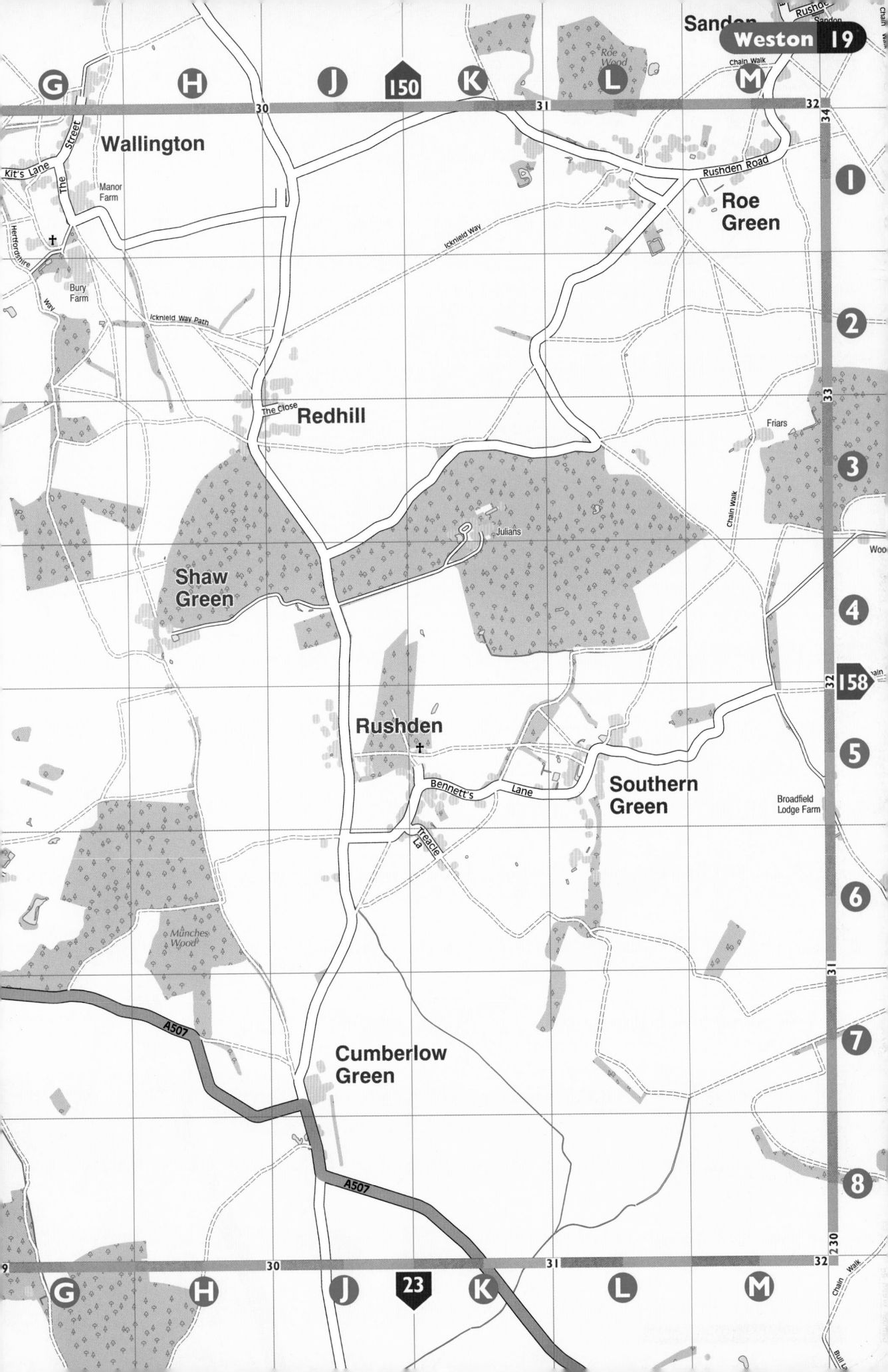

G   H   J   **150**   K   L   M

30   31   32

Wallington

Kit's Lane

Manor Farm

Hertfordshire

Way

Bury Farm

Icknield Way Path

The Close

Redhill

Icknield Way

Rushden Road

Roe Green

Roe Wood

Chain Walk

Friars

Chain Walk

Woo

Shaw Green

Julians

Rushden

Southern Green

Bennett's   Lane

Treacle La

Broadfield Lodge Farm

158

Munches Wood

A507

Cumberlow Green

A507

23

G   H   J   **23**   K   L   M

30   31   32

Chain Walk

Bull

G **H** **J** 17 **K** **L** **M**

24 25 26 30

Damask Green

The Snipe
Friars Road
Manor Ho
P.O Rw

Marlborough Cl
Woodlands Meade
Rowan Close
Damask Cl

I

2

29

3

Jack's Hill
Chesfield Downs Golf Club

How Wood

Golf Course

Tilekiln Farm

4

28

22

Hertfordshire Way

Manor Farm

Hertfordshire Way

5

Snowdonia Way

Havbur Way
Nevis
Gr Eables
Mrrck Cl
Cromdale
Grampian Pl

The Chilterns
Blackdown

Great

Church Lane

Graveley
Surgery

Chesfield Park

Number Court
Avon Dr W
Knm
Riccat Ct
Calder Dr

Mendip
Mendip Dr
Frfld Crs

Portcullis
Cl

Hertfordshire Way

Windrush Cl
Wnsm Rd

Brav Dr

The Beacons
Ashby Way

Cleveland Way
Fairfie
Gt Ashby

6

HIGH STREET

Dove Rd
Wnsm
Weston

Severn
Tees Close
Severn Way
Tamar

Great
Wansbeck
Cherwell Dr

Whitehorse

Round Diamond Primary School
Knott

27

B197

St Davids Cl
Old Bourne Way

St Nicholas Recreation Centre

Whitworth Road
Dgwood Court

Boulton Rd

Wedgwood Way

Wedgwe

7

St Andrews Drive
Weston Way
Manchester Rd

Leys Primary School
Salisbury Road
Winchester Cl
Lincoln Road
Beverley Rd

Wedgwood Gate Industrial Estate
Exeter Close

Pin Green Industrial Est

Cartwright

Underwood Road
Granby Road
Chouler Gardens
The Brambles

Ripon Road

Islington
Lancaster Way
Guildford
St Al Ln
Iona Close

St Nicholas Health Cen
Canterbury
York Rd

Surgery
Pilgrims Way

Southsea

Wedgwood Gate

Ely Close

Works

NORTH

Lister
Cl

Daltry Road

Turner Close
Arnold
Close
Wilson Close

Rook's Nest

Pilgrims Way

St Nicholas

Chester Road
Norwich Close

Martins Way
Ascot Crescent

Lingfi

8

Chancellors Road
Foster Close
Boswell Gardens

The Bury

Cemetery

York Road

The Giles Infant School
Durham Rd

Sefton Road

Martins Wood Primary School

26

Sandown Road

ROAD

Woodfield

Higgins Walk
Tudor Close
Nicholas Place
Chestnut Walk

A1072

Bader Close
Trafford Close
Trent Close

Trotts Hill Primary School
Jessop Road

Jessop Road
PO

Verity Way
Bradman

Martins Way

A1155

Chepstow

Wtherh

Derby Way

Mildmay Road

Mildmay Rd

23

G MARTINS WAY **H** Almond Hill School 24 **J** 33 **K** Wisden Road **L** **M** FAIRLANDS WAY

Barclay School
Cemetery
Grace Way
Vardon Road
Sutcliffe Close

Pin Green

Crescent

Cromwell Thomas Allevne
Frankl
Almonds
Providence Grove
25 26 Shirley
Dryden Rd

Weston

Weston Bury

Maiden Street

Munts Meadow

Manor Ho

Weston Works

Weston Primary School

Church End

Church La

Damask Green Rd

Damask Cl

A **B** **C** **18** **D** **E** **F**

5 26

30

27

28

I

Weston Park

2

29

Hertfordshire Way

3

Warren's Green

Weston Lodge

Fairclough Hall Farm

PH

Hall's Green

Dane End Lane

Hertfordshire Way

Warrensgreen Lane

4

Howells Farm

21

28

5

Dane End

Great Ashby

The Chilterns

Blackdown

Grampian

Cleveland Way

Ryders Wd

Quick

Fairfield Wy

Fairfield Wy

Grasmere

Lomond

6

Whitworth Road

Senate Place

Foye

Gt Ashby Wy

Heigh Cl

Lomond

Lowes

Wedgewood Court

Boulton Road

Wedgewood Park

Great Ashby Way

Serpentine

Windermere Cl

Wedgwood Gate

7

Stevenage Business Park

Pin Green Industrial Est

Ullswater Cl

Thirlmere Cl

Cartwright Road

Churchend Common

Works

Boxbury Farm

Box Wood

Manor Farm

Beech Lane

8

226

Ashby Crescent

Lingfield Road

Sandown

Gresley Way

Gordian Way

Trajan Gate

Julia Gate

Apollo Way

Augustus Gate

Valerian Way

Nerva

Emperor's Gate

Walkern

Froghall Lane

Brockwell Shott

Aubries

High St

Kitcheners Lane

B1037

Finches End

Cherry Tree Rise

Moors Ley

The Maltings

Monts Green Meadow

Walkern Primary School

Street

A **B** **C** **34** **D** STE GE ROAD **E** **F**

27 28

5 26

LANDS

Chepstow Close

Ayr Cl

Dorset

Tacitus Way

Cider

Fortuna Cl

Pastures

Boxfield

Dryden

G   H   J   K   156   L   M

1
2
3
4
30
5
6
7
8

Lilley Bottom
Hollybush
West Street
A505
BEECH HILL
HITCHIN RD
Dog Kennel Farm
Luton White Hill
Westbury Wood
Lilley Bottom
Putteridge Bury
University of Bedfordshire
Chalk Hill
Offley Chase
Putteridge High School
Recreation Centre
Putteridge J&I Sch
Putteridge Rd
Mangrove Green
Cockernhoe
Green La
Mangrove Rd
Cockernhoe Endowed Primary School
Chalk Hill
Stony Lane
Tea Green
Tankards Farm
Triggs Wy
Elmtree Av
Luton Road
Brickkiln Wood
Somerles J&I School
Slaughter's Wood
Wigmore
Rochford Drive
Claverley Gn
Tameton
Hedley
Lennox Gn
Rylands Heath
Cutlers Rise
Wandon End
Darle
LU2
Ashcroft High School
Buckingham Drive
Crawley Green
Warton Gn
Colwell Rise
Corbridge Dr
Emmer Gn
Superstore
Wigmore Primary School
Barford Rise
Hedley
Laxton Cl
Heaton Dell
The Dell
Bowbrook
Malthouse Gn
Darley Road
Lyneham Rd
Rowelfield
Mossbank
Airport Executive Industrial Park
Barratt Industrial Park
Winch Hill Farm
Hertfordshire
Lu

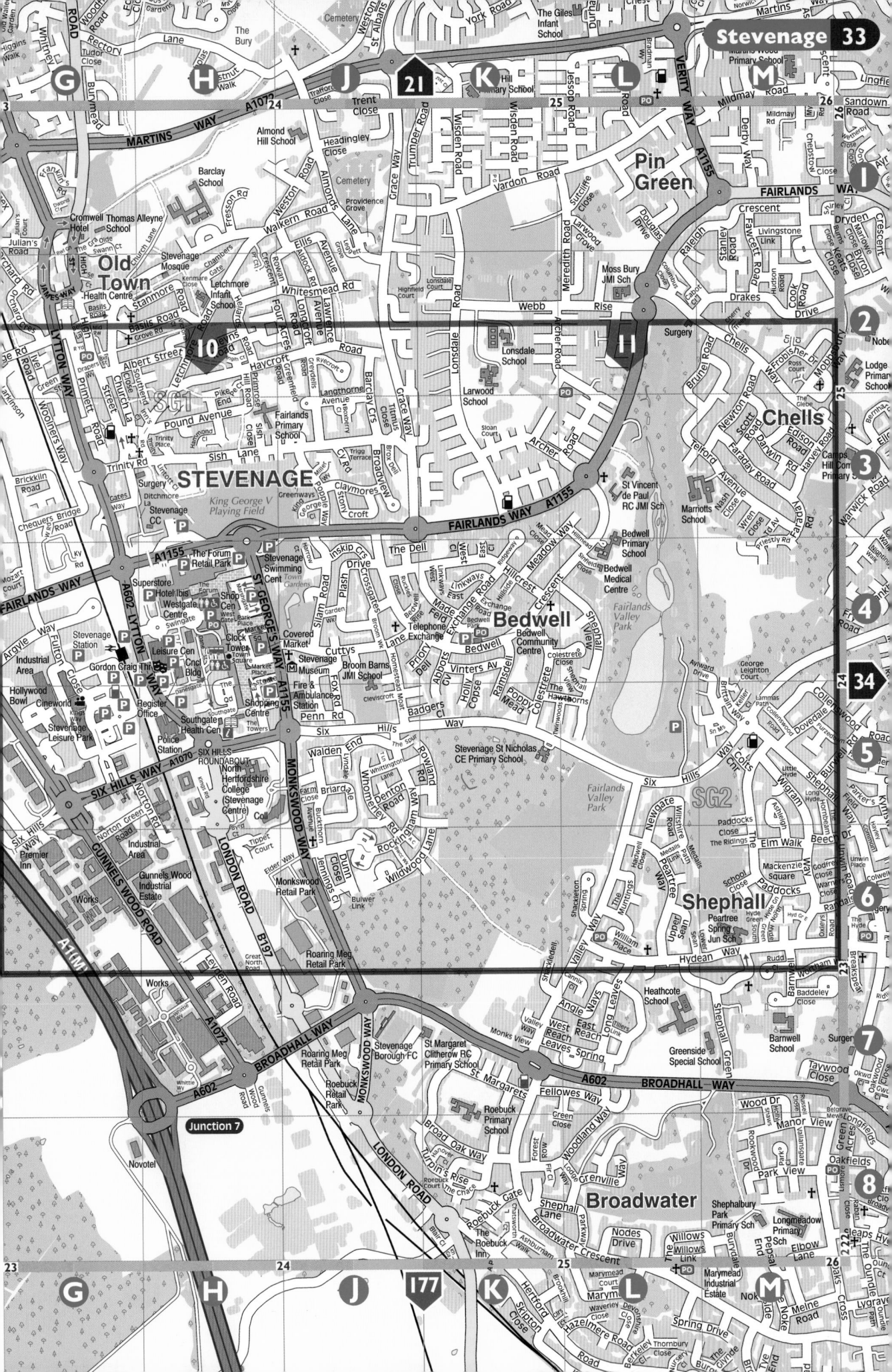

G H J 23 K L M
30 31 32 26

Walkern
Bury Farm

**Bassus
Green**

St-John's
Wood

1

2

25

Clay End
Road

Clay End

Walken Park
Farm

Holmes
Farm

3

Walkern
Hall

Walman's
Green

Bridge
Farm

SG2

4

24 162

Box
Hall

Old School Green

Lordship
Farm

Benington
Primary
School

Duck Lane

Benington

Benington
Park

5

Benington
Lordship

Three Stiles
Blacksmiths Hill

Town Lane

Town   Lane

6

23

Finches Farm

Whempstead Road

Chain Walk

Works
Braceys
Goodey
Meade

Hebing End

7

Benington
House

**Burn's
Green**

Cutting
Hill

8

222

Chain Walk

Lane

High   Elms   Lane

Idle
Hill

29 30 31 32
G H J K L M 179

Hempstead Road

'Comb's Wood'

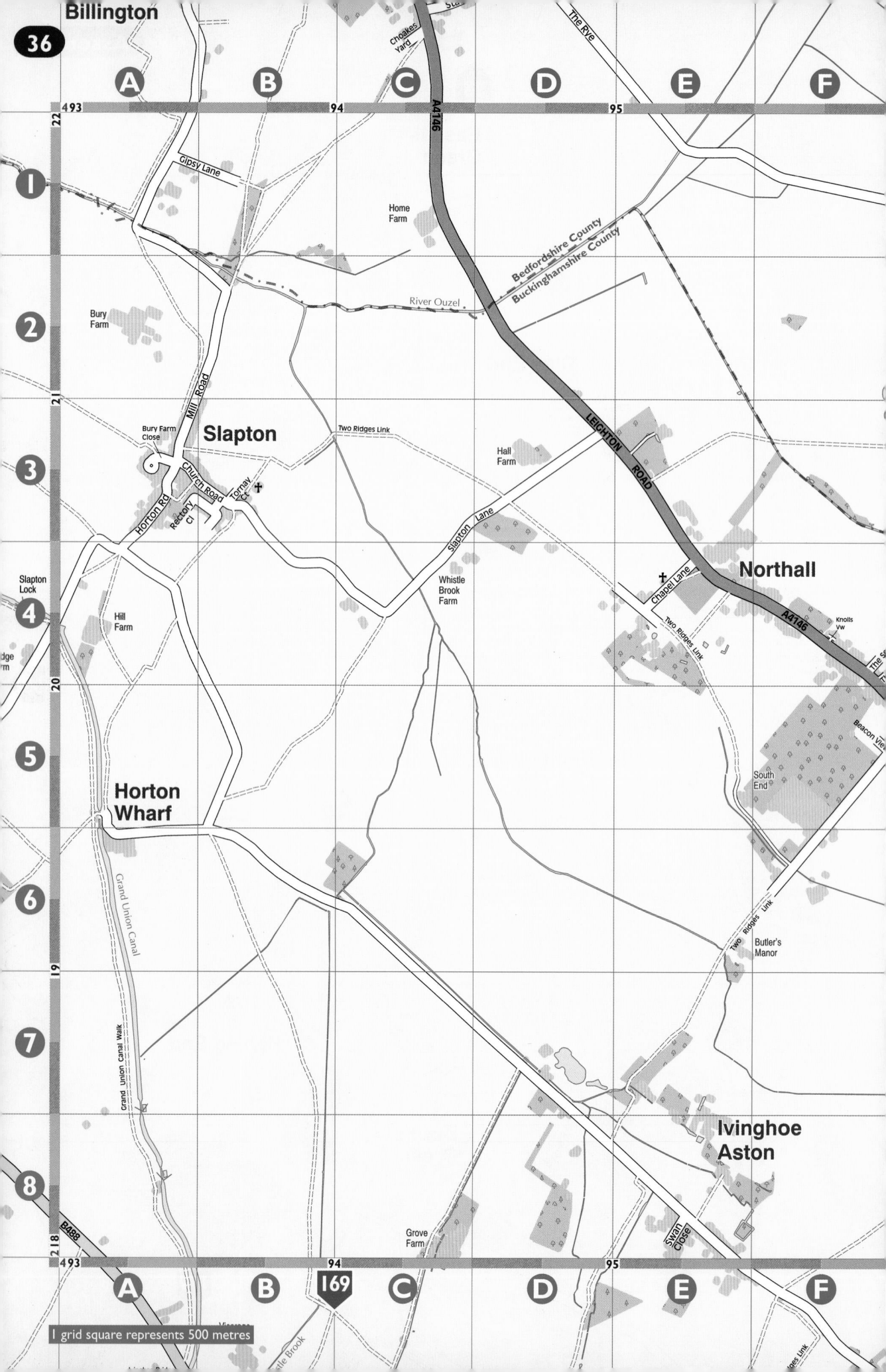

A · B · C · D · E · F

Gipsy Lane

Home Farm

A4146

Choakes Yard

The Rye

Bedfordshire County
Buckinghamshire County

River Ouzel

Bury Farm

Mill Road

LEIGHTON ROAD

Bury Farm Close

Slapton

Two Ridges Link

Hall Farm

Church Road

Horton Rd

Tornay Ct

Rectory Ct

Slapton Lane

Chapel Lane

Northall

Knolls Vw

A4146

Slapton Lock

Whistle Brook Farm

Hill Farm

Two Ridges Link

Beacon View

South End

Horton Wharf

Grand Union Canal

Two Ridges Link

Butler's Manor

Grand Union Canal Walk

Ivinghoe Aston

Swan Close

Grove Farm

B488

1 grid square represents 500 metres

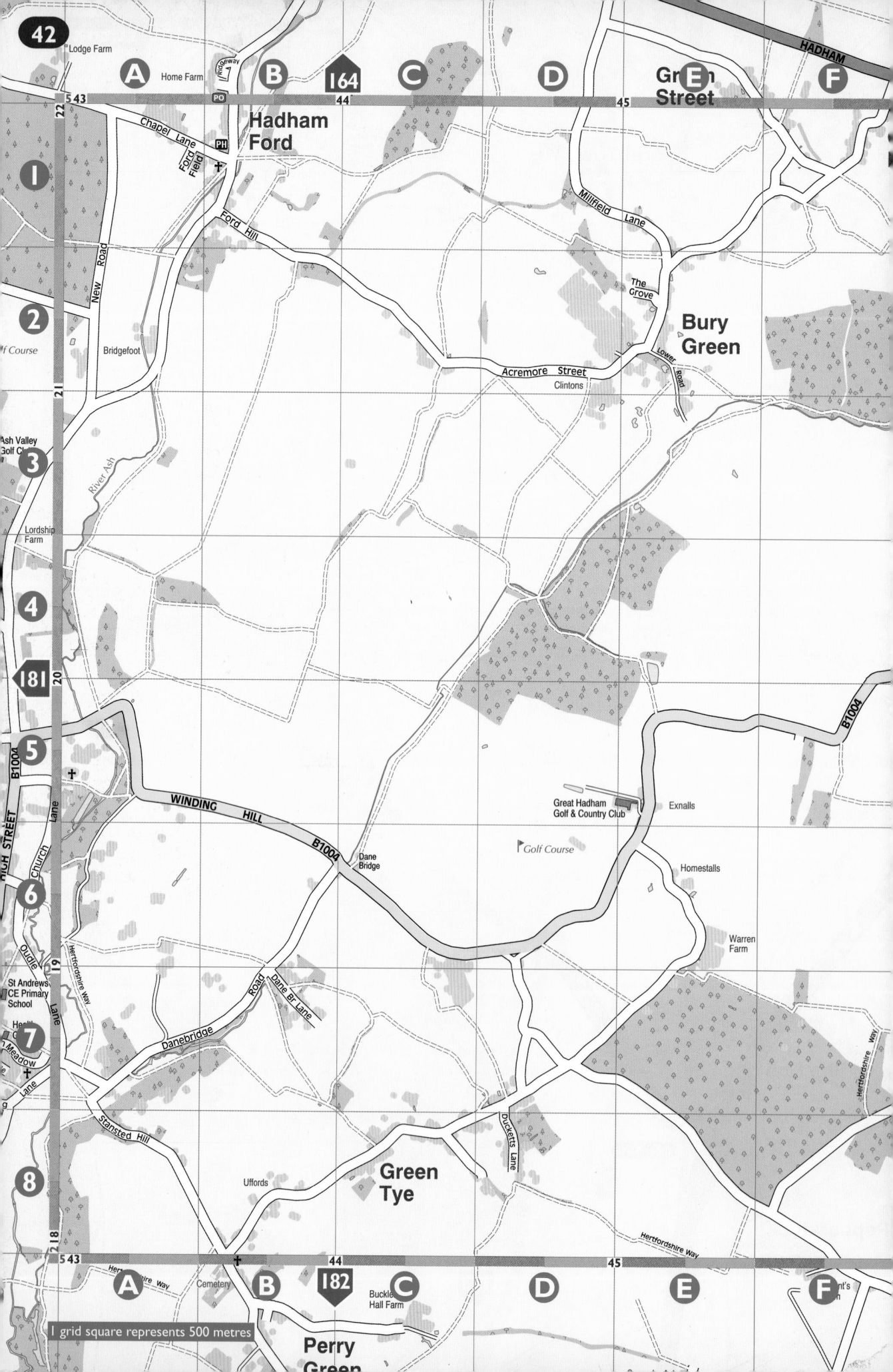

46

Kinsbourne
Green

HARPENDEN

Hatching
Green

1 grid square represents 500 metres

48

A   B   175   C   D   E   F

Gustard Wood

Golf Course

Mid Herts Golf Club

Delaport

Lamer Farm

Codicote Road

T Folly

Rose Lane

Garden Ct

CODICOTE RD

Waddling Lane

Lea Valley Walk

Dawes Lane

CORY-WRIGHT WAY

Lea Valley Walk

River Lea or Lee

B653

Kingfisher

PO

Mount Rd

Pl Farm

Meads La

East La

Meads La

Wheathampstead

Sheepcote La

B653

47

Ash Gv

Works

Kg Edward Pl

Cn Fld

Old Rectory

Bury Green

High Meads

Church St

St Helens Primary School

Surgery

Cmtry

St Thomas

Bracket VW

Necton Road

Marford Road

MARFORD ROAD

Four Limes

Garrard Way

Offas Way

Caesars

Conquerors Hl

Tudor Rd

Battleview

Brewhouse Hill

Lattimore Rd

Barton Rd

Maltings Dr

THE HILL

WICK

Nurseries Rd

Road

Hill Fort

Chalkdell Farm

Butterfield

High Ash Rd

Beech Hyde Primary School

Allen

Wright

Hewitt

Hill Dyke Rd

Davy's

Beech Cls

Vale Court

Beech Hyde Farm

Amwell

Road

Dyke Lane

Beech Hyde Lane

Nomansland

B651

Coleman Green Lane

Coleman Green

Ferrers Lane

Nomansland Common

Ferrers Lane

Nomansland Farm

Tower

Darplay Cl

Hill

Hillend Farm

A   B   66   C   D   E   F

1 grid square represents 500 metres

G   H   J   K   181   L   M

39   40   41   16

Babbs Green   Helham Green

Scholar's Hill   Scholar's Hill

Wareside   B1004

The Crown   Brook End   Hertfordshire Way   Hertfordshire Way

I

Wareside Primary School

Morley Hall   2

River Ash   15

B1004   3

Harcamlow Way   Harcamlow Way   Mardocks Farm

Watersplace Farm   4   Fillets Farm

182   14

5

Newgate Wood   Harcamlow Way

Easneye   Harcamlow Way   6

Bonningtons

13   H

Halfway House   HUNSDON ROAD

Hollycross Road   B180   7

Little Briggens   Olives Farm

Newlands   B180

Cappell Lane   Home Farm Industrial Estate   Harcamlow Way   8

12

38   39   40   41

St Margaret's Station   HIGH ST   STATION RD   PO   South St   Millers La   Andrews Primary School   ROYDON   HUNSDON ROAD   Stanstead Abbotts   Woodcott Avenue   Trotters Gap   The Maltings Industrial Estate   Chapelfields   Abbotts Way

A B C 168 D E F

I

Clinton

Weston Rd
Weston Rd
487
12
Burnhams
Parsley Cl
Road
Brook Street
Long
Pursham Dr
Aston Clinton School
Twitchel
Talbot
Turvey Cl
Chapel
Street
New
Overstrand
Beechwood
Rothchild Av
London
88
Road
Church Lane
Innkeeper's Lodge
Balloon Flights
Chestnut Gr
Tompkins Cl
Mount Cl
Dean Wy
Surgery
London Road
Blackmore Gate
Hedley Cl
London Rd
Drink Cl
Bs Rd
Thorne Wy
Wenwell Close
Buckland Road
89
Bucklandwharf

2

Green Park
Grand Union Canal (Wendover Arm, Disused)
Aylesbury Ring
Stablebridge
Wellonhead Bridge
Aylesbury Ring
Road
ICKNIELD
WAY
B4009
Lodge Farm
Gra
Dancer's End Lane

3

Grand Union Canal Walk
Aylesbury Ring
Harebridge
Lane
Chiltern Way
ICKNIELD
B4009
UPPER
Golf Course
Chiltern Forest Golf Club

4

Lower Farm
Officers Lawn Tennis Club
Chestnut End
Old School Cl
Church
Halton
McEwen
Ride
Rosemead
Road
Mansion Rd
Aylesbury Ring
10

5

The Orchard
Garden Cl
St Michaels Cl
Chestnut
Swann
Road
Clayfield Road
Avenue
Swann Rd
UPPER
ICKNIELD
WAY
Polish Av
Rd
Rd
Dacre
Rd
Halton Camp
High Moors
Halton Lane
Union Canal (Wendover Arm, Disused)

6

Rowborough Road
Halton Combined School
B4009
PO
Maitland
White Cr
Bonham
Carter
Rd
Stable Road
Road
Tittmus
Dacre
Road
Dacre Road
Haddington Hill
Wendover Woods
Dancersend

7

Portal Rd
Babington
Trenchard Av
High
Road
Linman Rd
Longcroft Rd
Scarlett Av
Road
Halton Wood
Halton Wood

8

Middle School
The John Hampden Wendover School
Wendover CE Junior School
John Colet School
Manor Road
Manor Crs
Bog Md
Haddington
The Beeches
Tring
Road
Beechwood Lane
Compton Rd
Colet Rd
Barlow Road
Woollerton Crs
Braddington Rd
The Maples
TRING
Ickfield Cl
Clay La
Wd Rd
Tedder Road
Halton
Ridgeway
Wharf
B4009
208
487
7
Back St
Grand
Hale

A 88 B C 89 D E F

1 grid square represents 500 metres

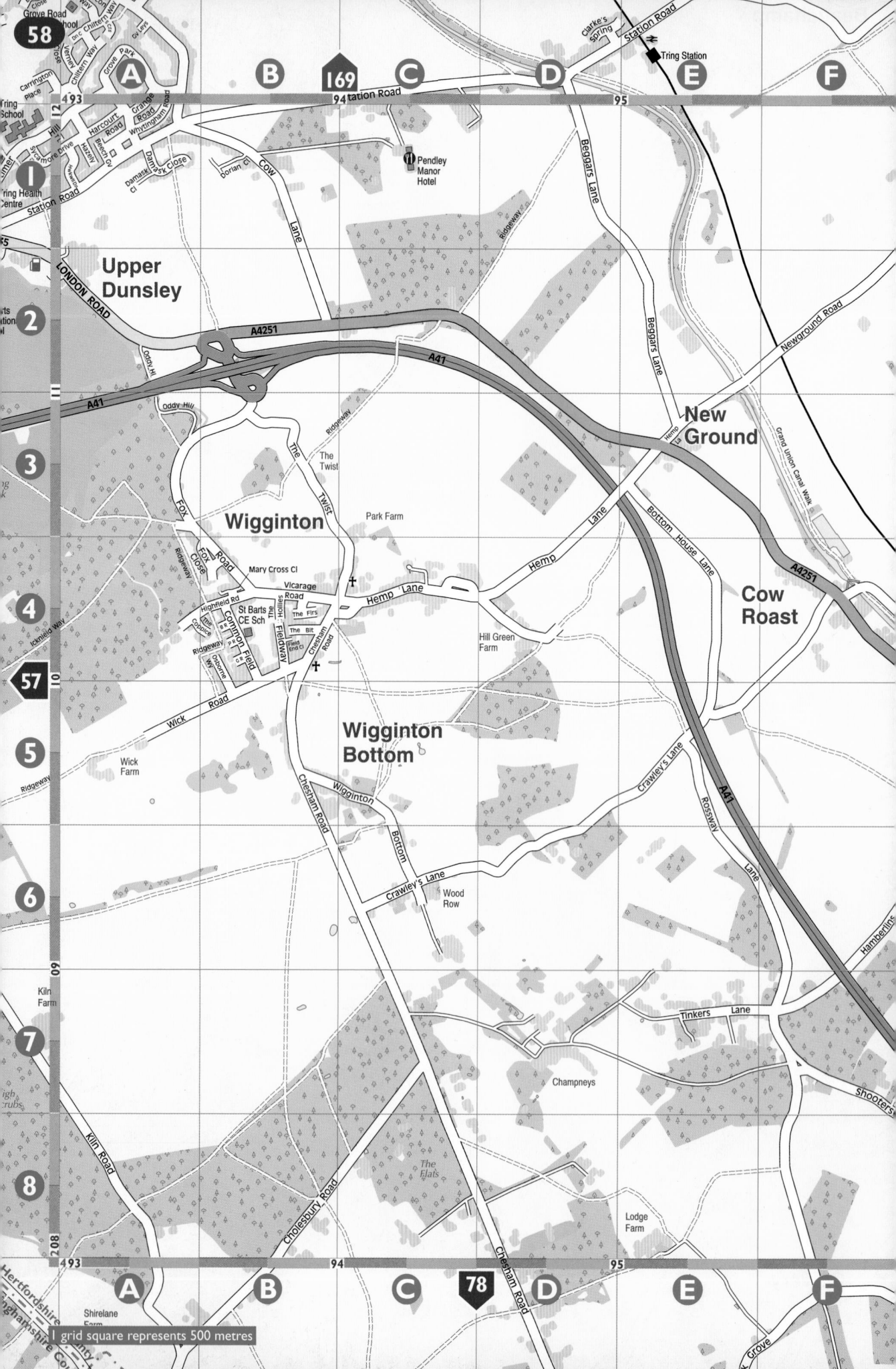

58

A B **169** C D E F
94 Station Road 95

I
2
3
4
57
5
6
7
8

A B **78** C D E F
493 94 95 208

Upper
Dunsley

Wigginton

Wigginton
Bottom

New
Ground

Cow
Roast

LONDON ROAD
A4251
A41
Oddy Hill
Ridgeway
The Twist
The Twist
Fox Road
Fox Close
Ridgeway
Mary Cross Cl
Vicarage Road
Highfield Rd
St Barts CE Sch
Common Field
The Fieldway
Wick Road
Ridgeway
Icknield Way
Osbourne Way
The Firs
The Bit
Field End Cl
Chesham Road
Hemp Lane
Hemp Lane
Hemp La
Park Farm
Hill Green Farm
Beggars Lane
Beggar's Lane
Ridgeway
Newground Road
Grand Union Canal Walk
Bottom House Lane
A4251
Crawley's Lane
Rossway Lane
A41
Chesham Road
Wigginton Bottom
Crawley's Lane
Wood Row
Tinkers Lane
Champneys
The Flats
Lodge Farm
Kiln Road
Cholesbury Road
Kiln Farm
Wick Farm
Hamberlins
shooters

Grove Road
Chiltern Way
Grove Park
Harcourt Road
Grange Road
Whytingham Road
Dorian Cl
Cow Lane
Damask Close
Pendley Manor Hotel
Clarke's spring
Station Road
Tring Station

Tring School
Tring Health Centre
Station Road
Sycamore Drive

Shirelane Farm
Hertfordshire County
Buckinghamshire County

I grid square represents 500 metres

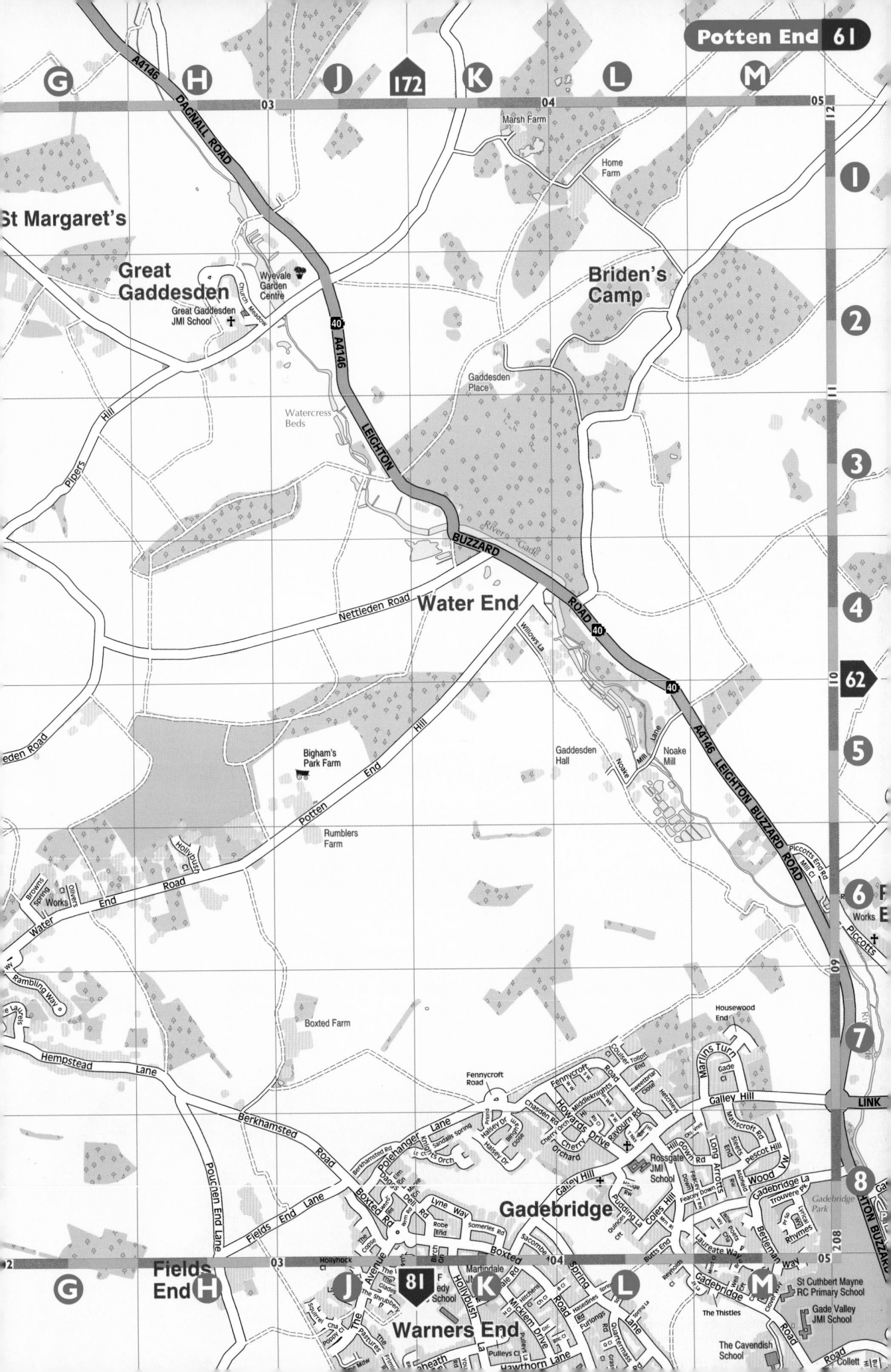

G H J 172 K L M

I
2
3
4
62
5
6
7
LINK
8

St Margaret's

Great Gaddesden

Wyevale Garden Centre

Great Gaddesden JMI School

A4146

DAGNALL ROAD

LEIGHTON

Watercress Beds

Marsh Farm

Home Farm

Briden's Camp

Gaddesden Place

River Gade

BUZZARD

Nettleden Road

Water End

ROAD

eden Road

Willows La

Gaddesden Hall

Noake Mill

Noake Mill Lane

A4146 LEIGHTON BUZZARD ROAD

Piccotts End Rd

Bigham's Park Farm

Potten

End

Hill

Road

Rumblers Farm

Hollybush Cl

Browns Spring Works

Olivers La

Water

End

Rambling Way

The Laurels

Hempstead Lane

Boxted Farm

Housewood End

Works

Piccotts

Berkhamsted

Road

Polehanger Lane

Berkhamsted Rd

Fennycroft Road

Fennycroft Rd

Howards Drive

Chasden Rd

Middleknights Hill

Cherry Orchard

Sweetbriar Close

Galley Hill

Martins Turn

Gade Cl

Rossgate JMI School

Long Arrotts

Manscroft Rd

Pescot Hill

Wood

Gadebridge La

Trouvere Pk

Gadebridge Park

Lynd Valral

Poulhen End Lane

Fields End Lane

Boxted Rd

Lyne Way

Someries Rd

Gadebridge

Galley Hill

Coles Hill

Pudding La

Butts End

Betteman La

Fields End H

G

J 81 K L M

St Cuthbert Mayne RC Primary School

Gade Valley JMI School

The Thistles

Gadebridge

Road

The Cavendish School

Warners End

G   H   Flamsteadbury Farm   J   **173**   K   L   M

09   10   11   12

AL3

St Albans

Gaddesden Lane

Church End

B487

Ramada Hotel

Aubrey Lane   ROAD   Flowers Farm

Little Revel End   HEMPSTEAD   Nicky Lane

Great Revel End Farm

End Lane

Brockswood Primary School   HEMEL   B487   Dane End Farm   Hill

Berkeley Sq   Cuffley Ct   Barford Cl   Shenley Road   Cherry Tree Lane   Nicky Line   M1   Hill Farm   **64**

Woodend Farm   Punch Bowl Lane

Lilly Lane   Punch Bowl Lane   Baker's Farm

Eaton Lodge   Southend Farm   Beech Hyde

Trees   Lane   Punch Bowl Lane   Old Jeromes

Boundary   Cherry Tree Lane   Butl Farm

Road   Buncefield Lane   Green Lane   Buncefield Oil Refinery   Hogg End Lane   Kettlewells Farm

Boundary Wy   Grovelands Business Centre   Maxted Cl   Enterprise Wy

End   Boundary Way   Woodwells Farm   09   10   11

G   Holme Place   Hales Pk   H   Green Lane   J   **83**   K   L   M

Cemetery

Gorhambury (Remains)

G H J **51** K L M

I

**Birch
Green**

2

3

4

70

5

6

60

7

8

2 08

G H **J** **89** K L M

**Little
Berkhamsted**

Sylvan Way
Sylvandale
Hurst
The Hole
The Shaws
Birchall Wood
Glebe
Birchall

Green Lane

B195
Holwell Hyde
Thistle Grove
Little Thistle

COLE GREEN LANE

BIRCHALL LANE B195

27

28

A414

29

12

igford
Cowper
Primary Sc

Birchall

The Old Coach Road

Birchall Lane

**Cole
Green**

Works

Station Road

Lea Valley Walk

Chain Walk

Chapel Lane

Woolmers Lane

Letty Green

Chain Walk

Burnside

HATFIELD ROAD A414

Holwell Court

ROAD

HOLWELL LANE B1455

Lea Valley Walk

LOW ROAD

B158

B158

Lea Valley Walk

Essendonbury
Farm

Howe
Green

Bedwell Avenue

Kennel
Hall
Farm

ESSENDON HILL B158

Bedwell Avenue

Church St
Rectory Cl
Glebe Cottages
Crib Cl
EST View
School Lane

Essendon

Chain Walk

Essendon Primary
School

West End

West End Lane

HIGH ROAD

Bedwellpark
Farm

Bedwell Av

27

Essendon

28

29

Little Berkhamsted La
Orchard Close
The Boundary

Bedwell
Park

Church

HERTFORD

Hertford Heath

Hertford Heath Primary School

Balls Wood

Swallow Grove Farm

Hertford C&CC Site

Jenningsbury Farm

LONDON ROAD B1197

Clements Farm

Edwards Green Farm

Dalmonds

Mangrove Lane

Highfield Wood

Monks Green

Brickendon Lane

Fanshaws

Brides Farm

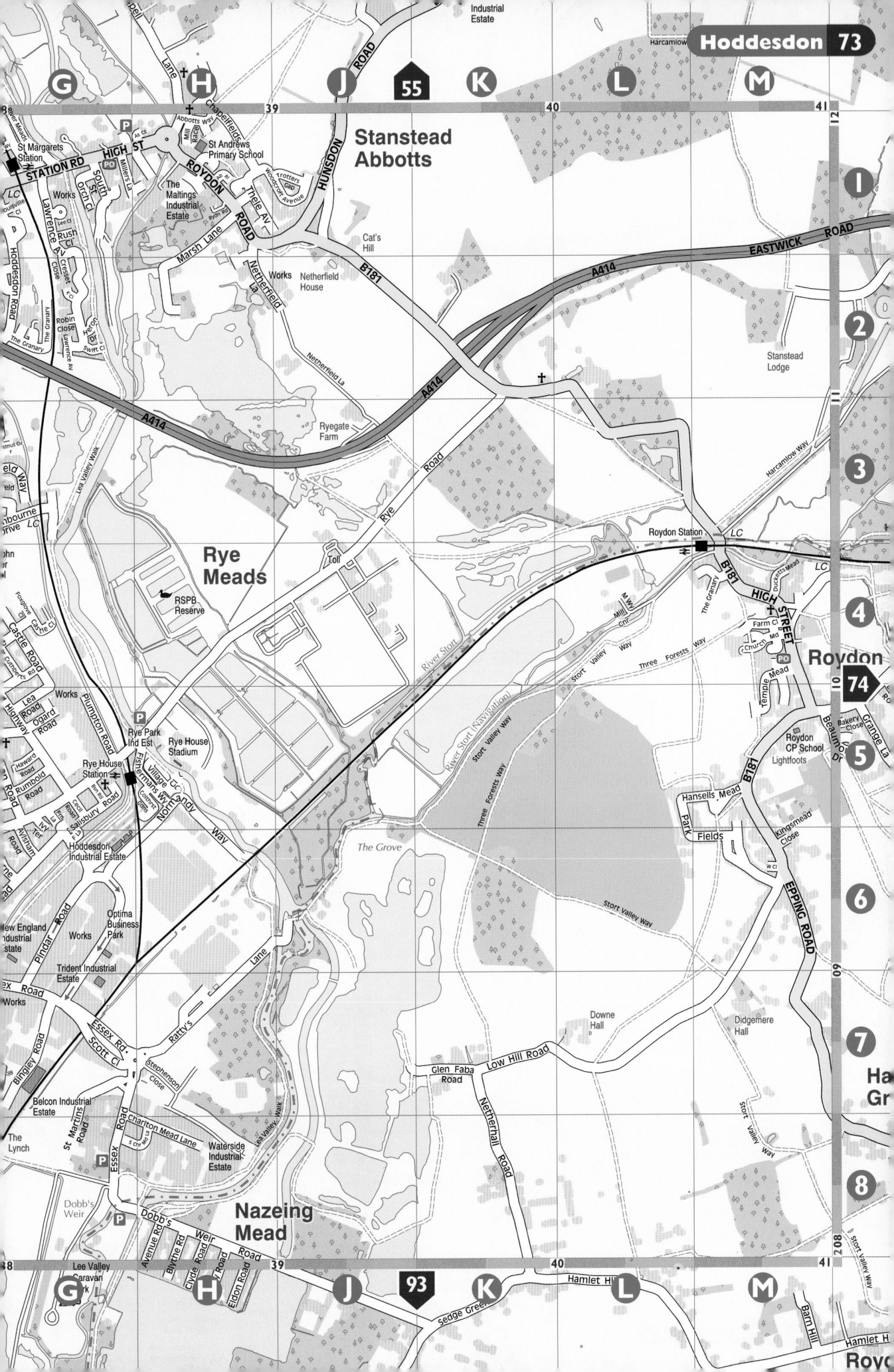

Stanstead Abbotts

Rye Meads

Nazeing Mead

Roydon **74**

Newnham's End

G   H   J   184   K   L   M

Housham Hall

Collin's Cross

Matching

1

Brick House

Harlow Road

Rainbow Road

Matching Tye

2

Harlow Tye

Stort Valley Way

Carter's Green

Matching Park

3

Forest Way

Housham Tye

Stort Valley Way

Way   Lane

New Way

Faggotters   Lane

Loyter's Green

Faggoters Farm

4

New Way

Faggoters Lane

10

5

Robins Acre

Stort Valley Way

High Laver Grange

6

Great Wilmores

Tilegate Road

High Laver

7

Tilegate Green

School Lane

Tilegate Road

Star Farm

8

Hall Farm

Magdalen Laver

Stort Valley Way

Rolls Farm

G   H   J   K   L   M

Ashlings Cottages

Crispins

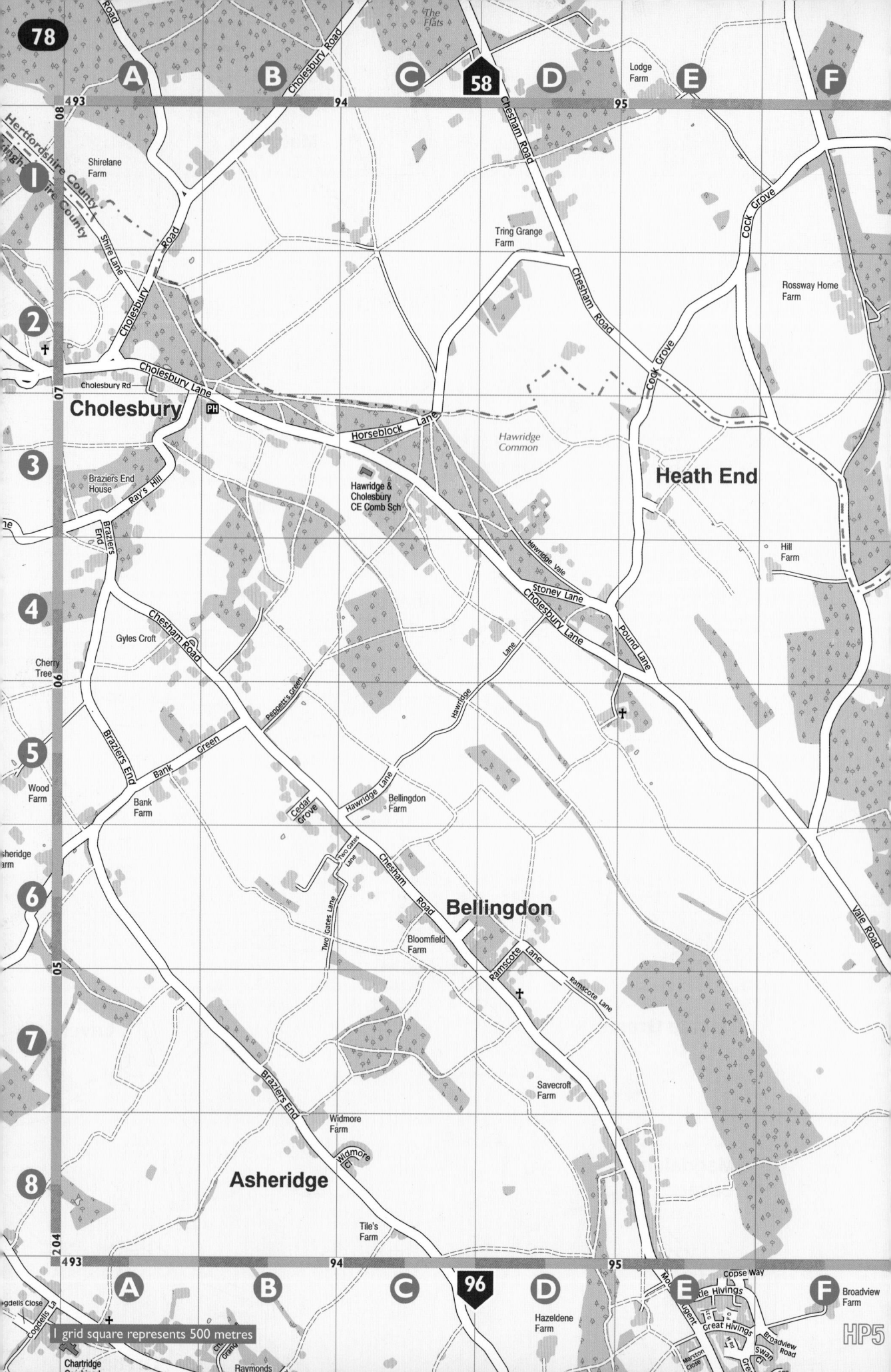

58

A B C D E F

I

Hertfordshire County

idge Hire County

Shirelane Farm

2

Shire Lane

Cholesbury Road

Cholesbury Rd

Cholesbury Lane

Cholesbury

PH

The Flats

Tring Grange Farm

Chesham Road

Lodge Farm

Cock Grove

Rossway Home Farm

3

Braziers End House

Ray's Hill

Braziers End

Horseblock Lane

Hawridge & Cholesbury CE Comb Sch

Hawridge Common

Heath End

Cock Grove

Hill Farm

4

Chesham Road

Gyles Croft

Cherry Tree

Pepperell's Green

Hawridge Vale

Stoney Lane

Cholesbury Lane

Lane

Pound Lane

06

5

Wood Farm

Braziers End

Bank Green

Cedar Grove

Hawridge Lane

Bank Farm

Hawridge Lane

Bellingdon Farm

sheridge arm

6

Two Gates Lane

Chesham Road

Bellingdon

Vale Road

05

Bloomfield Farm

Ramscote Lane

Ramscote Lane

7

Braziers End

Savecroft Farm

8

Asheridge

Widmore Farm

Widmore Cr

Tile's Farm

204 493

94 96 95

A B C 96 D E F

Copse Way

de Hivings

Broadview Farm

gdells Close

Chartridge

Hazeldene Farm

Great Hivings

Broadview Road

Swan

Marston Close

HP5

I grid square represents 500 metres

Raymonds

I grid square represents 500 metres

G   H   J   **63**   K   L   M

Boundary Way   09   10   08

Kettlewells Farm

Enterprise Wy

Woodwells Farm

Green Lane

Junction 8

Gorhambury (Remains)

I

2

End

Works

BREAKSPEAR WAY   A414

Buncefield La

Cemetery

Holme Place
Hales Pk
Crest Pk

Woodwells Farm

07

Wellbury Terrace
Datchworth Turn

St Margarets Way

Clinton End

Leverstock Green JMI School

Lombardy Cl

Westwick Row

Westwick Hall

3

Westwick
Row

Beechtree Lane

**Leverstock
Green**

A4147

LEVERSTOCK GREEN ROAD

Handpost Lodge Gdns

Hill End Farm

4

Leaside
PO

Bedmond Road

St David's Cl

A4147   **40** HEMEL   **40** HEMPSTEAD   **40** ROAD

Corner Farm

Junction 7

06

84

Special School

Chambersbury

The Horseshoe

Woodfield Dr

Blackwater Lane

Bunkers Lane

Well Farm

Bunkers Farm

5

Gt Furzefield Wood

Highwood Hall Farm

Cumberland Cl

6

Pimlico

Potterscrouch Plantations

05

Rose Acre

7

Hyde Farm

Hyde Lane

Harthall Lane

Bedmond Road

Bedmond Lane

Sergehill

8

Hyde Lane

Hart Hall Farm

Church Hill

St Albans Lane

Sergehill Lane

Featherbed Lane

Whitehse Farm

204

08   09   **101**   10   Whitehse

Redmond

Millhouse Lane

G   H   J   **101**   K   L   M

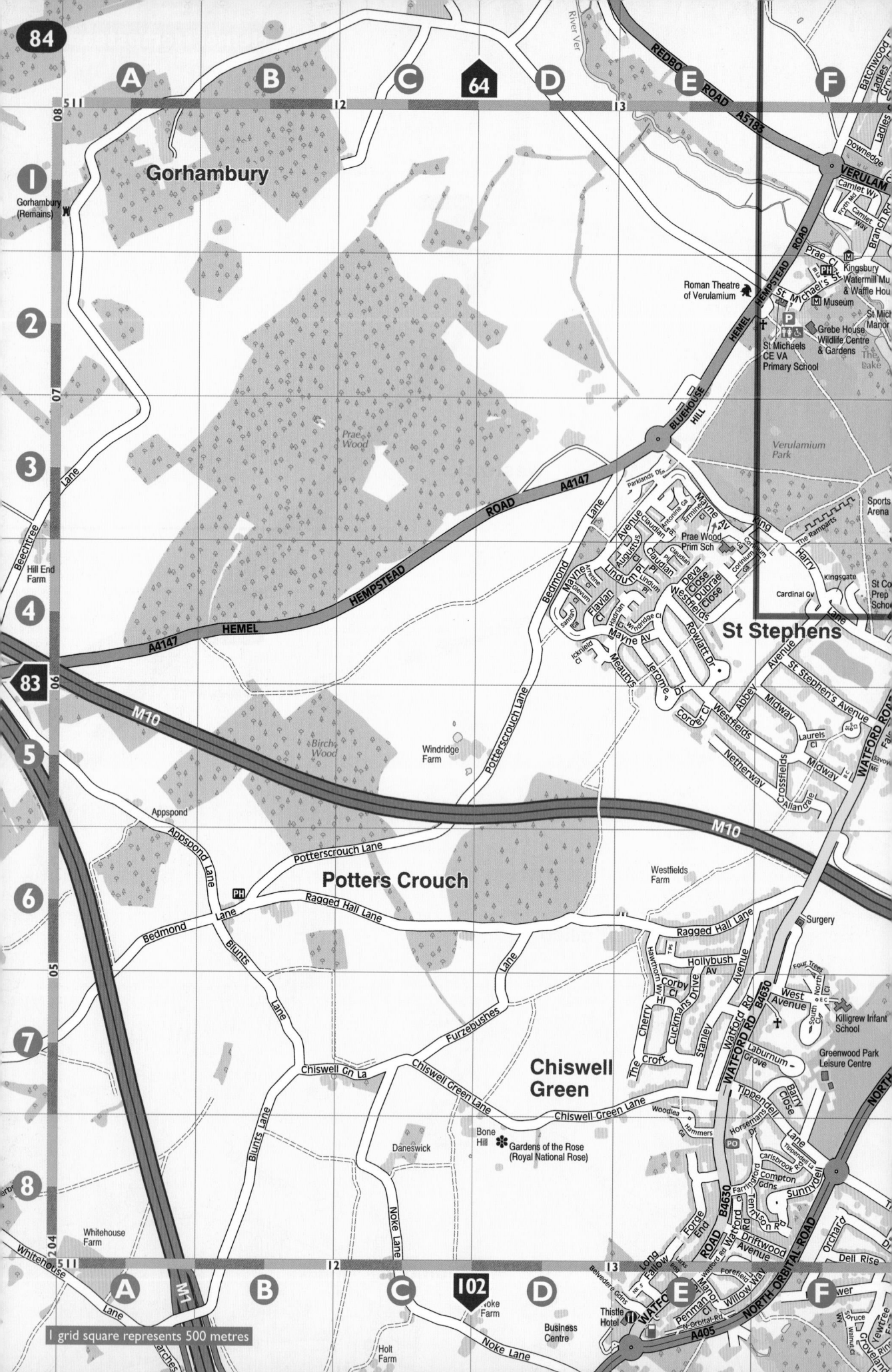

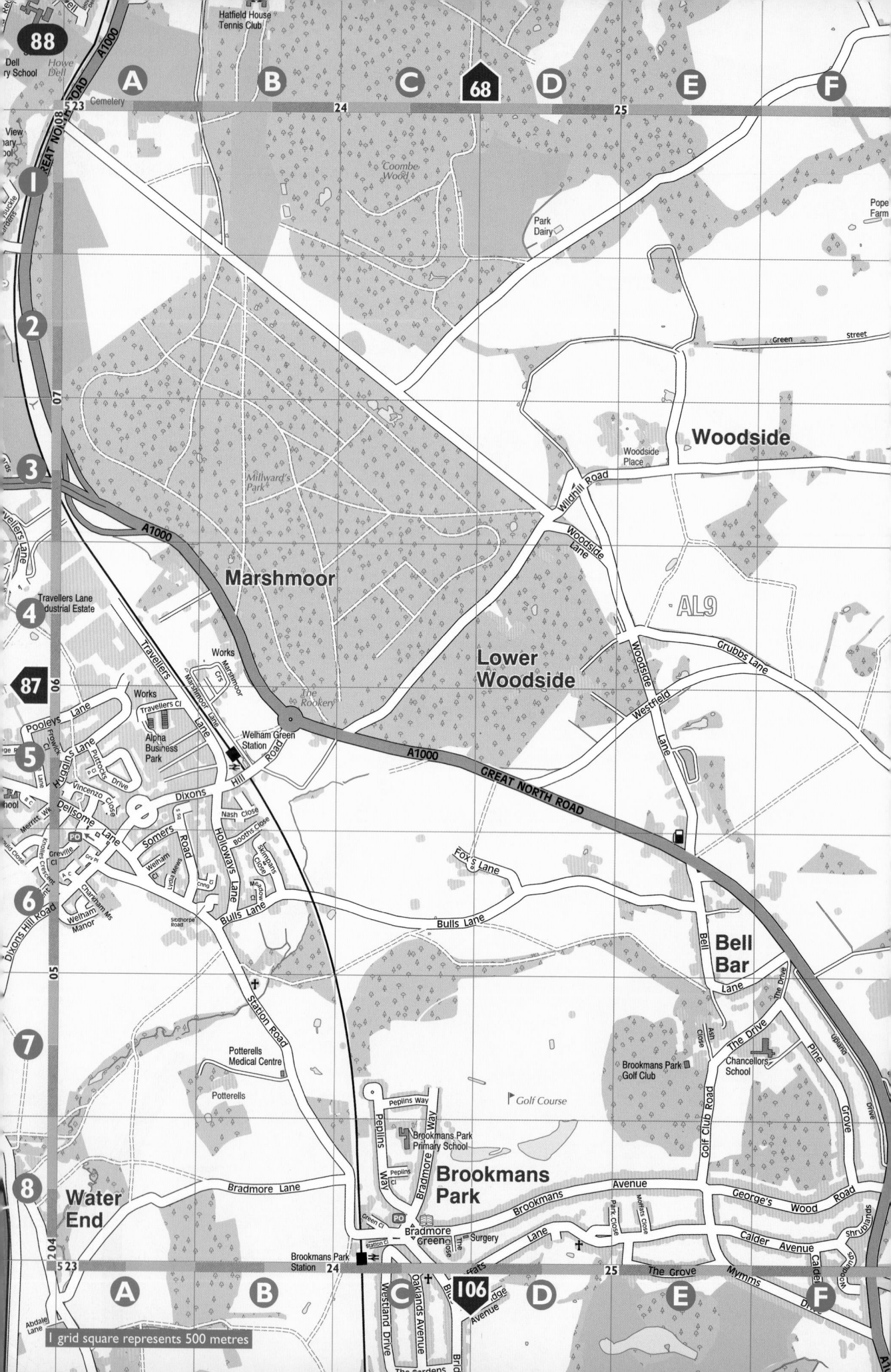

Farm
Bedwell Av

Church

Little Berkhamsted La
Orchard Close

Essendon Place

Bedwell Park

Golf Course

Hatfield London Country Club

Little Berkhamsted

I

Little Berkhamsted Lane

Chain

Bedwell Lodge Farm

2

Woodcock Lodge

Camfield Place

Cucumber Hall Farm

Wildhill

3

Kentish Lane

Hornbeam Lane

Cucumber Lane

Warrenwood Park

Tylers Causeway

Woodcock Farm

4

Tylers Caus

Woodhill House

90

Woodfield Lane

5

Grubbs Lane

Woodfield Farm

Coldharbour Farm

Kentish Lane Farm

Barbers Lodge Farm

New Farr

6

B158

Kentish Lane

7

Great Wood

Justice Hill

Great Wood Country Park

8

Grimes

B157

SHEPHERDS WAY

Lysley Pl
Ramsey Cl

Woodlands

THE RIDGEWAY

The Ridgeway

Th Ridgeway

B157

Fanshaws

G   H   J   71   K   L   M

33   34   35   08

Brickendon

Cowheath Wood

1

Cock

Broxbourne Wood National Nature Reserve

Broxbourne Wood

2

07

Cold Hall

Pembridge Lane

Wood House Lane

Ettriidge Farm

Paradise Wildlife Park

3

Carneles Green

White Stubbs Lane

Church Lane

Bencroft Wood

Emanual Pollards

4

06

Westlea

Wormley West End

West End Road

92

Holy Cross Hill

Wo 5 ley

Beaumont Road

Beaumont Manor

Bread and Cheese Lane

Thunderfield Grove

Park Lane Paradise

Factory Farm

6

05

Tanfield Stud Farm

7

Nightingale Rd

Dahlia Close

Bread & Cheese La

Hammondstreet Road

dstreet Road

Lovering Rd

Markham Road

Burgess Cl

Wilkinson Cl

Wells

Bloomfield Rd

Smiths Lane

Appleby Street

Pear Tree Walk

Sheldon Close

Maycroft Road

Spencer Avenue

Highfield Road

Willow Close

Hammond Close

Brandon Rd

Lower Shott

Upr Shott

Hilltop

Holbeck Lane

Wells Cleys

Adamsfield

Bencroft

Springwood

Cheshunt Park

8

04

Broadgreen Rd

Ferney Rd

Watercress Rd

Catisfield

Stockbridge

Nutwood Gdns

Oaklands Rd

Mountview Road

Smarts Cre

Fleming

Hammond Street

2

G   H   33   J   109   K   34   L   M   35

Argent Way

Crouch Lane

Biggs Gv

Jepps

Cacia Close

Peakes Way

Crouch

Rags Lane

Dig Dag Hill

Cavell Road

Caveli

Cowles

Byron

Longfield Lane

Spencer

Flamsted End Primary School

Rumsley

Blackdale

Park Lane

Mundens

Morse

Debenham Rd

St Pauls RC Primary School

Cheshunt Park Golf Club

Lucas

Fairfields Primary Sch

G
H
Nazeing Mead
J
73
K
L
M
I
Royd
Ham
39
40
41
08

P Esse
Dobb's Weir
P Dobb's
Avenue Rd
Blythe Rd
Clyde Road
Derby Road
Eldon Road
Road
Industrial Estate

Lee Valley Caravan Park

Hertfordshire County
Essex County

Broxbourne Sailing Club
Meadgate
Meadgate Road
Meadgate Works

Hamlet Hill
Sedge Green

Stoneshot Common

Hamlet Hil
Barn Hill

2
07

Sedge Green

Hoe Lane

3

Nazeing Glass Industrial Estate

Nazein

Peck's Hill
Maplecroft Lane
Lake Road
John Eliot Close
Highland Road
Banes down
North Street

Hillgrove Business Park

Shooters Drive
Palmers Grove Lane
Hoe Sunnyside
Hoe Lane

4
BACK

Old Nazeing Road

Western Road
Wheeler's Close
Barnfield Close
Worn

94
N P

Elizabeth Close
N Cl
PO
Middle St
Mayflower Close
Crooked Way
Hyde Mead

06

Elizabeth Close

Stort Valley Way

5

Lower Nazeing

Pound Close
Nazeing CP School
Barnard Acres
Tovey Close
Middle Street

Curtis Farm
Middle

Golf Cou

Tatsfield Avenue

Perry Hill

Perry Hill

Street

Nazeing Golf Club

6
05

St Leonards

Bumble's Green

Council Building

Na Ga

Paynes Lane

ST LEONARDS ROAD

St Leonards Road

Laundry Lane

Waltham Road
Allnams Cl
Bumbles Gn Lane
The Hts

7
204

Nazeing Long Green

Coleman's Lane

Felsteads

Waltham Road

8

Holyfield Hall Farm
38
39
Marsh Hill House
194
III
Galleyhill Green

G
H
MARSH H
J
III
K
L
M
40
41

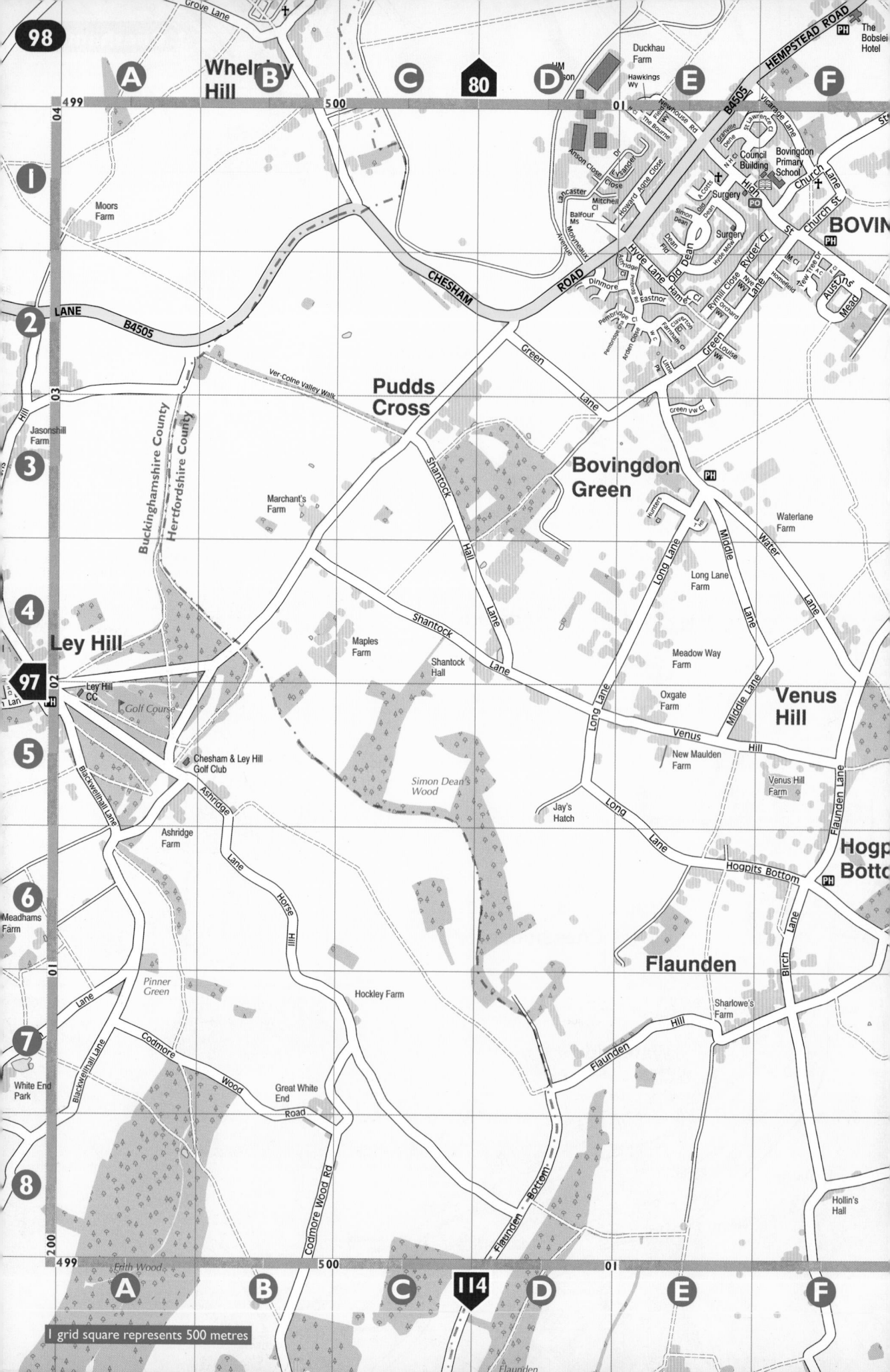

Grove Lane

Whelpley Hill

A   **B**   **C**   80   **D**   **E**   **F**

499   500   01

HEMPSTEAD ROAD   PH   The Bobslei Hotel

I

Moors Farm

04

LANE   B4505

2

Duckhau Farm

Hawkings Wy

UM son

Newhouse Rd

The Bourne

Granville Dene

St Lawrence La

Vicarage Lane

B4505

Anson Close/ Close

Council Building

Bovingdon Primary School

Church La

Lancaster Cl

Mitchell Cl

Balfour Ms

Howard Agne Close

A Cotts

Surgery

PO

High St

Church St

Dean Fld

Surgery

BOVIN

Maylands

Avenue

Hyde Lane

Ashridge more

Old Dean

simon Dean

Ryder Cr

Tew Tree Dr

PH

M Cl

03

CHESHAM

Dinmore

ROAD

Eastnor

Pembridge Cl

Pentridge Ct

Arden Close

Farnham

Hyde Mew

Ham Cl

Rymill Close Wy

Orchard

Green Wk

Louise Wk

Austins Mead

Homefield

Ver-Colne Valley Walk

Green

Pudds Cross

Lane

Green VW Cl

Hill

3

Jasonshill Farm

Shantock

Hall

Lane

Bovingdon Green

Hunters Cl

T Hill

PH

Waterlane Farm

Marchant's Farm

Long Lane

Middle

Water

Ley Hill

Maples Farm

Shantock

Lane

Long Lane Farm

Lane

4

Shantock Hall

02

Meadow Way Farm

Lane

Venus Hill

Ley Hill Lan

PH

Ley Hill CC

Golf Course

Oxgate Farm

Venus

Hill

97

Buckinghamshire County

Hertfordshire County

Venus Hill Farm

5

Chesham & Ley Hill Golf Club

New Maulden Farm

Middle Lane

Flaunden Lane

Blackwellhall Lane

Ashridge

Ashridge Farm

Simon Dean's Wood

Jay's Hatch

Long

Lane

Hogp Botto

Hogpits Bottom

PH

6

Meadhams Farm

01

Horse

Hill

Lane

Flaunden

Birch

Lane

Pinner Green

Hockley Farm

Sharlowe's Farm

7

Lane

Codmore

White End Park

Wood

Great White End Road

Codmore Wood Rd

Flaunden

Hill

Flaunden Bottom

8

Hollin's Hall

Erith Wood

200

499   500   01

A   **B**   **C**   114   **D**   **E**   **F**

Flaunden

1 grid square represents 500 metres

G H J **81** K L M 03 04 05

I

2

3

4

100

5

6

7

8

Phasels Wood

Rucklers Lane

DON

Longcroft Lane

Lane Farm

Flaunden Lane

Nuffield Farm

Copse Hill Cl

Chipperfield Rd

Bulstrode

Bulstrode Lane

Bulstrode Cl

Flaunden Lane

Rucklers Lane

Scatterdells Wood

Tower Hill

Wyevale Garden Centre

Tower Hill

New Road

Tenements Farm

Stoney Lane

Lane

Megg Lane

Wayside

Meggacres Farm

Cottingham Farm

Tuffs Farm

Chipperfield House

Scatterdells Lane

Croft Meadow

Croft End Rd

Croft Fld

Cft

Croft

Courtlands

Langley Road

Holly

Braziers Farm

Chapel Croft

Croft Lane

Alexandra Rd

Chipperfield

Hedges

Lane

Woodman's Wood

Pale Farm

The Two Brewers Hotel

The Street

Havenfield

Kings Lane

King's Cl

Lower Plantation

Woodmans Farm

Forge

St Pauls Prim School

PH

Belsize

Ollebertie Lane

Cherry Trees Farm

Dunny Lane

Rose Farm

Windmill Hill

Windmill Hl

Queen St

The Common

The Common

Chipperfield Common

Hollow Hedge

Ltl Windmill Hl

Penman's Green

Callipers Hall

Whitedell Farm

Flaunden

PH

Lane

Poles Hill

Belsize Farm

Hillmeads Farm

Bragmans

Lane

Rose Hall Farm

Plough Lane

PH

Quickmoor Lane

Moonshine Farm

Rosehall Woods

Great Sarratt Hall

Commonwood

Sarratt

G H J 83 K L M

Bedmond

Leavesden
Green

Abbots
Langley

Woodside

Kingswood

G H J 117 K L M Garst

1 2 3 4 W 102 5 6 7 8

G   H   J   93   K   L   M

I

Claverhambury

Holyfield Hall
Farm

2

Lee Valley
Park Farms

Hayes Hill
Farm

Galleyhill Green

Marsh Hill
House

MARSH HILL B194

Galleyhill
Wood

Aimes
Green

Claverhambury Road

Holyfield

HOLYFIELD ROAD B194

3

Monkhams
Hall

Claverhambury Road

Deerpark
Wood

EN9

CROOKED MILE B194

Dallance
House

Breach   Barns   Lane

Breach
Barns

4

Breaches
Farm

Galleyhill Road

Warlies
Park

5

P

6

Marle
Gardens

Valley Close

WALTHAM
ABBEY

Pick Hill
Farm

PICK

Amesbury

Homefield

Maple
Springs

Parklands

Hewins
Close

Drayson Close

Parvills

Newlesswell Dr

Paternoster Hill

Upshire
Road

Buxton Road

Princesfield Rd

St
Thomas's

Horse

Congreve Road

King Harold
School

Paternoster Close

Upshire
Ninefields

Upshire
Primary
School

VIEW B194

P

Crooked Mile

Waltham Holy
Cross Infant
School

Thaxted Way

The Gladeway

Broomstick Hall Road

Eastbrook Road

Rounton Road

Amwell Court

Badburgham
Court

Ninefields

Farmer Ct

7

Woodgre

Tudor Wy

Monkswood Avenue

Halfhides

Woodbrook
Gardens

Rosebank

Honey
Brook

Mason Cl

Cullings
Court

Mallion
Court

St Lawrence
CE Sch

Fullers

Stanway Rd

Abbots Dr

Theydon
Court

Surgery
Council
Building
Museum

Farm Hill Road

Quaker Lane

Howard Business
Park

Howard
Close

Rochford Avenue

Oak Road

Elm Close

Honey Lane

Meadowcross

Hillhouse CE VC
Primary
School

Hillhouse

Shernbroke Road

Peresfield
Rd

Osprey

Woodford

Read

8

Town Mead

Woollard
Street

Harveyfields

Denny Avenue

Roundhills

Springfields

Ruskin Av

Witham Cl

Morris Court

Haywood
Court

Gant Court

Caterham
Court

Shernbroke

Merlin

Farthingale Lane

Kestrel Rd

Wren Dr

Old Shire Lane

Honeypot

Cemetery

Caldbeck

The
Dale

Roundhills

Pinnacles

The Leverton
Infant Sch

The
Leverton
Junior Sch

Waltham Abbey
Marriott Hotel

the
Birches

Southend Lane

Cemetery

G   H   J   127   K   L   M

Works

Quinton Way

Waltham Abbey
Swimming Pool

Gilsland

M25

Lodge Lane

Beechfield Wk

M25

Honey Lane

HONE

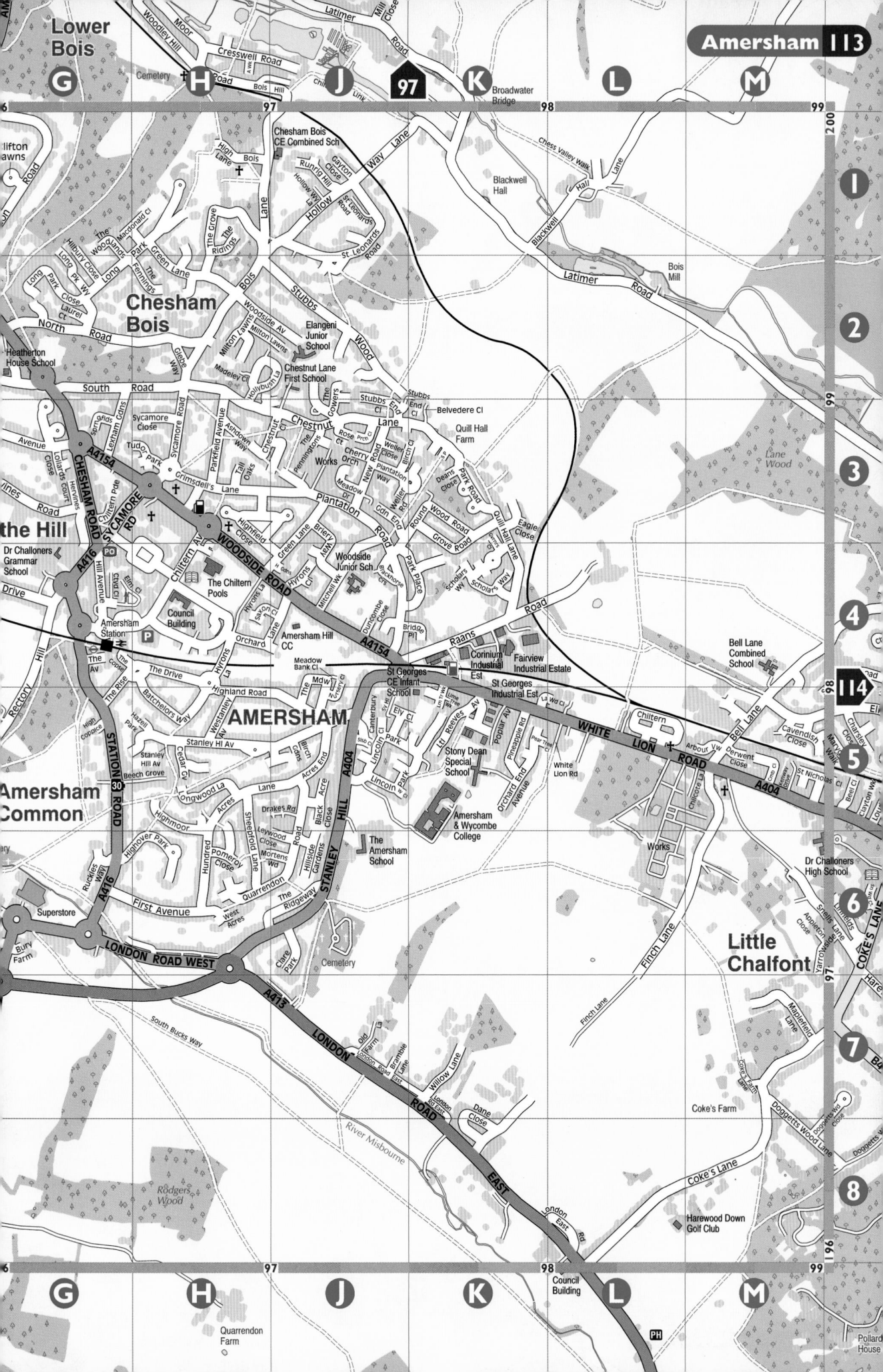

499 · 200 · 500 · 01

A · B · C · 98 · D · E · F

1

Frith Wood

2

Chess Valley Walk

The Chess

The Grove

The Ridings

Spring Close

The Grove

Latimer House

Flaunden Bottom

Flaunden Bottom

Martin Top Farm

Baldwin's Wood

3

Latimer Park Farm

Chess Valley Walk

Chess Valley Walk

Latimer

Mill Farm

Latimer Road

Latimer Road

Chenies Place

Chenies School

Chenies Manor House

Holloway

4

Chandos Close

Beechwood Avenue

Boughton

Pavilion Way

Chenies Ave

Avenue

Westwood Close

Chess Va Walk

Stoits Lane

Garden Centre

Bedford Cl

The Bed Hotel

Chandycroft Road

Kiln

Charsley

Elizabeth

Latimer Close

Westwood Drive

Farm Close

Chessfield Park

Westwood

5

Cavendish Close

Maryola Walk

Nicholas Cl

Beel Cl

Beechwood Cl

Russell Close

Chalfont Av

Bedford Avenue

Amersham Way

AMERSHAM ROAD

A404

Church Grove

Little Chalfont Primary School

Avenue

Oakington

Clayton Wy

Loudhams Road

Appenfield

Surg

PO

30

A404

Chalfont & Latimer Stn.

CHALFONT STN RD

Village Way

Little Chalfont Golf Club

6

Dr Challoners High School

Spells Lane

Linfields

The Hawthorns

COKE'S LANE

Burtons Lane

Loudhams Wood Lane

Golf Course

Lodge Lane

Lodge Farm

7

Maplefield

Appletree

Harewood Road

B4442

Burton's Way

Birkett Way

Burtons Lane

Park CV

Long Walk

New Road

Burtons Lane

Burton's Farm

Whitelands

8

Doggetts Wood Lane

Doggetts Way Close

Doggetts Wood Lane

Newhouse Farm

St Peters Way

Carpenters Wood Close

The Russell School

Blacketts Wd

Blacketts Dr

Grove Lane

Dovewood Close

Chalfont Lane

499 · 500 · 01

A · B · NIGHTINGALES · C · 128 · D · Burtons Lane · E · F

Chorleywood West

1 grid square represents 500 metres

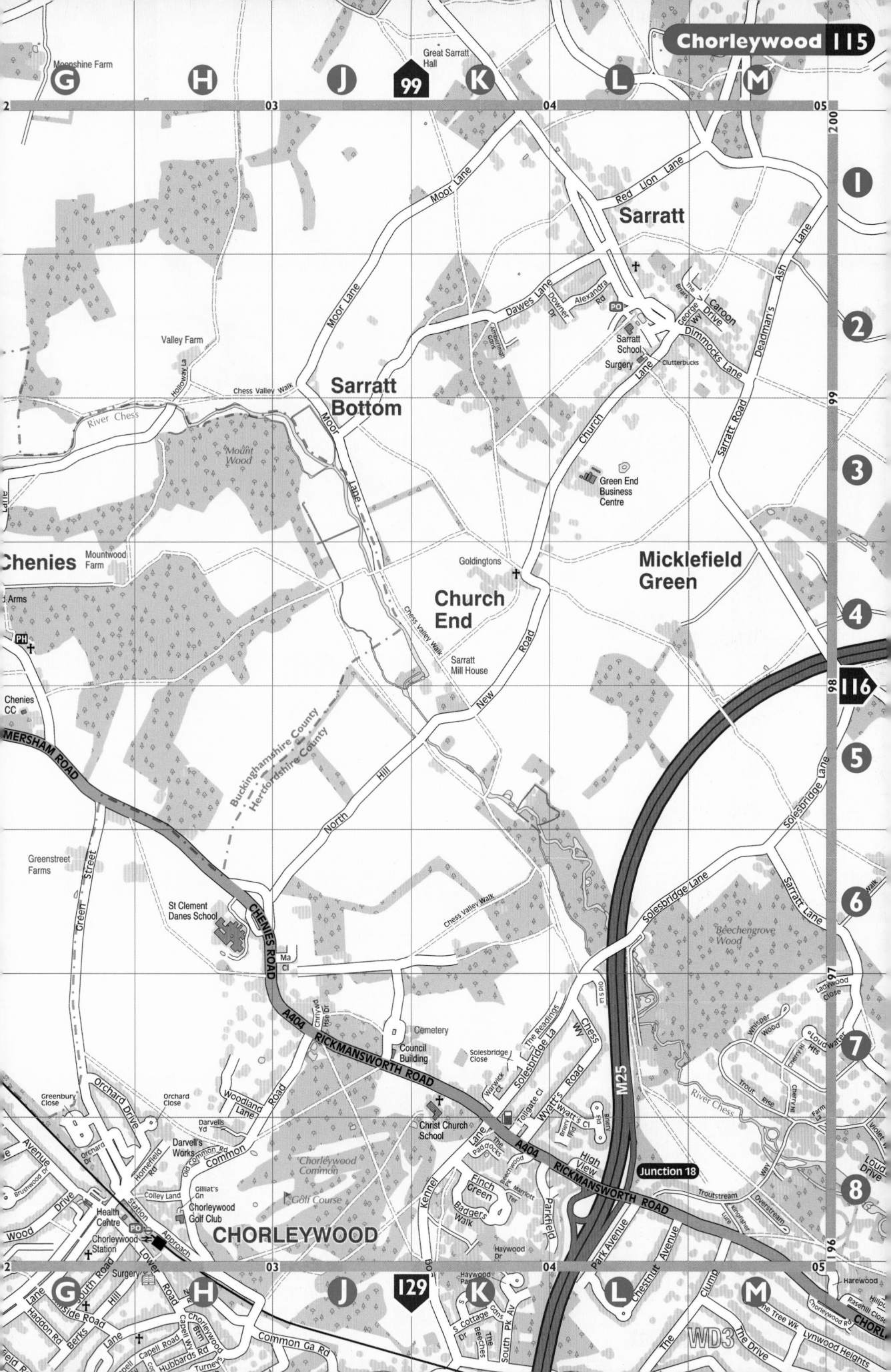

G H J 99 K L M

2 03 04 05 200

I

Moonshine Farm

Great Sarratt Hall

Sarratt

Red Lion Lane

2

Valley Farm

Chess Valley Walk

Holloway La

Dawes Lane

Downer W

Alexandra Rd

PO

George Dr

Caroon Drive

Ash Lane

Deadman's Lane

Dimmocks Lane

The Bratts

Sarratt Bottom

River Chess

Moor Lane

Mount Wood

Moor Lane

Sarratt School

Surgery

Clutterbucks

Sarratt Road

3

Mountwood Farm

Green End Business Centre

Micklefield Green

99

Chenies

Goldingtons

Church Road

4

Arms

PH

Chenies CC

Church End

Sarratt Mill House

New Road

98 116

MERSHAM ROAD

Buckinghamshire County

Hertfordshire County

North Hill

Solesbridge Lane

Sarratt Lane

5

Greenstreet Farms

Green Street

Chess Valley Walk

St Clement Danes School

Chenies Road

Beechengrove Wood

Solesbridge Lane

Walk

6

97

Ladywood Close

Greenbury Close

Orchard Drive

Orchard Close

A404 RICKMANSWORTH ROAD

Ma Cl

Cemetery

Council Building

Solesbridge Close

The Readings

Solesbridge La

Old S La

Chess Wy

M25

Whisper Wood

Loudwater Hts

Loudwater

River Chess

Trout Rise

Cherry Tree

Way

Violet Dr

7

Darvell's Yd

Darvell's Works

Old Common Rd

Common

Woodland Lane

Woodland Road

Christ Church School

Warrick Cl

Wyatt's Road

Wyatt's Cl

Briery Wy

Briery Fld

Chess Wy

Toolgate Cl

High View

Troutstream

Kingfisher

Overstream

8

96

Brunswick Dr

Avenue

Homefield Rd

Colley Land

Gilliat's Gn

Chorleywood Golf Club

Chorleywood Common

Golf Course

Kennel Lane

Finch Green

Badgers Walk

Marriott Ter

Paddocks

Parkfield

Junction 18

Park Avenue

Chestnut Avenue

Clump

The Drive

Chorleywood Heights

Health Centre

PO

Chorleywood Station

Surgery

Approach

Lower Road

Station Road

CHORLEYWOOD

Haywood Walk

Haywood Dr

A404 RICKMANSWORTH ROAD

CHORI

Rasehill Close

Harewood

Lynwood Heights

G H J 129 K L M

Wood

Haddon Rd

Berks Lane

Hill

Capell Rd

Chorleywood Bottom

Capell Way

Hubbards Rd

Common Ga Rd

Turneys

Field Rd

S Cottage Dr

The Beeches

S Park Av

Cons La

Gons La

The South

The Tree Wk

WD3

Chorleywood Cl

CHORL

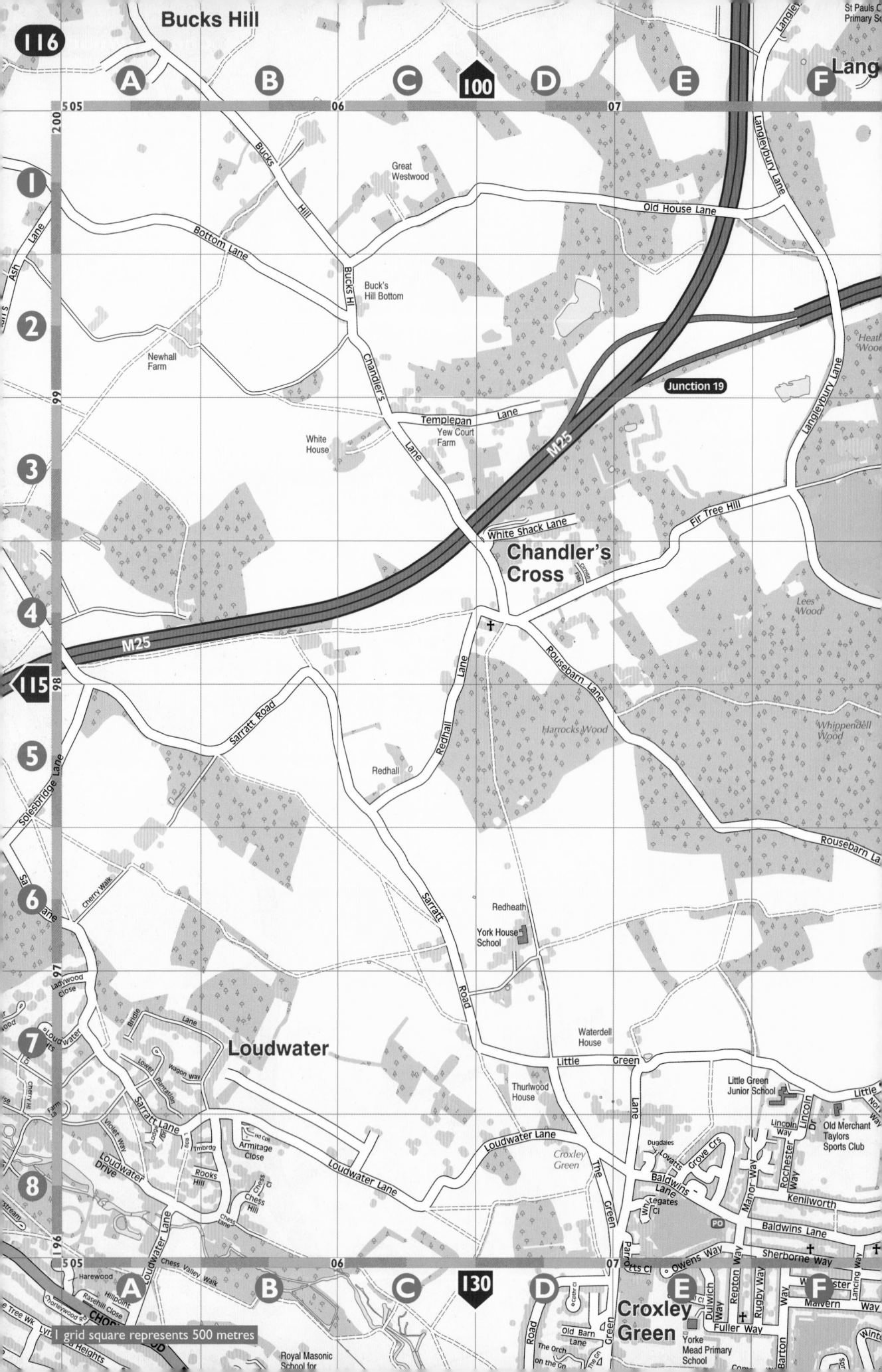

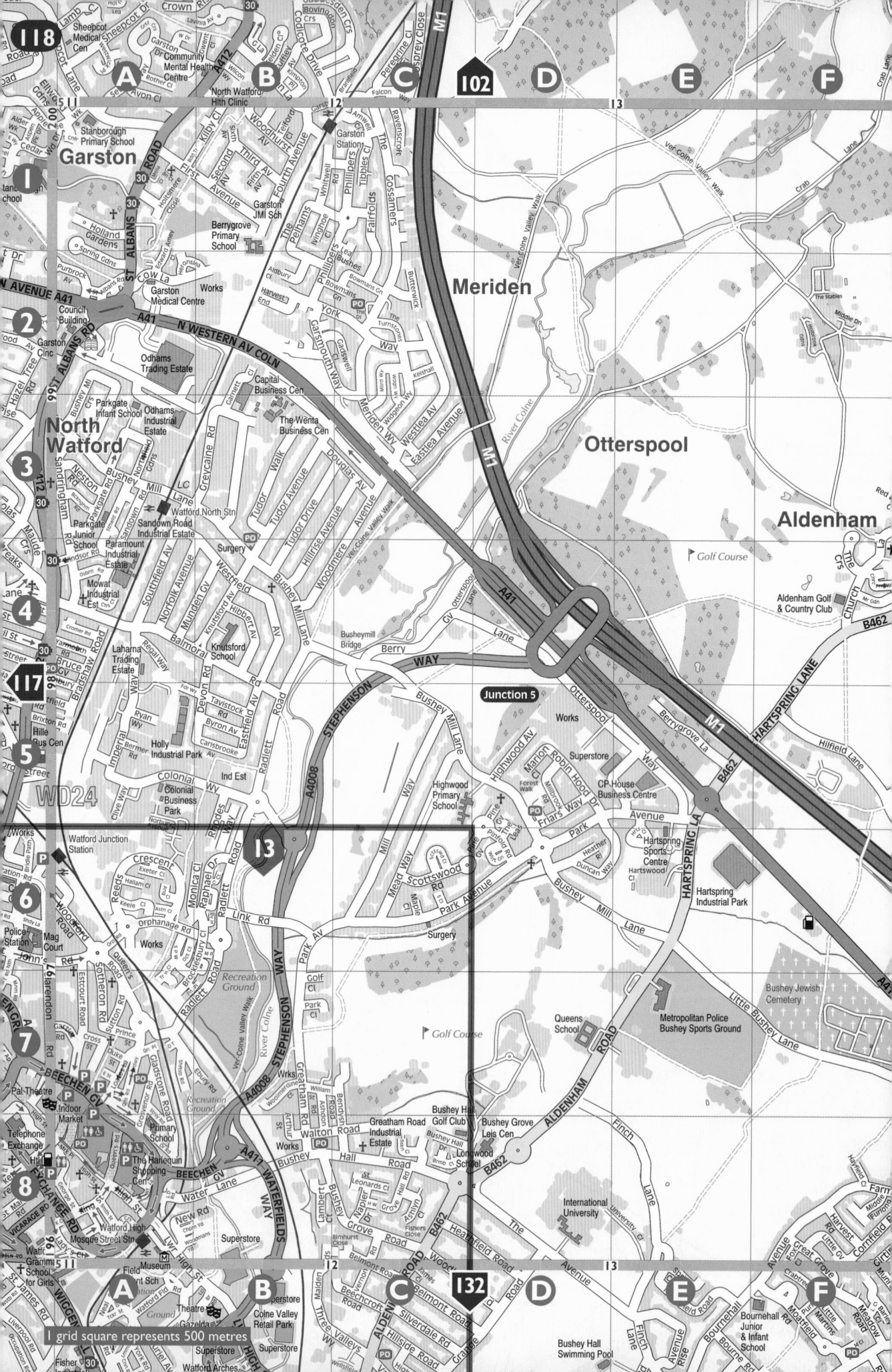

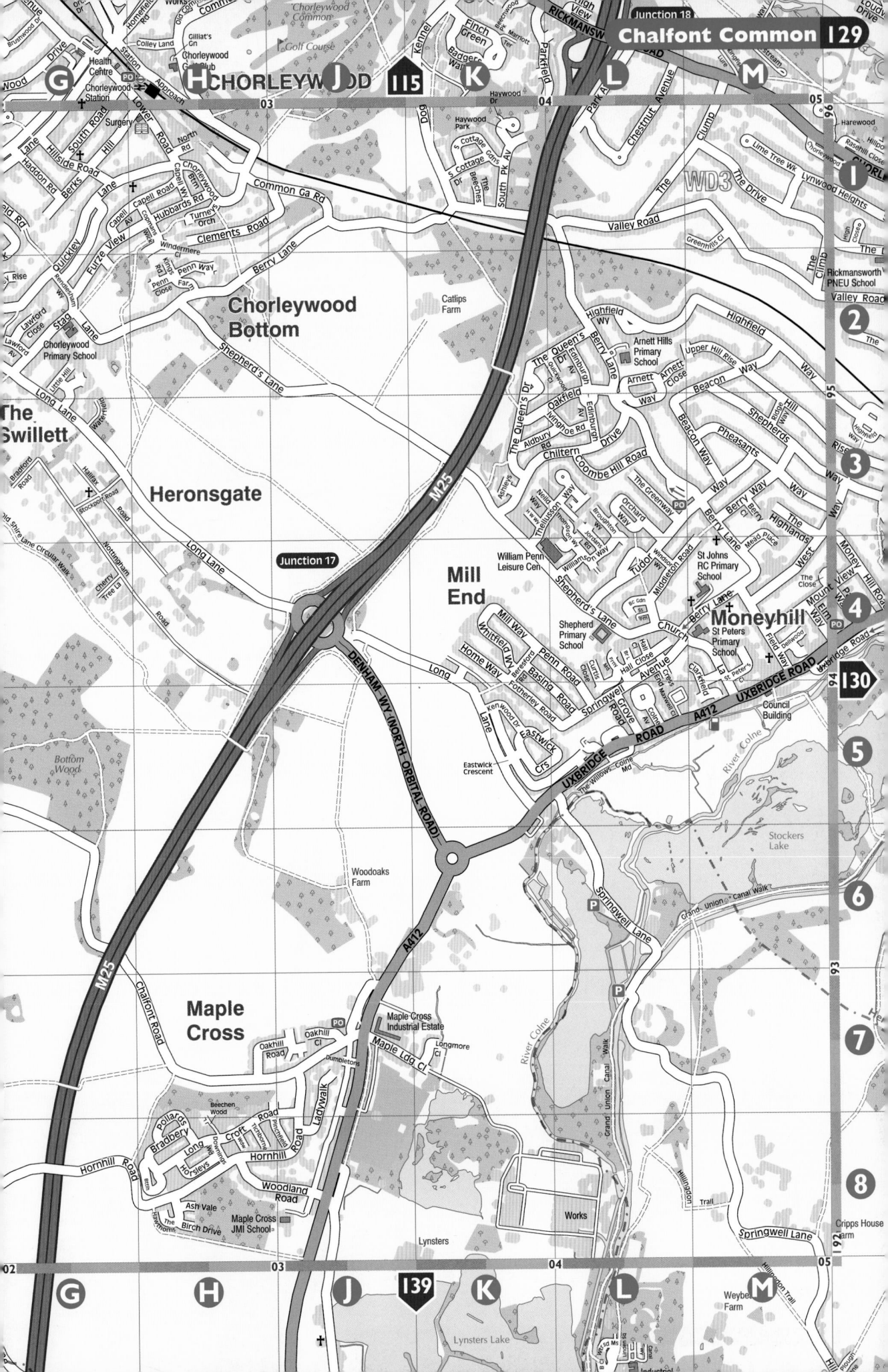

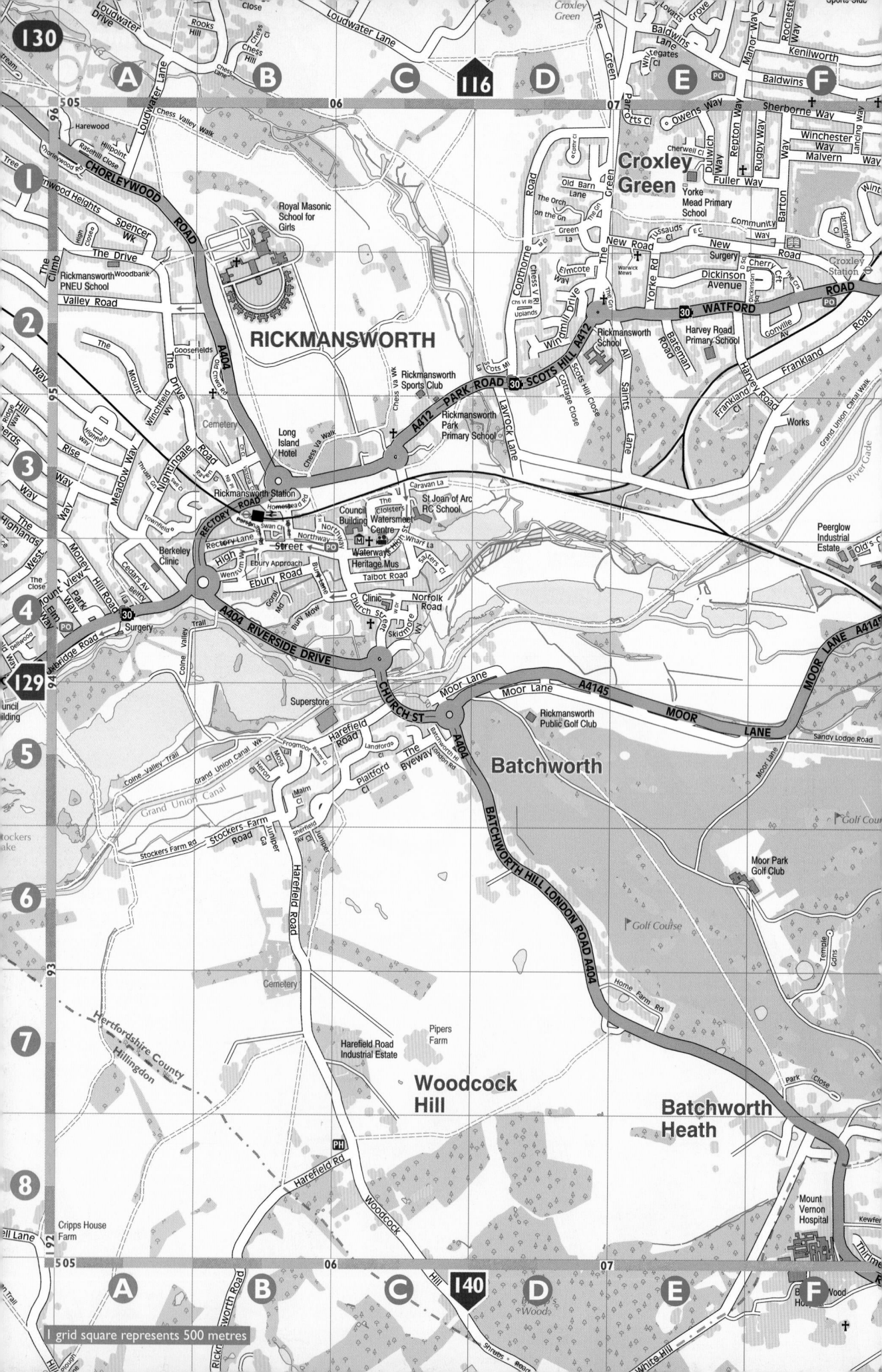

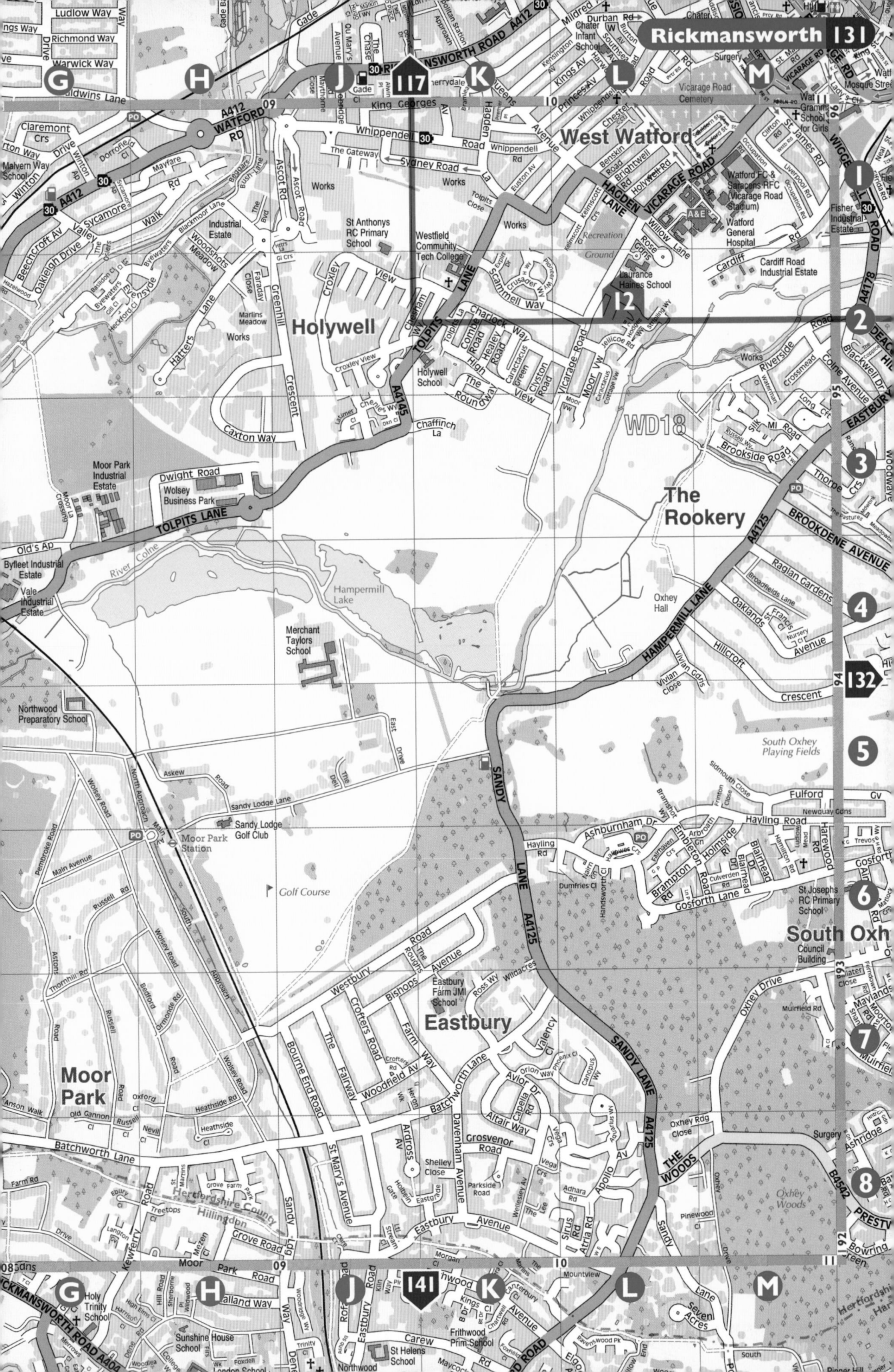

A   B   C   130   D   E   F

05   06   07

92

1   Plough Lane

Cripps House Farm

well Lane

Hill End

Rickmansworth Rd

Harefield Rd

Woodc

Hill

Bishop's Wood

Shrub Road

Northwood Rd

Winks Hill

Jackets Lane

Jackets Lane

Bishops Wood Hospital

Mount Vernon

Equestrian Centre

Manor Ho Drive

Hirst

A4180 DU

2   Harefield Grove

Sanctuary Close

Rickmansworth Rd

Hall Dr   Barden Cl   Hall Dr

Chapel Row   Cn

John Penrose Sports Centre   The Harefield Academy

John Penrose School

Northwood Road

Shepherds Hill House

Iveagh Cl

Ducks Hill Road

Kingfisher Cl

Fringewood Cl

Dykes Dr

3   unt   easant

Harefield Hospital

Harefield Health Centre

Newdigate Road

Park Rd   New

Vernon Drive

Newdigate Rd E

Adrian Close

Northwood Way

Ash Grove

Spring   Ash

Mossendew Cl

Ash Grove

Fallowfield Close

Harefield School

Olivia Gdns

Leys Close

Savoy   Cl

Gilbert Road   Cres

Sullivan   Knightscote Close

Dunster Cl

Harefield Inf Sch

Merle Av

Harefield CC

Pond

4   Dovedale Cl   High Street   Lewis Cl   Dexter Rd   Morse Cl

Childs Av

Manor Ct

Harefield

Knightscote Farm

5   139   Cntss Cl   Lovett

30

Breakspear Road North

Hillingdon Trail

Bourne Farm

Youngwood Farm

Breakspear House

6   Walk   St Mary's Road   St Mary's Close   Mary's Road   St Annes Road   Church Road   Church Hill   30

Broadwater La   Sedley Gv   Ivy Close   Gore Cl   Peerless   Harvil Road

Broadwater Gdns

Park Lodge Farm

Hillingdon Trail

Hillingdon Trail

Mad Bess Wood

Bayhurst Wood Country Park

Breakspear Road North

7   Peerless Drive   Widewater Business Centre   Road   P   PO   Dellside   Hillside   Harvil Road

Priory Av   Truesdale Drive   Priory Gdns

South Harefield

Fine Bush Lane

Hillin Bord FC

8   ornail   Grand Union Canal Walk

Harvil Road

Highway Farm

Newyears Green Lane

Greystoke

Glovers Grove

88

05   06   07

A   B   C   D   E   Newyears Green   F

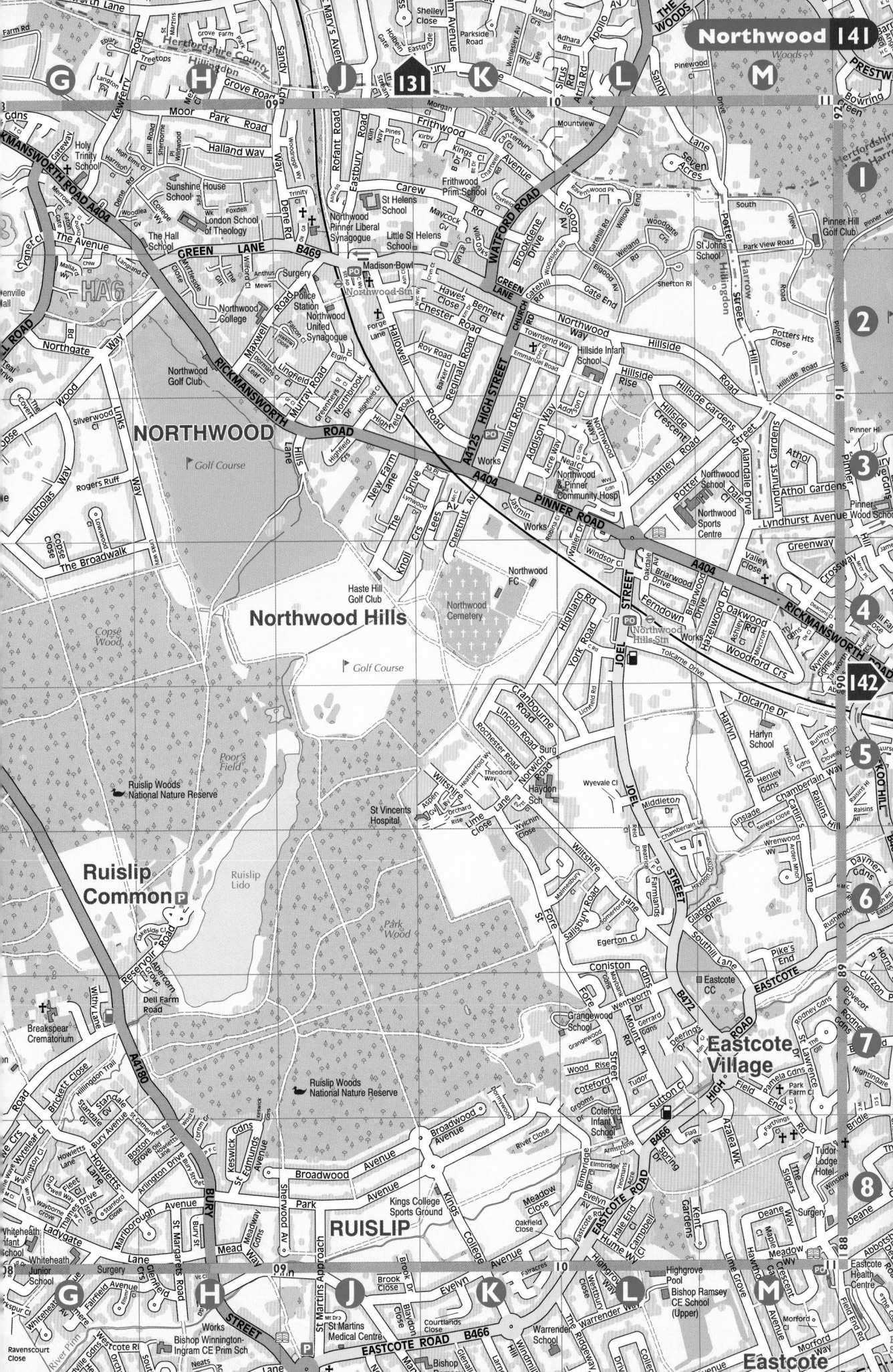

A B C D E F G H

5 22
46

1

West Sunderland
Farm

Sunderland
Hall Farm

Dunton
Fen

23

24

Sutton Road

Eyeworth

High Street

High Street

Sutton Road

2

45

3

Sutton Lane

Cambridge Road

Eyeworth Lodge
Farm

Newton

Boot Lane

Greenacres
Way

Kings Pond
Close

Lees
Close

Dunton

4

Park Corner
Farm

Lane

Biggleswade   Road

44

Dunton VC
Lower School

Hallpits

High Street

Church Street

Springfield

Lime Kiln
or
Fox Close

5

Millow Hall
Farm

Millow

6

43

Millowbury
Farm

7

8

42

Dunton Lodge
Farm

9

Bedfordshire County
Hertfordshire County

River River

River River

Edworth

Lower Farm

Manor
Farm

10

41

Manor
Farm

Hinxworth

Arnolds Lane

Ashwell
End

11

Francis Road

High Street

PH

Common

Love's
Lane

12

A1

40

5 22
A

23

24

Ashwell   Road

New Inn Road

Hinxworth Road

25

Love's
Farm

A B C D E F G H

Glebe
Farm

Pulter's
Farm

1 grid square represents 500 metres

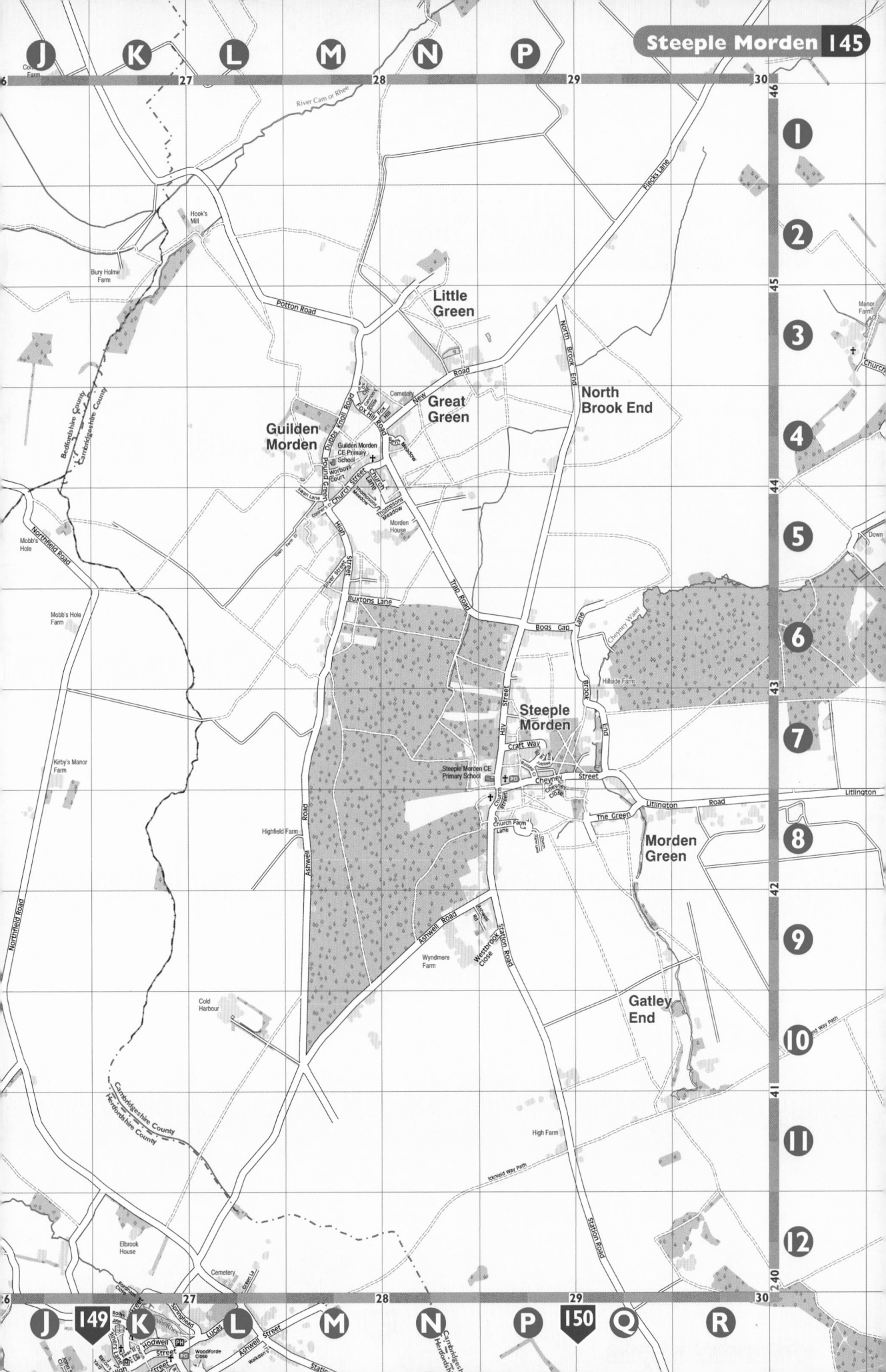

J K L M N P

1
2
3
4
5
6
7
8
9
10
11
12

Hook's Mill

Bury Holme Farm

Potton Road

Little Green

North Brook End

Great Green

North Brook End

Guilden Morden

Guilden Morden CE Primary School

Cemetery

Mobb's Hole

Mobb's Hole Farm

Buxtons Lane

Bogs Gap Lane

Cheyney Water

Hillside Farm

Steeple Morden

Kirby's Manor Farm

Highfield Farm

Steeple Morden CE Primary School

Craft Way

Cheyney Close

The Green

Litlington Road

Litlington

Morden Green

Church Farm Lane

Ashwell Road

Wyndmere Farm

Westbrook Close

Station Road

Gatley End

Cold Harbour

Northfield Road

Cambridgeshire County
Hertfordshire County

High Farm

Ichknield Way Path

Ickild Way Path

Elbrook House

Cemetery

J K L M N P **145** Q

End

Elbrook House

25   26   27   28

4   40

1

Love's Farm

Cambridgeshire County
Hertfordshire County

Surgery

High Street
Hodwell
Silver Street
Ashwell

2

39

Redlands Farm

Hinxworth Road

Colbron Cl

West End

Works

Ashwell Street

Dixie's Close

Partridge Hill

Newnham Way

Ickneild Way Path

Claybush Road

Kingsland Way

3

38

4

The Knoll

5

Pembroke Farm

Ashwell Road

Ickneild Way Path

SG7

6

Cat Ditch

Kingsland Way

37   **150**

Newnham Road

Newnham

PO

Hullockpit Hill

Ickneild Way Path

7

Park

Royston Road

70

A505

70

Bygrave

8

36

Manor House

9

Ashwell Road

Wedon Way

35

10

Lodge Farm

Ickneild Way Path

Great North Road

Blackhorse Farm

Royston Road

A505

Hall Way Farm

11

Salisbury Road
A507

Ashville Trading Estate

Marquis Business Centre

B656

Rhee Spring

Baldock Station

Yeomanry Drive

Royston Road

40

Orwell View

Wallington Road

12

234

Works

Ickneild Way

B656

Hartsfield Primary School

Cloth Common

24   25   26   27   **18**   28

J **17** K L M N P Q R

Baldock

I grid square represents 500 metres

A B C D E F G H

5 04   05   06   07

32

I

31   2

3

Harlington

30   4

5

29   6

7

28   8

Upper
Sundon   9

27   10

Lower Sundon   11

226   12

5 04   05   06   07

A B C D E F G H

Sampshill Road

Sampshill
Farm

Grange
Farm

Harlington Road

Harlington Upper
School

Lower
School
Wingate

Goswell End Road

Lincoln Way
Brian Road

Church Road
Barton Road

Cemetery

Manor
Close

Station Road

East End
Farms

Harlington Road

Sharpenhoe

Pyghtle
School

Priory
Farm

Barton Road

Brook End
Green Farm

Sharpenhoe Road

Faldo
Farm

Barton
Industrial
Estate

Faldo Road

Wood
Farm

Sundon Road

Dyer's Hall
Farm

Moleskin

Sharpenhoe Road

John Bunyan Trail

Icknield Way Path

Bartonhill
Cutting

Sundon Hills
Country Park

Icknield Way Path

Icknield
Way Path

Icknield Way Path

John Bunyan Trail

Church Road

Churchill Cl

Stanley

Streatley

Holtwood
Farm

Streatley Road

Sundon Road

Bury
Sharpenhoe Road

Sharpenhoe
Rd

Harlington Rd

Harlington Road

Common
La

State
Hall

Sundon
Lower
School

Hillside Vw
Church Road

Streatley Road

Manor Road

Luton Road A6

Luton Road A6

Barton Road

George
Wood

Manor Road

Manor
Farm

Sundon Road

Great
Bramingham
Farm

Great Bramingham Lane

John Bunyan Trail

Bramingham

Hayton
Close

LU3

Pinewood Cl

Chestnut
Way

Sundon Park Junior
School

Whitehaven

Whitehorse Vale

Bramingham
Primary
School

Chalton Cross
Farm

A B C D E F G H

5 04   05   06   07

27

J K L M N P Q

I
2
3
4
5
6
156
7
8
9
10
11
12

Westhey Manor

Higham Road

Hexton Common

Shillington Manor

Hertfordshire County

Bedfordshire County

Higham Road

York Close

Hanover Road
Windsor Road
Bedford Road
Sturt Road
Cumberland
Normal Road
Hastings Road
Dane Road

Manor Road

Grays Close

Dunstall Road

Arnold Close

BARTON-LE-CLAY

John Bunyan Trail

John Bunyan Trail

Mill Lane

Manor Farm

Hexton

Bury Farm

Hexton Manor

Pegsdon

B655

Ramsey Manor Lower School

Arnold Middle School

PH
PO

Hexton Primary School

HITCHIN RD
Pegsdon

B655

Orchard Close

B655 HEXTON ROAD

BARTON ROAD

BARTON ROAD

Orchard School

Cemetery

Church Road

John Bunyan Trail

Barton Hills National Nature Reserve

Ravensburgh Castle ✕

The Meg

Jeremiah's Tree

Gravel Hill

Fairy Hole

Bedfordshire County
Hertfordshire County

Ramsey Way Path

John Bunyan Trail

Barton Hill Farm

Morgrove Farm

John Bunyan Trail

Hexton Road

Lilley Hoo

Icknield Way Path

Hertfordshire County
Bedfordshire County

Lilley Manor Farm

New Farm

Pond Farm

Ward's Farm

Hexton Road

Golf Course

Icknield Way Path

John Bunyan Trail

Hertfordshire County
Bedfordshire County

Ward's Wood

Lilley

Gn Acres

South Bedfordshire Golf Club

John Bunyan Trail

West Street

Lilley Wood

BARTON ROAD

Turnpike

Cardinal Newman Catholic Secondary School

Warden Hill Rd

Dog Kennel Farm

A505

HILL

32 31 30 29 28 27 226

09   10   11   12

I grid square represents 500 metres

A   B   C   D   **151**   E   F   G   H

5 32   33   34   35

Rushden Rd

Rushden Road

Chain Walk

Sandon JM School

Slate Hall Farm

Bull Lane

HILL VIEW

Back Lane

Bucklan

1

Roe Green

Beckfield Lane

Green End

Whiteley Lane

Hodenhoe Manor

2

Beckfield Farm

Chain Walk

River Rib

Friars

3

Mill End

Hyde Hall Farm

A10

ERMINE STREET

Wood Farm

Lye End Farm

Chipping

4

The Sq

Royal Oak Cl

Chain Walk

19

32

Whitehall

5

Broadfield Lodge Farm

Ermine St

Steward's Ley

6

31

Chain Walk

Broadfield Hall

A10

7

Middle Farm

Lower Farm

Southfields Farm

Throcking Lane

8

30

Foxholes

Park Farm Industrial Estate

Throcking

Freman College

9

Coles Green Farm

Chain Walk

Throcking Road

Cottered Road

A10

Edwinstree School

The Pyghtle

Cottered

BALDOCK ROAD

Tylers Close

Longmead

BALDOCK ROA

10

PH

The Crescent

A507

A507

Buttermill Farm

The Fort

23

29

B1037

Brook End

Flanders Green

Tudor Stud

11

Chain Walk

12

Warren Lane

Spring Lane

Cottered Warren

Tannis Court

Aspende

2 28

5 32   33   34   35

Berkesdon Green

A   B   C   D   **162**   E   F   G   H

1 grid square represents 500 metres

J K L M 152 N P Q

LONDON ROAD

6 37 38 39 40 34

1

North End Farm

Barkway Equestrian Centre

Golf Course

Bandons Farm

2

Moats Rd

33

BIGGIN HILL

Biggin Manor

3

Anstey First School

Cave Gate Cottages

Sports La

B1368

River Quin

4

Snow Ed

Lincoln Hill

32

Wyddial

New Barns Cottages

5

Cherry Orchard Lane

Moles Lane

Beauchamps

Silkmead Farm

31

6

Silkmead Farm Industrial Estate

B1368

160

Moles Farm

7

Anderson's La

Bradbury Farm

Hall Lane

8

SG9

Halfacre Lane

B1038

Works

30

Hormead Primary School

Willow Green Park

Gt Ho

Vicarage Road

The Causeway

B1038

9

B1038

The

Layston First School

Garden Road

Hertfordshire Way

Cemetery

Hare Street Road

Hare Street

Great Hormead Bury

Hertfordshire Way

Baldock Road

Alswick Hall Farm

Hare Street Road

Horseshoe Lane

10

BUNTINGFORD

Little Hormead

Worsted Lane

Little Hormead Bury

Hertfordshire Way

Millfield First School

29

Mill Close

Snells Mead

The Street

Luynes

Knights Close

Owles Lane

Owles Hall

11

Watermill Industrial Estate

Owles Lane

London Road

B1368

Stonebury Farm

Dassel's Hill

Mutfords

12

A10

Hertfordshire Way

228

6 37 38 39 40

J K L M 163 N P Q R

Pinehill Farm

A   B   C   D   153   E   F   G   H

Langley
Lower
en
Waterwick Hill

New Farm

5 40   34   41   42   43

Essex County
Hertfordshire Cou

North
End Farm

I

River Stort

Bardons Farm

Scales Park

2   Cheapside

Montside

Anstey   Lower
Green

3   Anstey
First
School

33   Hertfordshire Way

Wood Lane

Snow   Coltsloot   Meesden   Mill
End   Lane

4   Lincoln
Hill

32   Anstey
Bury

New Barns
Cottages

5   Puttock's End

Cole
Green
Farm

6   Brick House
Farm

159   31   Brent Pelham   PUMP HILL

7   B1038   Borley Green
Cottage

Hartham
Common

8   CONDUIT LANE   B1038
Anderson's Lane
Hall Lane   The Causeway

Halfacre
Lane
30   B1038

Hormead
Primary
School   Great
Hormead

038   9   Willow Close   Park
Road
Hertfordshire   Way
Great
Hormead Bury   Hertfordshire   Way

Park   Road   Great
Hormead
Park   Whitebarns Lane

10   Little
Hormead Bury   Whitebarns

Lane   Little
Hertfordshire Way   Hormead

29   The   Street

11

River Ash

12   Mutfords   The   Street   Whitebarns Lane
Violets Lane
Hill
Furneux
Pelham

2 28   Hertfordshire Way

5 40   41   42   164   43   Barley
d

A   B   C   D   164   E   F   G   H

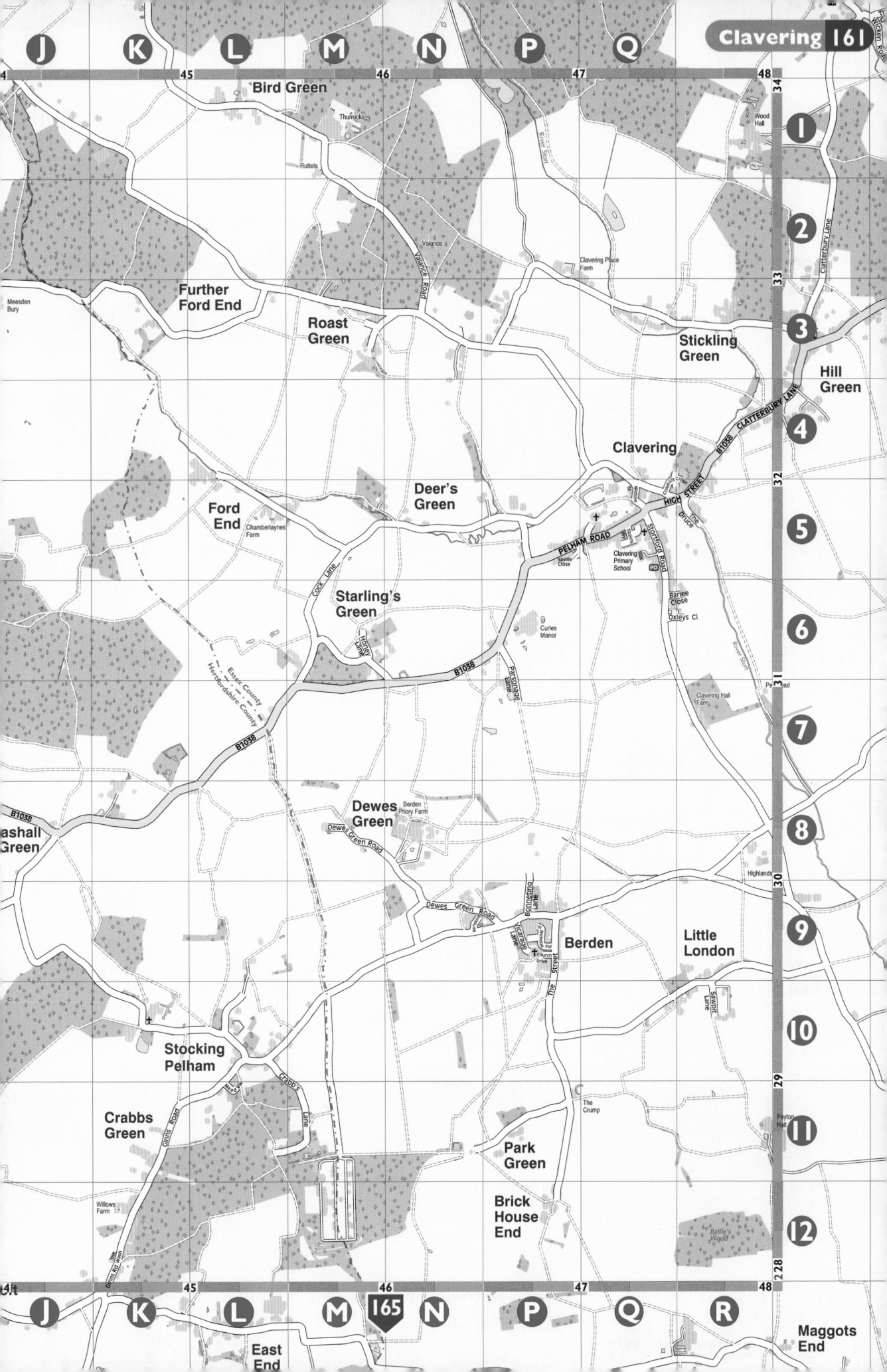

J K L M N P Q

45 46 47 48 34

Ficken Rd

Bird Green

Thurrocks

Wood Hall

1

Ruttels

2

Further Ford End

Meesden Bury

Valance

Clavering Place Farm

33

3

Roast Green

Stickling Green

Hill Green

Catterbury Lane

River Stort

Clavering

B1038 CLATTERBURY LANE

4

Deer's Green

Chamberlaynes Farm

Ford End

Cobbs Cross

HIGH STREET

The Bruce

Clatterbury Lane

32

5

Cock Lane

PELHAM ROAD

Saville Close

Clavering Primary School

Stortford Road

PO

Starling's Green

Horley Lane

Barlee Close

Oxleys Cl

6

Essex County

Hertfordshire County

B1038

Curles Manor

River Stort

31

7

B1038

Parsonage Lane

Clavering Hall Farm

Park Road

B1038

Berden Priory Farm

8

ashall Green

Dewes Green

Dewes Green Road

Highlands

30

Dewes Green Road

Bonsgrove Lane

Little London

9

Vicarage Lane

Berden

The Street

Sawn Lane

10

Church Drive

29

Stocking Pelham

Ginns Road

Crabb's Lane

The Crump

Peyton Hall

11

Crabbs Green

Park Green

12

Willows Farm

The Ginns Rd Nth

Brick House End

Battle's Wood

28

45 46 47 48

J K L M 165 N P Q R

East End

Maggots End

A   B   C   D   E   F   G   H

532   33   34   35

28

I

Warren Lane

Cottered Warren

Berkesdon Green

27

2

Gardners End

23

Moor Hall

3

Moor Green

Wakeley

Whatbarns Farm

26

4

Leycroft

Orange End

Peasefield

Cherry Gre

5

Chain Walk

Wood End

25

6

Rush Green

Mill Farm

7

en Park Farm

Sander's Green

Nasty

Stag Hall Farm

8

Chain Walk

Great Munden

24

The Old Bourne

Bugby's Farm

9

35

Libury Hall

10

Frogmore Hall Lane

Haultwick

23

II

The Street

Gifford's Lane

Dane End Tributary

Wentworth Cottages

12

Green End

Levens Green

222

Lordship's Farm

High Trees Farm

532   33   34   35

A   B   C   D   E   F   G   H

Munde Primary

Moor Common

Beggarman

Whempstead Road

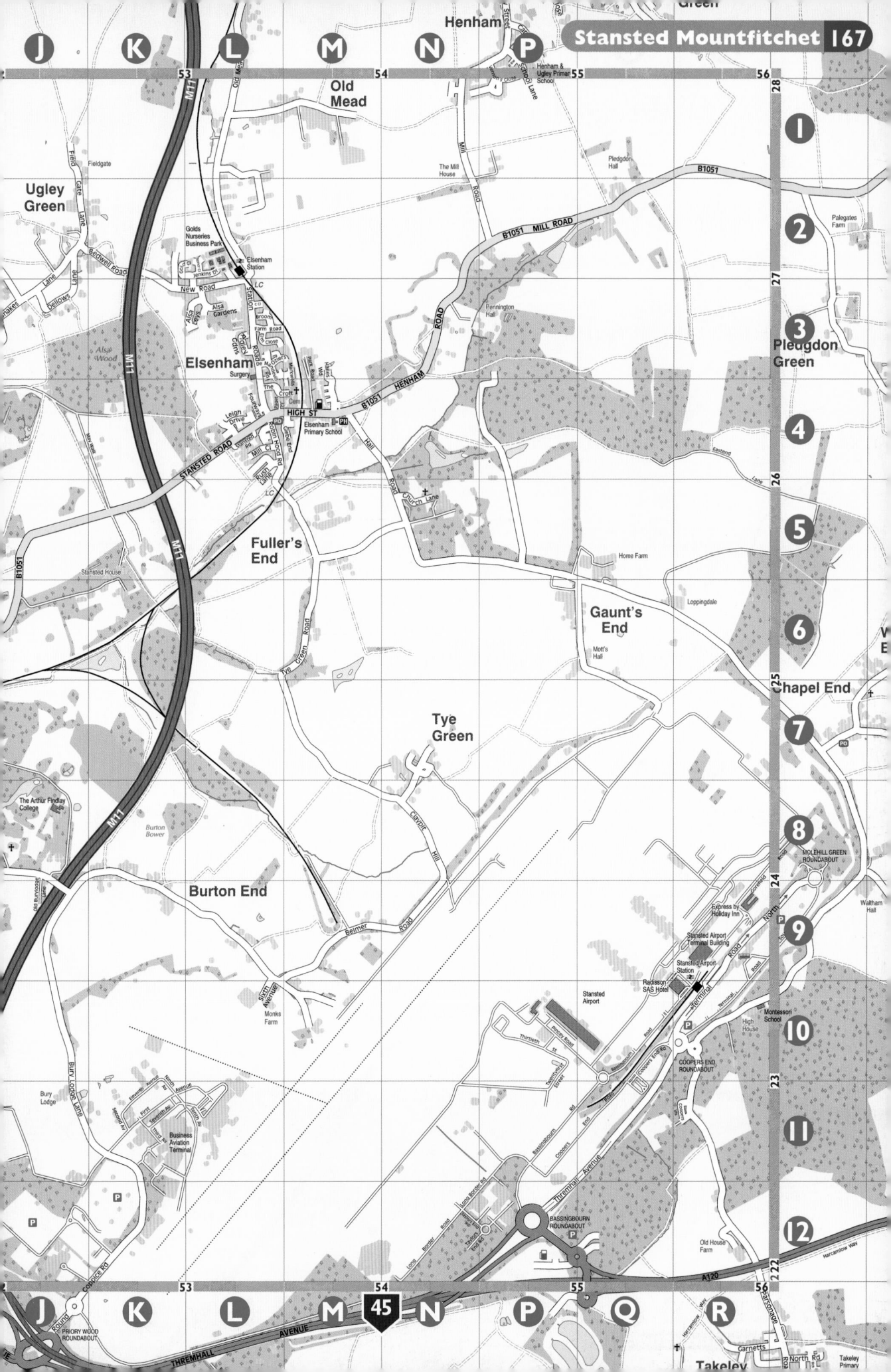

I grid square represents 500 metres

A   **B**   34   **C**   **D**   **E**   **F**   35   **G**   **H**

Green

527   28   29   30   High   Idle Hill   Elms

I

White
Hall

Bragbury
End

Gregory's
Farm

2

Golf Course

Blackwell

Stirling Close

3

Hook's
Cross

Leatherfield
Common

Astonbury
Wood

Frogmore

Arbury
Wood

Frogmore Hill

Frogmore
Hall

Blue
Hill

4

Raffin Green Lane

Bragbury Lane

Hazel
Farm

Walkern Road

A602

5

Staples Farm

River Beane

Beane
Road

Watton-at-Stone

Bardolphs

Bury Farm

Raffin Farm

Green   Lane

Broom Hall
Farm

Raffin
Green

Surgery

6

Datchworth

Watton-at-Stone
Station

177

7

Painter's
Green

Watton
Road

Watton-at-Stone
Primary School

Ware Road

Watton House

8

Hawkins Hall
Farm

Watton Road

Watkins Hall
Farm

Perrywood   Lane

9

Perrywood
Farm

Patchendon
Farm

Coltsfoot   Lane

10

Great Gobions
Farm

Stapleford

Green

Bu
Green

11

Burnham
Green

Burnham

Bramfield
Woods

Chain Walk

Warrenwood
Industrial
Estate

Desborough Drive

12

Tewin
Wood

West Riding

Firs

Row
Wood

Bramfield
House

527   28   29   30

A   **B**   51   **C**   **D**   **E**   **F**   52   **G**   **H**

Bramfield

J K L M **162** N P

End

32 33 34 35 22

1

2

Chapel Farm

Little Munden
CE Primary
School

21

Cutting

Chain Walk

Gomb's Wood

Egenton
Road

Kennedy

PO

Whitefield Road

Church Lane

Ship's
Farm

High Tree
Farm

Moorfield
Common

Dane End

Whitehill
Farm

3

Wd Cl
Potter's
Hall Farm

Whitehill
Golf Club

Cock's Wood

Rowney
Priory

4

Lowgate

Whempstead

Mill Lane

Whempstead Lane

*Brookfield
Common*

Lodge Farm

Golf Course

Rowney Lane

20

Bromley
Common

Sacombe
Hill Farm

Lowgate Lane

Lowgate Lane

**Sacombe
Green**

5

Sacombe Green Road

Marshall's Lane

6

Sacombe

WARE ROAD A602

Pound

Sacombe

Sacombebury
Farm

Sacombe
House

19 **180**

7

Heath Mount
Pre Prep School

*Woodhall
Park*

*The
Clumps*

8

Home
Farm

A602

Burrs
Green Farm

WARE ROAD

Chain Walk

Chelsing
Farm

18 Anchor

Hertfordshire Way

Bengeo Temple
Farm

Temple La

9

Lane

Hertfordshire Way

Temple

Hertfordshire Way

PH

Southend
Farm

Hertfordshire Way

Works

Stony Hills

The Orch

Temple

Chappell Ct

Tonwell

10

Bourns

Ware

17 Anchor

Stapleford
Primary Sch

Church Lane

Hertfordshire Way

Stonyhills

Tonwell St Marys
Primary School

Bourns
Road

Honour

Barleycroft

Anchor Lane

Poles

11

River Beane

Hertfordshire Way

**Chapmore
End**

WADESMILL ROAD

WESTMILL

Paynes
Hall

Poles Lane

A119

A602

A602

ROAD

216

12 Golf Course

Hanbury
Hotel &
Country Club

J K L M **53** N P Q R

32 33 34 35

Rickneys

Bullsmill

Standon
J   K   L   M   N   P   Q

164

Home Farm

40   41   42   43   22

Weston Green

Westland Green

Bromley

1

Bromley Hall

Bridgefoot

2

21

Westfield Bury

Golf Course

Ash Valley Golf Club

3

Standon Friars

Standon Business Park

High Street

Hadham Road

Standon Lane

River Rib

Latchford

Arches Hall

Standon Lodge

Balsams

Chaldean Farm

Lordship Farm

4

20

42

New Barns Lane

New Barns

B1004

The Sq

5

WINDING

Church Lane

High Street

Much Hadham

6

Biggin's Farm

Brand's Farm

St Andrews CE Primary School

Health Centre

19

Danebridge

7

Moor Place

Hadham Cross

Tower Hill

Ash Meadow

Kettle Green Road

Walnut Close

Malting Lane

Stansted Hill

Nimney Bourne

Rush Green

Kettle Green

Broadfield Way

SG10

8

Windmill Way

Station Rd

Widford Road

18

Nobland Green

182

Camwell Hall

Wynches

B1004

9

Hertfordshire Way

Castlebury Farm

Little Blakesware

Hadham Mill

10

17

Bakers End

Widford Road

Works

11

New Hall Farm

Blakesware Manor

Pegs Lane

High Street

Nether Street

12

16

Green   Helham Green   River Ash   Benningfield   Nether Street

55

J   K   L   M   N   P   Q   R

40   41   42   43   23

B1004 Ware Road

Widford

Bell La

J K L M N P

43
46 47 48 49

Spellbrook

Trims
Green

Allen's
+ Green

CM21

Shingle
Hall

Bursteads

Newhouse Farm

Sacombs Ash

Blount's
Farm

Hertfordshire Way

Tharbies

Hardings

Gangies Hill
Gangies

Crumps

Hoskins

West Road

West Road

Claylane
Farm

Clarklands
Industrial Estate

Parsonage
Farm

Cemetery

The Leventhorpe
School

Northfield Rd

Walnut Tree
Avenue

Crofters
End

Mandeville
Primary School

Sawbridgeworth
Station

SAWBRIDGEWORTH

Manor of
Groves Golf Club

Golf Course

Manor of
Groves Hotel

Jeffs

Bakers
Farm

MaCey's
Walk

**High
Wych**

High Wych
Primary School

Sayes Park
Farm

The Thomas Rivers
Medical Centre

Wisemans
Gardens
Newports

Pishiobury
Park

Rowney
Farm

Chaseways

Blenheim Cl

Rowney Gardens

Oak Drive

Pishiobury Drive

Fawbert & Barnard
Inf Sch

Eversley College

Hoestock
Road

Council
Building

Sheering
Fairway

Vantorts

East Drive

Three Forests Way

Reedings
Junior Sch

The
Forebury

The Maltings
Industrial Estate

Sappers
Close

**Lower
Sheering**

The Four
Acres

Newhouse

Rowneybury

Hertfordshire County
Essex County

Redricks Lane

Redricks
Farm

Pole Hole
Farm

Maple River
Industrial Park

Fort
Mill

Sarbie
Industrial Park

Harlow Mill
Station

Shenval
Industrial Estate

Gibberd
Garden

Aylmers
Farm

Durrington
Hall

Edinburgh Way

J K 75 L M N P 76 Q R
46 47 48 49

184

**Old
Harlow**

Cineworld

Jocelyns

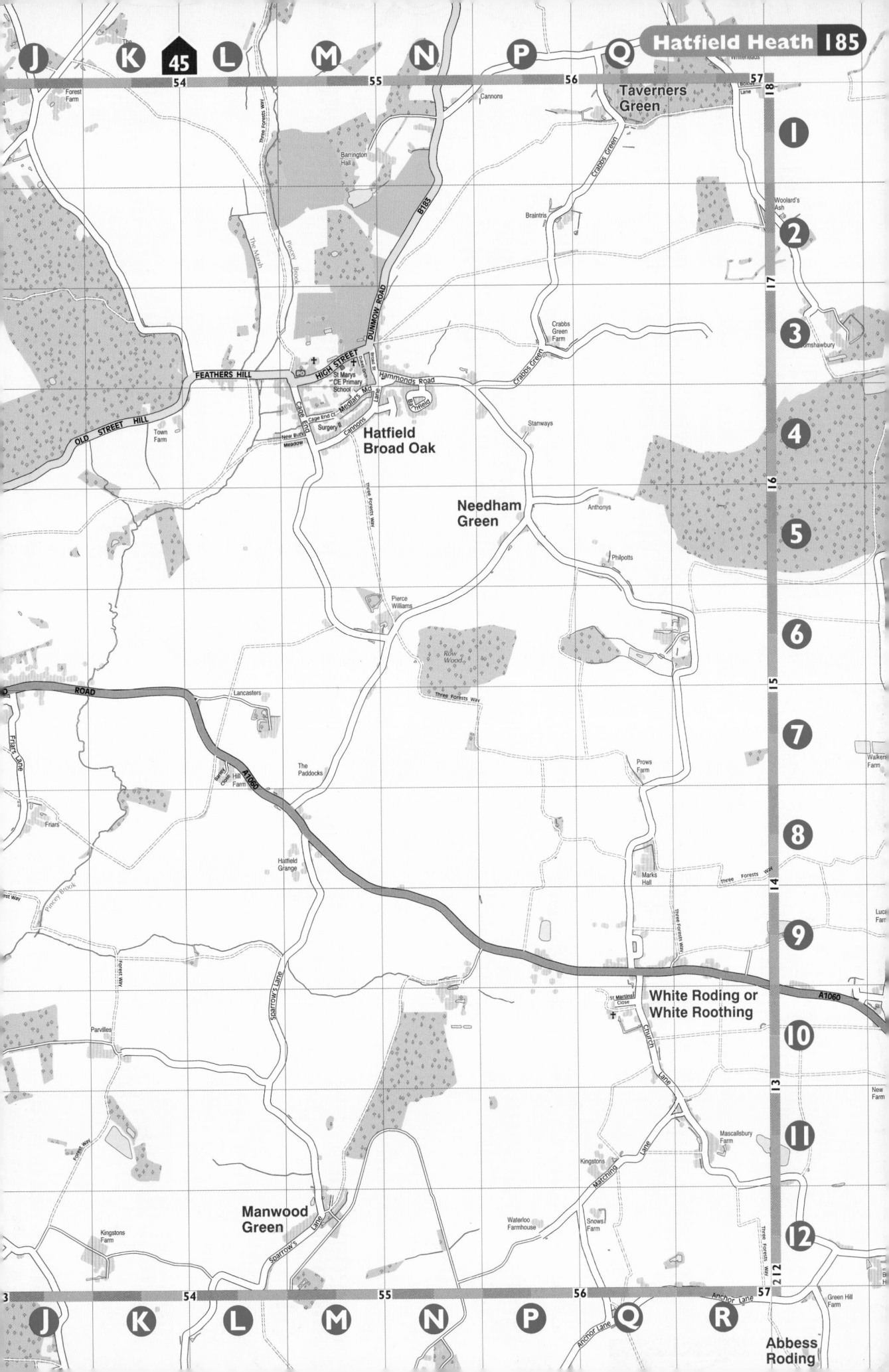

Abbots Langley ... 101 J6
Adeyfield ... 5 M2
Aimes Green ... 111 K2
Albury ... 164 G7
Albury End ... 164 F9
Aldbury ... 170 C11
Aldenham ... 118 F3
Aley Green ... 40 C8
Allen's Green ... 183 K3
Amersham ... 113 H5
Amersham Common ... 113 G5
Amersham Old Town ... 112 D6
Amersham on the Hill ... 112 F5
Amwell ... 48 A6
Ansells End ... 175 K7
Anstey ... 160 B3
Apsley ... 82 B6
Apsley End ... 146 A10
Ardeley ... 23 L6
Ardley End ... 184 H6
Arkley ... 135 M1
Arlesey ... 147 Q4
Asheridge ... 78 B8
Ashley Green ... 79 K6
Ashwell ... 149 Q1
Ashwell End ... 144 G12
Aspenden ... 158 H12
Aston ... 34 D7
Aston Clinton ... 168 A12
Aston End ... 34 C4
Astrope ... 168 F6
Astwick ... 148 D3
Ayot Green ... 49 K5
Ayot St Lawrence ... 176 B11
Ayot St Peter ... 49 K2
Ayres End ... 47 K8
Babbs Green ... 55 H1
Bakers End ... 181 J10
Baldock ... 17 K1
Ballingdon Bottom ... 172 A8
Barkway ... 152 F9
Barley ... 153 J3
Barleycroft End ... 164 H1
Barley End ... 170 C9
Barnet ... 136 D2
Barnet Gate ... 135 J2
Barton-le-Clay ... 155 K2
Barwick ... 180 G5
Bassingbourn ... 14 A1
Bassus Green ... 35 J1
Batchworth ... 130 D5
Batchworth Heath ... 130 E7
Batford ... 47 J2
Batlers Green ... 119 K4
Bayford ... 70 D8
Bedlar's Green ... 45 G4
Bedmond ... 101 J1
Bedwell ... 11 H5
Beecroft ... 38 C7
Bell Bar ... 88 E6
Bellingdon ... 78 C6
Belmont ... 143 L4
Belsize ... 99 J6
Bendish ... 175 L2
Bengeo ... 52 F5
Benington ... 35 J5
Bennetts End ... 5 L8
Bentfield Bury ... 166 D5
Bentfield Green ... 166 E5
Bentley Heath ... 122 D1
Berden ... 161 P7
Berkhamsted ... 79 L1
Bernards Heath ... 9 H1
Bidwell ... 25 L3
Birchanger ... 166 G11
Birch Green ... 70 H1
Birchwood ... 67 M6
Bird Green ... 161 L9
Biscot ... 28 A7
Bishop's Stortford ... 43 J2
Blackmore End ... 175 L11
Blue Hill ... 178 F4
Borehamwood ... 120 C7
Botany Bay ... 124 B2
Botley ... 97 L5
Bourne End ... 81 G4
Bovingdon ... 98 F1
Bovingdon Green ... 98 D3
Bower Heath ... 174 H11
Boxmoor ... 4 C7
Bozen Green ... 164 A2
Bragbury End ... 177 R2
Bramfield ... 52 A1
Bramingham ... 154 G12
Braughing ... 164 R7
Braughing Friars ... 164 D8
Brays Grove ... 3 L9
Breachwood Green ... 175 J1
Brent Pelham ... 160 E7
Brickendon ... 91 G1
Bricket Wood ... 102 D5
Brick House End ... 161 P12
Briden's Camp ... 61 L2
Brimsdown ... 126 C6
Broad Colney ... 104 B2
Broad Green ... 153 R2
Broadgreen Wood ... 70 E5
Broadley Common ... 94 B2
Broadoak End ... 52 D5
Broadwater ... 33 L8
Broken Green ... 164 C11
Bromley ... 181 N1
Brook End ... 158 A11
Brookmans Park ... 88 C8
Broxbourne ... 92 K2
Brunswick Park ... 137 L6
Buckland ... 158 H1
Buckland ... 168 D11
Bucklandwharf ... 56 E1
Bucks Hill ... 100 A8
Building End ... 153 Q6
Bulbourne ... 169 M9
Bullen's Green ... 87 J4
Bulls Cross ... 125 L2
Bull's Green ... 177 R10
Bulstrode ... 99 J2
Bumble's Green ... 93 L6
Buntingford ... 159 K10
Burge End ... 146 F12
Burnham Green ... 177 Q11
Burn's Green ... 35 K8
Burton End ... 167 L9
Bury Green ... 42 E2
Bury Green ... 109 M5
Bury Park ... 6 A3
Bushey ... 133 G3
Bushey Heath ... 133 J3
Butt's Close ... 157 N5
Bygrave ... 149 N8
Caddington ... 40 D5
Cadwell ... 147 Q12
Caldecote ... 148 H4
Caldecote Hill ... 133 K3

Campions ... 183 R12
The Camp ... 85 M3
Capability Green ... 41 J5
Carpenders Park ... 132 D5
Carter's Green ... 77 J3
Chalfont Common ... 128 D7
Chalfont St Peter ... 138 E2
Chandler's Cross ... 116 D4
Chapmore End ... 179 L12
Charlton ... 157 M8
Chartridge ... 96 A2
Chatter End ... 165 P6
Chaulden ... 81 H3
Chaul End ... 40 B2
Cheapside ... 60 B2
Cheddington ... 169 K3
Chells ... 11 M2
Chenies ... 115 G4
Cherry Green ... 162 H4
Chesham ... 97 G5
Chesham Bois ... 113 G2
Cheshunt ... 109 M4
Chessmount ... 97 J6
Cheverell's Green ... 172 F5
Childwick Bury ... 65 G4
Childwick Green ... 64 F3
Chiltern Green ... 174 E6
Chipperfield ... 99 M5
Chipping ... 158 H4
Chipping Barnet ... 136 C1
Chiswell Green ... 84 D7
Cholesbury ... 78 A3
Chorleywood ... 115 H8
Chorleywood Bottom ... 129 H2
Chorleywood West ... 128 E1
Church End ... 38 A3
Church End ... 63 L1
Church End ... 115 K4
Church End ... 147 R2
Church End ... 165 K11
Church End ... 169 Q7
Churchgate ... 109 M3
Churchgate Street ... 76 D2
Church Langley ... 76 B5
Clapgate ... 165 J7
Claverhambury ... 111 M1
Clavering ... 161 Q4
Clay End ... 35 J2
Clay Hill ... 125 G3
Clement's End ... 171 R6
Clothall ... 18 B5
Clothall Common ... 17 M1
Cockernhoe ... 29 H5
Cockfosters ... 137 J1
Codicote ... 176 F9
Codicote Bottom ... 176 D9
Codmore ... 97 J4
Cokenach ... 152 G8
Cold Christmas ... 180 E11
Cold Harbour ... 174 G12
Cole Green ... 69 L1
Coleman Green ... 180 E3
Colliers End ... 180 E3
Colney Heath ... 87 G4
Colney Street ... 103 J4
Commonwood ... 99 L8
Cooper's Green ... 66 F5
Cottered ... 158 A9
Counters End ... 81 L2
Cow Roast ... 58 E4
Crabbs Green ... 161 K11
Cradle End ... 42 F1
Crews Hill ... 124 F1
Cromer ... 23 H4
Cromer-Hyde ... 49 G8
Croxley Green ... 103 G1
Cuffley ... 108 D2
Cumberlow Green ... 19 J7
Cupid Green ... 62 F6
Dagnall ... 171 J3
Damask Green ... 21 M1
Dancers Hill ... 122 A1
Dane End ... 179 P2
Danesbury ... 177 J11
Darleyhall ... 30 A8
Dassels ... 163 P2
Datchworth ... 178 A6
Datchworth Green ... 177 Q8
Deacons Hill ... 134 C2
Deer's Green ... 161 N5
Denham Green ... 139 J8
Dewes Green ... 161 M8
Digswell ... 50 B2
Digswell Park ... 50 B4
Digswell Water ... 50 E3
Downside ... 39 J3
Drayton Beauchamp ... 168 G12
Driver's End ... 176 C5
Duck End ... 166 G12
Ducks Island ... 136 B3
Dudswell ... 59 H5
Dunstable ... 39 H1
Dunton ... 144 D4
East Barnet ... 137 H3
Eastbury ... 131 K7
Eastcote Village ... 141 M7
East End ... 74 C4
East End ... 165 L1
East End Green ... 70 A3
Easthall ... 31 M7
East Hyde ... 174 D9
Eastwick ... 74 F1
Eaton Bray ... 37 K3
Eaton Green ... 37 G2
Edgware ... 134 C7
Edlesborough ... 37 H5
Edworth ... 148 B10
Ellenbrook ... 67 G7
Elsenham ... 167 K3
Elstree ... 134 C2
Enfield ... 125 G8
Enfield Highway ... 126 A6
Enfield Island Village ... 126 F4
Enfield Lock ... 126 F4
Enfield Town ... 125 H7
Enfield Wash ... 126 C4
Epping Green ... 90 B4
Epping Green ... 94 E6
Epping Upland ... 95 G8
Essendon ... 69 K7
Eyeworth ... 144 F1
Farley Hill ... 6 A8
Farnham ... 166 B1
Farnham Green ... 165 P2
Fields End ... 81 L6
Fishers Green ... 18 B5
Flamstead ... 173 L1
Flamstead End ... 109 M2
Flaunden ... 98 L6
Fleetville ... 9 M3
The Folly ... 47 M3
Ford End ... 161 L5

Forty Hill ... 125 K5
Foster Street ... 76 D6
Freezy Water ... 126 C2
Friar's Wash ... 173 M6
Friern Barnet ... 137 J7
Frithsden ... 60 E5
Frithsden Gardens ... 60 C4
Frogmore ... 103 J2
The Frythe ... 49 L3
Fuller's End ... 167 L5
Furneux Pelham ... 160 G12
Further Ford End ... 161 K3
Gadebridge ... 61 K8
Ganwick Corner ... 122 F1
Garston ... 118 A1
Gaston Green ... 184 B5
Gatley End ... 145 Q10
Gaunt's End ... 167 Q6
Gilston ... 182 H12
Gilston Park ... 182 G11
Gilwell Park ... 127 G7
Goff's Oak ... 109 G2
Goose Green ... 72 A6
Gorhambury ... 84 A1
Gosmore ... 157 P10
Graveley ... 21 G5
Gravel Hill ... 138 D1
Gravesend ... 164 G5
Great Amwell ... 54 C8
Great Ashby ... 21 M6
Great Chishill ... 153 N3
Great Gaddesden ... 61 G2
Greatgap ... 169 P3
Great Green ... 145 N4
Great Hallingbury ... 96 E2
Great Hivings ... 96 E2
Great Hormead ... 160 B9
Great Munden ... 162 H8
Great Offley ... 156 F11
Great Parndon ... 74 F7
Great Wymondley ... 20 C3
Green End ... 18 A7
Green End ... 81 K5
Green End ... 158 B2
Green End ... 162 C12
Green End ... 163 P6
Greenhill ... 143 K7
Green Street ... 120 E3
Green Street ... 165 L12
The Green ... 171 M1
Green Tye ... 42 C8
Grovehill ... 62 B6
The Grove ... 117 G3
Gubblecote ... 168 H7
Guilden Morden ... 145 L4
Custard Wood ... 48 A1
Haddington Hill ... 56 C8
Hadham Cross ... 181 Q7
Hadham Ford ... 42 B1
Hadley ... 122 D7
Hadley Wood ... 123 H4
Hailey ... 72 D3
Haldens ... 50 E3
Hall Grove ... 68 F1
Hallingbury Street ... 45 H5
Halls Green ... 74 A7
Hall's Green ... 22 C3
Halton ... 56 B4
Hammerfield ... 4 B2
Hammond Street ... 91 G8
Handside ... 49 M8
Harefield ... 140 A4
Harefield Grove ... 140 B2
Hare Street ... 2 A9
Hare Street ... 23 K3
Hare Street ... 159 P9
Harlow ... 2 F6
Harmer Green ... 177 N12
Harpenden ... 46 D4
Harpenden Common ... 46 F6
Harrow ... 143 H8
Harrow Weald ... 143 J2
Hartham ... 53 G6
Hart Hill ... 7 M1
Hastoe ... 57 L6
Hatch End ... 142 C2
Hatching Green ... 46 D7
Hatfield ... 87 K1
Hatfield Broad Oak ... 185 M4
Hatfield Garden Village ... 67 J4
Hatfield Heath ... 184 H6
Hatfield Hyde ... 68 D2
Haultwick ... 162 D10
Hay Green ... 151 N7
Hay Street ... 163 Q4
Hazel End ... 166 C7
Headstone ... 142 F6
Heath End ... 78 E3
Hebing End ... 35 L7
Helham Green ... 55 K1
Hemel Hempstead ... 5 H3
Heronsgate ... 129 H3
Hertford ... 53 J8
Hertford Heath ... 71 M2
Hertingfordbury ... 52 E8
Hexton ... 155 P3
High Barnet ... 122 A7
High Beach ... 127 M5
High Cross ... 119 H1
High Cross ... 180 C7
Highfield ... 62 C8
High Laver ... 77 M7
The High ... 2 E6
High Town ... 6 F3
Highwood Hill ... 135 K5
High Wych ... 183 M8
Hill End ... 139 M1
Hilltop ... 97 H3
Hinxworth ... 144 C11
Hitchin ... 157 M6
Hitchin Hill ... 157 M8
Hobbs Cross ... 76 E4
Hobbs Hill ... 49 M1
Hockerill ... 44 B3
Hoddesdon ... 72 C7
Hogpits Bottom ... 98 F6
Holwell ... 147 K10
Holwellbury ... 147 K7
Holyfield ... 111 G2
Holywell ... 131 J2
Holywell ... 171 Q2
Honeywick ... 37 J1
Hoo End ... 175 P5
Hook's Cross ... 178 C3
Horn Hill ... 128 F7
Horton Wharf ... 36 A5
Houghton Regis ... 26 B4
Housham Tye ... 77 H3
Howe Green ... 44 M7
How Wood ... 103 G1
Hudnall ... 171 L10
Hudnall Corner ... 171 N10
Hunsdon ... 182 A8

Hunsdonbury ... 182 A11
Hunton Bridge ... 100 F7
Hyde Heath ... 96 A8
Ickleford ... 157 M1
Ivinghoe ... 169 R4
Ivinghoe Aston ... 36 E8
Jack's Hatch ... 94 F3
Jockey End ... 172 C9
Katherines ... 74 C8
Kelshall ... 151 K7
Kensworth ... 39 L8
Kensworth Lynch ... 39 L8
Kettle Green ... 181 N8
Keysers Estate ... 92 F4
Kimpton ... 175 P7
Kings Langley ... 100 E2
Kingsmoor ... 95 G2
King's Walden ... 30 D6
Kingswood ... 101 M8
Kinsbourne Green ... 173 K4
Kitt's End ... 122 C4
Knebworth ... 177 N5
Langley ... 32 D8
Langleybury ... 100 F8
Langley Lower Green ... 153 R12
Latchford ... 181 K4
Latchmore Bank ... 44 A1
Latimer ... 114 C3
Latton Bush ... 95 L1
Leagrave ... 27 G5
Leasey Bridge ... 47 K4
Lea Valley ... 47 K2
Leavesden Green ... 101 K8
Lemsford ... 49 K8
Letchmore Heath ... 119 J3
Letchworth Garden City ... 16 B3
Letty Green ... 69 L3
Level's Green ... 165 Q8
Levens Green ... 162 H12
Leverstock Green ... 83 G5
Lewsey Farm ... 26 D6
Ley Green ... 30 D4
Ley Hill ... 97 M4
Lilley ... 155 R11
Limbury ... 27 K4
Lippitts End ... 127 K6
Little Almshoe ... 157 Q12
Little Berkhamsted ... 89 L1
Little Chalfont ... 113 M6
Little Chishill ... 153 N6
Little Gaddesden ... 171 K10
Little Green ... 145 N3
Little Hadham ... 165 J11
Little Hallingbury ... 184 C1
Little Heath ... 60 E8
Little Heath ... 106 B7
Little Hormead ... 160 A10
Little London ... 161 R9
Little Offley ... 156 C7
Little Parndon ... 2 A4
Little Tring ... 169 J11
Little Wymondley ... 20 B5
London Colney ... 86 C8
Long Marston ... 168 F6
Loudwater ... 116 B7
Lower Bois ... 97 G8
Lower End ... 24 C8
Lower Green ... 147 N12
Lower Green ... 160 E2
Lower Nazeing ... 93 H5
Lower Sheering ... 184 A4
Lower Stondon ... 146 H6
Lower Sundon ... 154 C10
Lower Woodside ... 88 D4
Loyter's Green ... 77 K4
Lucas End ... 109 C1
Luffenhall ... 23 G1
Luton ... 7 H7
Lye Green ... 97 K2
Mackerye End ... 47 J1
Magdalen Laver ... 77 H8
Maggots End ... 166 A1
Mallows Green ... 165 Q3
Mangrove Green ... 29 K5
Mantles Green ... 112 E4
Manuden ... 166 B3
Manwood Green ... 185 L12
Maple Cross ... 129 H7
Mardlebury ... 177 P7
Mark Hall North ... 3 C5
Mark Hall South ... 3 C5
Markyate ... 172 H4
Marshalls Heath ... 47 L2
Marshalswick ... 65 L7
Marsh Farm ... 27 J2
Marshmoor ... 88 B4
Marsworth ... 169 L7
Matching ... 77 L1
Matching Tye ... 77 K2
Meesden ... 160 F4
Meppershall ... 146 D2
Meriden ... 118 C2
Merry Hill ... 132 F4
Mickleffield Green ... 115 L4
Mill End ... 129 K4
Mill End ... 158 C3
Mill Green ... 68 C5
Mill Hill ... 135 L8
Millow ... 144 C5
Moneyhill ... 129 M4
Monken Hadley ... 122 C6
Moor End ... 62 B3
Moor Green ... 162 B3
Moor Park ... 131 G7
Morden Green ... 145 Q8
Mott's Green ... 184 D3
Mount Pleasant ... 139 M3
Much Hadham ... 181 Q6
Nash Mills ... 82 E7
Nast Hyde ... 87 H1
Nasty ... 163 G1
Nazeing ... 93 M4
Nazeing Gate ... 94 A5
Nazeing Long Green ... 93 L7
Nazeing Mead ... 73 H8
Needham Green ... 185 N5
Nether Street ... 182 D4
Netteswell ... 3 H4
Nettleden ... 60 F3
New Barnet ... 136 F1
Newgate Street ... 90 C6
New Greens ... 65 G5
New Ground ... 58 E3
Newman's End ... 184 F12
New Mill ... 169 M11
New Mill End ... 174 B9
New Town ... 97 G3
Newtown ... 97 G3
New Town ... 7 G9
Nobland Green ... 181 L9
The Node ... 176 F4

Nomansland ... 48 A7
Northall ... 36 E4
Nothaw ... 107 L4
North Brook End ... 145 Q4
Northchurch ... 59 H7
North Harrow ... 142 E8
North Watford ... 117 M3
Northwood ... 141 G3
Northwood Hills ... 141 H4
Norton ... 148 F12
Norton Green ... 32 F6
Nup End ... 176 H5
Nuthampstead ... 153 K11
Oakfield ... 157 R7
Oaklands ... 177 N10
Oakleigh Park ... 137 G5
Odsey ... 150 C4
Old Hall Green ... 163 K12
Old Harlow ... 76 B1
Old Hatfield ... 68 C3
Old Knebworth ... 177 J3
Old Mead ... 167 M1
Old Town ... 33 G2
Orchard Green ... 97 M1
Otterspool ... 118 D3
Oxhey ... 132 B2
Oxlease ... 87 K3
Painter's Green ... 177 R7
Panshanger ... 50 E7
Park Green ... 161 P11
Parkside ... 26 A4
Park Street ... 85 C8
Park Town ... 7 J8
Passmores ... 75 H8
Patchetts Green ... 119 G5
Patient End ... 164 F2
Patmore Heath ... 165 K5
Peartree ... 50 C3
Pednor Bottom ... 96 A3
Pednormead End ... 96 E5
Pegsdon ... 155 Q4
Pepperstock ... 41 G8
Perry Green ... 182 F1
Peters Green ... 174 C6
Piccotts End ... 62 A6
Pimlico ... 83 J7
Pin Green ... 33 L1
Pinnacles ... 74 E5
Pinner ... 142 B6
Pinner Green ... 142 A4
Pinnerwood Park ... 142 A2
Pirton ... 156 F5
Pitstone ... 169 P6
Pitstone Green ... 169 G2
Pond Park ... 96 F3
Poplars ... 34 B6
Porter's End ... 175 L10
Potten End ... 60 E7
Potters Bar ... 107 J6
Potters Crouch ... 84 B6
Pottersheath ... 177 J8
Potter Street ... 76 B7
Pouchen End ... 81 H3
Presdales ... 54 C6
Preston ... 31 G3
Puckeridge ... 163 Q10
Pudds Cross ... 98 C2
Purwell ... 20 B1
Puttenham ... 168 D2
Rableyheath ... 177 J7
Radlett ... 120 A1
Radwell ... 148 G9
Redbourn ... 173 R11
Redbournbury ... 64 C3
Redhill ... 19 J3
Reed ... 152 B9
Reed End ... 151 Q2
Rickmansworth ... 130 B2
Ridge ... 105 K3
The Ridgeway ... 107 M1
Ringshall ... 170 H8
Roast Green ... 161 M3
Roe End ... 172 D5
Roe Green ... 19 M3
Roe Green ... 67 L8
Roestock ... 87 G5
The Rookery ... 131 L3
Rosedale ... 109 K2
Round Bush ... 119 H4
Round Green ... 28 C7
Rowley Green ... 121 K8
Roydon ... 73 M4
Roydon Hamlet ... 94 A1
Royston ... 14 C5
Rucklers Lane ... 82 C8
Ruislip ... 141 G6
Ruislip Common ... 141 G6
Rushden ... 19 J5
Rush Green ... 32 B5
Rush Green ... 54 A7
Rusling End ... 177 L7
The Ryde ... 68 B7
Rye Meads ... 73 H4
Rye Park ... 72 F6
Sacombe ... 179 L6
Sacombe Green ... 179 N6
St Albans ... 9 J5
St Ibbs ... 157 Q12
St Ippolitts ... 157 Q11
St Julians ... 85 G6
St Margarets ... 72 E1
St Margaret's ... 61 G1
St Nicholas ... 21 L7
St Paul's Walden ... 31 L8
St Stephens ... 84 E7
Sandon ... 150 H12
Sandridge ... 65 L3
Sarratt ... 115 L1
Sarratt Bottom ... 115 J3
Sawbridgeworth ... 183 M7
Sewardstone ... 127 G6
Sewell ... 25 H7
Shaftenhoe End ... 153 K5
Sharpenhoe ... 154 D3
Shaw Green ... 19 H4
Sheering ... 184 D1
Shenley ... 104 D8
Shenleybury ... 104 D8
Shephall ... 11 L9
Sherrardspark ... 49 M5
Shillington ... 146 A7
Shootersway ... 79 G8
Slapton ... 36 B9
Sleapshyde ... 87 G3
Slip End ... 41 G7
Slip End ... 150 B6
Smallford ... 86 F1
Smith's End ... 153 J5
Smug Oak ... 102 F4
Snailswell ... 147 M11
Snow End ... 160 A4
Sopwell ... 85 J3
South-end ... 182 F3

Southern Green	19	L5	The Swillett	129	G3	Tringford	169	J9	Waterdale	102	A4	White Hall	178	D1
South Harefield	140	B6	Symonds Green	32	E2	Tring Wharf	169	M10	Waterend	49	C5	White Roding or		
South Hatfield	87	M3	Takeley Street	45	M2	Trowley Bottom	173	K9	Water End	61	K4	White Roothing	185	Q10
South Mimms	105	M6	Taverners Green	185	Q1	Turnford	92	C7	Water End	88	A8	Whitwell	175	Q3
South Oxhey	131	M6	Tea Green	29	M6	Two Waters	4	D8	Watford	52	D3	Widford	182	C5
Spellbrook	183	Q1	Temple Fields	75	L1	Tye Green	35	H7	Waterside	97	H7	Wigginton	58	B3
Spitalbrook	92	E1	Tewin	51	J2	Tye Green	167	N7	Watford	12	F3	Wigginton Bottom	58	C5
Staines Green	70	A1	Tewin Wood	177	R12	Tylers Causeway	89	M4	Watford Heath	132	C3	Wildhill	89	G3
Stanborough	67	K2	Therfield	151	M6	Tyler's Hill	97	L5	Watton-at-Stone	178	E5	Willian	16	F7
Stanbridge	24	A4	Thorley	43	J7	Tyttenhanger	86	C5	Wealdstone	143	L5	Wilstone	168	H8
Stanbridgeford	24	B6	Thorley Houses	43	G4	Ugley Green	167	J2	Welham Green	87	M5	Wilstone Green	168	H9
Standon	163	Q12	Thorley Street	43	L6	Underhill	136	E2	Well End	121	G4	Windmill Hill	157	P6
Standon Green End	180	C5	Thornwood Common	95	M7	Uppend	165	P4	Wellpond Green	164	C12	Winsdon Hill	6	A6
Stanmore	133	M8	Threshers Bush	76	E6	Upper Dunsley	58	A2	Welwyn	176	G12	Woodcock Hill	130	C7
Stanstead Abbotts	73	J1	The Thrift	150	H2	Upper Stondon	146	G5	Welwyn Garden City	50	F5	Wood End	162	A6
Stansted Mountfitchet	166	E6	Throcking	158	C8	Upper Sundon	154	A9	Westbrook Hay	81	G6	Woodhall	68	C1
Stapleford	178	G10	Thundridge	180	B10	Upton End	146	B7	West End	69	H8	Woodrow	112	A8
Starling's Green	161	M6	Tilegate Green	77	H7	Upwick Green	165	L8	West Hyde	139	J2	Woodside	40	E7
Start Hill	45	G2	Tilekiln Green	44	F3	Venus Hill	98	F5	Westland Green	181	Q1	Woodside	88	C5
Startop's End	169	K8	Tilsworth	24	D3	Wadesmill	180	B9	Westmill	157	L4	Woodside	101	M6
Steeple Morden	145	P7	Titmore Green	20	C7	Wakeley	162	E3	Westmill	163	K3	Woodside Green	44	F8
Sevenage	10	C3	Todd's Green	20	E7	Walkern	22	F8	Weston	18	A8	Woodside Park	136	E7
Stewards	95	J2	Tolmers	90	C8	Wallington	19	G1	West Watford	12	C7	Woollensbrook	72	B4
Stickling Green	161	R3	Tonwell	179	P10	Walsworth	157	Q4	Westwick Row	83	J3	Woolmer Green	177	P7
Stocking Pelham	161	K10	Totteridge	136	E4	Waltham Abbey	111	H6	Wheathampstead	48	B4	World's End	124	E8
Stopsley	28	D6	Totteridge Green	136	A4	Waltham Cross	110	A7	Whelpley Hill	80	B8	Wormley	92	C6
Stotfold	148	E6	Totternhoe	37	M2	Wandon End	29	M8	Whempstead	179	L3	Wormleybury	91	M5
Streatley	154	F8	Tower Hill	99	K3	Ware	54	D3	Whetstone	136	F5	Wormley West End	91	L4
Studham	171	P4	Townsend	8	F1	Wareside	55	H1	Whippendell Bottom	100	A4	Wright's Green	184	D2
Sumners	94	E1	Travellers Rest	170	E1	Warners End	81	J1	Whipsnade	171	N1	Wyddial	159	L5
Sundon Park	27	G2	Trims Green	183	N2	Warren's Green	22	B3	Whitehall	158	C5	Wymondley Bury	20	D6
Swanley Bar	106	F2	Tring	57	M2	Washall Green	160	H8				Youngsbury	180	D9

USING THE STREET INDEX

Street names are listed alphabetically. Each street name is followed by its postal town or area locality, the Postcode District, the page number, and the reference to the square in which the name is found.

Standard index entries are shown as follows:

Abbey Av *STALW/RED* AL3 .... **84**   E5

Street names and selected addresses not shown on the map due to scale restrictions are shown in the index with an asterisk:

Abbots HI *HHS/BOV* HP3 * **82**   F7

GENERAL ABBREVIATIONS

ACC	ACCESS	CUTT	CUTTINGS	HOL	HOLLOW	NW	NORTH WEST	SKWY	SKYWAY
ALY	ALLEY	CV	COVE	HOSP	HOSPITAL	O/P	OVERPASS	SMT	SUMMIT
AP	APPROACH	CYN	CANYON	HRB	HARBOUR	OFF	OFFICE	SOC	SOCIETY
AR	ARCADE	DEPT	DEPARTMENT	HTH	HEATH	ORCH	ORCHARD	SP	SPUR
ASS	ASSOCIATION	DL	DALE	HTS	HEIGHTS	OV	OVAL	SPR	SPRING
AV	AVENUE	DM	DAM	HVN	HAVEN	PAL	PALACE	SQ	SQUARE
BCH	BEACH	DR	DRIVE	HWY	HIGHWAY	PAS	PASSAGE	ST	STREET
BLDS	BUILDINGS	DRO	DROVE	IMP	IMPERIAL	PAV	PAVILION	STN	STATION
BND	BEND	DRY	DRIVEWAY	IN	INLET	PDE	PARADE	STR	STREAM
BNK	BANK	DWGS	DWELLINGS	IND EST	INDUSTRIAL ESTATE	PH	PUBLIC HOUSE	STRD	STRAND
BR	BRIDGE	E	EAST	INF	INFIRMARY	PK	PARK	SW	SOUTH WEST
BRK	BROOK	EMB	EMBANKMENT	INFO	INFORMATION	PKWY	PARKWAY	TDG	TRADING
BTM	BOTTOM	EMBY	EMBASSY	INT	INTERCHANGE	PL	PLACE	TER	TERRACE
BUS	BUSINESS	ESP	ESPLANADE	IS	ISLAND	PLN	PLAIN	THWY	THROUGHWAY
BVD	BOULEVARD	EST	ESTATE	JCT	JUNCTION	PLNS	PLAINS	TNL	TUNNEL
BY	BYPASS	EX	EXCHANGE	JTY	JETTY	PLZ	PLAZA	TOLL	TOLLWAY
CATH	CATHEDRAL	EXPY	EXPRESSWAY	KG	KING	POL	POLICE STATION	TPK	TURNPIKE
CEM	CEMETERY	EXT	EXTENSION	KNL	KNOLL	PR	PRINCE	TR	TRACK
CEN	CENTRE	F/O	FLYOVER	L	LAKE	PREC	PRECINCT	TRL	TRAIL
CFT	CROFT	FC	FOOTBALL CLUB	LA	LANE	PREP	PREPARATORY	TWR	TOWER
CH	CHURCH	FK	FORK	LDG	LODGE	PRIM	PRIMARY	U/P	UNDERPASS
CHA	CHASE	FLD	FIELD	LGT	LIGHT	PROM	PROMENADE	UNI	UNIVERSITY
CHYD	CHURCHYARD	FLDS	FIELDS	LK	LOCK	PRS	PRINCESS	UPR	UPPER
CIR	CIRCLE	FLS	FALLS	LKS	LAKES	PRT	PORT	V	VALE
CIRC	CIRCUS	FM	FARM	LNDG	LANDING	PT	POINT	VA	VALLEY
CL	CLOSE	FT	FORT	LTL	LITTLE	PZ	PIAZZA	VIAD	VIADUCT
CLFS	CLIFFS	FTS	FLATS	LWR	LOWER	QD	QUADRANT	VIL	VILLA
CMP	CAMP	FWY	FREEWAY	MAG	MAGISTRATE	QU	QUEEN	VIS	VISTA
CNR	CORNER	FY	FERRY	MAN	MANSIONS	QY	QUAY	VLG	VILLAGE
CO	COUNTY	GA	GATE	MD	MEAD	R	RIVER	VLS	VILLAS
COLL	COLLEGE	GAL	GALLERY	MDW	MEADOWS	RBT	ROUNDABOUT	VW	VIEW
COM	COMMON	GDN	GARDEN	MEM	MEMORIAL	RD	ROAD	W	WEST
COMM	COMMISSION	GDNS	GARDENS	MI	MILL	RDG	RIDGE	WD	WOOD
CON	CONVENT	GLD	GLADE	MKT	MARKET	REP	REPUBLIC	WHF	WHARF
COT	COTTAGE	GLN	GLEN	MKTS	MARKETS	RES	RESERVOIR	WK	WALK
COTS	COTTAGES	GN	GREEN	ML	MALL	RFC	RUGBY FOOTBALL CLUB	WKS	WALKS
CP	CAPE	GND	GROUND	MNR	MANOR	RI	RISE	WLS	WELLS
CPS	COPSE	GRA	GRANGE	MS	MEWS	RP	RAMP	WY	WAY
CR	CREEK	GRG	GARAGE	MSN	MISSION	ROW	ROW	YD	YARD
CREM	CREMATORIUM	GT	GREAT	MT	MOUNT	S	SOUTH	YHA	YOUTH HOSTEL
CRS	CRESCENT	GTWY	GATEWAY	MTN	MOUNTAIN	SCH	SCHOOL		
CSWY	CAUSEWAY	GV	GROVE	MTS	MOUNTAINS	SE	SOUTH EAST		
CT	COURT	HGR	HIGHER	MUS	MUSEUM	SER	SERVICE AREA		
CTRL	CENTRAL	HL	HILL	MWY	MOTORWAY	SH	SHORE		
CTS	COURTS	HLS	HILLS	N	NORTH	SHOP	SHOPPING		
CTYD	COURTYARD	HO	HOUSE	NE	NORTH EAST				

POSTCODE TOWNS AND AREA ABBREVIATIONS

ABLGY	Abbots Langley	DUN/HR/TOD	Dunstable/	HLWW/ROY	Harlow west/Roydon	OXHEY	Oxhey	STAN	Stanmore
AMP/FLIT/BLC	Ampthill/Flitwick/		Houghton Regis/	HNLW	Henlow	PEND	Ponders End	STDN	Standon
	Barton-le-Clay		Toddington	HOD	Hoddesdon	PIN	Pinner	STHGT/OAK	Southgate/Oakwood
AMS	Amersham	DUN/WHIP	Dunstable/Whipsnade	HRW	Harrow	POTB/CUF	Potters Bar/Cuffley	STSD	Stansted
AMSS	Amersham south	EBAR	East Barnet	HTCH/STOT	Hitchin/Stotfold	RAD	Radlett	STVG	Stevenage
ARL/CHE	Arlesey/Church End	EDGW	Edgware	HTCHE/RSTV	Hitchin east/	RAYLNE/WEN	Rural Aylesbury	STVGE	Stevenage east
BAR	Barnet	EN	Enfield		Stevenage		north & east/Wendover	TRDG/WHET	Totteridge/Whetstone
BERK	Berkhamsted	ENC/FH	Enfield Chase/Forty Hill	KGLGY	Kings Langley	RBSF	Rural Bishop's Stortford	TRING	Tring
BGSW	Biggleswade	EPP	Epping	KNEB	Knebworth	RBSF	Rural Bishop's Stortford	WAB	Waltham Abbey
BLDK	Baldock	FBAR/BDGN	Friern Barnet/	KTN/HRWW/WS	Kenton/	RKW/CH/CXG	Rickmansworth/	WARE	Ware
BORE	Borehamwood		Bounds Green		Harrow Weald/		Chorleywood/	WAT	Watford
BRKMPK	Brookmans Park	GSTN	Garston		Wealdstone		Croxley Green	WATN	Watford north
BROX	Broxbourne	GTDUN	Great Dunmow	LBUZ	Leighton Buzzard	ROY	Royston	WATW	Watford west
BSF	Bishop's Stortford	GTMIS/PWD	Great Missenden/	LCOL/BKTW	London Colney/Bricket	RSLP	Ruislip	WCHMH	Winchmore Hill
BUNT	Buntingford		Prestwood		Wood	RYLN/HDSTN	Rayners Lane/	WGCE	Welwyn Garden City east
BUSH	Bushey	HARP	Harpenden	LOU	Loughton		Headstone	WGCW	Welwyn Garden City west
CFSP/GDCR	Chalfont St Peter/	HAT	Hatfield	LTN	Luton	SAFWS	Saffron Walden south	WLYN	Welwyn
	Gerrards Cross	HHNE	Hemel Hempstead northeast	LTNE	Luton east	SBW	Sawbridgeworth		
CHES/WCR	Cheshunt/Waltham Cross	HHS/BOV	Hemel Hempstead south/	LTNN/LIM	Luton north/Limbury	SDY/GAM/POT	Sandy/		
CHESW	Cheshunt west		Bovingdon	LTNW/LEA	Luton west/Leagrave		Gamlingay/Potton		
CHING	Chingford	HHW	Hemel Hempstead west	LWTH	Letchworth	SHFD	Shefford		
CHONG	Chipping Ongar	HLW	Harlow	MHAD	Much Hadham	STAL	St Albans		
CSHM	Chesham	HLWE	Harlow east	MLHL	Mill Hill	STALE/WH	St Albans east/		
CSTG	Chalfont St Giles	HLWS	Harlow south	NFNCH/WDSPK	North Finchley/		Wheathampstead		
DEN/HRF	Denham/Harefield				Woodside Park	STALW/RED	St Albans west/		
DEN/HRF	Denham/Harefield			NTHWD	Northwood		Redbourn		

Index - streets

A

Abbey Av STALW/RED AL3 84 E5
Abbey Cl PIN HA5 141 M5
Abbey Ct WAB EN9 110 F8
Abbey Dale Cl HLWE CM17 76 A6
Abbey Dr ABLGY WD5 101 L6
LTNE LU2 7 K2
Abbey Ms DUN/WHIP LU6 39 G3
STAL AL1 * 8 E7
Abbey Mill End STALW/RED AL3 8 C7
Abbey Mill La STALW/RED AL3 8 D7
Abbey Rd CHES/WCR EN8 110 C8
Abbey Vw MLHL NW7 135 K6
RAD WD7 119 K1
STAL AL1 8 E9
Abbeyview WAB EN9 110 F7
Abbey View Rd STALW/RED AL3 8 C5
Abbey Wk DUN/HR/TOD LU5 26 E8
Abbis Orch HTCH/STOT SG5 147 N12
Abbot John Ms STALE/WH AL4 48 B4
Abbots Av STAL AL1 85 J5
Abbots Av West STAL AL1 85 H5
Abbotsbury Gdns PIN HA5 142 A8
Abbots Cl KNEB SG3 177 R8
Abbots Gv STVG SG1 11 G5
Abbots Hl HHS/BOV HP3 * 82 F7
Abbots Pk STAL AL1 85 K4
Abbots Pl BORE WD6 120 F4
Abbots Ri KGLGY WD4 100 D1
Abbots Rd ABLGY WD5 101 G5
Abbots Vw KGLGY WD4 82 D8
Abbotsweld HLWS CM18 75 H8
Abbotswood Pde LTNE LU2 * 7 K2
Abbots Wood Rd LTNE LU2 7 K2
Abbotts Ct WARE SG12 73 H1
Abbotts Crs ENC/FH EN2 124 F6
Abbotts Dr WAB EN9 111 L7
Abbotts La WARE SG12 182 B5
Abbotts Ri WARE SG12 73 H1
Abbotts Rd BAR EN5 122 F8
LWTH SG6 16 B3
Abbotts V CSHM HP5 97 G2
Abbotts Wy BSF CM23 43 L6
WARE SG12 73 H1
Abdale La BRKMPK AL9 105 M1
Abel Cl HHNE HP2 5 M3
Abercorn Gv RSLP HA4 141 H6
Abercorn Rd LTNW/LEA LU4 26 D6
Abercrombie Dr EN EN1 125 L5
Abercrombie Wy
HLWW/ROY CM19 2 C9
Aberdale Gdns
POTB/CUF EN6 106 D7
Aberdare Rd PEND EN3 126 A8
Aberdeen Rd
KTN/HRWW/WS HA3 143 K4
Aberford Rd BORE WD6 120 E6
Abigail Cl LTNN/LIM LU3 28 B6
Abingdon Pl POTB/CUF EN6 106 F6
Abingdon Rd LTNW/LEA LU4 27 G6
Abinger Cl STVG SG1 10 F8
Abraham Cl OXHEY WD19 131 M7
Abridge Cl CHES/WCR EN8 126 B1
Abstacle Hl TRING HP23 57 K2
Acacia Cl CHESW EN7 109 J1
CSHM HP5 96 E4
STAN HA7 143 J1
Acacia Gv BERK HP4 79 M2
Acacia Rd ENC/FH EN2 125 H5
The Acacias EBAR EN4 * 137 H1
Acacia St HAT AL10 87 L3
Acacia Wk HARP AL5 47 H7
Acers LCOL/BKTW AL2 103 G2
Achilles Cl HHNE HP2 62 D8
Ackroyd Rd ROY SG8 14 F5
Acme Rd WATN WD24 117 L4
Acorn Cl ENC/FH EN2 124 E5
LTNE LU2 28 D6
STAN HA7 143 M2
Acorn Gld WLYN AL6 50 D1
Acorn La POTB/CUF EN6 108 C3
Acorn Pl WATN WD24 117 L3
Acorn Rd HHNE HP2 5 M5
The Acorns STALE/WH AL4 * 86 B2
Acorn St WARE SG12 182 B10
Acrefield Rd CFSP/GDCR SL9 138 B6
Acremore St STDN SG11 42 D2
Acre Piece HTCHE/RSTV SG4 157 Q7
Acres End AMSS HP7 113 J5
The Acres SHFD SG17 146 D4
Acre Wy NTHWD HA6 141 K3
Acre Wd HHNE HP2 5 J3
Acrewood Wy STALE/WH AL4 86 D2
Acton Cl CHES/WCR EN8 110 C5
Acworth Crs LTNW/LEA LU4 27 G4
Ada Cl FBAR/BDGN N11 137 K6
Adamsfield CHESW EN7 91 K8
Adams House HLW CM20 2 E5
Adams Wy TRING HP23 169 M12
Adderley Rd BSF CM23 43 M2
KTN/HRWW/WS HA3 143 K3
Addington Wy LTNW/LEA LU4 27 H6
Addis Cl PEND EN3 126 B5
Addiscombe Rd WATW WD18 12 E5
Addison Av STHGT/OAK N14 137 M2
Addison Cl NTHWD HA6 141 L3
Addison Rd CSHM HP5 97 G3
PEND EN3 126 A5
Addison Wy NTHWD HA6 141 K3
Adelaide Cl EN EN1 125 J4
STAN HA7 133 L7
Adelaide St LTN LU1 6 D6
STALW/RED AL3 8 F4
Adele Av WLYN AL6 50 D2
Aden Rd PEND EN3 126 C8
Adeyfield Gdns HHNE HP2 5 L1
Adeyfield Rd HHNE HP2 5 H2
Adhara Rd NTHWD HA6 131 L8
Admirals Cl STALE/WH AL4 87 J5
Admiral St HERT/BAY SG13 53 L7
Admirals Wk HOD EN11 92 E1
STAL AL1 85 L4
Admiral Wy BERK HP4 59 K7
Adrian Cl BAR EN5 136 B2
DEN/HRF UB9 140 B3
Adrian Rd ABLGY WD5 101 J5
Adstock Ms CFSP/GDCR SL9 * 138 B3
Adstone Rd LTN LU1 40 D6
Aidans Cl DUN/WHIP LU6 25 J8
Ailsworth Rd LTNN/LIM LU3 27 L3
Ainsdale Crs PIN HA5 142 E5
Ainsdale Rd OXHEY WD19 132 A6
Aintree Rd ROY SG8 15 G7
Aintree Wy STVG SG1 34 A1
Airedale HHNE HP2 62 C7
Airfield Wy GSTN WD25 101 K8
Airport Approach Rd
LTNE LU2 174 B1
Airport Wy LTN LU1 41 K5
LTNE LU2 174 A3
Aitken Rd BAR EN5 136 A1
Akeman Cl STALW/RED AL3 * 84 D4
Akeman St TRING HP23 57 L2
Alamein Cl BROX EN10 92 B2
Alandale Dr PIN HA5 141 M3
Alan Dr BAR EN5 136 C2
Alban Av STALW/RED AL3 8 E2
Alban Crs BORE WD6 120 F5
Alban Pk STALE/WH AL4 * 86 D2
Alban Rd LWTH SG6 17 G6
Albans Vw GSTN WD25 101 M7
Albany Cl BUSH WD23 133 H2
Albany Ga CSHM HP5 96 F4
Albany Ms LCOL/BKTW AL2 * 102 E1
WARE SG12 54 C4
Albany Pde PEND EN3 126 B4
Albany Pk PEND EN3 * 126 B4
Albany Park Av PEND EN3 126 A5
Albany Rd PEND EN3 126 B3
WGCE AL7 * 50 C7
Albany Ter TRING HP23 * 169 M11
Albemarle Av CHES/WCR EN8 110 A2
POTB/CUF EN6 106 F7
Albemarle Pk STAN HA7 134 A8
Albemarle Rd EBAR EN4 137 J3
Albeny Ga STAL AL1 8 F8
Albermarle Cl LTNW/LEA LU4 26 D6
Albert Ct DUN/WHIP LU6 39 G2
Albert Gdns HLWE CM17 76 B6
Albert Rd ARL/CHE SG15 147 Q5
CSHM HP5 97 G5
EBAR EN4 123 G8
LTN LU1 7 G9
MLHL NW7 135 K8
RYLN/HDSTN HA2 143 G5
Albert Rd North WAT WD17 12 F3
Albert Rd South WAT WD17 12 E3
Albert St NFNCH/WDSPK N12 137 G8
STAL AL1 8 E7
STALW/RED AL3 172 G4
STVG SG1 10 B1
TRING HP23 57 L2
Albion Cl HERT/BAY SG13 53 J7
Albion Ct LTNE LU2 6 F3
Albion Hl HHNE HP2 4 F4
Albion Rd LBUZ LU7 169 P4
LTNE LU2 6 F4
STAL AL1 9 K6
Albion St DUN/WHIP LU6 38 F1
Albion Ter CHING E4 * 126 F8
Albuhera Cl ENC/FH EN2 124 E5
Albury Cl LTNN/LIM LU3 154 G12
Albury Dr PIN HA5 142 A3
Albury Grove Rd
CHES/WCR EN8 110 B4
Albury Ride CHES/WCR EN8 110 B5
Albury Rd STDN SG11 165 J11
Albury Wk CHES/WCR EN8 110 A4
Alconbury BSF CM23 166 D12
WGCE AL7 51 J7
Alconbury Cl BORE WD6 120 D5
Aldbanks DUN/WHIP LU6 25 K8
Aldbury Cl GSTN WD25 118 B2
STALE/WH AL4 66 A5
Aldbury Gdns TRING HP23 * 169 M11
Aldbury Gv WGCE AL7 50 F7
Aldbury Rd
RKW/CH/CXG WD3 129 K3
Aldeburgh Cl STVG SG1 20 E8
Aldenham Av RAD WD7 119 L3
Aldenham Cl LTNW/LEA LU4 26 D6
Aldenham Gv RAD WD7 103 M8
Aldenham Rd OXHEY WD19 13 K9
RAD WD7 119 L1
Alden Md PIN HA5 * 142 E2
Alderbury Rd STSD CM24 166 G5
Alder Cl BLDK SG7 17 J2
BSF CM23 43 K5
HOD EN11 72 F5
LCOL/BKTW AL2 102 F2
Alder Crs LTNN/LIM LU3 27 L6
Alderley Ct BERK HP4 79 M2
Alderman Cl BRKMPK AL9 88 A6
Aldersbrook Av EN EN1 125 J6
Alders Cl EDGW HA8 135 G8
Alders End La HARP AL5 46 D3
Alders Rd EDGW HA8 135 G8
Alders Wk SBW CM21 183 Q7
Alderton Cl LTNE LU2 29 H8
Alderton Dr BERK HP4 170 G9
Alder Wk GSTN WD25 117 M1
Alderwood Ms EBAR EN4 123 G4
Aldhous Cl LTNN/LIM LU3 27 M4
Aldis Ms PEND EN3 126 E3
Aldock WGCE AL7 68 E1
Aldock Rd STVG SG1 33 J1
Aldridge Av EDGW HA8 134 F6
PEND EN3 126 E4
Aldridge Ct BLDK SG7 149 J12
Aldwickbury Crs HARP AL5 47 H4
Aldwick STAL AL1 85 M5
Aldwick Rd HARP AL5 47 J5
Aldwyke Ri WARE SG12 54 A2
Aldykes HAT AL10 67 K8
Alesia Rd LTNN/LIM LU3 27 J3
Alexander Cl EBAR EN4 123 H8
Alexander Ct BLDK SG7 * 17 J1
Alexander Ga STVG SG1 34 A1
Alexander Ms HLWE CM17 76 B7
Alexander Rd HERT/WAT SG14 52 E7
HTCH/STOT SG5 148 D7
LCOL/BKTW AL2 86 A7
Alexander St CSHM HP5 97 G4
Alexandra Av LTNN/LIM LU3 27 M6
Alexandra Gv
NFNCH/WDSPK N12 136 F8
Alexandra Ms WAT WD17 12 D1
Alexandra Rd BORE WD6 121 H4
HHNE HP2 4 F1
HLWE CM17 76 A4
HTCH/STOT SG5 157 P4
KGLGY WD4 99 L4
PEND EN3 126 B8
RKW/CH/CXG WD3 115 L2
STAL AL1 9 H6
WAT WD17 12 D1
Alexandra Wy CHES/WCR EN8 110 D8
Aleyn Wy BLDK SG7 149 M12
Alfred St DUN/HR/TOD LU5 39 G1
Alfriston Av RYLN/HDSTN HA2 142 E8
Alfriston Cl LTNE LU2 29 G6
Algar Cl STAN HA7 133 K8
Alicia Av KTN/HRWW/WS HA3 143 M6
Alicia Gdns
KTN/HRWW/WS HA3 143 M6
Alington La LWTH SG6 16 D6
Allandale HHNE HP2 62 B8
STALW/RED AL3 84 F5
Allandale Crs POTB/CUF EN6 106 C6
Allandale Rd PEND EN3 126 B2
Allard Crs BUSH WD23 133 G5
Allard Wy BROX EN10 92 C3
Alldicks Rd HHNE HP2 5 L6
Allenby Av DUN/HR/TOD LU5 26 E8
Allen Cl DUN/HR/TOD LU5 39 H1
RAD WD7 104 C6
STALE/WH AL4 48 B6
Allen Ct HAT AL10 * 87 M2
Allendale LTNN/LIM LU3 27 L1
Allerford Ct HRW HA1 142 F7
Allerton Cl BORE WD6 120 D4
Allerton Rd BORE WD6 120 C4
Alleyns Rd STVG SG1 10 C1
Allington Rd
RYLN/HDSTN HA2 143 G7
Allis Ms HLWE CM17 76 A4
Allison LWTH SG6 17 G4
Allison Cl WAB EN9 111 L7
Allmains Cl WAB EN9 93 M7
All Saints Cl BSF CM23 44 A1
Allsaints Crs GSTN WD25 102 B7
All Saints La
RKW/CH/CXG WD3 130 E2
All Saints Ms STAN HA7 143 J1
All Saints Rd DUN/HR/TOD LU5 25 M4
Allton Rd HNLW SG16 147 J5
Allum La BORE WD6 134 C1
Allum Wy TRDG/WHET N20 137 G4
Allwood Rd CHESW EN7 109 K1
Alma Cut STAL AL1 9 G8
Alma Link LTN LU1 6 E5
Alma Rd BERK HP4 59 J7
CSHM HP5 97 G3
PEND EN3 126 C7
STAL AL1 9 H7
Alma Rw
KTN/HRWW/WS HA3 * 143 H3
Alma St LTN LU1 6 E5
Almonds La STVG SG1 33 J1
The Almonds STAL AL1 85 M6
Almond Wy BORE WD6 120 F8
RYLN/HDSTN HA2 142 F4
Almshouse La EN EN1 125 M3
Alms La BLDK SG7 149 P1
Alnwick Dr TRING HP23 168 D2
Alpha Pl BSF CM23 43 M1
Alpha Rd PEND EN3 126 C8
Alpine Cl HTCHE/RSTV SG4 157 Q8
Alpine Wk BUSH WD23 133 J5
Alpine Wy LTNN/LIM LU3 27 H1
Alsa Gdns RBSF CM22 167 L3
Alsa Leys RBSF CM22 167 L3
Alsa St STSD CM24 166 H4
Alsop Cl DUN/HR/TOD LU5 25 M3
LCOL/BKTW AL2 104 C2
Alston Rd BAR EN5 122 C7
HHW HP1 4 A5
Altair Wy NTHWD HA6 131 K8
Altham Ct RYLN/HDSTN HA2 * 142 F3
Altham Gdns OXHEY WD19 132 B7
Altham Gv HLW CM20 3 J1
Altham Rd PIN HA5 142 C2
Althorp Cl BAR EN5 135 L3
Althorpe Rd HRW HA1 * 143 G7
Althorp Rd LTNN/LIM LU3 6 B1
STAL AL1 9 H4
Alton Av STAN HA7 143 K2
Alton Rd LTN LU1 7 H9
Altwood HARP AL5 47 H4
Alva Wy OXHEY WD19 132 B5
Alverstone Av EBAR EN4 137 H3
Alverton STALW/RED AL3 65 G7
Alveston Av
KTN/HRWW/WS HA3 143 M5
Alwin Pl WATW WD18 117 J8
Alwyn Cl BORE WD6 134 D2
LTNE LU2 28 C7
Alyngton BERK HP4 59 J6
Alzey Gdns HARP AL5 47 H5
Amberleigh Gdns
RKW/CH/CXG WD3 115 K2
Amberley Cl HARP AL5 46 F3
LTNE LU2 29 H5
PIN HA5 142 D5
Amberley Gn WARE SG12 54 A1
Amberry Ct HLW CM20 2 F4
Ambleside HARP AL5 * 47 H3
LTNN/LIM LU3 27 K4
Ambleside Crs PEND EN3 126 B7
Ambrose La HARP AL5 46 D1
Amenbury La HARP AL5 46 E4
Amersham Pl AMSS HP7 114 A5
Amersham Rd
CFSP/GDCR SL9 128 B7
Amersham Wy AMS HP6 114 C5
Amesbury WAB EN9 111 L6
Ames Cl LTNN/LIM LU3 154 F12
Amethyst Wk WGCW AL8 67 M1
Amhurst Rd LTNW/LEA LU4 26 D6
Amor Wy LWTH SG6 16 F3
Amwell Cl GSTN WD25 118 C1
Amwell Common WGCE AL7 50 F8
Amwell Ct HOD EN11 72 E6
WAB EN9 111 J7
Amwell End WARE SG12 54 B5
Amwell Hl WARE SG12 54 D7
Amwell La STALE/WH AL4 47 M6
WARE SG12 54 E7
Amwell St HOD EN11 72 E6
Amy La CSHM HP5 96 F6
Anchor Cl CHES/WCR EN8 110 B2
Anchor La HHW HP1 4 B6
WARE SG12 179 P11
Anchor Rd BLDK SG7 17 K2
Anchor St BSF CM23 43 M3
Anderson Cl BSF CM23 166 B3
DEN/HRF UB9 139 L3
Anderson Rd RAD WD7 104 E7
STVGE SG2 34 A3
Anderson's La BUNT SG9 160 A7
Andover Cl LTNW/LEA LU4 27 G3
Andrew Cl RAD WD7 104 D7
Andrewsfield WGCE AL7 51 G7
Andrew's La CHESW EN7 109 J2
Anelle Ri HHS/BOV HP3 82 D6
Angel Cl LTNW/LEA LU4 27 H6
Angell's Meadow BLDK SG7 149 P1
Angel Rd HRW HA1 143 J8
Angels La DUN/HR/TOD LU5 25 M4
Anglefield Rd BERK HP4 79 L1
Anglesey Cl BSF CM23 43 J2
Anglesey Rd OXHEY WD19 132 A8
PEND EN3 125 M8
Anglesmede Crs PIN HA5 142 E5
Anglesmede Wy PIN HA5 142 D5
Angle Ways STVGE SG2 33 K7
Anglian Cl WATN WD24 13 H1
Angotts Md STVG SG1 32 F3
Angus Cl LTNW/LEA LU4 26 E6
Anmer Gdns LTNW/LEA LU4 26 F5
Annables La HARP AL5 173 P5
Annette Cl
KTN/HRWW/WS HA3 143 J4
Anns Cl TRING HP23 57 J2
Anselm Rd PIN HA5 142 D2
Anson Cl HHS/BOV HP3 98 D1
STAL AL1 85 M4
STALE/WH AL4 66 A4
Anson Wk NTHWD HA6 131 G7
Anstee Rd LTNW/LEA LU4 26 F3
Anthony Cl MLHL NW7 135 J7
OXHEY WD19 132 B4
Anthony Gdns LTN LU1 6 D9
Anthony Rd BORE WD6 120 C6
Anthorne Cl POTB/CUF EN6 106 F5
Anthus Ms NTHWD HA6 141 H2
Antoinette Ct ABLGY WD5 * 101 K3
Antoneys Cl PIN HA5 142 B4
Antonine Ga STALW/RED AL3 84 E3
Anvil Cl HHS/BOV HP3 98 F2
Anvil Pl LCOL/BKTW AL2 * 84 E8
Apex Pde MLHL NW7 * 135 H7
Apex Point BRKMPK AL9 * 88 A4
Aplins Cl HARP AL5 46 D3
Apollo Av NTHWD HA6 131 L8
Apollo Cl DUN/HR/TOD LU5 39 H2
Apollo Wy HHNE HP2 62 C8
STVGE SG2 34 A1
Appleby Gdns DUN/WHIP LU6 38 F2
Appleby St CHESW EN7 91 J8
Apple Cots HHS/BOV HP3 98 E1
Applecroft BERK HP4 59 J7
HNLW SG16 147 J6
LCOL/BKTW AL2 102 F2
Applecroft Rd LTNE LU2 29 G5
WGCW AL8 49 M7
Applefield AMSS HP7 114 A5
Appleford's Cl HOD EN11 72 D5
Apple Glebe
AMP/FLIT/BLC MK45 155 J3
Apple Gv EN EN1 125 J7
The Apple Orchard HHNE HP2 62 D8
Appleton Av WARE SG12 181 J12
Appleton Cl AMSS HP7 113 M6
HLWW/ROY CM19 2 C8
Appleton Flds BSF CM23 43 L5
Appletree Dell
RKW/CH/CXG WD3 * 115 K8
Appletree Gdns EBAR EN4 123 J8
Appletree Gv STALW/RED AL3 173 R11
Appletrees HTCH/STOT SG5 * 157 M7
Appletree Wk CSHM HP5 97 H8
GSTN WD25 117 M1
Applewood Cl HARP AL5 46 C2
TRDG/WHET N20 137 J4
Appleyard Ter PEND EN3 * 126 A3
Approach La MLHL NW7 136 C8
Approach Rd EBAR EN4 123 G8
STAL AL1 9 H8
The Approach EN EN1 125 M6
POTB/CUF EN6 106 D6
Appspond La LCOL/BKTW AL2 84 A6
Apsley Cl BSF CM23 43 L5
HRW HA1 143 G7
Apsley End Rd
HTCH/STOT SG5 146 A12
Apton Ct BSF CM23 43 M2
Apton Flds BSF CM23 43 M3
Apton Rd BSF CM23 43 M2
Aquarius Wy NTHWD HA6 131 L8
Aragon Cl ENC/FH EN2 124 D4
HHNE HP2 63 G5
Aran Cl HARP AL5 47 H7
Arbour Cl LTNN/LIM LU3 154 G12
Arbour Rd PEND EN3 126 B8
The Arbour HERT/BAY SG13 71 H1
Arbour Vw AMSS HP7 113 M5
Arbroath Gn OXHEY WD19 131 L6
Arbroath Rd LTNN/LIM LU3 154 D12
The Arcade LTNW/LEA LU4 6 B2
Archer Cl KGLGY WD4 100 D3
Archer Rd STVG SG1 11 H1
Archers BUNT SG9 159 K9
HLWW/ROY CM19 94 E2
Archers Cl HERT/WAT SG14 53 G6
Archers Dr PEND EN3 126 A6
Archers Flds STAL AL1 9 J1
Archers Green La WLYN AL6 51 H5
Archers Ride WGCE AL7 68 F1
Archers Wy LWTH SG6 16 B3
Archery Cl
KTN/HRWW/WS HA3 143 K5
The Arches LWTH SG6 16 E2
Archfield WGCE AL7 50 C4
Archibald Cl PEND EN3 126 B2
Archive Cl RAYLNE/WEN HP22 168 B12
Archive Rd
RAYLNE/WEN HP22 168 B12
Arch Rd HTCHE/RSTV SG4 20 B5
Archway Pde LTNN/LIM LU3 * 27 K5
Archway Rd LTNN/LIM LU3 27 J5
Arden Cl BUSH WD23 133 K3
HHS/BOV HP3 98 E2
Arden Gv HARP AL5 46 F4
Arden Mhor PIN HA5 141 M6
Arden Pl LTNE LU2 7 G1
Arden Press Wy LWTH SG6 16 F3
Ardens Marsh STALE/WH AL4 * 66 C8
Ardens Wy STALE/WH AL4 66 B8
Ardleigh Gn LTNE LU2 29 J8
Ardley Cl DUN/WHIP LU6 39 G4
Ardley Crs RBSF CM22 184 H7
Ardross Av NTHWD HA6 131 J8
Arenson Wy DUN/HR/TOD LU5 25 M7
Argent Wy CHESW EN7 109 H1
Argyle Ct WATW WD18 * 12 A6
Argyle Rd BAR EN5 122 A8
NFNCH/WDSPK N12 136 E8
RYLN/HDSTN HA2 142 F8
Argyle Wy STVG SG1 10 A4
Argyll Av LTNN/LIM LU3 28 A7
Argyll Rd HHNE HP2 62 C5
Arkley Dr BAR EN5 121 L8
Arkley La BAR EN5 121 L7
Arkley Rd HHNE HP2 62 F5
Arkley Vw BAR EN5 121 M8
Arkwrights HLW CM20 3 J5
Arlesey New Rd LWTH SG6 16 A2
Arlesey Rd HTCH/STOT SG5 157 N1
Arlington NFNCH/WDSPK N12 136 E6
Arlington Crs CHES/WCR EN8 110 C8
Arlington Dr RSLP HA4 141 H8
Arlington Rd STHGT/OAK N14 137 M5
Armand Cl WAT WD17 117 K4
Armfield Rd ENC/FH EN2 125 H5
Armitage Cl
RKW/CH/CXG WD3 116 B8
Armitage Gdns LTNW/LEA LU4 27 H8
Armourers Cl BSF CM23 43 H5
Armour Ri HTCHE/RSTV SG4 157 R3
Armstrong Cl BORE WD6 121 G7
LCOL/BKTW AL2 104 C1
RSLP HA4 141 L8
Armstrong Crs EBAR EN4 123 H7
Armstrong Gdns RAD WD7 104 C6
Arnald Wy DUN/HR/TOD LU5 25 L5
Arncliffe Crs LTNE LU2 6 F1
Arnett Cl RKW/CH/CXG WD3 129 L2
Arnett Wy RKW/CH/CXG WD3 129 L2
Arnold Av East PEND EN3 126 E4
Arnold Av West PEND EN3 126 D4
Arnold Cl AMP/FLIT/BLC MK45 155 J3
HTCHE/RSTV SG4 157 R5
LTNE LU2 28 E6
STVG SG1 21 H8
Arnold Rd WAB EN9 127 G1
Arnolds La BLDK SG7 144 D11
Arnold Ter STAN HA7 * 133 K8
Arran Cl HHS/BOV HP3 83 G4
Arran Dr STAN HA7 134 A7
Arran Gn OXHEY WD19 * 132 B7
Arranmore Ct BUSH WD23 * 13 M5
Arretine Cl STALW/RED AL3 84 D4
Arrow Cl LTNN/LIM LU3 27 J3
Artesian Gv BAR EN5 123 G8
Arthur Gibbons Ct STVG SG1 * 21 L8
Arthur Rd STAL AL1 85 M2
Arthur St BUSH WD23 13 K5
LTN LU1 6 F8
Artichoke Dell
RKW/CH/CXG WD3 * 115 J8
Artisan Crs STALW/RED AL3 8 C3
Arundel Cl CHES/WCR EN8 109 M2
HHNE HP2 82 F1
STVGE SG2 34 C6
Arundel Dr BORE WD6 121 G8
Arundel Gv STALW/RED AL3 65 H6
Arundel Rd ABLGY WD5 101 L6
Arundel Rd EBAR EN4 123 J7
LTNW/LEA LU4 27 L7
Ascot Cl BORE WD6 134 E1
BSF CM23 44 C1
Ascot Ct RKW/CH/CXG WD3 * 130 F2
Ascot Crs STVG SG1 21 M8
Ascot Gdns PEND EN3 126 A3
Ascot Rd LTNN/LIM LU3 27 M7
ROY SG8 15 G7
WATW WD18 131 J1
Ascots La BRKMPK AL9 68 C4
Ascott Ct PIN HA5 * 141 L6
Ashanger La BLDK SG7 18 B5
Ashbourne Sq NTHWD HA6 141 J1
Ashbourne Av
TRDG/WHET N20 137 K5
Ashbourne Cl LWTH SG6 16 F5
NFNCH/WDSPK N12 136 F7
Ashbourne Ct STALE/WH AL4 86 A4
Ashbourne Gdns
HERT/BAY SG13 71 J1
Ashbourne Gv MLHL NW7 135 H8
Ashbourne Rd BROX EN10 92 D3
Ashbrook La HTCHE/RSTV SG4 157 R10
Ashburnam Wk STVGE SG2 33 K8
Ashburnham Cl
OXHEY WD19 * 131 L6
Ashburnham Dr OXHEY WD19 131 L6
Ashburnham Gdns HRW HA1 143 K8
Ashburnham Rd LTN LU1 6 A5
Ashbury Cl HAT AL10 67 J8
Ashby Ct HHNE HP2 62 F4
Ashby Dr AMP/FLIT/BLC MK45 155 J2
Ashby Gdns STAL AL1 85 H6
Ashby Ri BSF CM23 166 D12
Ashby Rd BERK HP4 59 H6
WATN WD24 117 L4
Ash Cl ABLGY WD5 101 H6
BRKMPK AL9 88 E7
DEN/HRF UB9 140 B3
EDGW HA8 135 G7
GSTN WD25 117 M1
STAN HA7 143 L1
Ashcombe WGCW AL8 50 C3
Ashcombe Gdns EDGW HA8 134 E7
Ash Copse LCOL/BKTW AL2 102 D5
Ashcroft DUN/WHIP LU6 25 K8
PIN HA5 142 E1
Ashcroft Cl HARP AL5 47 J5
Ashcroft Dr DEN/HRF UB9 139 K8
Ashcroft Rd LTNE LU2 28 F7
Ashdale BSF CM23 43 K5
Ashdale Gdns LTNN/LIM LU3 154 G12
Ashdale Gv STAN HA7 143 K1
Ashdales STAL AL1 85 H6
Ashdene PIN HA5 142 A5
Ashdon Rd BUSH WD23 13 K4
Ashdown LWTH SG6 148 C12
Ashdown Crs CHES/WCR EN8 110 C2
Ashdown Dr BORE WD6 120 D6
Ashdown Rd PEND EN3 126 A7
STVGE SG2 177 P2
Ashdown Wy AMS HP6 113 H3
Ash Dr HAT AL10 87 L3
HTCHE/RSTV SG4 157 Q9
HTCHE/RSTV SG4 * 175 K9
Ashendene Rd CHESW EN7 90 F7
HERT/BAY SG13 70 D8
Asheridge Rd CSHM HP5 96 D2
Ashfield Av BUSH WD23 132 F2
Ashfield Rd CSHM HP5 97 H3
Ashfields GSTN WD25 117 K1
Ashfield Wy LTNN/LIM LU3 27 L3
Ashford Crs PEND EN3 126 A6
Ashford Gn OXHEY WD19 132 B8
Ash Gv AMS HP6 112 E2
DEN/HRF UB9 140 B3
DUN/HR/TOD LU5 39 H1
HHS/BOV HP3 82 D6
STALE/WH AL4 48 A4

Ash Groves SBW CM21 ....184 A7
Ash Hill Cl BUSH WD23 ....132 F4
Ash Hill Dr PIN HA5 ....142 A5
Ashlea Rd CFSP/GDCR SL9 ....138 C4
Ashleigh STVGE SG2 ....11 M7
Ashley Cl HHNE HP2 ....5 L6
  LBUZ LU7 ....169 L1
  PIN HA5 ....141 M4
  WGCW AL8 ....50 A5
Ashley Dr BORE WD6 ....135 G4
Ashley Gdns HARP AL5 ....46 B2
Ashley Green Rd CSHM HP5 ....97 H1
Ashley Rd HERT/WAT SG14 ....52 E8
  PEND EN3 ....126 A6
  STAL AL1 ....86 A2
Ashleys RKW/CH/CXG WD3 ....129 J3
Ashlyn Cl BUSH WD23 ....13 M6
Ashlyns Ct BERK HP4 ....79 M2
Ashlyns Rd BERK HP4 ....79 M2
Ash Meadow MHAD SG10 ....181 M7
Ashmead Pl AMSS HP7 ....114 A5
Ash Mi ROY SG8 ....152 E10
Ashmore Gdns HHS/BOV HP3 ....82 D3
Ash Ride ENC/FH EN2 ....124 E1
Ashridge Cl HHS/BOV HP3 ....98 E2
Ashridge Dr LCOL/BKTW AL2 ....102 C4
  OXHEY WD19 ....132 A8
Ashridge Gdns PIN HA5 ....142 C6
Ashridge La CSHM HP5 ....98 B5
Ashridge Ri BERK HP4 ....59 K8
Ash Rd LTNW/LEA LU4 ....6 A3
  TRING HP23 ....57 L1
  WARE SG12 ....54 E2
Ashton Dr DUN/WHIP LU6 ....25 M8
  LTN LU1 ....6 F9
  PEND EN3 ....126 C2
Ashton's La BLDK SG7 ....17 J4
Ashton Sq DUN/WHIP LU6 ....38 F1
Ashtree Ct STAL AL1 ....9 J6
Ash Tree Fld HLW CM20 ....74 E3
Ash Tree Rd
  DUN/HR/TOD LU5 ....25 M3
  WATN WD24 ....117 M2
Ashtree Wy HHW HP1 ....81 L3
Ashurst Cl NTHWD HA6 ....141 M2
Ashurst Rd EBAR EN4 ....137 K1
  NFNCH/WDSPK N12 ....137 J3
Ash V RKW/CH/CXG WD3 ....129 H8
Ashville Wy BLDK SG7 ....149 L12
Ashwell Av LTNN/LIM LU3 ....27 G1
Ashwell Cl HTCHE/RSTV SG4 ....20 F5
Ashwell Common STVG SG1 ....20 F6
Ashwell Pk HARP AL5 ....47 H4
Ashwell Rd BLDK SG7 ....144 D12
Ashwell St ROY SG8 ....14 B3
  STALW/RED AL3 ....8 E1
Ashwells Wy CSTG HP8 ....128 A5
Ashwell Wk RKW/CH/TOD LU5 ....26 C3
Ashwood Dr CSHM HP5 ....96 F4
Ashwood Ms STAL AL1 ....8 E9
Ashwood Rd POTB/CUF EN6 ....106 F7
Ashworth Pl HLWE CM17 ....76 B5
Askew Rd NTHWD HA6 ....131 H5
Aspasia Cl STAL AL1 ....9 K8
Aspen Cl LCOL/BKTW AL2 ....102 C4
  STVGE SG2 ....177 P2
Aspenden Rd BUNT SG9 ....159 J12
Aspen Gv PIN HA5 ....141 M5
Aspen Park Dr GSTN WD25 ....117 M1
Aspen Pl STVGE SG2 ....177 M1
Aspens Pl HHW HP1 ....81 K5
The Aspens BSF CM23 ....166 D11
  HTCHE/RSTV SG4 ....157 G2
Aspen Wy PEND EN3 ....126 B1
  WGCE AL7 ....51 G8
Aspfield Rw HHW HP1 ....61 M8
Aspley Cl LTNW/LEA LU4 ....26 C6
Ass House La
  KTN/HRWW/WS HA3 ....132 F7
Astall Cl KTN/HRWW/WS HA3 ....143 H3
Aster Cl BSF CM23 ....43 K5
The Asters CHESW EN7 ....109 H2
Astley Gn LTNE LU2 ....29 H7
Astley Rd HLW CM20 ....4 D3
Aston Cl BUSH WD23 ....133 G1
  WATN WD24 ....13 H2
Aston End Rd STVGE SG2 ....34 C6
Aston Gra HERT/WAT SG14 ....53 H5
Aston La STVGE SG2 ....178 A2
Aston Ri HTCHE/RSTV SG4 ....157 R7
Aston Rd STDN SG11 ....163 P11
Astons Rd NTHWD HA6 ....131 G6
Aston Vw HHNE HP2 ....62 E4
Aston Wy POTB/CUF EN6 ....107 H6
Astral Cl HNLW WD16 ....147 K6
Astrope La TRING HP23 ....168 D2
Astwick Av HAT AL10 ....67 K5
Astwick Rd HTCH/STOT SG5 ....148 C4
Athelstan Rd HHS/BOV HP3 ....5 K9
Athelstan Wk North WGCE AL7 ....50 B8
Athelstone Rd
  KTN/HRWW/WS HA3 ....143 H4
Athenaeum Rd
  TRDG/WHET N20 ....137 G4
Athena Rd NTHWD HA6 ....141 M4
Athenia Cl CHESW EN7 ....96 A3
Atherstone Rd LTNW/LEA LU4 ....27 H8
Atherton End SBW CM21 ....72 D6
Atherton Pl RYLN/HDSTN HA2 ....143 G5
Athlone Cl RAD WD7 * 119 G2
Athol Cl PIN HA5 ....141 M3
Athol Gdns PIN HA5 ....141 M3
Atholl Cl LTNN/LIM LU3 ....27 H1
Atria Rd NTHWD HA6 ....131 L8
Attenborough Cl
  OXHEY WD19 ....132 C6
Attfield Cl TRDG/WHET N20 ....137 H5
Attimore Cl WGCW AL8 ....49 M8
Attimore Rd WGCW AL8 ....49 M8
Auber Cl HOD EN11 ....72 D4
Aubrey Av LCOL/BKTW AL2 ....86 F3
Aubrey Gdns LTNN/LIM LU4 ....26 E6
Aubrey La STALW/RED AL3 ....63 L5
Aubreys LWTH SG6 ....16 D7
Aubreys Rd HHW HP1 ....81 J3
Aubries STVGE SG2 ....34 F1
Auckland Cl EN1 EN1 ....125 M3
Auckland Rd POTB/CUF EN6 ....106 B6
Auden Dr BORE WD6 ....134 E7
Audley Cl BORE WD6 ....120 E7
Audley Gdns WAB EN9 ....111 G8
Audley Pl LTNE LU2 * 7 J2
Audley Rd ENC/FH EN2 ....124 E1
Audley St EBAR EN4 ....43 M6
Audwick Cl CHES/WCR EN8 ....110 B2
Augustine Rd
  KTN/HRWW/WS HA3 ....142 F3
Augustus St STALW/RED AL3 ....84 D1
  STAN HA7 ....134 A6

Augustus Ga STVGE SG2 ....34 A1
Austell Gdns MLHL NW7 ....135 J6
Austen Paths STVGE SG2 ....34 A1
Austenway CFSP/GDCR SL9 ....138 C5
Austenwood Cl
  CFSP/GDCR SL9 ....138 A4
Austenwood La
  CFSP/GDCR SL9 ....138 B4
Austin Rd LTNN/LIM LU3 ....27 M5
Austins Md HHS/BOV HP3 ....98 D3
Austins Pl HHNE HP2 ....82 B1
Austin Vls GSTN WD25 * 101 M5
Autumn Cl EN1 EN1 ....125 M6
Autumn Glades HHS/BOV HP3 ....83 G4
Autumn Gv WGCE AL7 ....68 F1
Avalon Cl ENC/FH EN2 ....124 E6
  WATN WD25 ....102 C6
Avebury Av LTNE LU2 ....7 G3
Avebury Rd HHNE HP2 ....62 E7
Avenue Ap KGLGY WD4 ....100 A4
Avenue Ct WLYN AL6 ....177 L10
Avenue Grimaldi LTNN/LIM LU3 ....27 M3
Avenue One LWTH SG6 ....17 G3
Avenue Ri BUSH WD23 ....132 E1
Avenue St Nicholas HARP AL5 ....46 B4
Avenue Ter OXHEY WD19 ....132 C2
The Avenue AMSS HP7 ....113 G4
  BAR EN5 ....122 C7
  BUSH WD23 ....118 D8
  DUN/WHIP LU6 ....38 C2
  FBAR/BDGN N11 ....137 M8
  HERT/WAT SG14 ....81 J1
  HHW HP1 ....92 D1
  HOD EN11 ....72 A6
  HTCH/STOT SG5 ....148 D7
  HTCHE/RSTV SG4 ....157 G6
  KTN/HRWW/WS HA3 ....143 K3
  LTNW/LEA LU4 ....27 H4
  NTHWD HA6 ....141 J5
  PIN HA5 ....141 M5
  PIN HA5 ....142 D8
  POTB/CUF EN6 ....106 D4
  RAD WD7 ....103 L8
  WAB EN9 ....94 A7
  WAT WD17 ....12 D2
  WLYN AL6 ....177 L10
Avery La LOU IG10 ....127 L4
Avia Cl HHS/BOV HP3 ....82 B6
Avior Dr NTHWD HA6 ....131 K7
Avocet Cl LWTH SG6 ....16 E4
Avocet Cl STALW/RED AL3 ....65 C7
Avon Cl GSTN WD25 ....142 E2
Avon Ct PIN HA5 * 142 E2
Avondale Av EBAR EN4 ....137 K4
  NFNCH/WDSPK N12 ....136 F8
Avondale Crs PEND EN3 ....126 C1
Avondale Rd
  KTN/HRWW/WS HA3 ....143 K5
  LTN LU1 ....6 B3
Avon Dr STVG SG1 ....21 K6
Avon Ms PIN HA5 ....142 D3
Avon Rd HNLW SG16 ....147 M5
Avon Sq HHNE HP2 ....62 D5
Axe Cl LTNN/LIM LU3 ....27 J3
Aycliffe Cl BORE WD6 ....120 D5
Aycliffe Rd BORE WD6 ....120 D5
Aydon Rd LTNN/LIM LU3 ....27 M3
Aylands Rd PEND EN3 ....126 D7
Aylesbury Ring TRING HP23 ....168 D7
Aylets Fld HLWS CM18 ....75 J8
Aylmer Cl STAN HA7 ....133 L7
Aylmer Dr STAN HA7 ....133 L7
Aylotts Cl BUNT SG9 ....158 H9
Aylsham Rd HOD EN11 ....72 G5
Aylward Dr STVGE SG2 ....11 L2
Aylward Gdns CSHM HP5 ....96 E4
Aylwards Ri STAN HA7 ....133 L7
Aynho St WATW WD18 ....12 B5
Aynscombe Cl DUN/WHIP LU6 ....38 D1
Aynsley Gdns HLWE CM17 ....76 C5
Aynsworth Av BSF CM23 ....166 C11
Ayot Gn WLYN AL6 ....49 K6
Ayot Little Green La WLYN AL6 ....49 K6
Ayot St Peter Rd WLYN AL6 ....49 H1
Ayr Cl STVG SG1 ....34 A1
Ayres End La HARP AL5 ....65 H1
Aysgarth Cl HARP AL5 ....46 F5
Aysgarth Rd STALW/RED AL3 ....173 Q11
Azalea Cl LCOL/BKTW AL2 ....104 A1
Azalea Wk PIN HA5 ....141 M1

B

Baas Hl BROX EN10 ....92 B3
Baas Hill Cl BROX EN10 ....92 C3
Baas La BROX EN10 ....92 C3
Babbage Rd STVG SG1 ....32 F4
Babington Rd
  RAYLNE/WEN HP22 ....56 B7
Back La BUNT SG9 ....158 H10
  GSTN WD25 ....119 J5
  HTCHE/RSTV SG4 ....31 K3
  RBSF CM22 ....184 B2
  ROY SG8 ....15 J1
  WAB EN9 ....93 M7
  WLYN AL6 ....51 J3
The Backs CSHM HP5 ....97 G5
Back St BLDK SG7 ....149 N7
  LTNE LU2 * 7 G6
The Back BERK HP4 ....60 F8
Bacons Dr POTB/CUF EN6 ....108 C7
Bacon's Yd BLDK SG7 ....149 P11
Badburgham Ct WAB EN9 ....111 K7
Baddeley Cl PEND EN3 ....126 E3
  STVGE SG2 ....33 J7
Bader Cl STVG SG1 ....21 J1
  WGCE AL7 ....51 G1
Badger Cl KNEB SG3 ....177 M1
Badgers BSF CM23 ....43 L5
Badgers Cl BORE WD6 * 120 D7
  ENC/FH EN2 ....124 D1
  HERT/BAY SG13 ....71 H2
  HRW HA1 ....143 H3
  STVG SG1 ....10 F5
Badgers Cft BROX EN10 ....92 C3
  HHNE HP2 ....83 J1
  TRDG/WHET N20 ....136 D7
Badgers Dene DUN/WHIP LU6 ....38 C1
Badgers Meadow
  RAYLNE/WEN HP22 ....56 A8
Badgers Wk
  RKW/CH/CXG WD3 ....115 K8
  WLYN AL6 ....177 Q12
Badger Wy HAT AL10 ....87 M2

Badingham Dr HARP AL5 ....46 C5
Badminton Cl BORE WD6 ....120 E6
  HRW HA1 * 143 J6
  STVGE SG2 ....177 J2
Badminton Dr BROX EN10 ....92 C2
Bagwicks Cl LTNN/LIM LU3 ....27 J2
Bailey St LTN LU1 ....7 H8
Baines La KNEB SG3 ....177 M1
Baird Cl BUSH WD23 ....132 F2
Baird Rd EN1 EN1 ....125 M7
Bairstow Ct BORE WD6 ....120 C5
Baker Cl STAL AL1 ....9 M3
Bakers Ct STVG SG1 ....10 A4
Bakerscroft CHES/WCR EN8 * 110 B2
Bakers Gv WGCE AL7 ....51 G8
Bakers Hi BAR EN5 ....122 F6
Baker's La HTCHE/RSTV SG4 ....176 B8
Bakers La ROY SG8 ....152 E4
Bakers Rd CHESW EN7 ....96 M4
Baker St BAR EN5 ....122 C1
  EN1 EN1 ....125 H6
  HERT/BAY SG13 ....71 M1
  LTN LU1 ....6 F9
  POTB/CUF EN6 ....106 D7
  STVG SG1 ....10 B3
Bakery Cl HLWW/ROY CM19 ....74 C1
Bakewell Cl LTNW/LEA LU4 ....27 H3
Balcary Gdns BERK HP4 ....79 J2
Balcombe Cl LTNE LU2 ....29 G5
Balcon Wy BORE WD6 ....121 G5
Baldock Cl LTNE LU2 ....29 G6
Baldock La BLDK SG7 ....17 J4
Baldock Rd BUNT SG9 ....158 F10
  HTCH/STOT SG5 ....148 B8
  LWTH SG6 ....16 F4
  ROY SG8 ....150 A4
Baldock St ROY SG8 ....14 B3
  WARE SG12 ....54 B3
Baldock Wy BORE WD6 ....120 D5
Baldwins WGCE AL7 ....50 F7
Baldwins La
  RKW/CH/CXG WD3 ....116 A3
Balfour Cl HARP AL5 ....47 H3
Balfour Rd TRDG/WHET N20 ....137 K6
Balfour Ms HHS/BOV HP3 ....98 C5
Balfour Rd HRW HA1 ....143 H7
Balfour St HERT/WAT SG14 ....53 G5
Baliol Rd HTCH/STOT SG5 ....157 P5
Ballards Rw
  RAYLNE/WEN HP22 * 168 B11
Ballater Cl OXHEY WD19 ....132 A7
Ballinger Ct BERK HP4 ....79 L2
Ballsough Hl
  HTCHE/RSTV SG4 ....175 P8
Balmoral Cl CHES/WCR EN8 ....110 A3
  STVGE SG2 ....177 J2
Balmoral Dr BORE WD6 ....121 H8
Balmoral Rd ABLGY WD5 ....101 J4
  HTCH/STOT SG5 ....157 N4
  PEND EN3 ....126 C1
  WATN WD24 ....118 A4
Balmore Crs EBAR EN4 ....137 L1
Balmore Wd LTNN/LIM LU3 ....154 H12
Balsams Cl HERT/BAY SG13 ....71 M3
Bampton Rd LTNW/LEA LU4 ....26 A3
Bamville Wd HARP AL5 * 47 H8
Banbury Cl ENC/FH EN2 ....124 F5
  LTNW/LEA LU4 ....27 K5
Banbury St WATW WD18 * 12 D7
Bancroft HTCH/STOT SG5 ....157 P6
Bancroft Gdns
  KTN/HRWW/WS HA3 ....143 G3
Bancroft Rd
  KTN/HRWW/WS HA3 ....143 G4
  LTNN/LIM LU3 ....27 M5
Bandley Ri STVGE SG2 ....34 A6
Banes Down WAB EN9 ....93 M4
Bank Cl LTNW/LEA LU4 ....27 K5
Bank Gn CSHM HP5 ....78 A5
Bank Mi BERK HP4 ....80 C1
Bankmill Br BERK HP4 ....80 C2
Bank Mill La BERK HP4 ....80 C2
Bankside ENC/FH EN2 ....124 C5
Bank Side ROY SG8 ....152 H5
Bankside Cl DEN/HRF UB9 ....139 L1
  DUN/HR/TOD LU5 ....25 L4
Bankside Down
  RKW/CH/CXG WD3 ....130 B2
Banks Rd BORE WD6 ....121 G6
Banton Cl EN1 EN1 ....125 M6
Barbaraville Camp
  BRKMPK AL9 * 68 D5
Barbel Cl CHES/WCR EN8 ....110 E8
Barberry Rd HHW HP1 ....81 L2
Barbers Wk TRING HP23 ....57 L2
Barchester Rd
  KTN/HRWW/WS HA3 ....143 H3
  WATW WD18 ....12 C9
Barclay Cl HERT/BAY SG13 ....71 M1
Barclay Rd HOD EN11 ....72 B7
Barclay Crs STVG SG1 ....10 C1
Barden Cl DEN/HRF UB9 ....140 A2
Bardwell Ct STAL AL1 ....8 E7
Bardwell Rd STAL AL1 ....8 E7
Barfield Av TRDG/WHET N20 ....137 K5
Barford Ri LTNE LU2 ....29 H5
Bargrove Av HHW HP1 ....81 L3
Barham Av BORE WD6 ....120 D6
Barham Rd STVGE SG2 ....34 A4
Baring Rd EBAR EN4 ....123 M8
Barker Cl NTHWD HA6 ....141 K6
Barkham Cl LBUZ LU7 ....169 K2
Barking Cl LTNW/LEA LU4 ....26 F5
Barkway Hl ROY SG8 ....152 G12
Barkway Rd ROY SG8 ....14 E8
Barlee Cl SAFWS CM21 ....161 G6
Barley Brow DUN/WHIP LU6 ....25 L1
  GSTN WD25 ....101 M3
Barley Cl BUSH WD23 ....132 F1
  RBSF CM22 ....185 L2
The Barleycorn LTNN/LIM LU3 * 6 D3
Barleycroft BUNT SG9 ....159 J11
Barley Cft HERT/WAT SG14 ....52 F2
  HHNE HP2 ....83 G2
  HLWS CM18 ....95 H3
  KNEB SG3 ....177 M1
Barleycroft Gn WGCW AL8 ....50 A5
Barley La RBSF CM22 ....185 M2
Barley Mow La STALE/WH AL4 ....86 D5
Barley Ponds Cl WARE SG12 ....54 D4
Barley Ponds Rd WARE SG12 ....54 D4
Barley Ri BLDK SG7 ....17 H4
Barleyvale LTNN/LIM LU3 ....27 L4
Barlings Rd HARP AL5 ....46 F8

Barlow Rd RAYLNE/WEN HP22 ....56 A8
Barmor Cl RYLN/HDSTN HA2 ....142 F7
Barnack Gv ROY SG8 ....14 D6
Barnacres Rd HHS/BOV HP3 ....82 D5
Barnard Acres WAB EN9 ....93 H5
Barnard Gn WGCE AL7 ....50 D8
Barnard Rd EN1 EN1 ....125 L5
  LTN LU1 ....40 D2
Barnard Wy HHNE HP2 ....5 M7
Barn Cl HHS/BOV HP3 ....5 H1
  RAD WD7 ....119 L1
  WGCW AL8 ....50 A5
Barncroft STDN SG11 ....165 A6
Barncroft Wy STAL AL1 ....9 M4
Barndell Cl HTCH/STOT SG5 ....148 E7
Barndicott WGCE AL7 ....51 G7
Barnes Av CSHM HP5 ....97 G6
Barnes Gv WGCE AL7 ....51 G7
Barnes Ri KGLGY WD4 ....100 A3
Barnes Rd HHS/BOV HP3 ....82 F5
Barnet By-Pass BORE WD6 ....135 G4
Barnet Gate La BAR EN5 ....135 G4
Barnet Hl BAR EN5 ....122 D6
Barnet La BORE WD6 ....134 D2
Barnet Rd BAR EN5 ....122 E3
  LCOL/BKTW AL2 ....104 C3
Barnet Wy (Barnet By-Pass)
  MLHL NW7 ....135 L9
Barnfield HHS/BOV HP3 ....5 L9
  RBSF CM22 ....185 N6
Barnfield Av LTNE LU2 ....28 A3
Barnfield Cl LTNE LU2 ....72 E5
  WAB EN9 ....93 H4
Barnfield Ct HARP AL5 ....47 G5
Barnfield Rd HARP AL5 ....47 H3
  STALE/WH AL4 ....66 A4
  WGCE AL7 ....68 C7
Barn Hl HLWW/ROY CM19 ....93 M1
Barnhill PIN HA5 ....142 A8
Barnhurst Pth OXHEY WD19 ....132 A8
Barn Lea RKW/CH/CXG WD3 ....129 K4
Barn Md HLWS CM18 ....75 H7
Barns Ct HLWW/ROY CM19 ....94 C1
Barnsdale Cl BORE WD6 ....120 D5
Barns Dene HARP AL5 ....46 C3
Barnside Ct WGCW AL8 ....50 A5
The Barns BGSW SG18 * 144 B10
Barns Ct HLWW/ROY CM19 ....94 C1
Barnsway KGLGY WD4 ....100 C2
Barnwell STVGE SG2 ....33 M7
Baron Cl FBAR/BDGN N11 ....137 M3
Baron Ct STVG SG1 ....20 F6
Barons Ga EBAR EN4 ....137 J2
Barons Md HRW HA1 ....143 H4
Baronsmere Ct BAR EN5 * 122 C7
The Barons BSF CM23 ....43 M4
Barra Cl HHS/BOV HP3 ....82 F5
Barrass Cl PEND EN3 ....126 E3
Barratt Wy
  KTN/HRWW/WS HA3 ....143 H5
Barrells Down Rd BSF CM23 ....166 A12
Barrett La BSF CM23 ....43 M2
Barrie Av DUN/WHIP LU6 ....25 L2
Barrington Park Gdns
  CSTG HP8 ....128 B4
Barrington Rd LWTH SG6 ....16 D5
Barrow Cl ENC/FH EN2 ....124 E1
Barrowdene Cl PIN HA5 ....142 C4
Barrow La CHESW EN7 ....109 K5
Barrow Point Av PIN HA5 ....142 C4
Barrow Point La PIN HA5 ....142 C4
Barr Rd POTB/CUF EN6 ....107 G7
Barry Cl LCOL/BKTW AL2 ....84 F7
Bartel Cl HHS/BOV HP3 ....83 H4
Bartholomew Gn
  STALW/RED AL3 ....172 G4
Bartholomew Rd BSF CM23 ....43 M3
Bartletts Md HERT/WAT SG14 ....53 H3
Barton Av RYLN/HDSTN HA2 ....142 F7
Barton Cl HARP AL5 ....47 G2
Barton Rd DUN/HR/TOD LU5 ....154 A3
  STALE/WH AL4 ....48 A3
The Bartons BORE WD6 ....134 B2
Barton Wy BORE WD6 ....120 E1
Bartop Cl CHESW EN7 ....109 H2
The Baulk LBUZ LU7 ....155 R11
Basildon Cl WATW WD18 ....131 G2
Basildon Sq HHNE HP2 ....62 D6
Basil Ms HLWE CM17 ....76 A4
Basils Rd STVG SG1 ....10 C1
Basing Rd RKW/CH/CXG WD3 ....129 K4
Baslow Cl
  KTN/HRWW/WS HA3 ....143 H3
Bassett Cl STALW/RED AL3 ....173 R12
Bassil Rd HHW HP1 ....2 G5
Bassingbourne Cl BROX EN10 ....92 D3
Bassingbourn Rd STSD CM24 ....167 R12
Bassingbourn Rbt STSD CM24 ....167 P12
Bassingburn Wk WGCE AL7 ....50 D8
Batchelors STDN SG11 ....163 P11
Batchelors Wy AMSS HP7 ....113 H5
  CSHM HP5 ....96 F3
Batchwood Dr STALW/RED AL3 ....8 B1
Batchwood Gdns
  STALW/RED AL3 ....65 H7
Batchwood Vw STALW/RED AL3 ....8 B1
Batchworth Hl
  RKW/CH/CXG WD3 ....130 C5
Batchworth Hill London Rd
  RKW/CH/CXG WD3 ....130 C5
Batchworth La NTHWD HA6 ....131 G8
Bateman Rd
  RKW/CH/CXG WD3 ....130 E2
Batford Cl WGCE AL7 ....50 E8
Batford Mi HARP AL5 * 47 H3
Batford Rd HARP AL5 ....47 H2
Bath Pl BAR EN5 ....122 C7
Bathurst Rd HHNE HP2 ....62 B7
Batley Rd ENC/FH EN2 ....123 M2
Batterdale BRKMPK AL9 ....68 C4
Battlefield Rd STAL AL1 ....8 E2
Battlers Green Dr RAD WD7 ....119 G3
Battleview STDN SG11 ....165 L11
Baud Cl STDN SG11 ....163 P11
The Baulk LBUZ LU7 ....155 R11
Bawdsey Cl STVG SG1 ....32 A1
Bawtry Rd TRDG/WHET N20 ....137 K6
Baxendale TRDG/WHET N20 ....137 G6
Baycroft Cl PIN HA5 ....142 A5
Bayford Cl HERT/BAY SG13 ....71 L5
  HHNE HP2 ....63 J9
Bayford Gn HERT/BAY SG13 ....70 D5
Bayford La HERT/BAY SG13 ....70 D5

Bayhurst Dr NTHWD HA6 ....141 K1
Baylam Dell LTNE LU2 ....29 J8
Bayley Hall Ms HERT/WAT SG14 ....53 H8
Bayley Md HHW HP1 * 4 C6
Baylie Ct HHNE HP2 ....82 C1
Baylie La HHNE HP2 ....82 C1
Bayne Cl EN1 EN1 ....125 L5
Bay Tree Wk WAT WD17 ....117 K4
Bayworth
  HERT/WAT SG14 * 16 F4
Beacon Av CFSP/GDCR SL9 ....38 C2
Beacon Ct HERT/BAY SG13 * 72 A2
Beacon Rd BERK HP4 ....170 F7
  WARE SG12 ....54 E3
Beaconsfield LTNE LU2 ....7 M4
Beaconsfield Cots
  TRDG/WHET N20 ....136 E6
Beaconsfield Rd
  FBAR/BDGN N11 ....137 L7
  HAT AL10 ....68 A3
  PEND EN3 ....168 E3
  RAYLNE/WEN HP22 ....168 C12
  STAL AL1 ....9 H6
  TRDG/WHET N20 ....137 K6
The Beacons STVG SG1 ....21 M6
Beacon Vw DUN/WHIP LU6 ....36 F5
  LBUZ LU7 ....24 B4
Beacon Wy
  RKW/CH/CXG WD3 ....129 L3
  TRING HP23 ....169 H12
The Beadles RBSF CM22 ....184 B1
Beadlow Rd LTNW/LEA LU4 ....26 D5
Beagle Cl RAD WD7 ....119 K3
Beale Cl STVGE SG2 ....34 A3
Beale St DUN/WHIP LU6 ....25 L7
Beamish Dr BUSH WD23 ....133 G4
Beane Av STVGE SG2 ....34 B3
Beane River Vw
  HERT/WAT SG14 ....53 G7
Beane Rd HERT/WAT SG14 ....52 F7
  HERT/WAT SG14 ....178 F5
The Beaneside
  HERT/WAT SG14 ....178 F5
Beanfield Rd SBW CM21 ....183 L5
Beanley Cl LTNE LU2 ....29 J7
Bear La BLDK SG7 ....149 P1
Bearton Av HTCH/STOT SG5 ....157 N5
Bearton Gn HTCH/STOT SG5 ....157 N4
Bearton Rd HTCH/STOT SG5 ....157 N4
Bearwood Cl POTB/CUF EN6 ....107 H6
Beasant House WATN WD24 ....13 J2
Beatham Ct WARE SG12 * 53 J1
Beatrice Cl PIN HA5 ....141 L6
Beatty Rd CHES/WCR EN8 ....110 D8
Beauchamp Gdns
  RKW/CH/CXG WD3 ....129 L4
Beauchamps WGCE AL7 ....50 F8
Beaufort Av
  KTN/HRWW/WS HA3 ....143 L6
Beaulieu Cl OXHEY WD19 ....132 A4
Beaulieu Dr PIN HA5 ....142 B8
  WAB EN9 ....110 F6
Beaumayes Cl HHW HP1 ....4 C5
Beaumonds STAL AL1 * 85 M1
Beaumont Av
  RYLN/HDSTN HA2 ....142 F8
  STAL AL1 ....85 M1
Beaumont Ga RAD WD7 ....119 L1
Beaumont Hall La
  STALW/RED AL3 ....63 M3
Beaumont Ms PIN HA5 * 142 C5
Beaumont Park Dr
  HLWW/ROY CM19 ....74 E5
Beaumont Pl BAR EN5 ....122 D5
Beaumont Rd BROX EN10 ....91 K6
  LTNN/LIM LU3 ....27 M7
Beaumont Vw CHESW EN7 ....91 H4
Beazley Cl WARE SG12 ....54 C3
Beckbury Cl LTNE LU2 ....29 J7
Becket Fold HRW HA1 ....143 K7
Becket Gdns WLYN AL6 ....51 A1
Beckets Sq BERK HP4 ....79 L1
Becketts Wk WARE SG12 * 54 B4
Becketts AV STALW/RED AL3 ....65 C7
Beckfield La BUNT SG9 ....158 A2
Beckham Cl LTNE LU2 ....29 J7
Becks Cl STALW/RED AL3 ....172 F4
Becmead Av
  KTN/HRWW/WS HA3 ....143 M7
Bedale Rd ENC/FH EN2 ....125 G4
Bede Cl PIN HA5 ....141 M4
Bedford Av AMS HP6 ....114 A5
  BAR EN5 ....122 C1
Bedford Cl HTCH/STOT SG5 ....146 A6
  RKW/CH/CXG WD3 ....126 C1
Bedford Crs PEND EN3 ....126 C1
Bedford Gdns LTNN/LIM LU3 ....9 J5
Bedford Park Rd STAL AL1 ....9 H5
Bedford Rd
  AMP/FLIT/BLC MK45 ....155 J1
  DUN/HR/TOD LU5 ....25 L3
  HNLW SG16 ....147 G8
  HRW HA1 ....143 C8
  HTCH/STOT SG5 ....147 L10
  MLHL NW7 ....135 J5
  NTHWD HA6 ....131 H7
  STAL AL1 ....9 H7
Bedford St BERK HP4 ....80 B1
  HTCH/STOT SG5 ....157 M6
  WATN WD24 ....117 M5
Bedmond La ABLGY WD5 ....83 L5
Bedmond Rd HHS/BOV HP3 ....83 H5
Bedwell Av HERT/BAY SG13 ....69 C7
Bedwell Cl WGCE AL7 ....50 C8
Bedwell Crs STVG SG1 ....10 C4
Bedwell Pk STVG SG1 ....10 F5
Bedwell Rd BROX EN10 ....91 M6
Beech Av ENC/FH EN2 ....124 E1
  RAD WD7 ....103 J3
  TRDG/WHET N20 ....137 J4
Beech Bottom STALW/RED AL3 ....65 H6
Beech Cl DUN/WHIP LU6 ....38 C1
  HARP AL5 ....47 L1
  WARE SG12 ....54 D5
Beech Crs STALE/WH AL4 ....80 A2
Beechcroft BERK HP4 ....79 M2
Beechcroft Av
  RKW/CH/CXG WD3 ....131 G2
  CSHM HP5 ....96 E4
Beech Dr BERK HP4 ....120 D6
  BORE WD6 ....120 D6
  SBW CM21 ....183 M9
  STVGE SG2 ....11 M8
Beechengrove PIN HA5 ....142 D5
Beechen Gv WAT WD17 ....12 F4

Beechen Wd
RKW/CH/CXG WD3 129 H7
The Beeches AMS HP6 112 E2
HTCHE/RSTV SG4 157 Q7
LCOL/BKTW AL2 103 H1
RAYLNE/WEN HP22 56 A8
RKW/CH/CXG WD3 129 K1
TRING HP23 * 58 A1
WATW WD18 * 12 E4
Beech Farm Dr STALE/WH AL4 66 D6
Beechfield HOD EN11 72 E3
KGLGY WD4 100 D4
SBW CM21 183 R7
Beechfield Cl BORE WD6 120 C6
STALW/RED AL3 * 173 R12
Beechfield Rd HHW HP1 4 C4
WARE SG12 54 D3
WGCE AL7 68 C1
Beechfield Wk WAB EN9 127 H1
Beech Gn DUN/WHIP LU6 25 K8
Beech Gv AMSS HP7 113 G5
TRING HP23 58 A1
Beech Hl EBAR EN4 123 H4
LTNE LU2 29 G2
LWTH SG6 16 B2
Beech Hill Av EBAR EN4 123 G5
Beech Hill Ct BERK HP4 60 B8
Beech Hill Gdns WAB EN9 127 M3
Beech Hyde La STALE/WH AL4 48 D6
Beeching Cl HARP AL5 46 F1
Beechlands BSF CM23 43 M4
Beech Lawns
NFNCH/WDSPK N12 * 137 H8
Beech Ms WARE SG12 54 B6
Beech Pk TRING HP23 * 58 D8
Beechpark Wy WAT WD17 117 J3
Beech Pl STALW/RED AL3 * 65 H7
Beech Rdg HARP AL5 * 173 R4
Beech Rd DUN/WHIP LU6 39 J4
LTN LU1 6 B3
STALW/RED AL3 65 J7
WATN WD24 117 L3
Beech Tree Cl STAN HA7 134 A8
Beechtree La STALW/RED AL3 83 M4
Beech Tree Wy
DUN/HR/TOD LU5 25 M4
Beechvale Cl
NFNCH/WDSPK N12 137 J8
Beech Wk MLHL NW7 135 H8
Beech Wy STALE/WH AL4 175 M11
Beechwood Av AMS HP6 114 A4
POTB/CUF EN6 106 F7
RKW/CH/CXG WD3 114 F8
STAL AL1 65 M8
Beechwood Cl AMS HP6 114 A5
BLDK SG7 17 K4
CHESW EN7 91 J8
HERT/BAY SG13 53 K7
HTCH/STOT SG5 157 M3
MLHL NW7 135 J8
Beechwood Ct DUN/WHIP LU6 38 D2
Beechwood Dr TRING HP23 170 D12
Beechwood La
RAYLNE/WEN HP22 56 B8
Beechwood Pk HHS/BOV HP3 81 K6
RKW/CH/CXG WD3 115 K8
Beechwood Ri WATN WD24 117 M2
Beechwood Rd LTNW/LEA LU4 27 K7
Beechwood Wy
RAYLNE/WEN HP22 168 C12
Beecroft La STVGE SG2 22 F7
Beecroft Wy DUN/WHIP LU6 38 D1
Beehive Cl BORE WD6 134 B2
Beehive Ct RBSF CM22 184 G6
Beehive Gn WGCE AL7 68 E1
Beehive La WGCE AL7 68 E2
Beehive Rd CHESW EN7 108 F2
Beel Cl AMSS HP7 114 A5
Beesonend La STALW/RED AL3 64 B3
Beeston Cl OXHEY WD19 132 B7
Beeston Dr CHES/WCR EN8 110 B1
Beeston Rd EBAR EN4 137 H2
Beethoven Rd BORE WD6 134 A3
Beeton Cl PIN HA5 142 E2
Beggarman's La STDN SG11 180 B1
Beggars Bush La WATW WD18 131 H1
Beggars La TRING HP23 58 D1
Beken Ct GSTN WD25 118 A1
Belcher Rd HOD EN11 72 E6
Belchers La WAB EN9 94 A6
Beldam Av ROY SG8 14 E8
Beldams Ga BSF CM23 44 C3
Beldams La BSF CM23 44 B4
Belfairs Gdn OXHEY WD19 132 B8
Belfairs Gn OXHEY WD19 132 B8
Belford Rd BORE WD6 120 D4
Belfry Av DEN/HRF UB9 139 L3
Belfry La RKW/CH/CXG WD3 130 A4
The Belfry LTNE LU2 28 C3
Belgrave Av WATW WD18 12 B8
Belgrave Cl MLHL NW7 135 H8
STALE/WH AL4 66 A6
Belgrave Dr KGLGY WD4 101 G2
Belgrave Gdns STAN HA7 134 A8
Belgrave Ms STVGE SG2 33 M7
Belgrave Rd LTNW/LEA LU4 27 H4
Belgravia Cl BAR EN5 122 D7
Belham Rd KGLGY WD4 100 D2
Bell Acre LWTH SG6 16 F5
Bell Acre Gdns LWTH SG6 16 F5
Bellamy Cl EDGW HA8 135 G6
KNEB SG3 177 M4
WAT WD17 117 L5
Bellamy Dr STAN HA7 143 M3
Bellamy Rd CHES/WCR EN8 110 C3
ENC/FH EN2 * 125 H6
Bellchambers Cl
LCOL/BKTW AL2 86 A8
Bell Cl ABLGY WD5 101 K1
HTCHE/RSTV SG4 157 R7
KNEB SG3 177 N4
PIN HA5 142 A5
Bellerby Ri LTNW/LEA LU4 26 F3
Belle Vue La BUSH WD23 133 H4
Bellevue Rd FBAR/BDGN N11 137 L7
WARE SG12 54 C4
Belle Vue Ter DEN/HRF UB9 * 139 L2
Bellfield Av
KTN/HRWW/WS HA3 143 H1
Bellfield Gdns HLWE CM17 76 A6
Bellgate HHNE HP2 62 C7
Bell Gn HHS/BOV HP3 * 98 F1
Bellingdon Rd CSHM HP5 96 F5
Bell La ABLGY WD5 101 L1
AMSS HP7 113 M5
BERK HP4 59 J8
BRKMPK AL9 88 E6
BROX EN10 92 C3
HERT/WAT SG14 53 H7
HOD EN11 72 E7
LCOL/BKTW AL2 104 C3
PEND EN3 126 B4
ROY SG8 153 K11
STVGE SG1 10 B1
WARE SG12 182 B5
Bell Md SBW CM21 183 Q7
Bellmount Wood Av
WAT WD17 117 J5
Bellows Mill La DUN/WHIP LU6 37 L5
Bell Rd EN EN1 125 H5
The Bell Rbt LCOL/BKTW AL2 104 E1
Bell Rw BLDK SG7 17 J1
Bells Cl HTCH/STOT SG5 146 B8
Bells Hl BAR EN5 136 B1
BSF CM23 43 L2
Bells Meadow ROY SG8 145 N4
Bell St SBW CM21 183 Q7
Bell Vw STALE/WH AL4 86 B2
Belmer Rd STSD CM24 167 M9
Belmers Rd TRING HP23 58 B4
Belmont Av EBAR EN4 137 K1
Belmont Cir
KTN/HRWW/WS HA3 * 143 M3
Belmont Cl EBAR EN4 123 K8
TRDG/WHET N20 136 F4
Belmont Hl STAL AL1 8 E7
Belmont Rd BUSH WD23 13 L7
CSHM HP5 96 F2
HHS/BOV HP3 5 H9
KTN/HRWW/WS HA3 143 K5
LTN LU1 6 B5
Belmor BORE WD6 134 E1
Belper Rd LTNW/LEA LU4 27 J7
Belsham Cl CSHM HP5 96 F2
Belsham Pl LTNE LU2 29 J7
Belsize Rd HHNE HP2 99 H7
Belsize Cl HHNE HP2 5 M5
STALE/WH AL4 66 A5
Belsize Rd HHNE HP2 5 M5
KTN/HRWW/WS HA3 143 H2
LTNW/LEA LU4 26 C6
Belswains La HHS/BOV HP3 82 C6
Beltona Gdns CHES/WCR EN8 110 B1
Belton Rd BERK HP4 59 L8
Belvedere Cl AMS HP6 113 K3
Belvedere Ct OXHEY WD19 132 B2
Belvedere Gdns
LCOL/BKTW AL2 102 D1
Belvedere Rd LTNN/LIM LU3 27 M4
Bembridge Gdns
LTNN/LIM LU3 27 K2
Bembridge Pl GSTN WD25 * 101 L7
Ben Austins STALW/RED AL3 63 L1
Benbow Cl STAL AL1 85 M4
Benchley Hl HTCHE/RSTV SG4 20 A1
Benchleys Rd HHW HP1 81 K3
Bench Manor Crs
CFSP/GDCR SL9 138 A4
Bencroft CHESW EN7 91 L8
Bencroft Rd HHNE HP2 5 H3
Bendish La HTCHE/RSTV SG4 175 P2
Bendysh Rd BUSH WD23 13 L4
Benedictine Ga
CHES/WCR EN8 110 C1
Benfleet Wy FBAR/BDGN N11 137 L5
Benford Rd HOD EN11 92 D1
Bengarth Dr
KTN/HRWW/WS HA3 143 H4
Bengeo Mdw
HERT/WAT SG14 * 53 G4
Bengeo Ms HERT/WAT SG14 * 53 G4
Bengeo St HERT/WAT SG14 53 G6
Ben Hale Cl STAN HA7 133 L8
Benham Cl CSHM HP5 96 F3
Benhooks Av BSF CM23 43 L4
Beningfield Dr
LCOL/BKTW AL2 103 L1
Benington Cl LTNE LU2 28 D4
Benington Rd STVGE SG2 34 D7
Bennett Cl NTHWD HA6 141 K2
WGCE AL7 68 D3
Bennett Ct LWTH SG6 16 E4
Bennetts CSHM HP5 97 H4
Bennetts Cl DUN/WHIP LU6 38 F2
STALE/WH AL4 87 H5
Bennetts End Cl HHNE HP2 * 5 L6
Bennetts End Rd HHNE HP2 5 K6
Bennett's La BUNT SG9 19 K5
Benning Av DUN/WHIP LU6 38 D1
Benningfield WARE SG12 182 B4
Benningfield Gdns BERK HP4 60 C7
Benningfield Rd WARE SG12 182 B5
Bennington Dr BORE WD6 120 B6
Benskin Rd WATW WD18 12 C7
Benskins Cl BSF CM23 161 N9
Bensley Cl FBAR/BDGN N11 137 K8
Benslow La HTCHE/RSTV SG4 157 Q6
Benslow Ri HTCHE/RSTV SG4 157 Q6
Benson Cl LTNN/LIM LU3 27 K1
Benstede STVGE SG2 177 Q1
Bentfield End Cswy
STSD CM24 166 F6
Bentfield Gdns STSD CM24 166 F6
Bentfield Rd STSD CM24 166 F6
Bentick Wy HTCHE/RSTV SG4 176 F7
Bentinck Cl CFSP/GDCR SL9 138 B7
Bentley Cl BSF CM23 43 M4
Bentley Dr HLWE CM17 76 A6
Bentley Heath La BAR EN5 122 C1
Bentley Rd HERT/WAT SG14 52 C6
Bentley Wy STAN HA7 133 L8
Benton Rd OXHEY WD19 132 B8
Bentons WAB EN9 * 93 J4
Bentsley Cl STALE/WH AL4 65 M6
Berceau Wk WAT WD17 117 J5
Berecroft HLWS CM18 95 H1
Berefeld HHNE HP2 62 B8
Beresford Av
TRDG/WHET N20 137 K5
Beresford Gdns EN EN1 125 J8
Beresford Rd HRW HA1 143 H7
LTNW/LEA LU4 27 L8
RKW/CH/CXG WD3 129 K4
STAL AL1 86 A3
Bericot Wy WGCE AL7 51 G7
Berkeley LWTH SG6 16 E5
Berkeley Av CSHM HP5 96 E4
Berkeley Cl ABLGY WD5 101 K6
BORE WD6 134 E1
CSHM HP5 96 E4
HTCH/STOT SG5 157 M5
POTB/CUF EN6 106 C6
STVGE SG2 177 N1
WARE SG12 54 A3
Berkeley Ct
RKW/CH/CXG WD3 * 131 H1
Berkeley Crs EBAR EN4 137 H1
Berkeley Pth LTNE LU2 6 F3
Berkeley Sq HHNE HP2 63 G4
Berkhampstead Rd CSHM HP5 97 G4
Berkhamsted Rd HHW HP1 61 H8
Berkley Av CHES/WCR EN8 110 B8
Berkley Cl LBUZ LU7 169 P6
STALE/WH AL4 66 A6
Berkley Pl CHES/WCR EN8 * 110 B8
Berks Hl RKW/CH/CXG WD3 129 G1
Bermer Rd WATN WD24 118 A5
Bernard Cl DUN/HR/TOD LU5 26 A8
Bernard Gv WAB EN9 110 F7
Bernard St STALW/RED AL3 8 F4
Berners Dr STAL AL1 85 H5
Berners Wy BROX EN10 92 D5
Bernhardt Crs STVGE SG2 34 A3
The Berries STALE/WH AL4 65 L6
Berrow Cl LTNE LU2 29 J7
Berry Av WATN WD24 117 M2
Berry Cl RKW/CH/CXG WD3 129 M3
Berryfield LBUZ LU7 169 K2
Berry Field Pk AMS HP6 112 F3
Berry Grove La GSTN WD25 118 D4
Berrygrove La GSTN WD25 118 E5
Berry Grove La WATN WD24 118 C4
Berry Hl STAN HA7 134 B7
Berry La RKW/CH/CXG WD3 129 H2
Berry Leys LTNN/LIM LU3 27 J2
Berrymead HHNE HP2 82 D1
Berry Wy RKW/CH/CXG WD3 129 M3
Berthold Ms WAB EN9 110 F7
Bertram Rd EN EN1 125 L8
Bert Wy EN EN1 125 K8
Berwick Cl CHES/WCR EN8 110 E8
STAN HA7 143 K1
STVG SG1 32 E1
Berwick Rd BORE WD6 120 D4
Besford Cl LTNE LU2 29 H7
Bessemer Cl HTCH/STOT SG5 157 N3
Bessemer Dr STVG SG1 32 F5
Bessemer Rd WGCW AL8 50 C3
Bethecar Rd HRW HA1 143 J7
Bethune Av FBAR/BDGN N11 137 K7
Bethune Cl LTN LU1 6 A8
Betjeman Cl CHESW EN7 109 L2
HARP AL5 * 47 G4
RYLN/HDSTN HA2 142 E6
Betjeman Rd ROY SG8 14 E6
Betjeman Wy HHW HP2 61 M8
Betony V ROY SG8 14 F8
Betstyle Rd FBAR/BDGN N11 137 M7
Bettespol Mdw
STALW/RED AL3 173 Q11
Betts La WAB EN9 94 A3
Betty's La TRING HP23 57 L1
Betula Ter CHES/WCR EN8 * 110 C6
Beulah Cl EDGW HA8 134 F6
Bevan Cl HHNE HP2 5 G6
Bevan Hl CSHM HP5 96 F3
Bevan Rd EBAR EN4 123 K8
Beverley Cl ROY SG8 14 C5
Beverley Gdns CHESW EN7 109 K5
STALE/WH AL4 66 B6
STAN HA7 143 L3
WGCE AL7 51 G7
Beverley Rd LTNW/LEA LU4 27 K8
STVG SG1 21 M7
Beverly Cl BROX EN10 92 C3
Bewcastle Gdns ENC/FH EN2 124 C8
Bewdley Cl HARP AL5 47 H7
Bewley Cl CHES/WCR EN8 110 B5
Bexhill Rd LTNE LU2 29 H7
Beyers Gdns HOD EN11 72 E4
Beyers Prospect HOD EN11 72 E4
Beyers Ride HOD EN11 72 E4
Bibbs Hall La
HTCHE/RSTV SG4 175 Q11
Bibshall Crs DUN/WHIP LU6 39 G3
Bicknoller Rd EN EN1 125 K5
Biddenham Turn GSTN WD25 118 A1
Bideford Gdns LTNN/LIM LU3 28 B5
Bideford Rd PEND EN3 126 D4
Bidwell Cl LWTH SG6 16 F4
Bidwell Hl DUN/HR/TOD LU5 25 L4
Biggin Hl BUNT SG9 159 P2
Biggin La HTCH/STOT SG5 157 N6
Biggleswade Rd BGSW SG18 144 A4
Biggs Grove Rd CHESW EN7 109 J1
Bignells Cnr POTB/CUF EN6 105 M8
Bigthan Rd DUN/HR/TOD LU5 39 G1
Billet La BERK HP4 59 L7
Billy Lows La POTB/CUF EN6 106 F5
Bilton Rd HTCHE/RSTV SG4 157 P3
Bilton Wy LTN LU1 27 K8
PEND EN3 126 D5
Bincote Rd ENC/FH EN2 124 D7
Binder Cl LTNW/LEA LU4 26 C5
Binder Ct LTNW/LEA LU4 * 26 C5
Bingen Rd HTCH/STOT SG5 157 L4
Bingham Cl HHW HP1 61 K8
Bingley Rd HOD EN11 73 G7
Binham Cl LTNE LU2 28 B2
Binyon Crs STAN HA7 133 K8
Birchall La HERT/WAT SG14 69 J1
Birchalls STSD CM24 166 G5
Birchall Wd WGCE AL7 51 G8
Birchanger La BSF CM23 166 F11
Birch Cl AMS HP6 113 J3
Birch Copse LCOL/BKTW AL2 102 C4
Birch Dr HAT AL10 87 L1
RKW/CH/CXG WD3 129 H8
Birchen Gv LTNE LU2 28 D6
Bircherley Ct HERT/WAT SG14 * 53 H7
Bircherley St HERT/WAT SG14 53 H7
Birches Cl PIN HA5 142 C7
The Birches BUSH WD23 133 G1
HHS/BOV HP3 81 K5
HTCHE/RSTV SG4 176 F9
LWTH SG6 16 C1
WAB EN9 111 K8
Birchfield Rd CHES/WCR EN8 109 M3
Birch Gdns AMSS HP7 113 J5
Birch Gn HHW HP1 81 K1
Birch Gv HNLW SG16 147 J6
POTB/CUF EN6 106 E6
WLYN AL6 177 L9
Birch La HHS/BOV HP3 98 F7
Birch Leys HHNE HP2 63 G5
Birch Link LTNW/LEA LU4 6 B2
Birchmead WAT WD17 117 K4
Birchmead Av PIN HA5 142 A6
Birchmead Cl STALW/RED AL3 * 65 H7
Birch Pk KTN/HRWW/WS HA3 143 G2
Birch Rd BERK HP4 59 H6
KNEB SG3 177 P8
Birch Side DUN/WHIP LU6 39 H3
Birch Tree Gv CSHM HP5 97 M4
Birch Tree Wk WAT WD17 117 K3
Birch Wk BORE WD6 * 120 E5
Birch Wy CSHM HP5 97 H3
HARP AL5 47 G5
Birchway HAT AL10 67 L6
Birch Wy LCOL/BKTW AL2 104 B1
Birchwood BSF CM23 166 F11
RAD WD7 104 E8
Birchwood Av HAT AL10 67 L6
Birchwood Cl HAT AL10 67 L6
Birchwood Wy
LCOL/BKTW AL2 102 F2
Birdcroft Rd WGCW AL8 50 B8
Birdie Wy HERT/BAY SG13 53 M6
Birds Cl WGCE AL7 68 F1
Birdsfoot La LTNN/LIM LU3 27 M3
Birds Hl LWTH SG6 16 E3
Birkbeck Rd ENC/FH EN2 125 H4
MLHL NW7 135 K8
NFNCH/WDSPK N12 137 G8
Birkdale Av PIN HA5 142 E5
Birkdale Gdns OXHEY WD19 132 B6
Birkett Wy CSTG HP8 114 B7
Birklands La LCOL/BKTW AL2 85 M7
Birklands Pk STAL AL1 * 85 M6
Birley Rd TRDG/WHET N20 137 G5
Birling Dr LTNE LU2 29 G4
Birstal Gn OXHEY WD19 132 B7
Birtley Cft LTNE LU2 29 J8
Biscot Rd LTNN/LIM LU3 6 C2
Bishop Ct ABLGY WD5 101 K5
Bishop Ken Rd
KTN/HRWW/WS HA3 143 K4
Bishop Rd STHGT/OAK N14 137 M3
Bishop's Av BSF CM23 43 M6
Bishops Av BORE WD6 134 D1
Bishops Av NTHWD HA6 131 J7
Bishops Cl BAR EN5 136 B2
EN EN1 125 M6
HAT AL10 67 K8
Bishop's Cl STALE/WH AL4 65 L6
Bishopscote Rd LTNN/LIM LU3 27 M6
Bishops Ct CHES/WCR EN8 * 109 M4
Bishopsfield HLWS CM18 75 J8
Bishops Fld RAYLNE/WEN HP22 56 E1
Bishops Md HHW HP1 4 C6
Bishops Park Wy BSF CM23 43 H3
Bishop Sq HAT AL10 67 J7
Bishops Ri HAT AL10 87 K4
Bishops Rd WLYN AL6 177 R11
Biskra WAT WD17 117 L5
Bisley Cl CHES/WCR EN8 110 B7
Bittacy Park Av MLHL NW7 136 B8
Bittern Cl CHESW EN7 90 F7
HHS/BOV HP3 82 D7
STVGE SG2 34 B7
Bittern Wy LWTH SG6 148 C12
The Bit TRING HP23 58 B4
Black Acre Cl AMSS HP7 113 J5
Blackberry Md STVGE SG2 34 B6
Blackbirds La GSTN WD25 103 G8
Black Boy Wd
LCOL/BKTW AL2 102 E4
Blackburn Rd
DUN/HR/TOD LU5 25 M6
Blackbury Cl POTB/CUF EN6 107 G5
Blackbushe BSF CM23 166 E12
Blackbush Spring HLW CM20 3 L4
Blackbush Springs HLW CM20 3 L4
Black Cut STAL AL1 9 H8
Blackdale CHESW EN7 109 L1
Black Ditch Rd WAB EN9 * 127 G2
Black Ditch Wy WAB EN9 126 F2
Blackdown Cl STVG SG1 21 M6
Blackett-ord Ct ROY SG8 * 14 E6
Blacketts Wood Dr
RKW/CH/CXG WD3 114 F8
Black Fan Cl ENC/FH EN2 125 G5
Black Fan Rd WGCE AL7 50 D6
Blackford Rd OXHEY WD19 132 B8
Black Green Wood Cl
LCOL/BKTW AL2 102 F3
Blackhill LBUZ LU7 24 D3
Black Horse Av CSHM HP5 97 H7
Blackhorse Cl
HTCHE/RSTV SG4 157 Q8
Blackhorse Crs AMS HP6 113 J4
Blackhorse La
HTCHE/RSTV SG4 157 Q9
POTB/CUF EN6 105 H4
STALW/RED AL3 173 Q11
Black Horse Pde PIN HA5 * 141 M7
Blackhorse Rd LWTH SG6 17 G1
Blackley Cl WAT WD17 117 K3
Black Lion Ct HLWE CM17 * 76 A1
Black Lion Hl RAD WD7 104 C6
Blackmoor La WATW WD18 131 H1
Blackmore LWTH SG6 16 F6
Blackmore Ct WAB EN9 111 L7
Blackmore Ga
RAYLNE/WEN HP22 56 E1
TRING HP23 168 C7
Blackmore Wy STALE/WH AL4 175 M11
Blacksmith Cl HTCH/STOT SG5 148 D6
Blacksmiths Cl BSF CM23 43 H6
Black Smiths Cl WARE SG12 54 E6
Blacksmiths Hl STVGE SG2 35 J5
Blacksmith's La ROY SG8 151 R8
STALW/RED AL3 8 A5
Blacksmiths Rw
STALW/RED AL3 * 172 G4
Blacksmiths Wy SBW CM21 183 M8
Black Swan Ct WARE SG12 * 54 B4
Black Swan La LTNN/LIM LU3 27 L4
Blackthorn Cl GSTN WD25 101 M6
STALE/WH AL4 66 A7
Blackthorn Dr LTNE LU2 29 G5
Blackthorne Cl HAT AL10 87 K3
Black Thorn Rd
DUN/HR/TOD LU5 26 A3
Blackthorn Rd WGCE AL7 50 E8
Blackwater La HHS/BOV HP3 83 J5
Blackwell Cl
KTN/HRWW/WS HA3 143 H2
Blackwell Dr OXHEY WD19 132 A2
Blackwell Gdns EDGW HA8 134 E7
Blackwellhall La CSHM HP5 98 A7
Blackwell Hall La CSHM HP5 113 K1
Blackwell Rd KGLGY WD4 100 E3
Bladon Cl HTCHE/RSTV SG4 20 D6
Bladon Gdns
RYLN/HDSTN HA2 142 F8
Blaine Cl TRING HP23 169 L11
Blair Cl BSF CM23 43 J2
HHNE HP2 62 F4
STVGE SG2 33 K8
Blairhead Dr OXHEY WD19 131 M6
Blake Cl ROY SG8 14 E4
STAL AL1 85 L5
Blakelands
AMP/FLIT/BLC MK45 155 K3
Blakemore End Rd
HTCHE/RSTV SG4 20 B6
Blakeney Cl TRDG/WHET N20 137 G4
Blakeney Dr LTNE LU2 28 A2
Blakeney Rd STVG SG1 32 E2
Blakes Wy WLYN AL6 177 J11
Blanchard Dr WATW WD18 117 J8
Blanchard Gv PEND EN3 126 E4
Blanche La POTB/CUF EN6 105 K8
Blandford Av LTNE LU2 28 B3
Blandford Rd STAL AL1 9 L5
The Blanes WARE SG12 54 A2
Blattner Cl BORE WD6 120 C8
Blawith Rd HRW HA1 143 J6
Blaydon Rd LTNE LU2 7 L4
Blegberry Gdns BERK HP4 79 J2
Blenheim Cl OXHEY WD19 132 A3
SBW CM21 183 M9
Blenheim Ct BSF CM23 43 J2
WGCE AL7 50 D6
Blenheim Crs LTNN/LIM LU3 28 A7
Blenheim Rd BAR EN5 122 B7
RYLN/HDSTN HA2 142 F8
STAL AL1 9 K3
Blenheim Wy STVGE SG2 177 Q2
Blenhiem Rd ABLGY WD5 101 L7
Blenkin Cl STALW/RED AL3 65 G6
Blind La BUNT SG9 23 K4
Blindman's La CHES/WCR EN8 110 B4
Bloomfield Av LTNE LU2 7 K1
Bloomfield Rd CHESW EN7 91 G7
HARP AL5 46 D2
Bloomsbury Gdns
DUN/HR/TOD LU5 26 B4
Blossom La ENC/FH EN2 125 G5
Blows Rd DUN/HR/TOD LU5 39 H2
Blucher St CSHM HP5 96 F5
Bluebell Cl HERT/BAY SG13 53 L7
HHW HP1 * 81 J3
Bluebell Dr ABLGY WD5 101 K1
CHESW EN7 109 H2
HNLW SG16 147 J6
Bluebells WLYN AL6 177 L10
Bluebell Wy HAT AL10 67 K4
Bluebell Wood Cl LTN LU1 40 D2
Blueberry Cl STALW/RED AL3 65 H6
Bluebird Wy LCOL/BKTW AL2 102 D4
Bluebridge Av BRKMPK AL9 106 C1
Blue Bridge Rd BRKMPK AL9 106 C2
Bluecoats Av HERT/WAT SG14 53 H7
Bluecoat Yd WARE SG12 54 B4
Bluehouse Hill
Hemel Hempstead Rd
STALW/RED AL3 84 E3
Bluett Rd LCOL/BKTW AL2 104 B1
Blundell Cl STALW/RED AL3 65 H6
Blundell Rd LTNN/LIM LU3 27 L6
Blunesfield POTB/CUF EN6 107 H5
Blunts La LCOL/BKTW AL2 84 B8
Blyth Cl BORE WD6 120 D5
STVG SG1 32 E2
Blythe Rd HOD EN11 93 H1
Blyth Pl LTN LU1 6 E8
Blythway WGCE AL7 50 D4
Blythwood Gdns STSD CM24 166 F7
Blythwood Rd PIN HA5 142 B3
Boardman Cl BAR EN5 136 C1
Bockings STVGE SG2 23 G8
Bodiam Cl EN EN1 125 H6
Bodmin Rd LTNW/LEA LU4 27 K5
Bodwell Cl HHW HP1 81 L1
Bogmoor Rd ROY SG8 152 H7
Bognor Gdns OXHEY WD19 * 132 A8
Bogs Gap La ROY SG8 145 P6
Bohemia HHNE HP2 82 C1
Bohun Gv EBAR EN4 137 J2
Bois Av AMS HP6 112 F2
Bois Hl CSHM HP5 97 H8
Bois La AMS HP6 113 H1
Bois Mi CSHM HP5 * 113 L2
Bois Moor Rd CSHM HP5 97 G8
Boissy Cl STALE/WH AL4 86 C3
Boleyn Av EN EN1 125 M5
Boleyn Cl HHNE HP2 63 G5
Boleyn Ct BROX EN10 92 C3
Boleyn Dr STAL AL1 85 H4
Boleyn Wy BAR EN5 123 G7
Bolingbroke Rd LTN LU1 6 A7
Bolingbrook STALE/WH AL4 65 L6
Bolney Gn LTNE LU2 29 H6
Bolton Rd HRW HA1 143 G6
LTN LU1 7 H6
Bonham Carter Rd
RAYLNE/WEN HP22 56 B6
Bonham Ct
RAYLNE/WEN HP22 168 B12
Boniface Gdns
KTN/HRWW/WS HA3 142 F2
Boniface Wk
KTN/HRWW/WS HA3 142 F2
Bonks Hl SBW CM21 183 P8
Bonnersfield Cl HRW HA1 143 L8
Bonnersfield La HRW HA1 143 K8
Bonneting La BSF CM23 161 P9
Bonney Gv CHESW EN7 109 L4
Bonnick Cl LTN LU1 6 C8
Booth Pl DUN/WHIP LU6 37 J3
Booths Cl BRKMPK AL9 88 B6
Boot La BGSW SG18 144 D4
Boreham Ms HOD EN11 72 E4
Bornedene POTB/CUF EN6 106 C5
Borough Rd DUN/HR/TOD LU5 39 H2
Borough Wy POTB/CUF EN6 106 C6
Borrell Cl BROX EN10 92 C2
Borrowdale Av DUN/WHIP LU6 39 G3
KTN/HRWW/WS HA3 143 L4
Borrowdale Ct HHNE HP2 62 C7
Borton Av HNLW SG16 147 K5
Bosanquet Rd HOD EN11 73 G5
Boscombe Ct LWTH SG6 * 16 F4
Boscombe Rd
DUN/HR/TOD LU5 26 B8
Bosmore Rd LTNN/LIM LU3 27 K4
Boston Gv RSLP HA4 141 G8
Boswell Cl RAD WD7 104 C6
Boswell Dr HTCH/STOT SG5 157 N1
Boswell Gdns STVG SG1 21 H8
Boswick La BERK HP4 59 H5
Bosworth Rd BAR EN5 122 E7
Botany Cl EBAR EN4 123 J8
Botley La CSHM HP5 97 L4
Botley Rd CSHM HP5 97 J4
HHNE HP2 62 E5
Bottom Dr DUN/WHIP LU6 38 B4
Bottom House La TRING HP23 58 E3
Bottom La KGLGY WD4 116 A1
Bottom Rd TRING HP23 57 G5
Boughton Wy AMS HP6 114 A5
Boulevard WATW WD18 * 131 H1
The Boulevard WATW WD18 131 H1
WGCE AL7 50 D5
Boulton Rd STVG SG1 22 A7
The Bounce HHNE HP2 62 B8
Boundary Cl BAR EN5 122 D5
Boundary Dr HERT/WAT SG14 53 H5
Boundary La WGCE AL7 68 C3
Boundary Pk HHNE HP2 * 4 F5
Boundary Rd BSF CM23 44 A4
CFSP/GDCR SL9 138 B2
PIN HA5 142 B8
STAL AL1 9 H2
The Boundary HERT/BAY SG13 90 A1
Boundary Wy GSTN WD25 101 M6
HHNE HP2 63 G7
Bourn Av EBAR EN4 137 H1
Bourne Cl BROX EN10 92 D2
WARE SG12 54 B3
Bourne End La HHW HP1 81 G4
Bourne End Rd NTHWD HA6 131 J7
Bournehall BUSH WD23 * 132 E2

Bournehall Av *BUSH* WD23 .... 132 E1
Bournehall La *BUSH* WD23 .... 132 E2
Bournehall Rd *BUSH* WD23 .... 132 E2
Bourne Honour *BUSH* WD23 .... 179 N10
Bournemead *BUSH* WD23 .... 132 E2
Bournemouth Rd *STVG* SG1 .... 32 F1
Bourne Rd *BERK* HP4 .... 59 K8
BUSH WD23 .... 132 E1
The Bourne *BSF* CM23 .... 44 A1
HARP AL5 .... 46 D3
HHS/BOV HP3 .... 98 E1
WARE SG12 .... 54 C4
Bournwell Cl *EBAR* EN4 .... 123 K6
Bouverie Rd *HRW* HA1 .... 143 C8
Bouvier Rd *PEND* EN3 .... 126 A4
Bovingdon Crs *GSTN* WD25 .... 102 B8
Bow Br *STALW/RED* AL3 .... 64 C7
Bowcock Wk *STVG* SG1 .... 10 F8
Bower Cl *DUN/WHIP* LU6 .... 37 K4
Bower Heath La *HARP* AL5 .... 174 C12
Bower La *DUN/WHIP* LU6 .... 37 K4
Bowershott *LWTH* SG6 .... 16 E5
Bowers Wy *HARP* AL5 .... 46 E3
Bowes Lyon Ms *STAL W/RED* AL3 .... 8 L6
Bowes Rd *FBAR/BDGN* N11 .... 137 M8
Bowgate *STAL* AL1 .... 9 H3
Bowland Crs *DUN/WHIP* LU6 .... 38 C7
Bowlers Md *BUNT* SG9 .... 158 H9
Bowles Gdn *EN* EN1 .... 125 M2
Bowling Cl *HARP* AL5 .... 46 F6
Bowling Gn *STVG* SG1 .... 33 G2
Bowling Green La *BUNT* SG9 .... 158 H9
LTNE LU2 .... 28 C7
Bowling Rd *WARE* SG12 .... 54 C4
Bowls Cl *STAN* HA7 .... 133 M8
Bowmans Av *HTCHE/RSTV* SG4 .... 157 R6
Bowmans Cl *DUN/WHIP* LU6 .... 39 G3
POTB/CUF EN6 .... 107 H6
WLYN AL6 .... 177 J10
Bowmans Ct *HHNE* HP2 .... 62 B8
Bowmans Gn *GSTN* WD25 .... 102 B8
Bowmans Wy *DUN/WHIP* LU6 .... 39 G2
Bowood Rd *PEND* EN3 .... 126 B6
Bowring Gn *OXHEY* WD19 .... 13 K6
Bowstridge La *CSTG* HP8 .... 138 A1
Bowyer Rd *DEN/HRF* UB9 .... 139 K8
Bowyers *HHNE* HP2 .... 62 B8
Bowyer's Cl *HTCH/STOT* SG5 .... 157 M4
Boxberry Cl *STVG* SG2 .... 10 F5
Boxelder Cl *EDGW* HA8 .... 135 G8
Boxfield *WCCE* AL7 .... 68 F2
Boxfield Gn *STVG* SG2 .... 34 B1
Boxgrove Cl *LTNE* LU2 .... 29 G4
Boxhill *HHW* HP1 .... 62 B8
Box La *HHS/BOV* HP3 .... 81 H7
HOD EN11 .... 72 C7
Boxley La *RBSF* CM22 .... 185 R1
Boxmoor Rd *KTN/HRWW/WS* HA3 .... 143 M6
Boxted Cl *LTNW/LEA* LU4 .... 27 G4
Boxted Rd *HHW* HP1 .... 61 J8
Box Tree Cl *CSHM* HP5 .... 97 H7
Boxtree La *KTN/HRWW/WS* HA3 .... 143 G3
Boxtree Rd *KTN/HRWW/WS* HA3 .... 143 H2
Boxwell Rd *BERK* HP4 .... 79 M1
Boxworth Cl *NFNCH/WDSPK* N12 .... 137 H4
Boyce Cl *BORE* WD6 .... 120 C5
Boyd Cl *BSF* CM23 .... 44 B1
Boyes Crs *LCOL/BKTW* AL2 .... 85 M8
Boyle Av *STAN* HA7 .... 143 L1
Boyle Cl *LTNE* LU2 .... 6 F3
Braceby Cl *LTNN/LIM* LU3 .... 27 K3
Brace Cl *CHESW* EN7 .... 90 F7
Braceys *STVG* SG2 .... 35 K7
Brache Cl *STALW/RED* AL3 .... 173 Q12
Bracken Cl *BORE* WD6 .... 120 F5
Brackendale *POTB/CUF* EN6 .... 106 F5
Brackendale Gv *HARP* AL5 .... 46 B2
LTNN/LIM LU3 .... 27 L3
Brackendene *LCOL/BKTW* AL2 .... 102 D4
Bracken Hl *BERK* HP4 .... 60 C8
Bracken La *WLYN* AL6 .... 177 M10
Brackenham Gdns *LTNE* LU2 .... 29 H6
Bracknell Cl *LTNW/LEA* LU4 .... 26 D6
Bracknell Pl *HHNE* HP2 .... 62 C6
Bradbery *RKW/CH/CXG* WD3 .... 129 J3
Bradbury Cl *BORE* WD6 .... 120 C5
Bradden La *HHNE* HP2 .... 172 A10
Braddon Ct *BAR* EN5 * 122 C4
Bradenham Rd *KTN/HRWW/WS* HA3 .... 143 M6
Bradford Rd *RKW/CH/CXG* WD3 .... 129 G3
Bradgate *POTB/CUF* EN6 .... 108 B1
Bradgate Cl *POTB/CUF* EN6 .... 108 B2
Bradley Common *BSF* CM23 .... 166 E10
Bradley Rd *LTNW/LEA* LU4 .... 27 H4
PEND EN3 .... 126 A7
Bradleys Cnr *HTCHE/RSTV* SG4 .... 20 A1
Bradman Wy *STVG* SG1 .... 21 L8
Bradmore Gn *BRKMPK* AL9 .... 88 D8
Bradmore La *BRKMPK* AL9 .... 88 B8
Bradmore Wy *BRKMPK* AL9 .... 88 C8
Bradshaw Ct *STVG* SG2 * 11 M8
Bradshaw Rd *WATN* WD24 .... 118 A3
Bradshaws *HAT* AL10 .... 87 K4
Bradshaws Cl *AMP/FLIT/BLC* MK45 .... 155 J2
Bradway *HTCHE/RSTV* SG4 .... 175 Q3
Braeburn Wk *ROY* SG8 .... 14 D6
Braemar *STVG* SG2 .... 177 R2
Braemar Turn *HHNE* HP2 .... 62 F4
Braeside *PIN* HA5 .... 142 F4
Bragbury Cl *STVG* SG2 .... 177 R2
Bragbury La *KNEB* SG3 .... 177 R5
STVG SG2 .... 177 R2
Bragmans La *RKW/CH/CXG* WD3 .... 99 H7
The Braid *CSHM* HP5 .... 97 J4
Brain Cl *HAT* AL10 .... 87 M7
Braintree Cl *LTNW/LEA* LU4 .... 26 D6
Braithwaite Rd *PEND* EN3 .... 126 D7
Braknybery *BERK* HP4 .... 59 J4
Brailings *CFSP/GDCR* SL9 .... 128 C3
Bramber Rd *NFNCH/WDSPK* N12 .... 137 L6
Bramble Cl *CFSP/GDCR* SL9 .... 138 C2
GSTN WD25 .... 101 G3
HARP AL5 .... 46 D2
LTNW/LEA LU4 .... 9 J6
Bramble La *AMSS* HP7 .... 113 J7
Bramble Ri *HLW* CM20 .... 2 B3
Bramble Rd *HAT* AL10 .... 87 G1
The Brambles *BSF* CM23 .... 43 J3
CHES/WCR EN8 .... 110 B5

ROY SG8 .... 14 F8
STAL AL1 .... 8 E9
STVG SG1 .... 21 H7
WARE SG12 .... 54 A4
WLYN AL6 .... 177 J9
Brambling Cl *BUSH* WD23 .... 13 M5
Brambling Ri *HHNE* HP2 .... 62 C7
Bramfield *GSTN* WD25 .... 102 C7
HTCHE/RSTV SG4 .... 157 R7
Bramfield Rd *HERT/WAT* SG14 .... 52 C5
Bramfield Pl *HHNE* HP2 .... 62 K4
Bramfield Rd *HERT/WAT* SG14 .... 52 C5
KNEB SG3 .... 177 M8
Bramham Ct *NTHWD* HA6 * 131 J8
Bramhanger Acre
LTNN/LIM LU3 .... 27 H2
Bramingham Rd *LTNN/LIM* LU3 .... 27 K3
Bramleas *WATW* WD18 .... 12 A7
Bramley Cl *BLDK* SG7 .... 149 K12
PIN HA5 .... 131 J6
STHGT/OAK N14 .... 137 M1
Bramley Ct *DUN/HR/TOD* LU5 .... 26 B4
Bramley Gdns *OXHEY* WD19 .... 142 A1
Bramley House Ct
ENC/FH EN2 * 125 H3
Bramley Pde *STHGT/OAK* N14 .... 124 C1
Bramley Rd *STHGT/OAK* N14 .... 137 M1
Bramley Shaw *WAB* EN9 .... 111 K7
Bramley Wy *STALW/RED* AL3 .... 8 L6
HARP AL5 .... 47 H4
Brampton Cl *CHESW* EN7 .... 109 L2
HARP AL5 .... 47 H4
Brampton Gv
KTN/HRWW/WS HA3 .... 143 L6
Brampton Park Rd
HTCH/STOT SG5 .... 157 N6
Brampton Ri *DUN/WHIP* LU6 .... 39 G3
Brampton Rd *OXHEY* WD19 .... 131 L6
ROY SG8 .... 15 G7
Brampton Ter *BORE* WD6 .... 120 E4
Bramshaw Gdns
OXHEY WD19 .... 132 B8
Bramshot Cl
HTCHE/RSTV SG4 .... 157 P9
Bramshott Cl *OXHEY* WD19 .... 131 L6
Branch Cl *HAT* AL10 .... 68 A1
Branch Rd *LCOL/BKTW* AL2 .... 103 H1
STALW/RED AL3 .... 9 H1
Brancroft Wy *PEND* EN3 .... 126 C5
Brandles Rd *LWTH* SG6 .... 16 E6
Brandon Cl *CHESW* EN7 .... 91 J6
Brandreth Av
DUN/HR/TOD LU5 .... 26 C8
Brandreth Ct *HRW* HA1 * 143 K8
Brand St *HTCH/STOT* SG5 .... 157 N6
Branksome Cl *HHNE* HP2 .... 82 K1
Branton Cl *LTNE* LU2 .... 29 J7
Brantwood Gdns *ENC/FH* EN2 .... 124 C8
Brantwood Rd *LTN* LU1 .... 6 C6
Bray Cl *BORE* WD6 .... 121 G5
Bray Dr *STVG* SG1 .... 35 J1
Brayes Ms *HTCH/STOT* SG5 .... 148 D7
Bray Ldg *CHES/WCR* EN8 * 110 C1
Brays Green La *AMS* HP6 .... 112 A1
Brays La *AMS* HP6 .... 96 A8
Brays Md *HLWS* CM18 .... 75 M7
Brays Meadow *AMS* HP6 .... 112 A1
Brays Rd *LTNE* LU2 .... 28 F6
Brayton Gdns *ENC/FH* EN2 .... 124 B8
Brazier Cl
AMP/FLIT/BLC MK45 .... 154 H2
Braziers End *CSHM* HP5 .... 78 A5
Braziers Rd *HERT/BAY* SG13 .... 53 K7
Braziers Quay *BSF* CM23 .... 44 A3
Breach Barns La *WAB* EN9 .... 111 L4
Bread & Cheese La *CHESW* EN7 .... 91 H4
Breadcroft La *HARP* AL5 .... 46 F3
Breakmead *WCCE* AL7 .... 68 F2
Breakspear Av *STAL* AL1 .... 9 K6
Breakspear Cl *WATN* WD24 .... 13 G6
Breakspear Ct *ABLGY* WD5 .... 101 K4
Breakspeare Rd *ABLGY* WD5 .... 101 J4
Breakspear Rd *RSLP* HA4 .... 140 F8
Breakspear Rd North
DEN/HRF UB9 .... 140 B5
Breakspear Wy *HHNE* HP2 .... 63 G5
Breaks Rd *HAT* AL10 .... 67 M8
Brecken Cl *STALE/WH* AL4 .... 65 L6
Brecon Cl *LTN* LU1 .... 4 D8
Brecon Rd *PEND* EN3 .... 126 A4
Brendon Av *LTNE* LU2 .... 29 J4
Brendon Ct *RAD* WD7 * 103 M8
Brent Pl *BAR* EN5 .... 136 E1
Brentwood Cl
DUN/HR/TOD LU5 .... 26 B3
Bressey Av *EN* EN1 .... 125 M1
Brett Rd *WATN* WD24 .... 117 L3
Brett Rd *BAR* EN5 .... 136 A1
Bretts Md *LTN* LU1 .... 4 C9
Brewers Cl *BSF* CM23 .... 43 J4
Brewers Hill Rd *DUN/WHIP* LU6 .... 25 P3
Brewery La *BLDK* SG7 .... 148 J12
STSD CM24 .... 166 G6
Brewery Rd *HOD* EN11 .... 72 E7
Brewhouse Hl *STALE/WH* AL4 .... 48 A1
Brewhouse La *HERT/WAT* SG14 .... 53 G7
Brian Rd *DUN/HR/TOD* LU5 .... 154 A3
Briants Cl *PIN* HA5 .... 142 C2
Briarcliff *HHW* HP1 .... 81 J1
Briar Cl *BERK* HP4 .... 60 E6
CHES/WCR EN8 .... 110 A3
LTNE LU2 .... 29 G5
Briardale *STVG* SG1 .... 10 C8
WARE SG12 .... 54 A2
Briarley Cl *BROX* EN10 .... 92 A5
Briar Patch La *LWTH* SG6 .... 16 B6
Briar Rd *GSTN* WD25 .... 101 J3
STALE/WH AL4 .... 66 A4
Briars Cl *HAT* AL10 .... 67 L8
Briars La *HAT* AL10 .... 67 L8
The Briars *CHES/WCR* EN8 .... 110 A5
HERT/BAY SG13 .... 53 L2
HLWS CM18 .... 75 J3
RKW/CH/CXG WD3 .... 115 Q5
Briarswood *CHESW* EN7 .... 109 J3
Briars Wd *HAT* AL10 .... 67 L8
Briar Wy *BERK* HP4 .... 80 A2
Briarwood Dr *NTHWD* HA6 .... 141 J9
Briary La *ROY* SG8 .... 14 D8
Briary Wy *HHNE* HP2 .... 82 K1
Briary Wood End *WLYN* AL6 .... 177 M9
Briary Wood La *WLYN* AL6 .... 177 M9
Brickcroft *BROX* EN10 .... 92 A6
Brickenden Ct *WAB* EN9 .... 111 K7
Brickendon La *HERT/BAY* SG13 .... 71 H8
Bricket Rd *STAL* AL1 .... 8 D3
Brickett Cl *RSLP* HA4 .... 141 H7
Brickfield *HAT* AL10 .... 67 L7
Brickfield Av *HHS/BOV* HP3 .... 64 A2
Brickfield La *BAR* EN5 .... 135 K2
The Brickfields *WARE* SG12 .... 53 M3

Brick Kiln La *LTN* LU1 .... 173 L1
Brick Kiln La *HTCH/STOT* SG5 .... 157 N6
Brickkiln Rd *STVG* SG1 .... 10 A7
Brick Knoll Pk *STAL* AL1 .... 185 A5
Brick La *LTN* LU1 .... 125 M6
Brickley La *LTNW/LEA* LU4 .... 26 F4
Brickmakers La *HHS/BOV* HP3 .... 82 F1
Brickwall Cl *WLYN* AL6 .... 49 L5
Brickyard La *ROY* SG8 .... 152 B2
Bride Hall La *WLYN* AL6 .... 48 E1
Bridewell Cl *BUNT* SG9 .... 159 J6
Bridge Cl *EN* EN1 .... 125 M6
Bridge Ct *RAD* WD7 * 119 M1
Bridge End *BUNT* SG9 .... 159 J9
Bridgefields *WCCE* AL7 .... 50 D6
Bridgefoot *BUNT* SG9 .... 159 J10
Bridge Foot *WARE* SG12 .... 54 B4
Bridgefoot La *POTB/CUF* EN6 .... 106 A7
Bridgeman Dr
DUN/HR/TOD LU5 .... 26 B4
Bridgend Rd *EN* EN1 .... 126 A1
Bridgenhall Rd *EN* EN1 .... 125 K5
Bridge Pl *AMS* HP6 .... 113 J4
WAT WD17 .... 13 G3
Bridger Cl *GSTN* WD25 .... 102 B7
Bridge Rd *KCLGY* WD4 .... 101 G7
KNEB SG3 .... 177 N7
LWTH SG6 .... 16 D3
STVG SG1 .... 32 F2
WGCW AL8 .... 50 B6
Bridge Rd East *WGCE* AL7 .... 50 C6
Bridge Rd West *STVG* SG1 .... 32 F2
Bridges Ct *HERT/WAT* SG14 .... 53 C7
Bridges Rd *STAN* HA7 .... 133 K8
Bridge St *BERK* HP4 .... 80 B1
BSF CM23 .... 44 A1
HHNE HP2 .... 2 C2
HTCH/STOT SG5 .... 157 N7
LTN LU1 .... 6 F4
PIN HA5 .... 142 B5
The Bridge
KTN/HRWW/WS HA3 .... 143 J4
Bridgewater Hl *BERK* HP4 .... 59 K6
Bridgewater Rd *BERK* HP4 .... 59 K6
Bridgewater Wy *BUSH* WD23 .... 132 C4
Bridgeways *HOD* EN11 .... 72 F7
Bridle Cl *HOD* EN11 .... 72 A8
PEND EN3 .... 126 D3
STALW/RED AL3 .... 9 H1
Bridle La *RKW/CH/CXG* WD3 .... 116 A2
Bridle Pth *WAT* WD17 .... 12 C1
Bridle Rd *PIN* HA5 .... 142 A4
Bridle Wy *BERK* HP4 .... 59 L7
HOD EN11 .... 72 A8
Bridleway *TRING* HP23 .... 57 J8
Bridle Wy *TRING* HP23 .... 57 H8
WARE SG12 .... 54 E7
Bridle Way (North) *HOD* EN11 .... 72 A8
Bridle Way (South) *HOD* EN11 .... 72 A8
Bridlington Rd *OXHEY* WD19 .... 132 B2
Brierley Ct *DUN/WHIP* LU6 .... 39 G4
LTNE LU2 .... 29 H1
Briery Rd *RKW/CH/CXG* WD3 .... 115 J7
Briery Wy *AMS* HP6 .... 113 J3
Brigadier Av *ENC/FH* EN2 .... 125 G5
Brigadier Hl *ENC/FH* EN2 .... 125 G5
Brighton Rd *WATN* WD24 .... 117 L4
Brighton Wy *STVG* SG1 .... 32 A5
The Brightside *BSF* CM23 .... 126 B5
Brightview Cl *LCOL/BKTW* AL2 .... 102 A1
Brightwell Av *DUN/WHIP* LU6 .... 38 A2
Brightwell Rd *WATW* WD18 .... 12 A7
Brightwen Gv *STAN* HA7 .... 133 L5
Brill Cl *LTNE* LU2 .... 29 H7
Brimfield Cl *LTNE* LU2 .... 29 H7
Brimsdown Av *PEND* EN3 .... 126 E4
Brimstone Wy *BERK* HP4 .... 59 K7
Brinklow Ct *STALW/RED* AL3 .... 84 F1
Brinley Cl *CHES/WCR* EN8 .... 110 B5
Brinsley Rd
KTN/HRWW/WS HA3 .... 143 H6
Brinsmead *LCOL/BKTW* AL2 .... 103 H1
Briscoe Cl *HOD* EN11 .... 72 D3
Briscoe Rd *HOD* EN11 .... 72 D3
Bristol Rd *LTNN/LIM* LU3 .... 27 L4
Britain St *LTNN/LIM* LU3 .... 10 G1
Britannia Av *STDN* SG11 .... 163 Q11
Britannia La *LTNN/LIM* LU3 .... 27 M4
Britannia Pl *BSF* CM23 .... 43 J4
Britannia Rd *CHES/WCR* EN8 .... 110 D8
CSHM HP5 .... 97 J3
NFNCH/WDSPK N12 .... 137 G6
Brittains Ri *HNLW* SG16 .... 146 A3
Brittain Wy *STVGE* SG2 .... 11 L8
Britten Cl *BORE* WD6 .... 134 D4
Britton Av *STALW/RED* AL3 .... 8 A1
Britwell Dr *BERK* HP4 .... 60 C1
Brive Rd *DUN/HR/TOD* LU5 .... 39 J2
Brixham Cl *STVG* SG1 .... 32 F2
Brixton Rd *WATN* WD24 .... 117 M5
Broad Acre *LCOL/BKTW* AL2 .... 102 A1
Broad Acres *HAT* AL10 .... 67 K5
Broadacres *LTNE* LU2 .... 29 K4
Broad Ct *WGCE* AL7 .... 50 C4
Broadcroft *HHNE* HP2 .... 64 A1
LWTH SG6 .... 16 A2
Broadfield *BSF* CM23 .... 166 B11
HLW CM20 .... 3 J7
Broadfield Cl *MHAD* SG10 .... 181 Q8
Broadfield Ct *BUSH* WD23 .... 133 J5
Broadfield Gdns
CHES/WCR EN8 .... 110 A5
Broadfield La *CHES/WCR* EN8 .... 109 M2
Broadfield Pl *WGCW* AL8 .... 49 M8
Broadfield Rd *HHNE* HP2 .... 5 K2
Broadfields *CHESW* EN7 .... 108 F3
HARP AL5 .... 46 D1
RYLN/HDSTN HA2 .... 142 F1
SBW CM21 .... 183 M4
Broadfields Hts *EDGW* HA8 .... 134 F6
Broadfields La *OXHEY* WD19 .... 131 M4
Broadfield Sq *EN* EN1 .... 125 M1
Broadfield Wy *MHAD* SG10 .... 181 Q8
Broadgate *WAB* EN9 .... 111 K7
Broadgates Av *EBAR* EN4 .... 122 F4
Broad Gn *HERT/BAY* SG13 .... 70 D5
Broadgreen Rd *CHESW* EN7 .... 91 M4
Broad Green Wd
HERT/BAY SG13 .... 70 D5
Broadhall Wy *STVG* SG1 .... 33 H6
Broadhurst *EDGW* HA8 .... 134 F6
Broad Md *LTNN/LIM* LU3 .... 27 M4
Broadlands Av *CSHM* HP5 .... 97 J4
PEND EN3 .... 126 B4
Broadlands Cl *PEND* EN3 .... 126 A4
Broadlawns Ct
KTN/HRWW/WS HA3 .... 143 J1
Broadleaf Av *BSF* CM23 .... 43 J4
Broadley Rd *HLWW/ROY* CM19 .... 94 D1
Broadmead *HTCHE/RSTV* SG4 .... 157 Q8
Broad Md *LTNN/LIM* LU3 .... 27 M4
Broadmead Cl *PIN* HA5 * 142 A1

Broadmeadow Ride
HTCHE/RSTV SG4 .... 157 Q9
Broadmeads *WARE* SG12 .... 54 B4
Broadoak Av *PEND* EN3 .... 126 B1
Broadoak End
HERT/WAT SG14 * 52 D4
Broad Oak Wy *STVGE* SG2 .... 33 K8
Broadstone Rd *HARP* AL5 .... 47 G5
Broad St *CSHM* HP5 .... 97 G4
HHNE HP2 .... 4 F2
RBSF CM22 .... 185 M3
Broadview *STVG* SG1 .... 10 A3
Broadview Rd *CSHM* HP5 .... 96 F1
Broadwalk *DUN/HR/TOD* LU5 * 38 E2
Broad Wk *HLW* CM20 .... 2 E5
Broadwalk *BERK* HP4 .... 60 G4
POTB/CUF EN6 .... 106 F4
Broadwater *BERK* HP4 .... 60 G4
POTB/CUF EN6 .... 106 F4
Broadwater Av *LWTH* SG6 .... 16 C6
WCCE AL7 .... 50 K8
Broadwater Crs *STVGE* SG2 .... 33 K8
Broadwater Dl *LWTH* SG6 .... 16 C6
Broadwater Gdns
DEN/HRF UB9 .... 139 M6
DEN/HRF UB9 .... 139 M6
STVGE SG2 .... 34 B3
Broadwater Pk
DEN/HRF UB9 * 139 L8
Broadwater Rd *WGCE* AL7 .... 50 B8
Broadway Av *HLWE* CM17 .... 75 M1
Broadway Av *LTNN/LIM* LU3 .... 112 F6
Broadway Pde
RYLN/HDSTN HA2 * 142 F7
The Broadway *AMSS* HP7 .... 112 F6
BRKMPK AL9 .... 68 A8
CFSP/GDCR SL9 * 138 C3
CSHM HP5 .... 96 F5
FBAR/BDGN N11 * 137 K8
KTN/HRWW/WS HA3 .... 143 J4
MLHL NW7 .... 135 J8
PIN HA5 .... 142 D2
POTB/CUF EN6 * 106 A1
STAL AL1 * 8 D5
STALE/WH AL4 .... 175 M12
STAN HA7 .... 134 A4
WAT WD17 .... 13 H4
Broadwood Av *RSLP* HA4 .... 141 J8
Brockenhurst Gdns
MLHL NW7 .... 135 J8
Brocket Rd *HOD* EN11 .... 72 E7
WGCW AL8 .... 67 K1
Brockett Cl *WGCW* AL8 .... 49 M7
Brockett Vw *STALE/WH* AL4 .... 44 A1
Brockhurst Cl *STAN* HA7 .... 143 K11
Brockhurst Rd *CSHM* HP5 .... 97 H3
Brocklesbury Cl *WATN* WD24 .... 13 H5
Brockles Md *HLWW/ROY* CM19 .... 95 G1
Brockley Av *STAN* HA7 .... 134 C1
Brockley Ct *STAN* HA7 .... 134 C1
Brockley Hl *STAN* HA7 .... 134 B5
Brockleyside *STAN* HA7 .... 134 B1
Brockswood La *WGCW* AL8 .... 49 M6
Brockton Cl *LTN* LU1 .... 40 E2
Brockwell Shott *STVGE* SG2 .... 22 F8
Brodewater Rd *BORE* WD6 .... 120 C4
Brodie Rd *ENC/FH* EN2 .... 125 G4
Bromborough Gn
OXHEY WD19 .... 132 A8
Bromefield *STAN* HA7 .... 134 A4
Bromet Cl *WAT* WD17 .... 117 K4
Bromleigh Cl *CHES/WCR* EN8 .... 110 C2
Bromley Gdns
DUN/HR/TOD LU5 .... 26 B4
Brampton Cl *LTNN/LIM* LU3 .... 27 K3
Bronte Av *HTCH/STOT* SG5 .... 148 A11
Bronte Crs *HHW* HP1 .... 81 H1
Bronte Paths *STVGE* SG2 .... 34 A3
Bronzewood Ct *CHES/WCR* EN8 .... 110 B7
Brook Cl *BORE* WD6 .... 120 F3
DUN/WHIP LU6 .... 39 G4
RAYLNE/WEN HP22 .... 168 B12
Brook Cots *STSD* CM24 .... 166 C4
Brook Ct *RAD* WD7 * 103 L7
Brookdene Av *OXHEY* WD19 .... 131 K2
Brookdene Dr *NTHWD* HA6 .... 141 M3
Brook Dr *HRW* HA1 .... 143 G6
RAD WD7 .... 103 K7
RSLP HA4 .... 141 J8
Brooke Cl *BUSH* WD23 .... 133 G3
Brooke End *STALW/RED* AL3 .... 63 L1
Brooke Gdns *BSF* CM23 .... 44 C2
Brook End *ROY* SG8 .... 145 P7
SBW CM21 .... 183 P7
Brooker Rd *WAB* EN9 .... 111 G8
Brooker Wy *BUSH* WD23 .... 133 G3
Brook Farm Cl *BSF* CM23 .... 43 J6
Brook Fld *STVGE* SG2 .... 34 C7
Brookfield *BORE* WD6 .... 120 D8
DUN/HR/TOD LU5 .... 26 A5
Brookfield Cl *TRING* HP23 .... 57 M1
Brookfield Gdns
CHES/WCR EN8 .... 110 B7
Brookfield La *CHES/WCR* EN8 .... 109 M2
STVGE SG2 .... 34 D5
Brookfield La East
CHES/WCR EN8 .... 110 A1
Brookfield La West
CHES/WCR EN8 .... 110 A1
Brookfield Pk *DUN/WHIP* LU6 * 37 L3
Brookfields *PEND* EN3 .... 126 B8
SBW CM21 .... 183 P8
Brookhill *STVGE* SG2 .... 177 N10
Brookhill Cl *EBAR* EN4 .... 137 H1
Brookhill Rd *EBAR* EN4 .... 137 H1
Brooklands Cl *LTNW/LEA* LU4 .... 27 G3
STAL AL1 * 134 A3
Brooklands Gdns
POTB/CUF EN6 .... 106 C2
Brook La *BERK* HP4 .... 59 M8
SBW CM21 .... 183 P7
Brooklane Fld *HLWS* CM18 .... 7 K8
Brookmans Av *BRKMPK* AL9 .... 88 D8
Brookmead *SHFD* SG17 .... 146 F7
Brook Meadow
NFNCH/WDSPK N12 .... 136 M7
Brookmill Cl *OXHEY* WD19 * 131 M4
Brook Pl *BAR* EN5 .... 123 N7
Brook Rd *BORE* WD6 .... 120 D5
CHES/WCR EN8 .... 110 D8
SBW CM21 .... 183 P8
Brooks Ct *STSD* CM24 * 166 C4
Brookshill *KTN/HRWW/WS* HA3 .... 143 J1
Brookshill Av *KTN/HRWW/WS* HA3 .... 133 H8
Brookshill Dr *KTN/HRWW/WS* HA3 .... 133 H8
Brookside *EBAR* EN4 .... 137 J2
HAT AL10 .... 67 H8
HERT/BAY SG13 .... 53 J8
HLWW/ROY CM19 .... 74 D7
HOD EN11 .... 72 E7
HTCH/STOT SG5 .... 146 E4
LWTH SG6 .... 16 D4
POTB/CUF EN6 .... 105 L6
WAB EN9 .... 111 J6
WATN WD24 .... 118 B2
Brookside Cl *BAR* EN5 .... 136 B2
Brookside Crs *POTB/CUF* EN6 .... 106 B1
Brookside Gdns *EN* EN1 .... 125 M3
Brookside Rd *OXHEY* WD19 .... 131 L3
Brookside South *EBAR* EN4 .... 137 L3
Brook St *DUN/WHIP* LU6 .... 37 L3
HTCH/STOT SG5 .... 148 C7
LTNN/LIM LU3 .... 7 G3
RAYLNE/WEN HP22 .... 168 B12
TRING HP23 .... 57 M1
Brook Vw *HTCHE/RSTV* SG4 .... 20 A3
Broom Cl *CHESW* EN7 .... 109 L1
HAT AL10 .... 87 K3
Broom Cnr *HARP* AL5 * 46 D1
Broomer Pl *CHES/WCR* EN8 .... 110 A3
Broom Farm Rd *RBSF* CM22 .... 185 M2
Broomfield *HLW* CM20 .... 3 H2
LCOL/BKTW AL2 .... 103 C3
Broomfield Av *BROX* EN10 .... 92 C8
Broomfield Cl *WLYN* AL6 .... 49 L6
Broomfield Ri *ABLGY* WD5 .... 101 H6
Broomfields *RBSF* CM22 .... 185 R6
Broom Gv *KNEB* SG3 .... 177 M4
WAT WD17 .... 117 L4
Broom Hl *HHW* HP1 .... 81 J3
WLYN AL6 .... 177 M4
Broomhills *WGCE* AL7 .... 50 E6
Broomleys *STALE/WH* AL4 .... 66 A7
Brooms Cl *WGCW* AL8 .... 50 B4
Broomstick Hall Rd *WAB* EN9 .... 111 J7
Broomstick La *CSHM* HP5 .... 97 L4
Broom Wk *STVG* SG1 .... 10 F5
Broughinge Rd *BORE* WD6 .... 120 F3
Broughton Av *LTNN/LIM* LU3 .... 28 A4
Broughton Hl *LWTH* SG6 .... 16 C2
Broughton Wy
RKW/CH/CXG WD3 .... 129 L3
Brownfields *WGCE* AL7 .... 50 D6
Brownfield Wy *STALE/WH* AL4 .... 175 M11
Browning Dr
HTCHE/RSTV SG4 .... 157 R5
Browning Rd *ENC/FH* EN2 .... 125 H4
HARP AL5 .... 46 E2
LTNW/LEA LU4 .... 26 E7
Brownings *LA HTCHE/RSTV* SG4 .... 30 B8
Brownlow Av *DUN/WHIP* LU6 .... 37 K6
Brownlow Cl *EBAR* EN4 .... 137 J2
Brownlow La *LBUZ* LU7 .... 169 K2
Brownlow Ri *DUN/WHIP* LU6 .... 37 L3
Brownlow Rd *BERK* HP4 .... 60 A8
BORE WD6 .... 120 C4
Browns Cl *LTNW/LEA* LU4 .... 27 H4
Browns Hedge *LBUZ* LU7 .... 169 K6
Browns Spring *BERK* HP4 .... 61 G6
The Brow *CSTG* HP8 .... 128 B6
GSTN WD25 .... 101 M7
Brox Dell *STVG* SG1 .... 10 F2
Broxley Md *LTNW/LEA* LU4 .... 26 D4
Broxbe Gdns *TRDG/WHET* N20 .... 137 K6
Bruce Gv *WATN* WD24 .... 13 G3
Bruce Rd *BAR* EN5 .... 122 C4
KTN/HRWW/WS HA3 .... 143 M3
Bruce Wy *CHES/WCR* EN8 .... 110 B7
Brunel Cl *LTNW/LEA* LU4 .... 26 C6
Brunel Rd *LTNW/LEA* LU4 .... 26 C6
STVG SG2 .... 11 K1
Brunswick Av
FBAR/BDGN N11 .... 137 M7
Brunswick Cl *PIN* HA5 .... 142 C8
Brunswick Crs
FBAR/BDGN N11 .... 137 L6
Brunswick Gv
FBAR/BDGN N11 .... 137 L6
Brunswick Park Gdns
FBAR/BDGN N11 .... 137 L5
Brunswick Park Rd
FBAR/BDGN N11 .... 137 L6
Brunswick Rd *PEND* EN3 .... 126 A4
Brunswick St *LTNE* LU2 .... 7 G3
Brunswick Wy
FBAR/BDGN N11 .... 137 M7
Brushmakers Ct *CSHM* HP5 .... 97 L4
Brushrise *WATN* WD24 .... 117 L2
Brushwood Dr
RKW/CH/CXG WD3 .... 115 Q8
Brushwood Rd *CSHM* HP5 .... 97 H3
Brussels Wy *LTNN/LIM* LU3 .... 13 D12
Bryan Rd *BSF* CM23 .... 43 M1
Bryanstone Rd
CHES/WCR EN8 .... 110 D8
Bryant Cl *BAR* EN5 .... 136 D1
Bryant Ct *HARP* AL5 .... 46 E2
Bryants Cl *HTCH/STOT* SG5 .... 148 B8
Bryce Cl *WARE* SG12 .... 54 B2
Bryn Wy *STALE/WH* AL4 .... 66 A7
Bryn-y-Mawr Rd *EN* EN1 .... 125 K8
Bryony Wy *DUN/WHIP* LU6 .... 25 J8
Buchanan Ct *BORE* WD6 .... 121 H4
Buchanan Dr *LTNE* LU2 .... 41 M1
Bucketsland La *BORE* WD6 .... 121 H4
Buckingham Av
TRDG/WHET N20 .... 137 G2
Buckingham Cl *EN* EN1 .... 125 K3
Buckingham Dr *LTNE* LU2 .... 29 G7
Buckingham Pde
CFSP/GDCR SL9 * 138 C2
STAN HA7 * 134 A8
Buckingham Rd *BORE* WD6 .... 120 F3
HRW HA1 .... 143 H7
TRING HP23 .... 57 M1
WATN WD24 .... 118 A3
Buckland Ri *PIN* HA5 .... 142 A8
Bucklands *RAYLNE/WEN* HP22 .... 168 E12
Bucklands *OXHEY* WD19 * 132 B2
Buckle Cl *LTNN/LIM* LU3 .... 27 L4
Bucklersbury *HTCH/STOT* SG5 .... 157 N7
Bucklers Cl *BROX* EN10 .... 92 D4
Bucknalls Cl *GSTN* WD25 .... 102 D5
Bucknalls Dr *LCOL/BKTW* AL2 .... 102 D5
Bucknalls La *GSTN* WD25 .... 102 C5
Bucks Aly *HERT/BAY* SG13 .... 90 B11
Bucks Av *OXHEY* WD19 .... 132 C3
Bucks Hl *KCLGY* WD4 .... 100 F3

Buckthorn Av STVG SG1 ... 10 E7
Buckton Rd BORE WD6 ... 120 D4
Buckwood Av
  DUN/HR/TOD LU5 ... 26 C8
Buckwood La DUN/WHIP LU6 ... 171 Q2
Buckwood Rd DUN/WHIP LU6 ... 172 G2
Budd Cl NFNCH/WDSPK N12 ... 136 F7
Buddcroft WGCE AL7 ... 50 F6
Bude Crs STVG SG1 ... 32 E3
Building End Rd ROY SG8 ... 153 R5
Bulbourne Cl BERK HP4 ... 59 K7
  HHW HP1 ... 4 A5
Bulbourne Ct TRING HP23 ... 169 L10
Bulbourne Rd TRING HP23 ... 169 M10
Bullace Cl HHW HP1 ... 81 K1
Bullbeggars La BERK HP4 ... 80 E1
Bullen's Green La
  STALE/WH AL4 ... 87 J5
Bullescroft Rd EDGW HA8 ... 134 A6
Bullfields SBW CM21 ... 183 Q5
Bullhead Rd BORE WD6 ... 121 G8
Bull La BUNT SG9 ... 158 A9
  CFSP/GDCR SL9 ... 138 B3
  SAFWS CB11 ... 153 R11
  STALE/WH AL4 ... 47 L3
Bullock's Hl HTCHE/RSTV SG4 ... 177 H6
Bullock's La HERT/BAY SG13 ... 71 G1
Bull Pln HERT/WAT SG14 ... 153 H7
Bull Pond La DUN/WHIP LU6 ... 38 F2
Bull Rd HARP AL5 ... 46 F5
Bullrush Cl HAT AL10 ... 87 M1
Bull's Cross EN EN1 ... 125 L2
Bulls Cross Ride
  ENC/FH EN2 ... 125 L1
Bullsland Gdns
  RKW/CH/CXG WD3 ... 128 F2
Bullsland La
  RKW/CH/CXG WD3 ... 128 F2
Bulls La BRKMPK AL9 ... 88 B6
Bullsmoor Cl CHES/WCR EN8 ... 126 A1
Bullsmoor Gdns
  CHES/WCR EN8 ... 125 M1
Bullsmoor La ENC/FH EN2 ... 125 L1
Bullsmoor Ride
  CHES/WCR EN8 ... 126 A1
Bull Stag Gn BRKMPK AL9 ... 68 A6
Bullwell Crs CHES/WCR EN8 ... 126 C3
Bulstrode Cl STDN SG11 ... 163 P9
Bulstrode La KGLGY WD4 ... 99 J3
Bulstrode Wy CFSP/GDCR SL9 ... 138 B7
Bulwer Gdns BAR EN5 ... 123 G8
Bulwer Link STVG SG1 ... 10 E8
Bulwer Rd BAR EN5 ... 122 F8
Bumbles Green La WAB EN9 ... 93 M7
Buncefield La HHNE HP2 ... 83 G1
Buncefield Terminal
  HHNE HP2 ... 63 H8
The Bungalows HARP AL5 ... 47 G2
Bunhill Cl DUN/WHIP LU6 ... 38 D1
Bunkers La HHS/BOV HP3 ... 82 E7
Bunnsfield WGCE AL7 ... 51 G6
Bunstrux TRING HP23 ... 57 K1
Buntingford Rd STDN SG11 ... 163 P9
Bunting Rd LTNW/LEA LU4 ... 26 E5
Bunyan Rd HTCH/STOT SG5 ... 156 F11
  TRING HP23 ... 169 M12
Bunyans La LTNN/LIM LU3 ... 27 L4
Burbage Cl CHES/WCR EN8 ... 110 C5
Burchell Ct BUSH WD23 ... 133 G3
Burfield Cl HAT AL10 ... 67 L6
Burfield Rd
  RKW/CH/CXG WD3 ... 128 F1
Burford Cl DUN/WHIP LU6 ... 39 H4
Burford Gdns HOD EN11 ... 72 F6
Burford St HOD EN11 ... 72 E5
Burford Wy HTCH/STOT SG5 ... 157 L3
Burgage End La
  HTCH/STOT SG5 ... 146 E12
Burges Cl DUN/WHIP LU6 ... 39 H4
Burgess Cl CHESW EN7 ... 91 G7
Burghley Av BORE WD6 ... 135 G1
  BSF CM23 ... 43 J2
Burghley Cl STVGE SG2 ... 177 N1
Burhill Gv PIN HA5 ... 142 C4
Burke Rd RAYLNE/WEN HP22 ... 56 A8
Burleigh Cl BUSH WD23 * ... 13 L5
Burleigh Md BRKMPK AL9 ... 68 A6
Burleigh Rd
  CHES/WCR EN8 * ... 110 C6
  EN EN1 ... 125 J4
  HERT/BAY SG13 ... 53 L6
  HHNE HP2 ... 83 G3
  STAL AL1 ... 85 M3
Burleigh Wy ENC/FH EN2 ... 125 H7
  POTB/CUF EN6 ... 108 C4
Burley LWTH SG6 ... 148 D12
Burley Hl HLWE CM17 ... 76 B6
Burley Rd BSF CM23 ... 44 A5
Burlington Cl PIN HA5 ... 141 M5
Burlington Ri EBAR EN4 ... 137 J4
Burlington Rd ENC/FH EN2 ... 125 H5
Burn Cl GSTN WD25 ... 119 H8
Burncroft Av PEND EN3 ... 126 A6
Burnell Ri LWTH SG6 ... 16 B4
Burnells Wy STSD CM24 ... 166 G6
Burnell Wk LWTH SG6 ... 16 C4
Burnet Cl HHNE HP2 ... 5 L1
Burnett Av HNLW SG16 ... 147 K5
Burnett Pk HLW/ROY CM19 ... 94 F2
Burnett Sq HERT/WAT SG14 ... 52 D6
Burnham Cl EN EN1 ... 125 J4
  KTN/HRWW/WS HA3 ... 143 L6
  WLYN AL6 ... 177 Q11
Burnham Green Rd WLYN AL6 ... 177 R11
Burnham Rd LTNE LU2 ... 28 F7
  STAL AL1 ... 9 M5
The Burnhams
  RAYLNE/WEN HP22 ... 168 A12
Burnley Cl OXHEY WD19 ... 132 A8
Burnsall Pl HARP AL5 ... 47 G7
Burns Cl HTCHE/RSTV SG4 ... 157 R5
  STVGE SG2 ... 33 N1
Burns Dr HHNE HP2 ... 62 F5
Burnside HERT/WAT SG14 ... 52 E8
  HOD EN11 ... 72 F7
  SBW CM21 ... 183 P7
  STAL AL1 ... 85 M4
Burnside Cl BAR EN5 ... 122 C4
Burns Rd ROY SG8 ... 14 D5
Burnt Cl LTNN/LIM LU3 ... 27 L2
Burntfarm Ride ENC/FH EN2 ... 108 F1
Burnt Mi HLW CM20 ... 2 D4
Buntmill Cl HLW CM20 ... 75 G2
Burntmill La HLW CM20 ... 75 G2
Burr Cl AMP/FLIT/BLC MK45 ... 155 J1
  LCOL/BKTW AL2 ... 104 C1
Burrell Cl EDGW HA8 ... 134 F5
The Burren AMS HP6 * ... 113 H11

Burrowfield WGCE AL7 ... 68 B1
Burrows Cha WAB EN9 ... 127 H2
Burrs La ROY SG8 ... 152 E10
Burr St DUN/WHIP LU6 ... 38 F1
  LTNE LU2 ... 7 G3
Bursland LWTH SG6 ... 16 B3
Bursland Rd PEND EN3 ... 126 B8
Burston Dr LCOL/BKTW AL2 ... 103 G3
Burton Av WATW WD18 ... 12 D5
Burton Cl STALE/WH AL4 ... 175 N12
Burton Dr PEND EN3 ... 126 E3
Burtonhole Cl MLHL NW7 ... 136 B7
Burtonhole La MLHL NW7 ... 136 B7
Burton La CHESW EN7 ... 109 J2
Burtons La CSTG HP8 ... 114 A6
Burton's Wy CSTG HP8 ... 114 A8
Burvale Ct WATW WD18 ... 112 D4
Burwell Rd STVGE SG2 ... 11 M7
Burwood Av PIN HA5 ... 142 A7
Burwood Pl EBAR EN4 ... 123 G5
Bury Av RSLP HA4 ... 141 G5
Burycroft WCCW AL8 ... 50 C4
Burydale STVGE SG2 ... 33 M8
Burydell La LCOL/BKTW AL2 ... 103 H1
Bury Farm AMSS HP7 ... 113 G6
Bury Farm Cl LBUZ LU7 ... 36 A3
Buryfield Wy SBW CM21 ... 54 A3
Bury Gn HHW HP1 ... 4 D1
  STALE/WH AL4 ... 47 L3
Bury Hl HHW HP1 ... 4 D1
Bury Hill Cl HHW HP1 ... 4 D1
Bury Holme BROX EN10 ... 92 D5
Bury La CHES/WCR EN8 ... 96 F5
  HERT/WAT SG14 ... 51 M1
  HTCHE/RSTV SG4 ... 176 D1
  KNEB SG3 ... 177 H6
  LTNN/LIM LU3 ... 154 C8
  RKW/CH/CXG WD3 ... 130 B4
Bury Lodge La STSD CM24 ... 45 J1
Bury Md ARL/CHE SG15 ... 147 G2
Burymead STVG SG1 ... 21 G8
Bury Mdw RKW/CH/CXG WD3 ... 130 B4
Bury Mead Rd
  HTCH/STOT SG5 ... 157 P3
Bury Park Rd LTN LU1 ... 6 C2
Bury Ri HHS/BOV HP3 ... 81 H7
  LBUZ LU7 ... 24 D4
Bury Rd CHING E4 ... 127 H8
  HAT AL10 ... 68 A2
  HHW HP1 ... 4 A1
  HLWE CM17 ... 77 J2
  HTCH/STOT SG5 ... 146 A2
Bury St RSLP HA4 ... 141 H8
The Bury CSHM HP5 * ... 96 F6
Burywick HARP AL5 ... 47 G7
Bushams CHESW EN7 ... 109 J3
Busby Av BROX EN10 ... 92 D4
Bushell Gn BUSH WD23 ... 133 H6
Bushel Whf TRING HP23 ... 169 L11
Bushey Cl WAB EN9 ... 127 G3
Bushey Cft HLWS CM18 ... 3 F7
Bushey Gn WGCE AL7 ... 50 F8
Bushey Grove Rd
  BUSH WD23 ... 13 J5
Bushey Hall Dr BUSH WD23 ... 13 M5
Bushey Hall Pk BUSH WD23 * ... 13 M5
Bushey Hall Rd BUSH WD23 ... 13 K5
Bushey Ley WGCE AL7 ... 51 G8
Busheymill Br WATN WD24 ... 118 C4
Bushey Mill Crs WATN WD24 ... 118 C3
Bushey Mill La BUSH WD23 ... 118 D6
  WATN WD24 ... 118 A3
Bushfield Cl EDGW HA8 ... 134 A1
Bushfield Crs EDGW HA8 ... 134 A1
Bushfield Rd HHS/BOV HP3 ... 81 G7
Bush Hall La BRKMPK AL9 ... 68 B5
Bushmead Rd LTNE LU2 ... 28 D8
Bush Spring BLDK SG7 ... 149 L12
Bushwood Cl BRKMPK AL9 ... 87 M5
Buslins La CSHM HP5 ... 96 C2
Butchers La HTCHE/RSTV SG4 ... 31 H3
Butely Rd LTNW/LEA LU4 ... 26 F1
Bute Sq LTN LU1 ... 6 F5
Bute St LTN LU1 ... 6 F5
Butlers Cl AMS HP6 ... 112 C3
Butlers Dr CHING E4 ... 127 C4
Butlers Yd BLDK SG7 ... 149 J12
Butlin Rd LTN LU1 ... 6 A5
  HAT AL10 ... 67 K4
Buttercup Cl DUN/WHIP LU6 ... 38 E1
  HAT AL10 ... 67 K4
Butterfield Green Rd LTNE LU2 ... 28 E3
Butterfield La STAL AL1 ... 85 J6
Butterfield Rd STALE/WH AL4 ... 48 A6
Butterfly La BORE WD6 ... 119 M7
Buttermere Av DUN/WHIP LU6 ... 39 G3
Buttermere Cl STAL AL1 ... 85 M3
Buttermere Ri SBW CM21 ... 183 Q8
Butterwick HLW CM20 ... 118 C2
Butterworth Pth LTNE LU2 ... 6 F3
Butt Field Vw STAL AL1 ... 85 G6
Butt La BSF CM23 ... 165 R3
Buttlehide RKW/CH/CXG WD3 ... 129 H6
Buttondene Crs BROX EN10 ... 92 F4
Butts End HHW HP1 ... 81 L1
Butts Gn HTCHE/RSTV SG4 * ... 18 A8
Buttsmead NTHWD HA6 ... 141 H4
The Butts BROX EN10 ... 92 C6
Buxted Rd
  NFNCH/WDSPK N12 ... 137 J8
Buxton Cl SHFD SG17 ... 146 E3
  STALE/WH AL4 ... 175 N11
Buxton Pth OXHEY WD19 * ... 132 A6
Buxton Rd LTN LU1 ... 6 D1
  WAB EN9 ... 111 L6
Buxtons La STVG SG1 ... 145 M6
Buzzard Rd LTNW/LEA LU4 ... 26 E1
Bycullah Av ENC/FH EN2 ... 124 F7
Bycullah Rd ENC/FH EN2 ... 124 F6
Byde St HERT/WAT SG14 ... 51 L8
Byers Cl POTB/CUF EN6 ... 107 G8
Byewaters WATW WD18 ... 131 G2
The Bye Wy
  KTN/HRWW/WS HA3 ... 143 J3
The Byeway
  RKW/CH/CXG WD3 ... 130 C5
Byfield WGCW AL8 ... 50 B6
Byfield Cl LTNW/LEA LU4 ... 26 F8
Bygrave Rd BLDK SG7 ... 149 K12
Bylands Cl BSF CM23 ... 43 K5
Byng Dr POTB/CUF EN6 ... 106 A4
Bynghams HLWW/ROY CM19 ... 74 D7
Byng Rd BAR EN5 ... 122 E4
Byngham St HERT/WAT SG14 ... 51 L8
Byers Cl POTB/CUF EN6 ... 107 G8
Byrd Ct STVG SG1 ... 10 D7
Byrd Wk BLDK SG7 ... 17 K3
Byre Rd STHGT/OAK N14 ... 137 G2
Byron Av BORE WD6 ... 134 C1
  WATN WD24 ... 118 B5
Byron Cl CHSW EN7 ... 109 J1
  HTCHE/RSTV SG4 ... 157 R5
  STVGE SG2 ... 34 C1

Byron Ct ENC/FH EN2 ... 124 F6
Byron Pl HHNE HP2 ... 62 F4
Byron Rd HARP AL5 ... 46 E3
  HRW HA1 ... 143 J8
  KTN/HRWW/WS HA3 ... 143 K4
  LTNW/LEA LU4 ... 26 F1
  MLHL NW7 ... 135 L8
  ROY SG8 ... 14 D4
Byslips Rd DUN/WHIP LU6 ... 171 K6
By The Wd OXHEY WD19 ... 132 B5
Byways BERK HP4 ... 60 C8
The Byway POTB/CUF EN6 ... 106 A3
By-wood End CFSP/GDCR SL9 ... 128 E8

C

Cabot Cl STVGE SG2 ... 33 L2
Caddington Cl EBAR EN4 ... 137 J1
Caddington Common
  STALW/RED AL3 ... 172 G1
Caddington Pk LTN LU1 * ... 26 G1
Caddis Cl STAN HA7 * ... 143 K2
Cade Cl LWTH SG6 ... 148 G12
Cades Cl LTN LU1 ... 40 E3
Cades Cl LTN LU1 ... 40 E3
Cadmore La CHES/WCR EN8 ... 110 C2
Cadwell La HTCHE/RSTV SG4 ... 157 P3
Caernarvon Cl HHNE HP2 ... 5 J3
  STVGE SG2 ... 177 G2
Caesars Rd STALE/WH AL4 ... 48 B5
Cage End RBSF CM22 ... 185 M4
Cage End Cl RBSF CM22 ... 185 M4
Cage Pond Rd RAD WD7 ... 104 C3
Cairns Cl STALE/WH AL4 ... 86 B3
Cairn Wy STAN HA7 ... 143 J1
Caishowe Rd BORE WD6 ... 120 F5
Caister Cl HHNE HP2 ... 5 J1
  STVG SG1 ... 20 E8
Calais Cl CHESW EN7 ... 91 H8
Calbury Cl STAL AL1 ... 85 M3
Calcutt Cl LTNW/LEA LU4 ... 26 E3
Caldbeck WAB EN9 ... 111 H8
Caldecot Av CHESW EN7 ... 109 K3
Caldecote Gdns BUSH WD23 ... 133 K3
Caldecote La BUSH WD23 ... 133 K3
Caldecote Rd BLDK SG7 ... 148 A5
Caldecot Wy BROX EN10 ... 92 D4
Calder Av BRKMPK AL9 ... 88 C5
Calder Wy STVG SG1 ... 21 L6
Calderwood Pl EBAR EN4 ... 122 F1
Caldwell Rd OXHEY WD19 ... 132 B7
Caleb Cl LTNW/LEA LU4 ... 27 M1
Caledon Rd LCOL/BKTW AL2 ... 86 A8
California BLDK SG7 ... 149 K12
California La BUSH WD23 ... 133 H4
The Callanders BUSH WD23 * ... 133 J4
Callisto Ct HHNE HP2 ... 62 D7
Callowland Pl WATN WD24 ... 117 M4
Calnwood Rd LTNW/LEA LU4 ... 26 F1
Calshot Wy ENC/FH EN2 ... 124 F7
Calthorpe Gdns EDGW HA8 ... 134 D8
Calton Av HERT/WAT SG14 ... 52 D6
Calton Rd BAR EN5 ... 137 G2
Calverley Cl BSF CM23 ... 43 L6
Calverton Rd LTNN/LIM LU3 ... 27 K3
Calvert Rd BAR EN5 ... 122 B6
Camberley Av EN EN1 ... 125 J8
Camberley Pl HARP AL5 ... 47 H7
Camborne Cl HHNE HP2 ... 62 C7
Cambrian Wy HHNE HP2 ... 62 C7
Cambridge Dr POTB/CUF EN6 ... 106 C5
Cambridge Gdns EN EN1 ... 125 L6
Cambridge Pde EN EN1 * ... 125 L6
Cambridge Rd BGSW SG18 ... 144 D3
  HLW CM20 ... 183 N11
  HTCHE/RSTV SG4 ... 157 R5
  ROY SG8 ... 152 F8
  RYLN/HDSTN HA2 ... 142 F7
  STAL AL1 ... 85 M3
  STDN SG11 ... 163 H11
  STSD CM24 ... 166 C5
  WATW WD18 ... 13 G6
Cambridge Ter BERK HP4 * ... 80 B1
Camden Rw HARP AL5 * ... 142 A5
Cameron Cl STVGE SG2 ... 11 M1
  TRDG/WHET N20 ... 137 J5
Cameron Ct WARE SG12 ... 54 A3
Cameron Dr CHES/WCR EN8 ... 110 B8
Cameron Rd CSHM HP5 ... 97 G4
Camfield WGCE AL7 ... 68 D3
Camford Wy LTNN/LIM LU3 ... 26 F1
Camlet Wy EBAR EN4 ... 122 F4
  STALW/RED AL3 ... 8 A9
Campania Gv LTNN/LIM LU3 ... 27 J7
Campbell Cl BUNT SG9 ... 158 H10
Camp Dr DUN/HR/TOD LU5 ... 25 M4
Campers Av LWTH SG6 ... 16 C4
Campers Wk LWTH SG6 ... 16 C4
Campfield Rd
  HERT/WAT SG14 ... 52 F7
  STAL AL1 ... 85 M4
Campfield Vw LWTH SG6 ... 16 A4
Campian Cl DUN/WHIP LU6 ... 38 J8
Campine Cl CHES/WCR EN8 ... 110 B2
Campion Cl GSTN WD25 ... 101 L3
Campion Rd HAT AL10 ... 67 K4
  HHW HP1 ... 81 J3
Campions Ct BERK HP4 ... 79 L2
The Campions BORE WD6 ... 120 B4
  STSD CM24 ... 166 G6
Campion Wy EDGW HA8 ... 135 G2
Campkin Md STVGE SG2 ... 34 B1
Camp Rd STAL AL1 ... 9 J6
Campton Rd SHFD SG17 ... 146 A3
Campus Five LWTH SG6 ... 17 G2
The Campus HHNE HP2 ... 62 F5
  WGCW AL8 ... 50 B6
Camp View Rd STAL AL1 ... 85 M3
Cam Sq HTCHE/RSTV SG4 ... 157 Q2
Canada La BROX EN10 ... 92 C7
The Canadas BROX EN10 ... 92 C7
Canalside DEN/HRF UB9 ... 139 L1
Canal Wy DEN/HRF UB9 ... 139 L1
Canberra Cl STALE/WH AL4 ... 65 K6
Canberra Gdns LTNN/LIM LU3 ... 26 E1
Candale Cl DUN/WHIP LU6 ... 39 G3
Candlefield HHS/BOV HP3 ... 5 M9
Canesworde Rd DUN/WHIP LU6 ... 38 G2
Canfield BSF CM23 ... 43 L1
Canford Cl ENC/FH EN2 ... 124 E6
Cangels Cl HHW HP1 ... 4 L4
Canham Cl HTCHE/RSTV SG4 ... 175 P8

Canning Rd
  KTN/HRWW/WS HA3 ... 143 J5
Cannix Cl STVGE SG2 ... 33 L7
Cannonbury Pk PIN HA5 ... 142 B8
Cannon La LTNE LU2 ... 28 C7
  PIN HA5 ... 142 C7
Cannon Mill Av CSHM HP5 ... 97 H7
Cannon Rd WATW WD18 ... 13 G8
Cannons Cl BSF CM23 ... 166 C12
Cannon's Cl ROY SG8 ... 145 M4
Cannons Ct STDN SG11 ... 163 P10
Cannons Meadow WLYN AL6 ... 51 J3
Cannon St STALW/RED AL3 ... 8 F4
Canonbury Rd EN EN1 ... 125 J5
Canon Mohan Cl
  STHGT/OAK N14 ... 137 L2
Canons Brook
  HLWW/ROY CM19 ... 74 E5
Canons Cl RAD WD7 ... 119 M1
  WLYN AL6 ... 177 L9
Canonsfield Rd WLYN AL6 ... 177 L9
Canons Ga CHES/WCR EN8 ... 92 D8
  HLW CM20 ... 7 L9
Canons Md STSD CM24 ... 166 C11
Canons Mill La BSF CM23 ... 166 C11
Canterbury Cl AMSS HP7 ... 113 J5
  LTNN/LIM LU3 ... 27 K5
  NTHWD HA6 ... 141 L5
Canterbury Rd BORE WD6 ... 120 E6
  HRW HA1 ... 142 F7
  WAT WD17 ... 12 F1
Canterbury Wy
  RKW/CH/CXG WD3 ... 117 G7
Cantilupe Cl DUN/WHIP LU6 ... 37 H3
Capel Cl TRDG/WHET N20 ... 137 G6
Capel Crs STAN HA7 ... 135 L5
Capel Gdns PIN HA5 ... 142 D6
Capell Av RKW/CH/CXG WD3 ... 129 G3
Capell Rd RKW/CH/CXG WD3 ... 129 G3
Capell Wy RKW/CH/CXG WD3 ... 129 H1
Capelvere Wk WAT WD17 ... 117 J3
Cape Rd STAL AL1 ... 85 M2
Capital Pl HLWW/ROY CM19 ... 74 E6
Caponfield WGCE AL7 ... 51 G8
Cappell La WARE SG12 ... 55 G8
Capron Rd DUN/HR/TOD LU5 ... 25 J5
  LTNW/LEA LU4 ... 27 J5
Capstan Ride ENC/FH EN2 ... 124 E6
Captain's Cl CSHM HP5 ... 96 E1
Captains Wk BERK HP4 ... 80 B2
Capuchin Cl STAN HA7 ... 143 M1
Caractacus Cottage Vw
  WATW WD18 ... 131 L3
Caractacus Gn WATW WD18 ... 131 K2
Caradoc Evans Cl
  FBAR/BDGN N11 * ... 137 M8
Caravan La RKW/CH/CXG WD3 ... 130 C3
Carbone Hl POTB/CUF EN6 ... 90 B8
Carde Cl HERT/WAT SG14 ... 52 D6
Cardiff Cl STVGE SG2 ... 177 P2
Cardiff Gv LTN LU1 ... 6 D2
Cardiff Rd LTN LU1 ... 6 D1
  PEND EN3 ... 125 M8
  WATW WD18 ... 12 E9
Cardiff Wy ABLGY WD5 ... 101 L3
Cardigan Ms LTN LU1 * ... 6 E4
Cardigan St LTN LU1 ... 6 E4
Cardinal Av BORE WD6 ... 120 F7
Cardinal Cl CHES/WCR EN8 ... 91 K8
Cardinal Gv STALW/RED AL3 ... 8 A9
Cardinal Wy
  KTN/HRWW/WS HA3 ... 143 J5
Cardrew Av
  NFNCH/WDSPK N12 ... 137 H8
Cardy Rd HHW HP1 * ... 4 B4
Carew Rd NTHWD HA6 ... 141 J1
Carew Wy OXHEY WD19 ... 132 D6
Careys Cft BERK HP4 ... 59 K6
Carfax Cl LTNW/LEA LU4 ... 26 C6
Carisbrook Cl EN EN1 ... 125 K5
Carisbrooke Av WATN WD24 ... 118 B5
Carisbrooke Rd HARP AL5 ... 47 G3
  LTNW/LEA LU4 ... 27 J8
Carleton Ri WLYN AL6 ... 176 H11
Carleton Rd CHES/WCR EN8 ... 110 B3
Carlisle Av STALW/RED AL3 ... 8 F2
  STAL AL1 ... 8 F2
Carlisle Cl DUN/WHIP LU6 ... 38 F3
Carlisle Pl FBAR/BDGN N11 * ... 137 M7
Carlton Av
  KTN/HRWW/WS HA3 ... 143 M7
Carlton Bank HARP AL5 * ... 46 F4
Carlton Cl BORE WD6 ... 121 H8
  EDGW HA8 ... 134 B4
Carlton Crs LTNN/LIM LU3 ... 28 A6
Carlton Rd FBAR/BDGN N11 * ... 137 L8
  HARP AL5 ... 46 E3
Carman Ct TRING HP23 ... 57 K2
Carmelite Rd
  KTN/HRWW/WS HA3 ... 143 M3
Carnaby Rd BROX EN10 ... 92 C2
Carnarvon Av EN EN1 ... 125 K6
Carnarvon Rd BAR EN5 ... 122 C7
Carnegie Cl PEND EN3 ... 126 F4
Carnegie Gdns LTNN/LIM LU3 ... 27 L1
Carnegie Rd STALW/RED AL3 ... 65 H6
Caro Ln HHS/BOV HP3 ... 82 F4
Carol Cl LTNN/LIM LU3 ... 27 M1
Caroline Ct STAN HA7 * ... 143 L1
Caroline Pl OXHEY WD19 ... 13 K9
Caroon Dr RKW/CH/CXG WD3 ... 115 M2
Carpenders Av OXHEY WD19 ... 132 C6
Carpenders Cl HARP AL5 ... 47 H8
Carpenters Arms La EPP CM16 ... 95 M7
The Carpenters BSF CM23 ... 44 B3
Carpenters Wood Dr
  RKW/CH/CXG WD3 ... 114 G6
Carpenter Wy POTB/CUF EN6 ... 107 G2
Carrigans BSF CM23 ... 43 L1
Carr Cl STAN HA7 ... 143 H1
Carrington Av BORE WD6 ... 134 C1
Carrington Cl BAR EN5 ... 135 G4
Carrington Sq
  KTN/HRWW/WS HA3 ... 143 G2
Carsdale Cl LTNN/LIM LU3 ... 27 L1
Carson Rd EBAR EN4 ... 123 K8

Carteret Rd LTNE LU2 ... 29 G8
Carterhatch La EN EN1 ... 125 K5
  PEND EN3 ... 125 L5
Carterhatch Rd PEND EN3 ... 126 C6
Carters Cl ARL/CHE SG15 ... 147 G2
  STVGE SG2 ... 36 A9
Cartersfield Rd WAB EN9 ... 111 G8
Carters Leys BSF CM23 ... 43 K5
Carters Md HLWE CM17 ... 75 M6
Carters Wk ARL/CHE SG15 ... 147 G2
Carters Wy ARL/CHE SG15 ... 147 G2
Carters Yd STAL AL1 * ... 8 G6
Cartmel Dr DUN/WHIP LU6 ... 38 F3
Cart Pth GSTN WD25 ... 102 A3
The Cart Tr HHS/BOV HP3 ... 82 D7
Cartwright Rd ROY SG8 ... 14 B4
Carve Ley WGCE AL7 ... 50 F8
Carvers Cft KNEB SG3 ... 177 J8
Cary Wk RAD WD7 ... 103 M8
Cashio La LWTH SG6 ... 148 E12
Caslon Wy LWTH SG6 ... 148 D12
Cassandra Ga CHES/WCR EN8 ... 110 D3
Cassiobridge Rd WATW WD18 ... 117 J3
Cassiobridge Ter
  RKW/CH/CXG WD3 ... 131 H1
Cassiobury Dr WAT WD17 ... 12 B1
Cassiobury Park Av
  WATW WD18 ... 117 J7
Cassio Pl WATW WD18 ... 117 J8
Cassio Rd WATW WD18 ... 12 C5
Cassio Whf WATW WD18 * ... 131 H1
Castellane Cl STAN HA7 ... 143 J1
Castle Gdns KGLGY WD4 ... 100 D3
Castle Cl BUSH WD23 ... 132 F5
  DUN/WHIP LU6 ... 73 L1
  HOD EN11 ... 73 G4
  LBUZ LU7 ... 169 P6
Castle Ct HTCH/STOT SG5 ... 157 M4
Castle Croft Rd LTN LU1 ... 40 E3
Castleford Cl BORE WD6 ... 120 D4
Castle Ga HERT/WAT SG14 ... 53 G8
Castle Gate Wy BERK HP4 ... 60 A7
Castle Hl BERK HP4 ... 60 A7
Castle Hill Cl BERK HP4 ... 59 M8
Castle Hill Ct BERK HP4 * ... 60 A7
Castle Hill Rd DUN/WHIP LU6 ... 37 M2
Castle Md HHW HP1 ... 4 C6
Castle Mead Gdns
  HERT/WAT SG14 ... 53 G7
Castles Cl HTCH/STOT SG5 ... 148 D6
Castle St BERK HP4 ... 80 A1
  BSF CM23 ... 43 M5
  HERT/WAT SG14 ... 53 G8
  LTN LU1 ... 6 F5
Castle Vw Rd BSF CM23 ... 44 A2
Castlewood Rd EBAR EN4 ... 123 H4
Catchacre DUN/WHIP LU6 ... 38 E2
Caterham Ct WAB EN9 ... 111 K8
Catesby Gn LTNN/LIM LU3 ... 154 G12
Catham Cl STAL AL1 ... 85 M4
Catherall Rd LTNN/LIM LU3 ... 27 M3
Catherine Cl HHNE HP2 ... 63 G5
Catherine Pl HRW HA1 ... 143 K7
Catherine Rd PEND EN3 ... 126 C3
Catherine St STALW/RED AL3 ... 8 F4
  EN EN1 ... 137 J2
Cathrow Ms HOD EN11 ... 72 E4
Catisfield Rd PEND EN3 ... 126 C3
Catkin Cl HHS/BOV HP3 ... 81 K1
Catlin's La PIN HA5 ... 141 M5
Catlin St HHS/BOV HP3 ... 81 K1
  HHW HP1 ... 4 B8
Catsbrook Rd LTNN/LIM LU3 ... 27 M3
Catsdell Bottom HHS/BOV HP3 ... 82 F5
Catsey La BUSH WD23 ... 133 G3
Catsey Wd BUSH WD23 ... 133 G3
Catterick Wy BORE WD6 ... 120 D5
Cattlegate Rd ENC/FH EN2 ... 108 C2
  POTB/CUF EN6 ... 108 C2
Cattley Cl BAR EN5 ... 122 C5
Cattlins Cl CHESW EN7 ... 109 J3
Cattsdell HHNE HP2 ... 62 E5
Causeway Cl POTB/CUF EN6 ... 107 H5
The Causeway BSF CM23 ... 43 M2
  BUNT SG9 ... 159 J9
  BUNT SG9 ... 158 E5
  POTB/CUF EN6 ... 107 G5
  ROY SG8 ... 151 M5
  STDN SG11 ... 164 B4
Cautherly La WARE SG12 ... 54 B8
Cavalier Cl LTNN/LIM LU3 ... 27 L3
Cavalier Ct BERK HP4 ... 80 A1
Cavan Dr STALW/RED AL3 ... 65 H5
Cavan Pl PIN HA5 ... 142 C3
Cavan Rd STALW/RED AL3 ... 173 Q11
Cavell Cl BSF CM23 ... 44 B3
Cavell Dr ENC/FH EN2 ... 124 E6
Cavell Rd CHESW EN7 ... 109 K1
Cavell Wk STVGE SG2 ... 35 A3
Cavendish Cl AMS HP6 ... 113 M5
Cavendish Ct
  RKW/CH/CXG WD3 * ... 131 H1
Cavendish Crs BORE WD6 ... 120 E8
Cavendish Rd BAR EN5 ... 122 A7
  CSHM HP5 ... 97 H6
  LTNN/LIM LU3 ... 27 M7
  STAL AL1 ... 9 K6
  STALW/RED AL3 ... 172 F3
  STVG SG1 ... 2 C4
Cavendish Wy HAT AL10 ... 67 K8
Cawkell Cl STSD CM24 ... 166 F6
Cawley Hatch
  HLWW/ROY CM19 ... 74 D5
Caxton Ga STVG SG1 * ... 32 C5
Caxton Hl HERT/BAY SG13 ... 53 J7
Caxton Pl STVG SG1 ... 32 C5
Caxton Rd HOD EN11 ... 72 F3
  WATW WD18 ... 131 H3
Cecil Av EN EN1 ... 125 K6
Cecil Cl BSF CM23 ... 44 D2
Cecil Ms EN EN1 * ... 125 K6
Cecil Pk PIN HA5 ... 142 C6
Cecil Rd CHES/WCR EN8 ... 110 B6
  ENC/FH EN2 ... 125 H4
  HERT/BAY SG13 ... 71 G3
  HLWS CM18 ... 75 G8
Cecil St WATN WD24 ... 13 G1

HOD EN11 ... 73 G5
KTN/HRWW/WS HA3 ... 143 J5
POTB/CUF EN6 ... 105 M6
STAL AL1 ... 9 K6
STHGT/OAK N14 ... 137 M4
Cecil St WATN WD24 ... 117 M4
Cedar Av CHES/WCR EN8 ... 110 B7
EBAR EN4 ... 137 J3
HTCH/STOT SG5 ... 157 N1
PEND EN3 ... 126 A6
Cedar Cl HERT/WAT SG14 ... 97 J4
HERT/WAT SG14 ... 52 F7
LTNW/LEA LU4 ... 26 C6
POTB/CUF EN6 ... 106 E4
SBW CM21 ... 183 D8
WARE SG12 ... 54 B5
Cedar Ct BSF CM23 ... 166 B12
STALE/WH AL4 ... 86 B2
Cedar Crs ROY SG8 ... 14 C7
Cedar Dr CSHM HP5 ... 96 C5
PIN HA5 ... 142 C1
Cedar Gn HOD EN11 ... 72 E8
Cedar Gv AMSS HP7 ... 113 H5
CSHM HP5 ... 78 D5
Cedar Lawn Av BAR EN5 ... 96 C1
Cedar Ldg CHES/WCR EN8 * ... 110 B2
Cedar Pk BSF CM23 ... 43 K5
Cedar Park Rd ENC/FH EN2 ... 125 C4
Cedar Rdg AMS HP6 ... 96 A8
Cedar Ri STHGT/OAK N14 ... 137 L3
Cedar Rd BERK HP4 ... 80 B2
ENC/FH EN2 ... 124 F4
HAT AL10 ... 87 L1
OXHEY WD19 ... 132 C2
Cedars Av RKW/CH/CXG WD3 ... 130 A4
Cedars Cl BORE WD6 ... 120 D8
CFSP/GDCR SL9 ... 128 C8
The Cedars BERK HP4 * ... 80 C1
DUN/WHIP LU6 ... 39 G2
HARP AL5 * ... 46 F4
Cedar Wk HHNE HP2 ... 4 F6
Cedar Wy BERK HP4 ... 80 B2
Cedar Wood Dr GSTN WD25 ... 117 M1
Cedarwood Dr STALE/WH AL4 ... 86 D2
Ceders Dell HTCHE/RSTV SG4 ... 157 P7
Celadon Cl PEND EN3 ... 126 C2
Celandine Dr LTNN/LIM LU3 ... 27 H4
Cell Barnes Cl STAL AL1 ... 85 M4
Cell Barnes La STAL AL1 ... 9 M8
Cemetery HI HHW HP1 ... 4
Cemetery Rd BSF CM23 ... 43 M4
DUN/HR/TOD LU5 ... 25 M5
Cemmaes Court Rd HHW HP1 * ... 4 D3
Cemmaes Meadow HHW HP1 * ... 4 D3
Centenary Cl MHAD SG10 ... 182 C3
Centenary Rd PEND EN3 ... 126 D8
Centenary Wk LOU IG10 ... 127 L7
Centennial Av BORE WD6 ... 133 M3
Centennial Pk BORE WD6 * ... 134 A3
Central Av CHES/WCR EN8 ... 110 C7
DUN/WHIP LU6 ... 171 L1
EN EN1 ... 125 L6
HNLW SG16 ... 147 K6
PIN HA5 ... 142 D8
Central Dr STAL AL1 ... 86 A1
WCCE AL7 ... 50 D5
Central Pde HRW HA1 ... 143 K7
PEND EN3 * ... 126 A4
Central Rd HLW CM20 ... 75 L1
Central Wy NTHWD HA6 ... 141 J2
Centre Wy WAT WD17 ... 13 H8
Centro HHNE HP2 ... 63 G8
Century Cl STALW/RED AL3 ... 8 D3
Century Ct WAT WD18 * ... 131 J3
Century Pk WAT WD17 ... 13 H8
Century Rd HOD EN11 ... 72 E6
WARE SG12 ... 54 B3
Cervantes Cl NTHWD HA6 ... 141 J2
Cestreham Crs CSHM HP5 ... 97 H3
Chace Av POTB/CUF EN6 ... 107 H6
The Chace STVGE SG2 ... 33 N4
Chad La STALW/RED AL3 ... 173 L4
Chadwell WARE SG12 ... 54 A4
Chadwell Cl LTNE LU2 ... 7 J1
Chadwell Ri WARE SG12 ... 54 A4
Chadwell Rd STVG SG1 ... 32 F5
Chadwick Cl DUN/WHIP LU6 ... 25 L8
Chaffinches Gn HHS/BOV HP3 ... 82 E6
Chaffinch La WATW WD18 ... 131 N3
Chagny Cl LTNW SG6 ... 16 C3
Chailey Av EN EN1 ... 125 K6
Chain Wk BUNT SG9 ... 158 A12
HERT/BAY SG13 ... 90 A4
HERT/WAT SG14 ... 178 F2
ROY SG8 ... 150 F2
WLYN AL6 ... 51 L1
Chalet Cl BERK HP4 ... 79 K1
Chalet Est MLHL NW7 * ... 135 L2
Chalfont Av AMS HP6 ... 114 B5
Chalfont Cl HHNE HP2 ... 62 F5
Chalfont La
RKW/CH/CXG WD3 ... 128 F1
RKW/CH/CXG WD3 ... 139 G2
Chalfont Pl STALW/RED AL3 * ... 9 C5
Chalfont Rd CSTG HP8 ... 128 F6
RKW/CH/CXG WD3 ... 129 G2
Chalfont Station Rd
AMSS HP7 ... 114 A6
Chalfont Wk PIN HA5 * ... 142 A4
Chalfont Wy LTNE LU2 ... 29 G7
Chalgrove WCCE AL7 ... 51 H6
Chalk Dl WCCE AL7 ... 50 F6
Chalk Acres DUN/HR/TOD LU5 ... 26 A5
Chalkdell Flds STALE/WH AL4 ... 65 L7
Chalkdell HI STALE/WH AL4 ... 5 J3
Chalkdown LTNE LU2 ... 28 B2
STVGE SG2 ... 34 B2
Chalk Fld LWTH SG6 ... 17 G6
Chalk HI CSHM HP5 ... 96 B3
LTNE LU2 ... 29 K5
OXHEY WD19 ... 13 L9
Chalk Hills BLDK SG7 ... 17 K4
Chalk La EBAR EN4 ... 123 K4
HLWE CM17 ... 76 A5
Chalkmill Dr EN EN1 ... 125 M7
Chalks Av SBW CM21 ... 183 P6
Chalkwell Park Av EN EN1 ... 125 L6
Challinor HLWE CM17 ... 76 C5
Challney Cl LTNW/LEA LU4 ... 27 G4
Chalton Rd LTNN/LIM LU3 ... 27 J4
Chamberlain Cl HLWE CM17 ... 76 A5
Chamberlaines HARP AL5 ... 173 Q4
Chamberlain La PIN HA5 ... 141 L6
Chambers Cl LTNN/LIM LU3 ... 141 M5
Chambersbury La
HHS/BOV HP3 ... 82 A7
Chambers Ga STVG SG1 ... 33 H2
Chambers Gv WCCE AL7 ... 51 J7
Chambers La HTCH/STOT SG5 ... 157 N1
Chambers' St HERT/WAT SG14 ... 53 G2
Champions Cl BORE WD6 ... 120 F3
Champions Wy HOD EN11 ... 72 E4

Champneys OXHEY WD19 * ... 132 C5
Chancellors ARL/CHE SG15 ... 147 R2
Chancellors Rd STVG SG1 ... 21 C8
Chancery Ct STALE/WH AL4 ... 85 B7
Chanctonbury Wy
NFNCH/WDSPK N12 ... 136 E7
Chandler's La
RKW/CH/CXG WD3 ... 116 C2
Chandlers Rd STALE/WH AL4 ... 66 A7
Chandos Av TRDG/WHET N20 ... 137 H4
Chandos Cl AMS HP6 ... 114 A4
Chandos Ct STAN HA7 ... 143 M1
Chandos Rd BORE WD6 ... 120 D6
HRW HA1 ... 143 G7
Chanfield Cl LTNW/LEA LU4 ... 26 D6
Chantry Cl BAR EN5 ... 135 K2
BSF CM23 ... 43 L1
ENC/FH EN2 ... 124 D1
KGLCY WD4 ... 100 E3
MLHL NW7 ... 135 K3
Chantry La HAT AL10 ... 87 K1
LCOL/BKTW AL2 ... 86 B8
STVG SG1 ... 20 D7
Chantry Pl
KTN/HRWW/WS HA3 ... 142 F1
Chantry Rd BSF CM23 ... 43 L1
KTN/HRWW/WS HA3 ... 142 F1
The Chantry HLW CM20 ... 3 L2
Chaomans LWTH SG6 ... 16 D6
Chapel Cl BERK HP4 ... 171 K11
GSTN WD25 ... 101 K3
LTNE LU2 ... 28 A1
STAL AL1 ... 85 H5
Chapel Cft KGLCY WD4 ... 99 L5
Chapel Crofts BERK HP4 ... 59 J7
Chapel Dr ARL/CHE SG15 ... 147 Q5
RAYLNE/WEN HP22 ... 168 C12
Chapel End La TRING HP23 ... 168 D9
Chapel Flds HLWE CM17 ... 76 A7
TRING HP23 ... 168 D5
Chapelfields WARE SG12 ... 55 H8
Chapel HI STSD CM24 ... 166 F6
Chapel La DUN/WHIP LU6 ... 37 G7
HERT/WAT SG14 ... 69 M3
HLWE CM17 ... 76 A7
PIN HA5 ... 142 F1
STDN SG11 ... 93 K4
TRING HP23 ... 168 F5
Chapel Pl HTCHE/RSTV SG4 ... 30 C8
SHFD SG17 ... 146 F4
STALW/RED AL3 ... 173 K7
Chapel Rw DEN/HRF UB9 ... 140 A3
HTCH/STOT SG5 * ... 157 P5
Chapel St BERK HP4 ... 80 A1
BCSW SG18 ... 144 D4
BLDK SG7 ... 144 C11
ENC/FH EN2 ... 125 C7
HHNE HP2 ... 82 B1
LTN LU1 ... 6 E7
TRING HP23 ... 57 K2
Chapel Viad LTN LU1 ... 6 E6
Chapel Wy ABLGY WD5 ... 101 K1
Chapman Cl LTNE LU2 ... 28 A1
Chapman Crs STVG SG1 ... 20 F8
Chapmans End STDN SG11 ... 163 P10
The Chapmans
HTCH/STOT SG5 * ... 157 N7
Chapmans Yd WAT WD17 ... 13 H6
Chappell Ct WARE SG12 ... 179 N10
Chappel Meadow TRING HP23 ... 169 M11
Chapter House Rd
LTNW/LEA LU4 ... 26 C7
Charcroft Gdns PEND EN3 ... 126 B8
Chard Dr LTNN/LIM LU3 ... 116 H12
Chardia Ter CHES/WCR EN8 * ... 110 B4
Charding Crs ROY SG8 ... 14 D6
Chardins Cl HHW HP1 ... 81 K1
Charkham Ms BRKMPK AL9 ... 88 A4
Charlbury Av STAN HA7 ... 134 B8
Charles Sevright Dr
MLHL NW7 ... 136 B8
Charles St BERK HP4 ... 79 M1
HHW HP1 ... 4 D5
LTNE LU2 ... 7 J2
TRING HP23 ... 57 L2
Charlesworth Cl HHS/BOV HP3 ... 5 K6
Charlock Wy WATW WD18 ... 12 B9
Charlotte La STALE/WH AL4 ... 86 C2
Charlton Cl HHNE HP2 ... 72 E7
Charlton Mead La HOD EN11 ... 73 D8
Charlton Rd HTCH/STOT SG5 ... 157 M8
Charlton Wy HOD EN11 ... 72 E8
Charlwood Cl
KTN/HRWW/WS HA3 ... 143 J1
Charlwood Rd LTNW/LEA LU4 ... 26 E5
Charmbury Ri LTNE LU2 ... 28 E5
Charmouth Cl STAL AL1 ... 65 L1
Charmouth Rd STAL AL1 ... 9 L1
Charndon Cl LTNN/LIM LU3 ... 154 H12
Charnwood Pl
TRDG/WHET N20 ... 137 G6
Charnwood Rd EN EN1 ... 125 M2
Charsley La AMS HP6 ... 114 A5
Charter Pl WAT WD17 ... 12 F4
Charters Cross HLWS CM18 ... 75 H8
Chartley Av STAN HA7 ... 143 K1
Chartridge OXHEY WD19 * ... 132 C5
Chartridge Cl BAR EN5 ... 135 L1
BUSH WD23 ... 133 L5
Chartridge Grange Dr
CSHM HP5 ... 96 B1
Chartridge La CSHM HP5 ... 96 B2
Chartridge Wy HHNE HP2 ... 83 G2
Chartwell Cl WAB EN9 ... 111 J7
Chartwell Dr LTNE LU2 ... 28 C6
Chartwell Rd NTHWD HA6 ... 141 J4
Charwood Cl RAD WD7 ... 104 C7
Chasden Rd HHW HP1 ... 61 K7
Chase Cl ARL/CHE SG15 ... 147 Q1
Chase Court Gdns
ENC/FH EN2 ... 125 C1
Chase Gn ENC/FH EN2 ... 125 G1
Chase Green Av ENC/FH EN2 ... 124 F1
Chase HI ENC/FH EN2 ... 125 G1
Chase Hill Rd ARL/CHE SG15 ... 147 Q2
Chase Ridings ENC/FH EN2 ... 125 E1
Chase Side ENC/FH EN2 ... 125 G2
STHGT/OAK N14 ... 137
Chase Side Av ENC/FH EN2 ... 125 G1
Chaseside LBUZ LU7 ... 169
Chase Side Cres ENC/FH EN2 ... 125 H1
Chase Side Pl ENC/FH EN2 ... 125 H1
Chase St LTN LU1 ... 6 B4
The Chase BSF CM23 * ... 43 M4
CHESW EN7 ... 108 F2

CSHM HP5 ... 96 F3
HERT/BAY SG13 ... 53 J4
HHNE HP2 ... 5 J4
HLWE CM17 ... 76 A4
PIN HA5 ... 142 A8
RAD WD7 ... 119 K5
WARE SG12 ... 54 A4
WLYN AL6 ... 177 M10
Chase Wy STHGT/OAK N14 ... 137 M4
Chaseways SBW CM21 ... 183 M9
Chasewood Av ENC/FH EN2 ... 124 F6
Chasten HI LWTH SG6 ... 16 B2
Chatsworth Cl WDGW WD6 ... 120 D7
BSF CM23 ... 43 J2
Chatsworth Ct STVGE SG2 ... 33 N8
Chatsworth Rd LTNW/LEA LU4 ... 27 H5
Chatteris Cl LTNW/LEA LU4 ... 27 H5
Chatterton LWTH SG6 ... 16 F4
Chatton Cl LTNE LU2 ... 29 J7
Chaucer Av BERK HP4 ... 59 K8
Chaucer Rd LTNN/LIM LU3 ... 28 A7
ROY SG8 ... 14 D5
Chaucer Wk HHNE HP2 ... 62 F4
Chaucer Wy HOD EN11 ... 72 E3
HTCHE/RSTV SG4 ... 20 A7
Chaulden House Gdns
HHW HP1 ... 81 K4
Chaulden La HHW HP1 ... 81 H4
Chaulden Ter HHW HP1 ... 81 K3
Chaul End Rd LTNW/LEA LU4 ... 26 F8
Chauncey Av POTB/CUF EN6 ... 107 J3
Chauncey Cl WARE SG12 ... 54 A2
Chauncy Gdns BLDK SG7 ... 149 M12
Chauncy Rd STVG SG1 ... 10 L8
Chaworth Gn LTNW/LEA LU4 ... 27 H3
Cheapside LTN LU1 ... 7 G5
Cheapside Sq LTN LU1 ... 6 F5
Chedburgh WGCE AL7 ... 51 H6
Cheddington La TRING HP23 ... 169 M4
Cheddington Rd LBUZ LU7 ... 169 M4
Cheffins Rd HOD EN11 ... 72 D4
Chells La STVGE SG2 ... 34 A1
Chells Wy STVGE SG2 ... 11 M1
Chelmsford Rd
HERT/WAT SG14 ... 52 E8
RBSF CM22 ... 184 H7
Chelsea Flds HOD EN11 ... 72 F3
Chelsea Gdns
DUN/HR/TOD LU5 ... 26 A4
HLWE CM17 ... 76 B4
Chelsing Ri HHNE HP2 ... 83 G3
Chelsworth Cl LTNE LU2 ... 29 J7
Chelveston WGCE AL7 ... 51 H6
Chelwood Av HAT AL10 ... 67 H6
Chelwood Cl NTHWD HA6 ... 141 G2
Chenduit Wy STAN HA7 ... 133 K8
Chene Dr STALW/RED AL3 ... 8 C2
Cheney Rd LTNN/LIM LU3 ... 27 G4
Cheney St PIN HA5 ... 142 A6
Chenies Av AMS HP6 ... 114 B5
Chenies Ct HHNE HP2 * ... 5 F5
Chenies Pde AMSS HP7 * ... 114 A6
Chenies Rd RKW/CH/CXG WD3 ... 115 H6
Chenies Wy WATW WD18 ... 131 J3
Chennells HAT AL10 ... 87 K1
Chennells Cl HTCHE/RSTV SG4 ... 157 R3
The Chennies HARP AL5 * ... 47 G5
Chepstow Cl STVG SG1 ... 33 M1
Chequer Ct LTN LU1 ... 7 G5
Chequer La STALW/RED AL3 ... 63 L1
Chequers BRKMPK AL9 ... 68 E5
BSF CM23 ... 43 J11
WGCE AL7 ... 68 B5
Chequers Bridge Rd STVG SG1 ... 10 D3
Chequers Cl BUNT SG9 ... 158 H9
HTCH/STOT SG5 ... 148 D7
LBUZ LU7 ... 169 N5
STDN SG11 ... 163 P9
Chequersfield WGCE AL7 ... 68 C2
Chequers HI STALW/RED AL3 ... 173 L1
Chequers La GSTN WD25 ... 31 H2
HTCHE/RSTV SG4 ... 169 N5
The Chequers DUN/WHIP LU6 ... 37 H3
PIN HA5 * ... 142 F2
Chequer St LTN LU1 ... 7 G5
STAL AL1 ... 8 E2
Cheriton Cl EBAR EN4 ... 123 N2
STALE/WH AL4 ... 66 F6
Cheshire Ct WCCE AL7 * ... 51 J4
Chesham Rd CSHM HP5 ... 78 A4
BSF CM23 ... 43 J5
GTMIS/PWD HP16 ... 96 B6

TRING HP23 ... 58 B5
Chesham Wy WATW WD18 ... 131 J2
Chessbury Cl CSHM HP5 ... 96 E5
Chessbury Rd CSHM HP5 ... 96 C5
Chess Cl CSHM HP5 ... 114 D2
Chess HI CSHM HP5 ... 114 D2
Chessington Ct PIN HA5 ... 142 D2
Chess La RKW/CH/CXG WD3 ... 116 D2
Chessmount Ri CSHM HP5 ... 97 H5
Chess Vale Ri
RKW/CH/CXG WD3 ... 130 D2
Chess Valley Wk CSHM HP5 ... 113 H5
RKW/CH/CXG WD3 ... 115 L7
Chesswood Ct
RKW/CH/CXG WD3 ... 130 B2
Chesswood Wy PIN HA5 ... 142 B3
Chester Av HARP AL5 ... 47 G4
Chester Cl LTNW/LEA LU4 ... 27 J6
Chester Dr RYLN/HDSTN HA2 ... 142 A8
Chesterfield Rd BAR EN5 ... 136 B1
PEND EN3 ... 126 C3
Chester Gibbons Gn
LCOL/BKTW AL2 ... 86 B8
Chester Pl NTHWD HA6 * ... 141 K2
Chester Rd BORE WD6 ... 121 K2
NTHWD HA6 ... 141 K4
STVG SG1 ... 21 L8
WATN WD18 ... 12 C1
Chesterton Cl HARP AL5 ... 47 G4
Chesterton Cl CSHM HP5 ... 97 H3
Chestnut Av CSHM HP5 ... 97 H3
HNLW SG16 ... 147 K6
LTNN/LIM LU3 ... 154 B12
NTHWD HA6 ... 141 K4
RAYLNE/WEN HP22 ... 56 A5
RKW/CH/CXG WD3 ... 129 L1
WARE SG12 ... 54 C2
Chestnut Cl AMS HP6 ... 113 H5
BERK HP4 ... 60 F7
BERK HP4 ... 171 J4
RAYLNE/WEN HP22 ... 168 D12
WARE SG12 ... 182 C5
Chestnut Cots
TRDG/WHET N20 * ... 136 C4
Chestnut Ct HTCH/STOT SG5 ... 157 M5
Chestnut Dr BERK HP4 ... 80 A4
KTN/HRWW/WS HA3 ... 143 K2
PIN HA5 ... 142 B1
RBSF CM22 ... 184 F6
STAL AL1 ... 65 M8
Chestnut End
RAYLNE/WEN HP22 ... 56 A4
Chestnut Gv EBAR EN4 ... 137 K1
HOD EN11 ... 72 F7
HLW CM20 ... 6 B1
TRDG/WHET N20 * ... 136 C4
Chestnut La
HHS/BOV HP3 ... 81 K6
HTCHE/RSTV SG4 ... 176 F7
PIN HA5 ... 142 D2
Chestnut Ri BUSH WD23 ... 132 F3
Chestnut Rd PEND EN3 ... 126 C1
The Chestnuts HERT/BAY SG13 ... 53 H8
HHS/BOV HP3 ... 81 K6
HTCHE/RSTV SG4 ... 176 F7
PIN HA5 ... 142 D2
Chestnut Wk
CFSP/GDCR SL9 * ... 138 C2
EPP CM16 ... 94 F7
HTCHE/RSTV SG4 ... 157 Q9
WATN WD24 ... 117 L3
WLYN AL6 ... 177 M9
Chetwynd Av EBAR EN4 ... 137 K4
Chevalier Cl STAN HA7 ... 134 B6
The Cheveralls DUN/WHIP LU6 ... 37 H3
Cheverells Cl STALW/RED AL3 ... 172 F4
Cheviot Cl BUSH WD23 ... 133 G2
LTNE LU2 ... 29 J6
Cheviot Rd LTNN/LIM LU3 ... 27 J4
Cheviots HAT AL10 ... 87 L3
HHNE HP2 ... 62 D7
Cheviot Wy STVG SG1 ... 21 L5
LBUZ LU7 ... 169 P5
WARE SG12 ... 54 C2
Cheyne Ct BUSH WD23 ... 13 L6
Cheyne Wk CSHM HP5 ... 97 H5
Cheyney Cl ROY SG8 ... 145 P7
Cheyney Rd ROY SG8 ... 145 P7
Chicheley Rd
KTN/HRWW/WS HA3 ... 143 G2
WGCW AL8 ... 50 B3
Chichester Cl
DUN/HR/TOD LU5 ... 39 H2
Chichester Wy HTCH/STOT SG5 ... 102 C7
Chicken La LCOL/BKTW AL2 ... 104 B1
Chiddingfold
NFNCH/WDSPK N12 ... 136 E6
Chilcote La AMSS HP7 ... 113 M5
Chilcott Rd WATN WD24 ... 117 J2
Chilcourt ROY SG8 ... 14 D7
Childs Av DEN/HRF UB9 ... 140 A4
Childwick Ct HHS/BOV HP3 ... 82 F5
Childwick Wy LWTH SG6 ... 16 A1
Chilham Cl HHNE HP2 ... 5 J5
Chiltern Av AMS HP6 ... 113 H4
BUSH WD23 ... 133 G3
DUN/WHIP LU6 ... 38 D7
Chiltern Cl BERK HP4 ... 59 L8
BORE WD6 ... 120 C3
BUSH WD23 ... 132 F3
CHESW EN7 ... 108 F1
WARE SG12 ... 54 B2
Chiltern Dene ENC/FH EN2 ... 124 D2
Chiltern Dr RKW/CH/CXG WD3 ... 129 K5
Chiltern Est WATN WD24 * ... 117 L5
Chiltern Gdns LTNW/LEA LU4 ... 27 H5
Chiltern Hts AMSS HP7 ... 113 L5
Chiltern Link CFSP/GDCR SL9 ... 138 C3
Chiltern Pde AMS HP6 ... 113 L5
Chiltern Pk DUN/HR/TOD LU5 ... 26 B7
Chiltern Park Av BERK HP4 ... 59 L8
Chiltern Ri LTN LU1 ... 6 D8
Chiltern Rd
AMP/FLIT/BLC MK45 ... 155 J2
AMS HP6 ... 96 A5
BLDK SG7 ... 17 K3
DUN/WHIP LU6 ... 38 D7
HTCHE/RSTV SG4 ... 157 Q6
PIN HA5 ... 142 A6
STALE/WH AL4 ... 66 A5
Chilterns HAT AL10 ... 87 L3
HHNE HP2 ... 62 D7
The Chilterns DUN/WHIP LU6 ... 172 B1
STVG SG1 ... 157 Q7
Chiltern Vw LWTH SG6 ... 16 B4
Chiltern Wy
RAYLNE/WEN HP22 ... 56 D3
TRING HP23 ... 169 N12

Chilton Gn WGCE AL7 ... 51 G7
Chilton Rd CSHM HP5 ... 97 G3
Chilvers Bank BLDK SG7 ... 17 J2
Chilworth Ga BROX EN10 ... 92 D4
Chime Sq STALW/RED AL3 ... 8 F3
Chindit Cl BROX EN10 ... 92 B2
Chinnery Cl EN EN1 ... 125 K4
Chinnery HI BSF CM23 ... 43 M4
Chipmunk Cha HAT AL10 ... 67 H6
Chippenham Cl PIN HA5 ... 141 H6
Chipperfield Rd HHS/BOV HP3 ... 98 C7
Chipping Cl BAR EN5 ... 122 C7
Chippingfield HLWE CM17 ... 76 A2
Chipstead CFSP/GDCR SL9 ... 138 A3
Chishill Rd ROY SG8 ... 153 J3
Chishill St ROY SG8 ... 153 P2
Chiswell St WATN WD24 ... 118 A4
Chiswick Green La
LCOL/BKTW AL2 ... 84 B7
Chittenden Cl HOD EN11 ... 72 F4
Chivenor Pl STALE/WH AL4 ... 86 H4
Chobham St LTN LU1 ... 7 H7
Chobham Wk LTN LU1 ... 7 H7
Cholesbury La CSHM HP5 ... 78 D4
Chorleywood Bottom
RKW/CH/CXG WD3 ... 129 H1
Chorleywood Cl
RKW/CH/CXG WD3 ... 130 B3
Chorleywood House Dr
RKW/CH/CXG WD3 ... 115 J7
Chorleywood Rd
RKW/CH/CXG WD3 ... 129 H1
Chouler Gdns STVG SG1 ... 21 H7
The Chowns HARP AL5 ... 46 E8
Christchurch Av
KTN/HRWW/WS HA3 ... 143 L6
Christchurch Cl ENC/FH EN2 ... 125 G6
STALW/RED AL3 ... 8 A3
Christchurch Crs RAD WD7 ... 119 L2
Christchurch Gdns
KTN/HRWW/WS HA3 ... 143 L6
Christ Church La BAR EN5 ... 122 C6
Christchurch Ldg EBAR EN4 ... 123 K8
Christchurch Rd HHNE HP2 ... 57 K1
TRING HP23 ... 57 K1
Christie Cl BROX EN10 ... 92 E2
Christie Ct WATW WD18 ... 12 C7
Christie Rd STVGE SG2 ... 34 A4
WAB EN9 ... 126 F1
Christopher Cl WARE SG12 * ... 54 B8
Christopher Pl STALW/RED AL3 ... 8 E6
Christy's Yd BLDK SG7 ... 144 D11
Church Av PIN HA5 ... 142 D4
Churchbury Cl EN EN1 ... 125 J6
Churchbury La EN EN1 ... 125 J7
Churchbury Rd EN EN1 ... 125 J6
Church Cl DUN/HR/TOD LU5 ... 39 G1
DUN/WHIP LU6 ... 171 P5
EDGW HA8 ... 135 G8
HTCHE/RSTV SG4 ... 176 F7
NTHWD HA6 ... 141 K2
POTB/CUF EN6 ... 108 C3
RAD WD7 ... 119 L2
ROY SG8 ... 152 A9
TRDG/WHET N20 ... 137 G6
Church Cn BROX EN10 ... 92 E2
Church Crs STALW/RED AL3 ... 8 A3
TRDG/WHET N20 ... 137 G6
Church Cft DUN/WHIP LU6 ... 37 H3
STALE/WH AL4 ... 86 A4
Church Dr BSF CM23 ... 161 P9
RYLN/HDSTN HA2 ... 142 E8
Church End ARL/CHE SG15 ... 147 Q2
DUN/HR/TOD LU5 ... 25 L4
DUN/WHIP LU6 ... 74 E7
HLWW/ROY CM19 ... 74 E7
ROY SG8 ... 153 J4
STALE/WH AL4 ... 63 L1
STALW/RED AL3 ... 172 F4
STDN SG11 ... 163 R6
STVGE SG2 ... 9 E9
Church Farm EBAR EN4 ... 137 K3
Church Farm La ROY SG8 ... 169 K6
TRING HP23 ... 169 K6
Church Farm Wy GSTN WD25 ... 47 G5
Churchfield HARP AL5 ... 47 G5
HLW CM20 ... 3 M3
ROY SG8 ... 153 J4
Church Fld WAT WD18 ... 53 M2
Churchfield Cl
RYLN/HDSTN HA2 ... 142 E8
Church Field Pth
CHES/WCR EN8 ... 110 A3
Churchfield Rd
CFSP/GDCR SL9 ... 138 B3
DUN/HR/TOD LU5 ... 25 M4
WLYN AL6 ... 51 G4
Church Flds RAD WD7 ... 119 L2
Churchfields BROX EN10 ... 92 E2
HERT/BAY SG13 ... 53 M4
STDN SG11 ... 163 Q11
STSD CM24 ... 166 F7
Churchfields La BROX EN10 ... 92 E2
Churchgate CHES/WCR EN8 ... 109 M3
Church Ga DUN/WHIP LU6 ... 37 J6
Churchgate Rd
CHES/WCR EN8 ... 109 M3
Churchgate St HLWE CM17 ... 76 C1
Church Gn DUN/WHIP LU6 ... 37 M2
HARP AL5 ... 46 E4
Church Green Ms HARP AL5 * ... 46 E4
Church Green Rw HARP AL5 * ... 46 E4
Church Gv AMS HP6 ... 114 C5
Church HI ABLGY WD5 ... 83 K8
DEN/HRF UB9 ... 140 A6
HARP AL5 ... 46 E4
HERT/BAY SG13 ... 71 M1
LBUZ LU7 ... 169 K1
Church Hill Rd EBAR EN4 ... 137 J2
Churchill Av
KTN/HRWW/WS HA3 ... 143 M8
Churchill Cl LTNN/LIM LU3 ... 154 F8
Churchill Rd
AMP/FLIT/BLC MK45 ... 155 H4
DUN/WHIP LU6 ... 39 H2
LTNW/LEA LU4 ... 26 C6
STAL AL1 ... 9 M3
Church La ARL/CHE SG15 ... 147 Q1
BERK HP4 ... 80 A1
BLDK SG7 ... 149 P1
BRKMPK AL9 ... 68 A4
BROX EN10 ... 91 M4
BSF CM23 ... 43 M7
CFSP/GDCR SL9 ... 138 B3
CHES/WCR EN8 ... 110 A3
ENC/FH EN2 ... 125 H1
HLW CM20 ... 37 H3
GSTN WD25 ... 118 F4
GTDUN CM6 ... 185 Q10
HERT/WAT SG14 ... 179 J11
HHS/BOV HP3 ... 98 F1
HTCHE/RSTV SG4 ...

HTCHE/RSTV SG4 ..... 21 G5
HTCHE/RSTV SG4 ..... 31 H3
HTCHE/RSTV SG4 ..... 175 P7
KGLGY WD4 ..... 100 E4
KTN/HRWW/WS HA3 ..... 143 K3
LBUZ LU7 ..... 169 L2
LOU IG10 ..... 127 M5
LWTH SG6 ..... 148 G12
MHAD SG10 ..... 181 R6
PIN HA5 ..... 142 C5
POTB/CUF EN6 ..... 107 K4
RBSF CM22 ..... 167 N5
RBSF CM22 ..... 184 D9
RKW/CH/CXG WD3 ..... 115 L3
RKW/CH/CXG WD3 ..... 129 L4
ROY SG8 ..... 145 M4
ROY SG8 ..... 151 M6
STALE/WH AL4 ..... 86 F4
STVG SG1 ..... 10 B1
TRING HP23 ..... 57 K6
TRING HP23 ..... 169 K8
WARE SG12 ..... 179 P1
Church Langley Wy
HLWE CM17 ..... 76 A5
Church Leys HLWS CM18 ..... 3 J9
Church Md DUN/WHIP LU6 ..... 171 P5
HLWW/ROY CM19 ..... 73 M4
Churchmead WAB EN9 * 93 G4
Churchmead Cl EBAR EN4 ..... 137 J2
Church Meadow HHW HP1 ..... 61 H2
Church Pas BAR EN5 * 122 D7
Church Pth HTCHE/RSTV SG4 ..... 20 D6
NFNCH/WDSPK N12 * 137 G8
Church Pl WLYN AL6 ..... 177 J12
Church Rd
AMP/FLIT/BLC MK45 ..... 155 J3
BERK HP4 ..... 171 J9
DEN/HRF UB9 ..... 140 A5
DUN/WHIP LU6 ..... 37 M3
DUN/WHIP LU6 ..... 171 P5
HERT/BAY SG13 ..... 90 A1
HERT/WAT SG14 ..... 52 F6
HHS/BOV HP3 * 83 G4
HLWE CM17 ..... 76 A8
HTCH/STOT SG5 ..... 148 D7
HTCHE/RSTV SG4 ..... 30 D6
LBUZ LU7 ..... 36 A3
LBUZ LU7 ..... 169 Q7
LOU IG10 ..... 127 L7
LTN LU1 ..... 41 G7
LTNN/LIM LU3 ..... 154 B10
NTHWD HA6 ..... 141 K2
POTB/CUF EN6 ..... 106 F4
RBSF CM22 ..... 44 C7
SHFD SG17 ..... 146 C5
STALW/RED AL3 ..... 173 K7
STAN HA7 ..... 133 M8
STSD CM24 ..... 166 H8
WAT WD17 ..... 117 L5
WGCW AL8 ..... 50 A7
Church St AMSS HP7 ..... 112 F6
BGSW SG18 ..... 144 D4
BLDK SG7 ..... 17 J1
BRKMPK AL9 ..... 68 A7
BRKMPK AL9 ..... 69 J7
BSF CM23 ..... 43 M2
BUNT SG9 ..... 159 J9
CSHM HP5 ..... 96 F5
DUN/HR/TOD LU5 ..... 39 G1
ENC/FH EN2 ..... 125 G7
HERT/WAT SG14 ..... 53 H7
HHNE HP2 ..... 62 B8
HHS/BOV HP3 ..... 98 F1
HTCH/STOT SG5 ..... 146 A9
LTN LU1 ..... 7 G5
RKW/CH/CXG WD3 ..... 130 C4
ROY SG8 ..... 145 P8
SBW CM21 ..... 183 Q7
STALE/WH AL4 ..... 48 B5
STALW/RED AL3 ..... 8 F1
WAB EN9 ..... 111 G7
WARE SG12 ..... 54 B4
WATW WD18 ..... 13 G5
WLYN AL6 ..... 177 J12
Church Vw BROX EN10 ..... 92 D2
RAYLNE/WEN HP22 ..... 56 A4
STALE/WH AL4 * 48 B5
TRING HP23 ..... 168 E5
Church View Av
HTCH/STOT SG5 ..... 146 A8
Church Wk BUSH WD23 ..... 132 E2
DUN/HR/TOD LU5 ..... 38 F1
SBW CM21 ..... 183 R7
Church Wy TRDG/WHET N20 ..... 137 J6
Church Yd TRING HP23 ..... 57 L1
The Chyne CFSP/GDCR SL9 ..... 138 D7
Cicero Dr LTNN/LIM LU3 ..... 27 L1
Cillocks Cl HOD EN11 ..... 72 E6
The Circuits PIN HA5 ..... 142 A6
Cissbury Ring North
NFNCH/WDSPK N12 ..... 136 D8
Cissbury Ring South
NFNCH/WDSPK N12 ..... 136 D8
City Pk WGCE AL7 * 50 E6
Claggy Rd HTCHE/RSTV SG4 ..... 175 M7
Claire Ct NFNCH/WDSPK N12 ..... 137 G6
Claire Gdns STAN HA7 ..... 134 A8
Clamp Hl STAN HA7 ..... 133 H7
Clapgate Rd BUSH WD23 ..... 132 F2
Clare Cl BORE WD6 ..... 134 D2
Clare Ct NTHWD HA6 ..... 131 J8
Clare Crs BLDK SG7 ..... 17 J3
Claremont CHESW EN7 ..... 109 K3
LCOL/BKTW AL2 ..... 102 E5
Claremont Crs
RKW/CH/CXG WD3 ..... 131 G1
Claremont House
WATW WD18 * 131 H2
Claremont Rd EBAR EN4 ..... 123 G4
KTN/HRWW/WS HA3 ..... 143 J4
LTNW/LEA LU4 ..... 27 M8
Clarence Cl BUSH WD23 ..... 133 K3
EBAR EN4 ..... 137 H1
Clarence Ct MLHL NW7 ..... 135 J8
Clarence Rd BERK HP4 ..... 79 K1
HARP AL5 ..... 46 E3
STAL AL1 ..... 9 K5
STSD CM24 ..... 166 G6
Clarenden Flds
RKW/CH/CXG WD3 ..... 116 D4
Clarendon Ms BORE WD6 * 120 E7
Clarendon Rd BORE WD6 ..... 120 E7
CHES/WCR EN8 ..... 110 B3
HARP AL5 ..... 46 F2
HRW HA1 ..... 143 J8
LTNE LU2 ..... 6 E2
WAT WD17 ..... 12 F3
Clare Pk AMSS HP7 ..... 113 J6
Clarion Cl HTCH/STOT SG5 ..... 156 E11
Clarke Gn GSTN WD25 ..... 117 L1
Clarkes Pightle
AMP/FLIT/BLC MK45 * 155 J3
Clarke's Rd HAT AL10 ..... 67 M6
Clarke's Spring TRING HP23 ..... 169 R12
Clarkes Wy DUN/HR/TOD LU5 ..... 26 A5
Clarke Wy GSTN WD25 ..... 117 L1
Clarkfield RKW/CH/CXG WD3 ..... 129 L4
Clarkhill HLWS CM18 ..... 75 J8
Clarks Cl WARE SG12 ..... 54 B2
Clark Rd ROY SG8 ..... 14 E6
Clarks Md BUSH WD23 ..... 133 G3
Clatterbury La SAFWS CB11 ..... 161 R4
Claudian Pl STALW/RED AL3 ..... 84 E3
Claudius Cl STAN HA7 ..... 134 B6
Claverhambury Rd WAB EN9 ..... 111 K3
Claverley Gn LTNE LU2 ..... 29 J7
Claverton Cl HHS/BOV HP3 ..... 98 E2
Clay Acre CSHM HP5 ..... 97 H4
Claybury BUSH WD23 ..... 132 F3
Claybush Rd BLDK SG7 ..... 149 P2
Claycroft WGCE AL7 ..... 50 F6
Claydon Cl LTNN/LIM LU3 ..... 28 A2
Claydon End CFSP/GDCR SL9 ..... 138 C5
Claydon La CFSP/GDCR SL9 ..... 138 C5
Claydown Wy LTN LU1 ..... 40 F8
Clay End Rd STVGE SG2 ..... 35 K3
Clayfield Rd
RAYLNE/WEN HP22 ..... 56 A5
Claygate Av HARP AL5 ..... 46 C3
Clay Hall Rd DUN/WHIP LU6 ..... 172 B2
Clay Hl ENC/FH EN2 ..... 125 G3
Clay La BUSH WD23 ..... 133 J3
RAYLNE/WEN HP22 ..... 56 A8
Claymore HHNE HP2 ..... 62 C6
Claymore Dr HTCH/STOT SG5 ..... 147 P12
Claymores STVG SG1 ..... 10 E3
Claypit Hl RBSF CM22 ..... 167 N8
Clayponds BSF CM23 ..... 44 A2
Clayton Dr HHS/BOV HP3 ..... 83 H4
Clayton Pde CHES/WCR EN8 * 110 B4
Clayton Wk AMSS HP7 ..... 114 A5
Cleall Av WAB EN9 ..... 111 G8
The Cleave HARP AL5 ..... 47 H4
Clementine Wy HHW HP1 ..... 4 B6
Clement Rd CHES/WCR EN8 ..... 110 C1
Clements Cl
NFNCH/WDSPK N12 ..... 136 F7
Clements End Rd
DUN/WHIP LU6 ..... 172 A7
Clements Rd
RKW/CH/CXG WD3 ..... 129 H1
Clements St WARE SG12 ..... 54 C4
Cleopatra Cl STAN HA7 ..... 134 B6
Clevedon Rd LTNE LU2 ..... 28 F7
Cleveland Crs BORE WD6 ..... 135 G1
Cleveland Rd HHNE HP2 ..... 62 F8
STALW/RED AL3 ..... 172 G4
Cleveland Wy HHNE HP2 ..... 62 F8
STVG SG1 ..... 22 A6
Cleves Rd HHNE HP2 ..... 62 F5
Cleviscroft STVG SG1 ..... 10 F6
Clewer Crs
KTN/HRWW/WS HA3 ..... 143 H3
Clifford Crs LTNW/LEA LU4 ..... 27 G4
Clifford Rd BAR EN5 ..... 122 F7
Clifton Av
KTN/HRWW/WS HA3 ..... 143 M4
Clifton Cl CHES/WCR EN8 ..... 110 C3
Clifton Gdns ENC/FH EN2 ..... 124 C8
Clifton Hatch HLWS CM18 ..... 75 L8
Clifton Lawns AMS HP6 ..... 113 G1
Clifton Rd AMS HP6 ..... 112 F1
DUN/WHIP LU6 ..... 25 L8
LTN LU1 ..... 6 A4
WATW WD18 ..... 12 F7
Clifton St STAL AL1 ..... 9 G4
Clifton Wy BORE WD6 ..... 120 E5
WARE SG12 ..... 54 B2
The Climb RKW/CH/CXG WD3 ..... 129 M2
Clinton Av LTNE LU2 ..... 28 D5
Clinton End HHNE HP2 ..... 83 G2
Clipped Hedge RBSF CM22 ..... 184 G6
Clitheroe Gdns OXHEY WD19 ..... 132 B6
Clive Cl POTB/CUF EN6 ..... 106 D5
Cliveden Cl
NFNCH/WDSPK N12 ..... 137 G7
Clive Rd EN EN1 ..... 125 L8
Clive Wy EN EN1 ..... 125 L8
WATN WD24 ..... 118 A5
Clockhouse Ms
RKW/CH/CXG WD3 * 115 J7
Cloister Gdns EDGW HA8 ..... 135 G8
Cloister Garth BERK HP4 ..... 80 A1
STAL AL1 ..... 85 J6
Cloister Lawns LWTH SG6 ..... 16 D5
Cloisters HARP AL5 * 47 G7
Cloisters Rd LTNW/LEA LU4 ..... 26 F6
LWTH SG6 ..... 16 D5
The Cloisters
DUN/HR/TOD LU5 * 39 G1
HHS/BOV HP3 * 5 M8
HTCH/STOT SG5 * 157 Q5
LTN LU1 ..... 173 L1
RKW/CH/CXG WD3 ..... 130 C3
WGCW AL8 ..... 50 B7
Cloister Wk HHNE HP2 * 62 B8
Clonard Wy PIN HA5 ..... 142 E1
Closemead Cl NTHWD HA6 ..... 141 G1
The Close BLDK SG7 ..... 17 J2
BLDK SG7 ..... 144 D11
BRKMPK AL9 * 68 B7
BRKMPK AL9 ..... 88 C8
BUNT SG9 ..... 19 H3
BUSH WD23 * 132 E2
EBAR EN4 ..... 137 K2
HARP AL5 ..... 46 B1
HHS/BOV HP3 * 99 G2
HTCHE/RSTV SG4 ..... 176 F8
LTNN/LIM LU3 ..... 27 L4
POTB/CUF EN6 ..... 106 E6
RAD WD7 ..... 103 K7
RBSF CM22 ..... 184 G6
RKW/CH/CXG WD3 ..... 129 M4
ROY SG8 ..... 15 G6
ROY SG8 * 151 M5
STAL AL1 ..... 85 G5
STALW/RED AL3 ..... 172 G4
STVG SG1 * 21 G8
TRDG/WHET N20 ..... 136 D5
WARE SG12 ..... 54 C4
Clothall Rd BLDK SG7 ..... 17 M3
Clovelly Cl PIN HA5 ..... 141 M5
Clovelly Wy STVG SG1 ..... 32 E2
Clover Av BSF CM23 ..... 43 H3
Clover Cl LTNW/LEA LU4 ..... 26 D6
Clover Fld HLWS CM18 ..... 75 L8
Cloverfield WGCE AL7 ..... 50 D4
The Clover Fld BUSH WD23 ..... 132 D2
Cloverland HAT AL10 ..... 87 K3
Clover Wk HAT AL10 ..... 67 K5
Clover Wy HHW HP1 ..... 81 M1
The Clump RKW/CH/CXG WD3 ..... 129 L1
Cluny Wy ARL/CHE SG15 ..... 147 Q4
Clusterbolts HERT/WAT SG14 ..... 179 J11
Clutterbucks
RKW/CH/CXG WD3 ..... 115 L2
Clydach Rd EN EN1 ..... 125 K8
Clyde Rd HOD EN11 ..... 93 H1
Clydesdale PEND EN3 ..... 126 B8
Clydesdale Cl BORE WD6 ..... 135 H1
Clydesdale Pth BORE WD6 * 135 H1
Clydesdale Rd LTNW/LEA LU4 ..... 26 E6
ROY SG8 ..... 14 F7
Clyde Sq HHNE HP2 ..... 62 D5
Clyde Ter HERT/BAY SG13 ..... 53 L7
Clyfton Cl BROX EN10 ..... 92 D5
Clyston Rd WATW WD18 ..... 131 K2
Coach Dr HTCHE/RSTV SG4 ..... 157 P8
Coachhouse Ms
HERT/WAT SG14 * 53 G6
The Coach House
AMP/FLIT/BLC MK45 ..... 155 J2
Coachman's La BLDK SG7 ..... 17 H1
Coach Ms STAL AL1 ..... 85 M2
Coalport Cl HLWE CM17 ..... 76 A6
Coates Dell GSTN WD25 ..... 102 C7
Coates Rd BORE WD6 ..... 134 B3
Coates Wy GSTN WD25 ..... 102 B6
Cobb Cl BORE WD6 ..... 135 G1
Cobbett Cl PEND EN3 ..... 126 A2
Cobbetts Ride TRING HP23 ..... 57 K2
Cobb Gn GSTN WD25 ..... 101 M6
Cobbinsbank WAB EN9 * 111 H7
The Cobbins WAB EN9 ..... 111 J6
Cobbins Wy HLWE CM17 ..... 76 C1
Cobb Rd BERK HP4 ..... 79 K1
Cobden Hl RAD WD7 ..... 119 M2
Cobden St LTNE LU2 ..... 7 G2
Cobham Cl EN EN1 ..... 125 L7
Cobham Rd WARE SG12 ..... 54 D3
Cob Lane Cl WLYN AL6 ..... 50 D1
Cobmead HAT AL10 ..... 67 M6
Cockbush Av HERT/BAY SG13 ..... 53 L6
Cockerell Cl STVG SG1 ..... 32 F3
Cocker Rd EN EN1 ..... 125 M2
Cockfosters Pde EBAR EN4 * 123 L8
Cockfosters Rd EBAR EN4 ..... 123 K4
Cock Gn HLWW/ROY CM19 ..... 74 F7
Cock Gv BERK HP4 ..... 78 E2
Cock La BROX EN10 ..... 92 A1
SAFWS CB11 ..... 161 M6
Cockle Wy RAD WD7 ..... 104 C7
Cockrobin La HLW CM20 ..... 182 E10
Codicote Dr GSTN WD25 ..... 102 B8
Codicote Rd HTCHE/RSTV SG4 ..... 175 R3
STALE/WH AL4 ..... 48 B4
WLYN AL6 ..... 49 G2
Codicote Rw HHNE HP2 ..... 62 E5
Codmore Crs CSHM HP5 ..... 97 J4
Codmore Wood Rd CSHM HP5 ..... 98 A7
Coe's Aly BAR EN5 ..... 122 C8
Cohen Cl CHES/WCR EN8 ..... 110 C6
Coke's Farm La CSTG HP8 ..... 113 M7
Coke's La CSTG HP8 ..... 113 M8
Colbron Cl BLDK SG7 ..... 149 N2
Colburn Av PIN HA5 ..... 142 C1
Colchester Dr PIN HA5 ..... 142 B7
Colchester Rd NTHWD HA6 ..... 141 L4
Cold Christmas La WARE SG12 ..... 180 B11
Coldham Gv PEND EN3 ..... 126 C3
Coldharbour La BUSH WD23 ..... 132 F2
HARP AL5 ..... 46 F1
Coldharbour Rd
HLWW/ROY CM19 ..... 74 E5
Coldmoreham Yd AMSS HP7 ..... 112 E5
Colebrook Av LTNN/LIM LU3 ..... 27 G2
Colebrook Wy
FBAR/BDGN N11 ..... 137 M8
Cole Green La WGCE AL7 ..... 68 D1
Cole Green Wy HERT/WAT SG14 ..... 70 E1
Colehills Cl SAFWS CB11 ..... 161 Q5
Coleman Green La
STALE/WH AL4 ..... 66 A2
Colemans Cl HTCH/STOT SG5 ..... 156 F1
Coleman's La WAB EN9 ..... 93 H8
Colemans Rd HTCHE/RSTV SG4 ..... 30 B8
Coleridge Cl CHESW EN7 ..... 109 K1
HTCHE/RSTV SG4 ..... 157 R5
Coleridge Crs HHNE HP2 ..... 62 F4
Coleridge Rd
NFNCH/WDSPK N12 ..... 137 G8
Coleridge Wy BORE WD6 ..... 120 E8
Cole Rd WAT WD17 ..... 117 M5
Colesdale POTB/CUF EN6 ..... 108 C4
Coles Gn BUSH WD23 ..... 133 G4
Coles Hl HHW HP1 ..... 61 L8
Colestrete STVG SG1 ..... 11 H6
Colestrete Cl STVG SG1 ..... 11 H5
Coleswood Rd HARP AL5 ..... 47 G6
Colet Rd RAYLNE/WEN HP22 ..... 56 A8
Colgate Pl PEND EN3 ..... 126 E3
Colgrove WGCW AL8 ..... 50 A8
Colindale Av STAL AL1 ..... 9 J9
Colin Rd LTNE LU2 ..... 28 D7
Collapit Cl HRW HA1 ..... 142 F8
College Av
KTN/HRWW/WS HA3 ..... 143 J3
College Cl BSF CM23 ..... 43 K2
KTN/HRWW/WS HA3 ..... 143 J2
STALW/RED AL3 ..... 173 K8
WARE SG12 ..... 54 B5
College Ct CHES/WCR EN8 ..... 110 A4
College Gdns ENC/FH EN2 ..... 125 H5
College Ga HLW CM20 ..... 2 D6
College Hill Rd
KTN/HRWW/WS HA3 ..... 143 J2
College La HAT AL10 ..... 87 J2
College Pl STALW/RED AL3 ..... 8 D5
College Rd ABLGY WD5 ..... 101 L5
CHES/WCR EN8 ..... 109 M4
ENC/FH EN2 ..... 125 H6
HERT/BAY SG13 ..... 72 A3
HRW HA1 ..... 143 J8
HTCH/STOT SG5 ..... 157 P5
KTN/HRWW/WS HA3 ..... 143 J3
STAL AL1 ..... 85 M3
College Rd North
RAYLNE/WEN HP22 ..... 168 A8
College Sq HLW CM20 ..... 2 D6
College St STALW/RED AL3 ..... 8 E5
College Wy NTHWD HA6 ..... 141 H1
WGCW AL8 ..... 50 B6
Collens Rd HARP AL5 ..... 46 F8
Collenswood Rd STVGE SG2 ..... 11 L6
Collet Cl CHES/WCR EN8 ..... 110 B2
Collett Rd HHW HP1 ..... 4 D3
WARE SG12 ..... 54 B3
Colley Land
RKW/CH/CXG WD3 ..... 115 H8
Collingdon St LTN LU1 ..... 6 D4
Collingtree LTNE LU2 ..... 28 F5
Collingwood Cl LTNW/LEA LU4 ..... 27 H6
Collingwood Dr
LCOL/BKTW AL2 ..... 86 B7
Collins Cross BSF CM23 ..... 166 D12
Collins Meadow
HLWW/ROY CM19 ..... 2 A7
Collins Wd LTN LU1 * 40 C5
Collinwood Av PEND EN3 ..... 126 A7
Collison Cl HTCHE/RSTV SG4 ..... 16 A7
Collyer Rd LCOL/BKTW AL2 ..... 104 B1
Colman Pde EN EN1 * 125 J7
Colmer Pl
KTN/HRWW/WS HA3 ..... 143 H2
Colmore Rd PEND EN3 ..... 126 A8
Colnbrook Cl LCOL/BKTW AL2 ..... 104 C1
Colne Av OXHEY WD19 ..... 131 M2
RKW/CH/CXG WD3 ..... 129 L5
Colne Gdns LCOL/BKTW AL2 ..... 104 C1
Colne Ldg BUSH WD23 * 13 K5
Colne Md RKW/CH/CXG WD3 ..... 129 L5
Colne Valley Trail
RKW/CH/CXG WD3 ..... 130 A4
Colne Wy HHNE HP2 ..... 62 D5
Colne Way Ct WATN WD24 * 118 B3
Colney Heath La
STALE/WH AL4 ..... 86 C3
Colonels Wk ENC/FH EN2 ..... 124 F6
Colonial Wy WATN WD24 ..... 118 A5
The Colonnades HAT AL10 ..... 68 A6
The Colonnade
CHES/WCR EN8 ..... 110 B2
STALW/RED AL3 * 8 E5
Colonsay HHS/BOV HP3 ..... 83 G4
Colston Crs CHESW EN7 ..... 108 F1
Colt Hatch HLW CM20 ..... 2 A4
Colthurst Gdns HOD EN11 ..... 73 H5
Colton Rd HRW HA1 ..... 143 J7
Colts Cnr STVGE SG2 ..... 11 L7
Colts Cft ROY SG8 ..... 153 N3
Coltsfield STSD CM24 ..... 166 G6
Coltsfoot WGCE AL7 ..... 68 F1
Coltsfoot Dr ROY SG8 ..... 14 F7
Coltsfoot Gn LTNW/LEA LU4 ..... 26 E4
Coltsfoot La KNEB SG3 ..... 177 R10
Coltsfoot Rd WARE SG12 ..... 54 C2
The Coltsfoot HHW HP1 ..... 81 J3
The Colts BSF CM23 ..... 43 L6
Columbia Rd BROX EN10 ..... 92 C8
Columbus Cl STVGE SG2 ..... 33 L2
Columbus Gdns NTHWD HA6 ..... 141 L3
Colvin Gdns CHES/WCR EN8 ..... 126 B1
Colwell Ri LTNE LU2 ..... 29 J7
Colwell Rd STVGE SG2 ..... 34 A6
Colwyn Cl STVG SG1 ..... 32 F1
Colyer Cl WLYN AL6 ..... 50 D2
Combe Rd WATW WD18 ..... 131 K2
Combe St HHNE HP2 ..... 4 E3
Comet Cl GSTN WD25 ..... 101 K8
Comet Rd HAT AL10 ..... 67 K8
Comet Wy HAT AL10 ..... 67 J8
Common Fld TRING HP23 ..... 58 B4
Commonfields HLW CM20 ..... 3 H3
Common Gdns BERK HP4 ..... 60 F7
Common Gate Rd
RKW/CH/CXG WD3 ..... 129 H1
Common La BLDK SG7 ..... 144 H11
GSTN WD25 ..... 119 J4
HARP AL5 ..... 174 H12
KGLGY WD4 ..... 100 D2
LTNN/LIM LU3 ..... 154 A9
ROY SG8 ..... 153 R6
Common Ri HTCHE/RSTV SG4 ..... 157 Q4
Common Rd DUN/WHIP LU6 ..... 171 N6
HTCH/STOT SG5 ..... 148 C5
RKW/CH/CXG WD3 ..... 115 H8
STAN HA7 ..... 133 H6
WAB EN9 ..... 94 C3
Commonside Rd HLWS CM18 ..... 95 K1
Commons La HHNE HP2 ..... 5 J1
The Commons WGCE AL7 ..... 68 E2
The Common BERK HP4 ..... 60 D7
HARP AL5 ..... 173 R5
HAT AL10 ..... 67 L7
KGLGY WD4 ..... 99 L6
RAD WD7 ..... 103 M5
RKW/CH/CXG WD3 * 129 J1
STALW/RED AL3 ..... 173 R12
STAN HA7 ..... 133 K5
Common Vw LWTH SG6 ..... 16 E1
Common Whf WARE SG12 ..... 54 C4
Community Wy
RKW/CH/CXG WD3 ..... 130 E1
Compania Gv LTNN/LIM LU3 ..... 27 L1
Compass Cl EDGW HA8 ..... 134 D7
Comp Ga DUN/WHIP LU6 ..... 37 J3
The Comp DUN/WHIP LU6 ..... 37 H3
Compton Av LTNW/LEA LU4 ..... 27 H5
Compton Gdns
LCOL/BKTW AL2 ..... 84 F8
Compton Pl OXHEY WD19 ..... 132 C7
Compton Ri PIN HA5 ..... 142 C7
Compton Rd
RAYLNE/WEN HP22 ..... 56 A8
Comreddy Cl ENC/FH EN2 ..... 124 F5
Comyne Rd WATN WD24 ..... 117 K2
The Comyns BUSH WD23 ..... 133 G4
Concorde Dr HHNE HP2 ..... 5 G2
Concorde St LTNE LU2 ..... 7 H3
Conduit La BUNT SG9 ..... 160 C8
HOD EN11 ..... 72 E7
Conduit La East HOD EN11 ..... 72 F7
Coney Cl HAT AL10 ..... 87 M2
Coneydale WGCW AL8 ..... 50 B5
Coneygate SHFD SG17 ..... 146 D4
Coney Gn SBW CM21 ..... 183 P6
Congreve Rd WAB EN9 ..... 111 J7
Conical Cnr ENC/FH EN2 ..... 125 G6
Conifer Cl CHESW EN7 ..... 109 K3
The Conifers GSTN WD25 ..... 118 A1
HHS/BOV HP3 * 81 K5
Conifer Wk STVGE SG2 ..... 34 A2
Coningesby Dr WAT WD17 ..... 117 J5
Coningsby Bank STAL AL1 ..... 85 G6
Coningsby Cl BRKMPK AL9 ..... 88 A6
Coningsby Ct RAD WD7 * 119 L2
Coningsby Dr POTB/CUF EN6 ..... 107 H7
Coniston Cl HHS/BOV HP3 ..... 83 G3
Coniston Gdns PIN HA5 ..... 141 L6
Coniston Rd KGLGY WD4 ..... 100 D2
LTNN/LIM LU3 ..... 27 K4
Connaught Av EBAR EN4 ..... 137 K4
EN EN1 ..... 125 J6
Connaught Cl EN EN1 ..... 125 J6
HHNE HP2 ..... 62 E8
Connaught Gdns BERK HP4 ..... 59 K6
Connaught Rd BAR EN5 ..... 136 B2
HARP AL5 ..... 46 F3
KTN/HRWW/WS HA3 ..... 143 K3
LTNW/LEA LU4 ..... 27 K6
STALW/RED AL3 ..... 8 D1
Connemara Cl BORE WD6 * 135 G2
Conner's Cl ROY SG8 ..... 145 M5
Connop Rd PEND EN3 ..... 126 B4
Conquerors Hl STALE/WH AL4 ..... 48 C5
Conquest Cl HTCHE/RSTV SG4 ..... 157 P8
Conquest Rd DUN/HR/TOD LU5 ..... 26 C4
Consort Cl FBAR/BDGN N11 ..... 137 K8
Constable Cl
DUN/HR/TOD LU5 ..... 26 B4
Constantine Cl STVG SG1 ..... 21 K8
Constantine Pl BLDK SG7 ..... 149 M12
Convent Cl HTCH/STOT SG5 ..... 157 P5
Conway Cl DUN/HR/TOD LU5 ..... 26 C4
STAN HA7 ..... 143 L1
Conway Gdns ENC/FH EN2 ..... 125 J4
Conway Rd LTNW/LEA LU4 ..... 27 M8
Conybury Cl WAB EN9 ..... 111 L6
Cony Cl CHESW EN7 ..... 109 J1
Conyers HLW CM20 ..... 2 C2
Cookfield Cl DUN/WHIP LU6 ..... 38 C1
Cook Rd STVGE SG2 ..... 33 M2
Cook's Hole Rd ENC/FH EN2 ..... 124 F4
Cooks Md BUSH WD23 ..... 132 F2
Cook's Meadow
DUN/WHIP LU6 ..... 37 J5
Cooks Spinney HLW CM20 ..... 3 L4
Cooks Vennel HHW HP1 ..... 61 L8
Cooks Wy HAT AL10 ..... 87 M2
HTCHE/RSTV SG4 ..... 157 Q4
Coombe Dr DUN/WHIP LU6 ..... 38 C2
Coombe Gdns BERK HP4 ..... 59 K8
Coombe Hill Rd
RKW/CH/CXG WD3 ..... 129 L3
Coombehurst Cl EBAR EN4 ..... 123 K6
Coombelands Rd ROY SG8 ..... 14 F5
Coombe Rd BUSH WD23 ..... 133 G3
ROY SG8 ..... 150 H4
Coombes Rd LCOL/BKTW AL2 ..... 86 A8
Cooper Cl HNLW SG16 ..... 146 G7
Coopers Cl BSF CM23 ..... 43 H5
Cooper's Cl HTCHE/RSTV SG4 ..... 175 M9
Coopers Cl STVGE SG2 ..... 34 B5
Coopers Ct WARE SG12 * 54 C4
Coopers Crs BORE WD6 ..... 121 G5
Coopers End Rd STSD CM24 ..... 167 P11
Coopers End Rbt STSD CM24 ..... 167 R10
Coopers Ga STALE/WH AL4 ..... 86 F4
Coopers Green La
STALE/WH AL4 ..... 66 D7
Cooper's Hl HTCHE/RSTV SG4 ..... 175 M8
Coopers La POTB/CUF EN6 ..... 107 J5
Coopers Lane Rd
POTB/CUF EN6 ..... 107 L7
Coopers Meadow
STALW/RED AL3 ..... 173 Q11
Coopers Rd POTB/CUF EN6 ..... 107 G4
Coopers Vls RBSF CM22 ..... 167 R11
Coopers Wy DUN/HR/TOD LU5 ..... 25 L5
Cooper Wy BERK HP4 ..... 80 B1
Cooters End La HARP AL5 ..... 46 D1
Copenhagen Cl LTNN/LIM LU3 ..... 27 H1
Copley Rd STAN HA7 ..... 134 A8
Copmans Wick
RKW/CH/CXG WD3 ..... 129 H1
The Coppens HTCH/STOT SG5 ..... 148 E8
Copper Beech Cl HHS/BOV HP3 ..... 81 K5
Copper Beeches HARP AL5 ..... 46 F4
WLYN AL6 ..... 177 K10
Copperfield Cl
HTCH/STOT SG5 ..... 148 A11
Copperfields LTNW/LEA LU4 ..... 26 F5
ROY SG8 ..... 14 D7
WGCE AL7 ..... 51 G8
Copperfields Cl
DUN/HR/TOD LU5 ..... 26 B5
The Copperfields ROY SG8 * 14 D7
Copperfield Wy PIN HA5 ..... 142 D6
Copperkins Gv AMS HP6 ..... 112 F2
Copperkins La AMS HP6 ..... 112 E1
Coppermill La
RKW/CH/CXG WD3 ..... 139 K2
Coppermill Lock
DEN/HRF UB9 * 139 L2
Copper Rdg CFSP/GDCR SL9 ..... 128 D8
Copperwood HERT/BAY SG13 ..... 53 K7
Coppice Cl HAT AL10 ..... 87 K4
RSLP HA4 * 141 G8
STAN HA7 ..... 143 K1
Coppice Hatch HLWS CM18 ..... 75 H7
Coppice Md HTCH/STOT SG5 ..... 148 C8
The Coppice BAR EN5 * 136 F2
BSF CM23 ..... 43 K4
ENC/FH EN2 ..... 124 F8
HHNE HP2 ..... 82 F1
OXHEY WD19 ..... 132 A2
TRING HP23 ..... 58 B4
Coppice Wk TRDG/WHET N20 ..... 136 E6
Coppies Gv FBAR/BDGN N11 ..... 137 M7
The Coppings HOD EN11 ..... 72 E4
Coppins Cl BERK HP4 ..... 79 J1
The Coppins
KTN/HRWW/WS HA3 ..... 143 J1
STALW/RED AL3 ..... 172 F4
Copse Cl NTHWD HA6 ..... 141 G3
Copse Hl HLWW/ROY CM19 ..... 74 F8
WLYN AL6 ..... 177 N9
Copse Hill Cl HHS/BOV HP3 ..... 99 H2
The Copse AMSS HP7 ..... 113 G4
BLDK SG7 * 17 K2
BSF CM23 ..... 44 C1
HERT/BAY SG13 ..... 53 L7
HHW HP1 ..... 61 J8
Copse Wy CSHM HP5 ..... 96 E1
LTNN/LIM LU3 ..... 27 H1
Copsewood Rd WATN WD24 ..... 117 M5
Copse Wood Wy NTHWD HA6 ..... 141 G3
Copshall Cl HLWS CM18 ..... 95 J1
Copthall Cl CFSP/GDCR SL9 ..... 138 D2
Copthall Cnr CFSP/GDCR SL9 ..... 138 C2
Copthall La CFSP/GDCR SL9 ..... 138 C2
Copthorne LTNE LU2 ..... 29 H6
Copthorne Av BROX EN10 ..... 92 D2
Copthorne Cl
RKW/CH/CXG WD3 ..... 130 D1
Copthorne Rd
RKW/CH/CXG WD3 ..... 130 D2
Copwood Cl
NFNCH/WDSPK N12 ..... 137 H7
Coral Cl DUN/WHIP LU6 * 37 J3
Coral Gdns HHNE HP2 ..... 5 K1
Corals Md WGCE AL7 ..... 50 B8
Coram Cl BERK HP4 ..... 80 A2
Corbar Cl EBAR EN4 ..... 123 H4
Corbridge Dr LTNE LU2 ..... 29 J7
Corby Cl LCOL/BKTW AL2 ..... 84 E7
Corby Crs ENC/FH EN2 ..... 124 C8
Cordell Cl CHES/WCR EN8 ..... 110 C2
Corder Cl STALW/RED AL3 ..... 84 E5
Coreys Mill La STVG SG1 ..... 20 F8
Corfe Cl BORE WD6 ..... 121 H7
HHNE HP2 ..... 5 J6
Corinium Gdns LTNN/LIM LU3 ..... 27 L1
Corinium Ga STALW/RED AL3 ..... 84 E3
Corncastle Rd LTN LU1 ..... 6 C8
Corncrake Cl LTNE LU2 ..... 29 G4
Corncroft HAT AL10 ..... 67 M6
Cornel Cl LTN LU1 ..... 40 E2
Cornerfield HAT AL10 ..... 67 M5
Corner Hall HHNE HP2 ..... 4 F7
Corner Hall Av HHNE HP2 ..... 4 F6
Corner Meadow HLWS CM18 ..... 95 L1
Corners WGCE AL7 ..... 50 E6
Corner Wd STALW/RED AL3 ..... 172 F4
Cornfield Crs BERK HP4 ..... 59 H6

Cornfield Rd BUSH WD23 118 F8
Cornfields STVGE SG2 34 A2
The Cornfields HHW HP1 4 C4
Cornflower Wy HAT AL10 67 J5
Cornhill Dr PEND EN3 126 C3
Corn Md WGCW AL8 50 A4
Cornmill WAB EN9 110 F7
Cornwall Cl CHES/WCR EN8 110 C7
Cornwall Rd HARP AL5 46 F3
PIN HA5 142 D2
STAL AL1 9 H9
Coronation Av ROY SG8 14 D8
Coronation Rd BSF CM23 43 L4
WARE SG12 54 B3
Coronation Rw ROY SG8 * 152 A8
Corringham Ct STAL AL1 9 J4
Corton Cl STVG SG1 32 F1
Corvus Cl ROY SG8 14 F5
Cory-wright Wy STALE/WH AL4 48 C4
Cosgrove Wy LTN LU1 27 H8
Cosne Ms HARP AL5 47 G6
Cotefield LTNW/LEA LU4 27 G6
Coteford Cl PIN HA5 141 L7
Cotesmore Rd HHW HP1 81 J3
Cotlandswick LCOL/BKTW AL2 86 A7
Cotney Cft STVGE SG2 34 B6
Cotsmoor STAL AL1 * 9 K6
Cotswold HHNE HP2 62 C7
Cotswold Av BUSH WD23 133 G2
Cotswold Business Pk LTN LU1 40 B7
Cotswold Cl STALE/WH AL4 66 A5
Cotswold Gdns LTNN/LIM LU3 27 G2
Cotswold Gn ENC/FH EN2 124 D8
Cotswolds HAT AL10 87 L2
Cotswold Wy ENC/FH EN2 124 D7
Cottage Cl RKW/CH/CXG WD3 130 D2
Cottage Gdns CHES/WCR EN8 110 B3
Cottered Rd BUNT SG9 158 D8
Cotterells HHW HP1 4 E4
Cotterells Hl HHW HP1 4 D3
Cotton Dr HERT/BAY SG13 53 M6
Cotton Fld HAT AL10 67 M6
Cottonham Cl
NFNCH/WDSPK N12 137 H8
Cottonmill Crs STAL AL1 8 F8
Cottonmill La STAL AL1 8 F9
Cotton Rd POTB/CUF EN6 107 G5
Coulser Cl HHW HP1 61 L7
Coulter Cl POTB/CUF EN6 108 B1
Counters Cl HHW HP1 81 L2
Countess Cl DEN/HRF UB9 140 A4
County Ga BAR EN5 136 F2
Coursers Rd LCOL/BKTW AL2 104 E1
STALE/WH AL4 87 G7
Courtaulds KGLGY WD4 99 M4
Court Dr DUN/HR/TOD LU5 25 M8
STAN HA7 134 C7
Courtenay Av
KTN/HRWW/WS HA3 142 F2
Courtfield Av HRW HA1 * 143 K7
Courtfield Cl BROX EN10 * 92 E2
Courtfield Crs HRW HA1 143 K7
Courtfields HARP AL5 47 H4
Courtland Av MLHL NW7 135 H6
Courtlands Cl WATN WD24 117 J1
Courtlands Dr WAT WD17 117 J2
Courtleigh Av EBAR EN4 123 H4
Court Ldg RAD WD7 * 104 E8
Courtside STALW/RED AL3 * 8 D2
The Courtway OXHEY WD19 132 C5
Courtyard Cl AMS HP6 113 G4
The Courtyards
WATW WD18 * 131 H3
The Courtyard HHS/BOV HP3 82 B8
STALE/WH AL4 86 D2
Covent Garden Cl
LTNW/LEA LU4 27 K6
Coventry Cl STVG SG1 21 M8
Coverdale HHNE HP2 62 C7
LTNW/LEA LU4 26 F3
Covert Cl BERK HP4 59 H7
Covert Rd BERK HP4 59 H6
The Covert NTHWD HA6 141 G2
Covey Wy EBAR EN4 123 G6
Cowards La HTCHE/RSTV SG4 176 F9
Cowbridge HERT/WAT SG14 53 G7
Cowdray Cl LTNE LU2 29 G6
Cowdrey Cl EN EN1 125 J6
Cowland Av PEND EN3 126 A8
Cow La BUSH WD23 * 132 E2
DUN/WHIP LU6 37 J5
GSTN WD25 118 A2
TRING HP23 58 B1
Cowles CHESW EN7 109 K1
Cowley Hl BORE WD6 120 E3
Cowlins HLWE CM17 76 B1
Cowper Ct STALW/RED AL3 172 F4
WATN WD24 117 L3
Cowper Crs HERT/WAT SG14 52 F4
Cowper Gdns STHGT/OAK N14 137 M2
Cowper Ri STALW/RED AL3 172 F4
Cowper Rd BERK HP4 79 M1
CSHM HP5 96 F3
HARP AL5 46 F4
HHW HP1 4 B4
STALW/RED AL3 172 F4
STHGT/OAK N14 137 M4
WGCE AL7 68 D1
Cowper St LTN LU1 6 F9
Cowpers Wy WLYN AL6 177 R12
Cowridge Crs LTNE LU2 7 L3
Cowslip Hl LWTH SG6 16 C2
Cox Cl RAD WD7 104 C6
Coxe Pl KTN/HRWW/WS HA3 143 L6
Coxfield Cl HHNE HP2 5 H4
Cox Ley RBSF CM22 184 G6
Coxs Gdns BSF CM23 43 L4
Cox's Wy ARL/CHE SG15 147 Q4
Coyney Gn LTNN/LIM LU3 6 B2
Cozens La East BROX EN10 92 D4
Cozens La West BROX EN10 92 C4
Cozens Rd WARE SG12 54 D3
Crabbe Crs CSHM HP5 97 H3
Crabbs Cl HTCH/STOT SG5 * 157 N6
Crabbs Gn RBSF CM22 185 P4
Crabb's La BUNT SG9 161 L10
Crab La GSTN WD25 102 F8
Crabtree Cl BUSH WD23 132 F1
HHS/BOV HP3 4 F7
Crabtree Dell LWTH SG6 17 G6
Crabtree La HARP AL5 46 F5
HHS/BOV HP3 5 G7
Crab Tree La HTCH/STOT SG5 156 F1
Crab Tree Rd KNEB SG3 177 M6
Crabtree Wk BROX EN10 92 C1
Crabtree Wy DUN/WHIP LU6 25 M8
Crackle Hill Rd SHFD SG17 146 D3
Crackley Meadow HHNE HP2 62 F5
Cracknell Cl EN EN1 125 M3
Craddock Rd EN EN1 125 K7
Cradock Rd LTNW/LEA LU4 26 F8
Crafton Gn STSD CM24 166 G6
Craft Wy ROY SG8 145 P7
Cragg Av RAD WD7 119 K2
Cragside STVGE SG2 177 Q2
Craigavon Rd HHNE HP2 62 D6
Craiglands STALE/WH AL4 66 B6
Craig Mt RAD WD7 119 M1
Craigs Wk CHES/WCR EN8 110 B2
Craigweil Av RAD WD7 119 M1
Craigweil Cl STAN HA7 134 B8
Craigweil Dr STAN HA7 134 B8
Crakers Md WATW WD18 * 12 E4
Cranborne Av
HTCH/STOT SG5 157 M7
Cranborne Cl HERT/BAY SG13 71 G2
POTB/CUF EN6 106 C5
Cranborne Crs POTB/CUF EN6 106 C5
Cranborne Gdns WGCE AL7 50 D8
Cranborne Pde
POTB/CUF EN6 * 106 B5
Cranborne Rd CHES/WCR EN8 110 B6
HAT AL10 67 M7
HOD EN11 72 F6
POTB/CUF EN6 106 C5
Cranbourne Av
POTB/CUF EN6 106 C4
Cranbourne Dr HARP AL5 47 G7
HOD EN11 72 F3
PIN HA5 142 B7
Cranbourne Rd NTHWD HA6 141 K5
Cranbrook Cl WARE SG12 54 B2
Cranbrook Dr LTNN/LIM LU3 27 H1
STALE/WH AL4 86 C2
Cranbrook La
FBAR/BDGN N11 137 M7
Cranbrook Rd EBAR EN4 137 H2
Cranefield Dr GSTN WD25 102 C6
Crane Md WARE SG12 54 C5
Cranes Wy BORE WD6 135 G1
Cranfield Crs POTB/CUF EN6 108 C3
Cranleigh Cl CHESW EN7 109 L2
Cranleigh Gdns LTNN/LIM LU3 28 A6
Cranmer Cl POTB/CUF EN6 107 G4
Cranmer Rd EDGW HA8 134 F6
Cranmore Cl RBSF CM22 167 L3
Cranwell Gdns BSF CM23 166 E12
Cravells Rd HARP AL5 47 G7
Crawford Rd HAT AL10 67 L6
Crawley Cl LTN LU1 40 G6
Crawley Dr HHNE HP2 62 D6
Crawley Green Rd LTNE LU2 7 K5
Crawley Rd LTN LU1 6 D3
Crawley's La TRING HP23 58 C6
Creamery Ct LWTH SG6 17 G6
Creasey Park Dr
DUN/WHIP LU6 25 K7
Creasy Cl ABLGY WD5 101 K5
Crecy Gdns STALW/RED AL3 173 Q11
Creighton Av STAL AL1 85 H6
Crescent East EBAR EN4 123 G4
Crescent Ri EBAR EN4 137 J1
LTNE LU2 7 H4
Crescent Rd BSF CM23 44 A3
EBAR EN4 123 H8
ENC/FH EN2 124 F8
FBAR/BDGN N11 137 K7
HHNE HP2 5 G2
LTNE LU2 7 H4
The Crescent ABLGY WD5 101 K4
BAR EN5 122 F7
BUNT SG9 158 A10
FBAR/BDGN N11 137 K7
GSTN WD25 118 F4
HLWE CM17 183 N11
HNLW SG16 147 K5
HTCH/STOT SG5 157 M4
HTCHE/RSTV SG4 157 Q10
LBUZ LU7 169 N5
LCOL/BKTW AL2 102 E4
LTN LU1 40 C5
LWTH SG6 16 E4
RKW/CH/CXG WD3 130 F2
TRING HP23 169 L8
WATW WD18 13 G6
WLYN AL6 50 A1
Crescent West EBAR EN4 123 G4
Cress End RKW/CH/CXG WD3 129 L4
Cresset Cl WARE SG12 73 G2
Cresswell Rd CSHM HP5 97 H8
Creswick HTCHE/RSTV SG4 175 Q2
Cresta Cl DUN/HR/TOD LU5 26 E7
Crest Dr PEND EN3 126 A4
Crest Pk HHNE HP2 83 G1
The Crest CHESW EN7 108 F1
DUN/HR/TOD LU5 26 C8
LTNN/LIM LU3 27 M2
POTB/CUF EN6 * 107 G5
SBW CM21 183 P7
WARE SG12 54 B1
WLYN AL6 177 K9
Crest Vw PIN HA5 142 B6
Creswick Ct WGCE AL7 * 50 B8
Crew Curve BERK HP4 59 K6
Crews Hl ENC/FH EN2 108 D8
Crib St WARE SG12 54 B3
Cricketers Arms Rd
ENC/FH EN2 * 125 G6
Cricketers Cl STALW/RED AL3 9 G3
Cricketer's Rd ARL/CHE SG15 147 Q4
Cricketfield La BSF CM23 43 K1
Crispin Fld LBUZ LU7 169 N5
Crispin Ter HTCH/STOT SG5 * 157 M6
Criss Gv CFSP/GDCR SL9 138 A4
Criss La CFSP/GDCR SL9 138 A4
Croasdaile Rd STSD CM24 166 G5
Croasdale Cl STSD CM24 166 G5
Crocus Fld BAR EN5 136 D2
Croft Cl KGLGY WD4 99 L4
MLHL NW7 135 J6
Croft Ct BORE WD6 121 H7
HARP AL5 * 46 F4
Croft End Rd KGLGY WD4 99 L4
Crofters SBW CM21 183 Q6
Crofters End SBW CM21 183 Q5
Crofters Rd NTHWD HA6 131 J7
Croft Fld HAT AL10 67 L8
KGLGY WD4 99 L4
Croft Gn DUN/WHIP LU6 38 D1
Croft La KGLGY WD4 99 L4
LWTH SG6 148 E12
Croft Meadow KGLGY WD4 99 L4
Croft Mdw LBUZ LU7 169 L2
Croft Ms NFNCH/WDSPK N12 137 G6
Crofton Wy BAR EN5 * 136 F2
ENC/FH EN2 124 E6
Croft Rd CFSP/GDCR SL9 138 C4
LTNE LU2 28 F6
PEND EN3 126 C6
WARE SG12 54 A3
Crofts Pth HHS/BOV HP3 82 F4
Crofts Rd HRW HA1 143 L8
The Crofts HHS/BOV HP3 82 F3
HTCH/STOT SG5 148 D10
The Croft BAR EN5 122 C8
BROX EN10 92 C5
LCOL/BKTW AL2 84 E7
LTNN/LIM LU3 27 H1
RBSF CM22 167 L4
WARE SG12 55 J1
WGCE AL7 68 D2
Croftwell HARP AL5 47 K5
Cromarty Rd EDGW HA8 134 F5
Cromdale Wk STVG SG1 21 M5
Cromer Cl BERK HP4 60 C1
Cromer Rd BAR EN5 123 G8
WATN WD24 118 A4
Cromer Wy LTNE LU2 28 B2
Crompton Pl PEND EN3 126 E4
Crompton Rd STVG SG1 32 E3
Cromwell Av CHESW EN7 109 M4
Cromwell Cl BSF CM23 43 H2
CSTG HP8 128 A6
STALE/WH AL4 66 B5
Cromwell Gn LWTH SG6 16 F1
Cromwell Hl LTNN/LIM LU3 6 E2
Cromwell Rd
AMP/FLIT/BLC MK45 155 J1
BORE WD6 120 C5
CHESW EN7 109 M2
HERT/BAY SG13 53 K6
LTNN/LIM LU3 6 D2
LWTH SG6 16 F1
STVGE SG2 34 A4
WARE SG12 54 D4
Cromwell Wy HTCH/STOT SG5 156 F1
Crooked Mile WAB EN9 111 G7
Crooked Wy WAB EN9 93 J4
Crookhams WGCE AL7 50 E5
Crop Common HAT AL10 67 M6
Crosby Cl DUN/WHIP LU6 39 G3
LTNW/LEA LU4 27 L7
STALE/WH AL4 86 A5
Crossbrook HAT AL10 87 J1
Crossbrook St CHES/WCR EN8 110 B5
Crossett Gn HHS/BOV HP3 83 G4
Crossfell Rd HHS/BOV HP3 82 F4
Crossfield Rd HOD EN11 72 F5
Crossfields STALW/RED AL3 84 F5
Crossfields Cl BERK HP4 79 K1
Crossgate EDGW HA8 134 E6
Crossgates STVG SG1 10 F4
Cross Gn BUNT SG9 * 158 A10
Crosslands LTN LU1 40 C6
Cross La HARP AL5 47 G8
HERT/WAT SG14 52 F7
Cross Lanes CFSP/GDCR SL9 128 D8
Cross Lanes Cl
CFSP/GDCR SL9 128 D8
Crossleys CSTG HP8 128 A7
LWTH SG6 148 D11
Crossleys Hl CSTG HP8 128 A6
Crossmead OXHEY WD19 131 M2
Cross Meadow CSHM HP5 96 D3
Cross Oak Rd BERK HP4 79 L2
Crossoaks La BORE WD6 105 H8
Crosspaths HARP AL5 46 A1
The Crosspath RAD WD7 119 L1
Cross Rd CHES/WCR EN8 110 C7
EN EN1 125 J8
FBAR/BDGN N11 137 M8
HERT/WAT SG14 53 G6
HRW HA1 143 H6
OXHEY WD19 13 M9
Cross Roads LOU IG10 127 M6
Cross St LTNE LU2 7 G3
LWTH SG6 16 D2
STALW/RED AL3 8 E5
WARE SG12 54 C4
WAT WD17 13 G3
Cross St North
DUN/WHIP LU6 * 25 L8
Crossway CSHM HP5 97 J4
Cross Wy HARP AL5 47 G2
Crossway HLWE CM17 76 B4
PIN HA5 141 M4
WGCW AL8 49 M3
Crossways BERK HP4 79 K2
DUN/HR/TOD LU5 26 A4
HHS/BOV HP3 82 F2
ROY SG8 152 H4
The Cross Wy
KTN/HRWW/WS HA3 143 J4
LTN LU1 6 B9
Crouchfield HERT/WAT SG14 53 G4
HHW HP1 4 B5
Crouchfield La WARE SG12 53 J1
Crouch Hall Gdns
STALW/RED AL3 173 Q11
Crouch Hall La
STALW/RED AL3 173 Q11
Crouch La CHESW EN7 109 G1
Crowborough Pth
OXHEY WD19 132 B7
Crow Furlong HTCH/STOT SG5 157 M7
Crowland Rd LTNE LU2 29 G4
Crow La ROY SG8 152 B8
Crown Cl MLHL NW7 135 K5
RBSF CM22 184 C9
Crownfield BROX EN10 92 E3
Crown Ga HLW CM20 2 E6
Crown Ri GSTN WD25 102 A8
Crown Rd BORE WD6 120 E5
EN EN1 125 L7
Crown Rose Ct TRING HP23 57 L2
Crown St STALW/RED AL3 173 R12
Crown Ter BSF CM23 44 A2
Crown Wk HHS/BOV HP3 82 C6
Croxdale Rd BORE WD6 120 D6
Croxley Vw WATW WD18 131 J2
Croxton Cl LTNN/LIM LU3 27 L2
Crozier Av BSF CM23 43 J1
Crusader Wy WATW WD18 12 B9
Crystal Wy HRW HA1 143 K7
Cuba Dr PEND EN3 126 A6
Cubbington Cl LTNN/LIM LU3 27 L2
Cubitt Cl HTCHE/RSTV SG4 20 A2
Cubitts Cl WLYN AL6 50 D2
Cublands HERT/BAY SG13 53 M7
Cuckmans Dr LCOL/BKTW AL2 84 E7
Cuckoo Hl PIN HA5 142 A5
Cuckoo Hill Dr PIN HA5 142 A5
Cuckoo Hill Rd PIN HA5 142 B6
Cucumber La BRKMPK AL9 89 K3
Cuffley Av GSTN WD25 102 B8
Cuffley Cl LTNN/LIM LU3 27 K6
Cuffley Ct HHNE HP2 63 G5
Cuffley Hl CHESW EN7 108 E3
Culgaith Gdns ENC/FH EN2 124 C8
Cullera Cl NTHWD HA6 141 K1
Cullings Ct WAB EN9 111 K7
Cullington Cl
KTN/HRWW/WS HA3 143 L6
Culloden Rd ENC/FH EN2 124 F6
Culrose Ct STVGE SG2 177 M1
Culverden Rd OXHEY WD19 131 M6
Culverhouse Rd LTNN/LIM LU3 28 A5
Culverlands Cl STAN HA7 133 M7
Culver Rd STAL AL1 9 H3
Culworth Cl LTN LU1 40 C6
Cumberland Cl AMSS HP7 113 M5
HERT/WAT SG14 52 F4
HHS/BOV HP3 83 J6
Cumberland Dr
STALW/RED AL3 173 R12
Cumberland Rd HRW HA1 142 F7
Cumberland St
DUN/HR/TOD LU5 25 M5
LTN LU1 7 G7
Cumberlow Pl HHNE HP2 83 G3
Cumbria Cl DUN/HR/TOD LU5 26 C4
Cundalls Rd WARE SG12 54 C3
Cunningham Av HAT AL10 67 H7
PEND EN3 126 C2
STAL AL1 9 K9
Cunningham Hill Rd STAL AL1 9 K9
Cunningham Pk HRW HA1 143 H7
Cunningham Rd
CHES/WCR EN8 110 C1
Cupid Green La HHNE HP2 62 E4
Curlew Cl BERK HP4 80 A2
LWTH SG6 148 C12
Curlew Ct BROX EN10 * 92 D5
Curlew Crs ROY SG8 14 F4
Curlew Rd LTNE LU2 29 G4
Curo Pk LCOL/BKTW AL2 103 J2
Currie St HERT/BAY SG13 53 J6
Curteys HLWE CM17 183 P12
Curthwaite Gdns ENC/FH EN2 124 B8
Curtis Cl RKW/CH/CXG WD3 129 L4
Curtis Rd HHS/BOV HP3 83 H3
Curtiss Dr GSTN WD25 101 K8
Curtis Wy BERK HP4 80 B2
Curzon Av STAN HA7 143 L3
Curzon Pl PIN HA5 142 A7
Curzon Rd LTNN/LIM LU3 6 C2
Cussen Pl LTNN/LIM LU3 * 27 H2
Cussons Cl CHESW EN7 109 L3
Cusworth Wy DUN/WHIP LU6 25 J8
Cutenhoe Rd LTN LU1 41 K4
Cutforth Rd SBW CM21 183 Q6
Cuthbert Cl CHESW EN7 109 K3
Cutlers Cl BSF CM23 43 J5
Cutlers Gn LTNE LU2 29 K7
Cutmore Dr STALE/WH AL4 86 F4
Cut Throat Av BERK HP4 171 L2
Cuttsfield Ter HHW HP1 81 K3
Cutts La HTCHE/RSTV SG4 175 P8
Cuttys La STVG SG1 10 E5
Cwmbran Ct HHNE HP2 62 D6
Cygnet Cl BORE WD6 121 G5
NTHWD HA6 141 G2
Cygnet Ct BSF CM23 43 M3
Cylers Thicket WLYN AL6 177 J11
Cymbeline Ct HRW HA1 * 143 K8
Cypress Av ENC/FH EN2 124 E1
WGCE AL7 51 G8
Cypress Cl WAB EN9 * 111 H8
Cypress Rd
KTN/HRWW/WS HA3 143 H4
Cypress Wk GSTN WD25 * 117 M1
Cyrils Wy STAL AL1 85 H5

D

Dacorum Wy HHNE HP2 4 E2
Dacre Crs HTCHE/RSTV SG4 175 N8
Dacre Gdns BORE WD6 135 H1
Dacre Gn ROY SG8 15 G7
Dacre Rd HTCH/STOT SG5 157 Q5
RAYLNE/WEN HP22 56 C6
Dads Wd HLW CM20 2 D7
Daffodil Cl HAT AL10 67 K4
Dagger La BORE WD6 133 L2
Daggs Dell Rd HHW HP1 61 J8
Dagnall Rd DUN/WHIP LU6 38 A7
HHW HP1 171 R12
Dagnalls LWTH SG6 16 D7
Dahlia Cl CHESW EN7 91 G7
LTNE LU2 28 F6
Daintrees WARE SG12 182 C5
Daintry Cl
KTN/HRWW/WS HA3 143 L6
Dairyglen Av CHES/WCR EN8 110 B5
Dairy Wy ABLGY WD5 101 K3
Daisy Ct LWTH SG6 16 E1
Daisy Dr HAT AL10 67 K5
Dalby Cl LTNW/LEA LU4 26 F5
Dale Av STALE/WH AL4 175 M12
Dale Cl BAR EN5 136 F2
DUN/HR/TOD LU5 26 D8
HTCHE/RSTV SG4 157 P9
PIN HA5 141 M3
Dale Ct GSTN WD25 * 101 L7
SBW CM21 183 P8
Dale Green Rd
FBAR/BDGN N11 137 M6
Dale Gv NFNCH/WDSPK N12 137 G8
Dale Rd DUN/HR/TOD LU5 26 D8
LTN LU1 6 B5
Daleside Dr POTB/CUF EN6 106 D6
Dales Pth BORE WD6 * 135 H1
Dales Rd BORE WD6 135 H1
The Dale LWTH SG6 16 C3
WAB EN9 111 J8
Dale Vw BAR EN5 * 122 D7
Dalewood HARP AL5 47 H4
WGCE AL7 51 H8
Dalkeith Gv STAN HA7 134 B8
Dalkeith Rd HARP AL5 47 G3
Dalling Dr DUN/HR/TOD LU5 26 A4
Dallow Rd LTN LU1 6 B4
Dalmeny Rd BAR EN5 137 G2
Dalton Cl LTNN/LIM LU3 154 H12
Dalton Gdns BSF CM23 43 L6
Dalton St STALW/RED AL3 8 E3
Dalton Wy HTCHE/RSTV SG4 175 Q3
WAT WD17 13 J9
Daltry Cl STVG SG1 21 G7
Daltry Rd STVG SG1 21 G7
Damask Cl HTCHE/RSTV SG4 21 M1
TRING HP23 58 A1
Damask Gn HHW HP1 81 J3
Damask Green Rd
HTCHE/RSTV SG4 21 M1
Dammersey Cl
STALW/RED AL3 172 H5
Damson Wk BLDK SG7 150 A2
Damson Wy STALE/WH AL4 66 A8
Dancers End La TRING HP23 57 G3
Dancers Hill Rd BAR EN5 122 B2
Dancote KNEB SG3 177 M4
Dane Acres BSF CM23 43 K1
Dane Br MHAD SG10 42 C6
Dane Bridge La MHAD SG10 42 B7
Danebridge Rd MHAD SG10 42 A7
Dane Cl AMSS HP7 113 K7
HARP AL5 47 G1
HTCH/STOT SG5 148 D5
Dane End ROY SG8 151 P8
Dane End La HTCHE/RSTV SG4 22 C4
Dane End Rd STDN SG11 180 B5
Danefield Rd HTCH/STOT SG5 156 E1
Daneland EBAR EN4 137 K2
Danemead HOD EN11 72 E4
Dane O'Coys Rd BSF CM23 43 K1
Dane Pk BSF CM23 43 K1
Dane Rd AMP/FLIT/BLC MK45 155 K2
LTNN/LIM LU3 27 M7
Danesbury La WLYN AL6 177 J9
Danesbury Pk HERT/WAT SG14 53 H6
WLYN AL6 177 K9
Danesbury Park Rd WLYN AL6 177 J10
Danescroft LWTH SG6 148 D12
Danes Ga HRW HA1 143 J5
Danesgate STVG SG1 10 C5
The Danes LCOL/BKTW AL2 103 G2
Dane St BSF CM23 44 A2
STVG SG1 10 D6
Daniells WGCE AL7 50 E6
Danvers Cft TRING HP23 169 N12
Danvers Dr LTNN/LIM LU3 155 J12
Danziger Wy BORE WD6 121 G5
Darblay Cl STALE/WH AL4 48 D8
Darby Dr WAB EN9 111 G7
WLYN AL6 177 L6
Darcy Cl CHES/WCR EN8 110 C5
TRDG/WHET N20 137 H5
Darkes La POTB/CUF EN6 106 E6
Dark La BUNT SG9 150 H12
CHESW EN7 109 L4
HARP AL5 47 H6
HTCHE/RSTV SG4 176 E9
Darlands Dr BAR EN5 136 B1
Darley Cft LCOL/BKTW AL2 * 102 F2
Darley Rd LTNE LU2 29 M8
Darnicle Hl CHESW EN7 90 E7
Darrington Rd BORE WD6 120 C5
Darr's La BERK HP4 59 H8
The Dart HHNE HP2 62 D5
Darvell Dr CSHM HP5 96 E3
Darvells Yd
RKW/CH/CXG WD3 115 H8
Darwin Cl FBAR/BDGN N11 137 M6
HHNE HP2 62 F4
STALW/RED AL3 65 J6
Darwin Gdns OXHEY WD19 132 A8
Darwin Rd STVGE SG2 11 L2
The Dashes HLW CM20 3 G4
Datchet Cl HHNE HP2 62 F5
Datchworth Turn HHNE HP2 83 G2
Davenham Av NTHWD HA6 131 K7
Davenport HLWE CM17 76 C6
Daventer Dr STAN HA7 143 K2
David Evans Ct LWTH SG6 16 B2
Davies St HERT/BAY SG13 53 J7
Davis Ct STAL AL1 * 9 G6
Davis Crs HTCH/STOT SG5 146 F12
Davison Cl CHES/WCR EN8 110 B2
Davison Dr CHES/WCR EN8 110 B2
Davis' Rw ARL/CHE SG15 147 Q5
Davys Cl STALE/WH AL4 48 C6
Dawes Cl CSHM HP5 96 F6
Dawes La RKW/CH/CXG WD3 115 K2
STALE/WH AL4 48 B4
Dawley WGCE AL7 50 D4
Dawley Ct HHNE HP2 62 D6
Dawlish Cl STVGE SG2 177 Q2
Dawlish Dr PIN HA5 142 C7
Dawlish Rd LTNW/LEA LU4 27 K6
Daws Hl CHING E4 127 G7
Daws La MLHL NW7 135 K8
Dawson Cl HNLW SG16 147 L4
Dayemead WGCE AL7 68 F2
Daymer Gdns PIN HA5 142 A6
Days Cl HAT AL10 67 K8
Day's Cl ROY SG8 14 D8
Days Md HAT AL10 67 K8
Deacon Cl STAL AL1 85 H6
Deacons Cl BORE WD6 120 E8
PIN HA5 141 M4
Deaconsfield Rd HHS/BOV HP3 5 G8
Deacons Hts BORE WD6 134 E2
Deacons Hl OXHEY WD19 132 A2
Deacon's Hill Rd BORE WD6 134 D1
Deacons Wy HTCH/STOT SG5 157 M4
Deadhearn La CSTG HP8 128 C4
Deadman's Ash La
RKW/CH/CXG WD3 115 M2
Dead Woman's La
HTCHE/RSTV SG4 31 G3
Deakin Cl WATW WD18 131 J3
Deanacre Cl CFSP/GDCR SL9 138 C1
Dean Ct GSTN WD25 * 102 B7
Deancroft Rd CFSP/GDCR SL9 138 C1
Deane Ct NTHWD HA6 * 141 J3
Deane Croft Rd PIN HA5 142 A8
Deane Wy RSLP HA4 141 M8
Dean Fld HHS/BOV HP3 98 E1
Dean Moore Cl STAL AL1 8 E7
Deans Cl ABLGY WD5 101 H6
AMS HP6 113 K3
TRING HP23 57 L1
Deanscroft KNEB SG3 177 M4
Dean's Dr EDGW HA8 135 H8
Deans Furlong TRING HP23 57 L1
Dean's Gdns STALE/WH AL4 65 L6
Deans Meadow BERK HP4 171 J4
Deansway HHS/BOV HP3 5 L9
CSHM HP5 96 F3
Deans Wy EDGW HA8 135 G8
Dean Wy RAYLNE/WEN HP22 56 D1
Deard's End La KNEB SG3 177 M4
Deards Wd KNEB SG3 177 M4
Dearne Cl STAN HA7 133 L8
Dearsley Rd EN EN1 125 L7
Debenham Rd CHESW EN7 109 M1
De Bohun Av STHGT/OAK N14 137 M2
Deep Acres AMS HP6 112 E2
Deepdene POTB/CUF EN6 106 B5
Deep Denes LTNE LU2 28 E7
Deeping Cl KNEB SG3 177 M5
Deer Cl HERT/BAY SG13 53 K7
Deerfield Cl WARE SG12 54 B3
Deerings Dr PIN HA5 141 L7
The Deerings HARP AL5 64 E1
Deer Pk HLWW/ROY CM19 74 E8
Deer Park Wk CSHM HP5 97 J2
Deer Park Wy WAB EN9 126 F2
Deerswood Av HAT AL10 87 M2
The Dee HHNE HP2 62 D5
Deeves Hall La POTB/CUF EN6 105 J7
De Havilland Cl STALE/WH AL4 87 G1
De Havilland Ct RAD WD7 * 104 C6
De Havilland Wy ABLGY WD5 101 K6
Deimos Dr HHNE HP2 62 E7
Delahay Ri BERK HP4 59 M7
Delamare Rd CHES/WCR EN8 110 D3
Delamere Gdns MLHL NW7 135 H8
Delamere Rd BORE WD6 120 F5
Delco Wy DUN/WHIP LU6 25 K7
Delfcroft WARE SG12 54 A2
Delfield Gdns LTN LU1 40 C5

Delius Cl BORE WD6 134 A2
Dell Cl CSHM HP5 96 D3
HARP AL5 46 F2
Dellcot Cl LTNE LU2 28 F4
Dellcott Cl WGCW AL8 49 M6
Dellcroft Wy HARP AL5 46 E7
Dellcut Rd HHNE HP2 62 E8
Dell Farm Rd RSLP HA4 141 H7
Dellfield CSHM HP5 96 E3
STAL AL1 9 K8
WARE SG12 180 B9
Dellfield Av BERK HP4 59 M7
Dellfield Cl BERK HP4 59 L7
RAD WD7 119 J1
WAT WD17 12 C1
Dellfield Rd HAT AL10 67 L8
Dell La BSF CM23 44 A2
RBSF CM22 184 A1
Dellmeadow ABLGY WD5 101 J4
Dell Meadow HHS/BOV HP3 82 C6
Dellmont Rd DUN/HR/TOD LU5 25 M4
Dellors Cl BAR EN5 136 B1
Dellows La RBSF CM22 167 J3
Dell Ri LCOL/BKTW AL2 84 F8
Dell Rd BERK HP4 59 H6
DUN/HR/TOD LU5 25 M4
PEND EN3 126 A4
WATN WD24 117 L3
Dellside DEN/HRF UB9 140 A7
Dell Side WATN WD24 117 L3
Dellsome La STALE/WH AL4 87 K5
Dell Springs BUNT SG9 159 J9
The Dells HHS/BOV HP3 82 F3
Dellswood Cl HERT/BAY SG13 53 J8
Dells Wood Cl HOD EN11 72 D4
The Dell BLDK SG7 17 J3
CFSP/GDCR SL9 138 C1
HERT/BAY SG13 71 G2
LTN LU1 40 C6
LTNE LU2 29 K8
NTHWD HA6 131 J5
PIN HA5 142 B4
RAD WD7 119 L2
ROY SG8 14 D8
STAL AL1 9 M2
STVG SG1 10 F4
WAB EN9 127 G2
Dellwood RKW/CH/CXG WD3 129 M4
Delmar Av HHNE HP2 83 H3
Delmeade Rd CSHM HP5 96 E6
Delmerend La
STALW/RED AL3 173 L8
Delphine Cl LTN LU1 40 E3
Delta Gain OXHEY WD19 132 B5
De Mandeville Ga EN EN1 125 L8
De Mandeville Rd RBSF CM22 167 L3
Demontfort Ri WARE SG12 54 A2
Denbigh Cl HHNE HP2 5 J5
Denbigh Rd LTNN/LIM LU3 27 M7
Denby LWTH SG6 16 F5
Denby Gra HLWE CM17 76 C5
Dencora Wy LTNN/LIM LU3 26 F1
Dendridge Cl EN EN1 125 M3
Dene Gdns STAN HA7 134 A8
Dene La STVGE SG2 34 C7
Dene Rd NTHWD HA6 141 G1
TRDG/WHET N20 137 K4
Denewood BAR EN5 137 G1
Denewood Cl WAT WD17 117 K3
Denham Cl HHNE HP2 62 E5
LTNN/LIM LU3 27 J1
Denham Garden Village
DEN/HRF UB9 * 139 K8
Denham Green La
DEN/HRF UB9 139 J7
Denham La CFSP/GDCR SL9 138 D2
Denham Rd TRDG/WHET N20 137 K5
Denham Wk CFSP/GDCR SL9 138 D1
Denham Wy BORE WD6 121 G5
Denham Way
(North Orbital Road)
RKW/CH/CXG WD3 139 J2
Denmark Cl LTNN/LIM LU3 154 E12
Denmark St WAT WD17 12 E2
Dennis Cl RAYLNE/WEN HP22 56 D1
Dennis Gdns STAN HA7 134 A8
Dennis La STAN HA7 133 M7
Denny Av WAB EN9 111 H8
Denny Ct BSF CM23 166 D11
Denny Ga CHES/WCR EN8 110 D1
Denny's La BERK HP4 79 K3
Densley Cl WGCW AL8 50 A5
Denton Cl BAR EN5 136 A1
LTNW/LEA LU4 26 F5
Denton Rd STVG SG1 10 F7
Dents Cl LWTH SG6 17 G6
Deodora Cl TRDG/WHET N20 137 J6
Derby Av KTN/HRWW/WS HA3 143 H3
NFNCH/WDSPK N12 137 G8
Derby Rd HOD EN11 93 H1
LTNW/LEA LU4 27 G7
WAT WD17 13 H5
Derby Wy STVG SG1 33 M1
Derry Leys HAT AL10 67 J6
Derwent Av EBAR EN4 137 K4
LTNN/LIM LU3 27 M2
MLHL NW7 135 H8
PIN HA5 142 C1
Derwent Cl AMSS HP7 113 M5
GSTN WD25 102 A7
Derwent Crs
NFNCH/WDSPK N12 137 G6
Derwent Dr DUN/WHIP LU6 39 G4
Derwent Rd HARP AL5 46 A1
HHS/BOV HP3 83 G3
HNLW SG16 147 K5
LTNE LU2 7 K3
Desborough Cl
HERT/WAT SG14 53 G4
WGCE AL7 68 F2
Desborough Dr WLYN AL6 177 Q12
Desborough Rd
HTCHE/RSTV SG4 20 A1
Desmond Rd WATN WD24 117 K2
De Soissons Cl WGCW AL8 67 M1
De Tany Ct STAL AL1 8 E8
Deva Cl STALW/RED AL3 84 E4
Devereux Dr WAT WD17 117 J4
De Vere Wk WAT WD17 117 J6
Devon Ct STAL AL1 9 H8
Devon Md HAT AL10 67 H6
Devon Rd LTNE LU2 7 M5
WATN WD24 118 B5
Devonshire Av AMS HP6 112 F3
Devonshire Cl STVGE SG2 177 N1
Devonshire Rd HARP AL5 46 F3
PIN HA5 142 A8
Dewars Cl WLYN AL6 177 J11
Dewes Green Rd BSF CM23 161 M8
Dewgrass Gv CHES/WCR EN8 126 B1
Dewhurst Rd CHES/WCR EN8 110 A3
Dewpond Cl STVG SG1 33 G1
Dewsbury Cl PIN HA5 142 C8
Dewsbury Rd LTNN/LIM LU3 27 M3
Dexter Cl LTNN/LIM LU3 154 H12
STAL AL1 9 L7
Dexter Rd BAR EN5 136 B2
DEN/HRF UB9 140 A4
Dharam Marg GSTN WD25 * 119 J5
Diamond Rd WATN WD24 117 L4
Dianne Wy EBAR EN4 123 J8
Dickens Bvd HTCH/STOT SG5 148 A11
Dickens Cl STALW/RED AL3 8 E3
Dickens Ct HHNE HP2 62 F4
Dickens La LBUZ LU7 24 E4
Dickenson Wy WARE SG12 54 B4
Dicker Mi HERT/BAY SG13 53 H6
Dicket Md WLYN AL6 177 J12
Dickins Cl CHESW EN7 109 L1
Dickinson Av
RKW/CH/CXG WD3 130 E2
Dickinson Quay HHS/BOV HP3 82 C7
Dickinsons Fld HARP AL5 47 G6
Dickinson Sq
RKW/CH/CXG WD3 130 E2
Dickson CHESW EN7 109 K1
Dickson Fold PIN HA5 142 B6
Dig Dag Hl CHESW EN7 109 K1
Digswell Cl BORE WD6 120 E4
Digswell Hl WGCW AL8 49 L4
Digswell La WGCE AL7 50 D3
Digswell Park Rd WGCW AL8 50 B2
Digswell Ri WGCW AL8 50 B5
Digswell Rd WGCW AL8 50 C4
Dimmocks La
RKW/CH/CXG WD3 115 L2
Dimsdale Crs BSF CM23 44 B4
Dimsdale St HERT/WAT SG14 53 G7
Dinant Link Rd HOD EN11 72 E6
Dingle Cl BAR EN5 135 K2
Dinmore HHS/BOV HP3 98 D2
Dinsdale Gdns BAR EN5 136 F1
Dione Rd HHNE HP2 62 D7
Dison Cl PEND EN3 126 B5
Ditchfield Rd HOD EN11 72 E4
Ditchling Cl LTNE LU2 29 G6
Ditchmore La STVG SG1 10 B2
Ditton Gn LTNE LU2 29 H7
Divot Pl HERT/BAY SG13 53 M6
Dixies Cl BLDK SG7 149 P2
Dixon Pl BUNT SG9 159 J10
Dixons Ct WARE SG12 * 54 C5
Dixon's Gap Br TRING HP23 168 H7
Dixons Hill Cl BRKMPK AL9 87 M7
Dixons Hill Rd BRKMPK AL9 87 M7
Dobbin Cl
KTN/HRWW/WS HA3 143 L4
Dobb's Weir Rd HOD EN11 73 H8
Docklands HTCH/STOT SG5 156 F1
Doctor's Commons Rd
BERK HP4 79 M2
Dodds La HHNE HP2 62 A5
Dodwood WGCE AL7 50 F8
Dogden La BSF CM23 166 A3
Doggetts Ct EBAR EN4 137 J1
Doggetts Wy STAL AL1 85 G4
Doggetts Wood Cl CSTG HP8 113 M8
Doggetts Wood La CSTG HP8 113 M7
Dog Kennel La HAT AL10 67 L7
RKW/CH/CXG WD3 129 K1
ROY SG8 14 E7
Dognell Gn WGCW AL8 49 M6
Dolesbury Dr WLYN AL6 177 L8
Dollimore Cl HTCHE/RSTV SG4 176 F8
Dollis Valley Dr BAR EN5 136 D1
Dollis Valley Green Wk
TRDG/WHET N20 136 F6
Dollis Valley Wy EBAR EN4 123 H8
Dolmans Pl DUN/WHIP LU6 38 F1
Dolphin Dr DUN/HR/TOD LU5 26 B4
Dolphin Sq TRING HP23 57 L2
Dolphin Wy BSF CM23 44 A1
Dolphin Yd STAL AL1 * 8 E6
WARE SG12 * 54 B4
Dominic Ct WAB EN9 110 F7
Dominion Pde HRW HA1 * 143 K7
Domville Cl TRDG/WHET N20 137 H5
Doncaster Cl STVG SG1 34 A1
Doncaster Gn OXHEY WD19 132 A8
Donkey La EN EN1 125 L6
TRING HP23 57 J2
Donnay Cl CFSP/GDCR SL9 138 B8
Donne Cl ROY SG8 14 D5
Dorchester Av HOD EN11 72 E5
RYLN/HDSTN HA2 143 G8
Dorchester Cl
DUN/HR/TOD LU5 25 M8
Dorchester Ct
RKW/CH/CXG WD3 * 131 G1
STHGT/OAK N14 137 M3
Dordans Rd LTNW/LEA LU4 27 J5
Dorel Cl LTNE LU2 28 D7
Dorian Cl TRING HP23 58 B1
Dorie Ms NFNCH/WDSPK N12 136 F7
Dormans Cl NTHWD HA6 141 H2
Dormer Cl BAR EN5 136 B1
Dormers HHS/BOV HP3 * 99 J1
Dormie Cl STALW/RED AL3 8 C1
Dormywood RSLP HA4 141 K7
Dorney End CSHM HP5 96 E4
Dorrien's Cft BERK HP4 59 K6
Dorrington Cl LTNN/LIM LU3 6 B1
Dorrofield Cl
RKW/CH/CXG WD3 131 G1
Dorset Cl BERK HP4 59 K8
Dorset Ct LTN LU1 7 H8
Dorset Rd HRW HA1 143 G8
Douglas Av WATN WD24 118 B3
Douglas Cl STAN HA7 133 L8
WLYN AL6 50 C2
Douglas Crs DUN/HR/TOD LU5 25 L6
Douglas Dr STVG SG1 33 L1
Douglas Gdns BERK HP4 59 K8
Douglas Rd HARP AL5 46 D3
LTNW/LEA LU4 27 L7
Douglas Wy WGCE AL7 51 G7
Doulton Cl HLWE CM17 76 C6
Dove Cl BSF CM23 43 L6
STSD CM24 166 G6
Dovecot Cl PIN HA5 142 A7
Dove Ct HAT AL10 87 L2
Dovedale LTNE LU2 28 C3
STVGE SG2 11 M6
WARE SG12 54 A2
Dovedale Cl DEN/HRF UB9 140 A4
Dove House Cl DUN/WHIP LU6 37 K5
Dovehouse Cft HLW CM20 3 L2
Dove House Dr HNLW SG16 147 M1
Dovehouse Hl LTNE LU2 28 F7
Dove House La
DUN/WHIP LU6 171 Q2
Dove La POTB/CUF EN6 106 F8
Dove Pk PIN HA5 142 D2
RKW/CH/CXG WD3 128 F1
Dover Cl LTNN/LIM LU3 27 L6
Dovercourt Gdns STAN HA7 134 C8
Doverfield CHESW EN7 109 G3
Dove Rd STVG SG1 21 K6
Dover Wy RKW/CH/CXG WD3 117 G8
Dowd Cl FBAR/BDGN N11 137 L5
Dowding Pl STAN HA7 143 L1
Dowding Wy GSTN WD25 101 K8
Dowley Wd WGCE AL7 50 F7
Dowling Ct HHS/BOV HP3 5 G8
Downalong BUSH WD23 133 H4
Downedge STALW/RED AL3 8 B3
Down Edge STALW/RED AL3 173 P12
Downer Dr RKW/CH/CXG WD3 115 K2
Downes Rd STALE/WH AL4 65 M6
Downfield Cl HERT/BAY SG13 72 A1
Downfield Ct WARE SG12 * 179 R12
Downfield Rd CHES/WCR EN8 110 C5
HERT/BAY SG13 72 A1
Downfields WGCW AL8 67 M1
Down Green La STALE/WH AL4 47 M6
Downhall Ley BUNT SG9 159 J11
Downhall Rd RBSF CM22 184 H11
Downhurst Av MLHL NW7 135 H8
Downing Cl RYLN/HDSTN HA2 143 G5
Downings Wd
RKW/CH/CXG WD3 129 H8
Downland Cl
TRDG/WHET N20 137 G4
Downlands BLDK SG7 149 L12
LTNN/LIM LU3 27 G2
ROY SG8 14 D7
STVGE SG2 34 B2
WAB EN9 111 J8
Downs Av PIN HA5 142 D8
Downsfield HAT AL10 87 L3
Downside HHNE HP2 5 H1
Downs La HAT AL10 87 L2
Downs Rd DUN/HR/TOD LU5 39 H1
EN EN1 125 J8
LTN LU1 6 B6
The Downs HAT AL10 87 L2
HLW CM20 3 H6
Downs Vw DUN/HR/TOD LU5 * 39 H3
Dowry Wk WAT WD17 117 K4
Dragon Rd HAT AL10 67 H7
Drakes Cl CHES/WCR EN8 110 B2
Drakes Dr NTHWD HA6 140 F3
STAL AL1 85 M5
STVGE SG2 33 M2
Drakes Rd AMSS HP7 113 H5
Drake St ENC/FH EN2 125 H5
Drakes Wy HAT AL10 87 M2
Drapers Ms LTNN/LIM LU3 * 6 C1
Drapers Rd ENC/FH EN2 124 F6
Drapers Wy STVG SG1 10 B1
Draycott Av
KTN/HRWW/WS HA3 143 M8
Draycott Cl
KTN/HRWW/WS HA3 143 M8
Drayman's Cl BSF CM23 43 H4
Drayson Cl WAB EN9 111 H6
Drayton Av POTB/CUF EN6 106 C6
Drayton Rd BORE WD6 120 E8
LTNW/LEA LU4 26 D6
The Drey CFSP/GDCR SL9 128 C8
Driftway ROY SG8 152 A9
The Driftway HHNE HP2 5 L3
Driftwood Av LCOL/BKTW AL2 84 E8
Drive Ct EDGW HA8 * 134 E8
Driver's End La
HTCHE/RSTV SG4 176 F5
The Drive AMSS HP7 113 H4
BAR EN5 122 C7
BRKMPK AL9 88 E7
CFSP/GDCR SL9 138 C2
CHESW EN7 108 F2
EDGW HA8 134 E8
ENC/FH EN2 125 H5
HARP AL5 46 E4
HERT/BAY SG13 * 90 C6
HERT/WAT SG14 53 G5
HLW CM20 3 H4
HOD EN11 72 E5
LCOL/BKTW AL2 85 L7
NTHWD HA6 141 J3
POTB/CUF EN6 106 D7
RAD WD7 103 L8
RKW/CH/CXG WD3 129 M1
SBW CM21 183 Q7
STALE/WH AL4 175 M10
WAT WD17 117 H3
WLYN AL6 177 N8
The Driveway HHW HP1 4 B6
POTB/CUF EN6 108 C2
Dromey Gdns
KTN/HRWW/WS HA3 143 K2
Drop La LCOL/BKTW AL2 102 F5
Drovers Wy BSF CM23 43 J4
DUN/WHIP LU6 38 D1
HAT AL10 67 M5
STAL AL1 8 E5
The Druce SAFWS CB11 161 R5
Drummond Dr STAN HA7 143 K2
Drummond Ride TRING HP23 169 L12
Drury Cl DUN/HR/TOD LU5 26 A4
Drury La DUN/HR/TOD LU5 26 A4
WARE SG12 182 B8
Drycroft WGCE AL7 68 C3
Drydell La CSHM HP5 96 D5
Dryden Crs STVGE SG2 34 A1
Dryden Rd
KTN/HRWW/WS HA3 143 K3
Drysdale Cl NTHWD HA6 141 J2
Dubbs Knoll Rd ROY SG8 145 M4
Dubrae Cl STALW/RED AL3 84 E4
Duchess Cl BSF CM23 43 H2
FBAR/BDGN N11 137 M8
Duchy Rd EBAR EN4 123 H4
Duck Aly CSHM HP5 96 F6
Ducketts La MHAD SG10 42 D8
Ducketts Md HLWW/ROY CM19 73 M4
Ducketts Wd WARE SG12 180 B10
Duck La STVGE SG2 35 J5
Duck Lees La PEND EN3 126 C8
Duckling La SBW CM21 183 Q7
Duckmore La TRING HP23 57 J4
Ducks Hill Rd NTHWD HA6 140 E4
Dudley Av CHES/WCR EN8 110 B6
Dudley Hill Cl WLYN AL6 177 L9
Dudley St LTNE LU2 6 F3
Dudswell La BERK HP4 59 H5
Dudswell Mi BERK HP4 * 59 G5
Duffield Cl HRW HA1 143 K7
Dugdale Hill La
POTB/CUF EN6 106 C7
Dugdales RKW/CH/CXG WD3 116 E8
Dukes Av DUN/WHIP LU6 171 L1
HRW HA1 143 J6
PIN HA5 142 D8
Duke's La HTCH/STOT SG5 157 N5
Dukes Orch RBSF CM22 185 M3
Dukes Ride BSF CM23 43 J2
Duke St HOD EN11 72 E6
LTNE LU2 7 G3
WAT WD17 13 G4
Dukes Wy BERK HP4 * 59 L7
Dulwich Wy
RKW/CH/CXG WD3 130 E1
Dumbarton Av
CHES/WCR EN8 110 B8
Dumbletons
RKW/CH/CXG WD3 129 J7
Dumfries Cl OXHEY WD19 131 L6
Dumfries St LTN LU1 6 E7
Duncan Cl BAR EN5 123 G8
WGCE AL7 50 C8
Duncan Wy BUSH WD23 118 D6
Duncombe Cl AMS HP6 113 J4
HERT/WAT SG14 53 G5
LTNN/LIM LU3 28 A3
Duncombe Dr
DUN/HR/TOD LU5 26 C7
Duncombe Rd BERK HP4 59 J7
HERT/WAT SG14 53 G6
Duncots Cl HTCH/STOT SG5 157 N2
Dundale Rd TRING HP23 57 L1
Dundas Ms PEND EN3 126 E3
Dundee Wy PEND EN3 126 C7
Dunhams Ct LWTH SG6 * 16 F3
Dunhams La LWTH SG6 16 F3
Dunlin LWTH SG6 148 C12
Dunlin Rd HHNE HP2 62 C5
Dunmow Rd BSF CM23 44 B2
Dunn Cl STVG SG1 10 E8
Dunnock Cl BORE WD6 120 E8
Dunny La RKW/CH/CXG WD3 99 K7
Dunraven Av LTN LU1 40 E1
Dunraven Dr ENC/FH EN2 124 E6
Dunsby Rd LTNN/LIM LU3 27 L3
Dunsley Pl TRING HP23 57 M2
Dunsmore OXHEY WD19 * 132 B5
Dunsmore Cl BUSH WD23 133 H2
Dunsmore Rd LTN LU1 6 B7
Dunsmore Wy BUSH WD23 133 G2
Dunstable Cl LTNW/LEA LU4 27 L8
Dunstable Pl LTN LU1 6 E6
Dunstable Rd BERK HP4 171 J3
DUN/HR/TOD LU5 25 M5
DUN/WHIP LU6 37 L4
DUN/WHIP LU6 171 P3
LBUZ LU7 24 D4
LTN LU1 6 B3
LTN LU1 39 L4
STALW/RED AL3 173 Q10
Dunstall Rd
AMP/FLIT/BLC MK45 155 J3
Dunstalls HLWW/ROY CM19 94 E1
Dunster Cl BAR EN5 122 B8
DEN/HRF UB9 139 M3
Dunster Ct BORE WD6 121 H7
Dunster Rd HHNE HP2 62 F4
Dunsters Md WGCE AL7 68 E1
Dunston Hl TRING HP23 57 L1
Dunwich Farm STVG SG1 32 E3
Durants Park Av PEND EN3 126 B8
Durants Rd PEND EN3 126 A8
Durban Rd East WATW WD18 12 D5
Durban Rd West WATW WD18 12 C5
Durbar Rd LTNW/LEA LU4 27 L8
Durham Cl SBW CM21 183 N8
WARE SG12 54 F8
Durham Rd BORE WD6 121 G7
HRW HA1 142 F7
LTNE LU2 7 L4
STVG SG1 21 L8
Durler Gdns LTN LU1 6 E9
Durley Av PIN HA5 142 C8
Durrants Dr
RKW/CH/CXG WD3 117 G7
Durrants Hill Rd HHS/BOV HP3 4 F9
Durrants La BERK HP4 79 J1
Durrants Rd BERK HP4 59 K8
Dury Rd BAR EN5 122 D5
Duxford Cl LTNN/LIM LU3 27 M2
Duxons Turn HHNE HP2 82 F1
Dwight Rd WATW WD18 131 H3
Dyers Rd DUN/WHIP LU6 37 H2
Dyes La HTCHE/RSTV SG4 32 D5
Dyke La STALE/WH AL4 48 C6
Dylan Cl BORE WD6 * 134 B3
Dymoke Gn STALE/WH AL4 65 L7
Dymoke Ms STVG SG1 * 33 G2
Dymokes Wy HOD EN11 72 E4
Dyrham La BAR EN5 121 L2
Dysons Cl CHES/WCR EN8 110 B7

E

Eagle Centre Wy
LTNW/LEA LU4 26 F2
Eagle Cl AMS HP6 113 K3
LTNW/LEA LU4 26 E5
PEND EN3 126 A8
WAB EN9 111 L8
Eagle Ct HERT/BAY SG13 53 M6
Eagle Wy HAT AL10 87 L2
Ealing Cl BORE WD6 121 H5
Earl Cl FBAR/BDGN N11 137 M8
Earls Cl BSF CM23 43 K3
Earls Cnr POTB/CUF EN6 * 105 L7
Earls Crs HRW HA1 143 J6
Earls Hill Gdns ROY SG8 14 D7
Earls La POTB/CUF EN6 105 J6
Earlsmead LWTH SG6 16 D6
Earls Meade LTNE LU2 6 E1
Earl St WAT WD17 13 G4
Earnshaw Dr HTCH/STOT SG5 148 A11
Easedale Cl DUN/WHIP LU6 39 G3
Easington Rd WARE SG12 179 N2
Easingwold Gdns LTN LU1 40 D1
East Barnet Rd BAR EN5 123 G8
Eastbourne Av STVG SG1 32 E3
Eastbrook Rd WAB EN9 111 J7
Eastbrook Wy HHNE HP2 5 J3
East Burrowfield WGCE AL7 68 B1
Eastbury Av EN EN1 125 J5
NTHWD HA6 131 J8
Eastbury Ct OXHEY WD19 * 132 A3
STAL AL1 9 J3
Eastbury Rd NTHWD HA6 141 J1
OXHEY WD19 132 A3
Eastcheap LWTH SG6 16 D4
East Cl EBAR EN4 123 L8
HTCHE/RSTV SG4 157 R4
LCOL/BKTW AL2 84 F7
STVG SG1 11 G4
East Common
CFSP/GDCR SL9 138 C8
Eastcote Dr HARP AL5 47 H7
Eastcote Rd PIN HA5 142 B7
RSLP HA4 141 L8
Eastcote Vw PIN HA5 142 A6
Eastcott Cl LTNE LU2 29 G8
East Crs FBAR/BDGN N11 137 K7
East Dr GSTN WD25 117 M2
LCOL/BKTW AL2 85 M8
NTHWD HA6 131 J5
SBW CM21 183 Q8
STALE/WH AL4 86 C1
East Duck Lees La PEND EN3 126 C8
East End DUN/HR/TOD LU5 26 A4
Eastend La RBSF CM22 167 R4
East End Wy PIN HA5 142 C5
Eastern Av CHES/WCR EN8 110 D7
DUN/HR/TOD LU5 26 B8
HNLW SG16 147 L6
Eastern Wy LWTH SG6 16 E1
Eastfield Av WATN WD24 118 B5
Eastfield Cl LTNE LU2 29 G5
Eastfield Ct STALE/WH AL4 66 B7
Eastfield Rd PEND EN3 126 B4
ROY SG8 14 F6
Eastfields PIN HA5 142 A7
East Flint HHW HP1 81 J1
East Ga HLW CM20 2 E5
Eastgate STVG SG1 10 D6
Eastglade NTHWD HA6 131 J8
Eastham Cl BAR EN5 136 C1
East Hl LTNN/LIM LU3 27 M3
Easthill Rd DUN/HR/TOD LU5 26 A4
Eastholm LWTH SG6 16 E1
Eastholm Gn LWTH SG6 16 E1
East La ABLGY WD5 101 L3
STALE/WH AL4 48 B4
Eastlea Av GSTN WD25 118 C3
East Lodge La ENC/FH EN2 124 B2
Eastman Wy HHNE HP2 62 E7
East Md WGCE AL7 68 F2
Eastmoor Pk HARP AL5 47 G7
East Mt STALE/WH AL4 48 B4
Eastnor HHS/BOV HP3 98 E2
Easton Gdns BORE WD6 121 J8
Eastor WGCE AL7 50 E4
East Pk HLWE CM17 75 M2
East Pole Cots
STHGT/OAK N14 * 124 B8
East Reach STVGE SG2 33 L7
East Ridgeway
POTB/CUF EN6 108 C2
East Riding WLYN AL6 177 R12
East Rd BSF CM23 44 B2
EBAR EN4 137 L4
HLW CM20 75 M1
PEND EN3 126 A4
East St CSHM HP5 96 F6
HHNE HP2 5 G1
LTNE LU2 155 R11
WARE SG12 54 B4
East Towers PIN HA5 142 B8
East Vw BAR EN5 122 D6
BRKMPK AL9 69 K7
HTCHE/RSTV SG4 20 A7
East Wk EBAR EN4 137 L4
HLW CM20 2 E5
East Wy WAB EN9 127 G2
Eastwick Crs
RKW/CH/CXG WD3 129 K5
Eastwick Hall La HLW CM20 74 E1
Eastwick Rd HLW CM20 74 F1
WARE SG12 73 M2
Eastwick Rw HHNE HP2 5 M4
Eaton Bray Rd DUN/WHIP LU6 37 G4
Eaton Cl STAN HA7 133 M7
Eaton Gdns BROX EN10 92 D4
Eaton Ga NTHWD HA6 141 G1
Eatongate Cl DUN/WHIP LU6 37 J5
Eaton Green Rd LTNE LU2 174 A1
Eaton Pk DUN/WHIP LU6 37 K3
Eaton Pl LTNE LU2 29 H8
Eaton Rd EN EN1 125 J7
HHNE HP2 62 F7
STAL AL1 85 M2
Eaton Valley Rd LTNE LU2 41 M1
Eaton Wy BORE WD6 120 D5
Ebberns Rd HHS/BOV HP3 5 H9
Ebenezer St LTN LU1 6 E7
Ebury Ap RKW/CH/CXG WD3 130 B4
Ebury Cl NTHWD HA6 131 G8
Ebury Rd WAT WD17 13 H3
Eccleston Cl EBAR EN4 137 J1
Echo Hl ROY SG8 14 D8
Eddington Crs WGCE AL7 68 B2
Eddiwick Av DUN/HR/TOD LU5 26 B2
Eddy St BERK HP4 59 L8
Eden Cl PEND EN3 126 E4
Edenhall Cl HHNE HP2 83 H3
Edens Cl BSF CM23 44 B2
Edenvale CHESW EN7 109 M3
Edgars Ct WGCE AL7 50 C8
Edgbaston Dr RAD WD7 104 C6
Edgcott Cl LTNN/LIM LU3 154 H12
Edgecote Cl LTN LU1 40 C6
Edgehill Gdns LTNN/LIM LU3 27 G1
Edgewood Dr LTNE LU2 29 G3
Edgeworth Cl STVGE SG2 34 A8
Edgeworth Rd EBAR EN4 123 J8
Edgwarebury Gdns
EDGW HA8 134 E8
Edgwarebury La BORE WD6 134 D3
EDGW HA8 134 E7
Edgware Way
(Watford By-Pass)
EDGW HA8 134 E7
Edinburgh Av
RKW/CH/CXG WD3 129 L2
Edinburgh Crs
CHES/WCR EN8 110 C7
Edinburgh Dr ABLGY WD5 101 L6
Edinburgh Ga DEN/HRF UB9 139 K8
Edinburgh Pl HLW CM20 75 L1
Edinburgh Wy HLW CM20 2 E1
Edingburgh Gdns BSF CM23 43 K3
Edington Rd PEND EN3 126 A6
Edison Cl STALE/WH AL4 86 A3
Edison Rd PEND EN3 126 D5
STVGE SG2 11 M2
Edkins Cl LTNE LU2 28 C4
Edlyn Cl BERK HP4 59 K8
Edmonds Dr STVGE SG2 34 B5
Edmund Beaufort Dr
STALW/RED AL3 8 F2
Edmund Ms KGLGY WD4 100 E3
Edmunds Rd HERT/WAT SG14 52 D6
Edridge Cl BUSH WD23 133 G1
Edson Cl GSTN WD25 101 K7
Edulf Rd BORE WD6 120 F6
Edward Amey Cl GSTN WD25 118 A2
Edward Cl ABLGY WD5 101 K6
STAL AL1 9 J7
Edward Ct HHS/BOV HP3 82 B6
WAB EN9 111 K7
Edward Gv EBAR EN4 137 H1
Edward Rd EBAR EN4 137 H1
RYLN/HDSTN HA2 143 G5
Edward St DUN/WHIP LU6 25 L8
LTNE LU2 7 H2
Edwin Ware Ct PIN HA5 * 142 A4
Edwyn Cl BAR EN5 136 A2

Egdon Dr LTNE LU2 28 B3
Egerton Cl PIN HA5 141 L6
Egerton Rd BERK HP4 59 L7
Egg Farm La KGLGY WD4 101 G4
Egglesfield Cl BERK HP4 59 J7
Eggleton Dr TRING HP23 169 L12
Eight Acres TRING HP23 57 L1
Eighth Av LTNN/LIM LU3 27 H2
Eisenberg Cl BLDK SG7 149 L12
Elaine Gdns LTN LU1 40 E8
Elbow La HOD EN11 71 M6
 STVG SG2 33 M8
Eldefield LWTH SG6 16 B2
Elderbeck Cl CHESW EN7 109 L2
Elderberry Cl LTNE LU2 28 F5
Elderberry Dr
 HTCHE/RSTV SG4 157 Q9
Elderberry Wy GSTN WD25 117 M1
Elder Cl TRDG/WHET N20 136 F5
Elder Ct BUSH WD23 133 J5
Elderfield HLWE CM17 76 B1
 WGCE AL7 50 F7
Elder Rd WARE SG12 54 D2
Elder Wy STVG SG1 10 D8
Eldon Av BORE WD6 120 E6
Eldon Rd HOD EN11 93 H1
 LTNW/LEA LU4 27 G7
Eleanor Av STALW/RED AL3 8 E1
Eleanor Crs MLHL NW7 136 B7
Eleanor Cross Rd
 CHES/WCR EN8 110 C8
Eleanor Gdns BAR EN5 136 B1
Eleanor Rd CFSP/GDCR SL9 138 A3
 CHES/WCR EN8 110 C7
 HERT/WAT SG14 53 G6
Eleanors Cl WARE SG12 180 B10
Eleanor's Cross DUN/WHIP LU6 38 F1
Eleanor Wy CHES/WCR EN8 110 D8
Eleventh Av STSD CM24 167 K11
Elfrida Rd WATW WD18 13 G8
Elgar Cl BORE WD6 134 A3
Elgar Pth LTNE LU2 6 F3
Elgin Av KTN/HRWW/WS HA3 143 M4
Elgin Dr NTHWD HA6 141 J2
Elgin Rd CHES/WCR EN8 110 A4
Elgiva La CSHM HP5 96 F5
Elgood Av NTHWD HA6 141 L1
Eliot Rd ROY SG8 14 E5
 STVGE SG2 34 A3
Elizabeth Av AMS HP6 114 A5
 ENC/FH EN2 124 F7
Elizabeth Cl BAR EN5 122 B7
 HERT/WAT SG14 52 D6
 WAB EN9 93 H4
 WGCE AL7 51 G7
Elizabeth Ct STALE/WH AL4 66 B7
Elizabeth Dr TRING HP23 169 M11
Elizabeth Rd BSF CM23 43 L4
Elizabeth St LTN LU1 6 E7
Elizabeth Wy HLW CM20 2 B2
 HLWW/ROY CM19 74 D6
Elkanette Ms
 TRDG/WHET N20 137 G5
Ellement Cl PIN HA5 142 B7
Ellenborough Cl BSF CM23 43 K4
Ellenbrook Cl WATN WD24 * 118 A5
Ellenbrook Crs HAT AL10 67 H8
Ellenbrook La HAT AL10 67 H8
Ellenhall Cl LTNN/LIM LU3 6 C1
Ellen Ms HHNE HP2 * 5 K1
Ellen Webb Dr
 KTN/HRWW/WS HA3 143 J5
Ellerdine Cl LTNN/LIM LU3 27 M5
Ellesborough Cl OXHEY WD19 132 A8
Ellesfield WLYN AL6 176 H12
Ellesmere Av MLHL NW7 135 H6
Ellesmere Cl DUN/WHIP LU6 38 A3
Ellesmere Gv BAR EN5 136 D1
Ellesmere Rd BERK HP4 80 B1
Ellingham Cl HHNE HP2 62 E8
Ellingham Rd HHNE HP2 82 D1
Elliott Cl WGCE AL7 68 B2
Elliott Rd STAN HA7 143 L1
Ellis Av CFSP/GDCR SL9 138 D3
 STVG SG1 33 J1
Ellis Cl HOD EN11 72 D3
Ellis Flds STALW/RED AL3 65 J6
Elliswick Rd HARP AL5 46 F8
Ellwood Gdns GSTN WD25 101 M8
Ellwood Ri CSTG HP8 128 A5
Elm Av LTN LU1 40 C6
 OXHEY WD19 132 C3
Elmbank Av BAR EN5 122 A8
Elmbridge HLWE CM17 76 D2
Elmbridge Cl RSLP HA4 141 L8
Elmbridge Dr RSLP HA4 141 L8
Elmbrook Dr BSF CM23 43 L6
Elm Cl AMS HP6 113 G4
 EPP CM16 94 F6
 RBSF CM22 167 L3
 RYLN/HDSTN HA2 142 F8
 WAB EN9 111 H8
Elmcote Wy
 RKW/CH/CXG WD3 130 D2
Elm Ct WAT WD17 * 12 F3
Elmcroft Crs
 RYLN/HDSTN HA2 142 E5
Elm Dr CHES/WCR EN8 110 C2
 HAT AL10 87 L1
 RYLN/HDSTN HA2 142 F8
 STALE/WH AL4 86 A2
Elmer Cl ENC/FH EN2 124 D7
Elmfield Cl POTB/CUF EN6 106 C7
Elmfield Rd POTB/CUF EN6 106 C7
Elm Gdns ENC/FH EN2 125 H4
 WGCW AL8 49 M7
Elmgate Gdns EDGW HA8 135 G8
Elm Gn HHW HP1 61 J8
Elm Gv BERK HP4 79 M1
 BSF CM23 44 B2
 WATN WD24 117 L3
Elmgrove Crs HRW HA1 143 K7
Elmgrove Gdns HRW HA1 143 L7
Elmgrove Rd HRW HA1 143 K7
Elm Hatch PIN HA5 142 D2
Elmhurst Cl BUSH WD23 133 L6
Elmhurst Gdns
 HTCH/STOT SG5 146 B8
Elmhurst Rd PEND EN3 126 A3
Elm Lawn Cl STAL AL1 9 H3
Elmoor Av WLYN AL6 176 H12
Elmoor Cl WLYN AL6 49 M1
Elmore Rd LTNE LU2 7 K1
 PEND EN3 126 B5
Elm Pk BLDK SG7 17 K1
 STAN HA7 133 M8
Elm Park Cl DUN/HR/TOD LU5 26 B3
Elm Park Rd PIN HA5 142 A4
Elm Rd BAR EN5 122 D8
 BSF CM23 43 L1
Elmroyd Av POTB/CUF EN6 106 D7
Elmroyd Cl POTB/CUF EN6 106 D7
Elms Cl HTCHE/RSTV SG4 20 C6
Elmscroft Gdns
 POTB/CUF EN6 106 D6
Elmside DUN/WHIP LU6 171 R1
Elmside Wk HTCH/STOT SG5 157 N6
Elmsleigh Av
 KTN/HRWW/WS HA3 143 M6
Elms Rd CFSP/GDCR SL9 138 C2
 KTN/HRWW/WS HA3 143 J2
 WARE SG12 54 E3
Elmstead Cl TRDG/WHET N20 136 E5
The Elms BORE WD6 * 120 E5
 HERT/BAY SG13 53 L7
 HTCHE/RSTV SG4 176 F7
 LOU IG10 * 127 K6
 NFNCH/WDSPK N12 * 137 J8
Elm Ter KTN/HRWW/WS HA3 143 H2
Elmtree Av LTNE LU2 29 J6
Elm Tree Dr ROY SG8 14 A1
Elmtree Hl CSHM HP5 96 F4
Elm Tree Wk
 RKW/CH/CXG WD3 * 115 K8
 TRING HP23 169 L12
Elm Wk RAD WD7 119 K2
 ROY SG8 15 G6
 STVGE SG2 11 L8
Elm Wy RKW/CH/CXG WD3 129 M4
Elmwood SBW CM21 183 R8
 WGCW AL8 49 M8
Elmwood Av BLDK SG7 17 K2
 BORE WD6 120 F8
 KTN/HRWW/WS HA3 143 L7
Elmwood Cl BLDK SG7 * 17 K1
Elmwood Crs LTNE LU2 28 C6
Elsinge Rd EN EN1 125 M2
Elstree Ga BORE WD6 * 121 H6
Elstree Hl North BORE WD6 134 B1
Elstree Hl South BORE WD6 134 A3
Elstree Pk BORE WD6 * 135 H2
Elstree Rd BUSH WD23 133 H4
 HHNE HP2 62 E4
Elstree Wy BORE WD6 121 G6
Elton Av BAR EN5 136 D1
Elton Pk WAT WD17 12 D1
Elton Rd HERT/WAT SG14 53 G6
Elveden Cl LTNE LU2 28 C3
Elvington Gdns LTNN/LIM LU3 154 H12
Elwood HLWE CM17 76 C6
Ely Cl AMSS HP7 113 J5
 HAT AL10 67 K7
 STVG SG1 21 M7
Ely Gdns BORE WD6 135 H1
Ely Rd STAL AL1 85 M3
Ely Wy LTNW/LEA LU4 27 H5
Embleton Rd OXHEY WD19 131 L6
Embry Cl STAN HA7 133 L7
Embry Dr STAN HA7 143 L1
Embry Wy STAN HA7 133 L8
Emerald Rd LTNW/LEA LU4 26 D7
Emerton Ct BERK HP4 59 J6
Emerton Garth BERK HP4 59 J6
Emily Ct HARP AL5 47 G6
Emmanuel Rd NTHWD HA6 141 K2
Emma Rothschild Ct
 TRING HP23 169 L12
Emmas Crs WARE SG12 72 F1
Emmer Gn LTNE LU2 29 K7
Emmitt Cl RAD WD7 104 C7
Emperor Cl BERK HP4 59 K6
Emperors Ga STVG SG1 34 B1
Empress Rd LTNN/LIM LU3 27 J5
Endeavour Cl HNLW SG16 146 H6
Endeavour Rd
 CHES/WCR EN8 110 C1
Enderby Rd LTNN/LIM LU3 28 A2
Enderley Rd
 KTN/HRWW/WS HA3 143 H3
Endersby Rd BAR EN5 136 A1
Endymion Ct HAT AL10 68 A7
Endymion Ms HAT AL10 68 A7
Endymion Rd HAT AL10 68 A7
Enfield Cl DUN/HR/TOD LU5 26 B3
Enfield Rd ENC/FH EN2 124 B8
England Av DUN/WHIP LU6 25 J6
Englands La DUN/HR/TOD LU5 39 G1
Englefield Cl ENC/FH EN2 124 E6
Englehurst HARP AL5 47 H4
Enid Cl LCOL/BKTW AL2 102 D5
Ennerdale Av DUN/WHIP LU6 38 F2
Ennerdale Cl STAL AL1 85 M4
Ennis Cl HARP AL5 47 H7
Ennismore Cl LWTH SG6 17 G6
Ennismore Gn LTNE LU2 29 K8
Enslow Cl LTN LU1 40 C6
Enstone Rd PEND EN3 126 C7
Enterprise Wy HHNE HP2 63 G8
 LTNN/LIM LU3 27 M1
Epping Gn HHNE HP2 62 F5
Epping New Rd LOU IG10 127 M8
Epping Rd EPP CM16 94 F6
 HLWW/ROY CM19 73 M6
Epping Wy LTNN/LIM LU3 154 C12
Ereswell Rd LTNN/LIM LU3 27 L2
Erin Cl LTNW/LEA LU4 27 G7
Ermine Cl CHESW EN7 109 M5
 ROY SG8 14 E5
 STALW/RED AL3 84 E3
Ermine Ct BUNT SG9 159 J9
Ermine St BUNT SG9 158 H7
 WARE SG12 180 B10
Errington Cl HAT AL10 67 J7
Escarpment Av
 DUN/WHIP LU6 171 K1
Escot Wy BAR EN5 136 A1
Esdaile La HOD EN11 72 E8
Eskdale LCOL/BKTW AL2 104 D1
 LTNW/LEA LU4 27 G4
Eskdale Av CSHM HP5 97 H4
Eskdale Ct HHNE HP2 62 C7
Essendon Gdns WGCE AL7 50 D7
Essendon Hl BRKMPK AL9 69 J7
Essex Cl LTN LU1 7 G8
Essex La KGLGY WD4 101 H7
Essex Md HHNE HP2 62 D4
Essex Rd BORE WD6 120 E7
 CSHM HP5 97 G3
 ENC/FH EN2 125 H8
 HOD EN11 72 C6
 STVG SG1 32 F1
 WAT WD17 12 D2
Essex St STAL AL1 9 G4
Estcourt Rd WAT WD17 13 G4
Ethelred Cl WGCE AL7 50 D8
Ethorpe Crs CFSP/GDCR SL9 138 C7
Etna Rd STALW/RED AL3 8 E4
Eton Av EBAR EN4 137 J2
Eunice Gv CSHM HP5 97 H7
Europa Rd HHNE HP2 62 D7
Euston Av WATW WD18 12 B4
Evans Av GSTN WD25 117 K1
Evans Cl DUN/HR/TOD LU5 26 B5
Evan's Cl RKW/CH/CXG WD3 130 E1
Evans Cl ROY SG8 14 E6
Evans Gv STALE/WH AL4 66 A6
Evans Wy TRING HP23 57 M1
Evans Whf HHS/BOV HP3 82 C6
Evedon Cl LTNN/LIM LU3 27 K3
Evelyn Av RSLP HA4 141 L8
Evelyn Dr PIN HA5 142 B2
Evelyn Rd DUN/HR/TOD LU5 26 D7
 EBAR EN4 123 K8
Evensyde WATW WD18 131 G2
Everard Cl STAL AL1 8 E9
Everest Cl ARL/CHE SG15 147 R4
Everest Gdns BSF CM23 43 K3
Everest Wy HHNE HP2 5 M2
Everett Cl BUSH WD23 133 J4
 CHESW EN7 91 G7
 PIN HA5 141 K5
Evergreen Cl KNEB SG3 177 N7
Evergreen Rd WARE SG12 54 D2
Evergreen Wk HHNE HP2 5 H6
Evergreen Wy LTNN/LIM LU3 27 L1
Everlasting La STALW/RED AL3 8 C2
Eversleigh Rd BAR EN5 137 G1
Exchange Rd STVG SG1 11 G4
 WATW WD18 12 F5
Executive Pk STAL AL1 * 85 M2
Exeter Cl STVG SG1 21 M7
 WATN WD24 13 H1
Exeter Rd PEND EN3 126 B7
 STHGT/OAK N14 137 M4
Explorer Dr WATW WD18 12 B9
Extension Rd HERT/BAY SG13 53 K7
Exton Av LTNE LU2 7 L2
Eyncourt Rd DUN/HR/TOD LU5 26 A7
Eynsford Ct HTCHE/RSTV SG4 157 P7
Eynsford Rd LTNW/LEA LU4 27 H6

F

Faggots Cl RAD WD7 120 A1
Faggotters La HLWE CM17 77 J4
Faints Cl CHESW EN7 109 K3
Fairacre HHS/BOV HP3 82 D6
Fairacres Cl POTB/CUF EN6 106 D7
Fairburn Cl BORE WD6 120 E5
Fair Cl BUSH WD23 132 F3
Faircross Wy STAL AL1 9 L2
Fairfax Av LTNN/LIM LU3 27 H2
Fairfax Rd HERT/BAY SG13 53 K6
Fairfield BUNT SG9 159 J11
Fairfield Av OXHEY WD19 132 A6
Fairfield Cl DUN/HR/TOD LU5 26 D8
 HARP AL5 47 H4
 NFNCH/WDSPK N12 137 G7
 PEND EN3 126 B8
 RAD WD7 119 J3
Fairfield Crs STVG SG1 21 M5
Fairfield Dr BROX EN10 92 D6
 RYLN/HDSTN HA2 143 G5
Fairfield Rd DUN/HR/TOD LU5 26 C8
 HOD EN11 72 E5
Fairfield Wy BAR EN5 136 E1
 HTCHE/RSTV SG4 20 A1
 STVG SG1 22 A6
Fairfolds GSTN WD25 118 C1
Fairford Av LTNE LU2 28 C4
Fairgreen EBAR EN4 123 K7
Fairgreen Ct EBAR EN4 * 123 K7
Fairgreen Rd LTN LU1 40 D6
Fairhaven LCOL/BKTW AL2 * 103 H1
Fairhaven Crs OXHEY WD19 131 L6
Fairhill HHS/BOV HP3 82 D6
Fairholme Ct PIN HA5 * 142 E1
Fairholme Rd HRW HA1 143 J7
Fairlands Wy STVG SG1 10 A4
Fairlawns PIN HA5 142 A4
 WAT WD17 117 K5
Fair Leas CSHM HP5 96 E3
Fairley Wy CHESW EN7 109 M2
Fairmead Av HARP AL5 47 G5
Fairmead Crs EDGW HA8 135 G7
Fairmead Rd LOU IG10 127 M7
Fair Oak Dr LTNE LU2 28 D6
Fairoaks Gv PEND EN3 126 B3
Fairseat Cl BUSH WD23 133 J5
Fairthorn Cl TRING HP23 57 J2
Fair Vw POTB/CUF EN6 106 F4
Fairview Dr WAT WD17 117 J2
Fairview Rd ENC/FH EN2 124 E5
 STVG SG1 10 A3
Fairview Wy EDGW HA8 134 E7
Fairway BSF CM23 44 C3
 HHS/BOV HP3 82 D6
 SBW CM21 183 R7
 WARE SG12 54 A5
Fairway Av BORE WD6 120 F6
Fairway Cl HARP AL5 46 E8
 LCOL/BKTW AL2 103 G1
Fairway Ct MLHL NW7 * 135 H6
Fairways CHES/WCR EN8 92 B8
The Fairways CHES/WCR EN8 * 92 B8
The Fairway ABLGY WD5 101 H6
 BAR EN5 136 F2
 HLWS CM18 75 K8
 MLHL NW7 135 H6
 NTHWD HA6 131 J7
 STHGT/OAK N14 137 M2
Faithfield BUSH WD23 * 13 L9
Faithorn Cl CSHM HP5 96 E4
Fakeswell La HNLW SG16 146 G7
Falcon Cl DUN/WHIP LU6 25 L8
 HAT AL10 87 L2
 NTHWD HA6 141 J2
 SBW CM21 183 N8
 STVGE SG2 34 B7
Falconer Rd BUSH WD23 132 E2
Falconers Fld HARP AL5 46 B2
Falconers Pk SBW CM21 183 P8
Falconers Rd LTNE LU2 28 F8
Falconer St BSF CM23 43 J4
Falcon Rdg BERK HP4 80 A2
Falcon Wy GSTN WD25 102 C8
 WGCE AL7 50 C5
Faldo Rd AMP/FLIT/BLC MK45 154 G1
Falkirk Gdns OXHEY WD19 132 B8
Falkland Av FBAR/BDGN N11 137 L7
Falkland Rd BAR EN5 122 C6
Fallow End WLYN AL6 177 K8
Fallowfield LTNN/LIM LU3 27 M5
 STAN HA7 133 L6
 STVGE SG2 34 A6
 WGCE AL7 50 D4
Fallowfield Cl DEN/HRF UB9 140 A3
Fallowfield Ct STAN HA7 133 L6
Fallow Ri HERT/BAY SG13 53 J7
Fallows Gn HARP AL5 46 F2
Falmer Rd EN EN1 125 J8
Falmouth Ct STALW/RED AL3 8 D2
Falstaff Gdns STAL AL1 84 F5
Falstone Gn LTNE LU2 29 J7
Fanhams Gra WARE SG12 * 54 E1
Fanhams Hall Rd WARE SG12 54 C2
Fanhams Rd WARE SG12 54 C3
Fanshaw Ct HERT/WAT SG14 52 F6
Fanshawe Crs WARE SG12 54 A3
Fanshawe St HERT/WAT SG14 52 F6
Fanshaws La HERT/BAY SG13 71 G8
Fantail La TRING HP23 57 K1
Faraday Cl LTNW/LEA LU4 27 G8
 WATW WD18 131 H2
Faraday Gdns HTCH/STOT SG5 148 A11
Faraday Rd STVGE SG2 11 L2
Far End HAT AL10 87 M3
Faringdon Rd LTNW/LEA LU4 27 G6
Faringford Cl POTB/CUF EN6 107 H5
Farland Rd HHNE HP2 82 F2
Farley Farm Rd LTN LU1 40 F4
Farley Hl LTN LU1 40 F5
Farm Av HARP AL5 46 B1
Farmbrook LTNE LU2 28 B2
Farm Cl AMS HP6 114 B5
 BAR EN5 135 M1
 BORE WD6 120 C4
 CHES/WCR EN8 110 A4
 DUN/HR/TOD LU5 26 A4
 HERT/WAT SG14 52 E7
 HLWW/ROY CM19 73 M4
 LWTH SG6 148 E12
 POTB/CUF EN6 108 C1
 RAD WD7 104 C4
 STVG SG1 10 E7
 WGCW AL8 50 A7
Farm Crs LCOL/BKTW AL2 85 L8
Farmer Ct WAB EN9 111 L7
Farmers Cl GSTN WD25 101 M7
Farmers Pl CFSP/GDCR SL9 138 A4
Farm Gn LTN LU1 41 G4
Farm Hill Rd WAB EN9 111 H8
Farmhouse Cl BROX EN10 * 92 D7
Farmhouse La HHNE HP2 62 E8
Farmlands ENC/FH EN2 124 E5
 PIN HA5 141 L6
Farm La HOD EN11 73 G5
 RKW/CH/CXG WD3 115 M7
 STDN SG11 180 E1
 STHGT/OAK N14 137 L2
Farm Pl BERK HP4 59 K8
Farm Rd EDGW HA8 135 G8
 LTN LU1 173 R2
 NTHWD HA6 131 G8
 RKW/CH/CXG WD3 114 E8
 STAL AL1 85 M1
Farmstead Rd
 KTN/HRWW/WS HA3 143 H3
Farm Wy BUSH WD23 118 F8
 NTHWD HA6 131 J7
Farnham Cl HHS/BOV HP3 98 E2
 SBW CM21 183 N8
 TRDG/WHET N20 137 G3
Farnley Gv LTNE LU2 7 K5
Farorna Wk ENC/FH EN2 124 E5
Farquhar St HERT/WAT SG14 53 G6
Farraline Rd WATW WD18 12 F6
Farrant Wy BORE WD6 120 C5
Farrer Top STALW/RED AL3 172 G4
Farriday Cl STALW/RED AL3 65 J6
Farrier Ct ROY SG8 14 D6
Farriers WARE SG12 54 E4
Farriers Cl BLDK SG7 149 J12
 HHS/BOV HP3 98 F2
 HTCHE/RSTV SG4 176 F8
Farriers End BROX EN10 92 D8
Farriers Wy BORE WD6 135 H2
 CSHM HP5 96 E2
 DUN/HR/TOD LU5 25 L5
Farringford Cl LCOL/BKTW AL2 84 E8
Farrow Cl LTNN/LIM LU3 154 H12
Farr Rd ENC/FH EN2 125 H5
Farr's La LTNE LU2 174 F8
Farthingale La WAB EN9 111 L8
Farthing Cl WAT WD17 13 H8
Farthing Dr LWTH SG6 17 G6
Farthings Cl PIN HA5 141 M8
Fauna Cl STAN HA7 134 B6
Faverolle Gn CHES/WCR EN8 110 B2
Faversham Cl TRING HP23 57 L1
Fawcett Rd STVGE SG2 33 M1
Fawn Ct BRKMPK AL9 68 A6
Fay Gn ABLGY WD5 101 H7
Feacey Down HHW HP1 61 L8
Fearney Md
 RKW/CH/CXG WD3 129 L4
Fearnley Rd WGCW AL8 50 A8
Fearnley St WATW WD18 12 E6
Featherbed La ABLGY WD5 83 M8
 HHS/BOV HP3 82 A6
Feather Dell HAT AL10 67 K8
Feathers Hl RBSF CM22 185 L3
Featherstone Gdns
 BORE WD6 121 H8
Featherston Rd STVGE SG2 34 A6
Federal Wy WATN WD24 118 A5
Felbridge Av STAN HA7 143 L3
Felbrigg Cl LTNE LU2 29 K7
Felden Cl GSTN WD25 102 B8
 PIN HA5 142 C2
Felden Dr HHS/BOV HP3 81 L6
Felden La HHS/BOV HP3 81 L6
Felden Lawns HHS/BOV HP3 81 L6
Felix Av LTNE LU2 28 E7
Fellowes La STALE/WH AL4 87 H5
Fellowes Wy STVGE SG2 33 K7
Fell Pth BORE WD6 * 135 H1
Fells Cl HTCH/STOT SG5 157 P5
Felmersham Ct LTN LU1 40 F2
Felmersham Rd LTN LU1 40 E2
Felmongers HLW CM20 75 M3
Felstead Cl LTNE LU2 * 28 D6
Felstead Rd CHES/WCR EN8 110 C6
Felstead Wy LTNE LU2 28 D7
Felton Cl BORE WD6 * 120 C4
 BROX EN10 92 D7
 LTNE LU2 29 H8
Fen End HTCH/STOT SG5 148 D5
Fennells HLWW/ROY CM19 94 F2
The Fennings AMS HP6 113 H2
Fennycroft Rd HHW HP1 61 K7
Fensome Dr DUN/HR/TOD LU5 26 C4
Fensomes Aly HHNE HP2 4 F1
Fenstanton Av
 NFNCH/WDSPK N12 137 H8
Fenton Gra HLWE CM17 76 A6
Fenwick Cl LTNN/LIM LU3 27 M4
Fenwick Rd DUN/HR/TOD LU5 26 C4
Ferguson Gv
 CHES/WCR EN8 * 110 B3
Fermor Crs LTNE LU2 29 G8
Fern Cl BROX EN10 92 D5
Ferndale MHAD SG10 181 R7
Ferndale Rd LTN LU1 40 F2
 PEND EN3 126 C3
Ferndale Ter HRW HA1 143 K6
Fern Dells HAT AL10 87 K1
Ferndene LCOL/BKTW AL2 102 D5
Ferndown NTHWD HA6 141 L4
Ferndown Cl PIN HA5 142 C2
Ferndown Rd OXHEY WD19 132 A6
Fern Dr HHNE HP2 5 H5
Fernecroft STAL AL1 85 G5
Ferney Rd CHESW EN7 91 H8
 EBAR EN4 137 L3
Fern Gv WGCW AL8 50 B3
Fernheath LTNN/LIM LU3 154 G12
Fernhill HLWS CM18 95 J1
Fern Hill La HLWS CM18 95 K1
Fernhills KGLGY WD4 101 H8
Fernleigh Ct
 RYLN/HDSTN HA2 142 F4
Fernley Cl PIN HA5 141 L6
Fernleys STALE/WH AL4 66 A7
Ferns Cl PEND EN3 126 C2
Fernside Av MLHL NW7 135 H6
Fernsleigh Cl CFSP/GDCR SL9 138 C1
The Ferns STALW/RED AL3 65 H6
Fernville La HHNE HP2 4 F2
Fern Wy GSTN WD25 117 M1
Fernwood Crs
 TRDG/WHET N20 137 K6
Ferny Hl EBAR EN4 123 K4
Ferrars Cl LTNW/LEA LU4 26 F8
Ferrers La HARP AL5 47 K8
Ferrier Rd STVGE SG2 34 A3
Ferryhills Cl OXHEY WD19 132 A6
Fesants Cft HLW CM20 75 M2
Fetherstone Cl
 POTB/CUF EN6 107 H6
Fiddle Bridge La HAT AL10 67 K7
Fidler Pl BUSH WD23 132 F2
Field Cl CSHM HP5 97 J2
 HARP AL5 47 H6
 STALE/WH AL4 65 L6
Field Crs ROY SG8 15 G6
Field End BAR EN5 121 M8
Field End Cl LTNE LU2 29 G5
 OXHEY WD19 132 C3
 TRING HP23 58 B4
Field End Rd PIN HA5 141 M7
Fielders Cl EN EN1 125 J8
Fielders Wy RAD WD7 104 C7
Fieldfare LWTH SG6 148 C12
 STVGE SG2 34 B6
Field Fare Gn LTNW/LEA LU4 26 E4
Fieldfares LCOL/BKTW AL2 104 B1
Fieldfare Wy ROY SG8 14 F5
Field Gate La RBSF CM22 167 J1
Fieldgate Rd LTNW/LEA LU4 27 H6
Fieldings Rd CHES/WCR EN8 110 D3
Field La LWTH SG6 16 D5
Field Rd HHNE HP2 82 E2
 OXHEY WD19 132 C2
Fields End TRING HP23 169 L11
Fields End La HHW HP1 61 H8
Fieldside Cots
 TRDG/WHET N20 * 136 D3
Field View Ri LCOL/BKTW AL2 102 C3
Field View Rd POTB/CUF EN6 106 E7
Field Wy CFSP/GDCR SL9 138 B2
 HHS/BOV HP3 98 E1
 HOD EN11 72 F3
 AMSS HP7 112 F7
 RKW/CH/CXG WD3 129 M4
Fieldway BERK HP4 80 C3
 TRING HP23 58 B4
 WARE SG12 72 F1
Fifth Av GSTN WD25 118 B1
 LWTH SG6 17 G3
Fifth Avenue Allende Av
 HLW CM20 2 E4
Fildyke Rd SHFD SG17 146 E3
Figtree Hill HHNE HP2 82 B1
Filey Cl STVG SG1 32 E2
Fillebrook Av EN EN1 125 J6
Fillingham Wy HAT AL10 67 J6
Filmer Rd LTNW/LEA LU4 27 J5
Finch Cl BAR EN5 136 E1
 HAT AL10 87 L2
 LTNW/LEA LU4 26 E5
Finchdale HHW HP1 4 A3
Finches End STVGE SG2 34 F1
The Finches HERT/BAY SG13 53 M7
 HTCHE/RSTV SG4 157 Q6
Finch Gn RKW/CH/CXG WD3 115 K8
Finch La AMSS HP7 113 L6
 BUSH WD23 132 E1
Finchley Pk
 NFNCH/WDSPK N12 137 G7
Finchley Vls
 NFNCH/WDSPK N12 * 137 H7
Finchmoor HLWS CM18 75 H8
Finch Rd BERK HP4 79 L1
Fine Bush La DEN/HRF UB9 140 F8
Finley Rd HARP AL5 47 H2
Finsbury Rd LTNW/LEA LU4 27 H4
Finucane Ri BUSH WD23 133 G5
Finway LTN LU1 40 E1
Finway Ct WATW WD18 * 12 B8
Finway Rd HHNE HP2 62 F6
Fiona Ct ENC/FH EN2 * 124 F7
Firbank WGCW AL8 * 50 A7
Firbank Cl ENC/FH EN2 125 G8
 LTNN/LIM LU3 27 G1
Firbank Dr OXHEY WD19 132 C3
Firbank Rd STALW/RED AL3 65 K6
Fir Cl STVGE SG2 33 K8
Firecrest LWTH SG6 148 C12
Firethorn Cl EDGW HA8 135 G7
Firlands BSF CM23 43 L3
Fir Pk HLWW/ROY CM19 74 F8
Firs Cl HAT AL10 87 M1
 HTCH/STOT SG5 157 M5
Firs Dr STALE/WH AL4 175 N12
Firs La POTB/CUF EN6 106 F7
The Firs Pk BRKMPK AL9 * 88 E5
First Av AMSS HP7 113 G6
 DUN/WHIP LU6 38 F2
 GSTN WD25 118 A1
 HLW CM20 3 G4
 STSD CM24 167 K11
First Avenue Mandela Av
 HLW CM20 2 E4
The Firs CHESW EN7 91 J8
 EDGW HA8 * 135 H7
 HARP AL5 * 47 H3
 STAL AL1 85 M6
 TRDG/WHET N20 137 H4
 TRING HP23 58 B4
 WGCW AL8 50 A3
Firs Wk NTHWD HA6 141 H1
 WLYN AL6 177 R12
Fir Tree Cl HHS/BOV HP3 82 E3
Fir Tree Ct BORE WD6 120 D8
Fir Tree Hl RKW/CH/CXG WD3 116 E3
Fir Tree Wk EN EN1 125 J7
Firway WLYN AL6 177 M10
Firway Cl WLYN AL6 177 M10
Firwood Av STALE/WH AL4 86 C2
Fisher Cl AMP/FLIT/BLC MK45 154 H2
 KGLGY WD4 100 E3
 PEND EN3 126 E3

Fishermans Wy HOD EN11.....73 H5
Fisher Rd
　KTN/HRWW/WS HA3.....143 K4
Fishers CI CHES/WCR EN8.....110 C8
　STDN SG13.....163 P10
Fishers Gn STVG SG1.....20 E8
Fisher's Green Rd STVG SG1.....3 F1
Fishers Hatch HLW CM20.....3 H5
Fishers Md STDN SG11.....163 P10
Fishponds Rd HTCH/STOT SG5.....157 N5
Fishery Pas HHW HP1.....4 B6
Fishery Rd HHW HP1.....4 A6
Fish HI ROY SG8.....14 E7
Fish Street Farm
　STALW/RED AL3.....173 R12
Fitzjohn Av BAR EN5.....136 C1
Fitzroy Av LTNE LU3.....27 M6
Fitzwarin CI LTNN/LIM LU3.....27 J2
Fitzwilliam CI
　TRDG/WHET N20.....137 K4
Fitzwilliams Ct HLWE CM17.....76 F4
Five Acres CSHM HP5.....97 H4
Five Acres Av LCOL/BKTW AL2.....102 C8
Five Fields CI OXHEY WD19.....132 C5
Five Oaks HAT AL10 *.....87 M3
　LTN LU1.....40 D5
Five Springs LTNN/LIM LU3.....27 J1
Flagstaff CI WAB EN9.....110 F7
Flagstaff Rd WAB EN9.....110 F7
The Flags HHNE HP2.....82 F2
Flag Wk PIN HA5.....141 L8
Flambard Rd HRW HA1.....143 L8
Flamstead Gn
　STALW/RED AL3.....63 L1
Flamstead End Rd
　CHES/WCR EN8.....109 M2
Flandrian CI PEND EN3.....126 E5
Flash La ENC/FH EN2.....125 G3
Flatfield Rd HHS/BOV HP3.....5 K5
The Flatlets HHNE HP2.....172 B9
Flaunden Bottom CSHM HP5.....114 C4
Flaunden HI HHS/BOV HP3.....98 D7
Flaunden La HHS/BOV HP3.....98 A8
Flavian CI STALW/RED AL3.....84 D4
Flax Ms STALW/RED AL3 *.....172 G4
Flecker CI STAN HA7.....133 K3
Flecks La ROY SG8.....145 Q2
Fleet CI RSLP HA4.....141 L8
The Fleet ROY SG8.....14 D7
Fleetwood Crs STVG SG1.....32 D2
Fleetwood Wy OXHEY WD19.....132 A7
Fleming CI CHEW EN7.....91 L4
Fleming Crs HERT/WAT AL7.....52 E7
Fleming Rd HTCH/STOT SG5.....148 A11
Fleming Wk HHNE HP2.....82 B2
Fletcher Wy HHNE HP2.....62 A8
Flexley Md WGCE AL7.....50 D4
Flex Meadow
　HLWW/ROY CM19.....74 C6
Flight Pth HNLW SG16.....147 K6
Flinders CI STAL AL1.....11 M9
　STVG SG2.....34 A4
Flint CI LTNN/LIM LU3.....27 J2
Flint Copse STALW/RED AL3.....46 A3
The Flintings HHNE HP2.....172 B9
Flint Rd LWTH SG6.....17 C1
Flint Wy STALW/RED AL3.....65 G6
Flitch Wy RBSF CM22.....45 K2
Flora CI STAN HA7.....134 B6
Flora Gv STAL AL1.....9 J7
Floral Dr LCOL/BKTW AL2.....86 B4
　LTNN/LIM LU3.....27 H3
Florence Av ENC/FH EN2.....125 G7
　LTNN/LIM LU3.....27 H3
Florence CI DUN/HR/TOD LU5.....26 C3
　GSTN WD25.....117 L1
　HLWE CM17.....76 A7
Florence Dr ENC/FH EN2.....125 G7
Florence St HTCH/STOT SG5.....157 P5
Florida CI BUSH WD23.....133 H5
Floriston CI STAN HA7.....143 M3
Floriston Gdns STAN HA7.....143 M3
Flower La MLHL NW7.....135 K8
Flowers Wy LTN LU1.....6 F6
Flowton Gv HARP AL5.....46 C4
Fogerty CI PEND EN3.....126 F3
Fold Cft HLW CM20.....2 A1
Foldingshott KNEB SG3.....177 R6
Folkington Cnr
　NFNCH/WDSPK N12.....136 D8
Follett Dr ABLGY WD5.....101 K5
Folly Av STALW/RED AL3.....8 D3
Folly CI HTCHE/RSTV SG4.....157 M2
　RAD WD7.....119 K2
Folly Flds STALW/WH AL4.....47 M3
Folly La LTN LU1.....40 B5
　STALW/RED AL3.....8 C4
Folly Pathway RAD WD7.....119 K1
The Folly BUNT SG9.....158 H10
　HERT/WAT SG14.....52 A6
Folly Vw WARE SG12.....54 F8
Fontmell CI STALW/RED AL3.....9 H1
Fontwell CI
　KTN/HRWW/WS HA3.....143 J2
Football CI BLDK SG7.....149 J12
Forbes Av POTB/CUF EN6.....107 H7
Force End HTCHE/RSTV SG4.....18 A8
Ford CI BUSH WD23.....119 G8
Fordham CI BLDK SG7.....145 K12
Fordham Rd EBAR EN4.....123 J4
　ROY SG8.....14 F8
Fordham Ter ROY SG8 *.....151 M6
Ford HI STDN SG11.....42 B1
Ford La STVG SG2.....34 D6
Ford St STDN SG11.....163 Q7
Fordwich CI HERT/WAT SG14.....52 C5
Fordwich HI HERT/WAT SG14.....52 C5
Fordwich Ri HERT/WAT SG14.....52 C5
Fordwich Rd WGCW AL8.....50 A8
Forebury Av SBW CM21.....183 R7
The Forebury SBW CM21.....183 R7
Forefield LCOL/BKTW AL2.....102 E1
Forelands Wy CSHM HP5.....97 C6
Forest Av HHS/BOV HP3.....5 G4
Forest CI WAB EN9.....127 M3
Forest CI CHESW EN7.....109 J4
Foresthall Rd STSD CM24.....166 F9
Forest La RAD WD7.....103 M5
Fore St BRKMPK AL9.....68 C7
　HERT/WAT SG14.....52 A6
　HLWE CM17.....76 A1
　HTCHE/RSTV SG4.....17 C2
　PIN HA5.....141 K6
Forest Rd CHES/WCR EN8.....110 D8
　GSTN WD25.....101 M7
　PEND EN3.....126 C2
Forest Rw STVG SG1.....33 K8
Forest Wk BUSH WD23.....118 D5

Forest Wy HLWE CM17.....76 F4
　HLWE CM17.....185 J11
　HLWS CM18.....95 M1
　RBSF CM22.....45 J3
　RBSF CM22.....185 J9
Forge CI HTCH/STOT SG5.....157 P5
　KGLGY WD4.....99 L5
Forge End LCOL/BKTW AL2.....84 B8
Forge La NTHWD HA6.....141 J2
　WLYN AL6.....176 H12
Form CI RAD WD7.....104 C5
Forres St HOD EN11.....72 A5
Forrest Crs LTNE LU2.....28 E6
Forresters Dr WGCE AL7.....51 G8
Fortnums Acre STAN HA7.....143 K1
Fortuna CI STAL AL1.....34 A1
Fortune La BORE WD6.....134 B2
The Fortunes HLWS CM18.....75 P7
Forty HI EN EN1.....125 K3
Forum PI HAT AL10 *.....67 L7
The Forum STVG SG1.....10 C4
Forward Cr
　KTN/HRWW/WS HA3.....143 J5
Foster CI CHES/WCR EN8.....110 B4
　STVG SG1.....21 G8
Foster Dr HTCHE/RSTV SG4.....157 P4
Foster Rd HHW HP1.....4 B6
Foster St HLWE CM17.....76 D7
Foston CI LTNN/LIM LU3.....27 K4
Fotheringham Rd EN EN1.....125 J7
Fotherley Rd
　RKW/CH/CXG WD3.....129 K5
Founceley Av WARE SG12.....179 P11
Foundary Ga CHES/WCR EN8.....110 C7
Founders Rd HOD EN11.....72 F4
Fountain Dr HERT/BAY SG13.....53 K6
Fountain Farm HLWS CM18.....75 K7
Fountain PI WAB EN9.....111 G8
Fountains Rd LTNN/LIM LU3.....28 A6
Fouracres LWTH SG6.....16 E7
　PEND EN3.....126 C5
Four Acres STVG SG1.....10 D1
　WGCE AL7.....68 C1
Fouracres Rd HHS/BOV HP3.....5 L7
The Four Acres SBW CM21.....184 A1
Fouracres Wk HHS/BOV HP3.....5 L7
Fourdrinier Wy HHS/BOV HP3.....5 C9
Four Limes STALW/WH AL4.....48 E1
Four Oaks CSHM HP5.....96 E1
Fourth Av GSTN WD25.....118 B3
　HLWW/ROY CM19.....2 B6
　LTNN/LIM LU3.....27 J1
　LWTH SG6.....17 G2
Four Trees LCOL/BKTW AL2.....84 F6
The Four Tubs BUSH WD23.....133 H3
Fourways RBSF CM22.....167 L4
Fovant CI HARP AL5.....47 G7
Fowlers Dr SHFD SC17.....146 D3
Fowley CI CHES/WCR EN8.....110 D8
Fowley Mead Pk
　CHES/WCR EN8 *.....110 D8
Foxbury CI LTNE LU2.....28 E6
Fox CI BGSW SG18.....144 D4
　BORE WD6.....134 B2
　BUSH WD23.....132 F1
　TRING HP23.....58 A4
Fox Cnr ROY SG8.....145 M4
Foxcroft STAL AL1.....11 M8
Foxdell HERT/WAT SG14.....70 A2
Fox Dells DUN/WHIP LU6.....39 G4
Foxdells HERT/WAT SG14.....70 A2
Foxdells La BSF CM23.....166 B11
Foxdell Wy CFSP/GDCR SL9.....128 C8
Foxes Dr CHESW EN7.....109 K3
Foxes La POTB/CUF EN6.....108 C2
Foxes Pde WAB EN9 *.....111 G7
Foxfield STVG SG2.....34 A6
Foxfield CI NTHWD HA6.....141 K1
Foxglove Bank ROY SG8.....15 G8
Foxglove CI BSF CM23.....43 J3
　HAT AL10.....87 M1
　HOD EN11.....73 C4
The Foxgloves HHW HP1.....81 J9
Foxglove Wy LTNN/LIM LU3.....28 B7
　WLYN AL6.....176 H12
Foxgrove Pth OXHEY WD19.....132 B8
Foxhill WATN WD24.....117 L2
　LTNE LU2.....28 C4
Fox HI ROY SG8.....145 M4
Fox Hill Rd ROY SG8.....145 M4
Foxholes Av HERT/BAY SG13.....53 L7
Foxhollows HAT AL10.....67 M6
　LCOL/BKTW AL2.....86 A8
Foxlands CI GSTN WD25.....101 L8
Foxley Dr BSF CM23.....44 C1
Foxley Gv WLYN AL6.....50 C1
Foxleys OXHEY WD19.....132 C6
Foxmead Ct ENC/FH EN2.....124 D7
Fox Rd STVG SG1.....10 C5
　TRING HP23.....58 A3
Fox's La BRKMPK AL9.....88 C2
Foxton Rd HOD EN11.....72 D7
Foxwood Cha WAB EN9.....127 G2
Foxwood CI MLHL NW7.....135 J7
Foyle CI STVG SG1.....22 A6
Framfield CI
　NFNCH/WDSPK N12.....136 D8
Frampton Rd POTB/CUF EN6.....107 G4
Frampton St HERT/WAT SG14.....53 H7
Frances St CSHM HP5.....97 G4
Franchise St CSHM HP5.....97 G4
Francis Av STALW/RED AL3.....8 H7
Francis CI HTCH/STOT SG5.....148 C11
　HTCHE/RSTV SG4.....17 M3
Francis Rd BLDK SG7.....144 C12
　PIN HA5.....141 K6
　WARE SG12.....54 B3
　WATW WD18.....13 H6
Francis St LTN LU1.....6 C4
Francis Yd CSHM HP5 *.....96 F5
Francklin Gdns EDGW HA8.....134 E6
Frankland CI
　RKW/CH/CXG WD3.....130 E3
Frankland Rd
　RKW/CH/CXG WD3.....130 F2
Frank Lester Wy LTNE LU2.....174 B1
Franklin Av
　AMP/FLIT/BLC MK45.....154 H2
　CHESW EN7.....109 J4
Franklin CI HHS/BOV HP3.....5 H9
　HTCH/STOT SG5.....156 H1
　STALE/WH AL4.....87 H1
　TRDG/WHET N20.....137 J3
Franklin Gdns
　HTCHE/RSTV SG4.....17 M3
Franklin Rd DUN/WHIP LU6.....38 D1
　WAT WD17.....13 G1
Franklin's Rd STVG SG1.....33 J1
Frank Martin Ct CHESW EN7.....91 M5
Franshams BUSH WD23 *.....133 J5

Fraser Cnr STVG SG2 *.....33 M2
Fraser Rd CHES/WCR EN8.....110 C2
Fraziers Ct PEND EN3.....126 A3
Frederick's PI
　NFNCH/WDSPK N12.....137 G2
Frederick CI LTNE LU2.....6 F3
Frederick Street Pas LTNE LU2 *.....6 F3
Fred Millard Ct STVG SG1 *.....10 F5
Freeman Av LTNN/LIM LU3.....27 M1
Freeman CI CSHM HP5.....97 C4
Freemans CI DUN/HR/TOD LU5.....25 P1
　HTCH/STOT SG5.....157 L4
Freewaters CI
　HTCH/STOT SG5.....157 N1
Freman Dr BUNT SG9.....158 H9
French Horn Ct WARE SG12 *.....54 B3
French Horn La HAT AL10.....67 M7
French's Av DUN/WHIP LU6.....25 J7
French's Ct LTNE LU2.....54 F8
French's Ga DUN/WHIP LU6.....25 J7
Frensham CHESW EN7.....91 K1
Frensham Dr HTCHE/RSTV SG4.....16 A7
Freshfield Dr STHGT/OAK N14.....137 M3
Freshwater CI LTNN/LIM LU3.....27 J2
Freshwaters HLW CM20.....3 H1
Fresson Rd STVG SG1.....21 G8
Freston Gdns EBAR EN4.....137 L1
Fretherne Chambers
　WGCW AL8 *.....50 B7
Fretherne Rd WGCW AL8.....50 B7
Friars Av TRDG/WHET N20.....137 J6
Friars CI LTN LU1.....6 A9
Friarscroft BROX EN10.....92 A3
Friars Fld HARP AL5.....59 J6
Friars La RBSF CM22.....184 H8
Friars Rd HTCHE/RSTV SG4.....17 M8
　STDN SG11.....164 C8
The Friars HLWW/ROY CM19.....74 F7
Friars Wk DUN/WHIP LU6.....38 F2
Friars Wash STALW/RED AL3 *.....173 P7
Friars Wy BUSH WD23.....118 D5
　KGLGY WD4.....100 E4
Friars Wd BSF CM23.....44 C1
Friary CI NFNCH/WDSPK N12.....137 J3
Friary Fld DUN/WHIP LU6.....38 F1
Friary Pk
　NFNCH/WDSPK N12 *.....137 J2
Friary Rd NFNCH/WDSPK N12.....137 H7
The Friary CHES/WCR EN8 *.....110 C8
Friary Wy NFNCH/WDSPK N12.....137 J7
Friday Furlong
　HTCH/STOT SG5.....157 L5
Friedberg Av BSF CM23.....43 H6
Friendless La STALW/RED AL3.....172 H4
Friends Av CHES/WCR EN8.....110 B6
Friern Barnet La
　TRDG/WHET N20.....137 H6
Friern Barnet Rd
　FBAR/BDGN N11.....137 L3
Friern CI CHESW EN7.....91 J4
Friern Mount Dr
　TRDG/WHET N20.....137 G3
Friern Pk NFNCH/WDSPK N12.....137 H8
Friern Watch Av
　NFNCH/WDSPK N12.....137 H7
Friesian CI LTNN/LEA LU4.....26 A5
Frimley Rd HHW HP1.....81 J1
Fringewood CI NTHWD HA6.....140 F3
Frinton CI OXHEY WD19.....131 M5
Friston Gn LTNE LU2.....29 H8
Frithsden Copse BERK HP4.....60 D5
Frithwood Av NTHWD HA6.....141 K1
Frobisher CI BUSH WD23.....132 C2
Frobisher Dr STVG SG2.....11 M1
Frobisher Ms ENC/FH EN2.....125 H8
Frobisher Rd STAL AL1.....86 A4
Frobisher Wy HAT AL10.....67 J1
Froghall La STVG SG2.....22 F8
Frogmoor La
　RKW/CH/CXG WD3.....130 D5
Frogmore LCOL/BKTW AL2.....103 J1
Frogmore HI HERT/WAT SG14.....178 C3
Frogmore Rd HHS/BOV HP3.....5 G9
Frogmore St TRING HP23.....57 L7
Frognal Av HRW HA1.....143 L8
Frogs Hall La STDN SG11.....162 D10
Frome CI LTNN/LEA LU4.....27 J5
Frome Sq HHNE HP2.....62 B3
Front St LTN LU1.....41 G8
The Front BERK HP4.....60 F4
Frowick CI BRKMPK AL9.....87 M5
Frowycke Crs POTB/CUF EN6.....105 J1
Fryer CI CSHM HP5.....97 H7
Fry Rd STVG SG2.....34 A3
Fryth Md STALW/RED AL3.....8 A4
Fulbeck Wy RYLN/HDSTN HA2.....143 L6
Fulbourne Ct LTNN/LEA LU4.....27 J7
Fulford Gv OXHEY WD19.....131 M5
Fuller CI BUSH WD23.....133 H5
Fuller Gdns WATN WD24.....117 K3
Fuller Rd WATN WD24.....117 K3
Fuller's CI HLWE CM17.....76 F6
Fullers CI LWTH SG6.....16 C2
Fuller's Md AMS HP6 *.....115 K7
Fullerton CI STALW/RED AL3.....172 G5
Fuller Wy RKW/CH/CXG WD3.....130 E1
Fulling Mill La WLYN AL6.....176 H12
Fulmar CI STVG SG1.....34 A1
Fulmer Wy CFSP/GDCR SL9.....138 C8
Fulmore CI HARP AL5.....47 H1
Fulton CI STVG SG1.....10 A5
Fulton Crs BSF CM23.....166 E12
Furham Fld PIN HA5.....142 A2
Furlay CI LWTH SG6.....16 B2
Furlong La DUN/WHIP LU6.....38 A2
Furlongs HHW HP1.....81 L1
The Furlong TRING HP23.....57 L7
Furlong Wy STVG SG12.....54 D7
Furmston Ct LWTH SG6.....16 C2
Furness Rd LTNN/LIM LU3.....39 G2
Furriers CI BSF CM23.....43 A4
The Furrows LTNN/LIM LU3.....27 M1
Furtherfield ABLGY WD5.....101 K5
Furthermost HHNE HP2.....82 F3
Furzebushes La
　LCOL/BKTW AL2.....84 C7
Furze CI LTNE LU2.....27 M8
　OXHEY WD19.....132 A8
Furzedown STVG SG2.....11 M6
Furzedown CI CHES/WCR EN8.....109 M2
Furzefield Ct POTB/CUF EN6 *.....106 C5
Furzefield Rd WGCE AL7.....50 C8
Furze Gv ROY SG8.....14 F8
Furzehill Pde BORE WD6.....120 B8
Furzehill Rd BORE WD6.....120 B8
Furzen CI DUN/WHIP LU6.....39 G4

Furzen Crs HAT AL10.....87 K3
Furze Rd HHW HP1.....81 J9
Furze Vw RKW/CH/CXG WD3.....129 G2
Fyfield Rd EN EN1.....125 J7

G

Gable CI ABLGY WD5.....101 J6
　PIN HA5.....142 D2
Gables Av BORE WD6.....120 D7
Gables CI CFSP/GDCR SL9.....128 C2
Gaddesden Crs GSTN WD25.....102 B8
Gaddesden Gv WGCE AL7.....50 F8
Gaddesden Rw BUSH WD23 *.....119 C8
Gade Av WATW WD18.....117 J8
Gade Bank RKW/CH/CXG WD3.....117 H8
Gade CI HHW HP1.....61 M7
　WATW WD18.....117 J8
Gade Valley CI KGLGY WD4.....100 E2
Gade View Gdns KGLGY WD4.....101 C6
Gade View Rd HHS/BOV HP3.....82 A6
Gadmore La TRING HP23.....57 J6
Gadswell CI GSTN WD25.....118 B2
Gage CI ROY SG8.....14 E5
Gainsborough Av STAL AL1.....9 J4
Gainsborough Dr
　DUN/HR/TOD LU5.....26 B4
Gainsborough Rd
　NFNCH/WDSPK N12.....136 F8
Gainsford Crs GSTN WD25.....102 B8
Gainswood WGCE AL7.....50 C8
Galdana Av BAR EN5.....123 G8
Gale Ct HARP/FLIT/BLC MK45.....155 J3
Gallants Farm Rd EBAR EN4.....137 J3
Gall End La STSD CM24.....166 H6
The Galleons AMSS HP7 *.....113 G4
Galley Gn HERT/BAY SG13.....72 E3
Galley HI HHW HP1.....61 L8
Galleyhill Rd WAB EN9.....111 J1
Galley La BAR EN5.....121 M7
Galliard CI LTNN/LIM LU3.....27 H1
Galloway CI BROX EN10.....92 A3
Galloway Rd BSF CM23.....43 M1
Galloway Pth HHNE HP2.....62 D7
Gallows HI KGLGY WD4.....101 G6
Gallows Hill La ABLGY WD5.....101 C6
Galston Rd LTNN/LIM LU3.....27 H1
Galva CI EBAR EN4.....123 L6
Games Rd EBAR EN4.....123 J7
Gammon CI HHW HP1.....5 L5
Gammons Farm CI
　WATN WD24.....117 K2
Gammons La WATN WD24.....117 J3
Gamnel Ms TRING HP23.....169 M11
Ganders Ash GSTN WD25.....101 L8
Gandhi Ct WATN WD24 *.....13 J1
Gangies HI SBW CM21.....183 L6
Gant Ct WAB EN9.....111 K8
Ganton Wk OXHEY WD19.....132 C7
Garamonde Pl HHNE HP2.....62 D7
Gaping La HTCH/STOT SG5.....157 L6
Garden CI LTNN/LIM LU3.....27 L5
　STALE/WH AL4.....48 B4
　WGCE AL7.....50 C6
Garden End AMS HP6.....113 J3
Garden Fld STVG SG2.....34 C7
Garden Field La BERK HP4.....80 D3
Gardenia Av LTNN/LIM LU3.....27 L5
Garden La ROY SG8.....14 E8
Garden Reach CSTG HP8.....114 B7
Garden Rw HTCH/STOT SG5.....157 P5
Gardens End
　DUN/HR/TOD LU5 *.....26 A4
The Gardens BLDK SG7.....17 J1
　BRKMPK AL9.....106 C1
　HRW HA1.....143 C8
　HTCH/STOT SG5.....148 C7
　PIN HA5.....142 D8
　WAT WD17.....12 A1
Garden Ter WARE SG12 *.....53 J1
Garden Terrace Rd HLWE CM17.....76 B7
Garden Wk ROY SG8.....14 F6
　STVG SG1.....10 E5
Gardiners La BLDK SG7.....149 P1
The Gardiners HLWE CM17.....75 M6
Gardner's CI DUN/WHIP LU6.....38 D1
Gardners CI FBAR/BDGN N11.....137 J3
Garfield St WATN WD24.....117 M4
Garland CI CHES/WCR EN8.....110 C5
Garland Rd STAN HA7.....143 M4
Garland Wy
　RAYLNE/WEN HP22.....168 C12
Garnault Rd EN EN1.....125 K4
Garner Dr BROX EN10.....92 C8
Garners CI CFSP/GDCR SL9.....138 C1
Garners End CFSP/GDCR SL9.....138 C1
Garners Rd CFSP/GDCR SL9.....138 C1
Garnett CI WATN WD24.....118 A2
Garnett Dr LCOL/BKTW AL2.....102 C3
Garrard Wy STALE/WH AL4.....48 A1
Garratts Rd BUSH WD23.....133 C3
Garrett CI CSHM HP5.....97 G6
Garretts Md LTNE LU2.....28 C7
Garsmouth Wy GSTN WD25.....118 B2
Garson Gv CSHM HP5.....96 E5
Garston Crs GSTN WD25.....102 A8
Garston Dr GSTN WD25.....102 A8
Garston La GSTN WD25.....102 A8
Garthland Dr BAR EN5.....135 M1
Garth Rd LWTH SG6.....16 C1
The Garth ABLGY WD5.....101 J6
　HHNE HP2.....82 F3
Gartlet Rd WAT WD17.....13 G3
Gascoyne Wy HERT/BAY SG13.....53 H8
Gas La AV1.....152 G10
Gatcombe Wy EBAR EN4.....123 K7
Gate CI BORE WD6.....134 C1
Gate Cots EDGW HA8 *.....134 C5
Gatecroft HHS/BOV HP3.....5 H9
Gate End NTHWD HA6.....141 L2
Gatehill Gdns LTNN/LIM LU3.....154 H12
Gatehill Rd NTHWD HA6.....141 K2
Gatehouse Ms BUNT SG9.....159 J10

Gater Dr ENC/FH EN2.....125 H5
Gatesbury Wy STVG SG11.....163 P10
Gatesdene CI BERK HP4.....171 J9
Gateshead Rd BORE WD6.....120 D6
Gates Orch
　RAYLNE/WEN HP22.....168 B12
Gates Wy STVG SG1.....10 D5
Gateway CI NTHWD HA6.....140 H2
The Gateways CHESW EN7.....109 H2
The Gateway WATW WD18.....131 J4
Gatwick CI BSF CM23.....166 D12
Gauldie Wy STDN SG11.....163 P11
Gaumont Ap WAT WD17.....12 F3
Gaunts Wy LWTH SG6.....148 D11
Gaveston Dr BERK HP4.....59 M7
Gawdrey CI CSHM HP5.....97 H5
Gawthorne Av MLHL NW7.....136 C8
Gayland Av LTNE LU2.....7 H4
Gayton CI AMS HP6.....113 J5
　LTNN/LIM LU3.....27 L5
Gayton Rd HRW HA1.....143 K8
Gaywood Av CHES/WCR EN8.....110 B4
Geddes Rd BUSH WD23.....119 G8
Geescroft Wk HARP AL5.....46 E7
Geisthorp Ct WAB EN9.....111 L6
Gelding CI LTNN/LEA LU4.....26 D4
The Generals Wk PEND EN3.....126 C3
Genotin Rd EN EN1.....125 H7
Gentleman's Rw ENC/FH EN2.....125 G7
Gentlemens Fld WARE SG12.....53 M2
George Gange Wy
　KTN/HRWW/WS HA3.....143 K8
George La ROY SG8.....14 E7
George Leighton Ct STVG SG2.....11 L6
George Lighton Ct STVG SG2 *.....11 L6
George Lovell Dr PEND EN3.....126 C3
Georges Md BORE WD6.....134 C2
George St BERK HP4.....80 B5
　CSHM HP5.....97 G4
　DUN/WHIP LU6.....25 J8
　HERT/WAT SG14.....53 G6
　HHNE HP2.....82 B3
　LTN LU1.....6 F4
　STALW/RED AL3.....8 E4
　STALW/RED AL3.....172 G4
　WATW WD18.....13 G6
George St West LTN LU1.....6 F6
George's Wood Rd
　BRKMPK AL9.....88 C3
George V Av PIN HA5.....142 D4
George V Wy
　RKW/CH/CXG WD3.....115 L2
George Wk WARE SG12.....54 B3
Georgewood Rd HHS/BOV HP3 *.....82 D7
Georgian CI STAN HA7.....143 L2
Gerard Av BSF CM23.....43 L5
Gerard Rd HRW HA1.....143 K8
Germains CI BUSH WD23.....96 F6
Germain St CSHM HP5.....96 F6
Gernon Rd LWTH SG6.....16 E4
Gernon Wk LWTH SG6.....16 E4
Gerrard Gdns PIN HA5.....141 L7
Gertrude Peake PI
　STALW/RED AL3 *.....173 R12
Gew's Cnr CHES/WCR EN8.....110 C5
Ghyll Gdns BERK HP4.....61 L5
Giant Tree HI BUSH WD23.....133 H5
Gibb Cft HLWS CM18.....95 J1
Gibbons CI BORE WD6.....120 C5
　STALE/WH AL4.....66 A4
Gibbons Wy KNEB SG3.....177 M5
Gibbs CI CHES/WCR EN8.....110 B5
Gibbs Couch OXHEY WD19.....132 B6
Gibbs Fld BSF CM23.....43 K4
Gibbs Gn EDGW HA8.....135 C7
Gibson CI HTCHE/RSTV SG4.....157 K6
Gidian Ct LCOL/BKTW AL2.....103 C1
Gifford's La STDN SG11.....162 E11
Gilbert Ct HARP AL5.....46 F1
Gilbert Rd DEN/HRF UB9.....140 B4
　PIN HA5.....141 K6
Gilbert St PEND EN3.....126 A3
Gilbert Wy BERK HP4.....79 L1
Gilbey Av BSF CM23.....44 B3
Gilbey Crs STSD CM24.....166 F5
Gildea CI PIN HA5.....142 C2
Gilded Acre DUN/WHIP LU6.....39 G4
Gilden CI HLWE CM17 *.....76 C1
Gilden Wy HLWE CM17.....76 B1
Gilder CI LTNN/LIM LU3.....27 L1
Gilderdale LTNN/LEA LU4.....26 E5
Gilders SBW CM21.....183 P7
Giles CI STALE/WH AL4.....66 A4
Gillam St LTN LU1.....7 G4
Gillan Gn BUSH WD23.....133 G5
Gill CI WATW WD18.....131 G2
Gillian Av STAL AL1.....85 C6
Gilliat's Gn RKW/CH/CXG WD3.....115 H8
Gillison CI LWTH SG6.....16 C1
Gills HI RAD WD7.....119 K1
Gills Hill La RAD WD7.....119 K1
Gills Hollow RAD WD7.....119 K1
Gillum Ct EBAR EN4.....137 K4
Gilmour CI CHESW EN7.....125 K1
Gilpin CI DUN/HR/TOD LU5.....26 B4
Gilpin Gn HARP AL5.....46 E1
Gilpin Rd WARE SG12.....54 C5
Gilpin's Gallop WARE SG12.....79 P7
Gilpin's Ride BERK HP4.....60 C8
Gilray Rd HHNE HP2.....82 C7
Gisland WAB EN9.....127 J1
Gilsted Ct STALW/RED AL3.....65 H6
Gilston Pk HLW CM20.....182 G10
Gilwell CI CHING E4.....127 L8
Gilwell La CHING E4.....127 L8
Gingers CI RAYLNE/WEN HP22.....168 C12
Ginns Rd BUNT SG9.....165 K1
Gippeswyck CI PIN HA5.....142 B1
Gipsy La BSF CM23.....166 E9
　KNEB SG3.....177 L6
　LBUZ LU7.....36 A1
Girdle Rd HTCHE/RSTV SG4.....157 Q3
Girons CI HTCHE/RSTV SG4.....157 R6
Girtin Rd BUSH WD23.....132 F1
Girton CI CHES/WCR EN8.....110 B5
Girton Rd RKW/CH/CXG WD3.....131 G1
Gisburne Wy WATN WD24.....117 L2
Gladback Wy ENC/FH EN2.....124 D7
Gladden Ct HLWS CM18.....95 J1
Gladding Rd CHESW EN7.....90 F7
Gladeside STALE/WH AL4.....66 B7
The Glades HHW HP1.....81 J1
The Glade ENC/FH EN2.....124 E7
　LWTH SG6.....16 F7
　NFNCH/WDSPK N12.....137 H7
　WGCW AL8.....50 A5
The Gladeway WAB EN9.....111 M4
Gladsdale Dr PIN HA5.....141 L6
Gladsmuir Rd BAR EN5.....122 C6
Gladstone Av LTN LU1.....6 E1

Gladstone Dr HTCH/STOT SG5 148 B11
Gladstone Pl BAR EN5 * 122 B8
Gladstone Rd CSHM HP5 97 G5
HOD EN11 72 F6
WARE SG12 54 A3
WARE SG12 179 P1
WAT WD17 13 H4
Gladstone Wy
KTN/HRWW/WS HA3 143 J5
Glaisdale LTNW/LEA LU4 27 G4
Glamis Cl CHESW EN7 109 L3
HHNE HP2 62 F4
Glamis Pl HHNE HP2 5 H1
Glanfield HHNE HP2 62 C7
Glanleam Rd STAN HA7 134 B7
Glanville Ms STAN HA7 133 L8
Gleave Cl STAL AL1 85 M1
Glebe Av ARL/CHE SG15 147 Q2
ENC/FH EN2 124 F7
Glebe Cl BRKMPK AL9 69 K7
CFSP/GDCR SL9 138 B3
HERT/WAT SG14 53 H5
HERT/WAT SG14 178 F6
HHS/BOV HP3 5 J9
LBUZ LU7 169 P4
Glebe Cots BRKMPK AL9 69 K7
Glebe Ct BSF CM23 44 B1
STAN HA7 134 A8
Glebe End RBSF CM22 167 L4
Glebelands HLW CM20 3 K1
Glebe La BAR EN5 135 L1
Glebe Rd CFSP/GDCR SL9 138 A3
HERT/WAT SG14 53 H5
LWTH SG6 16 E2
STAN HA7 134 A8
WLYN AL6 176 H12
The Glebe GSTN WD25 102 A7
HLW CM20 3 H4
HTCHE/RSTV SG4 * 20 A7
KGLGY WD4 100 E3
STVGE SG2 11 M2
Glebe Wy AMS HP6 113 H2
Gleed Av BUSH WD23 133 H5
Glemsford Cl LTNW/LEA LU4 26 F3
Glemsford Dr HARP AL5 47 H3
Glenbrook North ENC/FH EN2 124 D8
Glenbrook South ENC/FH EN2 124 D8
Glencoe Rd BUSH WD23 132 E2
Glencorse Gn OXHEY WD19 * 132 B7
Glendale HHW HP1 4 B3
Glendale Av EDGW HA8 134 D7
Glendevon Cl EDGW HA8 134 F6
Glendor Gdns MLHL NW7 135 H7
Gleneagles STAN HA7 143 M1
Gleneagles Cl OXHEY WD19 * 132 B8
Gleneagles Dr LTNE LU2 28 C3
Glenester Cl HOD EN11 72 E4
Glen Faba Rd
HLWW/ROY CM19 73 K7
Glenferrie Rd STAL AL1 9 L5
Glenfield Ct HERT/WAT SG14 52 D6
Glenfield Rd LTNN/LIM LU3 28 A3
Glengall Pl STAL AL1 * 85 J5
Glengall Rd EDGW HA8 134 F6
Glenhaven Av BORE WD6 120 E7
Glenhurst Rd
NFNCH/WDSPK N12 137 H7
Glenister Rd CSHM HP5 97 G2
Glenloch Rd PEND EN3 126 A6
Glen Luce CHES/WCR EN8 110 B4
Glenlyn Av STAL AL1 85 M3
Glenmore Gdns ABLGY WD5 101 L5
The Glen ENC/FH EN2 124 F8
LTN LU1 40 C6
NTHWD HA6 141 H2
PIN HA5 141 M7
Glenthorne Rd
FBAR/BDGN N11 137 K8
Glenview Rd HHW HP1 4 B3
Glenville Av ENC/FH EN2 125 G4
Glen Wy WAT WD17 117 J4
Glenwood BROX EN10 92 D1
WGCE AL7 51 G8
Glenwood Cl HRW HA1 143 K7
STVGE SG2 34 A7
Glenwood Rd MLHL NW7 135 J6
Glevum Cl STALW/RED AL3 84 D4
Globe Cl HARP AL5 47 G4
Globe Crs BSF CM23 165 R7
Glossop Wy ARL/CHE SG15 147 R2
Gloucester Av CHES/WCR EN8 110 C7
Gloucester Cl STVG SG1 21 J7
Gloucester Ct HAT AL10 67 K7
Gloucester Gdns EBAR EN4 123 L8
Gloucester Rd BAR EN5 136 F1
ENC/FH EN2 125 G4
HRW HA1 142 F7
LTN LU1 7 H6
Gloucester Ter LTN LU1 * 6 E4
Glover Cl CHESW EN7 * 109 K1
Glover Rd PIN HA5 142 B8
Glovers Cl HERT/BAY SG13 71 G1
Glyn Av EBAR EN4 123 H8
Glyn Ct STAN HA7 143 M1
The Glynde STVGE SG2 177 P1
Glyn Rd PEND EN3 126 A8
Glynswood CFSP/GDCR SL9 138 D2
Glynswood Pl NTHWD HA6 140 F2
Goat La EN EN1 125 K4
Gobions Wy POTB/CUF EN6 106 F2
Goblins Gn WGCE AL7 50 B8
Goddard End STVGE SG2 34 A8
Goddards Cl HERT/BAY SG13 90 A1
Godfrey Cl STVGE SG2 11 M8
Godfreys Ct LTN LU1 6 A7
Godfries Cl WLYN AL6 51 J2
Godwin Cl CHING E4 127 G4
Goffs Crs CHESW EN7 109 G3
Goff's La CHESW EN7 109 G3
Goff's Oak Av CHESW EN7 108 F2
Golda Cl BAR EN5 136 B2
Gold Cl BROX EN10 92 C2
RBSF CM22 167 K2
Gold Crest Cl LTNW/LEA LU4 26 E4
Goldcrest Wy BUSH WD23 133 G4
Goldcroft HHS/BOV HP3 82 E4
Golden Dell WGCE AL7 68 D3
Golders Cl EDGW HA8 134 F8
Goldfield Rd TRING HP23 57 K2
Goldfinch Wy BORE WD6 120 E8
Gold Hl East CFSP/GDCR SL9 138 B4
Gold Hl North
CFSP/GDCR SL9 138 A3
Gold Hl West CFSP/GDCR SL9 138 A3
Goldings BSF CM23 44 B1
Goldings Crs HAT AL10 67 M7
Goldings La HERT/WAT SG14 52 E4
Goldington Cl HOD EN11 72 D4
Goldon LWTH SG6 16 F5
Goldrill Dr FBAR/BDGN N11 137 L5
Goldring Wy LCOL/BKTW AL2 103 L1
Goldsdown Cl PEND EN3 126 C6
Goldsdown Rd PEND EN3 126 B6
Goldsmith Rd
FBAR/BDGN N11 137 K8
Goldsmith Wy STALW/RED AL3 8 D2
Goldstone Cl WARE SG12 54 B3
Goldstone Crs
DUN/HR/TOD LU5 26 B7
Golf Cl BUSH WD23 13 K3
Golf Club Rd BRKMPK AL9 88 E8
Golf Ride ENC/FH EN2 124 E1
Golfside Cl TRDG/WHET N20 137 J6
Gombards STALW/RED AL3 8 E4
Gomer Cl HTCHE/RSTV SG4 176 E8
Gonville Av
RKW/CH/CXG WD3 130 F2
Gonville Crs STVGE SG2 34 A7
Goodacre Cl POTB/CUF EN6 106 F6
Goodey Meade STVGE SG2 35 K7
Goodhall Cl STAN HA7 143 L1
Good Intent DUN/WHIP LU6 37 J5
Goodison Cl BUSH WD23 133 G1
Goodliffe Pk BSF CM23 166 D11
Goodrich Cl GSTN WD25 117 L1
Goodwin Ct CHES/WCR EN8 110 C2
Goodwins Md LBUZ LU7 169 L2
Goodwin Stile BSF CM23 43 K4
Goodwood Av PEND EN3 126 A3
WATN WD24 117 J1
Goodwood Cl HOD EN11 72 D6
Goodwood Rd ROY SG8 15 G7
Goodwyn Av MLHL NW7 135 J8
Goodyers Av RAD WD7 103 K7
Goose Acre CSHM HP5 97 L4
LBUZ LU7 169 L2
Gooseacre WGCE AL7 68 D1
Gooseberry Hl LTNN/LIM LU3 27 M2
Goosecroft HHW HP1 81 K1
Goosefields
RKW/CH/CXG WD3 130 A2
Goose La RBSF CM22 184 D2
Goral Md RKW/CH/CXG WD3 130 B4
Gordian Wy STVGE SG2 22 A8
Gordon Av STAN HA7 143 K1
Gordon Cl STAL AL1 9 M8
Gordon Hl ENC/FH EN2 125 G5
Gordon Rd CSHM HP5 97 G6
ENC/FH EN2 125 H5
KTN/HRWW/WS HA3 143 J5
WAB EN9 110 E8
Gordon St LTN LU1 6 E5
Gordons Wk HARP AL5 47 G5
Gordon Wy BAR EN5 122 D8
Gore Cl DEN/HRF UB9 139 M6
Gorefield Rd STSD CM24 167 R9
Gore Hl AMSS HP7 112 F8
Gorelands La CSTG HP8 128 B4
Gore La STDN SG11 180 G6
Gorham Dr STAL AL1 85 J5
Gorham Wy DUN/HR/TOD LU5 26 D7
Gorle Cl GSTN WD25 101 L8
Gorleston Cl STVG SG1 20 E8
Gorse Cl HAT AL10 87 K3
Gorse Cnr HARP AL5 * 47 G5
STALW/RED AL3 8 F1
Gorselands HARP AL5 46 F6
Gorseway HAT AL10 67 K4
Gorst Cl LWTH SG6 16 C4
Gosforth La OXHEY WD19 131 L6
Gosforth Pth OXHEY WD19 131 L6
Goshawk Cl LTNW/LEA LU4 26 E5
Gosling Av HTCH/STOT SG5 156 E11
Gosmore Ley Cl
HTCHE/RSTV SG4 157 P10
Gosmore Rd HTCHE/RSTV SG4 157 P8
The Gossamers GSTN WD25 118 C2
Gosse Cl HOD EN11 72 D4
Gosselin Rd HERT/WAT SG14 53 G5
Gossoms Ryde BERK HP4 59 L8
Gossoms's End BERK HP4 59 L8
Gothic Wy ARL/CHE SG15 147 Q4
Gough Rd EN EN1 125 M6
Gould Cl BRKMPK AL9 87 M6
Government Rw PEND EN3 126 E3
Governors Av DEN/HRF UB9 139 K7
Governors Cl AMS HP6 113 K3
Gowar Fld POTB/CUF EN6 105 L5
Gower Rd ROY SG8 14 D6
The Gowers AMS HP6 113 J3
HLW CM20 3 M2
Grace Av RAD WD7 104 B7
Grace Cl BORE WD6 121 H5
Grace Gdns BSF CM23 43 M5
Grace Wy STVG SG1 10 F1
Graeme Rd EN EN1 125 J6
Graemes Dyke Rd BERK HP4 79 L2
Grafton Cl STALE/WH AL4 86 B3
Grafton Pl STDN SG11 163 R12
Grafton Rd ENC/FH EN2 124 D7
HRW HA1 143 G7
Graham Av BROX EN10 92 D2
Graham Cl STAL AL1 85 H5
Graham Gdns LTNN/LIM LU3 28 A5
Graham Rd DUN/HR/TOD LU5 39 J2
KTN/HRWW/WS HA3 143 J5
Grailands BSF CM23 43 K1
Grammar School Wk
HTCH/STOT SG5 157 N6
Grampian Pl STVG SG1 21 M5
Grampian Wy LTNN/LIM LU3 27 G1
The Granaries WAB EN9 111 J8
Granary Cl STALE/WH AL4 48 B5
Granary La HARP AL5 46 F4
The Granary ARL/CHE SG15 147 Q4
HLWW/ROY CM19 73 M4
WARE SG12 73 H1
Granby Av HARP AL5 47 G3
Granby Park Rd CHESW EN7 109 K2
Granby Rd LTNW/LEA LU4 27 H6
STVG SG1 21 G7
Grandfield Av WAT WD17 117 L5
Grand Union Canal Wk
BERK HP4 59 J6
DEN/HRF UB9 139 M5
HHS/BOV HP3 82 D7
HHW HP1 4 A7
LBUZ LU7 169 N3
Grange Av EBAR EN4 137 J4
KTN/HRWW/WS HA3 143 M4
LTNW/LEA LU4 27 H5
NFNCH/WDSPK N12 137 G8
TRDG/WHET N20 136 G2
Grange Bottom ROY SG8 14 F8
Grange Cl CFSP/GDCR SL9 138 C3
HERT/WAT SG14 52 F7
HHNE HP2 5 G2
HTCHE/RSTV SG4 157 Q9
STALW/RED AL3 172 F3
WAT WD17 117 L5
Grange Ct HERT/WAT SG14 * 53 G6
LWTH SG6 * 148 E12
PIN HA5 * 142 C5
WAB EN9 111 G8
Grange Court Rd HARP AL5 47 G7
Grangedale Cl NTHWD HA6 141 J3
Grange Dr HTCH/STOT SG5 148 D8
Grange Flds CFSP/GDCR SL9 138 C3
Grange Gdns PIN HA5 142 D6
SHFD SG17 146 B1
WARE SG12 54 C5
Grange Hl EDGW HA8 135 G8
WLYN AL6 177 J11
Grange La GSTN WD25 119 H5
HLWW/ROY CM19 74 A5
Grange Pk BSF CM23 166 B12
Grange Ri HTCHE/RSTV SG4 176 F8
Grange Rd
AMP/FLIT/BLC MK45 154 H2
BORE WD6 134 D1
BSF CM23 44 A2
BUSH WD23 13 M8
CFSP/GDCR SL9 138 B3
HRW HA1 143 L8
LBUZ LU7 169 P5
LWTH SG6 16 D1
TRING HP23 168 G8
Grangeside BSF CM23 166 B11
Grange St STALW/RED AL3 8 F3
The Grange HOD EN11 * 72 E8
STALE/WH AL4 * 87 H5
STDN SG11 * 163 P10
STVG SG1 33 G1
Grangeview Rd
TRDG/WHET N20 137 G4
Grange Wk BSF CM23 44 A2
Grangeway
NFNCH/WDSPK N12 136 F7
Grangewood POTB/CUF EN6 106 F4
Grangewood Cl PIN HA5 141 L7
Gransden Cl LTNN/LIM LU3 27 L2
Grant Gdns HARP AL5 46 F3
Grantham Cl EDGW HA8 134 C6
ROY SG8 14 C5
Grantham Gdns WARE SG12 54 C3
Grantham Gn BORE WD6 135 G1
Grantham Ms BERK HP4 80 B1
Grantham Rd LTNW/LEA LU4 27 L8
Grant Rd KTN/HRWW/WS HA3 143 J5
Granville Dene HHS/BOV HP3 98 E1
Granville Gdns HOD EN11 72 E3
Granville Pl PIN HA5 142 B5
Granville Rd BAR EN5 122 A8
BERK HP4 59 J7
HTCHE/RSTV SG4 16 A8
LTN LU1 6 A4
STAL AL1 9 J6
WATW WD18 13 G6
Graphic Cl DUN/WHIP LU6 39 H3
Grasmere STVG SG1 22 A6
Grasmere Av HARP AL5 47 G3
LTNN/LIM LU3 27 M2
Grasmere Cl DUN/WHIP LU6 38 F2
GSTN WD25 101 M6
HHS/BOV HP3 82 F4
Grasmere Gdns
KTN/HRWW/WS HA3 143 L4
Grasmere Rd LTNN/LIM LU3 27 M2
STAL AL1 85 M4
WARE SG12 54 C2
Grassingham End
CFSP/GDCR SL9 138 C2
Grassingham Rd
CFSP/GDCR SL9 138 C2
Grassington Cl
LCOL/BKTW AL2 102 E4
Grass Mdw STVGE SG2 34 B2
Grass Warren WLYN AL6 51 J4
Grassy Cl HHW HP1 81 L1
Grasvenor Av BAR EN5 136 E2
Gravel Dr RAYLNE/WEN HP22 56 F2
Graveley Av BORE WD6 121 G8
Graveley Dell WGCE AL7 50 F8
Graveley La HTCHE/RSTV SG4 20 D4
Graveley Rd HTCHE/RSTV SG4 20 C3
STVG SG1 20 F6
Gravel Hl CFSP/GDCR SL9 138 C1
Gravelhill Ter HHW HP1 4 A4
Gravel La HHW HP1 4 A3
Gravelly Dell STDN SG11 163 Q5
Gravelly La STDN SG11 163 Q6
Gravel Pth BERK HP4 80 B1
Gravely Ct HHNE HP2 83 G3
Gravenhurst Rd
HTCH/STOT SG5 146 A5
Grayling Ct BERK HP4 59 K7
The Graylings ABLGY WD5 101 J7
Grays Cl AMP/FLIT/BLC MK45 155 J2
ROY SG8 14 D5
Grays Ct BSF CM23 43 L1
Graysfield WGCE AL7 68 E2
Gray's La HTCH/STOT SG5 157 M6
Grays Wk CSHM HP5 96 F3
The Grazings HHNE HP2 62 D8
Greatacre CSHM HP5 97 H4
Great Ashby Wy STVG SG1 21 L6
Great Augur St HLWE CM17 76 B4
Great Braitch La HAT AL10 67 J3
Great Bramingham La
LTNN/LIM LU3 154 H11
Great Brays HLWS CM18 3 L8
Great Break WGCE AL7 50 F8
Great Bushey Dr
TRDG/WHET N20 136 F4
Great Cambridge Rd EN EN1 125 L4
Great Conduit WGCE AL7 51 G6
Great Dell WGCW AL8 50 B5
Great Eastern Cl BSF CM23 44 A3
Great Elms Rd HHS/BOV HP3 82 D6
Greatfield Cl HARP AL5 46 A1
Great Gables STVG SG1 21 M5
Great Ganett WGCE AL7 68 F1
Great Gn HTCH/STOT SG5 156 F1
Great Gv BUSH WD23 118 F8
Great Groves CHESW EN7 109 J2
Great Hadham Rd BSF CM23 42 F4
Greatham Rd BUSH WD23 13 K4
Great Heath HAT AL10 67 M5
Great Hivings CSHM HP5 96 E1
Great Innings North
HERT/WAT SG14 178 F6
Great Innings South
HERT/WAT SG14 178 F6
Great Lawne KNEB SG3 177 R7
Great Ley WGCE AL7 68 C1
Great Leylands HLWS CM18 3 L9
Great Meadow BROX EN10 92 E4
Great Molewood
HERT/WAT SG14 52 F4
Great Northern Rd
DUN/HR/TOD LU5 39 G2
Great North Rd BAR EN5 122 D6
BLDK SG7 149 J11
BRKMPK AL9 67 M4
BRKMPK AL9 88 D5
STVG SG1 10 D9
WLYN AL6 177 K11
Great Palmers HHNE HP2 62 D5
Great Pk KGLGY WD4 100 E4
Great Plumtree HLW CM20 3 K2
Great Rd HHNE HP2 5 L1
Great Slades POTB/CUF EN6 106 D7
Great Stockwood Rd
CHESW EN7 91 H8
Great Sturgess Rd HHW HP1 81 K2
Great Westwood
KGLGY WD4 * 116 C1
Great Whites Rd HHS/BOV HP3 5 L7
Greenacre Cl BAR EN5 122 D4
Greenacres BUSH WD23 133 H5
HHNE HP2 83 H4
LBUZ LU7 169 N5
Green Acres LTNE LU2 155 R11
STVGE SG2 34 A8
WGCE AL7 * 68 D2
Greenacres Dr STAN HA7 143 M2
Greenacres Pk
DUN/WHIP LU6 * 172 B1
Greenall Cl CHES/WCR EN8 110 C4
Green Av MLHL NW7 135 H7
Greenbank CHES/WCR EN8 109 M2
Green Bank
NFNCH/WDSPK N12 136 F7
Greenbank Rd WAT WD17 117 H2
Greenbanks STAL AL1 9 K9
Greenbrook Av EBAR EN4 123 G5
Greenbury Cl
RKW/CH/CXG WD3 115 G7
ROY SG8 152 H4
Green Cl BRKMPK AL9 88 C8
CHES/WCR EN8 110 C6
EPP CM16 94 F6
LBUZ LU7 24 B4
LTNW/LEA LU4 26 F4
STVGE SG2 33 K8
Greencoates HERT/BAY SG13 53 J8
Greencroft EDGW HA8 135 G8
Green Cft HAT AL10 67 L5
Greencroft Gdns EN EN1 125 J7
Green Dell Wy HHS/BOV HP3 82 F2
Green Drift ROY SG8 14 C7
Greene Field Rd BERK HP4 80 A1
Green End WLYN AL6 49 M1
Green End Gdns HHW HP1 4 A4
Green End La HHW HP1 81 K2
Green End Rd HHW HP1 81 L2
Green End St
RAYLNE/WEN HP22 168 B12
Greenes Ct BERK HP4 60 A8
Greene Wk BERK HP4 80 B2
Greenfield BRKMPK AL9 68 B5
ROY SG8 14 C6
WGCW AL8 50 B4
Greenfield Av HTCH/STOT SG5 157 M1
OXHEY WD19 132 C5
Greenfield Cl DUN/WHIP LU6 25 J8
Greenfield End
CFSP/GDCR SL9 138 D2
Greenfield La HTCH/STOT SG5 157 N1
Greenfield Rd STVG SG1 10 E1
Greenfields HTCH/STOT SG5 146 A8
POTB/CUF EN6 * 108 C4
STSD CM24 166 G6
Greenfield St WAB EN9 111 G8
Greenfield Wy BGSW SG18 144 D4
RYLN/HDSTN HA2 142 F5
Greengage Cl ROY SG8 15 K1
Greengage Rd ROY SG8 15 K1
Greengate LTNN/LIM LU3 27 G1
Greenheys Cl NTHWD HA6 141 J3
Greenhill Av LTNE LU2 28 B6
Green Hill Cl STDN SG11 163 R7
Greenhill Ct BAR EN5 * 136 F1
Greenhill Crs WATW WD18 131 J2
Greenhill Pde BAR EN5 * 136 F1
Greenhill Pk BAR EN5 136 F1
BSF CM23 43 K4
Greenhill Rd HRW HA1 143 J8
Greenhills HLW CM20 3 G6
WARE SG12 54 A2
Greenhills Cl
RKW/CH/CXG WD3 129 M1
Greenhill Wy HRW HA1 143 J8
Greenland Rd BAR EN5 136 A2
Green La AMS HP6 113 H1
BLDK SG7 145 L12
BROX EN10 92 F5
CHING E4 * 127 J7
CSHM HP5 97 M7
DUN/WHIP LU6 37 H2
DUN/WHIP LU6 172 A1
EDGW HA8 134 D7
HHNE HP2 83 G3
HHS/BOV HP3 98 D2
HLWE CM17 76 F6
HTCHE/RSTV SG4 157 R4
LBUZ LU7 169 Q4
LTNE LU2 28 F5
LWTH SG6 148 F12
NTHWD HA6 141 H2
OXHEY WD19 132 A4
RKW/CH/CXG WD3 130 D1
STAL AL1 85 L6
STALW/RED AL3 65 G7
STALW/RED AL3 172 H5
STAN HA7 133 M7
STDN SG11 163 R6
WGCE AL7 69 G1
Green Lane Cl HARP AL5 47 J5
Green Lane Cots STAN HA7 * 133 M7
Green Lanes HAT AL10 67 K5
Greenleaf Wy
KTN/HRWW/WS HA3 143 K5
Green Meadow
POTB/CUF EN6 106 E4
Green Milverton LTNN/LIM LU3 27 L2
Greenmoor Rd PEND EN3 126 A6
Greenoak Pl EBAR EN4 123 K6
Green Oaks LTNE LU2 28 D6
Green Pth RAYLNE/WEN HP22 57 G1
Green Ride LOU IG10 127 M8
Greenriggs LTNE LU2 * 29 K7
Green Rd STHGT/OAK N14 137 M2
TRDG/WHET N20 137 G6
Greenside BORE WD6 120 E4
Greenside Cl TRDG/WHET N20 137 H5
Greenside Dr HTCH/STOT SG5 157 M5
Greenside Pk LTNE LU2 28 C6
Greensleeves Cl STALE/WH AL4 86 A3
Greenstead SBW CM21 183 Q8
Green St BORE WD6 120 E3
BRKMPK AL9 88 F2
HLWE CM17 76 B4
PEND EN3 126 A6
RKW/CH/CXG WD3 115 G6
ROY SG8 14 E5
STVG SG1 10 A1
Greensward BUSH WD23 132 F2
The Green BERK HP4 60 F7
BSF CM23 * 43 M5
CHES/WCR EN8 110 A2
DUN/HR/TOD LU5 26 A5
DUN/WHIP LU6 37 K5
HTCH/STOT SG5 148 D6
HTCHE/RSTV SG4 176 E8
KNEB SG3 176 H4
LCOL/BKTW AL2 * 104 B1
LTNE LU2 174 G6
LTNW/LEA LU4 27 G4
RKW/CH/CXG WD3 130 D1
ROY SG8 14 E6
ROY SG8 145 Q8
WAB EN9 111 G8
WARE SG12 54 B2
WLYN AL6 176 H12
Green Tiles La DEN/HRF UB9 139 K8
Green V WGCE AL7 50 E8
Green View Cl HHS/BOV HP3 98 E3
Greenway BERK HP4 79 L1
BSF CM23 44 C3
CSHM HP5 96 F2
HARP AL5 47 H5
HHNE HP2 82 F2
HLWW/ROY CM19 74 C5
LWTH SG6 16 E7
PIN HA5 141 M4
STVGE SG2 34 F1
TRDG/WHET N20 136 E5
Greenway Cl TRDG/WHET N20 136 E5
Green Way Gdns
KTN/HRWW/WS HA3 143 J4
Greenways ABLGY WD5 101 H5
BUNT SG9 158 H9
CHESW EN7 108 F3
DUN/WHIP LU6 37 H2
HERT/WAT SG14 52 F7
LTNE LU2 28 F4
STVG SG1 10 E2
WLYN AL6 50 C2
The Green Wy
KTN/HRWW/WS HA3 143 J3
The Greenway
CFSP/GDCR SL9 138 B5
PEND EN3 126 B1
PIN HA5 142 D8
POTB/CUF EN6 106 E7
RKW/CH/CXG WD3 129 L3
TRING HP23 169 K12
Greenwich Wy WAB EN9 127 G2
Greenwood Av CHESW EN7 109 M5
Greenwood Cl AMS HP6 * 113 J4
CHESW EN7 109 M5
Greenwood Dr GSTN WD25 101 M8
Greenwood Gdns RAD WD7 104 C6
The Greenwood
RAYLNE/WEN HP22 168 B12
Greenyard WAB EN9 111 G7
Greer Rd KTN/HRWW/WS HA3 143 G3
Gregories Cl LTNN/LIM LU3 6 E2
Gregory Av POTB/CUF EN6 107 G7
Gregory Cl SHFD SG17 146 D4
Gregory Ms WAB EN9 110 F6
Gregson Cl BORE WD6 121 G6
Grenadier Cl STALE/WH AL4 86 A3
Grenadine Cl CHESW EN7 109 K1
Grenadine Wy TRING HP23 169 L12
Grenfell Cl BORE WD6 121 G5
Grenville Av BROX EN10 92 D3
Grenville Cl CHES/WCR EN8 110 B6
Grenville Pl MLHL NW7 135 H8
Grenville Wy STVGE SG2 33 L8
Gresford Cl STALE/WH AL4 86 B2
Gresham Av TRDG/WHET N20 137 K7
Gresham Cl ENC/FH EN2 125 G7
LTNE LU2 29 H8
Gresham Ct BERK HP4 79 M2
Gresley Cl WGCW AL8 50 C5
Gresley Ldg ROY SG8 * 14 D6
Gresley Wy STVGE SG2 34 B3
Greville Cl BRKMPK AL9 87 M6
Greycaine Rd WATN WD24 118 B3
Greydells Rd STVG SG1 10 E1
Greyfell Cl STAN HA7 133 M8
Greyfriars WARE SG12 53 M2
Greyfriars La HARP AL5 46 E6
Greygoose Pk
HLWW/ROY CM19 74 E7
Greyhound La POTB/CUF EN6 105 L7
Greystoke Av PIN HA5 142 E5
Greystoke Cl BERK HP4 79 L2
Greystoke Dr RSLP HA4 140 F8
Greystoke Gdns ENC/FH EN2 124 B8
Griffiths Wy STAL AL1 8 D9
Griffon Wy GSTN WD25 101 K8
Grimsdells Cnr AMS HP6 * 113 H3
Grimsdell's La AMS HP6 113 H3
Grimsdyke Crs BAR EN5 122 A7
Grimsdyke Rd PIN HA5 142 C2
TRING HP23 58 B4
Grimstone Rd HTCHE/RSTV SG4 20 C5
Grimston Rd STAL AL1 9 H6
Grimthorpe Cl STALW/RED AL3 65 G7
Grindcobbe Cl STAL AL1 85 H5
Grinders End HTCHE/RSTV SG4 20 F5
Grindleford Av
FBAR/BDGN N11 137 L5
Grinstead La RBSF CM22 184 C3
Groom Rd BROX EN10 92 D8
Groomsby Dr LBUZ LU7 169 Q4
Grooms Cots CSHM HP5 97 M4
Grooms Dr PIN HA5 141 L7
Grosvenor Av KGLGY WD4 101 G2
Grosvenor Cl BSF CM23 43 K6
Grosvenor Ct
RKW/CH/CXG WD3 * 131 H1
Grosvenor Rd BLDK SG7 149 K12
BORE WD6 120 E7
BROX EN10 92 D2
LTNN/LIM LU3 27 M4
NTHWD HA6 131 K8
STAL AL1 9 H7
WAT WD17 13 H4
Grosvenor Rd West BLDK SG7 149 K12
Grosvenor Sq KGLGY WD4 101 G2
Grosvenor Ter HHW HP1 4 A5
The Grotto WARE SG12 54 B5
Ground La HAT AL10 67 M6
Grove Av HARP AL5 47 H6
PIN HA5 142 C6
Grove Bank OXHEY WD19 * 132 B4
Grovebury Cl DUN/WHIP LU6 39 H3
Grovebury Gdns
LCOL/BKTW AL2 103 G1
Grove Cl CFSP/GDCR SL9 138 A3
STHGT/OAK N14 * 137 M3
Grove Ct WAB EN9 110 F7
Grove Crs RKW/CH/CXG WD3 116 E8
Grovedale Cl CHESW EN7 109 K4
Grove End CFSP/GDCR SL9 138 A3
LTN LU1 6 A9
Grove Farm Pk NTHWD HA6 131 H8
Grove Gdns PEND EN3 126 B5
TRING HP23 169 M12
Grove Hall Rd BUSH WD23 13 L6
Grove Hl CFSP/GDCR SL9 138 A2

STSD CM24 166 G6
Grovelands HHNE HP2 63 G8
LCOL/BKTW AL2 102 F1
Grovelands Av
HTCHE/RSTV SG4 16 A7
Groveland Wy
HTCH/STOT SG5 148 E8
Grove La CSHM HP5 97 M1
Grove Lea HAT AL10 87 L3
Grove Leys TRING HP23 169 N12
The Grovells BERK HP4 * 171 M10
Grove Md HAT AL10 67 K8
Grove Meadow WGCE AL7 51 G7
Grove Mill La
RKW/CH/CXG WD3 117 G4
Grove Pk TRING HP23 169 N12
Grove Park Rd LTN LU1 40 E6
Grove Pl BRKMPK AL9 88 A6
GSTN WD25 * 118 F5
Grove Rd AMS HP6 113 K3
BORE WD6 120 E5
DUN/HR/TOD LU5 26 A2
DUN/HR/TOD LU5 39 H2
EBAR EN4 123 J7
FBAR/BDGN N11 137 M8
HARP AL5 47 H6
HHW HP1 81 L4
HTCH/STOT SG5 157 P4
LTN LU1 6 C5
NFNCH/WDSPK N12 137 H8
NTHWD HA6 131 H8
PIN HA5 142 D7
RKW/CH/CXG WD3 129 L5
STAL AL1 8 E8
STVG SG1 10 B1
TRING HP23 169 M12
WARE SG12 54 D3
Grove Rd West PEND EN3 126 A3
Grover Rd OXHEY WD19 132 B2
Groves Rd RAYLNE/WEN HP22 56 B6
Groves Wy CSHM HP5 96 D3
The Grove AMS HP6 113 H1
BRKMPK AL9 106 E1
CSHM HP5 114 B2
EDGW HA8 134 F7
ENC/FH EN2 124 E6
HARP AL5 * 47 J6
KGLGY WD4 * 100 A4
LTN LU1 6 A9
POTB/CUF EN6 107 G6
RAD WD7 103 L8
RBSF CM22 44 F5
RKW/CH/CXG WD3 * 116 E8
STDN SG11 42 E2
TRING HP23 * 169 N12
Grove Wk HERT/WAT SG14 53 G5
Grove Wy RKW/CH/CXG WD3 114 F8
Grovewood Cl
RKW/CH/CXG WD3 128 F1
Grubbs La BRKMPK AL9 88 E4
Guernsey Cl LTNW/LEA LU4 26 D6
Guessens Gv WGCW AL8 50 A7
Guessens Rd WGCW AL8 50 A7
Guessens Wk WGCW AL8 50 A6
Guildford Cl STVG SG1 21 J7
Guildford Rd STAL AL1 85 M3
Guildford St LTN LU1 6 F4
Guildown Av
NFNCH/WDSPK N12 136 F7
Guilfords HLWE CM17 183 P12
Guinery Gv HHS/BOV HP3 82 D6
Guinevere Gdns
CHES/WCR EN8 110 B4
Gulland Cl BUSH WD23 133 G1
Gullbrook HHW HP1 4 A3
Gullet Wood Rd GSTN WD25 117 L1
Gullicot Wy LBUZ LU7 169 P5
The Gulphs HERT/BAY SG13 53 H8
Gun La KNEB SG3 177 M4
Gun Meadow Av KNEB SG3 177 N5
Gunnels Wood Pk STVG SG1 * 10 C8
Gunnels Wood Rd STVG SG1 10 B8
Gunner Dr PEND EN3 126 E3
Gun Rd KNEB SG3 177 N5
Gun Road Gdns KNEB SG3 177 M5
Gurney Ct DUN/WHIP LU6 37 K3
Gurney Court Rd STAL AL1 9 K1
Gurney's La HTCH/STOT SG5 147 K10
Gustard Wd STALE/WH AL4 175 N12
Gwent Cl GSTN WD25 102 B8
Gwynfa Cl WLYN AL6 177 K10
Gwynne Cl TRING HP23 169 L12
Gwynns Wk HERT/BAY SG13 53 J7
Gypsy Cl WARE SG12 72 D1
Gypsy La KGLGY WD4 101 H7
WARE SG12 72 D1
WGCE AL7 68 D4
Gypsy Moth Av HAT AL10 67 J6

H

Hackforth Cl BAR EN5 135 M1
Hackney Cl BORE WD6 135 H1
Hadar Cl TRDG/WHET N20 136 E4
Haddenham Ct
OXHEY WD19 * 132 B6
Haddestoke Ga
CHES/WCR EN8 92 D8
Haddington Cl
RAYLNE/WEN HP22 56 B8
Haddon Cl BORE WD6 120 E6
HHS/BOV HP3 82 E3
STVGE SG2 177 Q2
Haddon Rd LTNE LU2 7 J4
RKW/CH/CXG WD3 129 G1
Hadham Ct BSF CM23 43 K1
Hadham Gv BSF CM23 43 J1
Hadham Rd STDN SG11 163 R12
Hadland Cl HHS/BOV HP3 80 E8
Hadleigh Cl RAD WD7 104 B4
Hadleigh Ct BROX EN10 92 D4
HARP AL5 47 J7
Hadley Cl BORE WD6 134 D1
Hadley Common BAR EN5 123 G6
Hadley Gra HLWE CM17 76 A5
Hadley Gn BAR EN5 122 D7
Hadley Green Rd BAR EN5 122 D6
Hadley Gn West BAR EN5 122 C6
Hadley Gv BAR EN5 122 C6
Hadley Highstone BAR EN5 122 D4
Hadley Pde BAR EN5 * 122 C7
Hadley Rdg BAR EN5 122 D7
Hadley Rd BAR EN5 122 F7
EBAR EN4 123 L4
Hadley Wood Rd BAR EN5 122 E6
Hadlow Down Cl
LTNN/LIM LU3 27 L4
Hadrian Av DUN/HR/TOD LU5 26 C7
Hadrian Cl STALW/RED AL3 84 D4
Hadrians Wk STVG SG1 34 A1
Hadrian Wy LWTH SG6 17 H2
Hadwell Cl STVGE SG2 11 K8
Hagdell Rd LTN LU1 41 G4
Hagden La WATW WD18 12 A6
Haggerston Rd BORE WD6 120 C4
Hagsdell Rd HERT/BAY SG13 53 H8
Haig Cl STAL AL1 85 M3
Haig Rd STAN HA7 134 A8
Hailes Wd RBSF CM22 167 M3
Hailey Av HOD EN11 72 E3
Hailey Cl HERT/BAY SG13 72 C3
Hailey La HERT/BAY SG13 72 B4
Hailey Pl SBW CM21 183 Q7
Hailsham Dr HRW HA1 143 H5
Haines Wy GSTN WD25 101 L8
Haldane Cl PEND EN3 126 F4
Haldens WGCE AL7 50 D4
Hale Cl EDGW HA8 135 G8
Hale End Cl RSLP HA4 141 L8
Hale Grove Gdns MLHL NW7 135 H8
Hale La EDGW HA8 135 G8
Hale Rd HERT/BAY SG13 53 H8
Hales Meadow HARP AL5 46 E3
Hales Pk HHNE HP2 83 G1
Hales Park Cl HHNE HP2 83 G1
Half Acre HTCH/STOT SG5 157 M7
Halfacre Hl CFSP/GDCR SL9 138 D3
Halfacre La BUNT SG9 160 A8
Half Acres BSF CM23 43 M1
Halfhide La CHES/WCR EN8 92 B8
Halfhides WAB EN9 111 H7
Half Moon La
DUN/HR/TOD LU5 39 H2
LTN LU1 173 L1
Half Moon Meadow HHNE HP2 63 G5
Half Moon Ms STAL AL1 8 F6
Half Moon Pl DUN/WHIP LU6 * 39 H3
Halford Ct HAT AL10 67 J7
Halfway Av LTNW/LEA LU4 27 H8
Halifax Cl GSTN WD25 101 K8
LCOL/BKTW AL2 102 D5
Halifax Rd ENC/FH EN2 125 G6
RKW/CH/CXG WD3 129 G3
Halifax Wy WGCE AL7 51 J7
Halings La DEN/HRF UB9 139 H6
Hallam Cl WATN WD24 13 H1
Hallam Gdns PIN HA5 142 C2
Halland Wy NTHWD HA6 131 H1
Hall Cl RKW/CH/CXG WD3 129 L4
Hall Dr DEN/HRF UB9 140 A3
Halley Rd WAB EN9 126 F2
Halleys Rdg HERT/WAT SG14 52 E8
Halley's Wy DUN/HR/TOD LU5 26 B5
Hall Farm Cl STAN HA7 133 M7
Hall Gdns STALE/WH AL4 87 H5
Hall Gv WGCE AL7 68 F1
Hall Heath Cl STAL AL1 65 M8
Halliday Cl RAD WD7 104 C6
Hallingbury Cl RBSF CM22 44 B8
Hallingbury Rd RBSF CM22 44 B5
SBW CM21 184 A5
Halling Hl HLW CM20 3 H3
Halliwick Court Pde
NFNCH/WDSPK N12 * 137 K8
Hall La BUNT SG9 160 A8
HTCHE/RSTV SG4 175 N9
KNEB SG3 177 N7
ROY SG8 153 P3
Hall Md LWTH SG6 16 A3
Hallmores BROX EN10 92 E1
Hallowell Rd NTHWD HA6 131 J2
Hallowes Crs OXHEY WD19 131 L6
Hall Pk BERK HP4 80 C2
Hall Park Ga BERK HP4 80 C3
Hall Park Hl BERK HP4 80 C2
Hall Pl STAL AL1 * 9 G4
Hall Place Cl STAL AL1 9 G4
Hall Place Gdns STAL AL1 9 G4
Hall Rd HHNE HP2 62 F8
RBSF CM22 167 M4
Halls Cl WLYN AL6 50 A1
Hallside BGSW SG18 144 C4
Hallside Rd EN EN1 125 K4
Hall St NFNCH/WDSPK N12 137 G8
The Hall Wk BERK HP4 * 80 B1
Hallwicks Rd LTNE LU2 28 F6
Hallworth Dr HTCH/STOT SG5 148 C7
Halsbury Cl STAN HA7 133 M8
Halsey Dr HHW HP1 61 K8
HTCHE/RSTV SG4 20 A3
Halsey Pk LCOL/BKTW AL2 104 D1
Halsey Pl WATN WD24 * 117 M4
Halsey Rd WATW WD18 12 E4
Halstead Hl CHESW EN7 109 J4
Halstead Rd EN EN1 125 J8
Halter Cl BORE WD6 135 H1
Halton Cl LCOL/BKTW AL2 103 G2
Halton Wood Rd
RAYLNE/WEN HP22 56 B8
Haltside HAT AL10 87 H1
Halwick Cl HHW HP1 4 B5
Halyard Cl LTNN/LIM LU3 27 M3
Hamberlins La TRING HP23 58 F6
Hambling Pl DUN/WHIP LU6 38 D1
Hamblings Cl RAD WD7 104 B7
Hambridge Wy
HTCH/STOT SG5 156 F1
Hambro Cl LTNE LU2 174 D10
Hamburgh Ct CHES/WCR EN8 110 B2
Hamels Dr HERT/BAY SG13 53 M6
Hamels La BUNT SG9 163 K6
Hamer Cl HHS/BOV HP3 98 E2
Hamilton Av HOD EN11 72 E5
Hamilton Cl EBAR EN4 123 J8
LCOL/BKTW AL2 102 E4
POTB/CUF EN6 105 L7
Hamilton Ct HAT AL10 * 87 M2
Hamilton Md HHS/BOV HP3 * 98 E1
Hamilton Rd BERK HP4 79 M1
EBAR EN4 123 J8
HRW HA1 143 J7
KGLGY WD4 101 G7
OXHEY WD19 131 M6
STAL AL1 9 M4
Hamilton St WATW WD18 13 H8
Hamlet Cl LCOL/BKTW AL2 102 D4
Hamlet Hl HLWW/ROY CM19 93 L1
The Hamlet BERK HP4 60 E6
Hamlin Crs PIN HA5 142 A7
Hamlyn Cl EDGW HA8 134 C6
Hammarskjold Rd HLW CM20 2 D4
Hammer La HHNE HP2 5 L1
Hammer Pde GSTN WD25 * 101 L7
Hammersfield Cl STDN SG11 163 P11
Hammers Ga LCOL/BKTW AL2 84 E8
Hammers La MLHL NW7 135 L7
Hammersmith Cl
DUN/HR/TOD LU5 26 A4
Hammersmith Gdns
DUN/HR/TOD LU5 26 A4
Hammond Cl BAR EN5 136 C1
CHESW EN7 91 K8
STVG SG1 10 C2
Hammond Ct LTN LU1 * 41 G8
Hammond End La HARP AL5 46 C8
Hammond Rd EN EN1 125 M7
Hammonds Hl HARP AL5 46 D8
Hammonds La STALE/WH AL4 66 E2
Hammonds Rd RBSF CM22 185 N3
Hammondstreet Rd
CHESW EN7 90 F7
Hammondswick HARP AL5 64 D1
Hammonde Cl EDGW HA8 134 F5
Hampden HTCHE/RSTV SG4 175 N8
Hampden Av CSHM HP5 96 E4
Hampden Cl LWTH SG6 16 F1
Hampden Crs CHESW EN7 109 M5
Hampden Hl WARE SG12 54 D4
Hampden Hill Cl WARE SG12 54 D3
Hampden Pl LCOL/BKTW AL2 103 J3
Hampden Ri ROY SG8 151 R1
Hampden Rd CFSP/GDCR SL9 138 B3
HTCHE/RSTV SG4 16 A8
KTN/HRWW/WS HA3 143 G3
Hampden Wy STHGT/OAK N14 137 M6
WAT WD17 117 J2
Hampermill La OXHEY WD19 131 L4
Hampshire Wy LTNN/LIM LU3 154 D12
Hampstead Cl
LCOL/BKTW AL2 102 D5
Hampton Cl BORE WD6 135 G1
FBAR/BDGN N11 137 L8
STVGE SG2 177 Q2
Hampton Gdns SBW CM21 183 M10
Hampton Rd LTNW/LEA LU4 6 A2
Hamstel Rd HLW CM20 2 B4
Hanaper Dr ROY SG8 152 H4
Hanbury Cl CHES/WCR EN8 110 B4
Hanbury Ct HRW HA1 * 143 K8
Hanbury Dr WARE SG12 180 A11
WCHMH N21 124 D8
Hanbury Ms WARE SG12 * 180 A12
Hancock Ct BORE WD6 121 G5
Hancock Dr LTNE LU2 28 C3
Hancroft Rd HHS/BOV HP3 5 L7
Handa Cl HHS/BOV HP3 82 F5
Handcross Rd LTNE LU2 29 H6
Hand La SBW CM21 183 N8
Handley Page Wy
LCOL/BKTW AL2 103 K4
Handpost Lodge Gdns
HHNE HP2 83 H3
Handside Cl WGCW AL8 50 A7
Handside Gn WGCW AL8 50 A6
Handside La WGCW AL8 49 M8
Handsworth Cl OXHEY WD19 131 L6
Hangar Rd DEN/HRF UB9 139 J6
Hangar Ruding OXHEY WD19 132 D6
Hanger Cl HHW HP1 4 C4
Hangmans La WLYN AL6 177 M9
Hankins La MLHL NW7 135 J5
Hanover Cl STVGE SG2 33 K8
Hanover Gdns ABLGY WD5 * 101 K4
Hanover Gra HARP AL5 46 C2
Hanover Gn HHW HP1 4 A6
Hanover Pl
AMP/FLIT/BLC MK45 155 J1
Hanover Wk HAT AL10 87 K3
Hansart Wy ENC/FH EN2 124 E5
Hanselin Cl STAN HA7 133 K8
Hansells Md HLWW/ROY CM19 73 L5
Hanswick Cl LTNE LU2 28 F7
Hanworth Cl LTNE LU2 28 B2
Hanyards La POTB/CUF EN6 108 B2
Harbert Gdns LCOL/BKTW AL2 102 F3
Harberts Rd HLWW/ROY CM19 2 B8
Harborne Cl OXHEY WD19 132 A8
Harbury Dell LTNN/LIM LU3 27 M2
Harcamlow Wy BSF CM23 165 Q6
HLW CM20 2 B1
HLWW/ROY CM19 73 M3
RBSF CM22 45 H5
RBSF CM22 166 E2
ROY SG8 153 R1
WARE SG12 180 E9
Harcourt Av EDGW HA8 135 G6
Harcourt Rd BUSH WD23 133 G1
TRING HP23 58 A1
Harcourt St LTN LU1 6 F9
Harding Cl GSTN WD25 102 A7
LTNN/LIM LU3 27 J2
STALW/RED AL3 173 R12
Harding Pde HARP AL5 * 46 F4
Harding Rd CSHM HP5 97 H4
Hardings WGCE AL7 51 G6
Hardings Cl HHS/BOV HP3 81 M5
HHW HP1 4 C9
Hardwick Cl STAN HA7 134 A8
STVGE SG2 177 Q2
Hardwicke Gdns AMS HP6 113 J4
Hardwicke Pl LCOL/BKTW AL2 104 B1
Hardwick Gn LTNN/LIM LU3 27 L2
Hardy Cl BAR EN5 136 C1
HTCHE/RSTV SG4 20 A2
Hardy Dr ROY SG8 14 E5
Hardy Rd HHNE HP2 5 K1
Hardy Wy ENC/FH EN2 124 E5
Harebell WGCE AL7 68 C3
Harebell Cl HERT/BAY SG13 53 M7
Harebridge La
RAYLNE/WEN HP22 56 C3
Hare Crs GSTN WD25 101 L6
Harefield HLW CM20 3 L5
STVGE SG2 34 A6
Harefield Cl ENC/FH EN2 124 E5
Harefield Pl STALE/WH AL4 66 B7
Harefield Rd LTN LU1 40 D1
RKW/CH/CXG WD3 130 B8
Hare La HAT AL10 87 M2
Harepark Cl HHW HP1 81 K1
Hare St HLWW/ROY CM19 2 B7
Hare Street Rd BUNT SG9 159 K10
Hare Street Springs
HLWW/ROY CM19 2 B7
Harewood RKW/CH/CXG WD3 130 A1
Harewood Rd CSTG HP8 114 A7
OXHEY WD19 131 M5
Harford Dr WAT WD17 117 J4
Harforde Ct HERT/BAY SG13 * 53 L7
Hargrave Cl STSD CM24 166 G5
Hargreaves Av CHESW EN7 109 M5
Hargreaves Cl CHESW EN7 109 M5
Hargreaves Rd ROY SG8 14 E8
Harkett Cl
KTN/HRWW/WS HA3 143 K4
Harkness CHESW EN7 109 M3
Harkness Rd HHNE HP2 5 G1
Harkness Wy HTCHE/RSTV SG4 16 A7
Harlech Rd ABLGY WD5 101 L5
The Harlequin WAT WD17 13 H5
Harlesden Rd STAL AL1 9 M5
Harlestone Cl LTNN/LIM LU3 154 G12
Harley Ct STALE/WH AL4 * 66 B6
Harley Crs HRW HA1 143 H6
Harley Rd HRW HA1 143 H6
Harling Rd DUN/WHIP LU6 37 L5
The Harlings HERT/BAY SG13 72 A3
Harlington Rd
DUN/HR/TOD LU5 154 B3
Harlow Common HLWE CM17 76 B8
Harlow Ct HHNE HP2 62 D6
Harlow Rd HLWE CM17 77 G2
HLWW/ROY CM19 74 A4
RBSF CM22 184 B10
SBW CM21 183 P9
Harlyn Dr PIN HA5 141 M5
Harmer Dell WLYN AL6 50 E1
Harmer Green La WLYN AL6 50 D1
Harmony Cl HAT AL10 67 L6
Harmsworth Wy
TRDG/WHET N20 136 D4
Harness Wy STALE/WH AL4 66 B7
Harold Cl HLWW/ROY CM19 74 D6
Harold Crs WAB EN9 111 G6
Harold Rd
AMP/FLIT/BLC MK45 155 J2
Harolds Rd HLWW/ROY CM19 74 D6
Harpenden La
STALW/RED AL3 173 R11
Harpenden Ri HARP AL5 46 C2
Harpenden Rd STALE/WH AL4 47 M5
STALW/RED AL3 9 G1
Harper Ct STVG SG1 * 11 G5
Harper La RAD WD7 104 A4
Harpsfield Broadway
HAT AL10 67 K7
Harptree Wy STAL AL1 9 L1
Harrier Wy WAB EN9 111 L8
Harries Cl CSHM HP5 96 F3
Harriescourt WAB EN9 111 L6
Harriet Walker Wy
RKW/CH/CXG WD3 129 K3
Harriet Wy BUSH WD23 133 H3
Harrington Hts
DUN/HR/TOD LU5 25 L4
Harris Cl ENC/FH EN2 124 F5
Harris Ct AMP/FLIT/BLC MK45 154 H1
Harris La HTCH/STOT SG5 156 F11
RAD WD7 104 E8
Harrison Cl HTCHE/RSTV SG4 157 P6
NTHWD HA6 141 G1
TRDG/WHET N20 137 J4
Harrison Rd WAB EN9 127 G1
Harrisons BSF CM23 166 F11
Harrison Wk CHES/WCR EN8 110 B4
Harris Rd GSTN WD25 117 L1
Harriss La WARE SG12 54 A3
Harrods Gn EDGW HA8 134 E8
Harrogate Rd OXHEY WD19 132 A6
Harrowband Rd HLWE CM17 76 A4
Harrow Ct STVG SG1 10 E4
Harrowdene STVGE SG2 34 A5
Harrowden Rd LTNE LU2 41 M1
Harrowes Meade EDGW HA8 134 E6
Harrow Vw HRW HA1 143 H6
Harrow Wy OXHEY WD19 132 C6
Harrow Weald Pk
KTN/HRWW/WS HA3 143 H1
Harrow Yd TRING HP23 57 L2
Harry Scott Ct LTNW/LEA LU4 27 G3
Harston Dr PEND EN3 126 E4
Hartcroft Cl HHS/BOV HP3 82 F3
Hartfield Av BORE WD6 120 E8
Hartfield Cl BORE WD6 134 E1
Hartford Av
KTN/HRWW/WS HA3 143 L5
Hartforde Rd BORE WD6 120 E6
Harthall La KGLGY WD4 100 F2
Hartham Common
HERT/WAT SG14 * 53 H6
Hartham La HERT/WAT SG14 53 G7
Hart Hill Dr LTNE LU2 7 J4
Hart Hill La LTNE LU2 7 J4
Hartland Cl EDGW HA8 134 E5
Hartland Dr EDGW HA8 134 E5
Hartland Rd CHES/WCR EN8 110 B4
FBAR/BDGN N11 137 K8
Hart La LTNE LU2 7 K2
Hartley Av MLHL NW7 135 K8
Hartley Cl MLHL NW7 135 K8
Hartley Rd LTNE LU2 7 H4
Hartmoor Ms PEND EN3 126 B3
Hart Rd HLWE CM17 183 N12
STAL AL1 8 F7
Hartsbourne Av BUSH WD23 133 G5
Hartsbourne Cl BUSH WD23 133 H5
Hartsbourne Rd BUSH WD23 133 H5
Hartsbourne Wy HHNE HP2 83 G3
Harts Cl BUSH WD23 118 E6
Hartsfield Rd LTNE LU2 28 E7
Hartspring La BUSH WD23 118 E6
GSTN WD25 118 F5
Hartsway PEND EN3 125 M8
Hartswood Cl BUSH WD23 118 E6
Hartswood Gn BUSH WD23 133 H5
Hart Wk LTNE LU2 7 K2
Hartwell Gdns HARP AL5 46 C4
Harvest Bank AMS HP6 96 A8
Harvest Cl LTNW/LEA LU4 26 E6
Harvest Ct LWTH SG6 * 17 G3
STALE/WH AL4 66 A6
WLYN AL6 177 L10
Harvest End GSTN WD25 118 B2
Harvesters Ms STALE/WH AL4 * 66 B6
Harvest La STVGE SG2 34 A2
Harvest Md HAT AL10 67 M7
Harvest Rd BUSH WD23 118 F8
Harveyfields WAB EN9 111 G8
Harvey Rd DUN/WHIP LU6 38 B2
LCOL/BKTW AL2 86 A8
RKW/CH/CXG WD3 130 E2
STVGE SG2 11 M3
Harvey's Hl LTNE LU2 28 D4
Harvil Rd DEN/HRF UB9 140 A6
Harwood Cl WGCW AL8 50 C3
WLYN AL6 51 J3
Harwood Hl WGCW AL8 50 C4
Harwoods Rd WATW WD18 12 C5
Hasedines Rd HHW HP1 81 L1
Haseldine Mdw HAT AL10 87 K1
Haseldine Rd LCOL/BKTW AL2 86 B8
Haselfoot LWTH SG6 16 C3
Haselwood Dr ENC/FH EN2 124 F8
Hasketon Dr LTNW/LEA LU4 26 F3
Haslemere BSF CM23 44 A5
Haslemere Av EBAR EN4 137 K4
Haslewood Av HOD EN11 72 E6
Haslingden Cl HARP AL5 46 B2
Hasluck Gdns BAR EN5 137 C2
Hastings Cl BAR EN5 123 G8
STVG SG1 32 E1
Hastings Rd
AMP/FLIT/BLC MK45 155 J2
Hastings St LTN LU1 6 E7
Hastings Wy BUSH WD23 13 L6
RKW/CH/CXG WD3 116 F8
Hastoe Hl TRING HP23 57 L4
Hastoe La TRING HP23 57 L3
Hatch Gn RBSF CM22 184 B1
Hatching Green Cl HARP AL5 46 E7
Hatch La BLDK SG7 17 K4
The Hatch PEND EN3 126 B5
Hatfield Av HAT AL10 67 J5
Hatfield Crs HHNE HP2 62 D6
Hatfield Rd BRKMPK AL9 69 J4
POTB/CUF EN6 107 G5
STAL AL1 9 G5
STALE/WH AL4 86 A2
WATN WD24 117 M5
Hatfield Tnl HAT AL10 67 K7
Hathaway Cl LTNW/LEA LU4 26 F7
STAN HA7 133 L8
Hathaway Ct STALE/WH AL4 86 C2
Hatherleigh Gdns
POTB/CUF EN6 107 H6
Hatherley Cha LTNE LU2 28 C7
Hatley Cl FBAR/BDGN N11 137 K8
Hatters La WATW WD18 131 H2
Hatters Wy LTN LU1 6 A3
Hatton Rd CHES/WCR EN8 110 B3
Havelock Pl HRW HA1 143 J8
Havelock Ri LTNE LU2 6 F1
Havelock Rd KGLGY WD4 100 D2
KTN/HRWW/WS HA3 143 J5
LTNE LU2 7 G1
Haven Cl HAT AL10 67 K7
Havenfield KGLGY WD4 99 M5
Havenhurst Ri ENC/FH EN2 124 E6
Havercroft Cl STALW/RED AL3 84 F4
Haverdale LTNW/LEA LU4 27 G5
Havers La BSF CM23 43 M4
Haward Rd HOD EN11 73 G5
Hawbush Cl WLYN AL6 49 M1
Hawbush Ri WLYN AL6 176 H12
Hawes Cl NTHWD HA6 141 K2
Hawes La CHING E4 127 G4
Haweswater Dr GSTN WD25 102 A7
Hawfield Gdns LCOL/BKTW AL2 85 H8
Hawk Cl WAB EN9 111 L8
Hawkenbury HLWW/ROY CM19 74 E7
Hawkes Dr STALW/RED AL3 173 R12
Hawkesley Ct RAD WD7 119 K1
Hawkesworth Cl NTHWD HA6 141 J2
Hawkfields LTNE LU2 28 C3
Hawkings Wy HHS/BOV HP3 80 E8
Hawkins Cl BORE WD6 121 G6
EDGW HA8 135 H8
Hawkins Hall La KNEB SG3 178 A7
Hawkshead La BRKMPK AL9 106 C2
Hawkshead Rd
POTB/CUF EN6 106 E3
Hawkshill STAL AL1 9 L7
Hawkshill Dr HHS/BOV HP3 81 J5
Hawksmead Cl PEND EN3 126 B2
Hawksmoor RAD WD7 104 E7
Hawkwell Dr TRING HP23 58 A1
Hawridge La CSHM HP5 78 C5
Hawridge V CSHM HP5 78 D4
Hawsley Rd HARP AL5 64 E1
Hawthorn Av LTNE LU2 28 F5
Hawthorn Centre HRW HA1 143 K6
Hawthorn Cl ABLGY WD5 101 K6
DUN/WHIP LU6 39 G2
HARP AL5 47 H6
HERT/WAT SG14 52 E6
HTCH/STOT SG5 157 M7
ROY SG8 15 G6
WAT WD17 117 K4
Hawthorn Crs LTN LU1 40 C6
Hawthorn Dr
RYLN/HDSTN HA2 142 E8
Hawthorne Av CHESW EN7 109 M4
KTN/HRWW/WS HA3 143 L8
RSLP HA4 141 M8
Hawthorne Cl CHESW EN7 109 M5
Hawthorne Rd RAD WD7 103 L8
Hawthornes HAT AL10 87 K2
Hawthorn Gv ENC/FH EN2 125 H4
Hawthorn Hl LWTH SG6 16 C2
Hawthorn La HHW HP1 81 K1
Hawthorn Ri BSF CM23 43 M6
Hawthorn Rd HOD EN11 72 F5
Hawthorns HLWS CM18 95 K1
WGCW AL8 50 B5
The Hawthorns BERK HP4 59 L8
CSTG HP8 114 A6
HHS/BOV HP3 81 K6
RKW/CH/CXG WD3 129 H8
STVG SG1 11 H6
WARE SG12 53 M2
Hawthorn Wy CSHM HP5 97 H3
HNLW SG16 146 G8
LCOL/BKTW AL2 84 E6
ROY SG8 15 G6
Hawtrees RAD WD7 119 K1
Haybluff Dr STVG SG1 21 L5
Haybourn Md HHW HP1 4 C5
Hay Cl BORE WD6 121 G6
Haycroft BSF CM23 44 C3
LTNE LU2 28 C3
Haycroft Rd STVG SG1 10 C1
Hayden Dell BUSH WD23 132 D2
Hayden Rd WAB EN9 127 G1
Haydens Rd HLW CM20 2 D6
Haydock Rd ROY SG8 15 G7
Haydon Dell Farm
BUSH WD23 * 132 D3
Haydon Dr PIN HA5 141 L6
Haydon Rd OXHEY WD19 13 M9
Hayes Cl LTNE LU2 28 F4
Hayfield STVGE SG2 34 B2
Hayfield Cl BUSH WD23 118 F8
Haygarth KNEB SG3 177 N5
Hay Gn ROY SG8 151 M7
Hayhurst Rd LTNW/LEA LU4 26 F7
Hay La HARP AL5 46 E4
Hayley Bell Gdns BSF CM23 43 M6
Hayley Common STVGE SG2 34 A5
Hayley Ct DUN/HR/TOD LU5 26 A4
Hayling Dr LTNE LU2 29 G6
Hayling Rd OXHEY WD19 131 K6
Haymarket Rd LTNW/LEA LU4 26 C5
Haymeads WGCW AL8 50 C4
Haymeads La BSF CM23 44 C3
Haymoor LWTH SG6 16 C2
Haynes Cl FBAR/BDGN N11 137 L6
WGCE AL7 50 E8
Haynes Md BERK HP4 59 L7
Haysman Cl LWTH SG6 16 E2
Hay St ROY SG8 145 P7
STDN SG11 163 Q3
Hayton Cl LTNN/LIM LU3 154 H11
Hay Wains KNEB SG3 177 P7
Hayward Rd TRDG/WHET N20 137 G5
Haywood Cl PIN HA5 142 B4
Haywood Copse
RKW/CH/CXG WD3 116 B8
Haywood Ct WAB EN9 111 K8
Haywood Dr
RKW/CH/CXG WD3 115 K8
Haywood La ROY SG8 151 N7
Haywood Pk
RKW/CH/CXG WD3 129 K1

Haywoods Dr HHS/BOV HP3 81 K5
Haywoods La ROY SG8 14 F6
Hazelbury Av ABLGY WD5 101 G6
Hazelbury Crs LTN LU1 6 B4
Hazel Cl CHESW EN7 91 J8
WLYN AL6 50 C2
Hazel Ct RKW/CH/CXG WD3 * 129 J7
Hazelcroft PIN HA5 142 E1
Hazeldell HERT/WAT SG14 178 F6
Hazeldell Link HHW HP1 * 81 J3
Hazeldell Rd HHW HP1 81 J3
Hazeldene CHES/WCR EN8 110 C6
Hazeldene Dr PIN HA5 142 A5
Hazelend Rd BSF CM23 166 D10
Hazel Gdns EDGW HA8 134 F7
Hazel Gv GSTN WD25 117 M1
HAT AL10 87 K3
HTCH/STOT SG5 148 C8
WGCE AL7 50 F6
Hazell Pk AMSS HP7 113 G5
Hazel Md BAR EN5 135 M1
Hazelmere Rd STALE/WH AL4 66 A7
STVGE SG2 177 N1
Hazel Rd BERK HP4 80 B2
LCOL/BKTW AL2 102 F2
Hazel Rw
NFNCH/WDSPK N12 * 137 H8
The Hazels WLYN AL6 * 51 J3
Hazel Tree Rd WATN WD24 117 M3
Hazelwood Cl CSHM HP5 97 H3
HTCH/STOT SG5 157 P5
LTNE LU2 28 F5
RYLN/HDSTN HA2 142 F6
Hazelwood Dr PIN HA5 141 M4
STALE/WH AL4 66 A8
Hazelwood La ABLGY WD5 101 H6
Hazelwood Rd
RKW/CH/CXG WD3 131 G2
Hazely TRING HP23 58 A1
Heacham Cl LTNW/LEA LU4 26 F5
Headingley Cl CHESW EN7 91 K8
RAD WD7 104 C6
STVG SG1 33 J1
Headlands Dr BERK HP4 60 C8
Headstone Dr HRW HA1 143 H6
KTN/HRWW/WS HA3 143 J5
Headstone Gdns
RYLN/HDSTN HA2 143 G6
Headstone La
RYLN/HDSTN HA2 142 F4
Headstone Pde HRW HA1 * 143 H6
Headstone Rd HRW HA1 143 J7
Healey Rd WATW WD18 131 K2
Hearleway HAT AL10 67 J6
Heath Av ROY SG8 14 D7
STALW/RED AL3 8 F2
Heathbourne Rd BUSH WD23 133 J5
Heath Brow HHW HP1 4 D6
Heathbrow Rd WLYN AL6 177 L9
Heathcliff Av HTCH/STOT SG5 147 R7
Heath Cl HARP AL5 46 F6
HHW HP1 4 D4
LTN LU1 6 A7
POTB/CUF EN6 106 F4
Heathcote Av HAT AL10 67 L6
Heathcote Gdns HLWE CM17 76 C5
Heathcroft WGCE AL7 51 G6
Heathdene Mnr WAT WD17 * 117 K5
Heath Dr POTB/CUF EN6 106 E4
WARE SG12 54 B2
Heather Cl ABLGY WD5 101 L6
BSF CM23 43 K3
Heather Dr ENC/FH EN2 124 F6
Heatherfold Wy PIN HA5 141 K5
Heather Gdns WAB EN9 127 G2
Heathermere LWTH SG6 148 D12
Heather Ri BUSH WD23 118 D6
Heather Rd WGCW AL8 68 A1
Heatherton Pk AMS HP6 112 F2
Heather Wk EDGW HA8 134 F8
Heather Wy HHNE HP2 82 B1
POTB/CUF EN6 106 D6
STAN HA7 143 K1
Heath Farm La STALW/RED AL3 9 G2
Heathfield ROY SG8 14 C7
Heathfield Cl LTN LU1 40 D5
OXHEY WD19 132 A3
POTB/CUF EN6 106 F4
Heathfield Rd BUSH WD23 13 M6
HTCH/STOT SG5 157 P3
LTNN/LIM LU3 28 A5
Heathgate HERT/BAY SG13 71 M2
Heath Hl HTCHE/RSTV SG4 176 D8
Heathlands WLYN AL6 177 M8
Heathlands Dr STALW/RED AL3 9 G1
Heath La HERT/BAY SG13 72 A3
HHW HP1 4 D6
HTCHE/RSTV SG4 176 E8
Heath Ldg BUSH WD23 * 133 H4
Heath Rd AMS HP6 96 A8
HTCHE/RSTV SG4 30 B8
OXHEY WD19 132 B3
POTB/CUF EN6 106 F4
STAL AL1 9 H3
WLYN AL6 177 M8
Heath Rw BSF CM23 166 D12
Heath's Cl EN EN1 125 H6
Heathside STAL AL1 9 H1
STALE/WH AL4 86 F5
Heathside Cl NTHWD HA6 131 H8
Heathside Rd NTHWD HA6 131 H7
The Heath HTCHE/RSTV SG4 30 B7
RAD WD7 103 L7
Heath Wy RAD WD7 104 A4
Heaton Dell LTNE LU2 29 J8
Heay Flds WGCE AL7 51 G6
Hebden Cl LTNW/LEA LU4 26 F5
Heckford Cl WATW WD18 131 G2
Heddon Court Av EBAR EN4 137 K1
Heddon Court Pde
EBAR EN4 * 137 L1
Heddon Rd EBAR EN4 137 K1
Hedgebrooms WGCE AL7 51 G6
Hedge Hl ENC/FH EN2 124 F5
Hedgeover CFSP/GDCR SL9 138 C1
Hedge Rw HHW HP1 61 L8
Hedgerow Cl STVGE SG2 34 B2
Hedgerow La BAR EN5 135 M1
Hedgerows SBW CM21 183 R7
The Hedgerows BSF CM23 44 B3
STVGE SG2 34 B1
The Hedgerow LTNW/LEA LU4 27 G4
Hedgerow Wk
CHES/WCR EN8 110 B4
Hedges Cl HAT AL10 67 M7
Hedgeside BERK HP4 60 E6
Hedley Cl RAYLNE/WEN HP22 56 E1
Hedley Ri LTNE LU2 29 J8
Hedley Rd STAL AL1 85 M2
Hedworth Av CHES/WCR EN8 110 B7
Heene Rd ENC/FH EN2 125 H6
Heighams HLWW/ROY CM19 74 D8
The Heights WAB EN9 93 M7
Helena Cl EBAR EN4 123 H3
Helens Ga CHES/WCR EN8 92 D8
Helions Rd HLWW/ROY CM19 2 A7
Hellards Rd STVG SG1 33 H2
Helmsley Cl LTNW/LEA LU4 26 F4
Helston Cl PIN HA5 142 D2
Helston Gv HHNE HP2 * 62 B5
Helston Pl ABLGY WD5 101 K6
Hemel Hempstead Rd
BERK HP4 171 M8
HHS/BOV HP3 83 J4
STALW/RED AL3 8 A5
STALW/RED AL3 63 H4
Hemingford Cl
NFNCH/WDSPK N12 137 H8
Hemingford Dr LTNE LU2 28 B4
Hemingford Rd WAT WD17 117 J2
Hemington Av
FBAR/BDGN N11 137 K8
The Hemmings BERK HP4 79 J2
Hemming Wy GSTN WD25 117 L1
Hemp La TRING HP23 58 C4
Hempstall WGCE AL7 68 F1
Hempstead La BERK HP4 61 G7
Hempstead Rd HHS/BOV HP3 80 F8
KGLGY WD4 100 D1
WAT WD17 12 C2
Henbury Wy OXHEY WD19 132 B6
Henderson Cl STALW/RED AL3 65 G6
Henderson Pl ABLGY WD5 101 K1
Hendon Wood La MLHL NW7 135 L3
Henge Wy LTNN/LIM LU3 27 H2
Henham Rd RBSF CM22 167 N4
Henley Cl DUN/HR/TOD LU5 26 C4
Henley Gdns PIN HA5 141 M5
Henry Cl ENC/FH EN2 125 J4
Henry Darlot Dr MLHL NW7 136 B8
Henry Rd EBAR EN4 137 H1
Henrys Grant STAL AL1 9 G8
Henry St HHS/BOV HP3 82 B6
TRING HP23 57 L2
Henry Wells Sq HHNE HP2 * 62 D6
Hensley Cl HTCHE/RSTV SG4 157 R7
WLYN AL6 177 J11
Henstead Pl LTNE LU2 29 H8
Heracles Cl LCOL/BKTW AL2 103 G2
Herald Cl BSF CM23 43 K3
Herberts Hole CSHM HP5 96 B4
Herbert St HHNE HP2 82 B1
Hereford Av EBAR EN4 137 K4
Hereford Gdns PIN HA5 142 C7
Hereford Rd LTNW/LEA LU4 26 E6
Hereward Cl WAB EN9 111 G6
Herga Ct WAT WD17 12 D1
Herga Rd
KTN/HRWW/WS HA3 143 K6
Heriots Cl STAN HA7 133 L7
Heritage Cl STALW/RED AL3 * 8 E6
Heritage Wk
RKW/CH/CXG WD3 * 115 J7
Herkomer Cl BUSH WD23 132 F2
Herkomer Rd BUSH WD23 132 E1
Hermitage Cl ENC/FH EN2 124 F6
Hermitage Cots STAN HA7 * 133 J8
Hermitage Ct POTB/CUF EN6 107 G7
Hermitage Rd
HTCH/STOT SG5 157 P6
The Hermitage ARL/CHE SG15 147 R1
Hermitage Wy STAN HA7 143 L3
Herne Ct BUSH WD23 * 132 G4
Herne Rd BUSH WD23 132 F2
STVG SG1 20 F8
Herneshaw HAT AL10 87 K2
Herns La WGCE AL7 50 F7
Herns Wy WGCE AL7 50 E5
Heron Cl HHS/BOV HP3 82 D7
RKW/CH/CXG WD3 130 B5
SBW CM21 183 P8
Heron Ct BSF CM23 44 A2
Heron Dr LTNE LU2 28 C3
WARE SG12 73 G2
Heronfield POTB/CUF EN6 107 G4
Herongate Rd CHES/WCR EN8 110 B1
Heron Md PEND EN3 126 E4
Heron Pl DEN/HRF UB9 139 L1
Herons Elm BERK HP4 59 J6
Heronsgate EDGW HA8 134 E8
Heronsgate Rd
RKW/CH/CXG WD3 128 F2
Heronslea GSTN WD25 118 A2
Heronslea Dr STAN HA7 134 C8
Herons Ri EBAR EN4 123 J8
Herons Wy STAL AL1 85 L6
Herons Wd HLW CM20 2 A2
Heronswood Pl WGCE AL7 50 E8
Heronswood Rd WGCE AL7 50 D7
Heron Wk NTHWD HA6 131 J7
Heron Wy HAT AL10 87 L2
HTCH/STOT SG5 148 C7
ROY SG8 14 F5
Herrongate Cl EN EN1 125 J6
Hertford Cl EBAR EN4 123 H7
Hertford End Ct
NTHWD HA6 * 131 J8
Hertford Rd BRKMPK AL9 68 B6
EBAR EN4 123 G7
HOD EN11 72 C5
PEND EN3 126 A5
STVGE SG2 177 M1
WARE SG12 72 D1
WLYN AL6 50 A1
WLYN AL6 51 K3
Hertford Road High St
PEND EN3 * 126 A8
Hertfordshire Wy BUNT SG9 160 A9
HERT/WAT SG14 179 J11
LWTH SG6 20 E2
SBW CM21 42 F7
Hertingfordbury Rd
HERT/WAT SG14 70 C1
Hertswood Ct BAR EN5 * 122 C8
Hervines Ct AMS HP6 113 G3
Hervines Rd AMS HP6 112 F3
Heswall Ct LTN LU1 7 H8
Heswell Gn OXHEY WD19 * 131 L6
Hetchleys HHW HP1 61 L7
Hever Cl LBUZ LU7 169 P7
Hewett Cl STAN HA7 133 M7
Hewins Cl WAB EN9 111 J6
Hewitt Cl STALE/WH AL4 48 B6
Hewlett Rd LTNN/LIM LU3 27 J5
Hexham Rd BAR EN5 122 F8
Hexton Rd
AMP/FLIT/BLC MK45 155 J3
HTCH/STOT SG5 156 G5
LTNE LU2 155 P9
Heybridge Ct HERT/WAT SG14 52 D6
Heybrigge Cl STALW/RED AL3 173 Q12
Heydon Rd ROY SG8 153 N3
Heydons Cl STALW/RED AL3 8 E1
Heyford End LCOL/BKTW AL2 103 G2
Heyford Rd RAD WD7 119 K3
Heyford Wy HAT AL10 68 A6
Heysham Dr OXHEY WD19 132 A8
Heywood Dr LTNE LU2 28 D6
Hibbert Av WATN WD24 118 B4
Hibbert Rd
KTN/HRWW/WS HA3 143 K4
Hibbert St LTN LU1 6 F8
Hibberts Wy CFSP/GDCR SL9 138 C5
Hickling Cl LTNE LU2 29 H8
Hickling Wy HARP AL5 47 G2
Hickman Cl BROX EN10 92 B2
Hicks Rd STALW/RED AL3 172 G4
Hidalgo Ct HHNE HP2 62 D8
The Hideaway ABLGY WD5 101 K5
Hide Rd HRW HA1 143 H6
The Hides HLW CM20 2 F4
Higgins Rd CHESW EN7 109 H1
Higgins Wk STVG SG1 21 G8
Higgin Wk STVG SG1 * 21 J8
High Acres ABLGY WD5 101 H6
Higham Dr LTNE LU2 29 H8
Higham Md CSHM HP5 97 G4
Higham Rd
AMP/FLIT/BLC MK45 155 J1
CSHM HP5 97 G4
High Ash Rd STALE/WH AL4 48 A6
High Av LWTH SG6 16 B4
High Banks LBUZ LU7 24 A4
Highbanks Rd PIN HA5 142 F1
Highbarns HHS/BOV HP3 82 E7
High Beech Rd LTNN/LIM LU3 27 H2
High Bois La AMS HP6 113 H1
Highbridge St WAB EN9 110 E8
Highbury Av HOD EN11 72 E5
Highbury Rd HTCHE/RSTV SG4 157 Q6
LTNN/LIM LU3 6 C2
Highbush Rd HTCH/STOT SG5 148 C8
High Canons BORE WD6 121 G3
Highclere Dr HHS/BOV HP3 82 F6
High Cl RKW/CH/CXG WD3 130 A1
High Coppice AMSS HP7 113 G5
Highcroft Rd HHS/BOV HP3 81 L7
Highcroft Trailer Gdns
HHS/BOV HP3 * 80 F8
High Cross GSTN WD25 119 H3
High Dane HTCHE/RSTV SG4 157 Q3
High Dells HAT AL10 87 K1
High Elms HARP AL5 46 E7
High Elms Cl NTHWD HA6 141 G1
High Elms La GSTN WD25 101 M5
STVGE SG2 178 G1
Highfield CSTG HP8 128 B5
HLWS CM18 3 L8
KGLGY WD4 100 C2
LWTH SG6 16 B5
OXHEY WD19 132 D6
Highfield Av BSF CM23 44 C3
HARP AL5 47 G5
PIN HA5 142 D7
Highfield Cl AMS HP6 113 H3
NTHWD HA6 141 J3
Highfield Ct STVG SG1 33 J2
Highfield Crs NTHWD HA6 141 J3
Highfield Dr BROX EN10 92 C3
Highfield La HHNE HP2 62 D8
STALE/WH AL4 86 A4
Highfield Ov HARP AL5 46 E2
Highfield Park Dr
STALE/WH AL4 86 A5
Highfield Rd BERK HP4 80 B2
BUSH WD23 13 L8
CHESW EN7 91 J8
CSHM HP5 96 F3
HERT/BAY SG13 71 H1
LTNW/LEA LU4 27 M8
NTHWD HA6 141 J3
STALE/WH AL4 65 M4
TRING HP23 57 J2
Highfields KGLGY WD4 * 100 C2
POTB/CUF EN6 108 C2
RAD WD7 119 K1
Highfields Cl DUN/HR/TOD LU5 26 E7
Highfields Wy POTB/CUF EN6 106 F5
RKW/CH/CXG WD3 129 L2
High Firs RAD WD7 119 L1
High Firs Crs HARP AL5 47 H5
Highgate Gv SBW CM21 183 P7
High Gv STALW/RED AL3 8 E1
WGCW AL8 49 M6
Highgrove Cl FBAR/BDGN N11 137 L8
Highgrove Wy RSLP HA4 141 L8
Highland Dr BUSH WD23 132 F3
HHS/BOV HP3 82 F2
Highland Rd AMSS HP7 113 H5
BSF CM23 43 M6
NTHWD HA6 141 L4
WAB EN9 93 J4
Highlands BRKMPK AL9 68 A5
OXHEY WD19 132 A4
ROY SG8 14 F7
Highlands Cl CFSP/GDCR SL9 138 D2
Highlands End
CFSP/GDCR SL9 138 D2
Highlands La CFSP/GDCR SL9 138 D1
Highlands Ldg SHFD SG17 * 146 A2
Highlands Rd BAR EN5 136 E1
The Highlands BAR EN5 136 E1
POTB/CUF EN6 107 G5
RKW/CH/CXG WD3 129 M3
High La RBSF CM22 184 E11
STSD CM24 166 G5
High Md HRW HA1 143 J7
LTNN/LIM LU3 27 L6
Highmead STSD CM24 166 G5
High Meadow Cl PIN HA5 141 M6
High Meads STALE/WH AL4 48 A5
Highmoor AMSS HP7 113 H5
HARP AL5 46 E1
High Oak Rd WARE SG12 54 B3
High Oaks ENC/FH EN2 124 D4
STALW/RED AL3 65 G5
High Oaks Rd WGCW AL8 49 M6
Highover Cl LTNE LU2 7 M2
Highover Pk AMSS HP7 113 G6
Highover Rd LWTH SG6 16 B4
Highover Wy
HTCHE/RSTV SG4 157 R4
High Pastures RBSF CM22 184 D9
High Plash STVG SG1 * 10 E5
High Rdg HARP AL5 46 C2
LTNE LU2 29 G8
POTB/CUF EN6 108 C1
High Ridge Cl HHS/BOV HP3 82 B7
Highridge Cl RAD WD7 103 K7
Highridge Pl ENC/FH EN2 * 124 D4
High Ridge Rd HHS/BOV HP3 82 B7
High Rd BRKMPK AL9 69 J8
BROX EN10 92 D1
BUSH WD23 133 H4
EPP CM16 95 M6
FBAR/BDGN N11 137 M8
GSTN WD25 101 K8
HERT/WAT SG14 178 H11
HTCH/STOT SG5 146 A10
KTN/HRWW/WS HA3 143 J3
TRDG/WHET N20 136 F3
High Road Broxbourne
BROX EN10 92 D3
High Road Eastcote PIN HA5 141 M7
High Road Turnford
CHES/WCR EN8 92 C8
High Road Wormley
BROX EN10 92 D6
High St ABLGY WD5 101 K4
AMSS HP7 112 E5
ARL/CHE SG15 147 Q5
BAR EN5 122 C7
BERK HP4 59 J6
BGSW SG18 144 D4
BLDK SG7 17 K1
BLDK SG7 144 C11
BLDK SG7 149 P1
BSF CM23 43 M2
BUNT SG9 159 J10
BUSH WD23 132 E2
CFSP/GDCR SL9 138 C3
CHES/WCR EN8 110 B7
CSHM HP5 96 F5
CSTG HP8 128 A6
DEN/HRF UB9 140 A4
DUN/HR/TOD LU5 25 M5
DUN/WHIP LU6 37 J6
FBAR/BDGN N11 137 M8
HARP AL5 46 E3
HERT/WAT SG14 178 F5
HHNE HP2 82 B1
HHS/BOV HP3 98 E1
HLWE CM17 76 A1
HLWW/ROY CM19 73 M4
HOD EN11 92 E1
HTCH/STOT SG5 148 D7
HTCH/STOT SG5 156 E10
HTCH/STOT SG5 156 F1
HTCH/STOT SG5 157 N6
HTCHE/RSTV SG4 21 G5
HTCHE/RSTV SG4 157 P10
HTCHE/RSTV SG4 175 N8
HTCHE/RSTV SG4 176 F8
KGLGY WD4 100 E3
KTN/HRWW/WS HA3 143 J5
LBUZ LU7 169 L2
LCOL/BKTW AL2 86 A7
LTNW/LEA LU4 27 G5
MHAD SG10 181 R6
MLHL NW7 135 M8
NTHWD HA6 141 K3
PIN HA5 142 C5
POTB/CUF EN6 107 G6
RBSF CM22 167 M4
RBSF CM22 185 M3
RKW/CH/CXG WD3 130 B4
ROY SG8 145 M5
ROY SG8 152 A8
ROY SG8 152 H3
SAFWS CB11 161 Q5
SDY/GAM/POT SG19 144 F1
SHFD SG17 146 D4
STALE/WH AL4 48 B4
STALE/WH AL4 65 M4
STALE/WH AL4 86 F4
STALW/RED AL3 8 E6
STALW/RED AL3 172 F3
STDN SG11 163 P10
STVG SG1 33 G2
STVGE SG2 34 F1
TRING HP23 57 L2
WARE SG12 73 G1
WARE SG12 182 B8
WAT WD17 12 F4
WLYN AL6 177 J12
High Street Gn HHNE HP2 62 E7
High St South DUN/WHIP LU6 39 G1
The High HLW CM20 2 D5
High Town Rd LTNE LU2 7 G4
High Trees EBAR EN4 137 J1
High Vw BSF CM23 166 E10
CSTG HP8 128 B5
HAT AL10 87 K2
HTCH/STOT SG5 157 M7
PIN HA5 142 A6
RKW/CH/CXG WD3 115 L8
STALW/RED AL3 172 G5
WATW WD18 131 K2
Highview Av EDGW HA8 135 G7
Highview Cl POTB/CUF EN6 107 G7
Highview Gdns EDGW HA8 135 G8
POTB/CUF EN6 107 G7
STALE/WH AL4 66 A5
The Highway STAN HA7 143 K3
High Wickfield WGCE AL7 51 G8
Highwood Av BUSH WD23 118 D5
NFNCH/WDSPK N12 137 G7
High Wood Cl LTN LU1 40 D2
Highwood Gv MLHL NW7 135 H8
Highwoodhall La
HHS/BOV HP3 82 E7
Highwood Hl MLHL NW7 135 K5
High Wood Rd HOD EN11 72 D4
High Wych La SBW CM21 183 L7
High Wych Rd SBW CM21 183 J11
High Wych Wy HHNE HP2 62 E4
Hilberry Ct BUSH WD23 * 132 F3
Hilbury HAT AL10 87 K1
Hilbury Cl AMS HP6 113 G1
Hilfield La GSTN WD25 118 F5
Hiljon Crs CFSP/GDCR SL9 138 C3
Hillary Cl LTNN/LIM LU3 27 H2
Hillary Crs LTN LU1 6 B7
Hillary Ri ARL/CHE SG15 147 R4
BAR EN5 122 E8
Hillary Rd HHNE HP2 5 M1
Hill Av AMS HP6 113 G4
Hillborough Crs
DUN/HR/TOD LU5 26 A2
Hillborough Rd LTN LU1 6 D8
Hillbrow LWTH SG6 16 B4
Hillbury Av
KTN/HRWW/WS HA3 143 M7
Hill Cl BAR EN5 136 A1
HARP AL5 47 G1
LTNN/LIM LU3 28 A2
STAN HA7 133 M7
Hill Common HHS/BOV HP3 82 E6
Hill Crs HRW HA1 143 L7
TRDG/WHET N20 136 F5
Hill Crest HTCHE/RSTV SG4 175 Q3
POTB/CUF EN6 107 G8
Hillcrest BLDK SG7 17 K2
HAT AL10 87 L1
STALW/RED AL3 * 8 B9
STVG SG1 10 F4
Hillcrest Av EDGW HA8 134 F7
LTNE LU2 28 A1
PIN HA5 142 B6
Hillcrest Pk LWTH SG6 * 16 A3
Hillcrest Rd RAD WD7 104 E7
Hillcroft DUN/WHIP LU6 25 J8
Hillcroft Av PIN HA5 142 D8
Hill Croft Cl LTNW/LEA LU4 26 F3
Hillcroft Crs OXHEY WD19 131 M4
Hillcroft Rd CSHM HP5 97 H3
Hilldown Rd HHW HP1 61 L8
Hill Dyke Rd STALE/WH AL4 48 B6
Hill End Farm La
HTCHE/RSTV SG4 31 M5
Hill End La STAL AL1 86 A5
Hill End Rd DEN/HRF UB9 139 M1
Hillersdon Av EDGW HA8 134 D8
Hill Farm Av GSTN WD25 101 L7
Hill Farm La STALW/RED AL3 63 M4
WLYN AL6 176 A11
Hill Farm Rd CFSP/GDCR SL9 138 C2
CSHM HP5 97 H8
Hillfield HAT AL10 67 M5
Hillfield Av HTCHE/RSTV SG4 157 Q3
Hillfield Cl RYLN/HDSTN HA2 143 G6
Hillfield Ct HHNE HP2 5 H3
Hillfield La South BUSH WD23 133 J2
Hillfield Rd CFSP/GDCR SL9 138 C2
HHNE HP2 5 G3
Hillfield Sq CFSP/GDCR SL9 138 C2
Hillfoot Rd HTCH/STOT SG5 146 A8
Hillgate HTCHE/RSTV SG4 157 Q2
Hillhouse WAB EN9 111 K7
Hill House Av STAN HA7 143 K2
Hill House Cl CFSP/GDCR SL9 138 C2
Hilliard Rd NTHWD HA6 141 K3
Hillier Cl BAR EN5 136 F2
Hillingdon Rd GSTN WD25 101 L8
Hillingdon Trail DEN/HRF UB9 139 L4
Hill Ley HAT AL10 67 K8
Hill Leys POTB/CUF EN6 108 C2
Hill Md BERK HP4 79 L2
Hillmead STVG SG1 11 J3
Hillpoint RKW/CH/CXG WD3 130 A1
Hill Ri CFSP/GDCR SL9 138 B4
LTNN/LIM LU3 27 G2
POTB/CUF EN6 107 G8
POTB/CUF EN6 108 B1
RKW/CH/CXG WD3 129 M3
Hillrise Av WATN WD24 118 B4
Hill Rise Crs CFSP/GDCR SL9 138 C4
Hill Rd HRW HA1 143 L7
HTCHE/RSTV SG4 176 E8
NTHWD HA6 141 H1
PIN HA5 142 C8
Hillsborough Gn
OXHEY WD19 * 131 L6
Hillshott LWTH SG6 16 E3
Hill Side BAR EN5 137 G1
LBUZ LU7 169 K3
Hillside BAR EN5 * 135 L1
CSHM HP5 96 E2
DEN/HRF UB9 140 A7
DUN/HR/TOD LU5 25 M4
HAT AL10 67 L8
HLWE CM17 76 A7
HOD EN11 72 D6
HTCHE/RSTV SG4 176 F8
ROY SG8 14 E8
STVG SG1 11 H4
WARE SG12 54 B5
WGCE AL7 68 F2
Hillside Av BORE WD6 120 F8
BSF CM23 44 A2
CHES/WCR EN8 110 B5
Hillside Cl ABLGY WD5 101 J6
CFSP/GDCR SL9 138 C1
HTCH/STOT SG5 146 A8
Hillside Crs CHES/WCR EN8 110 B5
ENC/FH EN2 125 H4
NTHWD HA6 141 L3
OXHEY WD19 132 B2
WARE SG12 72 F1
Hillside Gdns AMSS HP7 113 J6
BAR EN5 122 C8
BERK HP4 80 B2
EDGW HA8 134 D7
NTHWD HA6 141 L2
Hillside La WARE SG12 54 E8
Hillside Pk BLDK SG7 * 17 L2
Hillside Ri NTHWD HA6 141 L2
Hillside Rd BUSH WD23 13 L8
DUN/HR/TOD LU5 39 H2
HARP AL5 46 D2
HTCH/STOT SG5 146 A8
LTNN/LIM LU3 6 D2
NTHWD HA6 141 L2
RAD WD7 119 M1
RKW/CH/CXG WD3 129 G1
STAL AL1 9 H4
Hillside Ter HERT/BAY SG13 71 G1
Hillside Wy WLYN AL6 177 N9
Hills La NTHWD HA6 141 J3
Hill St STALW/RED AL3 8 C5
Hills Vw LTNN/LIM LU3 154 B9
The Hill HLWE CM17 76 A1
STALE/WH AL4 48 B6
Hill Top BLDK SG7 17 J2
Hilltop STALW/RED AL3 173 P11
Hilltop Cl CHESW EN7 91 K8
Hilltop Rd BERK HP4 80 A2
KGLGY WD4 101 H1
Hilltop Vw SHFD SG17 146 D3
Hilltop Wk HARP AL5 47 H5
Hilltop Wy STAN HA7 133 L6
Hill Tree Cl SBW CM21 183 P8
Hill Vw BERK HP4 59 L7
BUNT SG9 158 H1
HTCHE/RSTV SG4 175 Q3
Hillview Cl PIN HA5 142 D1
Hillview Crs LTNN/LIM LU3 28 A2
Hillview Gdns CHES/WCR EN8 110 C1
RYLN/HDSTN HA2 142 E5
Hillview Rd MLHL NW7 136 B7
PIN HA5 142 D2
Hill Wy AMSS HP7 112 F7
Hill Waye CFSP/GDCR SL9 138 D8
Hilly Fld HLWS CM18 95 K1
Hillyfields DUN/WHIP LU6 39 G3
Hilly Flds WGCE AL7 51 G6
Hilmay Dr HHW HP1 4 C4
Hilton Av DUN/WHIP LU6 38 F3
NFNCH/WDSPK N12 137 H8
Hilton Cl STVG SG1 32 F2
Himalayan Wy WATW WD18 12 B9
Hindes Rd HRW HA1 143 J7
Hindhead Gn OXHEY WD19 132 A8
Hine Wy HTCH/STOT SG5 157 L4
Hinkley Cl DEN/HRF UB9 140 A6
Hinton Wk DUN/HR/TOD LU5 26 C3
Hinwick Cl ARL/CHE SG15 147 R2
Hinxworth Rd BLDK SG7 148 F3
Hipkins BSF CM23 43 L5
Hipkins Pl BROX EN10 92 C2
Hispano Ms PEND EN3 126 E3
Hitchens Cl HHW HP1 81 K1
Hitches Yd WARE SG12 * 54 B4
Hitchin Hl HTCHE/RSTV SG4 157 N7
Hitchin Rd HNLW SG16 147 J5

Name	Area	Page	Grid
HTCH/STOT SG5		155	R4
HTCHE/RSTV SG4		175	P7
LTNE LU2		7	H3
LWTH SG6		16	C6
SHFD SG17		146	H2
STVG SG1		20	F1
Hitchin St *BLDK* SG7		17	J1
Hitchwood La *HTCHE/RSTV* SG4		31	K4
Hitherbaulk *WGCE* AL7		68	B1
Hither Fld *HHNE* HP2		54	C2
Hitherfield La *HARP* AL5		46	E3
Hither Meadow *CFSP/GDCR* SL9 *		138	C3
Hitherway *WGCW* AL8		50	B3
Hitherwell Dr *KTN/HRWW/WS* HA3		143	H5
Hive CI *HHNE* HP2		133	H5
Hive Rd *BUSH* WD23		133	H5
Hiving's HI *CSHM* HP5		96	E2
Hivings Pk *CSHM* HP5		96	F3
Hobart CI *TRDG/WHET* N20		137	J5
Hobart Wk *STALW/RED* AL3		65	K6
Hobbs CI *CHES/WCR* EN8		110	B3
STALE/WH AL4		86	C3
Hobbs Cross Rd *HLWE* CM17		76	D2
Hobbs HI *WLYN* AL6		50	A1
Hobbs Rd *HHS/BOV* HP3		82	C6
Hobbs Wy *WCCW* AL8		50	A8
Hobby Horse CI *CHES* EN7		91	H6
Hobletts Rd *HHNE* HP2		82	D1
Hobsons CI *HOD* EN11		72	D4
Hobsons Wk *TRING* HP23		169	G8
Hobtoe Rd *HLWW* CM20		74	E4
Hockeridge Vw *BERK* HP4		79	K2
Hockerill *HERT/WAT* SG14		178	G6
Hockerill St *BER* SG23		44	H2
Hocklands *WGCE* AL7		51	G6
Hockwell Ring *LTNW/LEA* LU4		26	F4
Hoddesdon Rd *WARE* SG12		73	G1
Hodds Wood Rd *CSHM* HP5		97	G7
Hodges Wy *WATW* WD18		131	H8
Hodgkins Ms *STAN* HA7		133	L8
Hodings Rd *HLW* CM20		2	F1
Hodson PI *PEND* EN3		126	E4
Hodwell *BLDK* SG7		149	P5
Hoecroft *WAB* EN9		93	K4
Hoe La *EN* EN1		125	M4
WAB EN9		93	K4
WARE SG12		54	B5
Hoestock Rd *SBW* CM21		183	P7
The Hoe *OXHEY* WD19		132	B9
Hogg End La *STALW/RED* AL3		63	L8
Hogg La *BORE* WD6		119	J3
Hog Hall La *BERK* HP4		170	C4
Hog La *CSHM* HP5		78	F4
Hogpits Bottom *HHS/BOV* HP3		98	E6
Hogsdell La *HERT/BAY* SG13		71	M1
Holbeck La *CHESW* EN7		91	K9
Holbein Ga *HTCH/HA6*		131	J4
Holborn CI *STALE/WH* AL4		66	B5
Holborn CI *EN* EN1		125	K5
Holcombe HI *MLHL* NW7		135	L6
Holcroft *HARP* AL5		47	H2
Holdbrook *HTCHE/RSTV* SG4		157	R6
Holden Av *NFNCH/WDSPK* N12		136	F8
Holden CI *HERT/BAY* SG13		51	J8
HTCHE/RSTV SG4		20	A2
Holden Rd *NFNCH/WDSPK* N12		136	F7
Holders La *STVGE* SG2		34	C4
The Holdings *BRKMPK* AL9		68	B8
Holecroft *WAB* EN9		111	J8
Holford Wy *LTNW/LIM* LU3		154	H12
Holgate Dr *LTNW/LEA* LU4		26	F6
Holkham CI *LTNW/LEA* LU4		26	E5
Holland Ct *BAR* EN5		137	M8
STAN HA7		133	M8
Holland Gdns *GSTN* WD25		118	A4
Holland Rd *LTNW/LEA* LU4		27	M7
Holland's Cft *WARE* SG12		182	B8
Holland Wk *STAN* HA7		133	L8
Hollick's La *DUN/WHIP* LU6		39	H7
Holliday St *BERK* HP4		80	B1
Holliers Wy *HAT* AL10		67	L8
Hollies CI *ROY* SG8		14	F7
Hollies End *HHNE* NW7		135	M8
The Hollies *BAR* EN5		135	L4
HHS/BOV HP3		98	E6
KTN/HRWW/WS HA3		143	L6
STAL AL1 *		9	G3
TRING HP23		58	B9
Hollies Wy *POTB/CUF* EN6		107	G5
Holliwick Rd *DUN/HR/TOD* LU5		26	D7
Holloway La *RKW/CH/CXG* WD3		114	F4
Holloways La *BRKMPK* AL9		88	B5
The Holloway *RAYLNE/WEN* HP22		57	G1
Hollow La *HTCHE/RSTV* SG4		157	P6
Hollow Wy *CSHM* HP5		96	C4
Hollow Way La *AMS* HP6		113	J4
Hollybush Av *LCOL/BKTW* AL2		84	E6
Hollybush CI *BERK* HP4		61	H6
KTN/HRWW/WS HA3		143	J3
OXHEY WD19		132	A3
WLYN AL6		177	L9
Hollybush HI *LTNE* LU2		156	B12
Hollybush Rd *AMS* HP6		113	K4
HARP AL5		81	K1
HHW HP1		81	K1
HTCHE/RSTV SG4		175	M1
KNEB SG3		177	Q6
STALW/RED AL3		173	J6
WGCE AL7		68	D3
Hollybush Rd *CSHM* HP5		96	E1
LTNE LU2		29	E1
Hollybush Rw *TRING* HP23 *		58	B5
Hollybush Wy *CHESW* EN7		109	L2
Holly CI *HAT* AL10		87	K1
Holly Copse *STVG* SG1		11	G6
Holly Cft *HERT/WAT* SG14		52	D6
Hollycross Rd *WARE* SG12		55	G1
Holly Dell *HERT/BAY* SG13		71	G1
Holly Dr *BORE* WD6		123	B2
POTB/CUF EN6		106	F7
Holly Farm CI *LTN* LU1		6	C9
Holly Fld *HLWW/ROY* CM19		75	G8
Hollyfield *HAT* AL10		87	L3
TRING HP23		169	N12
Hollyfield Av *FBAR/BDGN* N11		137	J4
Hollyfield CI *TRING* HP23		169	N12
Hollyfields *BROX* EN10		97	M8
Hollyhock *BUSH* WD23		133	H3
Hollyhock CI *HHW* HP1		81	J1
Holly Gv *PIN* HA5		142	C3
Holly Grove Rd *HERT/WAT* SG14		52	A2
Holly Hall CI *WLYN* AL6		177	J12
Holly Hedges La *HHS/BOV* HP3		99	G4
Hollyhock CI *HHW* HP1		81	J1
Holly La *HARP* AL5		175	J10

Holly Leys *STVGE* SG2		177	P1
Holly Park Rd *FBAR/BDGN* N11		137	J8
Holly Rd *KNEB* SG3		177	N8
PEND EN3		126	B2
Holly Shaws *STVGE* SG2		33	M7
Holly St *LTN* LU1		6	B1
Hollytree CI *CFSP/GDCR* SL9		128	C2
CSHM HP5		97	M5
Holly Tree Ct *HHNE* HP2		82	F2
Holly Wk *HARP* AL5		47	H4
WGCW AL8		50	A8
Holmbridge Gdns *PEND* EN3		126	B8
Holmbrook Av *LTNN/LIM* LU3		28	A4
Holmbury CI *BUSH* WD23		133	J5
Holmdale *LWTH* SG6		16	C6
Holmdale CI *BORE* WD6		120	D6
Holmdene Av *RYLN/HDSTN* HA2		142	F5
Holmebury CI *BUSH* WD23		133	J5
HAT AL10		67	K5
Holme Lea *GSTN* WD25		102	A8
Holme Rd *BORE* WD6		120	D6
Holme PI *HHNE* HP2		83	G1
Holme Rd *HAT* AL10		67	K5
Holmes Av *MLHL* NW7		136	C8
Holmesdale *CHES/WCR* EN8		126	A1
Holmes Meadow *HLWW/ROY* CM19		94	F3
Holme Wy *STAN* HA7		143	K1
Holmfield CI *LTNE* LU2		6	D7
Holm Oak Pk *WATW* WD18 *		12	C5
Holmscroft Rd *LTNN/LIM* LU3		27	K3
Holmshill La *BORE* WD6		121	K3
Holmside Ri *OXHEY* WD19		131	M6
Holmwood CI *RYLN/HDSTN* HA2		143	C5
Holmwood Gv *MLHL* NW7		135	H8
Holmwood Rd *PEND* EN3		126	B2
Holroyd Crs *BLDK* SG7		17	J2
Holsworth CI *RYLN/HDSTN* HA2		143	C7
Holt CI *BORE* WD6		120	D8
Holts Meadow *STALW/RED* AL3		173	R11
LTNE LU2		29	H8
Holtsmere CI *GSTN* WD25		118	A1
Holtsmere End La *STALW/RED* AL3		62	F1
The Holt *HHNE* HP2		5	J4
WGCE AL7		51	H8
Holtwhite Av *ENC/FH* EN2		125	G6
Holtwhite's HI *ENC/FH* EN2		124	D5
Holwell Hyde *WGCE* AL7		69	G1
Holwell La *BRKMPK* AL9		69	J1
Holwell PI *PIN* HA5		142	C6
Holwell Rd *HTCH/STOT* SG5		146	H11
WGCE AL7		50	D8
Holy Cross HI *BROX* EN10		91	L5
Holyfield Rd *WAB* EN9		91	M5
Holyrood Crs *STAL* AL1		85	H6
Holyrood Rd *BAR* EN5		137	G2
Holywell CI *DUN/WHIP* LU6		171	P3
Holywell HI *STAL* AL1		8	B7
Holywell Rd *DUN/WHIP* LU6		171	P2
WATW WD18		12	D8
Home CI *BROX* EN10		92	D6
HLW CM20		3	J6
HTCH/STOT SG5		148	D7
LTNW/LEA LU4		27	G5
STDN SG11		180	C7
Home Ct *LTNW/LEA* LU4 *		27	H7
Homedale Dr *LTNW/LEA* LU4		27	H7
Home Farm *TRING* HP23		57	L3
Home Farm Ct *STDN* SG11 *		163	P10
Home Farm Rd *BERK* HP4		59	H6
RKW/CH/CXG WD3		130	E7
Homefield *BERK* HP4		60	F6
BLDK SG7		144	D11
HHS/BOV HP3		98	B4
WAB EN9		111	L6
Homefield Ct *HTCHE/RSTV* SG4		32	D7
Homefield Rd *BUSH* WD23		132	E1
HHNE HP2		5	M9
RAD WD7		119	K3
RKW/CH/CXG WD3		115	H8
WARE SG12		54	C3
Homeleigh Ct *CHES/WCR* EN8		109	M4
Home Ley *WGCE* AL7		68	C3
Home Meadow *WGCE* AL7		50	C7
Home Park Mill Link Rd *KGLGY* WD4		100	F5
Home Pastures *RBSF* CM22		184	A7
Homerfield *WGCW* AL8		50	A7
Homerswood La *WLYN* AL6		49	L3
Homerton Rd *LTNN/LIM* LU3		27	L3
Homestead CI *LCOL/BKTW* AL2		103	G1
Homestead La *WCCE* AL7		68	D1
Homestead Rd *HAT* AL10		68	D2
Homestead Moat *STVG* SG1		10	F5
Homestead Paddock *STHGT/OAK* N14		137	M1
Homestead Wy *HAT* AL10		67	J8
Home Wy *RKW/CH/CXG* WD3		129	K4
Homewood *POTB/CUF* EN6		108	C1
Homewood La *POTB/CUF* EN6		108	A1
Homewood Rd *STAL* AL1		65	M7
Honeybourne *BSF* CM23		43	L5
Honey Brook *WAB* EN9		111	J9
Honeycroft *WGCW* AL8		50	A8
Honeycroft Dr *STALE/WH* AL4		86	A5
Honeycross Rd *HHW* HP1		81	J3
Honeygate *LTNE* LU2		28	C5
Honey La *BUSH* SG9		159	J9
SAFWS CB11		161	M6
WAB EN9		111	J8
Honeymeade *STVG* SG1 *		183	N10
Honeysuckle CI *BSF* CM23		43	J3
HERT/BAY SG13		53	L7
Honeysuckle Fld *CSHM* HP5		97	G4
Honeysuckle Gdns *HAT* AL10		87	M1
Honeyway Rd *DUN/WHIP* LU6		37	J1
Honeywick CI *DUN/WHIP* LU6		37	J1
Honeywood CI *POTB/CUF* EN6		108	H7
Honister CI *STAN* HA7		143	M3
Honister Gdns *STAN* HA7		143	M2
Honister PI *STAN* HA7		143	M3
Honiton Ms *LTNN/LIM* LU3		27	J3
Honor St *HLWE* CM17		76	D4
Honours Md *HHS/BOV* HP3 *		98	E1
Hood CI *STHGT/OAK* N14		137	M2
Hook Fld *HLWS* CM18		7	G6
Hook Ga *LTNE* LU2		125	M3
Hooking Gn *RYLN/HDSTN* HA2		142	F5
Hook La *POTB/CUF* EN6		107	K6
The Hook *BAR* EN5		137	H2

Hoopers Ms *BUSH* WD23		132	F4
Hoops La *ROY* SG8		151	M7
Hoo Rd *SHFD* SG17		146	F2
Hoo St *LTN* LU1		7	G9
The Hoo *HLWE* CM17		183	N12
Hope Gn *GSTN* WD25		101	N7
Hopewell Rd *SHFD* SG17		17	H1
Hop Garden Wy *GSTN* WD25		102	A5
Hopground CI *STAL* AL1		85	L4
Hopkins Crs *STALE/WH* AL4		65	M4
Hopkins Yd *STAL* AL1		9	F7
Hoppit Rd *WAB* EN9		110	F6
Hopton Rd *STVG* SG1		32	E2
Hoptree CI *NFNCH/WDSPK* N12 *		136	F7
Hopwood CI *WAT* WD17		117	H2
Horace Gay Gdns *LWTH* SG6		16	C4
Hordle Gdns *STAL* AL1		9	K8
Hornbeam CI *BORE* WD6		120	E5
MLHL NW7		135	K6
Hornbeam La *BRKMPK* AL9		89	J3
Hornbeams *LCOL/BKTW* AL2		103	H2
WGCE AL7		50	F8
Hornbeam Av *LTN* LU1		6	A5
Hornbeam Spring *KNEB* SG3		177	M5
The Hornbeams *HLW* CM20		2	M7
STVGE SG2		11	M7
Hornbeam Wy *CHESW* EN7		109	K3
The Hornets *WATW* WD18		12	E6
Horn HI *HTCHE/RSTV* SG4		175	Q3
Hornhill Rd *RKW/CH/CXG* WD3		129	G8
Hornsby CI *LTNE* LU2		29	G8
Horns CI *HERT/BAY* SG13		71	G1
Horns End PI *PIN* HA5		142	A6
Hornsfield *WGCE* AL7		51	G6
Horns Mill Rd *HERT/BAY* SG13		70	F2
Horns Rd *HERT/BAY* SG13		53	G8
Horrocks CI *WARE* SG12		54	B2
Horsa Gdns *HAT* AL10		67	H7
Horselock La *CSHM* HP5		78	C5
Horsecroft Rd *HHW* HP1		4	A6
HLWW/ROY CM19		74	C6
Horse Cross *STDN* SG11		164	B9
Horse HI *CSHM* HP5		98	A9
Horselers *HHS/BOV* HP3		5	M9
Horsemans Dr *LCOL/BKTW* AL2		84	E8
Horseshoe HI *BGSW* SG18		144	D4
LBUZ LU7		169	K2
ROY SG8		152	H4
WAB EN9		111	L8
Horseshoe La *BUNT* SG9		159	R10
ENC/FH EN2		125	J4
GSTN WD25		101	M6
TRDG/WHET N20		136	B4
The Horseshoe *HHS/BOV* HP3		83	G4
Horsham Av *NFNCH/WDSPK* N12		137	J8
Horsham CI *LTNE* LU2		29	H6
Horsler CI *AMP/FLIT/BLC* MK45		155	J7
Horsleys *RKW/CH/CXG* WD3		129	H8
Horton Gdns *HHNE* HP2		62	B4
Horton Rd *LBUZ* LU7		36	A3
Hospital Circular Rd *RAYLNE/WEN* HP22		56	B7
Hospital HI *CSHM* HP5		97	G6
Hospital Rd *ARL/CHE* SG15		147	P6
Houghton Pde *DUN/HR/TOD* LU5		25	L7
Houghton Park Rd *DUN/HR/TOD* LU5		26	C3
Houghton Rd *DUN/HR/TOD* LU5		25	L6
Housden CI *STALE/WH* AL4		86	A5
Housefield Wy *STALE/WH* AL4		86	A5
House La *ARL/CHE* SG15		147	Q2
STALE/WH AL4		66	A4
Housewood End *HHW* HP1		61	M7
Housman Av *ROY* SG8		14	D4
Howard CI *BUSH* WD23		133	J3
FBAR/BDGN N11		137	L5
HTCH/STOT SG5 *		148	D8
LTNN/LIM LU3		27	L1
STAL AL1		86	A5
WAB EN9		111	H8
Howard Dr *BORE* WD6		121	H8
LWTH SG6		16	F6
Howarde Ct *STVG* SG1		10	B2
Howard Ga *LWTH* SG6		16	F5
Howard PI *DUN/HR/TOD* LU5		39	H2
Howard Rd *CSHM* HP5		96	F2
Howards HI *PIN* HA5		141	M4
Howardsgate *WGCW* AL8		50	B6
Howards Wd *LWTH* SG6		16	F6
Howard Wy *BAR* EN5		136	B1
HLW CM20		3	J1
Howberry Gn *ARL/CHE* SG15		147	P6
Howe CI *RAD* WD7		104	C6
Howe Dell *HAT* AL10		67	M8
Howe Rd *HHS/BOV* HP3		5	M7
How Fld *HARP* AL5		46	C2
Howfield Gn *HOD* EN11		72	D4
Howicks Gn *WGCE* AL7		68	E2
Howland Ct *PIN* HA5		142	E1
Howland Garth *STAL* AL1		85	G6
Howlands *WGCE* AL7		68	A5
Howletts La *RSLP* HA4		141	G8
Howse Rd *WAB* EN9		126	F1
Howton PI *BUSH* WD23		133	H4
How Wd *LCOL/BKTW* AL2		102	F2
Hoylake Gdns *OXHEY* WD19		132	B7
Hubbards Rd *RKW/CH/CXG* WD3		129	H1
Huckleberry CI *LTNN/LIM* LU3		27	L1
Hucklesby Wy *LTNN/LIM* LU3		6	E3
Hudnall La *BERK* HP4		171	K11
Hudson CI *STAL* AL1		85	G5
WATN WD24		117	K2
Hudson Av *DEN/HRF* UB9		139	K8
Huggins La *BRKMPK* AL9		87	M5
Hughenden Av *KTN/HRWW/WS* HA3		143	M7
Hughenden Rd *STALE/WH* AL4		65	M7
Hughes Ct *NFNCH/WDSPK* N12		137	J8
Hugo CI *WATW* WD18		117	M8
Hull CI *CHESW* EN7		91	H8
Hull Gv *HLWW/ROY* CM19		94	E2
Hull La *STDN* SG11		163	Q6
Humber Ct *STVG* SG1		21	K5
Humberstone CI *LTNN/LEA* LU4		27	G1
Humberstone Rd *LTNN/LEA* LU4		27	G1
Hume Wy *RSLP* HA4		141	L1
Humphrey Talbot Av *DUN/WHIP* LU6		171	M2

Humphrys Rd *DUN/HR/TOD* LU5		26	B6
Hundred Acres *CHES/WCR* EN8 *		110	E8
Hundred Acres La *AMSS* HP7		113	H6
Hunsdon *WGCE* AL7		51	H7
Hunsdon Rd *WARE* SG12		73	J1
WARE SG12		182	B5
Hunston CI *LTNW/LEA* LU4		26	F4
Hunters CI *STALE/WH* AL4		66	M4
Hunter CI *BORE* WD6		135	G1
POTB/CUF EN6		106	F7
Huntercrombe Gdns *OXHEY* WD19		132	A8
Hunters CI *CSHM* HP5		96	E4
HHS/BOV HP3		98	E4
HTCH/STOT SG5		148	C7
STVGE SG2		34	B2
TRING HP23		169	M12
Hunter's La *GSTN* WD25		101	M3
Hunters Oak *HHNE* HP2		62	F5
Hunters Pk *BERK* HP4		60	C8
Hunters Reach *CHESW* EN7		96	E4
Hunters Ride *LCOL/BKTW* AL2		102	C5
Hunters Wy *ENC/FH* EN2		124	E5
ROY SG8		14	F7
WGCE AL7		68	D2
Huntingdon CI *BROX* EN10		92	C6
Huntingdon Rd *STVG* SG1		32	E4
Hunting Ga *HHNE* HP2		62	C6
HTCHE/RSTV SG4		157	R2
Hunting Gate CI *ENC/FH* EN2		124	E1
Hunton Bridge HI *KGLGY* WD4		101	L3
Hunts CI *LTN* LU1		6	C8
Huntsman CI *STDN* SG11		163	P10
Huntsmans CI *BERK* HP4		171	J4
Hunts Md *PEND* EN3		126	B3
Huntsmill Rd *HHW* HP1		81	J3
Hurlock CI *DUN/WHIP* LU6		38	E3
Hurlock Wy *LTNW/LEA* LU4		26	F5
Hurn Gv *BSF* CM23		166	E12
STSD CM24		166	G7
Huron Rd *BROX* EN10		92	C8
Hurricane Wy *ABLGY* WD5		101	L7
Hurst CI *BLDK* SG7		149	L12
BSF CM23		43	L2
WGCE AL7		51	G8
Hurst Dr *CHES/WCR* EN8		110	B8
Hurstlings *WGCE* AL7		68	F1
Hurst PI *NTHWD* HA6		140	F4
Hurst Ri *BAR* EN5		122	E7
Hurst Wy *LTNN/LIM* LU3		27	J1
Hutton CI *HERT/WAT* SG14		52	E7
LTNW/LEA LU4		27	H1
Hutton Gv *NFNCH/WDSPK* N12		136	F8
Hutton La *KTN/HRWW/WS* HA3		143	G2
Hutton Wk *KTN/HRWW/WS* HA3		143	G2
Hyatts Yd *CSHM* HP5 *		96	F6
Hyburn CI *HHS/BOV* HP3		82	F3
LCOL/BKTW AL2		102	D4
Hydean Wy *STVGE* SG2		11	J9
Hyde Av *HTCH/STOT* SG5		148	C8
POTB/CUF EN6		106	F7
Hyde CI *BAR* EN5		122	D7
HARP AL5		46	A4
Hyde Gn *STVGE* SG2		11	M9
Hyde Gn East *STVGE* SG2		11	M9
Hyde Gn North *STVGE* SG2		11	M9
Hyde Gn South *STVGE* SG2		11	M9
Hyde La *HHS/BOV* HP3		98	D6
LCOL/BKTW AL2		103	J2
LTNE LU2		174	D7
Hyde Md *WAB* EN9		93	J5
Hyde Mdw *HHS/BOV* HP3		98	D6
Hyde Rd *LTN* LU1		40	D5
The Hyde *STVGE* SG2		34	A6
Hyde Va *WGCE* AL7		68	D3
Hyde View Rd *HARP* AL5		46	A4
Hyde Wy *WGCE* AL7		50	C7
Hyperion Ct *HHNE* HP2		62	D7
Hyrons CI *AMS* HP6		113	J4
Hyrons La *AMS* HP6		113	H4
Hyver HI *BAR* EN5		135	H2

I

Ibberson Wy *HTCHE/RSTV* SG4		157	Q6
Ibsley Wy *EBAR* EN4		137	J1
Iceni Ct *LWTH* SG6		16	F2
Ickleford Rd *HTCH/STOT* SG5		157	P5
Icklefield CI *LTNW/LEA* LU4		26	F4
Icknield CI *HTCH/STOT* SG5		157	N1
RAYLNE/WEN HP22		56	A8
STALW/RED AL3		84	D4
Icknield Gn *LWTH* SG6		16	C3
Icknield Wy *LTNW/LEA* LU4		169	L11
Icknield St *DUN/WHIP* LU6		27	K5
Icknield Wk *ROY* SG8		38	F7
BERK HP4		14	F6
Icknield Wy *BERK* HP4		170	C4
BLDK SG7		149	J12
DUN/WHIP LU6		37	L8
LTNN/LIM LU3		27	K2
ROY SG8		14	A3
STVG SG1		151	P3
Icknield Wy East *BLDK* SG7		149	K12
Icknield Way Pth *BLDK* SG7		18	L1
BLDK SG7		149	N2
HTCH/STOT SG5		156	B5
LTNN/LIM LU3		154	E6
LTNW/LEA LU4		27	G1
ROY SG8		14	A3
STVG SG1		145	P11
The Icon *STVG* SG1 *		10	D5
Ilford CI *LTNE* LU2		29	G6
Ilkley Rd *OXHEY* WD19		132	B8
Imberfield *LTNW/LEA* LU4		26	E4
Imperial CI *RYLN/HDSTN* HA2		142	E8
Imperial Dr *RYLN/HDSTN* HA2		142	E8
Imperial PI *BORE* WD6 *		120	C8
Imperial Wy *WATW* WD24		118	A5
Indells *HAT* AL10		87	K1
Index Dr *DUN/WHIP* LU6		39	J1
Ingelheim Ct *STVG* SG1		10	B3
Ingersoll Rd *PEND* EN3		126	A4
Ingle CI *PIN* HA5		142	A1
Inglefield *POTB/CUF* EN6		106	E4
Ingles *WGCE* AL7		68	D3
Ingleside Dr *STVG* SG1		20	F8
Inglewood Gdns *LCOL/BKTW* AL2		85	K7
Ingram Ct *STAL* AL1		134	A4
Ingram Gdns *LTNE* LU2		28	B3
Ingle Rd *CSHM* HP5		96	D4
Inkerman Rd *STAL* AL1		9	G7

Inkerman St *LTN* LU1		6	E5
Inkerman Ter *CSHM* HP5		96	D4
Inkwell CI *NFNCH/WDSPK* N12		137	G6
Innes Ct *HHS/BOV* HP3		5	L9
Innova Wy *PEND* EN3		126	D2
Inn's CI *STVG* SG1		10	C2
Inskip Crs *STVG* SG1		10	F4
Inverforth Rd *FBAR/BDGN* N11		137	M8
Inverness Av *EN* EN1		125	J5
Iona CI *STVG* SG1		21	K7
Ionian Wy *HHNE* HP2		62	D7
Iredale Vw *BLDK* SG7		149	L12
Ireton CI *STVG* SG1		10	C7
Irkdale Av *EN* EN1		125	K5
Iron Dr *HERT/BAY* SG13		53	M6
Irvine Av *KTN/HRWW/WS* HA3		143	L5
Irvine CI *TRDG/WHET* N20		137	J5
Irving CI *BSF* CM23		43	J3
Irving Crs *LBUZ* LU7		169	L1
Isabel CI *HOD* EN11		72	F5
Isabel Ga *CHES/WCR* EN8		92	D8
Isabelle CI *CHESW* EN7		109	G3
Isenburg Wy *HHNE* HP2		62	D7
Isherwood CI *ROY* SG8		14	D6
Isis CI *RSLP* HA4		141	G4
Island Centre Wy *PEND* EN3		126	E4
Isle of Wight La *DUN/WHIP* LU6		38	F6
Islington Wy *STVG* SG1		21	K7
Ivanhoe Dr *KTN/HRWW/WS* HA3		143	M4
Ivatt CI *HTCHE/RSTV* SG4		20	E2
Iveagh CI *NTHWD* HA6		140	F7
Ivel CI *AMP/FLIT/BLC* MK45		155	K2
Ivel Rd *STVG* SG1		10	A1
Ivel Wy *BLDK* SG7		149	G7
HTCH/STOT SG5		148	D5
Ivere Dr *BAR* EN5		136	F2
Ives Rd *HERT/WAT* SG14		52	F5
Ivinghoe Br *LBUZ* LU7		169	N1
Ivinghoe CI *EN* EN1		125	J6
GSTN WD25		118	B1
STALW/RED AL3		66	A5
Ivinghoe Rd *BUSH* WD23		133	H2
RKW/CH/CXG WD3		129	L4
Ivinghoe Wy *DUN/WHIP* LU6		37	J9
Ivory CI *STALW/RED* AL3		84	A4
Ivory Ct *HHS/BOV* HP3		5	M8
Ivybridge *BROX* EN10		92	E1
Ivy CI *DUN/WHIP* LU6		25	J3
Ivy Lea *RKW/CH/CXG* WD3		129	L4
Ivy Rd *LTN* LU1		6	B9
Ivy House La *BERK* HP4		80	C1
Ivy Ter *HOD* EN11		73	G5
Ivy Wk *NTHWD* HA6 *		141	H4

J

Jackdaw CI *STVGE* SG2		34	B5
Jackdaws *WGCE* AL7		51	G7
Jackets La *NTHWD* HA6		140	E2
Jacketts Fld *ABLGY* WD5		101	K5
Jackman's PI *LWTH* SG6		16	F5
Jacks Hill Pk *HTCHE/RSTV* SG4		21	G3
Jacks La *DEN/HRF* UB9		139	L7
Jackson Rd *EBAR* EN4		137	J2
Jacksons CI *DUN/WHIP* LU6		37	J5
Jacksons Dr *CHESW* EN7		109	L2
Jackson's La *ROY* SG8		152	M1
Jackson St *BLDK* SG7		149	J12
Jack Stevens CI *HLWE* CM17 *		76	D4
Jakes Vw *LCOL/BKTW* AL2		103	G1
James Bedford CI *PIN* HA5		142	A4
James CI *BUSH* WD23		13	M7
James Ct *LTN* LU1		6	D7
James Lee Sq *PEND* EN3		126	E4
James Martin CI *DEN/HRF* UB9		139	L8
Jameson Rd *HARP* AL5		46	F2
James Wy *OXHEY* WD19		132	B7
STVG SG1		33	G2
Jane CI *HHNE* HP2		62	F5
Jarden *LWTH* SG6		17	G5
Jardine Wy *DUN/HR/TOD* LU5		39	J2
Jarman CI *HHNE* HP2		5	K9
Jarman Wy *HHNE* HP2		5	K9
ROY SG8		14	C6
Jarvis Cleys *CHESW* EN7		91	H3
Jarvis CI *BAR* EN5		136	B1
Jasmin CI *BSF* CM23		43	J3
NTHWD HA6		141	K3
Jasmine Dr *HERT/BAY* SG13		53	L7
Jasmine Gdns *HAT* AL10		67	K6
Jasmine Wk *CSHM* HP5		96	E4
Jasmin Wy *HHW* HP1		81	J1
Jasons HI *CSHM* HP5		97	M3
Jasper Ct *PEND* EN3		126	A4
Jay CI *LWTH* SG6		16	C1
Jaycroft *ENC/FH* EN2		124	E5
Jays CI *LCOL/BKTW* AL2		103	G2
Jaywood *LTNE* LU2		29	G4
Jeans La *BSF* CM23		43	L2
Jeans Wy *DUN/HR/TOD* LU5		39	J1
Jeffery CI *ROY* SG8		14	D5
Jeffreys Rd *PEND* EN3		126	D8
Jeffries Rd *WARE* SG12		73	G1
Jellicoe Gdns *STAN* HA7		143	K1
Jellicoe Rd *WATW* WD18		131	L2
Jenkins Av *LCOL/BKTW* AL2		102	C4
Jenkins Dr *RBSF* CM22		167	L2
Jenkins La *RBSF* CM22		44	B5
Jennings CI *STVG* SG1		10	E8
Jennings Rd *STAL* AL1		9	K3
Jennings Wy *BAR* EN5		122	A7
HHNE HP2		5	J6
Jenning Wd *WLYN* AL6		177	M10
Jepps CI *CHESW* EN7		91	M3
Jepps La *ROY* SG8		14	E7
Jeremiah CI *AMP/FLIT/BLC* MK45		155	J2
Jerome Dr *STALW/RED* AL3		84	C4
Jerounds *HLWW/ROY* CM19		74	F7
Jersey Av *KTN/HRWW/WS* HA3		143	M4
Jersey La *HOD* EN11		72	G4
Jersey La *STAL* AL1		85	L1
Jersey Ms *LTNW/LEA* LU4		26	C5
Jervis Av *PEND* EN3		126	C1
Jervis Rd *BSF* CM23		43	M3
Jesmond Wy *STAN* HA7		134	C9
Jessop Rd *STVG* SG1		10	C4
Jeve CI *BLDK* SG7		149	L12
Jill Grey PI *HTCHE/RSTV* SG4		157	P7
Jillifer Rd *LTNW/LEA* LU4		26	E6
The Jinnings *WGCE* AL7		68	F2
Jocelyns *HLWE* CM17		76	A1
Jocketts HI *HHW* HP1		81	K2
Jocketts Rd *HHW* HP1		81	K3
Joel St *NTHWD* HA6		141	L4

PIN HA5 ... 141 L5
John Barker Pl
  HTCH/STOT SC5 ... 157 L4
John Bunyan Trail
  LTNN/LIM LU3 ... 154 E6
  SHFD SG17 ... 146 D1
Johnby Cl PEND EN3 ... 126 C3
John Dyde Cl BSF CM23 ... 44 A3
John Eliot Cl WAB EN9 ... 93 J4
John Gooch Dr ENC/FH EN2 ... 124 F5
John Howland Cl HNLW SG16 ... 147 M1
John Lamb Ct
  KTN/HRWW/WS HA3 ... 143 L3
John Sale Cl BLDK SG7 ... 149 N1
Johns La CSHM HP5 ... 79 H4
Johnson Ct HHNE HP2 ... 5 H7
Johns Rd BSF CM23 ... 166 C12
John St LTN LU1 ... 7 G5
  ROY SG8 ... 14 E7
John Tate Rd HERT/BAY SG13 ... 53 K8
Joiner's Cl CFSP/GDCR SL9 ... 138 C2
Joiners Cl ARL/CHE SG15 ... 138 C5
Joiners Wy CFSP/GDCR SL9 ... 138 C2
The Joint ROY SG8 ... 152 C7
Jones Rd CHESW EN7 ... 108 F4
Jonquil Cl WGCE AL7 ... 68 F1
Jordan Cl GSTN WD25 ... 117 K1
Jordans WGCE AL7 ... 51 G6
Jordans Rd
  RKW/CH/CXG WD3 ... 129 L3
Jordan's Wy LCOL/BKTW AL2 ... 102 C4
Joshua Wk CHES/WCR EN8 ... 110 C5
Joslyn Cl PEND EN3 ... 126 A4
Joyce Ct WAB EN9 ... 111 H8
Joyners Fld HLWS CM18 ... 95 G1
Jubilee Av LCOL/BKTW AL2 ... 86 B8
  WARE SG12 ... 54 D3
Jubilee Cl HNLW SG16 ... 147 K6
Jubilee Cl DUN/WHIP LU6 ... 25 J8
Jubilee Crs ARL/CHE SG15 ... 147 G7
Jubilee End ROY SG8 ... 145 P7
Jubilee Rd LWTH SG6 ... 17 G2
  STVG SG1 ... 2 F1
  WATN WD24 ... 117 L4
Jubilee St LTNE LU2 ... 7 H3
Jubilee Wy ROY SG8 ... 145 P7
Judge's HI POTB/CUF EN6 ... 107 V3
Judge WATN WD24 ... 117 M4
Jules Thorn Av EN EN1 ... 125 L7
Julia Gdns STVGE SG2 ... 34 A1
Julian Cl BAR EN5 ... 122 F7
Julian's Ct STVG SG1 ... 33 L5
Julian's Rd STVG SG1 ... 32 F1
Julius Caesar Wy STAN HA7 ... 134 A6
Julius Gdns LTNN/LIM LU3 ... 27 J2
Junction Rd HRW HA1 ... 143 H8
Juniper Av LCOL/BKTW AL2 ... 102 C5
Juniper Cl BAR EN5 ... 136 B3
  BROX EN10 ... 92 D7
  LTNW/LEA LU4 ... 27 J7
  RKW/CH/CXG WD3 ... 130 B6
Juniper Ct
  KTN/HRWW/WS HA3 * ... 143 K3
  NTHWD HA6 ... 141 L3
  WLYN AL6 ... 177 L10
Juniper Gdns RAD WD7 ... 104 C7
Juniper Ga RKW/CH/CXG WD3 ... 130 B6
Juniper Gn HHW HP1 ... 81 J2
Juniper Gv WAT WD17 ... 117 L4
Jupiter Dr HHNE HP2 ... 62 D8
Jupiter Ga STVGE SG2 ... 34 B7
Juson's Glebe
  RAYLNE/WEN HP22 ... 56 A8
Jute La PEND EN3 ... 126 C6
Juxon Cl KTN/HRWW/WS HA3 ... 142 F3

K

Kaduna Cl PIN HA5 ... 141 M7
Kardwell Cl HTCHE/RSTV SC4 ... 157 Q7
Kates Cl BAR EN5 ... 135 L5
Katescroft WGCE AL7 ... 68 C3
Katherine Cl HHS/BOV HP3 ... 5 J8
Katherine Dr DUN/HR/TOD LU5 ... 26 C1
Katherine's
  HLWW/ROY CM19 ... 74 D3
Katherine's Wy
  HLWW/ROY CM19 ... 74 D3
Katrine Sq HHNE HP2 ... 62 B6
Kay Cl TRING HP23 ... 169 L12
Kay Wk STALE/WH AL4 ... 86 B1
Keaton Cl DUN/HR/TOD LU5 ... 26 B4
Keats Cl HHNE HP2 ... 62 F4
  ROY SG8 ... 14 D5
  STVGE SG2 ... 33 M1
Keats Wy HTCHE/RSTV SC4 ... 20 A2
Keble Ter ABLGY WD5 ... 101 K6
Kecksy's SBW CM21 ... 183 R5
Keeble Cl LTNE LU2 ... 29 J8
Keele Cl WATN WD24 ... 13 G2
Keely Cl EBAR EN4 ... 137 J1
Keepers Cl LBUZ LU7 ... 169 L2
  LTNE LU2 ... 29 J8
Keiths Rd HHNE HP2 ... 5 M5
Keiths Wd KNEB SG3 ... 177 M4
Kelbys WGCE AL7 ... 51 G6
Keller Cl STVGE SG2 ... 11 L6
Kelling Cl LTNE LU2 ... 28 A1
Kelly Cl BORE WD6 ... 121 H6
Kelman Cl CHES/WCR EN8 ... 110 B5
Kelmscott Crs WATW WD18 ... 12 C4
Kelshall GSTN WD25 ... 118 C2
Kelshall St ROY SG8 ... 151 L9
Kelvin Cl LTN LU1 ... 6 F8
Kelvin Crs
  KTN/HRWW/WS HA3 ... 143 J2
Kemble Cl POTB/CUF EN6 ... 107 H7
Kemble Pde POTB/CUF EN6 * ... 107 G6
Kempe Cl STAL AL1 ... 85 G6
Kempe Rd EN EN1 ... 125 M2
Kemp Pl WATN WD23 ... 132 E2
Kemprow GSTN WD25 ... 119 H9
Kemps Dr NTHWD HA6 ... 141 K2
Kempsey Cl LTNE LU2 ... 29 H7
Kendal Cl LTNN/LIM LU3 ... 27 L2
  TRDG/WHET N20 ... 137 J5
Kendale HHS/BOV HP3 ... 82 F3
Kendale Rd HTCHE/RSTV SC4 ... 157 P7
  LTNW/LEA LU4 ... 26 F7
Kendall Cl WGCE AL7 ... 68 C3
Kendal Md WD23 ... 133 L1
Kendals Cl RAD WD7 ... 119 J2
Kenerne Dr BAR EN5 ... 136 C1
Kenetic Cl CHES/WCR EN8 ... 110 D2
Kenetic Crs PEND EN3 ... 126 D2
Kenford Cl GSTN WD25 ... 101 M6
Kenilworth Cl HHNE HP2 ... 5 J5
  STVG SG1 ... 2 C7
Kenilworth Ct WAT WD17 ... 117 G5
Kenilworth Crs EN EN1 ... 124 A3
Kenilworth Dr BORE WD6 ... 121 G7
  RKW/CH/CXG WD3 ... 116 F8

Kenilworth Gdns
  OXHEY WD19 ... 132 A8
Kenilworth Rd EDGW HA8 ... 135 G5
  LTN LU1 ... 6 B4
Kenley Cl EBAR EN4 ... 123 J8
Kenmare Cl STVG SG1 ... 33 H2
Kenmare St STVG SG1 ... 21 K6
Kenmore Av
  KTN/HRWW/WS HA3 ... 143 L7
Kennard Rd FBAR/BDGN N11 ... 137 L8
Kennedy Av HOD EN11 ... 72 D7
Kennedy Cl CHES/WCR EN8 ... 110 C2
  LCOL/BKTW AL2 ... 86 B8
  PIN HA5 ... 141 L8
Kennedy Rd WARE SG12 ... 179 N2
Kennel La HARP AL5 ... 173 Q4
Kennelwood La HAT AL10 ... 67 M7
Kenneth Av WATW WD18 ... 12 B6
Kenneth Gdns STAN HA7 ... 143 L8
Kenneth Rd LTNE LU2 ... 7 K1
Kennett Wy STVG SG1 ... 21 L6
Kenning Rd HOD EN11 ... 72 E5
Kennington Rd LTNN/LIM LU3 ... 27 M7
Kensington Av WATW WD18 ... 12 A6
Kensington Cl
  DUN/HR/TOD LU5 ... 26 C5
  FBAR/BDGN N11 * ... 137 L8
  STAL AL1 ... 85 L4
Kensington Wy BORE WD6 ... 121 H7
Kensworth Rd
  DUN/WHIP LU6 ... 171 Q5
Kent Cl BORE WD6 ... 121 H4
Kent Crs BSF CM23 ... 43 L5
Kent Dr EBAR EN4 ... 123 L5
Kent Gdns HARP AL5 ... 141 L8
Kentish La BRKMPK AL9 ... 89 G6
Kenton Gdns STAL AL1 ... 9 J1
Kenton La
  KTN/HRWW/WS HA3 ... 143 K2
Kenton Rd
  KTN/HRWW/WS HA3 ... 143 L8
Kent Rd DUN/HR/TOD LU5 ... 26 B3
  LTN LU1 ... 4 B3
Kents Av HHS/BOV HP3 ... 82 B6
Kent's La STDN SG11 ... 163 Q11
Kenway Dr AMSS HP7 ... 113 M5
Kenwood Dr
  RKW/CH/CXG WD3 ... 129 K5
Kenworth Cl CHES/WCR EN8 ... 110 D4
Kenyon Pl WGCE AL7 ... 68 C2
Kerdistone Cl POTB/CUF EN6 ... 106 E1
Kerr Cl BAR EN5 ... 122 A8
Kerri Cl BAR EN5 ... 122 A8
Kerril Cft HLW CM20 ... 74 E4
Kerry Av STAN HA7 ... 134 A7
Kerry Ct STAN HA7 ... 134 B7
Kershaw Cl LTNN/LIM LU3 ... 27 L1
Kershaw's HI
  HTCHE/RSTV SC4 ... 157 P7
Kessingland Av STVG SG1 ... 20 B8
Kesters Rd CSHM HP5 ... 97 H6
Keston Ms WAT WD17 ... 12 C1
Kestral Wy ROY SG8 ... 14 F5
Kestrel Cl BERK HP4 ... 80 A2
  GSTN WD25 ... 102 C8
  STVGE SG2 ... 34 B7
Kestrel Gdns BSF CM23 ... 43 J3
Kestrel Gn HAT AL10 ... 87 L1
The Kestrels LCOL/BKTW AL2 ... 102 C6
Kestrel Wk LWTH SG6 ... 16 F6
Kestrel Wy LTNW/LEA LU4 ... 26 A4
  WGCE AL7 ... 50 D5
Keswick Cl DUN/WHIP LU6 ... 38 F2
  STAL AL1 ... 85 M3
Keswick Dr PEND EN3 ... 126 A2
Keswick Gdns RSLP HA4 ... 141 H7
Kettering Rd PEND EN3 ... 126 B3
Kettle Green Rd MHAD SG10 ... 181 Q7
Ketton Cl LTNE LU2 ... 7 L6
Kewferry Cl NTHWD HA6 ... 141 G1
Kewferry Rd NTHWD HA6 ... 141 G1
Keyfield STAL AL1 ... 8 F7
Keyfield Ter STAL AL1 ... 8 F7
Keymer Cl LTNE LU2 ... 29 J8
Keynton St HERT/WAT SG14 ... 52 D6
Keysers Rd BROX EN10 ... 92 B4
Kibes La WARE SG12 ... 54 B4
Kidner Cl LTNE LU2 ... 29 J8
Kilbride Cl HHNE HP2 ... 62 D6
Kilby Rd STVG SG1 ... 10 A3
Kilfillan Gdns BERK HP4 ... 79 L2
Kilmarnock Dr LTNE LU2 ... 28 C4
Kilmarnock Rd OXHEY WD19 ... 132 B7
Kiln Av AMS HP6 ... 114 A4
Kiln Cl BERK HP4 ... 79 H6
Kilncroft HHS/BOV HP3 ... 82 F4
Kiln Ground HHS/BOV HP3 ... 82 C3
Kiln House Cl WARE SG12 ... 97 L5
Kiln La CSHM HP5 ... 97 J5
Kiln Rd HHS/BOV HP3 ... 82 B6
Kiln Rd TRING HP23 ... 57 L6
Kiln Wy DUN/HR/TOD LU5 ... 26 B3
  NTHWD HA6 ... 141 J1
Kilsmore La CHES/WCR EN8 ... 110 B2
Kilvinton Dr ENC/FH EN2 ... 125 H4
Kilworth Cl WGCE AL7 ... 68 F1
Kimberley LWTH SG6 ... 148 D11
Kimberley Cl BSF CM23 ... 44 A4
  LTNW/LEA LU4 ... 26 C1
Kimberley Gdns EN EN1 ... 125 K7
Kimberley Rd STALW/RED AL3 ... 8 D3
Kimble Cl WATW WD18 ... 131 J2
Kimble Crs BUSH WD23 ... 133 K6
Kimbolton Crs STVGE SG2 ... 177 N1
Kimbolton Gn BORE WD6 ... 121 H5
Kimps Wy HHS/BOV HP3 ... 5 M8
Kimpton Cl HHNE HP2 ... 62 D6
  KNEB SG3 ... 177 N7
Kimpton Pl GSTN WD25 ... 102 B8
Kimpton Rd HTCHE/RSTV SC4 ... 175 J7
  LTNE LU2 ... 7 J4
  STALE/WH AL4 ... 175 N11
  WLYN AL6 ... 176 C7
Kimptons Cl POTB/CUF EN6 ... 106 B7
Kimptons Md POTB/CUF EN6 ... 106 B7
Kindersley Cl WLYN AL6 ... 177 J11
Kindersley Wy ABLGY WD5 ... 101 K5
King Arthur Ct CHES/WCR EN8 ... 110 C5
King Charles Rd RAD WD7 ... 104 C6
King Croft Rd HARP AL5 ... 173 Q8
King Edgar Yd ROY SG8 * ... 153 P7
King Edward Pl WAB EN9 * ... 111 L8
King Edward Rd BAR EN5 ... 122 F4
  CHES/WCR EN8 ... 110 C5
  OXHEY WD19 ... 13 G4
  RAD WD7 ... 104 C6
King Edward's Rd PEND EN3 ... 126 B4
  WARE SG12 ... 54 C3

King Edward St HHS/BOV HP3 ... 82 B6
Kingfisher Cl
  KTN/HRWW/WS HA3 ... 143 K2
  NTHWD HA6 ... 140 F9
  STALE/WH AL4 ... 86 B4
  WARE SG12 ... 73 Q3
Kingfisher Ct HTCHE/RSTV SC4 ... 157 Q7
Kingfisher Dr HHS/BOV HP3 ... 82 D7
Kingfisher Lure KGLGY WD4 ... 100 C3
  RKW/CH/CXG WD3 ... 115 M8
Kingfisher Meadow
  RBSF CM22 ... 45 M2
Kingfisher Ri STVGE SG2 ... 34 B7
Kingfisher Wy BSF CM23 ... 44 A2
King George Av BUSH WD23 ... 132 F2
King George Rd WAB EN9 ... 111 G8
  WARE SG12 ... 54 C3
King Georges Av WATW WD18 ... 12 A6
King Georges Cl
  HTCH/STOT SC5 ... 157 M3
King George's Wy
  HTCHE/RSTV SC4 ... 175 Q3
Kingham Rd WARE SG12 ... 181 J12
Kinghamway LTNE LU2 ... 6 F1
King Harry La STALW/RED AL3 ... 84 F5
King Harry St HHNE HP2 ... 4 F1
King Henry Ct WAB EN9 * ... 127 G1
King Henry's Ms PEND EN3 ... 126 E3
King James Av
  POTB/CUF EN6 ... 108 C3
King James Wy ROY SG8 ... 14 C7
Kingley Pk KGLGY WD4 * ... 100 F5
Kings Av HHS/BOV HP3 ... 82 D1
  WATW WD18 ... 12 B6
Kingsbridge Rd BSF CM23 ... 44 A1
Kingsbury Av
  DUN/HR/TOD LU5 ... 26 C8
  STALW/RED AL3 ... 8 A1
Kingsbury Ct
  DUN/HR/TOD LU5 ... 39 G1
Kingsbury Gdns
  DUN/HR/TOD LU5 ... 26 D8
Kingsclere PI ENC/FH EN2 ... 125 G6
Kings Cl CSTG HP8 ... 128 B5
King's Cl KGLGY WD4 ... 99 M5
Kings Cl NTHWD HA6 ... 141 G9
  WATW WD18 ... 13 G6
Kings College Rd RSLP HA4 ... 141 H8
Kings Ct BSF CM23 ... 44 A1
Kingscroft WGCE AL7 ... 50 F7
Kingscroft Av
  DUN/HR/TOD LU5 ... 25 M8
Kingsdale Rd BERK HP4 ... 79 L2
Kingsdon La HLWE CM17 ... 76 A4
Kingsdown HTCHE/RSTV SC4 ... 157 N6
Kingsdown La LTNN/LIM LU3 ... 28 B3
Kings Farm Rd
  RKW/CH/CXG WD3 ... 129 N7
Kingsfield HOD EN11 ... 72 E5
  RYLN/HDSTN HA2 ... 142 F7
Kingsfield Ct OXHEY WD19 ... 132 B3
Kingsfield Dr PEND EN3 ... 126 B1
Kingsfield Rd OXHEY WD19 ... 132 B3
  WARE SG12 ... 179 N2
Kingsfield Wy PEND EN3 ... 126 B1
Kingsgate STALW/RED AL3 ... 8 B3
Kings Heath Pk HARP AL5 ... 174 G11
Kings Hedges HTCH/STOT SC5 ... 157 L5
Kingshill Av
  KTN/HRWW/WS HA3 ... 143 M6
  STALE/WH AL4 ... 65 M7
Kingshill Ct BAR EN5 * ... 122 C8
Kingshill Dr
  KTN/HRWW/WS HA3 ... 143 M4
Kingshill Wy BERK HP4 ... 79 L3
Kingsland HLWS CM18 ... 75 G7
Kingsland Cl DUN/HR/TOD LU5 ... 26 D8
Kingsland Ct LTN LU1 ... 7 H5
Kingsland Rd HHW HP1 ... 4 A6
  LTN LU1 ... 7 H5
Kingsland Wy BLDK SG7 ... 149 Q2
Kings La KGLGY WD4 ... 99 L5
Kingsley Av BORE WD6 ... 120 D6
  CHES/WCR EN8 ... 109 M3
Kingsley Ct EDGW HA8 * ... 134 F5
  WGCE AL7 ... 68 C3
Kingsley Rd LTNN/LIM LU3 ... 27 L4
  PIN HA5 ... 142 C6
Kingsley Wk TRING HP23 ... 57 L1
Kings Md DUN/WHIP LU6 ... 38 F2
Kingsmead BAR EN5 ... 122 E8
  CHES/WCR EN8 ... 110 B2
  POTB/CUF EN6 ... 108 C2
  SBW CM21 ... 183 Q8
  STALE/WH AL4 ... 66 B7
  WAB EN9 * ... 93 J4
Kingsmead Cl
  HLWW/ROY CM19 ... 73 M6
Kings Meadow KGLGY WD4 ... 100 E3
Kingsmill Ct HAT AL10 ... 87 M2
Kingsmoor Rd
  HLWW/ROY CM19 ... 74 F8
Kings Pond Cl BGSW SG18 ... 144 D4
Kings Rd BAR EN5 ... 122 A7
  BERK HP4 ... 79 H6
King's Rd CSTG HP8 ... 128 B5
King's Rd HERT/BAY SG13 ... 53 L6
  HTCH/STOT SC5 ... 157 M3
  LCOL/BKTW AL2 ... 86 A8
  STALW/RED AL3 ... 8 B3
Kings Rd STVG SG1 ... 10 C7
Kings Sq HAT AL10 * ... 67 H5
Kingston PI
  KTN/HRWW/WS HA3 ... 143 M2
Kingston Rd EBAR EN4 ... 137 H1
  LTNE LU2 ... 28 A1
Kingston V ROY SG8 ... 14 F1
King St BSF CM23 ... 43 M2
  CSHM HP5 ... 96 F5
  DUN/HR/TOD LU5 ... 25 M5
  LTN LU1 ... 6 F5
  ROY SG8 ... 14 E7
  STALW/RED AL3 ... 172 G4
  TRING HP23 ... 169 J3
  WATW WD18 ... 13 G4
Kings Walden Ri STVGE SG2 ... 34 A2
King's Walden Rd
  HTCH/STOT SC5 ... 156 D11
Kings Wk ROY SG8 * ... 14 C7
Kings Wy HRW HA1 ... 143 H2
  LBUZ LU7 ... 24 C1
  STVG SG1 ... 21 L8
Kingsway CFSP/GDCR SL9 ... 138 C4
  DUN/HR/TOD LU5 ... 26 A8
  LTNN/LIM LU3 ... 27 J4
  POTB/CUF EN6 ... 108 C7
  ROY SG8 ... 14 E7
  STALW/RED AL3 ... 8 B3
  WARE SG12 ... 54 C3

Kingsway Crs
  RYLN/HDSTN HA2 ... 143 G6
Kingsway Gdns
  HTCH/STOT SC5 ... 148 G8
Kingsway North Orbital Rd
  GSTN WD25 ... 101 L8
Kingswell Ride
  POTB/CUF EN6 ... 108 C7
Kingswood Av
  HTCHE/RSTV SC4 ... 20 B1
Kingswood Cl BAR EN5 ... 137 G2
Kingswood Cl GSTN WD25 ... 101 M8
Kings Yd RKW/CH/CXG WD3 * ... 130 C4
Kingwell Rd EBAR EN4 ... 123 H4
King William Cl
  AMP/FLIT/BLC MK45 ... 155 K1
King William Ct WAB EN9 * ... 127 G1
Kinmoor Cl LTNN/LIM LU3 ... 27 H1
Kinross Cl LTNN/LIM LU3 ... 27 H1
Kinsbourne Crs HARP AL5 ... 46 A1
Kinsbourne Cl HARP AL5 ... 46 B1
Kinsbourne Green La
  HARP AL5 ... 173 R6
Kipling Cl HTCHE/RSTV SC4 ... 20 A2
Kipling Gv HHNE HP2 ... 62 F4
Kipling Rd ROY SG8 ... 14 F4
The Kipling LTNN/LIM LU3 ... 27 M3
Kipling Wy HARP AL5 ... 46 B1
Kirby Cl NTHWD HA6 ... 141 K4
Kirby Dr LTNN/LIM LU3 ... 154 F12
Kirby Rd DUN/WHIP LU6 ... 38 C1
Kirkcaldy Gn OXHEY WD19 ... 132 A6
Kirkdale Rd BERK HP4 ... 79 M1
Kirkland Dr ENC/FH EN2 ... 123 M8
Kirklands WGCW AL8 ... 50 C3
Kirkstone Dr DUN/WHIP LU6 ... 38 F3
Kirkwick Av HARP AL5 ... 46 A1
Kirkwood Rd LTNW/LEA LU4 ... 26 D6
Kirtle Rd CSHM HP5 ... 97 G5
Kitchen Garden Ct
  HTCH/STOT SC5 ... 157 N7
Kitching La STVG SG1 ... 32 D4
Kite Fld BERK HP4 ... 59 J6
Kite Wy LWTH SG6 ... 16 C1
Kitsbury Rd BERK HP4 ... 79 M1
Kitsbury Ter BERK HP4 ... 79 M1
Kit's La BLDK SG7 ... 19 C1
Kitson Wy HLW CM20 ... 2 D1
Kitswell Wy RAD WD7 ... 103 K7
Kitt's End Rd BAR EN5 ... 122 C3
Knap Cl LWTH SG6 ... 17 G1
Knebworth Ga STVGE SG2 ... 33 K8
Knebworth La STVGE SG2 ... 33 K8
Kneesworth St ROY SG8 ... 14 D6
Knella Gn WGCE AL7 ... 50 E7
Knella Rd WGCE AL7 ... 50 D7
Knifton Ct POTB/CUF EN6 * ... 106 C7
Knightsbridge Wy HHNE HP2 ... 5 J1
Knights Cl BSF CM23 ... 43 H1
  BUNT SG9 ... 159 J11
  DUN/WHIP LU6 ... 37 J4
Knights Fld LTNE LU2 ... 6 E1
Knightsfield WGCW AL8 ... 50 B3
Knightscote Cl DEN/HRF UB9 ... 140 B4
Knights Orch HHW HP1 ... 61 K8
  STALW/RED AL3 ... 8 C1
Knights Rd STAN HA7 ... 134 A7
Knights Rw BSF CM23 ... 43 L3
Knights Templars Gn
  STVGE SG2 ... 34 A1
Knight St SBW CM21 ... 183 Q7
Knights Wood Cl EDGW HA8 ... 135 G5
Knightswood Cl EDGW HA8 ... 135 G5
Knoll Crs NTHWD HA6 ... 141 J4
Knoll Dr STHGT/OAK N14 ... 137 L3
Knolles Crs BRKMPK AL9 ... 87 M6
Knoll Gn HHNE HP2 * ... 62 C8
Knoll Rd LTNE LU2 ... 28 C5
Knolls Vw DUN/WHIP LU6 ... 36 F4
The Knoll HERT/BAY SG13 ... 53 M6
  DUN/WHIP LU6 ... 38 D2
  PIN HA5 * ... 142 B4
Knott Cl STVGE SG2 ... 21 M6
Knotts Cl DUN/WHIP LU6 ... 39 G4
Knowle Dr HARP AL5 ... 47 H6
The Knowle HOD EN11 ... 72 E8
Knowl Dr BORE WD6 ... 134 C1
Knowl Wy BORE WD6 ... 134 C1
Knowl Piece HTCHE/RSTV SC4 ... 157 M3
Knutsford Av WATN WD24 ... 118 B4
Koh-i-Noor Av BUSH WD23 ... 132 C2
Kristiansand Wy LWTH SG6 ... 17 G1
Kymberley Rd HRW HA1 * ... 143 J3
Kymswell Rd STVGE SG2 ... 34 A5
Kynance Cl LTNE LU2 ... 28 E6
Kynaston Cl
  KTN/HRWW/WS HA3 ... 143 H2
Kynaston Rd ENC/FH EN2 ... 125 H4
Kynaston Wd
  KTN/HRWW/WS HA3 ... 143 H2
Kyrkeby LWTH SG6 ... 17 G5
Kytes Dr GSTN WD25 ... 102 B7

L

Laburnum Cl CHES/WCR EN8 ... 110 B5
  LTNN/LIM LU3 ... 28 A2
  RBSF CM22 ... 184 C9
Laburnum Gv LCOL/BKTW AL2 ... 86 E7
  LTNN/LIM LU3 ... 27 M7
  RSLP HA4 ... 141 H8
Laburnum Rd HOD EN11 ... 72 F5
Lacemaker Ct AMSS HP7 * ... 113 Q6
Lacey Dr EDGW HA8 ... 134 C7
Laceys Wy LCOL/BKTW AL2 ... 86 C7
Lachbury Cl LTN LU1 ... 40 E3
Lackmore Rd EN EN1 ... 109 A1
Lacre Wy LWTH SG6 ... 17 G5
Ladbrooke Cl POTB/CUF EN6 ... 106 E6
Ladbrooke Dr POTB/CUF EN6 ... 106 E6
Ladies Gv STALW/RED AL3 ... 8 B3
Ladyalesford Av STAN HA7 ... 133 M8
Ladygate La RSLP HA4 ... 141 H6
Ladygrove WGCE AL7 ... 68 C3
Ladyhill LTNW/LEA LU4 ... 26 F3
Lady Margaret Gdns
  WARE SG12 ... 54 C3
Ladysmith Rd EN EN1 ... 125 K6
  KTN/HRWW/WS HA3 ... 143 H1
  LBUZ LU7 ... 169 K2
  STALW/RED AL3 ... 8 E3
Ladywalk RKW/CH/CXG WD3 ... 129 J8
Ladywell Prospect SBW CM21 ... 183 R8

Ladywood Cl
  RKW/CH/CXG WD3 ... 115 M7
Ladywood Rd HERT/WAT SG14 ... 52 C7
Lagley Meadow BERK HP4 ... 59 L8
Laidon Sq HHNE HP2 ... 62 B6
Lake Dr BUSH WD23 ... 133 G5
Lakeland Cl
  KTN/HRWW/WS HA3 ... 143 H1
Lake Rd WAB EN9 ... 93 H3
Lakeside ENC/FH EN2 ... 124 B8
  TRING HP23 ... 169 L12
Lakeside Cl RSLP HA4 ... 141 H6
Lakeside Crs EBAR EN4 ... 137 K2
Lakeside Pl LCOL/BKTW AL2 ... 104 B2
Lakeside Rd CHES/WCR EN8 ... 110 A2
The Lake BUSH WD23 ... 133 H4
Lake Vw EDGW HA8 ... 134 D8
  KGLGY WD4 ... 100 F2
  POTB/CUF EN6 ... 107 G7
Laleham Av NW7 ... 135 H6
Lalleford Rd LTNE LU2 ... 29 L8
Lamb Cl GSTN WD25 ... 102 D8
  HAT AL10 ... 87 M1
Lamb Ct STALE/WH AL4 * ... 48 E1
Lambe RAYLNE/WEN HP22 ... 56 C7
Lambert Cl BUSH WD23 ... 118 F8
Lambert Rd
  NFNCH/WDSPK N12 ... 137 H8
Lambert Wy
  NFNCH/WDSPK N12 ... 137 G8
Lamb La STALW/RED AL3 ... 173 R12
Lamb Meadow ARL/CHE SC15 ... 147 P6
Lambourn Cha RAD WD7 ... 119 J2
Lambourn Cl ENC/FH EN2 ... 123 G3
Lambourne Gdns EN EN1 ... 125 K6
Lambourn Gdns HARP AL5 ... 46 D2
Lambs Cl DUN/HR/TOD LU5 ... 26 B8
  POTB/CUF EN6 ... 108 D3
Lambscroft Wy
  CFSP/GDCR SL9 ... 138 C4
Lambs Gdns STVGE SG2 ... 182 B5
Lambs Wk ENC/FH EN2 ... 125 G6
Lambton Av CHES/WCR EN8 ... 110 B8
Lamer La LTNE LU2 ... 28 F7
Lamers Rd LTNE LU2 ... 29 L7
Lammasmead BROX EN10 ... 92 D5
Lammas Pth STVGE SG2 ... 11 L6
Lammas Rd HERT/WAT SG14 ... 178 F5
  LBUZ LU7 ... 169 L2
  WATW WD18 ... 13 G8
Lammas Wy LWTH SG6 ... 17 G5
Lamorna Cl LTNN/LIM LU3 ... 27 K3
  RAD WD7 ... 103 M8
Lampits HOD EN11 ... 72 F7
Lampitts Cross LTNN/LIM LU3 * ... 27 L4
Lamplighters Cl WAB EN9 ... 111 L8
Lamsey Rd HHNE HP2 ... 5 L8
Lancaster Av EBAR EN4 ... 123 H4
  HTCH/STOT SC5 ... 157 M5
  LTNN/LIM LU3 ... 28 A1
Lancaster Cl
  AMP/FLIT/BLC MK45 ... 155 K1
  STVG SG1 ... 21 J7
Lancaster Dr HHS/BOV HP3 ... 98 D1
Lancaster Rd EBAR EN4 ... 123 H4
  ENC/FH EN2 ... 125 H5
  HTCH/STOT SC5 ... 157 N5
  RYLN/HDSTN HA2 ... 142 E7
  STAL AL1 ... 9 J2
Lancaster Wy ABLGY WD5 ... 101 K5
  BSF CM23 ... 43 H1
Lancelot Gdns EBAR EN4 ... 137 L3
Lancing Rd LTNE LU2 ... 29 L8
Lancing Wy RKW/CH/CXG WD3 ... 130 F1
Lancot Av DUN/WHIP LU6 ... 38 D2
Lancotbury Cl DUN/WHIP LU6 ... 38 C2
Lancot Dr DUN/WHIP LU6 ... 38 C1
Landau Wy BROX EN10 ... 92 D7
Landford Cl
  RKW/CH/CXG WD3 ... 130 C5
Landmead Rd CHES/WCR EN8 ... 110 C3
Landrace Rd LTNW/LEA LU4 ... 26 C5
Landridge Dr EN EN1 ... 125 M4
Lands' End BORE WD6 ... 134 B2
Lane Ap MLHL NW7 ... 136 C8
Lane End BERK HP4 ... 79 L3
  HAT AL10 ... 87 K3
  HLWE CM17 ... 76 A4
Lanefield Wk WGCW AL8 ... 50 A7
Lane Gdns BUSH WD23 ... 133 J4
Lanercost Cl WLYN AL6 ... 177 M10
Laneside EDGW HA8 ... 135 G8
Lane Wood Cl AMSS HP7 ... 113 K5
Langbridge Cl
  HTCHE/RSTV SC4 ... 157 Q8
Langdale Av HARP AL5 ... 47 H3
Langdale Cl DUN/WHIP LU6 ... 39 G2
Langdale Ct HHNE HP2 ... 62 C7
Langdale Gdns PEND EN3 ... 126 B1
Langdale Rd DUN/WHIP LU6 ... 38 F2
Langdale Ter BORE WD6 * ... 121 H4
Langdon St TRING HP23 ... 57 L2
Langfield Cl WAB EN9 ... 93 J4
Langford Cl STALE/WH AL4 ... 66 A8
Langford Crs EBAR EN4 ... 123 L5
Langford Dr LTNE LU2 ... 28 E6
Langford Rd STALE/WH AL4 ... 66 A8
Langham Cl LTNE LU2 ... 28 B2
  STALE/WH AL4 ... 66 A8
Langholme BUSH WD23 ... 133 G4
Langland Ct NTHWD HA6 ... 141 G2
Langland Dr PIN HA5 ... 142 C2
Langleigh Wk ROY SG8 * ... 148 D12
Langley Av HHS/BOV HP3 ... 5 J8
  TRDG/WHET N20 ... 137 G3
Langley Cl CHESW EN7 ... 108 F3
Langley Ct CHESW EN7 ... 109 G3
Langley Crs EDGW HA8 ... 135 G5
  KGLGY WD4 ... 100 E4
  STALW/RED AL3 ... 8 D1
Langley Gn WAB EN9 * ... 93 H4
Langley Gv STALE/WH AL4 ... 66 B7
Langley Hi KGLGY WD4 ... 100 D3
Langley Hill Cl KGLGY WD4 ... 100 D3
Langley La ABLGY WD5 ... 101 K5
  HTCHE/RSTV SC4 ... 157 R8
Langley Lodge La KGLGY WD4 ... 100 C5
Langley Rd ABLGY WD5 ... 99 M4
  WAT WD17 ... 12 D5
Langley Rw BAR EN5 ... 122 D2
Langley Sidings STVG SG1 ... 33 J7
Langley St LTN LU1 ... 7 G7
Langley Wy WAT WD17 ... 117 K5
Langley Whf KGLGY WD4 ... 100 E4
Langmead Dr BUSH WD23 ... 133 H4
Langstone Ley WGCE AL7 ... 51 H6
Langthorne Av STVG SG1 ... 10 B6
Langton Av TRDG/WHET N20 ... 137 G2
Langton Gv NTHWD HA6 ... 131 G4
Langton Rd HOD EN11 ... 72 D7
  KTN/HRWW/WS HA3 ... 143 H1

Langwood Gdns WAT WD17 117 L5
Lankers Dr RYLN/HDSTN HA2 142 D8
Lankester Rd ROY SG8 14 D8
Lannock LWTH SG6 17 G5
Lannock Hl HTCHE/RSTV SG4 17 H7
Lanrick Copse BERK HP4 60 C8
Lansbury Rd PEND EN3 126 B5
Lansdowne Ct BROX EN10 * 92 E2
Lansdowne Rd CSHM HP5 97 G3
LTNN/LIM LU3 6 C1
Lansdown Rd CFSP/GDCR SL9 138 B3
Lanterns La STVGE SG2 34 B3
The Lanterns ROY SG8 * 14 E7
Lanthorn Cl BROX EN10 92 C1
Laporte Wy LTNW/LEA LU4 27 K8
Lapwing Cl HHNE HP2 62 C6
Lapwing Dell LWTH SG6 16 F7
Lapwing Pl GSTN WD25 * 102 A6
Lapwing Ri STVGE SG2 34 B7
Lapwing Rd LTNW/LEA LU4 26 E5
Lapwing Wy ABLGY WD5 101 L5
Larch Av HTCHE/RSTV SG4 157 Q9
LCOL/BKTW AL2 102 C4
Larch Cl CHESW EN7 109 J1
Larches Av EN EN1 126 A1
The Larches BERK HP4 59 H8
BUSH WD23 13 L8
LTNE LU2 6 E2
STALE/WH AL4 66 B6
WARE SG12 54 A1
Larch Ri BERK HP4 59 L8
Larchwood BSF CM23 43 K4
Larchwood Rd HHNE HP2 62 D8
Larken Cl BUSH WD23 133 G4
Larken Dr BUSH WD23 133 G4
Larkens Cl STDN SG11 163 P10
Larkfield Av
KTN/HRWW/WS HA3 143 M5
Larkin Pl ROY SG8 14 E4
Larkins Cl BLDK SG7 149 K12
Larkins La MHAD SG10 181 R8
Larkinson STVG SG1 10 A1
Lark Ri HAT AL10 87 L2
Larksfield WARE SG12 54 C2
Larksfield Gv EN EN1 125 M5
Larkspur Cl BSF CM23 43 K3
HHW HP1 81 J1
Larkspur Gdns LTNW/LEA LU4 27 K7
Larkspur Gv EDGW HA8 135 G7
Larks Rdg LCOL/BKTW AL2 84 E8
Larks Ri CSHM HP5 97 H7
Larksway BSF CM23 43 J3
Larkswood HLWE CM17 76 A7
Larkswood Ri PIN HA5 142 A6
STALE/WH AL4 66 A5
Larmans Rd PEND EN3 126 A2
Larsen Dr WAB EN9 111 H8
Larwood Gv STVG SG1 33 L1
Latchford Ms STALE/WH AL4 48 B4
Latchmoor Av
CFSP/GDCR SL9 138 B6
Latchmoor Gv
CFSP/GDCR SL9 138 B6
Latchmoor Wy
CFSP/GDCR SL9 138 B6
Latchmore Bank RBSF CM22 44 B7
Latchmore Cl
HTCHE/RSTV SG4 157 P8
Latimer Cl AMS HP6 114 A5
HHNE HP2 62 F5
PIN HA5 142 A3
WATW WD18 131 J3
Latimer Gdns PIN HA5 142 A3
WGCE AL7 50 F7
Latimer Rd BAR EN5 122 F7
CSHM HP5 97 J8
LTN LU1 7 G8
RKW/CH/CXG WD3 114 D4
Latium Cl STAL AL1 8 E8
Lattimore Rd STAL AL1 9 G7
STALE/WH AL4 48 A5
Latton Gn HLWS CM18 95 K1
Latton Hall Cl HLW CM20 3 M4
Latton House HLWS CM18 75 M8
Latton St HLWE CM17 75 M6
Lauderdale Rd KGLGY WD4 101 G7
Launceston
RKW/CH/CXG WD3 128 F2
Laundry La WAB EN9 93 K7
Launton Cl LTNN/LIM LU3 154 H12
Laureate Wy HHW HP1 61 M8
Laurel Av POTB/CUF EN6 106 D6
Laurel Bank HHS/BOV HP3 81 K5
NFNCH/WDSPK N12 * 137 G7
Laurel Bank Rd ENC/FH EN2 125 G5
Laurel Cl HHNE HP2 5 K1
LBUZ LU7 24 B4
OXHEY WD19 132 B3
Laurel Ct AMS HP6 113 G2
Laureldene MHAD SG10 181 R8
Laurel Flds POTB/CUF EN6 106 D5
Laurel Gdns MLHL NW7 135 H6
Laurel Pk
KTN/HRWW/WS HA3 143 K2
Laurel Rd CFSP/GDCR SL9 138 B3
STAL AL1 9 K5
Laurels Cl STALW/RED AL3 84 F5
The Laurels BERK HP4 60 F7
BORE WD6 * 120 E5
BUSH WD23 * 133 J5
CHESW EN7 109 J1
Laurel Vw TRDG/WHET N20 136 F6
Laurel Wy HTCH/STOT SG5 157 N2
TRDG/WHET N20 136 E6
Lauries Cl HHW HP1 80 F4
Laurimel Cl STAN HA7 143 M1
Laurino Pl BUSH WD23 133 G5
Lavender Cl BSF CM23 43 K3
CHESW EN7 109 K1
HAT AL10 67 K5
HLW CM20 3 H4
LTNE LU2 28 C2
Lavender Ct BLDK SG7 149 J12
Lavender Crs STALW/RED AL3 8 D1
Lavender Gdns ENC/FH EN2 124 F4
KTN/HRWW/WS HA3 143 J1
Lavender Hl ENC/FH EN2 124 E5
Lavender Rd ENC/FH EN2 125 H5
Lavender Wy HTCH/STOT SG5 157 M6
Lavinia Av GSTN WD25 102 A8
Lavrock La RKW/CH/CXG WD3 130 D3
Lawford Av
RKW/CH/CXG WD3 129 G2
Lawford Cl LTN LU1 6 C7
RKW/CH/CXG WD3 129 G2
Law Hall La HTCHE/RSTV SG4 175 L1
Lawley Rd STHGT/OAK N14 137 M3
Lawn Av HTCHE/RSTV SG4 175 N8
Lawn Gdns LTN LU1 6 E9
Lawn La HHNE HP2 4 F7
Lawns Cl HTCH/STOT SG5 156 E11
The Lawns BROX EN10 92 D4
The Lawns HHW HP1 81 J1
PIN HA5 142 F2
RAD WD7 104 C7
STALW/RED AL3 8 C4
STVGE SG2 34 B5
WGCW AL8 50 B4
Lawnswood BAR EN5 * 136 C1
Lawn V PIN HA5 142 B4
Lawrance Gdns
CHES/WCR EN8 110 B2
Lawrance Rd STALW/RED AL3 65 G6
Lawrence Av LWTH SG6 16 E5
MLHL NW7 135 J7
SBW CM21 183 Q5
STVG SG1 33 J2
Lawrence Campe Cl
TRDG/WHET N20 137 H6
Lawrence Cl HERT/WAT SG14 52 C6
Lawrence Ct MLHL NW7 135 J8
OXHEY WD19 * 132 B6
Lawrence End Rd LTNE LU2 174 G6
Lawrence Gdns MLHL NW7 135 K6
Lawrence Md
HTCHE/RSTV SG4 * 20 D5
Lawrence Moorings
SBW CM21 183 R7
Lawrence Rd PIN HA5 142 B7
Lawrence St MLHL NW7 135 K7
Lawrence Wy DUN/WHIP LU6 25 K7
Lawson Gdns PIN HA5 141 M5
Lawson Rd PEND EN3 126 A5
Lawton Rd EBAR EN4 123 H7
Laxton Cl LTNE LU2 29 J8
Laxton Gdns BLDK SG7 17 J2
Layard Rd EN EN1 125 K5
Lay Brook STALE/WH AL4 65 L6
Layham Dr LTNE LU2 29 H8
Layston Meadow BUNT SG9 159 K11
Layston Pk ROY SG8 14 E8
Layter's Av CFSP/GDCR SL9 138 A4
Layter's Av South
CFSP/GDCR SL9 138 A4
Layter's Cl CFSP/GDCR SL9 138 A4
Layter's End CFSP/GDCR SL9 138 A4
Layters Wy CFSP/GDCR SL9 138 B7
Lea Bushes GSTN WD25 118 C1
Leachcroft CFSP/GDCR SL9 138 A3
Lea Cl BSF CM23 166 D12
BUSH WD23 132 F1
Leadbeaters Cl
FBAR/BDGN N11 137 K8
Leaf Cl NTHWD HA6 141 H2
Leafield LTNN/LIM LU3 27 K5
Leafields DUN/HR/TOD LU5 26 A3
Leaford Crs WATN WD24 117 K3
Leaforis Rd CHESW EN7 109 L2
Leaf Rd DUN/HR/TOD LU5 25 M3
Leaf Wy STAL AL1 85 H5
Leafy La TRING HP23 57 J4
Leagrave High St
LTNW/LEA LU4 26 D6
Leagrave Rd LTNN/LIM LU3 27 L6
LTNW/LEA LU4 6 A1
Lea Gn BRKMPK AL9 * 68 C5
Lea Gv BSF CM23 166 D12
Leahoe Gdns HERT/BAY SG13 53 G8
Leaholme Waye RSLP HA4 140 F8
Leamington Rd LTNN/LIM LU3 27 L2
Lea Mt CHESW EN7 109 J2
Leander Gdns GSTN WD25 * 118 C3
Lea Rd ENC/FH EN2 125 H5
HARP AL5 46 F2
HOD EN11 73 G5
LTN LU1 7 H6
WAB EN9 110 E8
WATN WD24 * 117 M4
Leasey Bridge La HARP AL5 47 K4
Leasey Dell Dr STALE/WH AL4 47 K3
Leaside HHNE HP2 83 G3
The Leas BLDK SG7 17 J2
BUSH WD23 118 D6
HHS/BOV HP3 82 E6
Leat Cl SBW CM21 183 R6
Leathersellers Cl BAR EN5 * 122 C7
Leathwaite Cl LTNN/LIM LU3 27 K4
Lea Valley Wk BRKMPK AL9 68 A3
BROX EN10 92 E8
HARP AL5 47 G2
HOD EN11 73 H8
LTN LU1 174 A4
PEND EN3 126 E7
WARE SG12 54 A4
Leavesden Rd STAN HA7 143 L1
WATN WD24 117 M4
Leaves Spring STVGE SG2 33 K7
Leaview WAB EN9 110 F7
Lea Wk HARP AL5 47 G1
Lebanon Cl WAT WD17 117 H2
Le Corte Cl KGLGY WD4 100 D3
Lectern La STAL AL1 85 J6
Leda Av PEND EN3 126 B5
Ledgemore La HHNE HP2 172 B11
Ledwell Rd LTN LU1 40 D6
Leeches Wy LBUZ LU7 169 L2
Lee Cl HERT/BAY SG13 71 G1
WARE SG12 71 G1
Leecroft Rd BAR EN5 122 C8
Lee Farm Cl CSHM HP5 97 L4
Leefe Wy POTB/CUF EN6 108 B2
Leeming Rd BORE WD6 120 D5
Lees Av NTHWD HA6 141 K3
Lees Cl BGSW SG18 144 D4
Leeside BAR EN5 136 C1
POTB/CUF EN6 107 H6
Leete Pl ROY SG8 14 D6
The Lee NTHWD HA6 131 K8
Lee Vw ENC/FH EN2 124 F5
Leggatts Cl WATN WD24 117 K2
Leggatts Ri GSTN WD25 117 L1
Leggatts Wy WATN WD24 117 L2
Leggatts Wood Av
WATN WD24 117 M2
Leggett Gv STVG SG1 33 J1
Leggfield Ter HHW HP1 81 K2
Leghorn Crs LTNW/LEA LU4 26 E6
Legions Wy BSF CM23 44 A1
Legra Av HOD EN11 72 E7
Leicester Rd BAR EN5 136 F1
LTNW/LEA LU4 27 J8
Leigh Common WGCE AL7 68 C1
Leigh Ct BORE WD6 * 121 H6
Leigh Dr RBSF CM22 167 L4
Leigh Rodd OXHEY WD19 132 C6
Leighton Av PIN HA5 142 C8
Leighton Buzzard Rd HHNE HP2 4 E3
Leighton Ct DUN/WHIP LU6 38 E1
Leighton Rd DUN/WHIP LU6 36 D3
KTN/HRWW/WS HA3 143 H4
Lemonfield Dr GSTN WD25 102 C6
Lemon Field Dr GSTN WD25 102 C7
Lemsford Ct BORE WD6 121 G8
Lemsford La WGCW AL8 49 M8
Lemsford Rd HAT AL10 67 K7
STAL AL1 9 J4
Lemsford Village WGCW AL8 49 K8
Lennox Gn LTNE LU2 29 K7
Lensbury Cl CHES/WCR EN8 110 C2
Leonard's Cl WLYN AL6 177 L9
Lesbury Cl LTNE LU2 29 J8
Leslie Cl STVGE SG2 34 A7
Lester Ms LTNE LU2 * 6 F2
Leston Cl DUN/WHIP LU6 39 H4
Letchfield CSHM HP5 97 M5
Letchford Ter
KTN/HRWW/WS HA3 * 142 F3
Letchmore Cl STVG SG1 10 C2
Letchmore Rd RAD WD7 119 L2
STVG SG1 10 B2
Letchworth Cl OXHEY WD19 132 B8
Letchworth Ga LWTH SG6 16 F6
Letchworth La LWTH SG6 16 D6
Letchworth Point LWTH SG6 * 16 F3
Letchworth Rd BLDK SG7 17 H2
LTNN/LIM LU3 27 K5
Levenage La WARE SG12 182 C6
Leven Cl CHES/WCR EN8 * 110 B7
OXHEY WD19 * 132 B8
Levendale LTNW/LEA LU4 27 G4
Leven Dr CHES/WCR EN8 110 B7
Leven Wy HHNE HP2 62 B6
Leveret Cl GSTN WD25 101 L8
Leverstock Green Rd
HHNE HP2 82 F2
Leverton Wy WAB EN9 111 G7
Lewes Rd
NFNCH/WDSPK N12 137 J8
Lewes Wy RKW/CH/CXG WD3 116 F8
Lewins Rd CFSP/GDCR SL9 138 B5
Lewis Cl DEN/HRF UB9 140 A4
Lewis La ARL/CHE SG15 147 Q3
CFSP/GDCR SL9 138 C3
Lewsey Park Ct
LTNW/LEA LU4 * 26 E5
Lewsey Rd LTNW/LEA LU4 26 F6
Lexden Ter WAB EN9 * 111 G8
Lexham Gdns AMS HP6 113 G3
Lexington Cl BORE WD6 120 D7
Lexington Ct POTB/CUF EN6 106 B5
Lexington Wy BAR EN5 122 B8
Leyburne Rd LTNN/LIM LU3 27 M3
Leycroft Wy HARP AL5 47 J6
Leyden Rd STVG SG1 10 C9
Leygreen Cl LTNE LU2 7 L3
Leyhill Dr LTN LU1 40 F5
Leyland Av PEND EN3 126 C6
STAL AL1 85 H4
Leyland Cl CHES/WCR EN8 110 A3
Leys Av LWTH SG6 16 D3
Leys Cl DEN/HRF UB9 140 B3
HRW HA1 143 H6
Leysdown WGCE AL7 51 H7
Leys Gdns EBAR EN4 137 L1
Leys Rd HHS/BOV HP3 5 K7
Leys Rd East PEND EN3 126 C5
The Leys AMS HP6 112 F1
RAD WD7 119 L3
STALE/WH AL4 66 B7
TRING HP23 57 M1
Leyton Gn HARP AL5 46 E4
Leyton Rd HARP AL5 46 E4
Ley Wk WGCE AL7 51 G7
Leywood Cl AMSS HP7 113 H5
Liberty Cl HERT/BAY SG13 71 G1
Liberty Wk STAL AL1 86 A3
Library Rd LTN LU1 6 F5
Lichfield Cl EBAR EN4 123 K7
Lichfield Pl STAL AL1 * 9 J3
Lichfield Rd NTHWD HA6 141 L5
Lichfield Wy BROX EN10 92 D4
Liddel Cl LTNN/LIM LU3 27 L6
Lidgate Cl LTNW/LEA LU4 26 F3
Lieutenant Ellis Wy
CHESW EN7 109 K5
Life Cl LTNW/LEA LU4 26 D5
Lighthorne Ri LTNN/LIM LU3 27 L2
Lightswood Cl CHESW EN7 109 H1
Lilac Av EN EN1 126 A2
Lilac Cl CHESW EN7 109 M5
Lilac Gv LTNN/LIM LU3 154 C12
Lilac Rd HOD EN11 72 F5
Lilac Wy HARP AL5 47 H7
Lilbourne Dr HERT/BAY SG13 53 L6
Lilley Bottom LTNE LU2 29 L2
Lilley Bottom Rd
HTCHE/RSTV SG4 30 C6
Lilleyhoo La HTCH/STOT SG5 156 B11
Lilley La MLHL NW7 * 135 J8
Lilliard Cl HOD EN11 72 F3
Lilly La HHNE HP2 63 H6
The Limberlost WLYN AL6 176 H10
Limbrick Rd HARP AL5 46 F7
Limbury Rd LTNN/LIM LU3 27 K5
Lime Av LTNW/LEA LU4 26 F6
STALE/WH AL4 175 M11
Lime Cl AMP/FLIT/BLC MK45 155 J2
KTN/HRWW/WS HA3 143 L4
OXHEY WD19 132 B3
STVGE SG2 34 B5
WARE SG12 54 C3
Limedene Cl PIN HA5 142 B3
Lime Gv ROY SG8 14 F5
RSLP HA4 141 M8
TRDG/WHET N20 136 C4
Limekiln Cl ROY SG8 14 F8
Limekiln La BLDK SG7 17 K2
STSD CM24 166 E7
Lime Pk BSF CM23 44 A3
Limes Av NFNCH/WDSPK N12 137 G7
The Limes Av
FBAR/BDGN N11 137 M8
Limes Ct HOD EN11 72 E7
Limes Crs BSF CM23 44 A2
Limes Rd CHES/WCR EN8 110 B6
The Limes AMS HP6 112 F1
ARL/CHE SG15 147 Q1
HTCH/STOT SG5 157 M7
RKW/CH/CXG WD3 * 130 A4
STALW/RED AL3 9 G2
WGCE AL7 68 E1
Limetree Av LTN LU1 173 Q2
Lime Tree Cl LTNN/LIM LU3 154 C12
Limetree Ct PIN HA5 142 E2
Lime Tree Ct LCOL/BKTW AL2 85 M8
PIN HA5 * 142 E2
Lime Tree Dr BGSW SG18 144 D4
Lime Tree Pl STAL AL1 9 H8
Lime Tree Wk AMSS HP7 113 K5
BUSH WD23 133 J4
ENC/FH EN2 125 G4
RKW/CH/CXG WD3 129 M1
Limewalk DUN/HR/TOD LU5 39 H1
Lime Wk HHS/BOV HP3 5 L6
Lime Wy RAD WD7 104 A4
Linacres LTNW/LEA LU4 27 H5
Linbridge Wy LTNE LU2 29 J7
Linces Wy WGCE AL7 68 F1
Lincoln Cl BSF CM23 43 K4
DUN/HR/TOD LU5 39 J3
RYLN/HDSTN HA2 142 D7
WGCE AL7 51 G6
Lincoln Ct BERK HP4 79 M1
BORE WD6 135 H1
Lincoln Dr OXHEY WD19 132 A6
RKW/CH/CXG WD3 116 F8
Lincoln Pk AMSS HP7 113 J5
Lincoln Rd CFSP/GDCR SL9 138 C3
EN EN1 125 J8
LTNW/LEA LU4 27 M8
NTHWD HA6 141 K5
RYLN/HDSTN HA2 142 D7
STVG SG1 21 M7
Lincoln's Cl STALE/WH AL4 66 A5
The Lincolns MLHL NW7 135 K6
Lincoln Wy DUN/HR/TOD LU5 154 A3
RKW/CH/CXG WD3 116 F8
Lincot La HTCHE/RSTV SG4 176 C2
Lindbergh WGCE AL7 51 G7
Linden Av EN EN1 125 L5
WATW WD18 12 A5
Linden Cl CHESW EN7 109 M4
DUN/HR/TOD LU5 26 D8
STAN HA7 133 M8
Linden Ct DUN/HR/TOD LU5 25 M5
HARP AL5 46 F5
Linden Crs STAL AL1 86 A2
Lindencroft LWTH SG6 148 E12
Linden Dr CFSP/GDCR SL9 138 C3
Linden Gdns EN EN1 125 L5
Linden Gld HHW HP1 4 B4
Linden Lea GSTN WD25 101 L7
PIN HA5 * 142 D2
Linden Rd DUN/HR/TOD LU5 26 D7
FBAR/BDGN N11 137 K5
LTNW/LEA LU4 27 J5
STALW/RED AL3 173 Q11
Linden Sq DEN/HRF UB9 139 L1
The Lindens BSF CM23 43 M3
DUN/HR/TOD LU5 25 M5
HAT AL10 * 67 K7
HHS/BOV HP3 81 K5
NFNCH/WDSPK N12 * 137 H8
STVG SG1 10 F6
Lindhill Cl PEND EN3 126 B6
Lindiswara Ct
RKW/CH/CXG WD3 * 130 E2
Lindley Cl HARP AL5 46 E1
Lindlings HHW HP1 81 J3
Lindo Cl CSHM HP5 96 F4
Lindsay Av HTCHE/RSTV SG4 157 R8
Lindsay Cl ROY SG8 14 D4
Lindsay Pl CHESW EN7 109 M4
Lindsey Cl BSF CM23 166 B12
Lindsey Rd BSF CM23 166 B12
LTNE LU2 29 H8
Lindum Pl STALW/RED AL3 84 D4
Linfield Ct HERT/WAT SG14 52 D6
Linfields AMSS HP7 114 A6
Linford Cl HLWW/ROY CM19 75 G7
Linford End HLWW/ROY CM19 75 G7
Lingfield Cl NTHWD HA6 141 J2
Lingfield Rd ROY SG8 14 F7
STVG SG1 22 A8
Lingfield Wy WAT WD17 117 K4
Lingholm Wy BAR EN5 136 B1
Lingmoor Dr GSTN WD25 102 A7
Linington Av CSHM HP5 97 L4
Link Cl HAT AL10 67 M8
Link Dr HAT AL10 67 M8
Linkfield WGCE AL7 68 C3
Link Rd BSF CM23 43 M1
FBAR/BDGN N11 137 L7
HHW HP1 62 A7
WATN WD24 13 J2
WLYN AL6 177 M10
Links Av HERT/BAY SG13 53 M6
Links Dr BORE WD6 120 D7
RAD WD7 103 K7
TRDG/WHET N20 136 E4
Linkside Cl ENC/FH EN2 124 D7
Linkside Gdns ENC/FH EN2 124 D7
Linkside Rd BSF CM23 44 C3
Links Side ENC/FH EN2 124 D7
The Links CHES/WCR EN8 92 B8
Links Vw STALW/RED AL3 8 B2
Links View Cl STAN HA7 143 L1
Links Wy LTNE LU2 28 A1
NTHWD HA6 141 G3
Linksway NTHWD HA6 141 H3
Links Wy RKW/CH/CXG WD3 117 G7
The Link PEND EN3 126 C5
PIN HA5 142 A8
Link Wy BSF CM23 43 L3
DEN/HRF UB9 139 L8
Linkway PIN HA5 142 B3
Linkways East STVG SG1 11 G4
Linkways West STVG SG1 11 G4
The Linkway BAR EN5 136 E2
Linley Dell LTNE LU2 29 H7
Linnet Cl BUSH WD23 133 G4
LTNW/LEA LU4 26 E5
LWTH SG6 16 C1
Linnet Rd ABLGY WD5 101 L5
Linney Head DUN/WHIP LU6 * 171 P3
Linnins Pond STALW/RED AL3 173 K8
Linsey Cl HHS/BOV HP3 82 E6
Linslade Cl PIN HA5 141 M5
Linster Gv BORE WD6 135 G1
Linten Cl HTCHE/RSTV SG4 20 A3
Linthorpe Rd EBAR EN4 123 J7
Linton Av BORE WD6 120 D6
Lintons Cl HOD EN11 72 F6
Lintott Cl STVG SG1 10 C2
Linwood SBW CM21 * 183 Q7
Linwood Crs EN EN1 125 L5
Linwood Rd HARP AL5 47 G6
WARE SG12 54 D2
Lion Ct BORE WD6 121 G5
Liphook Rd OXHEY WD19 132 B7
Lippitts Hl LOU IG10 127 J6
LTNE LU2 28 C4
Liscombe Rd DUN/HR/TOD LU5 26 C8
Lismore HHS/BOV HP3 83 G4
STVGE SG2 34 A8
Lister Av HTCHE/RSTV SG4 157 P8
Lister Cl STVG SG1 21 G7
Liston Cl LTNW/LEA LU4 26 F4
Litlington Rd ROY SG8 145 Q8
Little Acre STALW/RED AL3 8 E1
Little Acres WARE SG12 54 B5
Little Almshoe Rd
HTCHE/RSTV SG4 31 L1
Little Berkhamsted La
BRKMPK AL9 89 K2
Little Berries LTNN/LIM LU3 27 J2
Little Brays HLWS CM18 3 L9
Little Bridge Rd BERK HP4 * 80 B1
Littlebrook Gdns
CHES/WCR EN8 110 B4
Little Brook Rd
HLWW/ROY CM19 74 A5
Little Burrow WGCE AL7 68 B1
Littlebury Cl HTCH/STOT SG5 148 E8
Little Bushey La BUSH WD23 118 E7
Little Catherells HHW HP1 61 J8
Little Cattins HLWW/ROY CM19 94 D1
Little Cedars
NFNCH/WDSPK N12 137 G7
Little Chishill Rd ROY SG8 153 L5
Little Church Rd LTNE LU2 28 F6
Little Common STAN HA7 133 L6
Littlecote Pl PIN HA5 142 C3
Little Dell WGCW AL8 50 B5
Littlefield Rd LTNE LU2 28 F6
Little Foxes HOD EN11 * 72 A7
Little Ganett WGCE AL7 68 F1
Little Graylings ABLGY WD5 101 J7
Little Greencroft CSHM HP5 96 E1
Littlegreen La LTN LU1 40 C7
Little Green La
RKW/CH/CXG WD3 116 D7
Little Gv BUSH WD23 118 F8
Littlegrove EBAR EN4 137 J2
Little Grove Av CHESW EN7 109 J1
Little Grove Fld
HLWW/ROY CM19 2 C6
Little Hardings WGCE AL7 51 G6
Little Hayes KGLGY WD4 100 E3
Little Heath RBSF CM22 184 F6
Little Heath La HHW HP1 80 F3
Little Hl RKW/CH/CXG WD3 129 G2
Little Hivings CSHM HP5 96 E1
Little Hoo TRING HP23 57 K1
Little How Cft ABLGY WD5 101 G5
Little Hyde STVGE SG2 11 M7
Little Lake WGCE AL7 68 F2
Little La HARP AL5 47 G7
HTCH/STOT SG5 146 F12
Little Ley WGCE AL7 68 C2
Little Martins BUSH WD23 132 F1
Little Md HAT AL10 67 M5
Little Meadow LTN LU1 * 40 F6
Little Mimms HHNE HP2 82 C1
Little Moss La PIN HA5 142 C4
Little Mundells WGCE AL7 50 D6
Little Orchard Cl ABLGY WD5 101 H5
PIN HA5 * 142 C4
Little Oxhey La OXHEY WD19 132 C8
Little Pk HHS/BOV HP3 98 E2
Little Park Gdns ENC/FH EN2 125 G7
Little Piper's Cl CHESW EN7 108 F3
Little Potters BUSH WD23 133 H3
Little Pynchons HLWS CM18 75 K8
Little Reeves Av AMSS HP7 113 K5
Little Rdg WGCE AL7 50 E7
Little Rivers WGCE AL7 50 E6
Little Rd HHNE HP2 82 C1
Little Shardeloes AMSS HP7 112 E6
Little Spring CSHM HP5 96 F2
Little Stock Rd CHESW EN7 91 H8
Little Stream Cl NTHWD HA6 131 J8
Little St WAB EN9 127 G2
Little Thistle WGCE AL7 69 G1
Little Tring Rd TRING HP23 169 K11
Little Wade WGCE AL7 68 D2
Little Wk HLW CM20 2 E5
Little Widbury WARE SG12 54 D4
Little Widbury La WARE SG12 54 D4
Little Windmill Hl KGLGY WD4 99 J6
Little Wood Cft LTNN/LIM LU3 27 J2
Little Youngs WGCW AL8 50 A7
Liverpool Rd LTN LU1 6 D5
STAL AL1 9 G6
WATW WD18 12 F7
Livingstone Link STVGE SG2 33 M1
Livingstone Wk HHNE HP2 62 D6
Llanbury Cl CFSP/GDCR SL9 138 C2
Lloyd Ct PIN HA5 142 B7
Lloyd Ms PEND EN3 126 E4
Lloyd-Taylor Cl STDN SG11 164 H11
Lloyd Wy HTCHE/RSTV SG4 175 N8
Loates La WAT WD17 13 G4
Loates Pasture STSD CM24 166 F5
Local Board Rd WAT WD17 13 J7
Locarno Av LTNW/LEA LU4 27 G3
Lochnell Rd BERK HP4 59 K7
Lockers Park La HHW HP1 4 C3
Locket Rd
KTN/HRWW/WS HA3 143 K4
Locket Road Ms
KTN/HRWW/WS HA3 143 J4
Lockfield Av PEND EN3 126 C6
Lockhart Cl DUN/WHIP LU6 39 H3
Lockington Crs
DUN/HR/TOD LU5 26 C7
Lockley Crs HAT AL10 67 M6
Lockleys Dr WLYN AL6 177 J12
Lockyer Cl PEND EN3 126 F4
Lodge Av BORE WD6 134 D1
Lodge Cl HERT/WAT SG14 53 G5
LBUZ LU7 169 L2
Lodge Ct HTCH/STOT SG5 157 N2
Lodge Crs CHES/WCR EN8 110 B8
Lodge Dr BRKMPK AL9 68 B5
RKW/CH/CXG WD3 116 A8
Lodge End RAD WD7 103 M8
RKW/CH/CXG WD3 117 H8
Lodge Fld WGCE AL7 50 C4
Lodge Gdns HARP AL5 46 E3
Lodge Hall HLWS CM18 95 J1
Lodge La CSTG HP8 114 D6
NFNCH/WDSPK N12 137 G8
WAB EN9 127 H1
Lodge Rd RKW/CH/CXG WD3 117 H8
Lodge Wy STVGE SG2 33 L8
Loftus Cl LTNW/LEA LU4 26 F5
Logan Cl PEND EN3 126 B5
The Logans BAR EN5 * 122 B7
Loire Ms HARP AL5 47 G6
Lollard Cl LTNW/LEA LU4 26 C6
Lollards Cl AMS HP6 113 G3
Lombard Av PEND EN3 126 A5
Lombard Rd FBAR/BDGN N11 137 M8
Lombard Vls
FBAR/BDGN N11 * 137 M8
Lombardy Cl HHNE HP2 83 H3
Lombardy Dr BERK HP4 80 B2
Lombardy Wy BORE WD6 120 C5
Lomond Rd HHNE HP2 62 B6
Lomond Wy STVG SG1 22 A6
London Loop BORE WD6 134 F2
CHING E4 127 H8
EN EN1 125 M3
London Rd BERK HP4 80 B1
BLDK SG7 17 K3
BSF CM23 43 M6
BUNT SG9 159 K11
BUSH WD23 132 D2
CSTG HP8 128 A5
DUN/WHIP LU6 39 H2
ENC/FH EN2 125 H8
HERT/BAY SG13 53 J7
HHW HP1 4 A7
HLWE CM17 75 M6

HLWE CM17 95 M4
HTCHE/RSTV SG4 157 P8
KNEB SG3 177 N4
RAD WD7 104 D7
RAYLNE/WEN HP22 168 B12
ROY SG8 151 R3
SBW CM21 183 Q7
STAL AL1 8 F7
STALW/RED AL3 172 G4
STAN HA7 134 A8
STVG SG1 10 D7
STVGE SG2 33 J8
TRING HP23 57 M2
WARE SG12 54 C6
WLYN AL6 50 A1
London Rd East AMSS HP7 113 J7
London Rd West AMSS HP7 113 G6
London Rw ARL/CHE SG15 147 Q6
Londrina Ter BERK HP4 80 B1
Long Acre HLWE CM17 75 M1
Longacres STALE/WH AL4 86 B2
Long Arrotts HHW HP1 61 M8
Long Banks HLWS CM18 75 H8
Long Barn Cl GSTN WD25 101 L6
Long Border Rd STSD CM24 167 N12
Longbridge Cl TRING HP23 169 L11
Longbrooke DUN/HR/TOD LU5 26 B5
Long Buftlers HARP AL5 47 K5
Long Chaulden HHW HP1 81 J3
Longcliffe Pth OXHEY WD19 131 L6
Long Cl HNLW SG16 146 G7
LTNE LU2 29 G6
Long Cft OXHEY WD19 131 M3
Longcroft RAYLNE/WEN HP22 168 D12
Long Cft STSD CM24 166 F5
Longcroft Av HARP AL5 46 D4
RAYLNE/WEN HP22 56 B7
Longcroft Dr
AMP/FLIT/BLC MK45 154 H3
Long Croft Dr CHES/WCR EN8 110 D8
Longcroft Gdns WGCW AL8 50 B8
Longcroft Gn WGCW AL8 68 B1
Longcroft La HHS/BOV HP3 99 G2
WGCW AL8 50 B8
Long Croft Rd LTN LU1 40 E2
RKW/CH/CXG WD3 129 H8
Longcroft Rd STVG SG1 33 J2
Long Cutt STALW/RED AL3 173 Q11
Longdean Pk HHS/BOV HP3 82 E6
Long Elmes
KTN/HRWW/WS HA3 142 F3
Long Elms ABLGY WD5 101 H7
Long Elms Cl ABLGY WD5 101 H7
Long Fallow LCOL/BKTW AL2 102 E1
Longfield HHS/BOV HP3 82 F4
HLWS CM18 75 L7
Longfield Av PEND EN3 126 A3
Longfield Dr AMS HP6 112 F4
LTNW/LEA LU4 27 H8
Longfield Gdns TRING HP23 57 J2
Longfield La CHESW EN7 109 K1
Longfield Rd CSHM HP5 96 D3
HARP AL5 47 G6
TRING HP23 57 J2
Longfields STVGE SG2 34 A8
Long Grove Cl BROX EN10 92 C1
Long Hale LBUZ LU7 169 N6
Long Hedge DUN/HR/TOD LU5 39 H1
LBUZ LU7 169 N5
Long Hyde STVGE SG2 11 M7
Long John HHNE HP2 5 L6
Longland Dr TRDG/WHET N20 136 F6
Longlands HHNE HP2 5 L1
Longlands Cl CHES/WCR EN8 110 B6
Longlands Rd WGCE AL7 68 D1
Long La HHS/BOV HP3 98 D5
HTCHE/RSTV SG4 175 L2
RKW/CH/CXG WD3 129 G2
STVGE SG2 34 C4
Long Leaves STVGE SG2 33 L7
Long Ley HLW CM20 3 K6
LBUZ LU7 169 L2
WGCE AL7 51 G7
Longley Rd HRW HA1 143 H7
Longmans Cl WATW WD18 131 G2
Long Marston La LBUZ LU7 169 K2
Long Marston Rd TRING HP23 169 J7
Long Md DUN/HR/TOD LU5 25 M3
Longmead BUNT SG9 158 H10
HAT AL10 67 L5
KNEB SG3 177 N7
LWTH SG6 16 C2
Long Meadow BSF CM23 43 K3
CSHM HP5 97 G2
DUN/WHIP LU6 38 E1
HERT/WAT SG14 * 178 F5
STALW/RED AL3 172 G4
Longmeadow Dr
HTCH/STOT SG5 147 N12
Long Mimms HHNE HP2 82 C1
Long Moor CHES/WCR EN8 110 C3
Longmore Av BAR EN5 137 G2
Longmore Cl
RKW/CH/CXG WD3 129 K7
Longmore Gdns WGCE AL7 50 D7
Long Pk AMS HP6 113 G2
Long Park Cl AMS HP6 113 G2
Long Park Wy AMS HP6 113 G1
Long Plough
RAYLNE/WEN HP22 168 B12
Longridge RAD WD7 103 M8
Long Rdg STVGE SG2 34 B8
Long Spring STALW/RED AL3 65 J5
Longspring WATN WD24 117 M3
Long Vw BERK HP4 59 L7
Long Wk CSTG HP8 114 C7
Long Wd HLWS CM18 95 H2
Longwood La AMSS HP7 113 H5
Longwood Rd HERT/WAT SG14 52 D6
The Loning PEND EN3 126 A4
Lonsdale HHNE HP2 62 C7
Lonsdale Cl LTNN/LIM LU3 27 L4
Lonsdale Ct STVG SG1 33 K2
Lonsdale Dr ENC/FH EN2 124 B8
Lonsdale Rd STVG SG1 11 G1
Loom La RAD WD7 119 K3
Loop Rd WAB EN9 110 F6
Lord Mead La WLYN AL6 176 C10
Lords Av BSF CM23 43 H2
Lords Cl LBUZ LU7 24 C4
RAD WD7 104 C6
Lordship La LWTH SG6 16 F5
Lordship Rd CHESW EN7 109 M4
Lords Md DUN/WHIP LU6 37 J3
Lords Meadow
STALW/RED AL3 173 Q12
Lords Mill Ct CSHM HP5 97 G6
Lords Ter DUN/WHIP LU6 * 37 J3
Lord St HOD EN11 72 C7
WAT WD17 13 G4
Lords Wd WGCE AL7 51 G7
Lorian Cl NFNCH/WDSPK N12 136 F7
Loring Rd BERK HP4 80 A2
DUN/WHIP LU6 38 D1
TRDG/WHET N20 137 J5
Lorne Rd KTN/HRWW/WS HA3 143 K4
Lorraine Pk
KTN/HRWW/WS HA3 143 J2
Lorrimer Cl LTNE LU2 28 C3
Lothair Rd LTNE LU2 28 E5
Loudhams Rd AMSS HP7 114 A5
Loudhams Wood La CSTG HP8 114 B6
Loudwater Dr
RKW/CH/CXG WD3 116 A8
Loudwater Hts
RKW/CH/CXG WD3 115 M7
Loudwater La
RKW/CH/CXG WD3 130 A1
Loudwater Rdg
RKW/CH/CXG WD3 116 A8
Louise Wk HHS/BOV HP3 98 E2
Louisville Cl WARE SG12 73 G1
Louvain Wy GSTN WD25 101 M6
Lovatts RKW/CH/CXG WD3 116 E8
Lovelace Rd EBAR EN4 137 J3
Love La BLDK SG7 144 G12
KGLGY WD4 100 C3
PIN HA5 142 C5
Lovel Cl HHW HP1 81 L2
Lovel End CFSP/GDCR SL9 138 A2
Lovell Cl HTCHE/RSTV SG4 157 Q7
Lovell Rd EN EN1 125 M1
Lovel Md CFSP/GDCR SL9 138 A2
Lovel Rd CFSP/GDCR SL9 138 A2
Lovering Rd CHESW EN7 91 G7
Lovers' Wk DUN/HR/TOD LU5 39 G1
Lovet Rd HLWW/ROY CM19 74 E6
Lovett Gn
AMP/FLIT/BLC MK45 154 C2
Lovett Rd DEN/HRF UB9 140 A5
LCOL/BKTW AL2 85 L8
Lovett Wy DUN/HR/TOD LU5 26 B6
Lowbell La LCOL/BKTW AL2 104 C1
Lower Adeyfield Rd HHNE HP2 5 G1
Lower Barn HHS/BOV HP3 5 K9
Lower Bourne Gdns
WARE SG12 54 A2
Lower Clabdens WARE SG12 54 D4
Lower Dagnall St
STALW/RED AL3 8 D5
Lower Derby Rd WAT WD17 13 H6
Lower Emms HHNE HP2 63 G5
Lowerfield WGCE AL7 50 E8
Lower Gower Rd ROY SG8 14 E5
Lower Harpenden Rd LTN LU1 41 M4
Lower Hatfield Rd
HERT/BAY SG13 70 D4
Lower High St WAT WD17 13 H6
Lower Icknield Wy
RAYLNE/WEN HP22 168 E12
Lower Innings
HTCH/STOT SG5 157 M5
Lower Island Wy WAB EN9 126 F1
Lower Kings Rd BERK HP4 79 M1
Lower King St ROY SG8 14 E7
Lower Luton Rd HARP AL5 47 G1
STALE/WH AL4 47 L3
Lower Mardley Hl WLYN AL6 177 M9
Lower Meadow
CHES/WCR EN8 110 B1
HLWS CM18 95 J1
Lower Paddock Rd
OXHEY WD19 13 L9
Lower Park Crs BSF CM23 43 M4
Lower Paxton Rd STAL AL1 9 G7
Lower Plantation
RKW/CH/CXG WD3 116 A7
Lower Rd CFSP/GDCR SL9 138 C5
HHS/BOV HP3 82 E8
HTCHE/RSTV SG4 30 D8
RBSF CM22 184 C2
RKW/CH/CXG WD3 115 H8
STDN SG11 42 E2
WARE SG12 54 D7
Lower Sales HHW HP1 81 K3
Lower Sean STVGE SG2 11 K9
Lower Shott CHESW EN7 91 K8
Lower St STSD CM24 166 G7
Lower Tail OXHEY WD19 132 C6
Lower Titmore Gn
HTCHE/RSTV SG4 20 C8
Lower Tub BUSH WD23 133 H3
Lower Yott HHNE HP2 5 J4
Lowes Cl STVG SG1 22 A7
Lowestoft Rd WATN WD24 117 M5
Loweswater Cl GSTN WD25 102 A7
Lowfield SBW CM21 183 Q8
Lowfield La HOD EN11 72 E7
Lowgate La WARE SG12 179 Q5
Low Hill Rd HLWW/ROY CM19 73 K7
Lowick Rd HRW HA1 143 J6
Lowlands BRKMPK AL9 68 A5
Lowndes Av CSHM HP5 96 F4
Low Rd BRKMPK AL9 69 K5
Lowry Dr DUN/HR/TOD LU5 26 B4
Lowson Gv OXHEY WD19 132 C3
Lowswood Cl NTHWD HA6 141 G3
Lowther Cl BORE WD6 134 D1
Lowther Dr ENC/FH EN2 124 C8
Lowther Rd DUN/WHIP LU6 39 G3
Loxley Ct WARE SG12 * 54 C4
Loxley Rd BERK HP4 59 J7
Lucan Rd BAR EN5 122 C7
Lucas Ct WAB EN9 111 K7
Lucas Gdns LTNN/LIM LU3 27 M1
Lucas La BLDK SG7 149 Q1
HTCH/STOT SG5 157 M6
Lucern Cl CHESW EN7 109 J1
Lucerne Wy LTNN/LIM LU3 28 A5
Lucks Hl HHW HP1 81 J2
Ludgate TRING HP23 57 K1
Ludlow Av LTN LU1 41 J5
Ludlow Md OXHEY WD19 131 M6
Ludlow Wy
RKW/CH/CXG WD3 117 G8
Ludun Cl DUN/HR/TOD LU5 39 J1
Ludwick Cl WGCE AL7 * 68 D1
Ludwick Gn WGCE AL7 * 50 D8
Ludwick Wy WGCE AL7 50 D7
Lukes La TRING HP23 168 H6
Lukes Lea TRING HP23 169 L8
Lullington Cl LTNE LU2 29 G6
Lullington Garth BORE WD6 * 135 G1
Lulworth Av CHESW EN7 108 F3
Lumbards WGCE AL7 50 E4
Lumen Rd ROY SG8 14 E6
Lunardi Ct STDN SG11 163 N10
Lundin Wk OXHEY WD19 * 132 B7
Luther Cl EDGW HA8 135 G5
Luther King Rd
HLWW/ROY CM19 2 D7
The Luton Dr LTN LU1 41 L4
Luton La STALW/RED AL3 173 Q9
Luton Rd AMP/FLIT/BLC MK45 154 H4
DUN/HR/TOD LU5 39 H1
HARP AL5 46 C1
HTCH/STOT SG5 156 C11
HTCHE/RSTV SG4 175 L7
LTNE LU2 29 J6
LTNN/LIM LU3 154 H8
STALW/RED AL3 172 G2
Luton White Hl LTNE LU2 29 L1
Luxembourg Cl LTNN/LIM LU3 27 H1
Luxford Pl SBW CM21 183 R8
Luynes Ri BUNT SG9 159 J11
Lybury La STALW/RED AL3 173 N10
Lycaste Cl STAL AL1 9 K7
Lych Ga GSTN WD25 102 B7
Lycrome La CSHM HP5 97 H2
Lycrome Rd CSHM HP5 97 J2
Lydia Ms BRKMPK AL9 88 A6
Lye Green Rd CSHM HP5 97 J4
Lye Hl HTCHE/RSTV SG4 174 H2
Lye La LCOL/BKTW AL2 102 E4
The Lye BERK HP4 171 K11
Lygean Av WARE SG12 54 C4
Lygetun Dr LTNN/LIM LU3 27 J3
Lygrave STVGE SG2 177 Q1
Lyles La WGCW AL8 50 C5
Lyle's Rw HTCHE/RSTV SG4 157 P7
Lymans Rd ARL/CHE SG15 147 Q3
Lyme Av BERK HP4 59 H6
Lymington Ct GSTN WD25 * 101 L8
Lymington Rd STVG SG1 32 F1
Lynch Hl DUN/WHIP LU6 172 C1
The Lynch HOD EN11 72 F7
Lyncroft Av PIN HA5 142 B7
Lyndale STVG SG1 10 E6
Lyndhurst Av PIN HA5 141 M3
Lyndhurst Cl HARP AL5 47 G3
Lyndhurst Dr HARP AL5 47 G3
Lyndhurst Gdns EN EN1 125 J8
PIN HA5 141 M3
Lyndhurst Rd CSHM HP5 96 F2
LTN LU1 6 C5
Lyndon Av PIN HA5 142 C1
Lyndon Md STALE/WH AL4 66 A3
Lyndsey Pl CHESW EN7 * 109 M4
Lyne Wy HHW HP1 61 K8
Lynford Cl BAR EN5 135 K1
Lynford Gdns EDGW HA8 134 F6
Lynmouth Rd WGCE AL7 50 D7
Lynn Cl KTN/HRWW/WS HA3 143 H4
Lynn St ENC/FH EN2 125 H5
Lynsey Cl STALW/RED AL3 173 Q10
Lynton Av ARL/CHE SG15 147 Q4
NFNCH/WDSPK N12 137 H7
STAL AL1 86 A3
Lynton Md TRDG/WHET N20 136 E6
Lynton Pde CHES/WCR EN8 110 B4
Lynton Rd CSHM HP5 96 F2
Lynwood Av LTNE LU2 28 E6
Lynwood Dr NTHWD HA6 141 J3
Lynwood Hts
RKW/CH/CXG WD3 129 M1
Lyon Rd HRW HA1 143 K8
Lyonsdown Av BAR EN5 137 G2
Lyonsdown Rd BAR EN5 137 G1
Lyon Wy STALE/WH AL4 86 E2
Lyrical Wy HHW HP1 61 M8
Lysander Cl HHS/BOV HP3 98 D1
Lysander Wy ABLGY WD5 101 L6
WGCE AL7 51 H6
Lys Hill Gdns HERT/WAT SG14 52 F5
Lysley Pl BRKMPK AL9 107 G1
Lytchet Wy PEND EN3 126 A5
Lytham Av OXHEY WD19 132 B8
Lytton Av LWTH SG6 16 D4
PEND EN3 126 C4
Lytton Flds KNEB SG3 177 M4
Lytton Gdns WGCW AL8 50 B7
Lytton Rd BAR EN5 123 G8
PIN HA5 142 C2
Lyttons Wy HOD EN11 72 E4
Lytton Wy STVG SG1 10 A1

M

Mabbutt Cl LCOL/BKTW AL2 102 C4
Mabey's Wk SBW CM21 183 M8
Macaret Cl TRDG/WHET N20 136 F3
Macaulay Rd LTNW/LEA LU4 26 E7
Macdonald Cl AMS HP6 113 G1
Macdonald Rd
FBAR/BDGN N11 137 K8
Macdonnell Gdns GSTN WD25 117 K1
Macer's La BROX EN10 92 D6
Macintosh Cl CHESW EN7 91 H8
Mackenzie Sq STVGE SG2 11 M8
Mackerel Hall ROY SG8 14 C7
Maddesfield Ct RAD WD7 104 C7
Maddles LWTH SG6 17 H5
Maddox Rd HHNE HP2 82 F2
HLW CM20 3 G4
Made Feld STVG SG1 11 G4
Madeley Cl AMS HP6 113 H2
Madgeways Cl WARE SG12 * 54 D8
Madgeways La WARE SG12 54 D8
Mafeking Rd EN EN1 125 K7
Magdalene Cl BGSW SG18 144 D4
Magellan Cl STVGE SG2 34 B4
Magna Cl HARP AL5 47 H7
Magnaville Rd BSF CM23 43 L5
BUSH WD23 133 J3
Magnolia Av ABLGY WD5 101 K6
Magnolia Cl HERT/BAY SG13 53 L7
LCOL/BKTW AL2 85 H8
Magnolia Gdns EDGW HA8 135 G7
Magpie Cl EN EN1 125 L5
Magpie Crs STVGE SG2 34 B5
Magpie Hall Rd STAN HA7 133 J5
Magpie Pl GSTN WD25 * 102 A6
Magpies EPP CM16 94 E6
The Magpies LTNE LU2 28 B3
Mahon Cl EN EN1 125 K5
Maidenbower Av
DUN/WHIP LU6 25 K8
Maidenhall Rd LTNW/LEA LU4 27 L7
Maidenhead St
HERT/WAT SG14 53 H7
Maidenhead Yd
HERT/WAT SG14 53 H7
Maidens Br ENC/FH EN2 * 125 L3
Maidensfield WGCW AL8 50 B4
Maiden St HTCHE/RSTV SG4 18 A8
Mailers La BSF CM23 166 B3
Main Av NTHWD HA6 131 G6
Main Dr CFSP/GDCR SL9 138 A7
Main Rd HERT/WAT SG14 52 A2
Main Rd North BERK HP4 170 G2
Main Rd South BERK HP4 171 J4
Maitland Rd
RAYLNE/WEN HP22 56 B6
STSD CM24 166 G7
Major Haddock Cl ROY SG8 14 D6
Malcolm Ct STAN HA7 134 A8
Malden Flds BUSH WD23 13 K6
Malden Rd BORE WD6 120 E7
WAT WD17 12 D2
Maldon Ct HARP AL5 46 F3
Malham Cl LTNW/LEA LU4 27 K6
Malins Cl BAR EN5 * 135 M1
Malkin Dr HLWE CM17 76 C6
Malkin Wy WATW WD18 117 J8
Mallard Cl BAR EN5 * 137 H2
Mallard Gdns LTNN/LIM LU3 27 L4
Mallard Ms HARP AL5 47 G2
Mallard Rd ABLGY WD5 101 L5
ROY SG8 14 D7
STVGE SG2 34 B7
Mallards Ct OXHEY WD19 132 D6
Mallards Ri HLWE CM17 76 A5
The Mallards HHS/BOV HP3 82 D7
Mallard Wy GSTN WD25 118 C2
NTHWD HA6 141 G2
Mallion Ct WAB EN9 111 K7
Mallory Gdns EBAR EN4 137 L3
Mallows Gn HLWW/ROY CM19 94 E1
Mallows Green Rd BSF CM23 165 Q3
The Mallow LTNN/LIM LU3 * 27 K6
Mallow Wk CHESW EN7 109 H2
ROY SG8 14 F8
The Mall DUN/HR/TOD LU5 26 A8
LCOL/BKTW AL2 103 G1
Malm Cl RKW/CH/CXG WD3 130 B5
Malmesbury Cl PIN HA5 141 K6
Malmes Cft HHS/BOV HP3 83 G4
Malms Cl DUN/WHIP LU6 39 H8
Malmsdale WGCW AL8 50 B3
Malpas Dr PIN HA5 142 B7
Maltby Dr EN EN1 125 M4
Malthouse Gn LTNE LU2 29 K8
Malthouse La HTCH/STOT SG5 148 E6
Malthouse Ms DEN/HRF UB9 * 140 A3
The Malthouse
HERT/WAT SG14 * 53 H7
Malting La MHAD SG10 181 R7
STDN SG11 163 Q6
TRING HP23 170 D12
Malting Md HAT AL10 * 68 A7
Malting Ms HERT/BAY SG13 * 53 G8
Maltings Cl BLDK SG7 149 L12
ROY SG8 14 D6
Maltings Dr STALE/WH AL4 48 A6
Maltings La ROY SG8 153 N3
The Maltings Norton Hall Farm
LWTH SG6 * 148 G12
Maltings Orch
HTCH/STOT SG5 156 F2
The Maltings AMSS HP7 * 112 F5
HERT/BAY SG13 * 53 J7
KGLGY WD4 101 G7
ROY SG8 * 14 D6
STVGE SG2 34 F1
Maltmans La CFSP/GDCR SL9 138 A5
Malus Cl HHNE HP2 82 E1
Malvern Cl BUSH WD23 133 G2
HAT AL10 67 K7
STALE/WH AL4 65 M6
Malvern Rd LTN LU1 6 A5
PEND EN3 126 C3
Malvern Wy HHNE HP2 62 C8
RKW/CH/CXG WD3 130 F1
Malzeard Rd LTNN/LIM LU3 6 C2
Manan Cl HHS/BOV HP3 83 G4
Manchester Cl STVG SG1 21 K6
Manchester Pl DUN/WHIP LU6 25 M8
Manchester St LTN LU1 6 E5
Mancroft Rd LTN LU1 40 D8
Mandela Av HLW CM20 3 H3
Mandela Pl WATN WD24 13 J2
Mandelyns BERK HP4 59 J6
Mandeville STVGE SG2 34 A8
Mandeville Cl BROX EN10 92 D2
HERT/BAY SG13 71 G2
WAT WD17 117 K4
Mandeville Dr STAL AL1 85 H5
Mandeville Ri WGCW AL8 50 B5
Mandeville Rd HERT/BAY SG13 71 G2
PEND EN3 126 C2
POTB/CUF EN6 107 G6
STHGT/OAK N14 137 M5
Mangrove Dr HERT/BAY SG13 71 J1
Mangrove La HERT/BAY SG13 71 K6
Mangrove Rd
HERT/BAY SG13 53 J8
LTNE LU2 29 G6
Manhattan Av WATW WD18 12 A5
Manland Av HARP AL5 47 G3
Manland Wy HARP AL5 47 G3
Manley Hwy HTCH/STOT SG5 157 K6
Manley Rd HHNE HP2 5 J1
Manly Dixon Dr PEND EN3 126 C3
Mannicotts WGCW AL8 49 M7
Manning Pl LTNE LU2 29 J7
Manor Av HHS/BOV HP3 4 F9
Manor Cl BAR EN5 122 C8
BERK HP4 * 80 A1
HARP AL5 46 E7
HAT AL10 67 K5
HERT/WAT SG14 53 H5
HTCH/STOT SG5 157 N2
LWTH SG6 16 D6
MLHL NW7 * 135 H8
Manor Cots NTHWD HA6 141 K3
Manor Ct CHES/WCR EN8 * 110 B5
DEN/HRF UB9 140 A4
EN EN1 125 M2
HRW HA1 * 143 K8
POTB/CUF EN6 * 106 D6
RAD WD7 119 K3
Manor Crs HTCHE/RSTV SG4 157 R7
RAYLNE/WEN HP22 56 A8
Manor Croft Pde
CHES/WCR EN8 * 110 B4
Manor Dr AMS HP6 112 F2
LCOL/BKTW AL2 102 E1
MLHL NW7 135 H8
TRDG/WHET N20 137 J6
Manor Farm Cl
AMP/FLIT/BLC MK45 155 J2
LTNW/LEA LU4 27 G6
Manor Farm Rd EN EN1 125 M1
Manor Farm Stables
KNEB SG3 177 J4
Manor Hatch HLWS CM18 3 M9
Manor Hatch Cl HLWS CM18 75 M6
Manor House Dr NTHWD HA6 140 F2
STVGE SG2 34 B2
Manor House Gdns
ABLGY WD5 101 H5
Manor Links BSF CM23 44 C2
Manor Pde HAT AL10 67 K5
HRW HA1 * 143 K8
Manor Pk DUN/HR/TOD LU5 25 M5
Manor Park Dr
RYLN/HDSTN HA2 142 F5
Manor Park Gdns EDGW HA8 134 E8
Manor Pl BORE WD6 * 121 G7
Manor Pound Rd LBUZ LU7 169 L2
Manor Rd
AMP/FLIT/BLC MK45 155 K3
BAR EN5 122 C8
BSF CM23 44 A2
CSHM HP5 96 F3
ENC/FH EN2 125 H6
HAT AL10 67 K5
HLWE CM17 183 N12
HOD EN11 72 E5
HRW HA1 143 L8
LBUZ LU7 169 K2
LCOL/BKTW AL2 86 A8
LOU IG10 127 M4
LTN LU1 7 H7
LTN LU1 40 C6
LTNN/LIM LU3 154 B10
POTB/CUF EN6 106 D5
RAYLNE/WEN HP22 56 A8
STAL AL1 9 H4
STALE/WH AL4 47 K3
STSD CM24 166 G8
TRING HP23 169 L12
WAB EN9 111 H7
WAT WD17 117 M5
Manorside BAR EN5 122 C8
Manor St BERK HP4 80 B1
Manor Vw STVGE SG2 33 M8
Manorville Rd HHS/BOV HP3 82 A6
Manor Wy BORE WD6 121 G8
CSHM HP5 97 H4
LWTH SG6 16 D7
POTB/CUF EN6 106 E4
RKW/CH/CXG WD3 116 E8
RYLN/HDSTN HA2 142 F6
Mansard Cl PIN HA5 142 B5
TRING HP23 57 L2
Manscroft Rd HHW HP1 61 M8
Mansdale Rd STALW/RED AL3 63 K1
Mansefield Cl CSHM HP5 96 F2
Mansells La HTCHE/RSTV SG4 176 E6
Mansfield SBW CM21 183 L8
Mansfield Av EBAR EN4 137 K2
Mansfield Gdns
HERT/WAT SG14 53 G5
Mansfield Rd BLDK SG7 17 J2
LTNW/LEA LU4 27 M8
Mansion Dr TRING HP23 57 M2
Mansion Hl RAYLNE/WEN HP22 56 C5
Manston Cl CHES/WCR EN8 110 A4
Manston Dr BSF CM23 166 D12
Manston Rd HLW CM20 3 H7
Manston Wy STALE/WH AL4 86 B3
Manton Dr LTNE LU2 28 B5
Manton Rd DUN/WHIP LU6 38 B4
HTCHE/RSTV SG4 157 R7
PEND EN3 126 E3
Manus Wy TRDG/WHET N20 137 G5
Manx Cl LTNW/LEA LU4 27 L7
Maple Av BSF CM23 43 K1
STALW/RED AL3 65 G6
Maple Cl BSF CM23 43 K1
BUSH WD23 13 M2
HAT AL10 87 L1
HNLW SG16 146 G7
RSLP HA4 141 M8
Maplecroft La WAB EN9 93 J3
Maplefield LCOL/BKTW AL2 102 F3
Maplefield La CSTG HP8 113 M7
Maple Gn HHW HP1 61 J8
Maple Gv BSF CM23 43 K1
WAT WD17 117 L5
WGCE AL7 50 D4
Maple Leaf Cl ABLGY WD5 101 L6
Maple Lodge Cl
RKW/CH/CXG WD3 129 J7
Maple Rd HARP AL5 46 D4
Maple Rd East LTNW/LEA LU4 6 A3
Maple Rd West LTNW/LEA LU4 40 F1
Maple Spring BSF CM23 43 J1
Maple Springs WAB EN9 111 L7
The Maples CHESW EN7 109 J2
HLWW/ROY CM19 94 F2
HTCHE/RSTV SG4 157 P8
RAYLNE/WEN HP22 56 A8
STVGE SG2 * 177 P1
Mapleton Crs PEND EN3 126 A4
Mapleton Rd EN EN1 125 M6
Maple Wy DUN/HR/TOD LU5 26 C3
DUN/WHIP LU6 172 A1
ROY SG8 14 F5
Maplewood WARE SG12 54 A2
Maran Av WLYN AL6 50 A1
Marbury Pl LTNN/LIM LU3 * 27 K5
Marchmont Gn HHNE HP2 62 B8
Marconi Pl FBAR/BDGN N11 137 M7
Marconi Wy STALE/WH AL4 86 B2
Mardale Av DUN/WHIP LU6 39 G3
Mardle Cl LTN LU1 40 C7
Mardley Av WLYN AL6 177 M9
Mardleybury KNEB SG3 177 N8
Mardleybury Ct KNEB SG3 * 177 N7
Mardleybury Rd KNEB SG3 177 N8
Mardley Dell WLYN AL6 177 M8
Mardley Hts WLYN AL6 177 N9
Mardley Hl WLYN AL6 177 M9
Mardley Wd WLYN AL6 177 M8
Mardyke Rd HLW CM20 3 L3
Marford Rd STALE/WH AL4 48 D5
WGCW AL8 49 H7
Margaret Av STALW/RED AL3 8 E1
Margaret Cl ABLGY WD5 101 K6
POTB/CUF EN6 107 G7
WAB EN9 111 H7
Margaret Rd EBAR EN4 123 H8
Margeholes OXHEY WD19 132 C5
Margery Wd WGCE AL7 50 E3
Margherita Pl WAB EN9 111 K8
Margrave Gdns BSF CM23 43 L4
Marguerite Wy BSF CM23 43 J3
Marian Gdns GSTN WD25 101 M7
Maricas Av
KTN/HRWW/WS HA3 143 H3
Marigold Pl HLWE CM17 * 75 M1
Marina Dr DUN/WHIP LU6 38 C2
Marina Gdns CHES/WCR EN8 110 A4
Mariner Wy HHNE HP2 5 M4
Marion Cl BUSH WD23 118 D5
Marion Rd MLHL NW7 135 L8
Marion Wk HHNE HP2 * 62 D5
Marish La DEN/HRF UB9 139 G6
Mark Dr CFSP/GDCR SL9 128 B7
Markeston Gn OXHEY WD19 132 B7
Market Chambers
ENC/FH EN2 * 125 H7
Market Hl BUNT SG9 159 J10
ROY SG8 14 E7
Market Oak La HHS/BOV HP3 82 E6
Market Pl CFSP/GDCR SL9 138 B3
HAT AL10 67 M7
HERT/WAT SG14 53 H7
HTCH/STOT SG5 157 N6
STALW/RED AL3 8 E6
STVG SG1 10 D5

WAT WD17 .... 13 G5
Market Sq BSF CM23 .... 43 M2
  HLW CM20 .... 2 A1
  LTN LU1 .... 40 F3
  STVG SG1 .... 10 D5
Market St HERT/WAT SG14 .... 53 H7
  HLWE CM17 .... 76 A1
  WATW WD18 .... 12 F6
Market Wk AMSS HP7 * 112 F4
Markfield CI LTNN/LIM LU3 .... 28 A3
Mark Hall Moors HLW CM20 .... 3 M1
Markham Dr BORE WD6 .... 120 D7
Markham Crs
  DUN/HR/TOD LU5 .... 26 C7
Markham Rd CHESW EN7 .... 91 G8
  LTNN/LIM LU3 .... 28 A1
Mark Rd HHNE HP2 .... 62 E8
Markwells RBSF CM22 .... 167 M3
Markwell Wd
  HLWW/ROY CM19 .... 94 F3
Markyate Rd STALW/RED AL3 .... 173 J1
Marlands SBW CM21 .... 183 R5
Marlborough Av EDGW HA8 .... 134 D4
  RSLP HA4 .... 141 G8
Marlborough CI BSF CM23 .... 43 M4
  HTCHE/RSTV SG4 .... 21 M1
  TRDG/WHET N20 .... 137 K6
  WLYN AL6 .... 177 M9
Marlborough Gdns
  TRDG/WHET N20 .... 137 K6
Marlborough Ga STAL AL1 .... 9 G6
Marlborough HI HRW HA1 .... 143 H8
Marlborough Pk HARP AL5 .... 47 G6
Marlborough Ri HHNE HP2 .... 62 C7
Marlborough Rd LTNN/LIM LU3 .... 6 C1
  STAL AL1 .... 34 A4
  STVGE SG2 .... 34 A4
  WATW WD18 .... 12 E5
Marle Gdns WAB EN9 .... 111 G6
Marley Rd WGCE AL7 .... 68 E1
Marlin CI BERK HP4 .... 59 K8
Marlin Copse BERK HP4 .... 79 L2
Marlin Ct LTNW/LEA LU4 .... 26 C5
Marlin HI TRING HP23 .... 57 L4
Marlin Rd LTNW/LEA LU4 .... 26 C5
Marlins CI RKW/CH/CXG WD3 .... 115 J6
Marlins End BERK HP4 .... 79 L2
Marlins Meadow WATW WD18 .... 131 H2
Marlin Sq ABLGY WD5 .... 101 K5
The Marlins NTHWD HA6 .... 141 K1
Marlins Turn HHW HP1 .... 61 M7
Marlow Av LTN LU1 .... 40 F3
Marlowe CI STVGE SG2 .... 34 A1
Marlowes HHNE HP2 .... 4 F3
Marmet Av LWTH SG6 .... 16 E3
Marne Av FBAR/BDGN N11 .... 137 M2
Marnham Ri HHW HP1 .... 61 L8
Marquis CI BSF CM23 .... 43 H3
  HARP AL5 .... 47 H3
Marquis HI HTCH/STOT SG5 .... 146 C8
Marquis La HARP AL5 .... 47 H3
Marrilyne Av PEND EN3 .... 126 C4
  LTNN/LIM LU3 .... 27 M3
Marriott Rd BAR EN5 .... 122 B7
Marriotts Wy HHNE HP2 .... 5 C6
Marriotts Yd BAR EN5 * 122 B7
Marriott Ter
  RKW/CH/CXG WD3 .... 115 K4
Marryat Rd EN EN1 .... 125 M1
Marschefield HTCH/STOT SG5 .... 148 C7
Marsden CI WGCW AL8 .... 67 M1
Marsden Gn WGCW AL8 .... 49 M8
Marsden Rd WGCW AL8 .... 49 M8
Marshall Av STALW/RED AL3 .... 65 J7
Marshall CI FBAR/BDGN N11 .... 137 M7
Marshall Est MLHL NW7 .... 135 L1
Marshall Rd LTNE LU2 .... 29 G7
Marshalls Av HTCH/STOT SG5 .... 146 B8
Marshalls Heath La HARP AL5 .... 175 L12
Marshall's La STDN SG11 .... 180 B7
  WARE SG12 .... 179 Q5
Marshalls Wy STALE/WH AL4 .... 47 L1
Marshal's Dr STAL AL1 .... 65 L7
Marshalswick La STAL AL1 .... 65 L7
Marsham La CFSP/GDCR SL9 .... 138 C8
Marsham Ldg CFSP/GDCR SL9 .... 138 C8
Marsham Wy CFSP/GDCR SL9 .... 138 C7
Marshbarns BSF CM23 .... 43 J1
Marsh CI CHES/WCR EN8 .... 110 D7
  MLHL NW7 .... 135 K6
Marshcroft Dr
  CHES/WCR EN8 .... 110 C4
Marshcroft La TRING HP23 .... 169 P11
Marshe CI POTB/CUF EN6 .... 107 H4
Marshgate STVG SG1 .... 10 D4
Marshgate Dr HERT/BAY SG13 .... 53 J1
Marsh HI WAB EN9 .... 111 J1
Marsh La HLWE CM17 .... 76 Q12
  MLHL NW7 .... 135 J6
  STAN HA7 .... 134 A4
  WARE SG12 .... 73 H2
Marshmoor Crs BRKMPK AL9 .... 88 B4
Marshmoor La BRKMPK AL9 .... 88 A4
Marsh Rd LTNN/LIM LU3 .... 27 J4
  PIN HA5 .... 142 C1
The Marsh ROY SG8 * 152 A4
Marsom Gv LTNN/LIM LU3 .... 27 M1
Marston CI CSHM HP5 .... 96 E1
Marston Ct TRING HP23 .... 168 F3
Marston Gdns LTNE LU2 .... 28 D5
Marston Rd HOD EN11 .... 72 C6
Marsworth Av PIN HA5 .... 142 B3
Marsworth Rd LBUZ LU7 .... 169 P5
Marten Ga STALE/WH AL4 .... 65 L6
Marthorne Crs
  KTN/HRWW/WS HA3 .... 143 H4
Martian Av HHNE HP2 .... 62 D7
Martin CI HAT AL10 .... 87 L2
Martindale Rd HHW HP1 .... 81 K1
The Martindales LTNE LU2 * 7 J3
Martinfield WCCE AL7 .... 50 D6
Martingale Rd ROY SG8 .... 14 F7
Martini Dr PEND EN3 .... 126 E3
Martins CI RAD WD7 .... 119 J2
Martins Dr CHES/WCR EN8 .... 110 C2
  HERT/BAY SG13 .... 53 M7
Martins Mt BAR EN5 .... 122 C4
Martins Wy STVG SG1 .... 33 G1
Martin Wy LWTH SG6 .... 16 B4
Martlesham WGCE AL7 .... 51 J7
Martock CI
  KTN/HRWW/WS HA3 .... 143 L6
Martock Gdns
  FBAR/BDGN N11 .... 137 K8
Martyr CI STAL AL1 .... 85 H6
Marwood CI KGLGY WD4 .... 100 D3
Mary Cross CI TRING HP23 .... 58 B4
Marygold Wk AMS HP6 .... 113 H2
Maryland HAT AL10 .... 67 K8
Mary McArthur PI STSD CM24 .... 166 G5
Marymead Ct STVGE SG2 .... 177 N1
Marymead Dr STVGE SG2 .... 177 N1

Mary Park Gdns BSF CM23 .... 43 M5
Maryport Rd LTNW/LEA LU4 .... 27 L7
Mary Proud CI WLYN AL6 * 177 L10
Maryrose Wy
  TRDG/WHET N20 .... 137 H4
Mary Wy OXHEY WD19 .... 132 A7
Marywells SHFD SG17 .... 146 D5
Masefield CI BORE WD6 .... 134 F1
  STAN HA7 .... 133 K8
Masefield Ct HARP AL5 .... 46 F1
Masefield Rd HARP AL5 .... 46 F2
Masefield Wy ROY SG8 .... 14 E8
Mason CI BORE WD6 .... 121 H6
  WAB EN9 .... 111 K8
Masons Av
  KTN/HRWW/WS HA3 .... 143 J5
Masons Ct BSF CM23 .... 43 L2
Masons Pde CHESW EN7 * 109 G2
Masons Rd EN EN1 .... 125 M2
  HHNE HP2 .... 82 F1
Mason Wy WAB EN9 .... 111 J7
Massey CI FBAR/BDGN N11 .... 137 M8
Masters CI LTN LU1 .... 40 A6
Matching La BSF CM23 .... 43 K1
  GTDUN CM6 .... 185 Q12
Matching Rd HLWE CM17 .... 76 D1
  RBSF CM22 .... 184 C10
Mathams Dr BSF CM23 .... 43 K4
Mathews CI STVG SG1 .... 21 H8
Matlock CI BAR EN5 .... 136 B1
Matlock Crs LTNW/LEA LU4 .... 27 G8
  OXHEY WD19 .... 132 A6
Matthew Ga HTCHE/RSTV SG4 .... 21 L4
Matthew St DUN/WHIP LU6 .... 38 F1
Mattocke Rd HTCH/STOT SG5 .... 117 L4
Maude Crs WATN WD24 .... 117 M3
Maud Jane's CI LBUZ LU7 .... 169 Q4
Maulden Ct LTNE LU2 .... 29 G8
Maundsey CI DUN/WHIP LU6 .... 39 G4
Maunds Hatch HLWS CM18 .... 95 H1
Maurice Browne CI
  NTHWD HA6 .... 141 J8
Maxfield CI TRDG/WHET N20 .... 137 J2
Maxted CI HHNE HP2 .... 63 G8
Maxted Cnr HHNE HP2 * 62 F7
Maxted Rd HHNE HP2 .... 62 F7
Maxwell CI RKW/CH/CXG WD3 .... 129 L5
Maxwell Ri OXHEY WD19 .... 132 C3
Maxwell Rd BORE WD6 .... 120 F7
  NTHWD HA6 .... 141 H2
  STAL AL1 .... 85 M3
  STVG SG1 .... 32 F4
Maxwelton Av MLHL NW7 .... 135 H8
Maxwelton CI MLHL NW7 .... 135 H8
Mayall CI PEND EN3 .... 126 E3
Maybank Gdns PIN HA5 .... 141 L7
Maybury Av CHES/WCR EN8 .... 109 M2
Maybury Ct EN EN1 .... 125 M4
May CI DUN/WHIP LU6 .... 37 K4
  STALW/RED AL3 .... 8 F2
Maycock Gv NTHWD HA6 .... 141 K1
Maycroft SWLT SG6 .... 148 E12
  PIN HA5 .... 141 M4
Maydencroft La
  HTCH/STOT SG5 .... 157 M9
Maydwell Ldg BORE WD6 .... 120 D6
Mayer Wy DUN/HR/TOD LU5 .... 25 L6
Mayes CI BSF CM23 .... 44 D1
Mayfair Ct EDGW HA8 .... 134 D8
Mayfare RKW/CH/CXG WD3 .... 131 H1
Mayfield Av
  KTN/HRWW/WS HA3 .... 143 M7
  NFNCH/WDSPK N12 .... 137 G7
  HLWE CM17 .... 76 D1
Mayfield Crs HNLW SG16 .... 146 C7
Mayfield Dr PIN HA5 .... 142 D6
Mayfield Pk BSF CM23 .... 43 K6
Mayfield Rd DUN/WHIP LU6 .... 39 H3
  LTNE LU2 .... 28 F5
  PEND EN3 .... 126 B6
Mayflower Av HHNE HP2 .... 5 L1
Mayflower CI HERT/WAT SG14 .... 70 C1
  HTCHE/RSTV SG4 .... 176 F1
  RSLP HA4 .... 141 G8
  WAB EN9 .... 93 J5
Mayflower Gdns BSF CM23 .... 43 H3
Mayflower Rd
  LCOL/BKTW AL2 .... 102 F1
May Gdns BORE WD6 .... 134 B2
Mayhall La AMS HP6 .... 112 F1
Mayhill Rd BAR EN5 .... 136 C1
Maylands Av HHNE HP2 .... 62 F8
Maylands Rd OXHEY WD19 .... 132 A7
Mayles CI STVG SG1 .... 32 F2
Maylin CI HTCHE/RSTV SG4 .... 20 A1
Maylins Dr SBW CM21 .... 183 P7
Maynard Dr STAL AL1 .... 85 H5
Maynard PI POTB/CUF EN6 .... 108 C3
Maynard Rd HHNE HP2 .... 4 F4
Mayne Av LTNW/LEA LU4 .... 27 G8
Mayo CI CHES/WCR EN8 .... 110 A2
Mayo Gdns HHW HP1 .... 61 M6
Maypole St HLWE CM17 .... 76 A4
Maypole Yd DUN/WHIP LU6 * 38 F1
Mayshades CI KNEB SG3 .... 177 N7
May's La BAR EN5 .... 135 M3
May St LTN LU1 .... 7 G3
  ROY SG8 .... 153 N1
Maythorne CI WATW WD18 .... 117 J8
Maytree CI EDGW HA8 .... 135 G6
Maytree Crs WATN WD24 .... 117 K2
Maytrees HTCHE/RSTV SG4 .... 143 N1
  RAD WD7 .... 119 J3
May Wk STSD CM24 .... 167 J4
Maze Green Hts BSF CM23 .... 43 J3
Maze Green Rd BSF CM23 .... 43 J4
Mazoe CI BSF CM23 .... 43 M4
Mazoe Rd BSF CM23 .... 43 M4
McAdam CI HOD EN11 .... 72 E5
McAdam Dr ENC/FH EN2 .... 124 C1
McDonald Ct HAT AL10 .... 87 L2
McDougall Rd BERK HP4 .... 80 D1
McEwen Ride
  RAYLNE/WEN HP22 .... 56 B4
McGredy CHESW EN7 .... 109 J4
Mc Kellar CI WGCW AL8 .... 133 C5
Mc Kenzie Rd BROX EN10 .... 92 D7
Mead CI KTN/HRWW/WS HA3 .... 143 H5
  STVG SG1 .... 11 H2
Meades La CSHM HP5 .... 96 H6
Meadfield EDGW HA8 .... 134 D5
Meadgate Rd WAB EN9 .... 93 H2
Meadhook Dr
  AMP/FLIT/BLC MK45 .... 154 H2
Mead La HERT/BAY SG13 .... 53 H4

Meadow Av RAD WD7 .... 104 A5
Meadowbank
  HTCHE/RSTV SG4 .... 157 R4
  KGLGY WD4 .... 100 E4
  OXHEY WD19 .... 132 A3
Meadow Bank CI AMSS HP7 .... 113 J4
Meadowbank CI BORE WD6 .... 135 K1
Meadowbanks BAR EN5 .... 135 K1
Meadowbrook TRING HP23 .... 169 M12
Meadow CI BAR EN5 .... 136 D2
  BRKMPK AL9 .... 88 B6
  CSHM HP5 .... 96 E1
  HERT/BAY SG13 .... 53 K6
  KNEB SG3 .... 177 R7
  LCOL/BKTW AL2 .... 102 E3
  PEND EN3 .... 126 C5
  RAD WD7 .... 104 A4
  RSLP HA4 .... 141 G8
  STALE/WH AL4 .... 66 A4
  TRING HP23 .... 57 L1
Meadow Cft HAT AL10 .... 67 K8
Meadowcroft BERK HP4 .... 59 H6
  BUSH WD23 * 132 F2
  CFSP/GDCR SL9 .... 138 B4
  STAL AL1 .... 85 L5
  STSD CM24 .... 166 G5
Meadowcross WAB EN9 .... 111 H6
Meadow Dell HAT AL10 .... 67 K8
Meadow Gn WGCW AL8 .... 50 A7
Meadowlands BAR EN5 .... 135 K1
  BSF CM23 .... 166 C12
Meadow La DUN/HR/TOD LU5 .... 25 M4
  LBUZ LU7 .... 169 Q6
Meadow Rd BERK HP4 .... 59 H4
  BORE WD6 .... 120 F6
  BUSH WD23 .... 132 F2
  GSTN WD25 .... 101 L8
  HHS/BOV HP3 .... 82 E7
  LTNN/LIM LU3 .... 27 M5
  PIN HA5 .... 142 B6
Meadow Road CI BERK HP4 .... 59 L7
Meadowside GSTN WD25 .... 101 M5
The Meadows AMSS HP7 .... 113 J4
  BSF CM23 .... 43 L4
  HHW HP1 .... 81 J1
  HTCHE/RSTV SG4 .... 30 C8
  SBW CM21 .... 184 A1
Meadowsweet HNLW SG16 .... 146 H1
Meadowsweet CI BSF CM23 .... 43 L5
The Meadow HERT/BAY SG13 .... 72 C3
  STALW/RED AL3 .... 173 R3
  STALW/RED AL3 .... 173 Q9
  WGCE AL7 .... 51 G7
Meadow Vw BUNT SG9 .... 158 H11
  HTCHE/RSTV SG4 .... 157 R4
  STALW/RED AL3 .... 173 Q9
Meadow Wk HARP AL5 .... 47 G5
  STSD CM24 .... 163 Q11
Meadow Wy AMS HP6 .... 112 A1
  HHS/BOV HP3 .... 81 K5
  HTCH/STOT SG5 .... 148 C7
  HTCHE/RSTV SG4 .... 156 E10
  LTN LU1 .... 40 C5
  LWTH SG6 .... 16 D4
  POTB/CUF EN6 .... 106 C8
  RKW/CH/CXG WD3 .... 130 A3
  ROY SG8 .... 151 N7
  RSLP HA4 .... 141 G8
  SBW CM21 .... 184 A8
  STVG SG1 .... 11 H4
The Meadow Wy
  KTN/HRWW/WS HA3 .... 143 J3
Mead PI RKW/CH/CXG WD3 .... 129 M4
Meads CI DUN/HR/TOD LU5 .... 25 M4
Meads Ctyd STVGE SG2 * 34 A2
Meads La WARE SG12 .... 48 B4
Meads Rd PEND EN3 .... 126 C5
The Meads BERK HP4 .... 59 K7
  DUN/WHIP LU6 .... 37 H3
  LCOL/BKTW AL2 .... 102 D3
  LTNN/LIM LU3 .... 27 L6
  LWTH SG6 .... 16 C3
The Mead BROX EN10 * 92 F3
Meadvale Rd WARE SG12 .... 54 A5
Mead Vw BUSH WD23 .... 13 L2
  RSLP HA4 .... 141 G8
Meadway BAR EN5 .... 122 E8
  BERK HP4 .... 60 A4
  DUN/WHIP LU6 .... 38 E2
  HARP AL5 .... 47 G5
  HOD EN11 .... 92 E1
  KNEB SG3 .... 177 M5
  PEND EN3 .... 126 B2
  STALE/WH AL4 .... 87 H5
  STVG SG1 .... 32 E8
  WGCE AL7 .... 68 D1
Meadway CI BAR EN5 .... 122 E7
  PIN HA5 .... 142 F1
Meadway Gdns RSLP HA4 .... 141 G8
The Meadway POTB/CUF EN6 .... 108 D2
Meautys STALW/RED AL3 .... 84 D4
Medalls Link STVGE SG2 .... 11 K8
Medalls Pth STVGE SG2 .... 11 K8
Medcalf Rd PEND EN3 .... 126 D3
Medina Rd LTNW/LEA LU4 .... 27 L4
Medlars Md RBSF CM22 .... 184 C8
Medley CI DUN/WHIP LU6 .... 37 K4
Medlows HARP AL5 .... 46 C3
Medow Md RAD WD7 .... 103 J4
Medway CI GSTN WD25 .... 102 A8
Medway Rd HHNE HP2 .... 62 D5
Medwick Ms HHNE HP2 .... 62 D5
Mees CI LTNN/LIM LU3 .... 154 F12
Meeting Aly WAT WD17 * 13 G4
Meeting House La BLDK SG7 * 149 J12
  BUNT SG9 .... 159 J10
Megg La KGLGY WD4 .... 99 M3
Melbourne Av PIN HA5 .... 142 F5
Melbourne CI BUSH WD23 .... 132 F1
  STALW/RED AL3 .... 65 K1
Melbourne Ct WGCW AL8 .... 49 M8
Melbourne Rd BUSH WD23 .... 132 F1
Melbourn Rd ROY SG8 .... 14 C1
Melbourn St ROY SG8 .... 14 E7
Melford CI LTNE LU2 .... 29 H7
Melia CI GSTN WD25 .... 118 A1
The Melings HHNE HP2 .... 62 E6
Melling Dr EN EN1 .... 125 L5
Melne Rd STVGE SG2 .... 36 E5
Melrose Av BORE WD6 .... 134 F1
  POTB/CUF EN6 .... 106 F7
Melrose PI WAT WD17 .... 117 K4
Melson St LTN LU1 .... 7 G3
Melsted Rd HHW HP1 .... 62 A2
Melton Wk DUN/WHIP LU6 .... 26 C3
Melvern CI STVGE SG2 .... 177 P2

Melvyn CI CHESW EN7 .... 108 F2
Memorial Rd LTNN/LIM LU3 .... 27 K5
Mendip CI STALE/WH AL4 .... 66 A1
Mendip Rd BUSH WD23 .... 133 G2
Mendip Wy HHNE HP2 .... 62 A4
Mentley La STVG SG1 .... 21 L6
Mentley La East STDN SG11 .... 163 P9
Mentley La West STDN SG11 .... 163 P9
Mentmore Crs DUN/WHIP LU6 .... 39 G4
Mentmore Rd LBUZ LU7 .... 169 K1
  STAL AL1 .... 85 H4
Mentmore Vw TRING HP23 .... 169 K12
Mepham Crs
  KTN/HRWW/WS HA3 .... 143 G2
Mepham Gdns
  KTN/HRWW/WS HA3 .... 143 G2
Meppershall Rd
  HTCH/STOT SG5 .... 146 C6
Mercer PI PIN HA5 .... 142 A4
Mercers HHNE HP2 .... 62 C8
  HLWW/ROY CM19 .... 74 E8
Mercers Av BSF CM23 .... 43 H5
Mercers Rw STAL AL1 .... 85 G4
Merchant Dr HERT/BAY SG13 .... 53 K6
Merchants Wk BLDK SG7 .... 149 M12
Mercia Rd BLDK SG7 .... 17 L1
Mercury Wk HHNE HP2 .... 62 D7
Meredith Rd STVG SG1 .... 33 L2
Merefield SBW CM21 .... 183 Q8
Meriden Wy GSTN WD25 .... 118 C3
Meridian CI MLHL NW7 .... 135 H7
Meridian Wy WAB EN9 .... 110 E8
  WARE SG12 .... 54 F8
Merle Av DEN/HRF UB9 .... 140 A4
Merlewood DEN/HRF UB9 .... 111 L8
Merling Cft BERK HP4 .... 59 J7
Merlin CI GSTN WD25 .... 101 L8
  HTCHE/RSTV SG4 .... 157 R6
  LTNN/LIM LU3 .... 27 M5
  STDN SG11 .... 42 D7
Merrick PI STVG SG1 .... 21 M5
Merrifield CI WGCE AL7 .... 68 D2
Merring Wy WAB EN9 .... 94 D3
Merrion Av STAN HA7 .... 134 B8
Merritt Wk BRKMPK AL9 .... 87 M5
Merrow Dr HHW HP1 .... 81 J1
Merrows CI NTHWD HA6 .... 141 G1
Merryfield Gdns STAN HA7 .... 134 A4
Merryfields STALE/WH AL4 .... 86 C2
Merry Hill Mt BUSH WD23 .... 132 F4
Merry Hill Rd BUSH WD23 .... 132 E4
Merryhills Dr ENC/FH EN2 .... 124 C4
Mersey PI HHNE HP2 .... 62 D5
Merton Rd ENC/FH EN2 .... 125 H4
  WATW WD18 .... 12 A4
Metford Crs PEND EN3 .... 126 E4
Metropolitan Ms WATW WD18 .... 117 J8
Metropolitan Station Ap
  WATW WD18 .... 12 A5
Meux CI CHES/WCR EN8 .... 109 L7
The Mews Norton Hall Farm
  LWTH SG6 * 148 G12
The Mews HARP AL5 .... 46 F1
  NFNCH/WDSPK N12 * 136 F8
  RBSF CM22 .... 44 A8
  SBW CM21 .... 183 Q6
  WATW WD18 * 13 G4
Meyer Gn EN EN1 .... 125 L4
Meyrick Av LTN LU1 .... 6 B7
Mezen CI NTHWD HA6 .... 131 H8
Michaels Rd BSF CM23 .... 166 C11
Michigan CI BROX EN10 .... 92 C3
Michleham Down
  NFNCH/WDSPK N12 .... 136 D7
Micholls Av CFSP/GDCR SL9 .... 128 C3
Mickelfield Rd HHNE HP2 .... 83 G2
Mickelfield Wy BORE WD6 .... 120 C3
Micklem Dr HHW HP1 .... 81 K1
Midcot Wy BERK HP4 .... 59 K7
Mid Cross La CFSP/GDCR SL9 .... 128 D8
Middle Dene MLHL NW7 .... 135 H6
Middle Down GSTN WD25 .... 118 C2
Middle Drift ROY SG8 .... 152 A8
Middlefield HAT AL10 .... 67 L7
Middlefield Av HOD EN11 .... 72 E5
  STALE/WH AL4 .... 66 A4
Middlefield Rd HOD EN11 .... 72 E5
Middlefields Ct LWTH SG6 * 148 D12
Middle Furlong BUSH WD23 .... 118 F8
Middlehill HHW HP1 .... 81 J2
Middleknights HI HHW HP1 .... 61 L8
Middle La HHS/BOV HP3 .... 98 C8
Middle Ope WATN WD24 .... 117 M3
Middle Rd BERK HP4 .... 79 M1
  EBAR EN4 .... 137 J2
  WAB EN9 .... 110 F6
Middle Rw BSF CM23 .... 43 M5
  STVG SG1 .... 10 B1
Middlesborough CI STVG SG1 .... 21 K7
Middle St SAFWS CB11 .... 161 Q5
  WAB EN9 .... 93 J4
Middleton Dr PIN HA5 .... 141 L5
Middleton Rd LTNE LU2 .... 29 H7
  RKW/CH/CXG WD3 .... 129 L4
Middle Wy WATN WD24 .... 117 M3
The Middle Wy
  KTN/HRWW/WS HA3 .... 143 K4
Midhurst WGCE AL7 .... 16 C1
Midhurst Gdns LTNN/LIM LU3 .... 28 A1
Midland Rd HHNE HP2 .... 4 F2
  LTNE LU2 .... 6 E1
Midland Wy HNLW SG16 .... 147 K6
Midway STALW/RED AL3 .... 84 C7
Milburn CI LTNN/LIM LU3 .... 154 F12
Mildmay Rd STVG SG1 .... 33 M1
Mildred Av BORE WD6 .... 134 B3
  WATW WD18 .... 12 B6
Mile CI WAB EN9 .... 111 G4
Mile House CI STAL AL1 .... 85 L5
Mile House La STAL AL1 .... 85 L5
Miles CI HLWW/ROY CM19 .... 2 B7
Milespit HI MLHL NW7 .... 135 M8
Milestone CI STVGE SG2 .... 34 B5
Milestone Rd HLWE CM17 .... 76 A1
Miles Wy TRDG/WHET N20 .... 137 L5
Miletree Crs DUN/WHIP LU6 .... 39 H3
Milford CI STALE/WH AL4 .... 66 B6
Milford HI HARP AL5 .... 47 H1
Milksey La HTCHE/RSTV SG4 .... 20 C4
Millacres WARE SG12 * 54 C1
Milland Ct STVG SG1 .... 21 M5
Millard Ct BORE WD6 .... 121 H5
Millard Wy HTCHE/RSTV SG4 .... 16 A1
Millbank HHS/BOV HP3 .... 82 B6

Mill Br BAR EN5 * 136 D1
  HERT/WAT SG14 .... 53 D1
Millbrook Rd BUSH WD23 .... 118 D5
Mill CI BUNT SG9 .... 159 J10
  CSHM HP5 .... 97 J8
  HHS/BOV HP3 .... 82 E7
  HHW HP1 .... 61 M6
  HTCH/STOT SG5 .... 148 E7
  HTCHE/RSTV SG4 .... 20 B1
  RBSF CM22 .... 167 L4
  WARE SG12 .... 54 A4
  WGCW AL8 .... 49 G8
Mill Cnr BAR EN5 .... 122 D5
  HLWW/ROY CM19 .... 73 D4
  ROY SG8 * 152 A8
Millcrest Rd CHESW EN7 .... 108 D3
Millcroft BSF CM23 .... 166 C12
Mill End AMP/FLIT/BLC MK45 * 154 C2
  STDN SG11 .... 163 R11
Mill End CI DUN/WHIP LU6 .... 37 K5
Millennium Whf
  RKW/CH/CXG WD3 * 130 C4
Miller Av PEND EN3 .... 126 C4
Miller CI STALW/RED AL3 .... 173 R12
Miller PI CFSP/GDCR SL9 .... 138 C4
Millers CI BSF CM23 .... 43 J4
  MLHL NW7 .... 135 J4
Millersdale HLWW/ROY CM19 .... 94 F1
Millers Green CI ENC/FH EN2 .... 124 F7
Millers La WARE SG12 .... 73 J4
Millers Lay DUN/HR/TOD LU5 .... 26 D7
Millers Ri STAL AL1 .... 9 G8
Millers Vw MHAD AL5 .... 181 Q8
Millers Wy DUN/HR/TOD LU5 .... 26 C7
Millers Yd HERT/WAT SG14 .... 53 H7
Mill Farm CI PIN HA5 .... 142 A4
Mill Fld HLWE CM17 .... 76 A1
Millfield BERK HP4 .... 60 B8
  WARE SG12 .... 54 C9
  WGCE AL7 .... 51 G6
Millfield La HTCHE/RSTV SG4 .... 157 P9
  LTN LU1 .... 40 A4
  STDN SG11 .... 42 D7
Millfield Ms LTN LU1 * 40 B7
Millfield Rd LTNN/LIM LU3 .... 27 M6
Millfields CSHM HP5 .... 97 J8
  SBW CM21 .... 183 R6
  STSD CM24 .... 166 G2
Millfield Wk HHS/BOV HP3 .... 82 E5
Millfield Wy LTN LU1 .... 40 A4
Mill Gdns TRING HP23 .... 57 M1
Mill Green La BRKMPK AL9 .... 68 C8
Mill Green Rd WGCE AL7 .... 50 C8
Mill HI BSF CM23 .... 166 A4
  ROY SG8 .... 152 A1
  STSD CM24 .... 166 F7
Millhouse La ABLGY WD5 .... 101 L1
Millhurst Ms HLWE CM17 .... 76 C1
Milligan CI LTNW/LEA LU4 .... 27 H5
Milliners Ct STAL AL1 * 9 G5
Milliners Wy BSF CM23 .... 43 J5
  LTNN/LIM LU3 .... 27 J4
Mill La AMP/FLIT/BLC MK45 .... 154 H2
  AMSS HP7 .... 112 G5
  ARL/CHE SG15 .... 147 P5
  BROX EN10 .... 92 D3
  BUNT SG9 .... 160 G4
  CFSP/GDCR SL9 .... 138 D8
  CHES/WCR EN8 .... 110 C2
  CHING E4 .... 126 F7
  HERT/WAT SG14 .... 52 F1
  HLWE CM17 .... 76 C1
  HTCH/STOT SG5 .... 155 P2
  HTCHE/RSTV SG4 .... 18 A8
  KGLGY WD4 .... 100 E3
  RBSF CM22 .... 184 F5
  ROY SG8 .... 151 M5
  SBW CM21 .... 183 R6
  SHFD SG17 .... 146 C1
  STALW/RED AL3 .... 173 J8
  STDN SG11 .... 179 J2
  WARE SG12 .... 55 J7
  WLYN AL6 .... 177 H12
Mill Lane CI BROX EN10 .... 92 D3
Millmarsh La PEND EN3 .... 126 C6
Mill Race WARE SG12 .... 73 H1
Mill Rdg EDGW HA8 .... 134 D8
Mill Rd DUN/HR/TOD LU5 .... 25 L5
  HERT/WAT SG14 .... 53 H7
  HTCHE/RSTV SG4 .... 157 P10
  LBUZ LU7 .... 169 K1
  RBSF CM22 .... 167 N1
  ROY SG8 .... 14 E6
Mill Side STSD CM24 .... 166 F4
Millson CI TRDG/WHET N20 .... 137 H5
Millstream CI HERT/WAT SG14 .... 53 H5
  HTCHE/RSTV SG4 .... 157 Q3
Mill St BERK HP4 .... 80 C4
  BLDK SG7 .... 149 P11
  HHS/BOV HP3 .... 82 B6
  HLWE CM17 .... 76 C1
  LTN LU1 .... 6 E4
The Mill TRING HP23 .... 168 G8
Millthorne CI
  RKW/CH/CXG WD3 .... 130 D1
Mill View Rd TRING HP23 .... 57 K1
Millwards HAT AL10 .... 87 M3
Mill Wy MLHL NW7 .... 135 J8
  RKW/CH/CXG WD3 .... 129 K4
  BUSH WD23 .... 13 L1
Millway CI HTCHE/RSTV SG4 .... 30 B7
Milman CI PIN HA5 .... 142 B5
Milne Fld PIN HA5 .... 142 E2
Milner CI GSTN WD25 .... 101 M8
Milner Ct BUSH WD23 .... 132 F2
Milneway DEN/HRF UB9 .... 139 M3
Milton Av BAR EN5 .... 136 D1
  CFSP/GDCR SL9 .... 138 B6
Milton CI ROY SG8 .... 14 D8
Milton Ct WAB EN9 .... 111 G8
Milton Dene HHNE HP2 .... 62 D5
Milton Dr BORE WD6 .... 120 F8
Milton Lawns AMS HP6 .... 113 H2
Milton Rd
  HARP AL5 .... 46 F4
  HRW HA1 .... 143 J7
  LTN LU1 .... 6 B7
  MLHL NW7 .... 135 J8
  RAYLNE/WEN HP22 .... 168 D12
  STVG SG1 .... 2 A8
  WARE SG12 .... 54 B3
Milton St WATN WD24 .... 117 M5
Milton Vw HTCHE/RSTV SG4 .... 21 L4
Milton Wy DUN/HR/TOD LU5 .... 26 B5
Milverton Gn LTNN/LIM LU3 .... 27 L2
Milwards HLWW/ROY CM19 .... 94 D3
Mimas Rd HHNE HP2 .... 62 D7

Mimms Hall Rd
POTB/CUF EN6 106 B5
Mimms La RAD WD7 104 E7
Mimram Cl HTCHE/RSTV SG4 175 Q2
Mimram Pl WLYN AL6 177 J12
Mimram Rd HERT/WAT SG14 52 F8
WLYN AL6 177 J12
Minall Cl TRING HP23 57 K1
Minchen Rd HLW CM20 3 K3
Minehead Wy STVG SG1 32 E2
Mineral Cl BAR EN5 136 A2
Mineral La CSHM HP5 97 G6
Minerva Cl STVGE SG2 22 A8
Minerva Dr WAT WD17 117 J2
The Minims HAT AL10 67 L6
Minister Ct LCOL/BKTW AL2 103 J2
Minoan Dr HHS/BOV HP3 82 C6
Minorca Wy LTNW/LEA LU4 26 E6
Minsden Rd STVGE SG2 34 B6
Minster Cl HAT AL10 87 L2
Minster Rd ROY SG8 14 D5
Minton La HLWE CM17 76 A5
Mirrie La DEN/HRF UB9 139 G7
Misbourne Av CFSP/GDCR SL9 128 C8
Misbourne Cl CFSP/GDCR SL9 128 C8
Misbourne Ct AMSS HP7 * 112 F6
Missden Dr HHS/BOV HP3 83 G4
Missenden Rd CSHM HP5 96 D6
Miss Joans Ride BERK HP4 171 L2
Mistletoe Hl LTNE LU2 174 A1
Mistley Rd HLW CM20 3 L2
Miswell La TRING HP23 57 K2
Mitchell Cl ABLGY WD5 101 L6
HHS/BOV HP3 98 D1
STAL AL1 85 H6
WGCE AL7 51 G7
Mitchell Wk AMS HP6 113 J4
Mitre Ct HERT/WAT SG14 * 53 H7
Mitre Gdns BSF CM23 44 A5
Mixes Hill Rd LTNE LU2 28 D5
The Mixies HTCH/STOT SG5 148 C7
The Moakes LTNN/LIM LU3 27 J2
Moat Cl BUSH WD23 132 F1
Moat Dr HRW HA1 143 G6
Moatfield Rd BUSH WD23 132 F1
Moat La LTNN/LIM LU3 27 M5
Moatside BUNT SG9 160 A2
Moat Side PEND EN3 126 A8
The Moat STDN SG11 163 P10
Moatwood Gn WGCE AL7 50 C8
Mobbsbury Wy STVGE SG2 11 M1
Mobley Gn LTNE LU2 28 F6
Moelyn Ms HRW HA1 143 L7
Moffats Cl BRKMPK AL9 88 E8
Moffats La BRKMPK AL9 106 C1
Moira Cl LTNN/LIM LU3 27 G3
Molescroft HARP AL5 46 B1
Moles La BUNT SG9 159 L6
Molesworth HOD EN11 72 E3
Molewood Rd HERT/WAT SG14 52 F6
Mollison Av PEND EN3 126 C6
Molteno Rd WAT WD17 117 L5
Molyneaux Av HHS/BOV HP3 98 D1
Mompies Rd HLW CM20 3 M5
Monarch's Wy
CHES/WCR EN8 110 C7
Monarch Wk RAD WD7 * 104 D7
Monastery Cl STALW/RED AL3 8 D6
Monastery Gdns ENC/FH EN2 125 H6
Moneyhill Ct
RKW/CH/CXG WD3 * 129 M4
Money Hill Rd
RKW/CH/CXG WD3 130 A4
Money Hole La WLYN AL6 51 J6
Monica Cl WATN WD24 13 J2
Monkfrith Av STHGT/OAK N14 137 M2
Monkfrith Wy
STHGT/OAK N14 137 M3
Monklands LWTH SG6 16 B3
Monks Av BAR EN5 137 G2
Monksbury HLWS CM18 75 L8
Monks Cl BROX EN10 92 E2
DUN/HR/TOD LU5 26 C8
ENC/FH EN2 125 G6
LWTH SG6 16 A3
STAL AL1 85 J4
STALW/RED AL3 173 R12
Monks Horton Wy STAL AL1 9 M2
Monksmead BORE WD6 121 G8
Monks Ri WGCW AL8 50 B3
Monks Rd ENC/FH EN2 124 F6
Monks Rw WARE SG12 54 B3
Monks Vw STVGE SG2 33 K7
Monks Wk BUNT SG9 158 H10
Monkswick Rd HLW CM20 3 H3
Monkswood WGCW AL8 50 A3
Monkswood Av WAB EN9 111 H7
Monkswood Dr BSF CM23 43 K3
Monkswood Gdns BORE WD6 135 H1
Monkswood Wy STVG SG1 10 E7
Monmouth Rd WAT WD17 12 F3
Monroe Crs EN EN1 125 M5
Monro Gdns
KTN/HRWW/WS HA3 143 J2
Mons Av BLDK SG7 17 K3
Mons Cl HARP AL5 47 H7
Monson Rd BROX EN10 92 D2
Montacute Rd BUSH WD23 133 J3
Montague Av LTNW/LEA LU4 27 G3
Montague Cl BAR EN5 122 D8
Montague Hall Pl BUSH WD23 132 E2
Montague Rd BERK HP4 79 M1
Montayne Rd CHES/WCR EN8 110 B6
Montesole Ct PIN HA5 142 A4
Montfitchet Wk STVGE SG2 34 B2
Montgomerie Cl BERK HP4 59 L7
Montgomery Av HHNE HP2 5 M1
Montgomery Dr
CHES/WCR EN8 110 C2
Monton Cl LTNN/LIM LU3 27 K3
Montrose Av LTNN/LIM LU3 27 M6
Montrose Rd
KTN/HRWW/WS HA3 143 J4
Monument La CFSP/GDCR SL9 138 C1
Moolintock Pl PEND EN3 126 F3
Moon La BAR EN5 122 D7
Moorcroft Wy PIN HA5 142 C7
Moore Crs DUN/HR/TOD LU5 26 A5
Moor End DUN/WHIP LU6 37 K4
Moorend WGCE AL7 68 E2
Moor End Cl DUN/WHIP LU6 37 K5
Moor End La DUN/WHIP LU6 37 K4
Moor End Rd HHNE HP2 4 E5
Moore Rd BERK HP4 59 K7
Moorfield Rd DEN/HRF UB9 139 L8
PEND EN3 126 A5
Moorfields HLWS CM18 95 G2
Moor Hall La BSF CM23 43 H6
Moorhall Rd DEN/HRF UB9 139 M7
Moor Hall Rd HLWE CM17 76 D1
Moorhen Wy HLWW/ROY CM19 73 L4
Moorhurst Av CHESW EN7 108 F3
The Moorings BSF CM23 44 A3
Moorland Gdns LTNE LU2 6 E3
Moorland Rd HARP AL5 46 F1
HHW HP1 81 K4
Moorlands LCOL/BKTW AL2 * 103 J2
WGCE AL7 68 E2
Moorlands Reach SBW CM21 183 R8
Moor La RKW/CH/CXG WD3 115 J2
Moor Lane Crossing
WATW WD18 131 G3
Moormead Cl HTCH/STOT SG5 157 M7
Moormead Hl HTCH/STOT SG5 157 L7
Moor Mill La LCOL/BKTW AL2 103 J3
Moor Park Gdns
NTHWD HA6 * 131 G5
Moor Park Rd NTHWD HA6 141 H1
Moor Rd CSHM HP5 97 G7
Moorside WGCE AL7 68 E2
Moors Ley STVGE SG2 22 E8
The Moors WGCE AL7 50 E6
Moor St LTN LU1 6 C4
Moors Wk WGCE AL7 50 F6
Moortown Rd OXHEY WD19 132 A7
Moor Vw WATW WD18 131 L3
Moorymead Cl
HERT/WAT SG14 178 F6
Moran Cl LCOL/BKTW AL2 102 D5
Moray Cl EDGW HA8 * 134 F5
Morcambe Cl LTNW/LEA LU4 26 F6
Morcom Rd DUN/HR/TOD LU5 39 J3
Morecambe Cl STVG SG1 32 F2
Morecambe Gdns STAN HA7 134 B7
Morefields TRING HP23 169 L11
Moreland Dr CFSP/GDCR SL9 138 D8
Moremead WAB EN9 111 H7
Moreton Av HARP AL5 46 D3
Moreton Cl CHESW EN7 109 M1
Moreton End Cl HARP AL5 46 D3
Moreton End La HARP AL5 46 D3
Moreton Pl HARP AL5 46 D2
Moreton Rd North LTNE LU2 28 E7
Moreton Rd South LTNE LU2 28 E7
Morgan Cl LTNW/LEA LU4 27 J6
NTHWD HA6 131 K8
STVG SG1 21 H8
Morgan Gdns GSTN WD25 118 F4
Morgans Cl HERT/BAY SG13 71 H1
Morgan's Rd HERT/BAY SG13 71 H1
Morgan's Wk HERT/BAY SG13 71 H2
Morice Rd HOD EN11 72 D5
Morland Cl DUN/WHIP LU6 38 E3
Morland Wy CHES/WCR EN8 110 C2
Morley Crs EDGW HA8 135 G5
Morley Gv HLW CM20 2 C3
Morley Hl ENC/FH EN2 125 H4
Mornington WLYN AL6 50 E1
Mornington Rd RAD WD7 103 L8
Morningtons HLWW/ROY CM19 95 G1
Morpeth Av BORE WD6 120 D4
Morpeth Cl HHNE HP2 5 J5
Morrel Cl BAR EN5 123 G7
Morrell Cl LTNN/LIM LU3 27 L2
Morrell Ct WGCE AL7 * 50 D6
Morrello Gdns
HTCHE/RSTV SG4 157 Q8
Morris Cl CFSP/GDCR SL9 138 D3
HNLW SG16 147 L4
LTNN/LIM LU3 27 J1
Morris Ct WAB EN9 111 K8
Morriston Cl OXHEY WD19 132 A8
Morris Wy LCOL/BKTW AL2 86 B8
Morse Cl DEN/HRF UB9 140 A4
Mortain Dr BERK HP4 59 K7
Mortens Wd AMSS HP7 113 H6
Mortimer Cl BUSH WD23 132 F2
LTN LU1 40 D3
Mortimer Ga CHES/WCR EN8 110 D1
Mortimer Hl TRING HP23 57 M1
Mortimer Ri TRING HP23 57 M1
Mortimer Rd ROY SG8 14 F7
Morton Cl LBUZ LU7 169 N5
Morton St ROY SG8 14 E5
Morven Cl POTB/CUF EN6 107 G5
Mosquito Wy HAT AL10 67 J7
Mossbank Av LTNE LU2 174 A1
Moss Cl PIN HA5 142 D4
RKW/CH/CXG WD3 130 B5
Mossdale Ct LTNW/LEA LU4 * 27 G4
Mossendew Cl DEN/HRF UB9 140 B3
Moss Gn WGCE AL7 68 C1
Moss La PIN HA5 142 C4
Mossman Dr LTN LU1 40 C5
Moss Rd GSTN WD25 101 M8
Moss Side LCOL/BKTW AL2 102 D4
Moss Wy HTCH/STOT SG5 157 L4
Mostyn Rd BUSH WD23 133 G1
LTNN/LIM LU3 27 J5
Motts Cl HERT/WAT SG14 178 E5
Mott St CHING E4 127 J5
Moules Yd BLDK SG7 149 P1
Moulton Ri LTNE LU2 7 H4
Mountbatten Cl STAL AL1 85 M5
Mountbel Rd STAN HA7 * 143 L4
Mount Cl EBAR EN4 123 L8
HHW HP1 81 K2
RAYLNE/WEN HP22 56 D1
Mount Dr LCOL/BKTW AL2 85 H7
RYLN/HDSTN HA2 142 D7
STSD CM24 166 G8
Mounteagle ROY SG8 14 E8
Mountfield Rd HHNE HP2 5 H2
LTNE LU2 28 C7
Mountfitchet Rd STSD CM24 166 G8
Mount Garrison
HTCHE/RSTV SG4 157 P6
Mount Grace Rd LTNE LU2 29 G3
POTB/CUF EN6 106 E5
Mount Gv EDGW HA8 135 G6
Mountjoy HTCHE/RSTV SG4 16 A8
Mount Nugent CSHM HP5 96 E1
Mount Pde EBAR EN4 * 123 J8
Mount Park Rd PIN HA5 141 L7
Mount Pleasant
DEN/HRF UB9 139 L3
EBAR EN4 123 K8
HERT/BAY SG13 72 A1
HTCH/STOT SG5 157 M7
STALW/RED AL3 8 C5
Mount Pleasant Cl
BRKMPK AL9 68 A5
Mount Pleasant La
BRKMPK AL9 68 A5
LCOL/BKTW AL2 102 C4
Mount Pleasant Rd
LTNN/LIM LU3 27 J4
Mount Rd EBAR EN4 137 J1
HERT/WAT SG14 52 E8
STALE/WH AL4 48 B4
Mountside
KTN/HRWW/WS HA3 143 K3
Mountsorrel HERT/BAY SG13 53 K7
The Mount CHESW EN7 91 H8
LTNN/LIM LU3 6 E3
POTB/CUF EN6 106 F4
RKW/CH/CXG WD3 130 A2
ROY SG8 152 G4
TRDG/WHET N20 137 G5
Mount Vw ENC/FH EN2 124 D4
LCOL/BKTW AL2 104 C1
Mountview MLHL NW7 135 H6
NTHWD HA6 141 L1
Mount Vw RKW/CH/CXG WD3 129 M4
Mountview Av
DUN/HR/TOD LU5 39 J3
Mountview Rd CHESW EN7 91 J8
Mountway POTB/CUF EN6 106 E4
Mount Wy WGCE AL7 68 D2
Mountway Cl WGCE AL7 68 D2
Mowbray Crs HTCH/STOT SG5 148 D7
Mowbray Gdns
HTCHE/RSTV SG4 157 Q8
Mowbray Rd BAR EN5 123 G8
EDGW HA8 134 E7
HLW CM20 3 K2
Moxes Wd LTNN/LIM LU3 27 J2
Moxom Av CHES/WCR EN8 110 C4
Moxon St BAR EN5 122 D7
Mozart Ct STVG SG1 10 A4
Muddy La LWTH SG6 16 D6
Mud La HARP AL5 47 H8
Muirfield LTNE LU2 28 C3
Muirfield Cl OXHEY WD19 * 132 A8
Muirfield Gn OXHEY WD19 132 A7
Muirfield Rd OXHEY WD19 131 M7
Muirhead Wy KNEB SG3 177 M4
Mulberry Cl BROX EN10 92 D6
EBAR EN4 123 H8
LCOL/BKTW AL2 102 F2
LTN LU1 6 A5
TRING HP23 169 L12
WAT WD17 117 J2
Mulberry Ct BSF CM23 44 A4
Mulberry Gdns RAD WD7 104 C7
Mulberry Gn HLWE CM17 76 B1
Mulberry Md HAT AL10 67 J4
Mulberry Pl STALW/RED AL3 * 63 M1
Mulberry Wy HTCH/STOT SG5 157 M3
Mullion Cl
KTN/HRWW/WS HA3 142 F3
LTNE LU2 28 F5
Mullion Wk OXHEY WD19 132 B7
Mulready Wk HHS/BOV HP3 82 C6
Mundells CHESW EN7 109 L1
WGCE AL7 50 D6
Munden Gv WATN WD24 118 D8
Munden Rd WARE SG12 179 N2
Mundesley Cl STVG SG1 20 F8
Mundesly Cl OXHEY WD19 132 A8
Mungo-Park Cl BUSH WD23 * 133 G5
Munro Rd BUSH WD23 132 F1
The Muntings STVGE SG2 11 J8
Munts Meadow
HTCHE/RSTV SG4 18 A8
Murchison Rd HOD EN11 72 F5
Muriel Av WATW WD18 13 H8
Murray Crs PIN HA5 142 B3
Murray Rd BERK HP4 60 A8
NTHWD HA6 141 J3
Murrell La HTCH/STOT SG5 148 E8
Murton Ct STAL AL1 9 H4
Musca Cl LTNW/LEA LU4 * 27 K8
Musgrave Cl EBAR EN4 123 G5
Muskalls Cl CHESW EN7 109 L1
Muskham Rd HLW CM20 3 M1
Musk Hl HHW HP1 81 J3
Musleigh Mnr WARE SG12 54 D4
Musley Hl WARE SG12 54 C3
Musley La WARE SG12 54 C3
Mussenden Ct WATN WD24 * 117 M5
Mussons Pth LTNE LU2 6 F3
Muswell Cl LTNN/LIM LU3 27 M3
Mutchetts Cl GSTN WD25 102 C7
Mutford Cft LTNE LU2 29 H8
Mutton La POTB/CUF EN6 106 B5
Myddelton Av EN EN1 125 J4
Myddelton Pk
TRDG/WHET N20 137 H6
Myddleton Cl STAN HA7 133 L5
Myddleton Rd WARE SG12 54 B5
Myers Cl RAD WD7 104 C6
Myles Ct CHESW EN7 109 G3
Mylne Cl CHES/WCR EN8 110 A1
Mymms Dr BRKMPK AL9 106 E1
Myrtle Cl EBAR EN4 137 K4
Myrtle Gdns HNLW SG16 147 J6
Myrtle Gv ENC/FH EN2 125 H4
Myrtleside Cl NTHWD HA6 141 H2
Myson Wy BSF CM23 44 B2

N

Nags Head Rd PEND EN3 126 A8
Nails La BSF CM23 43 M2
Nairn Cl HARP AL5 47 H7
Nairn Gn OXHEY WD19 131 L6
Nalders Rd CSHM HP5 97 H3
Nan Clark's La MLHL NW7 135 K5
Nancy Downs OXHEY WD19 132 A3
Nansen Village
NFNCH/WDSPK N12 * 136 F7
Napier Cl LCOL/BKTW AL2 86 B7
Napier Dr BUSH WD23 13 L6
Napier Rd LTN LU1 6 D6
Nappsbury Rd LTNW/LEA LU4 27 H4
Napsbury Av LCOL/BKTW AL2 86 A8
Napsbury La STAL AL1 85 L7
The Nap KGLGY WD4 100 E3
Nascot Pl WAT WD17 12 E1
Nascot Rd WAT WD17 12 E1
Nascot St WAT WD17 12 E1
Nascot Wood Rd WAT WD17 117 K3
Naseby Rd LTN LU1 6 A5
Nash Cl BORE WD6 120 D8
BRKMPK AL9 88 B5
DUN/HR/TOD LU5 26 B4
KNEB SG3 178 A7
STVGE SG2 11 L3
Nashleigh Hl CSHM HP5 97 H3
Nash Mills La HHS/BOV HP3 82 D8
Nash Rd ROY SG8 14 E8
Nash Wy KTN/HRWW/WS HA3 143 M8
Nathaniel Wk TRING HP23 169 L12
Nathans Cl WLYN AL6 177 J10
Nayland Cl LTNE LU2 29 J8
Naylor Rd TRDG/WHET N20 137 G5
Nazeingbury Cl WAB EN9 93 H4
Nazeingbury Pde WAB EN9 * 93 H4
Nazeing Common WAB EN9 94 A5
Nazeing New Rd BROX EN10 92 E3
Neagh Cl STVG SG1 22 A6
Neagle Cl BORE WD6 121 G5
Neal Cl NTHWD HA6 141 L3
Neal Ct HERT/WAT SG14 53 G7
WAB EN9 111 K7
Neal St WATW WD18 13 G7
Necton Rd STALE/WH AL4 48 C5
Needham Rd LTNW/LEA LU4 26 F3
Neild Wy RKW/CH/CXG WD3 129 K3
Nell Gwynn Cl RAD WD7 104 C6
Nelson Av STAL AL1 85 M5
Nelson Rd BERK HP4 171 J4
BSF CM23 44 A4
Nelson St HERT/WAT SG14 52 F6
Nene Rd HNLW SG16 147 K5
Neptune Ct BORE WD6 * 120 E7
Neptune Dr HHNE HP2 62 C8
Neptune Ga STVGE SG2 22 B8
Neptune Rd HRW HA1 143 H8
Nesbitts Aly BAR EN5 * 122 D7
Neston Rd WATN WD24 118 A3
Netherby Cl TRING HP23 169 M11
Netherby Gdns ENC/FH EN2 124 C8
Nethercott Cl LTNE LU2 29 G8
Netherfield La WARE SG12 73 H2
Netherfield Rd HARP AL5 64 F1
NFNCH/WDSPK N12 136 F8
Netherhall Rd
HLWW/ROY CM19 73 K7
Netherlands Rd BAR EN5 137 H2
Netherstones HTCH/STOT SG5 148 D6
Nether St NFNCH/WDSPK N12 136 F8
WARE SG12 182 C4
Netherway STALW/RED AL3 84 E5
Netley Dell LWTH SG6 16 F6
Netteswellbury Farm
HLWS CM18 3 J8
Netteswell Orch HLW CM20 2 E4
Netteswell Rd HLW CM20 3 G2
Nettle Cl LTNW/LEA LU4 26 C6
Nettlecroft HHW HP1 4 B5
WGCE AL7 50 F6
Nettleden Rd BERK HP4 171 J10
Nevell's Gn LWTH SG6 16 D2
Nevells Rd LWTH SG6 16 D3
Nevil Cl NTHWD HA6 131 H8
Neville Cl POTB/CUF EN6 106 D5
Neville Rd LTNN/LIM LU3 27 L4
Nevilles Ct LWTH SG6 * 16 F2
Nevill Gv WATN WD24 117 M5
Nevis Rd STVG SG1 21 L5
The New Ar HERT/WAT SG14 * 53 H7
Newark Cl ROY SG8 14 D5
Newark Gn BORE WD6 121 H7
Newark Rd LTNW/LEA LU4 27 L7
New Barnes Av STAL AL1 85 L5
New Barn La RBSF CM22 44 C8
New Barns La MHAD SG10 181 Q5
New Bedford Rd LTN LU1 6 E4
Newberries Av RAD WD7 119 M1
Newbiggin Pth OXHEY WD19 132 A7
Newbold Rd LTNN/LIM LU3 27 M2
Newbolt Rd STAN HA7 143 K1
Newbury Av PEND EN3 126 D3
Newbury Cl BSF CM23 43 L1
LTNW/LEA LU4 27 J7
STVG SG1 21 H8
New Bury Meadow
RBSF CM22 185 M4
Newbury Rd DUN/HR/TOD LU5 26 C3
Newby Cl EN EN1 125 J6
Newcastle Cl STVG SG1 21 K7
New Chilterns AMSS HP7 * 113 J5
New Cl KNEB SG3 177 M3
Newcombe Pk MLHL NW7 135 J8
Newcombe Rd LTN LU1 6 B5
Newcome Rd RAD WD7 104 E8
New Cots BRKMPK AL9 106 A2
New Ct KNEB SG3 * 177 N7
Newdigate Gn DEN/HRF UB9 140 B3
Newdigate Rd DEN/HRF UB9 140 A3
Newdigate Rd East
EN/HRF UB9 140 B3
Newell La STVGE SG2 23 G2
Newell Ri HHS/BOV HP3 5 J9
Newell Rd HHS/BOV HP3 5 H9
Newells LWTH SG6 17 H5
Newells Hedge LBUZ LU7 169 P4
New England Cl
HTCHE/RSTV SG4 157 P9
New England St
STALW/RED AL3 8 D5
New Farm La NTHWD HA6 141 J3
New Fiddlers Hl HARP AL5 * 174 A12
Newfield La HHNE HP2 5 K3
Newfields WGCW AL8 49 M8
Newfield Wy STALE/WH AL4 86 A4
Newford Cl HHNE HP2 82 F1
New Ford Rd CHES/WCR EN8 110 D8
Newgate STVGE SG2 11 K8
Newgate Cl STALE/WH AL4 66 B7
Newgatestreet Rd CHESW EN7 90 F8
Newgate Street Village
HERT/BAY SG13 90 B5
New Greens Av
STALW/RED AL3 65 H5
Newground Rd TRING HP23 58 F2
New Hall Cl HHS/BOV HP3 98 E1
Newhall Cl HHS/BOV HP3 * 98 E1
Newhall Ct WAB EN9 111 K7
Newhouse Crs GSTN WD25 101 M7
New House Pk STAL AL1 85 L5
Newhouse Rd HHS/BOV HP3 80 E8
New Inn Rd BLDK SG7 148 H1
New Kent Rd STAL AL1 8 F6
Newland Cl PIN HA5 142 C1
STAL AL1 85 L5
Newland Dr EN EN1 125 M5
Newland Gdns HERT/BAY SG13 53 J7
Newlands LWTH SG6 16 E6
Newlands Av RAD WD7 103 K8
Newlands Cl EDGW HA8 134 C6
Newlands Cl East
HTCHE/RSTV SG4 157 P9
Newlands Cl West
HTCHE/RSTV SG4 157 P9
Newlands La
HTCHE/RSTV SG4 157 P9
Newlands Pk ABLGY WD5 * 83 K8
Newlands Pl BAR EN5 136 B1
Newlands Rd HHW HP1 81 J1
LTN LU1 41 H7
Newlands Wk GSTN WD25 102 B7
Newlands Wy POTB/CUF EN6 106 F4
Newlyn Cl LCOL/BKTW AL2 102 C4
STVG SG1 32 E3
Newlyn Rd BAR EN5 122 D8
Newman Av ROY SG8 15 G7
Newmans Dr HARP AL5 46 D3
Newman's Wy EBAR EN4 123 G6
Newmarket Ct STALW/RED AL3 8 D3
Newmarket Rd ROY SG8 14 F7
Newminster Ct ENC/FH EN2 * 124 A12
Newnham Cl LTNE LU2 29 H8
Newnham Pde
CHES/WCR EN8 * 110 B4
Newnham Rd BLDK SG7 148 H8
Newnham Wy BLDK SG7 149 L4
New Pde RKW/CH/CXG WD3 * 130 D2
New Park Dr HHNE HP2 82 F1
New Park La STVGE SG2 34 C7
New Park Rd DEN/HRF UB9 140 A3
HERT/BAY SG13 90 A6
New Pl WLYN AL6 49 M1
Newport Cl PEND EN3 126 C3
Newport Md OXHEY WD19 * 132 B7
Newports SBW CM21 183 N8
Newquay Gdns OXHEY WD19 131 M5
New River Av WARE SG12 72 F1
New River Cl HOD EN11 72 F6
New Rd AMSS HP7 112 D8
BERK HP4 59 J7
BORE WD6 134 B2
BROX EN10 92 D1
CSTG HP8 114 C7
GSTN WD25 119 J5
HERT/WAT SG14 53 H5
HLWE CM17 76 B1
KGLGY WD4 99 K4
KNEB SG3 177 P6
POTB/CUF EN6 105 L7
RAD WD7 104 E8
RAD WD7 119 J2
RBSF CM22 167 K3
RKW/CH/CXG WD3 115 K5
RKW/CH/CXG WD3 130 D1
ROY SG8 15 M1
ROY SG8 145 N4
STDN SG11 42 A2
TRING HP23 168 G8
WARE SG12 54 C4
WAT WD17 13 H6
WGCW AL8 67 L2
WLYN AL6 50 D2
Newstead HAT AL10 87 K3
New St BERK HP4 80 B1
LBUZ LU7 169 K2
LTN LU1 6 E7
SBW CM21 183 Q6
WAT WD17 13 G5
Newteswell Dr WAB EN9 111 H6
Newton Cl HARP AL5 47 H7
HOD EN11 72 F3
Newton Crs BORE WD6 121 G8
Newtondale LTNW/LEA LU4 27 G4
Newton Dr SBW CM21 183 P8
Newton Rd
KTN/HRWW/WS HA3 143 J3
STVGE SG2 11 L2
Newtons Wy
HTCHE/RSTV SG4 157 P7
New Town HTCHE/RSTV SG4 176 F8
Newtown Rd BSF CM23 43 M3
New Town Rd LTN LU1 7 G8
New Town St LTN LU1 7 G8
New Wk HTCH/STOT SG5 146 A8
New Way La HLWE CM17 76 F6
New Wd WGCE AL7 51 G6
New Woodfield Gn
DUN/HR/TOD LU5 39 J3
Newyears Green La
DEN/HRF UB9 140 D8
Niagara Cl CHES/WCR EN8 110 B3
Nibthwaite Rd HRW HA1 143 J7
Nicholas Cl STALW/RED AL3 65 H7
WATN WD24 117 M3
Nicholas La HERT/WAT SG14 53 H7
Nicholas Pl STVG SG1 21 H8
Nicholas Rd BORE WD6 134 D2
Nicholas Wy DUN/WHIP LU6 * 38 F1
NTHWD HA6 141 G3
Nicholls Cl
AMP/FLIT/BLC MK45 154 H2
STALW/RED AL3 173 P12
Nicholls Fld HLWS CM18 75 M6
Nichols Cl LTNE LU2 28 F7
Nicholson Dr BUSH WD23 133 G4
Nickleby Wy HTCH/STOT SG5 148 A11
Nicky Line HHNE HP2 5 H1
Nicola Cl KTN/HRWW/WS HA3 143 H4
Nicol Cl CFSP/GDCR SL9 138 A3
Nicol End CFSP/GDCR SL9 138 A3
Nicoll Wy BORE WD6 135 H1
Nicol Rd CFSP/GDCR SL9 138 A3
Nidderdale HHNE HP2 62 D7
Nightingale Cl ABLGY WD5 101 L5
LTNE LU2 29 G3
PIN HA5 142 A7
RAD WD7 119 K2
Nightingale Ct LTNN/LIM LU3 * 6 D3
Nightingale La STAL AL1 86 A5
Nightingale Pl
RKW/CH/CXG WD3 130 B3
Nightingale Rd BUSH WD23 132 E1
CHESW EN7 91 G7
CSHM HP5 96 F3
HTCH/STOT SG5 157 P5
RKW/CH/CXG WD3 130 A3
Nightingales La CSTG HP8 128 B4
Nightingale Ter
ARL/CHE SG15 147 Q6
Nightingale Wk STVGE SG2 34 A4
Nightingale Wy BLDK SG7 17 J3
DEN/HRF UB9 139 K8
ROY SG8 14 F5
Nightingles BSF CM23 44 B3
Nimbus Wy HTCHE/RSTV SG4 20 A2
Nimmo Dr BUSH WD23 133 H3
Nimrod Cl STALE/WH AL4 66 A8
Nimrod Dr HAT AL10 67 H7
Nine Acre La HAT AL10 87 K1
Nine Ashes WARE SG12 182 B10
Ninefields WAB EN9 111 K7
Ninesprings Wy
HTCHE/RSTV SG4 20 A3
Ninian Rd HHNE HP2 62 C5
Ninnings Cots HARP AL5 * 46 E5
Ninning's La WLYN AL6 177 K7
Ninnings Rd CFSP/GDCR SL9 138 D2
Ninnings Wy CFSP/GDCR SL9 138 D2
Ninth Av LTNN/LIM LU3 27 H2
STSD CM24 167 K10
Niton Cl BAR EN5 136 B2
Niven Cl BORE WD6 121 G5
Noahs Court Gdns
HERT/BAY SG13 53 H8
Noake Mill La HHW HP1 61 L5
The Nobles BSF CM23 43 K3
Nodes Dr STVGE SG2 33 L8
Node Way Gdns WLYN AL6 50 A2
Noke La LCOL/BKTW AL2 84 C8
Noke Shot HARP AL5 47 G1
Noke Side LCOL/BKTW AL2 102 E1
Nokeside STVGE SG2 177 P1
The Nokes HHW HP1 61 L8
The Noke STVGE SG2 177 P1
The Nook WARE SG12 72 F1
Norbury Av WATN WD24 13 H1
Norbury Gv MLHL NW7 135 J6
Norcott Cl DUN/HR/TOD LU5 39 H2
Norfolk Av WATN WD24 118 A4

Norfolk Cl EBAR EN4 123 L8
Norfolk Ct BAR EN5 * 122 C8
Norfolk Gdns BORE WD6 121 H8
Norfolk House
RKW/CH/CXG WD3 * 130 C4
Norfolk Rd BAR EN5 122 E7
BUNT SG9 158 H9
DUN/HR/TOD LU5 39 J3
HRW HA1 142 F7
LTNE LU2 7 L5
RKW/CH/CXG WD3 130 C4
Norfolk Wy BSF CM23 43 M4
Norgrove Pk
CFSP/GDCR SL9 138 C6
Norman Av BSF CM23 43 K3
Norman Cl STAL AL1 85 J5
WAB EN9 111 H7
Norman Ct POTB/CUF EN6 107 G4
Norman Crs PIN HA5 142 A3
Normandy Av BAR EN5 136 D1
Normandy Ct HHNE HP2 5 G2
Normandy Dr BERK HP4 59 L8
Normandy Rd STALW/RED AL3 8 E3
Normandy Wy HOD EN11 73 H5
Norman Rd
AMP/FLIT/BLC MK45 155 J2
LTNN/LIM LU3 27 M7
WLYN AL6 49 M2
Normans Cl LWTH SG6 148 D12
Normansfield Cl BUSH WD23 132 F3
Norman's La ROY SG8 14 E8
Normans La WLYN AL6 177 L7
Norman's Wy STSD CM24 166 G6
Norman Wy DUN/WHIP LU6 38 C1
Norrington End
STALW/RED AL3 173 N8
Norris Cl BSF CM23 44 C2
LCOL/BKTW AL2 85 M8
Norris Gv BROX EN10 92 C2
Norris La HOD EN11 72 E6
Norris Ri HOD EN11 72 D6
Norris Rd HOD EN11 72 E7
Norrys Cl EBAR EN4 137 K1
Norrys Rd EBAR EN4 123 K8
Northall Cl DUN/WHIP LU6 37 H3
Northall Rd DUN/WHIP LU6 37 H4
Northampton Rd PEND EN3 126 C8
North Ap GSTN WD25 101 L8
NTHWD HA6 131 G5
North Av LWTH SG6 16 F1
RAD WD7 104 C6
RYLN/HDSTN HA2 142 F8
Northaw Cl HHNE HP2 62 F5
Northaw Pl POTB/CUF EN6 * 107 J4
Northaw Rd West
POTB/CUF EN6 107 L4
North Barn BROX EN10 92 F4
North Bridge Rd BERK HP4 59 K7
Northbrook Dr NTHWD HA6 141 J3
Northbrook End ROY SG8 145 P5
Northbrook Rd BAR EN5 136 C2
Northbrooks HLWW/ROY CM19 2 B8
Northchurch La CSHM HP5 79 G3
Northcliffe DUN/WHIP LU6 37 J3
Northcliffe Dr
TRDG/WHET N20 136 D4
North Cl BAR EN5 136 A1
LCOL/BKTW AL2 84 F7
ROY SG8 14 D6
North Common Rd
STALW/RED AL3 63 L1
Northcourt
RKW/CH/CXG WD3 * 129 L4
North Dene MLHL NW7 135 H6
Northdown Rd
CFSP/GDCR SL9 138 C1
HAT AL10 87 L3
North Drift Wy LTN LU1 6 A7
North Dr HAT AL10 68 A6
HTCH/STOT SG5 148 A10
STALE/WH AL4 66 C8
STDN SG11 180 D8
Northend HHS/BOV HP3 82 F4
Northern Av HNLW SG16 147 K6
Northfield STDN SG11 163 R6
Northfield Av PIN HA5 142 B6
Northfield Gdns WATN WD24 118 A3
Northfield Rd BLDK SG7 145 J9
BORE WD6 120 F5
CHES/WCR EN8 110 C6
EBAR EN4 123 J7
HARP AL5 47 G1
SBW CM21 183 Q5
TRING HP23 169 Q9
Northfields DUN/HR/TOD LU5 25 K6
LWTH SG6 148 D12
North Ga HLW CM20 2 D5
Northgate NTHWD HA6 141 G2
Northgate End BSF CM23 43 M1
Northgate Pth BORE WD6 120 D4
North Gv HLWS CM18 3 M8
North Hl RKW/CH/CXG WD3 115 H6
Northiam NFNCH/WDSPK N12 136 E7
Northlands POTB/CUF EN6 107 H5
North Mt TRDG/WHET N20 * 137 G5
Northolm EDGW HA8 135 H7
Northolt Av BSF CM23 166 D12
North Orbital Rd
DEN/HRF UB9 139 K6
LCOL/BKTW AL2 102 C4
North Orbital Road
St Albans Rd GSTN WD25 102 B7
North Pk CFSP/GDCR SL9 138 C5
North Pl HLW CM20 183 L12
WAB EN9 110 F7
North Ride WLYN AL6 177 J11
Northridge Wy HHW HP1 81 K3
North Riding LCOL/BKTW AL2 102 E4
North Rd AMS HP6 113 G2
BERK HP4 79 M1
CHES/WCR EN8 110 C7
HERT/WAT SG14 52 E6
HOD EN11 72 E6
RKW/CH/CXG WD3 129 H1
STVG SG1 21 G7
North Road Av
HERT/WAT SG14 52 E6
North Road Gdns
HERT/WAT SG14 52 F7
North St BSF CM23 43 M1
LTNE LU2 6 F3
WAB EN9 93 J4
North Ter BSF CM23 43 M1
Northumberland Av EN EN1 125 M4
Northumberland Rd BAR EN5 137 G2
RYLN/HDSTN HA2 142 D7
Northview Rd
DUN/HR/TOD LU5 25 L7
LTNE LU2 28 D7
North Wy PIN HA5 142 A5
Northway RKW/CH/CXG WD3 130 B3
WGCE AL7 50 D4
Northway Crs MLHL NW7 135 J7
Northwell Dr LTNN/LIM LU3 27 K1
North Western Av
WATN WD24 117 K1
North Western Avenue
Colne WATN WD24 118 A2
North Western Avenue
Gade Side WAT WD17 117 H1
Northwick Av
KTN/HRWW/WS HA3 143 L8
Northwick Park Rd HRW HA1 143 K8
Northwick Rd OXHEY WD19 132 A7
Northwold Dr PIN HA5 142 A5
Northwood WGCE AL7 51 H7
Northwood Cl CHESW EN7 109 K1
Northwood Gdns
NFNCH/WDSPK N12 137 H8
Northwood Rd DEN/HRF UB9 140 C3
Northwood Wy DEN/HRF UB9 140 B3
NTHWD HA6 141 L2
Nortoft Rd CFSP/GDCR SL9 138 D1
Norton Bury La LWTH SG6 148 G11
Norton Cl BORE WD6 120 E5
Norton Crs BLDK SG7 17 J1
Norton Gn STVG SG1 * 32 F6
Norton Green Rd STVG SG1 10 B7
Norton Rd LTNN/LIM LU3 27 K5
LWTH SG6 16 E1
STVG SG1 10 B7
Norton Street La
HTCHE/RSTV SG4 176 A3
Norton Wy North LWTH SG6 16 E1
Norton Wy South LWTH SG6 16 E4
Norvic Rd TRING HP23 169 L8
Norwich Cl STVG SG1 21 M8
Norwich Rd NTHWD HA6 141 K5
Norwich Wy
RKW/CH/CXG WD3 116 F7
Norwood Cl HERT/WAT SG14 52 D6
Norwood Ct AMSS HP7 * 112 F6
Norwood Dr
RYLN/HDSTN HA2 142 D8
Norwood Rd CHES/WCR EN8 110 C4
Nottingham Cl GSTN WD25 101 L8
Nottingham Rd
RKW/CH/CXG WD3 129 G4
Novello Wy BORE WD6 121 H5
Nower Hl PIN HA5 142 D6
Nugents Ct PIN HA5 * 142 C3
Nugent's Pk PIN HA5 142 C3
Numbers Farm KGLGY WD4 * 101 G3
Nunnery Cl STAL AL1 9 G9
Nunnery La LTNN/LIM LU3 27 M4
Nunnery Stables STAL AL1 8 F9
Nunn's Rd ENC/FH EN2 125 G6
Nunsbury Dr BROX EN10 92 C7
Nun's Cl HTCH/STOT SG5 157 N6
Nuns La STAL AL1 85 J6
Nupton Dr BAR EN5 136 A2
Nurseries Rd STALE/WH AL4 48 C6
The Nurseries DUN/WHIP LU6 37 J5
Nursery Cl AMSS HP7 113 J5
DUN/WHIP LU6 38 E1
OXHEY WD19 131 M4
PEND EN3 126 B5
STVGE SG2 177 N1
Nursery Crs LWTH SG6 16 D3
Nursery Flds SBW CM21 183 P7
Nursery Gdns CHESW EN7 109 H2
PEND EN3 126 B5
TRING HP23 57 M1
WARE SG12 54 C4
WGCE AL7 50 C4
Nursery Hl WGCE AL7 50 C4
Nurserymans Rd
FBAR/BDGN N11 137 L5
Nursery Pde LTNN/LIM LU3 * 27 J4
Nursery Rd BROX EN10 * 92 C7
BSF CM23 43 M3
HOD EN11 72 F4
LTNN/LIM LU3 27 K4
PIN HA5 142 A5
WAB EN9 93 H4
Nursery Rw BAR EN5 * 122 C7
Nutcroft KNEB SG3 177 R7
Nutfield WGCE AL7 50 E4
Nut Gv WGCW AL8 50 B4
Nuthampstead Rd ROY SG8 152 F11
Nutkins Wy CSHM HP5 97 G3
Nutleigh Gv HTCH/STOT SG5 157 M4
Nut Slip BUNT SG9 159 J11
Nuttfield Cl
RKW/CH/CXG WD3 * 130 F2
Nutt Gv EDGW HA8 134 B5
Nutwood Gdns CHESW EN7 91 J8
Nye Wy HHS/BOV HP3 98 E2
Nymans Cl LTNE LU2 29 H6

O

Oak Av ENC/FH EN2 124 D5
LCOL/BKTW AL2 102 E4
Oak Cl DUN/HR/TOD LU5 39 H1
HHS/BOV HP3 82 D6
STHGT/OAK N14 137 M3
WAB EN9 111 H8
Oakcroft Cl PIN HA5 141 M4
Oakdale STHGT/OAK N14 137 M4
WGCW AL8 50 B3
Oakdale Av NTHWD HA6 141 L4
Oakdale Cl OXHEY WD19 132 A7
Oakdale Rd OXHEY WD19 132 A6
Oakdene CHES/WCR EN8 110 C4
Oakdene Cl PIN HA5 142 D2
Oakdene Rd HHS/BOV HP3 82 D6
WATN WD24 117 M2
Oakdene Wy STAL AL1 86 A2
Oak Dr BERK HP4 80 B2
SBW CM21 183 N9
Oak End BUNT SG9 158 H11
HLWS CM18 * 75 K7
Oak End Wy CFSP/GDCR SL9 138 D7
Oaken Gv WGCE AL7 68 C2
Oak Farm BORE WD6 135 G1
Oak Fld CSHM HP5 96 F4
Oakfield RKW/CH/CXG WD3 129 L3
Oakfield Av HTCHE/RSTV SG4 157 R8
KTN/HRWW/WS HA3 143 M5
Oakfield Cl POTB/CUF EN6 106 D5
RSLP HA4 141 K8
Oakfield Ct BORE WD6 * 120 F8
Oakfield Rd HARP AL5 46 D8
Oakfields STVGE SG2 33 M8
Oakfields Av KNEB SG3 177 N3
Oakfields Cl STVGE SG2 34 A8
Oakfields Rd KNEB SG3 177 N3
Oak Gld NTHWD HA6 140 F3
Oak Gn ABLGY WD5 101 J6
Oak Gv HAT AL10 67 K8
HERT/BAY SG13 71 J1
Oakhill LWTH SG6 17 H5
Oakhill Av PIN HA5 142 C4
Oakhill Cl RKW/CH/CXG WD3 129 J7
Oakhill Dr WLYN AL6 176 G11
Oakhill Rd RKW/CH/CXG WD3 129 H7
Oakhurst Av EBAR EN4 137 J3
HARP AL5 46 D7
Oakhurst Pl WATW WD18 * 12 A6
Oakhurst Rd PEND EN3 126 B2
Oakington WGCE AL7 51 H7
Oakington Av AMS HP6 114 C5
Oaklands BERK HP4 79 L1
Oaklands Av BRKMPK AL9 106 C1
OXHEY WD19 131 M4
Oaklands Cl BSF CM23 166 D11
Oaklands Ct WAT WD17 117 L5
Oaklands Dr BSF CM23 166 D12
HLWE CM17 76 A6
Oaklands Ga NTHWD HA6 141 J1
Oaklands Gv BROX EN10 92 C6
Oaklands La BAR EN5 121 M8
STALE/WH AL4 66 D8
Oaklands Pk BSF CM23 166 D11
Oaklands Ri WLYN AL6 177 M10
Oaklands Rd CHESW EN7 91 J8
TRDG/WHET N20 136 D3
Oaklands Wd HAT AL10 67 L8
Oakland Vw WLYN AL6 177 M9
Oak La HTCHE/RSTV SG4 20 F5
POTB/CUF EN6 108 D2
Oaklea WLYN AL6 177 L10
Oaklea Cl WLYN AL6 177 L9
Oaklea Wd WLYN AL6 177 L10
Oakleigh Av TRDG/WHET N20 137 H4
Oakleigh Cl TRDG/WHET N20 137 K6
Oakleigh Crs TRDG/WHET N20 137 J6
Oakleigh Dr
RKW/CH/CXG WD3 131 G2
Oakleigh Gdns EDGW HA8 134 D8
TRDG/WHET N20 137 G4
Oakleigh Ms TRDG/WHET N20 137 G5
Oakleigh Pk North
TRDG/WHET N20 137 H4
Oakleigh Pk South
TRDG/WHET N20 137 J4
Oakleigh Rd PIN HA5 142 D1
Oakleigh Rd North
TRDG/WHET N20 137 H5
Oakleigh Rd South
FBAR/BDGN N11 137 L7
Oakley Cl LTNW/LEA LU4 27 H5
Oakley Rd HARP AL5 47 H6
HRW HA1 143 J8
LTNW/LEA LU4 27 H5
Oak Lodge Cl STAN HA7 134 A8
Oakmeade PIN HA5 142 E1
Oakmead Gdns EDGW HA8 135 H7
Oakmere Av POTB/CUF EN6 107 G7
Oakmere Cl POTB/CUF EN6 107 H5
Oakmere La POTB/CUF EN6 107 G6
Oak Piece WLYN AL6 177 K10
Oakridge LCOL/BKTW AL2 102 D3
Oakridge Av RAD WD7 103 K7
Oak Rd KNEB SG3 177 P8
LTNW/LEA LU4 6 A3
Oakroyd Av POTB/CUF EN6 106 D7
Oakroyd Cl POTB/CUF EN6 106 D8
Oaks Cl HTCHE/RSTV SG4 157 P8
RAD WD7 119 K1
Oaks Cross STVGE SG2 177 P1
The Oaks BERK HP4 79 L1
BORE WD6 * 120 E5
LTN LU1 41 G8
NFNCH/WDSPK N12 136 F7
OXHEY WD19 132 A4
Oak St BSF CM23 43 M3
HHS/BOV HP3 82 D6
Oak Tree Cl ABLGY WD5 101 H6
Oaktree Cl BSF CM23 43 M2
CHESW EN7 109 G2
Oak Tree Cl HAT AL10 67 L7
HERT/BAY SG13 72 A2
LWTH SG6 16 C5
STVGE SG2 35 K6
Oak Tree Ct BORE WD6 * 134 B2
WLYN AL6 * 177 L9
Oak Tree Dr TRDG/WHET N20 136 F4
Oaktree Gdns HLWE CM17 76 B6
Oaktree Garth WGCE AL7 50 C8
Oakview WATW WD18 117 J7
Oakview Cl CHESW EN7 109 M2
HARP AL5 46 D8
OXHEY WD19 132 A2
Oakway AMS HP6 112 F1
DUN/WHIP LU6 171 P2
Oak Wy HARP AL5 46 E8
STHGT/OAK N14 137 L3
Oakway Pl RAD WD7 103 L8
Oakwell Cl DUN/WHIP LU6 38 D2
STVGE SG2 177 R2
Oakwell Dr POTB/CUF EN6 107 M7
Oak Wd BERK HP4 79 K2
Oakwood Av BORE WD6 120 F8
DUN/HR/TOD LU5 39 J2
Oakwood Cl STVGE SG2 34 A7
Oakwood Dr HARP AL5 46 D8
LTNN/LIM LU3 27 G1
STALE/WH AL4 86 A1
Oakwood Ms HLWE CM17 76 A1
Oakwood Rd LCOL/BKTW AL2 102 D3
PIN HA5 141 M4
Oak Yd WAT WD17 * 13 G5
Oatfield Cl LTNW/LEA LU4 26 D5
Oatlands Rd PEND EN3 126 A5
Oban Ter LTN LU1 6 A4
Oberon Cl BORE WD6 121 G5
Obrey Wy BSF CM23 43 L6
Observer Dr WATW WD18 117 J8
Occupation Rd WATW WD18 12 E7
Octavia Ct WATN WD24 13 H2
Oddy Hl TRING HP23 58 A2
Odeon Pde
RKW/CH/CXG WD3 * 130 C4
Odsey Mdw BLDK SG7 * 150 C4
Odyssey Rd BORE WD6 120 F5
Offa Rd STALW/RED AL3 8 C5
Offas Wy STALE/WH AL4 48 B5
Offham Slope
NFNCH/WDSPK N12 136 D8
Offley Hl HTCH/STOT SG5 156 E10
Offley Rd HTCH/STOT SG5 157 M7
Ogard Rd HOD EN11 73 G5
Okeford Cl TRING HP23 57 K1
Okeford Dr TRING HP23 57 K1
Okeley La TRING HP23 57 J2
The Old Bakery LTN LU1 * 7 G9
Old Barn La
RKW/CH/CXG WD3 130 D1
Old Bedford Rd LTNE LU2 6 E1
Old Bell Cl STSD CM24 166 F7
Old Bells Ct CSHM HP5 96 F6
Old Bourne Wy STVG SG1 21 L6
Old Brewery Cl
HTCH/STOT SG5 148 D6
Old Burylodge La STSD CM24 167 J9
Oldbury Rd EN EN1 125 L6
Old Chantry La STVG SG1 20 E7
Old Charlton Rd
HTCH/STOT SG5 157 N7
Old Chorleywood Rd
RKW/CH/CXG WD3 130 B2
Old Church La STAN HA7 143 M1
WARE SG12 180 C10
The Old Coach Rd
HERT/WAT SG14 69 K2
Old Common Rd
RKW/CH/CXG WD3 115 H8
Old Crabtree La HHNE HP2 5 J5
Old Cross HERT/WAT SG14 53 G7
Old Dairy Ct DUN/HR/TOD LU5 26 D7
Old Dean HHS/BOV HP3 98 E1
The Old Dr WGCW AL8 49 M8
Old Earls La POTB/CUF EN6 105 L7
Olden Md LWTH SG6 16 F6
Olde Swann Ct STVG SG1 33 G1
Old Farm LBUZ LU7 169 P5
Old Farm La AMSS HP7 113 J7
Old Farm Yd RBSF CM22 184 C9
Old Field Cl AMS HP6 114 C5
Oldfield Cl STAN HA7 133 L8
Oldfield Farm Rd HNLW SG16 147 K5
Oldfield Ri HTCHE/RSTV SG4 175 Q2
Oldfield Rd HHW HP1 81 J3
LCOL/BKTW AL2 86 B7
Old Fishery La HHW HP1 81 K4
Old Fold Cl BAR EN5 * 122 D5
Old Fold La BAR EN5 122 D5
Old Fold Vw BAR EN5 122 A7
Old Forge Cl GSTN WD25 101 L7
STAN HA7 133 L7
WLYN AL6 50 D3
Old Forge Rd EN EN1 125 K4
Old Forge Rw
HERT/BAY SG13 * 71 M2
Old French Horn La HAT AL10 67 M7
Old Gannon Cl NTHWD HA6 131 G7
Old Garden Ct STALW/RED AL3 8 D5
Old Grove Cl CHESW EN7 91 H8
Old Hale Wy HTCH/STOT SG5 157 N4
Old Hall Cl PIN HA5 142 C3
Old Hall Dr PIN HA5 142 C3
Old Hall Ri HLWE CM17 76 C5
Oldhall St HERT/WAT SG14 53 H7
Old Harpenden Rd
STALW/RED AL3 65 J6
Old Herns La WGCE AL7 51 G5
Old Hertford Rd BRKMPK AL9 68 A6
Old Hwy HOD EN11 72 F5
Oldhill DUN/WHIP LU6 39 G3
Oldhouse Ct HHNE HP2 5 K2
Oldhouse Cft HLW CM20 3 H3
Old House La HLWW/ROY CM19 74 B8
KGLGY WD4 116 E1
Old House Rd HHNE HP2 5 K2
Old Howletts La RSLP HA4 141 H8
Oldings Cnr BRKMPK AL9 67 M4
Old Knebworth La KNEB SG3 177 J3
Old La KNEB SG3 177 P4
Old Leys HAT AL10 87 L4
Old Library La
HERT/WAT SG14 * 53 G7
Old Lodge Wy STAN HA7 133 L8
Old London Rd HERT/BAY SG13 53 J7
STAL AL1 8 F7
The Old Maltings BSF CM23 44 A2
HERT/BAY SG13 * 53 G8
Old Maple HHNE HP2 62 D4
Old Md CFSP/GDCR SL9 138 C1
Old Meadow Cl BERK HP4 79 L3
Old Mead Rd RBSF CM22 167 L1
Old Mill Gdns BERK HP4 80 B1
Old Mill La RBSF CM22 184 B3
Old Mill Rd KGLGY WD4 101 G8
Old Nazeing Rd BROX EN10 92 E3
Old North Rd ROY SG8 14 C3
Old Nursery Wy WLYN AL6 176 G10
Old Oak STAL AL1 85 J5
Old Oak Cl ARL/CHE SG15 147 Q1
Old Oak Gdns BERK HP4 * 59 J6
Old Oaks WAB EN9 111 J6
Old Orch HLWS CM18 75 H7
LCOL/BKTW AL2 85 H8
LTN LU1 6 E9
Old Orchard Cl EBAR EN4 123 H4
Old Orchard Ms BERK HP4 80 A2
Old Park Av ENC/FH EN2 125 G8
Old Parkbury La
LCOL/BKTW AL2 103 K4
Old Park Gv ENC/FH EN2 125 G8
Oldpark Ride CHESW EN7 109 H6
Old Park Rd ENC/FH EN2 124 F7
HTCH/STOT SG5 157 N6
Old Park Rd South
ENC/FH EN2 124 F8
Old Park Vw ENC/FH EN2 124 E7
Old Rectory Cl HARP AL5 46 E3
Old Rectory Dr HAT AL10 67 M8
Old Rectory Gdns
STALE/WH AL4 48 B4
Old Redding
KTN/HRWW/WS HA3 132 F8
Old River La BSF CM23 43 M2
Old Rd AMP/FLIT/BLC MK45 155 J4
HLWE CM17 183 N11
PEND EN3 126 A5
Old's Ap WATW WD18 131 G4
Old Sax La CSHM HP5 96 B1
Old School Cl
HTCHE/RSTV SG4 176 F8
RAYLNE/WEN HP22 56 A4
Old School Ct DUN/WHIP LU6 37 K3
Old School Gdns
AMP/FLIT/BLC MK45 155 J2
Old School Gn STVGE SG2 35 J4
Old School Wk ARL/CHE SG15 147 Q5
Old's Cl WATW WD18 130 F4
Old Shire La
RKW/CH/CXG WD3 128 E3
WAB EN9 111 L8
Old Shire Lane Circular Wk
CSTG HP8 128 E5
DEN/HRF UB9 139 H4
Old Solesbridge La
RKW/CH/CXG WD3 115 L7
Old Sopwell Gdns STAL AL1 8 F9
Old South Cl PIN HA5 142 B3
Old Street Hl RBSF CM22 185 J4
Old Uxbridge Rd
RKW/CH/CXG WD3 139 J2
Old Vicarage Gdns
STALW/RED AL3 172 F3
The Old Walled Gdn STVG SG1 21 G8
Old Watford Rd
LCOL/BKTW AL2 102 C4
Old Watling St
STALW/RED AL3 173 K5
Oldwood WLYN AL6 177 L10
Olive Cl STAL AL1 85 M3
Oliver Cl HHS/BOV HP3 82 C6
HOD EN11 72 F5
LCOL/BKTW AL2 103 H1
Oliver Ct WARE SG12 * 53 J1
Oliver Ri HHS/BOV HP3 82 C6
Oliver Rd HHS/BOV HP3 82 D6
Olivers Cl BERK HP4 61 G6
Oliver's La HTCH/STOT SG5 148 D6
Olivia Gdns DEN/HRF UB9 140 A3
Olleberrie La
RKW/CH/CXG WD3 99 J6
Olma Rd DUN/HR/TOD LU5 25 L7
Olwen Ms PIN HA5 142 B4
Olyard Ct LTN LU1 40 F4
Olympic Cl LTNN/LIM LU3 154 E12
Olympus Rd HNLW SG16 147 K5
Omega Ct WARE SG12 * 54 B3
Omega Maltings WARE SG12 * 54 C4
One Tree Pl AMS HP6 * 113 G4
Onslow Cl HAT AL10 67 M8
Onslow Pde STHGT/OAK N14 * 137 M4
Onslow Rd LTNW/LEA LU4 27 H4
Ontario Cl BROX EN10 92 C7
On The Hl OXHEY WD19 132 C5
The Opening
HTCHE/RSTV SG4 176 F9
Openshaw Wy LWTH SG6 16 E3
Oram Pl HHS/BOV HP3 5 G8
Orbital Crs GSTN WD25 117 K1
Orchard Av BERK HP4 79 L1
GSTN WD25 101 M5
HARP AL5 46 D4
TRDG/WHET N20 137 H5
Orchard Cl
AMP/FLIT/BLC MK45 155 J4
BORE WD6 120 D8
BUSH WD23 133 H4
DUN/HR/TOD LU5 25 M6
HERT/BAY SG13 90 A1
HHNE HP2 62 D8
HTCHE/RSTV SG4 157 P10
LTN LU1 40 C5
LWTH SG6 16 D1
POTB/CUF EN6 108 C2
RAD WD7 119 J3
RBSF CM22 184 C9
RKW/CH/CXG WD3 115 H7
SHFD SG17 146 E3
STAL AL1 9 K8
WARE SG12 54 B3
WARE SG12 73 G1
WAT WD17 12 B1
Orchard Crs EDGW HA8 135 G8
EN EN1 125 K5
STVG SG1 33 G2
Orchard Cft HLW CM20 3 L3
Orchard Dr EDGW HA8 134 D8
LCOL/BKTW AL2 84 F8
RAYLNE/WEN HP22 56 C1
RKW/CH/CXG WD3 115 G7
STDN SG11 163 Q11
WAT WD17 117 K5
Orchard End DUN/WHIP LU6 37 J5
Orchard End Av AMSS HP7 113 K5
Orchard Gdns WAB EN9 110 F8
Orchard Gv CFSP/GDCR SL9 138 A3
Orchard House La STAL AL1 8 E7
Orchard La AMS HP6 113 H4
Orchardleigh Av PEND EN3 126 A6
Orchard Md HAT AL10 67 K8
The Orchard on The Gn
RKW/CH/CXG WD3 130 D1
Orchard Pde POTB/CUF EN6 * 106 B5
Orchard Pl CHES/WCR EN8 110 B4
Orchard Ri PIN HA5 141 K5
Orchard Rd BAR EN5 122 C8
BLDK SG7 17 J1
BSF CM23 166 D12
CSTG HP8 128 A5
HTCHE/RSTV SG4 157 R4
ROY SG8 14 C6
STVG SG1 32 F1
WLYN AL6 177 J12
WLYN AL6 177 Q12
Orchard Sq BROX EN10 92 D6
The Orchards DUN/WHIP LU6 37 J3
LTN LU1 41 G7
SBW CM21 183 Q6
TRING HP23 57 K2
Orchard St HHS/BOV HP3 82 B6
STALW/RED AL3 8 D7
The Orchard BLDK SG7 17 K1
BROX EN10 * 92 E2
HERT/WAT SG14 52 F4
HTCHE/RSTV SG4 176 E8
KGLGY WD4 100 E3
RAYLNE/WEN HP22 56 A5
TRDG/WHET N20 136 F4
TRING HP23 * 57 K2
WARE SG12 179 N10
WGCW AL8 50 B5
Orchard Vw BLDK SG7 150 A2
Orchard Wy CHESW EN7 108 F1
DUN/WHIP LU6 37 K4
EN EN1 125 J7
HHS/BOV HP3 98 E2
HNLW SG16 147 J6
HTCHE/RSTV SG4 30 C8
KNEB SG3 177 L4
LBUZ LU7 24 B4
LBUZ LU7 169 Q4
LTNW/LEA LU4 27 G5
LWTH SG6 16 D1
POTB/CUF EN6 106 F2
RKW/CH/CXG WD3 129 L3
ROY SG8 14 D5
Orchehill Av CFSP/GDCR SL9 138 B6
Orchehill Ri CFSP/GDCR SL9 138 C7
Orchid Cl CHESW EN7 109 G4
DUN/WHIP LU6 25 J8
HAT AL10 67 K4
LTNN/LIM LU3 27 G3
Ordelmere LWTH SG6 148 D12
Ordnance Rd PEND EN3 126 B3
Oregon Wy LTNN/LIM LU3 27 L1
Organ Hall Rd BORE WD6 120 C5
Orient Cl STAL AL1 9 H9
Oriole Cl ABLGY WD5 101 L5
Oriole Wy BSF CM23 43 J3
Orion Wy NTHWD HA6 131 K7
Orlando Cl HTCHE/RSTV SG4 157 Q7
Ormesby Dr POTB/CUF EN6 106 B6
Ormonde Rd NTHWD HA6 131 H7
Ormsby Cl LTN LU1 41 J4
Ormskirk Rd OXHEY WD19 132 B7
Oronsay HHS/BOV HP3 82 F4
Orphanage Rd WAT WD17 13 G2
Orpington Cl LTNW/LEA LU4 26 E6
Orton Cl STALE/WH AL4 65 L6
Orton Gv EN EN1 125 K5
Orwell Av STVG SG1 21 K6
Orwell Ct WATN WD24 13 J3
Orwell Vw BLDK SG7 149 M12

Phoenix Cl *NTHWD* HA6 .... 131 K7
The Phygtle *CFSP/GDCR* SL9 .. 138 C1
Piccotts End La *HHNE* HP1 ...... 62 A7
Piccotts End Rd *HHW* HP1 .... 61 M6
Pickets Cl *BUSH* WD23 .... 133 H4
Pickford Hl *HARP* AL5 .... 47 G2
Pickford Rd *STALE/RED* AL3 ..... 172 B1
Pick Hl *WAB* EN9 .... 111 L6
Picknage Rd *ROY* SG8 .... 14 F5
Pie Cnr *STALE/RED* AL3 .... 173 L8
Pie Gdn *STALE/RED* AL3 .... 173 L8
Pietley Hl *STALE/RED* AL3 .... 173 J8
Pigeonwick *HARP* AL5 .... 46 E2
Piggottshill La *HARP* AL5 .... 47 G6
Piggotts La *LTNW/LEA* LU4 ...... 27 H5
Piggotts Orch *AMSS* HP7 .... 112 C6
Piggotts Wy *BSF* CM23 .... 43 L4
Piggy La *RKW/CH/CXG* WD3 ..... 128 C2
Pightle Cl *ROY* SG8 .... 14 D6
The Pightle *LBUZ* LU7 .... 169 P6
Pig La *RBSF* CM22 .... 44 A6
Pigotts Wy *BSF* CM23 .... 43 L3
Pike End *STVG* SG1 .... 10 C1
Pike's End *PIN* HA5 .... 141 M6
Pikes Leap *STALE/WH* AL4 .... 48 A8
Pilgrim Cl *GSTN* WD25 .... 102 A7
Pilgrim's Ri *BDEN* EN4 .... 137 J1
Pilgrims Wy *STVG* SG1 .... 21 M7
Pilkingtons *HLWE* CM17 .... 76 B5
Piltdown Rd *OXHEY* WD19 .... 132 B7
Pinceybrook Rd *HLWS* CM18 .... 95 G1
Pincey Rd *STSD* CM24 .... 167 P10
Pinchfield *RKW/CH/CXG* WD3 ... 129 H8
Pinchpools Rd *BSF* CM23 .... 166 C6
Pindar Rd *HOD* EN11 .... 73 C6
Pineapple Rd *AMSS* HP7 .... 113 C6
Pine Cl *BERK* HP4 .... 79 M1
   CHES/WCR EN8 .... 110 A4
   STAN HA7 .... 133 M7
Pine Crest *WLYN* AL6 .... 177 L9
Pinecroft *HHS/BOV* HP3 .... 82 D6
Pinecroft Crs *BAR* EN5 .... 122 C4
Pine Gv *BRKMPK* AL9 .... 88 F7
   BSF CM23 .... 43 J8
   BUSH WD23 .... 118 D5
   LCOL/BKTW AL2 .... 102 D4
   TRDG/WHET N20 .... 136 D4
Pinehurst Cl *ABLGY* WD5 .... 101 J6
Pinelands *BSF* CM23 .... 166 B12
Pine Rdg *STAL* AL1 .... 85 L5
Pine Rd *DUN/WHIP* LU6 .... 170 F1
   FBAR/BDGN N11 .... 137 L5
   PIN HA5 .... 141 L8
   STALE/WH AL4 .... 86 A2
   WAT WD17 .... 13 H5
Pinewood Dr *POTB/CUF* EN6 ... 106 D5
Pinewood Gdns *HHNE* HP2 ...... 5 J8
   HHW HP1 .... 4 C2
Pinewood Ldg *BUSH* WD23 * .. 133 H4
Pinewoods *STVG* SG2 * 3 J8
Pinfold Dell *LTNE* LU2 .... 70 E1
Pinfold Rd *BUSH* WD23 .... 118 D6
Pinnacles *WAB* EN9 .... 111 J8
Pinnate Pl *WGCE* AL7 .... 68 C3
Pinner Ct *PIN* HA5 .... 142 E6
Pinner Gn *PIN* HA5 .... 142 A4
Pinner Gv *PIN* HA5 .... 142 C6
Pinner Hl *PIN* HA5 .... 141 M2
Pinner Hill Rd *PIN* HA5 .... 142 A3
Pinner Park Av
   RYLN/HDSTN HA2 .... 143 G4
Pinner Park Gdns
   RYLN/HDSTN HA2 .... 143 G4
Pinner Rd *HRW* HA1 .... 142 F7
   NTHWD HA6 .... 140 A8
   OXHEY WD19 .... 13 K9
   PIN HA5 .... 142 D6
Pinner Vw *HRW* HA1 .... 143 G7
   RYLN/HDSTN HA2 .... 143 G6
Pinnocks La *BLDK* SG7 .... 17 K2
Pinto Cl *BORE* WD6 * 135 H2
Pioneer Wy *WATW* WD18 .... 12 B9
Pipers Av *HARP* AL5 .... 47 H6
Pipers Cl *STALE/RED* AL3 .... 173 Q11
Pipers Cft *DUN/WHIP* LU6 .... 38 D2
Pipers Green La *STAN* HA7 ..... 134 C6
Pipers Hl *HHW* HP1 .... 61 J3
Pipers La *HARP* AL5 .... 47 J6
   STALE/RED AL3 .... 172 C1
Pipit Cl *ROY* SG8 .... 14 F5
Pippens *WGCW* AL8 .... 50 C4
Pippin Cl *RAD* WD7 .... 104 C7
Pippin Gv *ROY* SG8 .... 14 D6
The Pippins *GSTN* WD25 * 102 A8
Pirton Cl *HTCH/STOT* SG5 ...... 157 N6
   STALE/WH AL4 .... 66 A5
Pirton Rd *HTCH/STOT* SG5 ..... 147 J11
   LTNW/LEA LU4 .... 27 G4
Pishiobury Dr *SBW* CM21 .... 183 P9
Pitfield Wy *PEND* EN3 .... 126 B1
Pitsfield *WGCE* AL8 .... 50 B4
Pitstone Cl *STALE/WH* AL4 ..... 66 A5
Pitt Dr *STALE/WH* AL4 .... 86 A5
Pittman's Fld *HLW* CM20 .... 3 H4
Pix Ct *ARL/CHE* SG15 .... 147 Q1
Pix Farm La *HHW* HP1 .... 80 E7
Pixies Hill Crs *HHW* HP1 .... 81 K4
Pixies Hill Rd *HHW* HP1 .... 81 K3
Pixmore Av *LWTH* SG6 .... 16 D4
Pixmore Est *LWTH* SG6 * 16 E4
Pixmore Wy *LWTH* SG6 .... 16 D4
Pix Rd *HTCH/STOT* SG5 .... 148 C8
   LWTH SG6 .... 16 E3
Place Farm *STALE/WH* AL4 ..... 48 A4
Plaistow Wy *ROY* SG8 .... 153 N3
Plaiters Cl *TRING* HP23 .... 57 L8
Plaiters Wy *DUN/HR/TOD* LU5 .. 25 L4
Plaitford Cl
   RKW/CH/CXG WD3 .... 130 C5
Plantagenet Pl *WAB* EN9 .... 110 F4
Plantation Rd *AMS* HP6 .... 113 J3
   LTNW/LIM LU3 .... 27 H2
Plantation Wk *HHW* HP1 .... 61 L8
Plantation Wy *AMS* HP6 .... 113 J3
Plash Dr *STVG* SG1 .... 10 E4

Plashes Cl *STDN* SG11 .... 163 P11
Plashes Dr *BUNT* SG9 .... 159 K11
Plashets *RBSF* CM22 .... 184 C8
The Plashets *RBSF* CM22 ...... 184 C9
Platt Cl *LTNW/LEA* LU4 .... 27 H5
Platts Rd *PEND* EN3 .... 126 A5
The Platt *AMSS* HP7 .... 112 F6
Plaw Hatch La *BSF* CM23 .... 44 B1
Playford Sq *LTNW/LEA* LU4 * ... 27 H4
Playhouse Sq *HLW* CM20 .... 2 D7
The Pleasaunce *BAR* EN5 ...... 86 B1
Pleasant Pl
   RKW/CH/CXG WD3 * 139 J2
Pleasant Ri *BRKMPK* AL9 .... 68 A5
Pleasant Dr *BSF* CM23 .... 43 L1
The Pleasaunce
   RAYLNE/WEN HP22 .... 168 C12
Plewes Cl *LTNW/LEA* LU6 * 172 A1
Plomer Av *HOD* EN11 .... 72 D4
Plough Cl *LTNW/LEA* LU4 .... 26 C5
Plough Ct *LTNW/LEA* LU4 * 26 C5
Plough Farm *RSLP* HA4 .... 141 M8
Plough Hl *POTB/CUF* EN6 .... 108 C4
Plough La *BERK* HP4 .... 60 F6
   DEN/HRF UB9 .... 156 F6
   HTCHE/RSTV SG4 .... 30 E4
   RKW/CH/CXG WD3 .... 99 J6
Ploughmans Cl *BSF* CM23 ..... 43 J4
Ploughmans End *WGCE* AL7 ... 51 J6
Plover Cl *BERK* HP4 .... 80 A2
Ployters Rd *HLWW/ROY* CM19 . 95 G5
Plummers La *LTNE* LU2 * 174 H8
Plumpton Cl *LTNE* LU2 .... 70 C5
Plumpton Rd *HOD* EN11 .... 73 G5
Plum Tree La *HNLW* SG16 ...... 147 K6
Pluto Ri *HHNE* HP2 .... 62 C8
Plymouth Cl *LTNE* LU2 .... 28 F7
Poets Cha *HHW* HP1 .... 61 M8
Poets Ga *HARP* AL5 .... 46 F4
Poets Gn *LTNW/LEA* LU4 .... 109 H2
Poets Gn *LTNW/LEA* LU4 .... 26 C5
Poets Wy *HRW* HA1 * 143 J6
Polayn Garth *WGCW* AL8 .... 50 A4
Polegate *LTNE* LU2 .... 29 H7
Polehanger La *HHW* HP1 .... 61 J8
Poles Hl *CSHM* HP5 .... 96 E3
   RKW/CH/CXG WD3 .... 99 J7
Poles La *WARE* SG12 .... 54 A2
Poles Pk *WARE* SG12 .... 180 A11
Police Rw *ROY* SG8 .... 151 M6
Polish Av *RAYLNE/WEN* HP22 .. 56 C5
Pollard Gdns *STVG* SG1 .... 33 K1
Pollard Hatch
   HLWW/ROY CM19 .... 74 F8
Pollard Rd *TRDG/WHET* N20 ... 137 J5
Pollards *RKW/CH/CXG* WD3 .... 129 H8
Pollards Cl *CHESW* EN7 .... 109 G3
Pollards Wy *HNLW* SG16 .... 147 J6
   HTCH/STOT SG5 .... 156 E1
Pollywick Rd *TRING* HP23 ...... 58 B4
Polsten Ms *PEND* EN3 .... 126 E3
Polzeath Cl *LTNE* LU2 * 174 A1
Pomeroy Cl *AMSS* HP7 .... 113 J6
Pomeroy Crs *WATN* WD24 ..... 117 M2
Pomeroy Gv *LTNE* LU2 .... 28 C4
Pomfret Av *LTNE* LU2 .... 7 J5
Pond Cl *DEN/HRF* UB9 .... 140 A4
   LTNW/LEA LU4 .... 26 F4
   STVG SG1 .... 33 J2
Pond Ct *HTCHE/RSTV* SG4 * ... 176 F8
Pond Cft *HAT* AL10 .... 89 H1
   WGCE AL7 .... 50 C8
Pondcroft Rd *KNEB* SG3 .... 177 H5
Pondfield Crs *STALE/WH* AL4 .. 65 M7
Pond La *BERK* HP4 .... 171 L10
   BLDK SG7 .... 17 J1
   RBSF CM22 .... 184 C6
Pond Park Rd *CSHM* HP5 .... 96 F3
Pond Rd *HHS/BOV* HP3 .... 82 E7
Pondside *HTCHE/RSTV* SG4 ... 21 C5
Pondsmeade *STALW/RED* AL3 . 173 R12
Pondwick Rd *HARP* AL5 .... 47 H7
Pondwicks *AMSS* HP7 .... 112 F5
Pondwicks Cl *STAL* AL1 .... 8 D7
Pondwicks Rd *LTNE* LU2 .... 5 G3
Pooleys La *BRKMPK* AL9 .... 87 M5
Popes La *WATN* WD24 .... 117 M3
Pope's Rd *ABLGY* WD5 .... 101 J3
Popes Rw *WARE* SG12 .... 54 C3
Popis Gdns *WARE* SG12 .... 54 C3
Poplar Av *AMSS* HP7 .... 113 G5
   HTCH/STOT SG5 .... 67 H8
   LTNW/LIM LU3 .... 28 A1
Poplar Cl *CSHM* HP5 .... 97 G2
   HTCHE/RSTV SG4 .... 157 Q2
   PIN HA5 .... 142 B3
   ROY SG8 .... 14 B8
   STDN SG11 .... 180 D8
Poplar Dr *ROY* SG8 .... 14 B8
Poplar Rd *DUN/WHIP* LU6 ...... 172 A1
Poplars *WGCE* AL7 .... 50 C8
Poplars Cl *GSTN* WD25 .... 101 M6
   HAT AL10 .... 67 H8
   LTNE LU2 .... 28 B8
Poplar Shaw *WAB* EN9 .... 111 K7
The Poplars *ARL/CHE* SG15 .... 147 Q1
   BORE WD6 .... 120 E5
   CHESW EN7 .... 91 J8
   DEN/HRF UB9 .... 140 A3
   HHW HP1 .... 4 B1
   HTCH/STOT SG5 .... 147 P12
   RAYLNE/WEN HP22 .... 56 A1
   STAL AL1 .... 85 M6
   STHGT/OAK N14 .... 137 M1
Popple Wy *STVG* SG1 .... 10 E3
Poppy Cl *HHW* HP1 .... 81 J1
   LTNW/LIM LU3 .... 28 B7
Poppyfields *WGCE* AL7 .... 51 G7
Poppy Md *STVG* SG1 .... 11 N1
Poppy Wk *CHESW* EN7 .... 109 H2
Porch Wy *TRDG/WHET* N20 .... 137 K6
Porlock Dr *LTNE* LU2 .... 29 G3
Portal Rd *RAYLNE/WEN* HP22 .. 56 B5
Portcullis Lodge Rd *EN* EN1 ... 125 H7
Porters Cl *BUNT* SG9 .... 159 J9
Porters Hl *HARP* AL5 .... 47 G1
Porter's Ms *HTCHE/RSTV* SG4 .176 F8
Porters Park Dr *RAD* WD7 ...... 104 C6
Portland La *CHESW* EN7 .... 109 L5
Portland Rd *STALW/RED* AL3 ... 65 K6
Portland Cl *STALE/WH* AL4 ..... 86 A5
Portland Ct *LTNW/LEA* LU5 * ... 27 H5
Portland Dr *CHESW* EN7 .... 109 L5
Portland Pl *BSF* CM23 * 43 M2
   HERT/BAY SG13 .... 72 A1
Portland Ride
   DUN/HR/TOD LU5 .... 25 M7
Portland Rd *BSF* CM23 .... 43 M2
   LTNW/LEA LU4 .... 27 H5

Portland St *STALW/RED* AL3 ... 8 C5
Port La *RBSF* CM22 .... 44 B7
Portman Cl *HTCH/STOT* SG5 ... 157 M4
   STALE/WH AL4 .... 66 A5
Portmill La *HTCH/STOT* SG5 ... 157 P6
Portobello Cl
   AMP/FLIT/BLC MK45 .... 155 J3
   CSHM HP5 .... 96 B5
Port V *HERT/WAT* SG14 .... 53 G7
Porz Av *DUN/HR/TOD* LU5 ...... 26 B6
Postfield *WGCE* AL7 .... 50 E4
Post Office Rd *EN/CH/FH* EN2 .. 124 E6
Post Office Rw
   HTCHE/RSTV SG4 .... 17 M8
Post Office Wk
   HERT/WAT SG14 * 53 H7
Post Wood Gn *HERT/BAY* SG13 72 A2
Post Wood Rd *WARE* SG12 ..... 54 C6
Potash La *TRING* HP23 .... 168 D5
Potten End Hl *HHW* HP1 .... 61 J5
Potterells *BRKMPK* AL9 * 88 B7
The Potteries *BAR* EN5 .... 136 E1
Potters Bar Station Yd
   POTB/CUF EN6 * 106 E5
Potterscrouch La
   LCOL/BKTW AL2 .... 84 B6
Potters Fld *EN* EN1 * 125 J8
   HLWE CM17 .... 76 B7
   STALW/RED AL3 .... 65 J6
Pottersheath Rd *WLYN* AL6 .... 177 K8
Potters Heights Cl *PIN* HA5 .... 141 M2
Potters La *BAR* EN5 .... 122 E6
Potters La *BORE* WD6 .... 121 G5
   STVG SG1 .... 32 F5
Potters Rd *BAR* EN5 .... 122 F6
Potter St *BSF* CM23 .... 43 M2
   HLWE CM17 .... 76 A6
   NTHWD HA6 .... 141 L3
Potter Street Hl *PIN* HA5 .... 141 M1
Potters Wood Cl *WARE* SG12 .. 180 A5
Pottery Cl *LTNW/LIM* LU3 ...... 27 K2
Potton Rd *ROY* SG8 .... 145 L3
Pouchen End La *HHW* HP1 ..... 81 J7
Poulteney Rd *STSD* CM24 ...... 166 C5
Poultney Cl *HOD* EN11 .... 73 J5
Pound Av *STVG* SG1 .... 10 C2
Pound Cl *STALE/WH* AL4 * 66 A3
Pound Gn *ROY* SG8 .... 145 M4
Pound La *CSHM* HP5 .... 78 D4
   RAD WD7 .... 104 D7
Poundwell *WGCE* AL7 .... 50 E4
Powdermill La *WAB* EN9 .... 110 E4
Powdermill Ms *WAB* EN9 .... 110 F4
Powdermill Wy *WAB* EN9 .... 110 F6
Power Cl *LTN* LU1 .... 7 H5
Power Dr *PEND* EN3 .... 126 D2
Powis Ct *BUSH* WD23 * 133 H4
   POTB/CUF EN6 .... 107 G8
Powys Cl *BORE* WD6 .... 121 H7
Poynders Hl *HHW* HP1 * 83 G5
Poynders Meadow
   HTCHE/RSTV SG4 .... 176 F8
Poynings Cl *HARP* AL5 .... 47 K5
Poynings Wy
   NFNCH/WDSPK N12 .... 136 B2
Poynters Rd *LTNW/LEA* LU4 ... 26 C5
Prae Cl *STALW/RED* AL3 .... 8 A4
Praetorian Ct *STAL* AL1 .... 85 G5
Prebendal Dr *BROX* EN10 * 92 D2
The Precinct *BROX* EN10 * 92 D2
Premier Pl *WATW* WD18 .... 12 B7
Prentice Wy *LTNE* LU2 * 174 B2
Prescott Cl *HTCH/STOT* SG5 ... 54 B5
Prescott Rd *CHES/WCR* EN8 ... 110 C1
Presdales Dr *WARE* SG12 .... 54 B5
President Wy *LTNE* LU2 .... 174 B1
Preslent Cl *HTCH/STOT* SG5 ... 146 B8
Prestatyn Cl *STVG* SG1 .... 32 F2
Preston Ct *BAR* EN5 .... 123 C4
Preston Gdns *LTNE* LU2 .... 28 D7
   PEND EN3 .... 126 C3
Preston Hl *CSHM* HP5 .... 97 H3
Preston Pth *LTNE* LU2 .... 28 D7
Prestwick Cl *LTNE* LU2 .... 28 C4
Prestwick Dr *BSF* CM23 .... 166 D12
Prestwick Rd *OXHEY* WD19 .... 132 A4
Prestwood Av
   KTN/HRWW/WS HA3 .... 143 M6
Prestwood Cl
   KTN/HRWW/WS HA3 .... 143 M6
Pretoria Rd *WATW* WD18 .... 12 D6
Pricklers Hl *BAR* EN5 .... 136 F1
Priestland Gdns *BERK* HP4 ..... 60 C7
Priestley Ln *LTN* LU1 .... 40 E2
Priestly Rd *STVG* SG2 .... 3 N2
Primary Rd *ARL/CHE* SG15 ..... 147 Q5
Primett Rd *STVG* SG1 .... 10 B2
Primley La *RBSF* CM22 .... 184 C8
Primrose Av *ENC/FH* EN2 ...... 125 H5
Primrose Cl *ARL/CHE* SG15 .... 147 Q5
   BSF CM23 .... 43 J3
   HAT AL10 .... 67 H8
   HHW HP1 .... 81 J3
   LTNW/LIM LU3 .... 28 A1
Primrose Cl *STVG* SG1 .... 10 D1
Primrose Dr *HERT/BAY* SG13 .. 53 M7
Primrose Fld *HLWS* CM18 ...... 75 K8
Primrose Gdns *BUSH* WD23 ... 132 E5
Primrose Hl *KGLGY* WD4 .... 100 F2
Primrose La *ARL/CHE* SG15 .... 147 P5
   GSTN WD25 .... 119 H4
Primrose Vw *ROY* SG8 .... 15 G4
Prince Andrew's La *ROY* SG8 .. 14 E8
Prince Charles Av
   HTCH/STOT SG5 .... 148 E7
Prince Edward St *BERK* HP4 ... 80 A1
Prince Edward Wy
   HTCH/STOT SG5 .... 148 B8
Prince of Wales Cl
   ARL/CHE SG15 .... 147 Q5
Prince Pk *HHW* HP1 .... 81 J3
Princes Av *PEND* EN3 .... 126 C2
   WATW WD18 .... 12 B7
Princes Cl *BERK* HP4 .... 59 L7
   EDGW HA8 .... 134 B4
Princes Dr *HRW* HA1 .... 143 J2
Princesfield Rd *WAB* EN9 ...... 111 M7
Princes Ga *STALW/RED* AL3 ... 23 J2
Princes Ms *DUN/WHIP* LU6 .... 38 E1
Princes Rd *POTB/CUF* EN6 * ... 106 D2
Princess Diana Dr
   STALE/WH AL4 .... 86 A3
Princess St *LTN* LU1 .... 6 C1
Princes St *DUN/WHIP* LU6 ..... 38 E1
Prince's St *HTCH/STOT* SG5 ... 148 D6

Princes St *WARE* SG12 .... 54 B3
Prince St *WAT* WD17 .... 13 G3
Prince Wy *LTNW/LEA* LU4 ...... 174 B1
Printers Wy *DUN/WHIP* LU6 * .. 38 B1
Prior Gv *CSHM* HP5 .... 97 G4
Priors Cl *HERT/BAY* SG13 ...... 71 M2
Priors Hl *HTCH/STOT* SG5 ...... 156 E1
Priors Md *EN* EN1 .... 125 J5
Priors Wood Rd
   HERT/BAY SG13 .... 72 A2
   HLWE CM17 .... 183 N12
Priory Av *DEN/HRF* UB9 .... 140 A6
   HLWE CM17 .... 183 N12
Priory Cl *BROX* EN10 .... 92 C5
   DEN/HRF UB9 .... 139 M6
   HLWE CM17 .... 72 A7
   ROY SG8 .... 14 F7
   STAN HA7 .... 143 H1
   STHGT/OAK N14 .... 137 M1
   TRDG/WHET N20 .... 136 D3
Priory Ct *BSF* CM23 .... 43 L2
   HLWS CM18 .... 15 M8
Priory Dell *STVG* SG1 .... 10 F5
Priory Dr *STAN* HA7 .... 133 K6
Priory End *HTCHE/RSTV* SG4 .. 157 P8
Priory Field Dr *EDGW* HA8 ..... 134 F7
Priory Flds *WAT* WD17 .... 117 K5
Priory Gdns *BERK* HP4 .... 80 A5
   DEN/HRF UB9 .... 140 A6
   LTNE LU2 .... 28 B6
Priory Ga *HTCHE/RSTV* SG4 ... 20 D5
Priory Orch *STALW/RED* AL3 ... 173 K7
Priory Rd *CFSP/GDCR* SL9 ..... 138 A5
   DUN/HR/TOD LU5 .... 39 G1
   St HERT/WAT SG14 .... 53 H7
   WARE SG12 .... 54 A8
The Priory *STALW/RED* AL3 .... 173 R12
Priory Vw *BUSH* WD23 .... 133 J3
Priory Wk *STAL* AL1 .... 9 H9
Priory Wood Rbt *RBSF* CM22 .. 45 C1
Pritchett Cl *PEND* EN3 .... 126 F3
Proctors Wy *BSF* CM23 .... 44 A5
Proctor Wy *LTNE* LU2 .... 174 A2
Progress Pk *LTNW/LEA* LU4 * .. 26 F3
Progress Wy *LTNW/LEA* LU4 ... 26 F3
The Promenade *EDGW* HA8 * .. 134 C8
Prospect La *HARP* AL5 .... 64 D1
Prospect Pl *WLYN* AL6 .... 177 J12
Prospect Rd *BAR* EN5 .... 122 F4
   CHES/WCR EN8 .... 110 A3
   STAL AL1 .... 8 E9
Prospect Wy *LTNE* LU2 .... 174 A2
Protea Wy *LWTH* SG6 .... 16 F4
Providence Gv *STVG* SG1 ...... 33 J1
Providence Wy *BLDK* SG7 ...... 17 K2
Provost Wy *LTNE* LU2 .... 174 A1
Prowse Av *BUSH* WD23 .... 133 G5
Pryor Cl *ABLGY* WD5 .... 101 K6
Pryor Gdns *HTCH/STOT* SG5 .. 148 D5
Pryor Rd *BLDK* SG7 .... 42 A3
Pryors Cl *BSF* CM23 .... 44 A3
Pryor Wy *LWTH* SG6 .... 17 H4
Puddephat's La
   STALW/RED AL3 .... 172 F10
Pudding La *HHW* HP1 .... 61 L8
   ROY SG8 .... 153 J4
Puddingstone Dr
   STALE/WH AL4 .... 86 A4
The Pudgell *ROY* SG8 .... 153 N3
Pulham Av *BROX* EN10 .... 92 C2
Puller Rd *BAR* EN5 .... 122 B6
   HHW HP1 .... 81 J1
Pulleys Cl *HHW* HP1 .... 81 K1
Pulleys La *HHW* HP1 .... 81 K1
Pullfields *CSHM* HP5 .... 96 E4
Pullman Cl *STAL* AL1 .... 9 H9
Pullman Dr *HTCHE/RSTV* SG4 . 157 N6
Pulpit Cl *CSHM* HP5 .... 96 E3
Pulter's Wy
   HTCHE/RSTV SG4 .... 157 Q7
Pump Hl *BUNT* SG9 .... 160 C6
Pump La *CSHM* HP5 .... 97 J7
   EPP CM16 .... 94 F6
Punchard Crs *PEND* EN3 .... 126 F4
Punch Bowl La *CSHM* HP5 ..... 97 G6
   HHNE HP2 .... 63 H7
Punchbowl Pk *HHNE* HP2 * 63 H7
Purbrock Av *GSTN* WD25 .... 118 A2
Purcell Cl *BORE* WD6 .... 120 B5
   WLYN AL6 .... 177 R11
Purcell Rd *WGCE* AL7 .... 68 C2
Purdom Rd *WGCE* AL7 .... 51 G7
Purford Gn *HLWS* CM18 .... 3 M9
Purkiss Rd *HERT/BAY* SG13 .... 71 G2
Purlings Rd *BUSH* WD23 .... 132 F1
Pursley Gdns *BORE* WD6 .... 120 F4
Purway Cl *LTNN/LIM* LU3 .... 27 J1
Purwell La *HTCHE/RSTV* SG4 .. 28 A1
Putnams Dr
   RAYLNE/WEN HP22 .... 168 B12
Putney Rd *PEND* EN3 .... 126 B2
Puttenham Cl *WATW* WD18 ... 132 A6
Putteridge Pde *LTNE* LU2 * 28 F5
Putteridge Rd *LTNE* LU2 .... 28 F5
Putters Cft *HHNE* HP2 .... 62 F5
Puttocks Cl *WAB* EN9 .... 88 A5
Puttocks Dr *BRKMPK* AL9 ...... 88 A5
Pycombe Cnr
   NFNCH/WDSPK N12 .... 136 D7
Pye Gdns *BSF* CM23 .... 43 K1
Pyenest Rd *HLWW/ROY* CM19 . 74 F7
Pyghtle La *LTNN/LIM* LU3 ...... 28 A1
The Pyghtle *BUNT* SG9 .... 158 H9
The Pyghtle *LTN* LU1 .... 40 E2
Pyghtle *HTCH/STOT* SG5 .... 147 H1
Pym Cl *EBAR* EN4 .... 137 H1
Pymmes Brook Trail
   EBAR EN4 .... 137 J1
Pymmes Green Rd
   FBAR/BDGN N11 .... 137 M7
Pymms Brook Dr *EBAR* EN4 ... 123 J8
Pyms Cl *LWTH* SG6 .... 16 F1
Pynchbek *BSF* CM23 .... 43 L3
Pynchon Paddocks
   RBSF CM22 .... 184 D2
Pynders La *DUN/HR/TOD* LU5 . 26 D2
Pynest Green La *LOU* IG10 ..... 127 L3
Pynnacles Cl *STAN* HA7 .... 133 M8
Pyot Pth *BORE* WD6 .... 120 D3
Pytchley Cl *LTNE* LU2 .... 28 C4
Pytt Fld *HLWE* CM17 .... 75 M7

Q

The Quadrangle *WGCW* AL8 ... 50 A6

The Quadrant
   DUN/HR/TOD LU5 .... 26 A6
   LWTH SG6 .... 16 D3
   ROY SG8 .... 14 D5
   RYLN/HDSTN HA2 * 143 H5
   STALE/WH AL4 .... 65 M7
   STVG SG1 .... 10 D5
Quail Wk *ROY* SG8 .... 14 E8
Quaker La *WAB* EN9 .... 111 G8
Quaker Rd *WARE* SG12 .... 54 C2
Quakers La *POTB/CUF* EN6 .... 106 F4
Quantock Cl *LTNN/LIM* LU3 .... 27 M1
   STALE/WH AL4 .... 66 A4
   STVG SG1 .... 22 B6
Quantock Ct *LTNN/LIM* LU3 * .. 27 M1
Quantock Ri *LTNN/LIM* LU3 .... 27 M1
Quantocks *HHNE* HP2 .... 62 D7
Quarrendon Rd *AMSS* HP7 .... 113 H6
Quarry Spring *HLW* CM20 ...... 3 J5
Quarry Wk *DUN/WHIP* LU6 .... 38 C2
Quartermass Cl *HHW* HP1 ..... 81 L1
Quartermass Rd *HHW* HP1 .... 81 L1
Queen Anne's Cl
   HTCH/STOT SG5 .... 148 D3
Queen Bee Ct *HAT* AL10 .... 67 H6
Queen Elizabeth Ct
   WAB EN9 .... 127 L1
Queen Hoo La *KNEB* SG3 ...... 178 B11
Queen Mary's Av *WATW* WD18 117 L8
Queen Marys Ct *WAB* EN9 * ... 127 L1
Queen Mother's Dr
   DEN/HRF UB9 .... 139 K8
Queens Cl *KTN/HRWW/WS* HA3 143 M5
   TRDG/WHET N20 .... 137 H5
   WATW WD18 .... 12 B4
Queen's Cl *EDGW* HA8 .... 134 B4
   SBW CM21 .... 183 K8
Queens Crs *BSF* CM23 .... 43 L4
   STALE/WH AL4 .... 65 M7
Queens Dr *ABLGY* WD5 .... 101 K6
   EN EN1 .... 125 H8
   HERT/BAY SG13 .... 71 H1
The Queen's Dr
   RKW/CH/CXG WD3 .... 129 K2
Queens Pde
   FBAR/BDGN N11 * 137 K8
Queens Parade Cl
   FBAR/BDGN N11 * 137 K8
Queen's Pl *WAT* WD17 .... 13 H4
Queens Rd *BAR* EN5 .... 59 L8
   BERK HP4 .... 59 L8
   CSHM HP5 * 97 G4
   HARP AL5 .... 46 F6
   ROY SG8 .... 14 E6
   WARE SG12 .... 54 D3
Queen's Rd *CHES/WCR* EN8 ... 110 C4
   EN EN1 .... 125 J8
   HERT/BAY SG13 .... 71 H1
The Queen's Sq *HHNE* HP2 .... 5 G5
Queen St *DUN/HR/TOD* LU5 ... 25 M9
   HTCH/STOT SG5 .... 148 D7
   HTCHE/RSTV SG4 .... 157 P7
   KGLGY WD4 .... 99 L5
   LBUZ LU7 .... 169 P8
   STALW/RED AL3 .... 8 C3
   TRING HP23 .... 57 L2
Queens Wy *HRW* HA1 .... 143 J6
Queens Wy *RAD* WD7 .... 104 C5
   CHES/WCR EN8 .... 110 D8
Queensway *DUN/WHIP* LU6 ... 25 M8
   HAT AL10 .... 67 L8
   HHNE HP2 .... 4 E1
   PEND EN3 .... 126 A8
   ROY SG8 .... 14 E6
   STVG SG1 .... 10 D5
Queensway Pde
   DUN/WHIP LU6 * 25 M8
The Queensway
   CFSP/GDCR SL9 .... 138 B6
Queens Well Av
   TRDG/WHET N20 .... 137 J3
Queenswood Crs *GSTN* WD25 . 101 L7
Queenswood Dr
   HTCHE/RSTV SG4 .... 16 A8
Quendell Wk *HHNE* HP2 * 5 G5
Quendon Dr *WAB* EN9 .... 111 H7
Quickbeams *WGCE* AL7 .... 50 C4
Quickberry Pl *AMSS* HP7 * 113 G5
Quickley Brow
   RKW/CH/CXG WD3 .... 128 F2
Quickley La
   RKW/CH/CXG WD3 .... 129 G2
Quickley Ri *RKW/CH/CXG* WD3.. 128 F2
Quickly Brow
   RKW/CH/CXG WD3 .... 128 F2
Quickmoor La *KGLGY* WD4 .... 99 M7
Quickswood *LTNN/LIM* LU3 .... 28 A1
Quickwood Cl
   RKW/CH/CXG WD3 .... 129 K2
Quill Hall La *AMS* HP6 .... 113 H3
Quills *LWTH* SG6 .... 17 H5
Quilter Cl *LTNN/LIM* LU3 .... 27 K5
Quinces Cft *HHW* HP1 .... 61 L8
Quincey Rd *WARE* SG12 .... 54 A2
Quin Ct *STDN* SG11 .... 163 R6
Quinn Wy *LWTH* SG6 .... 17 G4
Quinta Dr *BAR* EN5 .... 135 M1
Quinton Wy *WAB* EN9 .... 127 L1

R

Raans Rd *AMS* HP6 .... 113 K4
Raban Cl *STVG* SG2 .... 34 A8
Rabley Heath Rd *WLYN* AL6 ... 176 G8
Rackman Dr *LTNN/LIM* LU3 .... 28 A4
Radbourne Ct
   KTN/HRWW/WS HA3 * 143 M8
Radburn Cl *HLWS* CM18 .... 95 L1
Radburn Wy *LWTH* SG6 .... 16 F5
Radburn Wy *LWTH* SG6 .... 16 F5
Radcliffe Av *ENC/FH* EN2 ...... 125 G5
Radcliffe Rd *HTCH/STOT* SG5 . 157 Q5
   KTN/HRWW/WS HA3 .... 143 L4
Radlett La *BORE* WD6 .... 104 D8
Radlett Park Rd *RAD* WD7 ..... 103 M8
Radlett Rd *GSTN* WD25 .... 119 G4
   LCOL/BKTW AL2 .... 103 J3
   WAT WD17 .... 13 H7
Radnor Av *HRW* HA1 .... 143 H7
Radnor Gdns *EN* EN1 .... 124 C2
Radnor Hall *BORE* WD6 .... 134 C1
Radnor Rd
   LTNW/LEA LU4 .... 26 D5
Radstock Cl
   KTN/HRWW/WS HA3 .... 143 L5
Radstock Cl *FBAR/BDGN* N11 . 137 J8
Radstone Pl *LTNE* LU2 .... 29 J8
Radwell La *BLDK* SG7 .... 19 G9

Raebarn Gdns BAR EN5 135 M1
Raffin Cl KNEB SG3 177 R6
Raffin Green La
HERT/WAT SG14 178 B4
KNEB SG3 178 A6
Raffin Pk KNEB SG3 178 A6
Ragged Hall La
LCOL/BKTW AL2 84 B6
Raglan Av CHES/WCR EN8 110 B8
Raglan Cl LTNW/LEA LU4 * 26 D6
Raglan Gdns OXHEY WD19 131 M4
Rags La CHESW EN7 109 J1
Railway Ap HRW HA1 143 K6
Railway Pl HERT/BAY SG13 53 J7
Railway Rd CHES/WCR EN8 110 D7
Railway St HERT/BAY SG13 71 H2
Railway Ter KGLGY WD4 100 E1
Rainbow Cl STALW/RED AL3 173 P12
Rainbow Ct OXHEY WD19 132 A2
Rainbow Rd HLWE CM17 77 J2
Rainer Cl CHES/WCR EN8 110 B3
Rainsford Rd STSD CM24 166 F5
Raisins Hl PIN HA5 141 M5
Raleigh Crs STVGE SG2 33 L2
Raleigh Dr TRDG/WHET N20 137 J6
Raleigh Gv LTNW/LEA LU4 27 H8
Raleigh Rd ENC/FH EN2 125 H8
The Rally ARL/CHE SG15 147 Q2
Ralston Wy OXHEY WD19 132 B5
Ramblers La HLWE CM17 76 B4
Ramblers Wy WGCE AL7 50 F8
Rambling Wy BERK HP4 60 F7
Ramerick Gdns ARL/CHE SG15 147 P7
Ram Gorse HLW CM20 2 A3
Ramillies Rd MLHL NW7 135 J5
Ramney Dr PEND EN3 126 C2
The Ramparts STALW/RED AL3 8 A9
Ramridge Rd LTNE LU2 28 E7
Ramsay Cl BROX EN10 92 C3
Ramsbury Rd STAL AL1 9 G8
Ramscote La CSHM HP5 78 D7
Ramsdell STVG SG1 11 H6
Ramsden Rd FBAR/BDGN N11 137 K8
Ramsey Cl BRKMPK AL9 107 H1
LTNW/LEA LU4 26 D6
STAL AL1 9 M9
Ramsey Lodge Ct STAL AL1 * 9 H4
Ramsey Rd
AMP/FLIT/BLC MK45 155 J2
Ramson Ri HHW HP1 81 J3
Randalls Ri HHNE HP2 62 C8
Randalls Wk LCOL/BKTW AL2 102 D5
Randals Hl STVGE SG2 11 M9
Randon Cl RYLN/HDSTN HA2 142 F4
Rand's Meadow
HTCH/STOT SG5 147 K10
Ranelagh Cl EDGW HA8 134 E7
Ranelagh Dr EDGW HA8 134 E7
Ranelagh Rd HHNE HP2 82 F2
Ranleigh Wk HARP AL5 47 H7
Ranmoor Cl HRW HA1 143 H6
Ranmoor Gdns HRW HA1 143 H6
Rannoch Cl EDGW HA8 134 F5
Rannoch Wk HHNE HP2 62 B6
Ranock Cl LTNN/LIM LU3 27 H1
Ranskill Rd BORE WD6 120 E5
Ransom Cl HTCHE/RSTV SG4 157 P9
OXHEY WD19 132 A3
Ranston Cl DEN/HRF UB9 139 K8
Rant Meadow HHS/BOV HP3 5 M7
Ranulf Cl HLWE CM17 183 N11
Ranworth Av HOD EN11 72 F3
STVGE SG2 177 Q2
Ranworth Cl HHNE HP2 5 G6
Ranworth Gdns
POTB/CUF EN6 106 B5
Raphael Cl RAD WD7 104 C6
Raphael Dr WATN WD24 13 J2
Rasehill Cl RKW/CH/CXG WD3 130 A1
Rasper Rd TRDG/WHET N20 137 G5
Rathlin HHS/BOV HP3 82 F4
Rat's La LOU IG10 127 M4
Ratty's La HOD EN11 73 H7
Ravenbank Rd LTNE LU2 29 G4
Raven Cl RKW/CH/CXG WD3 130 A3
Raven Ct HAT AL10 87 L2
Ravenhill Wy LTNW/LEA LU4 26 E5
Ravensburgh Cl
AMP/FLIT/BLC MK45 154 H2
Ravens Cl EN EN1 125 J6
Ravenscourt DUN/WHIP LU6 25 K6
Ravens Ct TRING HP23 168 F5
Ravenscraig Rd
FBAR/BDGN N11 137 M7
Ravenscroft BROX EN10 * 92 D2
GSTN WD25 118 C1
HARP AL5 47 H7
Ravenscroft Cots BAR EN5 * 136 E2
Ravenscroft Pk BAR EN5 122 B7
Ravensdale Av
NFNCH/WDSPK N12 137 G7
Ravensdell HHW HP1 81 K1
Ravens La BERK HP4 80 B1
Ravensmead CFSP/GDCR SL9 128 D8
Ravensthorpe LTNE LU2 28 F5
Ravenswood Pk NTHWD HA6 141 L1
Rawdon Dr HOD EN11 72 E8
Rayburn Rd HHW HP1 61 L8
Raydean Rd BAR EN5 136 E1
Rayfield WGCW AL8 50 B4
Ray Gdns STAN HA7 133 M8
Raylands Md CFSP/GDCR SL9 138 A7
Raymer Cl STAL AL1 9 H3
Raymond Cl ABLGY WD5 101 H6
Raymonds Cl WGCE AL7 * 68 C1
Raymonds Pln WGCE AL7 68 C1
Rayners La PIN HA5 142 D8
Raynham Rd BSF CM23 44 B1
Raynham St HERT/BAY SG13 53 J6
Raynham Wy LTNE LU2 29 H8
Raynsford Rd WARE SG12 54 C4
Raynton Rd PEND EN3 126 B3
Ray's Hl CSHM HP5 78 A3
Read Ct WAB EN9 111 L7
Readers Ct DUN/WHIP LU6 25 L7
The Readings HLWS CM18 75 K8
RKW/CH/CXG WD3 115 K7
Reading Wy MLHL NW7 136 B8
Reaper Cl LTNW/LEA LU4 26 C5
Recreation Gnd STSD CM24 166 F7
Recreation Rd
DUN/HR/TOD LU5 26 A3
Rectory Cl BRKMPK AL9 69 J7
BSF CM23 43 K6
LBUZ LU7 36 A3
STAN HA7 143 M1
WARE SG12 182 B9
Rectory Fld HLWW/ROY CM19 74 F7
Rectory Gdns HAT AL10 67 M8
Rectory Hl AMSS HP7 113 G5
Rectory La AMSS HP7 112 F5
BERK HP4 80 A1
BSF CM23 165 Q7
BUSH WD23 132 E2
HERT/WAT SG14 178 F6
HLWW/ROY CM19 74 F7
KGLGY WD4 100 E2
KNEB SG3 177 Q7
LTNE LU2 155 R11
RAD WD7 104 D7
RKW/CH/CXG WD3 130 B4
STAN HA7 133 M8
STVG SG1 21 G8
Rectory Mnr
HTCH/STOT SG5 * 156 E1
Rectory Rd
RKW/CH/CXG WD3 130 B3
SHFD SG17 146 D4
WGCW AL8 50 A3
Rectory Wd HLW CM20 2 C4
Redan Rd WARE SG12 54 C2
Redbournbury La
STALW/RED AL3 64 B3
Redbourn La HARP AL5 46 C7
Redbourn Rd HHNE HP2 62 E6
STALW/RED AL3 64 C6
Redcar Dr STVG SG1 32 E3
Redcote La HARP AL5 46 E6
Redding Dr AMS HP6 112 F3
Redding La STALW/RED AL3 173 N9
Reddings HHS/BOV HP3 5 M7
WGCW AL8 50 A6
Reddings Av BUSH WD23 132 F1
Reddings Cl MLHL NW7 135 K7
The Reddings BORE WD6 120 D7
MLHL NW7 135 K6
Redditch Ct HHNE HP2 62 D6
Redferns Cl LTN LU1 40 E3
Redfield Cl DUN/WHIP LU6 25 J8
STALW/RED AL3 173 Q12
Redgrave Gdns
LTNN/LIM LU3 27 K1
Redhall Cl HAT AL10 87 K3
Redhall Dr HAT AL10 87 K3
Redhall La RKW/CH/CXG WD3 116 C5
Redheath Cl GSTN WD25 117 K1
Redhill Rd HTCH/STOT SG5 157 L5
Redhoods Wy East LWTH SG6 16 C3
Redhoods Wy West LWTH SG6 16 C3
Red House Cl WARE SG12 54 C6
Redlands BLDK SG7 * 149 M9
Redlands Rd PEND EN3 126 C5
Red Lion Cl GSTN WD25 118 F3
Red Lion Crs HLWE CM17 76 A7
Red Lion La HHS/BOV HP3 82 D8
HLWE CM17 76 A7
RKW/CH/CXG WD3 115 L1
LWTH SG6 16 E3
Red Lion Pde PIN HA5 * 142 C5
Red Lion St CSHM HP5 96 F6
Red Lodge Gdns BERK HP4 79 L2
Redmire Cl LTNW/LEA LU4 26 F3
Redoubt Cl HTCHE/RSTV SG4 157 Q4
Red Rails LTN LU1 6 B9
Redricks La SBW CM21 183 K11
Red Rd BORE WD6 120 D7
Redvers Cl BSF CM23 166 C11
Red White & Blue Rd
BSF CM23 166 D11
Red Willow HLWW/ROY CM19 74 D8
Redwing Cl STVGE SG2 34 A5
Redwing Gv ABLGY WD5 101 L5
Redwing Ri ROY SG8 14 F5
Redwood Cl OXHEY WD19 132 A7
Redwood Dr HHNE HP2 5 H6
LTNN/LIM LU3 27 G1
Redwood Ri BORE WD6 120 E3
Redwoods HERT/WAT SG14 53 G6
WGCW AL8 50 B2
Redwood Wy BAR EN5 136 B1
Reed Cl LCOL/BKTW AL2 104 B1
Reedham Cl LCOL/BKTW AL2 102 E3
Reedings Wy SBW CM21 183 R5
Reed Pl HARP AL5 * 46 D2
Reeds Crs WAT WD17 13 G2
WATN WD24 13 G1
Reedsdale LTNE LU2 29 K7
The Reeds WGCE AL7 50 B8
Reenglass Rd STAN HA7 * 134 B7
Rees Dr STAN HA7 134 C7
Reeves Av LTNN/LIM LU3 27 M5
Reeves La HLWW/ROY CM19 94 A1
Reeves Pightle ROY SG8 153 P2
Regal Cl STDN SG11 163 Q11
Regal Dr FBAR/BDGN N11 137 M8
Regal Wy WATN WD24 118 A4
Regency Cl BSF CM23 43 L2
Regency Ct DUN/WHIP LU6 39 G2
HLWS CM18 75 L8
Regent Cl KGLGY WD4 100 E3
NFNCH/WDSPK N12 137 G8
STALE/WH AL4 66 A6
WGCE AL7 50 C8
Regent Ct HTCH/STOT SG5 148 D6
Regents Cl RAD WD7 103 L8
Regent St DUN/WHIP LU6 25 M8
HTCH/STOT SG5 148 D7
LTN LU1 6 E6
WATN WD24 117 M4
Reginald Ms HLWE CM17 76 A4
Reginald Rd NTHWD HA6 141 K3
Reginald St LTNE LU2 6 F2
Regis Rd LTNW/LEA LU4 26 C5
Reid Cl PIN HA5 141 L5
Remus Cl STAL AL1 85 H6
Rendlesham Av RAD WD7 119 K3
Rendlesham Cl WARE SG12 53 M3
Rendlesham Rd ENC/FH EN2 124 F5
Rendlesham Wy
RKW/CH/CXG WD3 129 G2
Rennison Cl CHESW EN7 109 K1
Renshaw Cl LTNE LU2 29 J7
Repton Cl LTNN/LIM LU3 27 K1
Repton Gn STALW/RED AL3 65 M7
Repton Pl AMSS HP7 * 113 L5
Repton Wy
RKW/CH/CXG WD3 130 E1
Reservoir Rd RSLP HA4 141 G7
Reson Wy HHW HP1 4 B5
Reston Cl BORE WD6 120 E4
Retford Cl BORE WD6 120 E4
The Retreat AMS HP6 114 C5
DUN/HR/TOD LU5 26 D8
Revels Cl HERT/WAT SG14 53 H5
Revels Rd HERT/WAT SG14 53 H5
Reynard Copse BSF CM23 166 B12
Reynards Rd WLYN AL6 176 H10
Reynard's Wy LCOL/BKTW AL2 102 D2
Reynard Wy HERT/BAY SG13 53 L7
Reynolds Cl HHW HP1 81 L1
Reynolds Crs STALE/WH AL4 65 M5
Reynolds Yd CSHM HP5 96 F6
Rhee Spring BLDK SG7 149 M12
Rhodes Av BSF CM23 43 M4
Rhodes Wy WATN WD24 13 J1
Rhymes HHW HP1 61 M8
Ribbledale LCOL/BKTW AL2 104 D1
Ribblesdale HHNE HP2 62 C7
Rib Cl STDN SG11 163 Q11
Ribocon Wy LTNW/LEA LU4 26 F2
Ribston Cl RAD WD7 104 B7
Rib V HERT/WAT SG14 53 H4
Rib Wy BUNT SG9 159 J10
Riccat La STVG SG1 21 K6
Richards Cl BUSH WD23 133 H3
HRW HA1 143 L7
LTN LU1 40 F3
Richardson Cl LCOL/BKTW AL2 104 C1
Richardson Crs CHESW EN7 90 F7
Richardson Pl STALE/WH AL4 86 F4
Richards St HAT AL10 67 H6
Richard Stagg Cl STAL AL1 85 M4
Richard St DUN/HR/TOD LU5 39 G1
Richfield Rd BUSH WD23 133 G3
Richmond Cl BORE WD6 135 H1
BSF CM23 43 J2
WARE SG12 53 M2
Richmond Ct BROX EN10 92 D2
DUN/WHIP LU6 37 J3
LTNE LU2 7 H1
POTB/CUF EN6 * 107 G5
Richmond Dr WAT WD17 117 J6
Richmond Gdns
KTN/HRWW/WS HA3 143 K2
Richmond Hl LTNE LU2 7 H1
Richmond Rd BAR EN5 136 F1
POTB/CUF EN6 107 G5
Richmond Wy
RKW/CH/CXG WD3 117 G8
Rickfield Cl HAT AL10 87 L2
Rickmansworth La
CFSP/GDCR SL9 138 C1
Rickmansworth Rd
RKW/CH/CXG WD3 115 J7
WAT WD17 12 E3
Rickyard Cl LTNE LU2 28 F6
Rickyard Meadow
STALW/RED AL3 173 Q12
The Rickyard Norton Hall Farm
LWTH SG6 * 148 G12
The Rickyard BLDK SG7 149 P1
Riddell Gdns BLDK SG7 17 K1
Riddings La HLWS CM18 95 K1
Riddy Hill Cl
HTCHE/RSTV SG4 * 157 Q7
Riddy La LTNN/LIM LU3 27 M4
The Riddy HTCHE/RSTV SG4 176 F9
The Ride DUN/WHIP LU6 37 M3
PEND EN3 126 A7
Ridge Av HARP AL5 46 C1
LWTH SG6 16 E3
Ridge Crest ENC/FH EN2 124 D5
Ridgedown STALW/RED AL3 173 Q12
Ridgefield WAT WD17 117 J3
Ridgehurst Av GSTN WD25 101 K7
Ridge La WAT WD17 117 J2
Ridge Lea HHW HP1 81 K3
Ridgemont Gdns EDGW HA8 135 G7
Ridgemount End
CFSP/GDCR SL9 128 C8
Ridgemount Gdns
ENC/FH EN2 124 F7
Ridge Rd LWTH SG6 16 E3
Ridge St WATN WD24 117 M4
The Ridge BAR EN5 * 136 D1
Ridgeview LCOL/BKTW AL2 104 D2
Ridge Vw TRING HP23 169 N12
Ridgeview Cl BAR EN5 136 B2
Ridgeview Rd
TRDG/WHET N20 136 F6
Ridgeway BERK HP4 79 K1
DUN/WHIP LU6 172 A1
HARP AL5 * 46 C1
LBUZ LU7 170 A7
RAD WD7 104 A5
Ridge Wy
RKW/CH/CXG WD3 129 M3
Ridgeway STDN SG11 164 H12
STVG SG1 11 H4
WGCE AL7 50 F8
Ridgeway Av
DUN/HR/TOD LU5 26 B7
EBAR EN4 137 K2
Ridgeway Cl CSHM HP5 96 F2
HHS/BOV HP3 82 D7
Ridgeway Dr
DUN/HR/TOD LU5 26 C8
Ridgeway Rd CSHM HP5 96 F2
Ridgeways HLWE CM17 76 C5
ROY SG8 * 15 G6
The Ridgeway AMSS HP7 113 J6
ENC/FH EN2 124 A2
FBAR/BDGN N11 137 K7
HERT/WAT SG14 52 D6
HTCH/STOT SG5 157 M7
HTCHE/RSTV SG4 176 F8
MLHL NW7 135 M7
POTB/CUF EN6 107 L1
POTB/CUF EN6 123 K1
RAD WD7 119 K3
RYLN/HDSTN HA2 142 D7
STALE/WH AL4 65 L6
WARE SG12 54 A2
WAT WD17 117 J3
Ridgewood Dr HARP AL5 46 C2
Ridgewood Gdns HARP AL5 46 C1
Ridgmont Rd STAL AL1 9 H8
Ridgway Rd LTNE LU2 7 H2
Ridings Av WCHMH N21 124 F8
The Ridings AMS HP6 113 H1
BSF CM23 43 K5
CSHM HP5 114 B2
EBAR EN4 * 137 J3
HERT/WAT SG14 52 E8
LTNN/LIM LU3 6 B1
STALW/RED AL3 172 G3
STVGE SG2 11 L8
Ridler Rd EN EN1 125 J4
Ridley Gdns RBSF CM22 167 L3
Ridlins End STVGE SG2 34 A7
Rigby Pl PEND EN3 126 E3
Rigery La STDN SG11 180 D3
Rigeway Vw LBUZ LU7 169 P5
Riley Rd PEND EN3 126 A4
Ringlewell Cl EN EN1 125 M6
Ringshall Dr BERK HP4 170 H9
Ringshall Rd BERK HP4 170 H6
Ringtale Pl BLDK SG7 149 M12
Ringway Rd LCOL/BKTW AL2 102 F1
Ringwood Cl PIN HA5 * 142 A5
Ringwood Rd LTNE LU2 28 B3
Ripley Rd ENC/FH EN2 125 G5
LTNW/LEA LU4 27 G8
Ripley Wy CHESW EN7 109 M4
HHW HP1 81 J1
Ripon Rd STVG SG1 21 K7
Ripon Wy BORE WD6 135 G1
STALE/WH AL4 66 B6
Risdens HLWS CM18 95 G1
Risedale Cl HHNE HP2 5 J8
Risedale Hl HHNE HP2 5 J8
Risedale Rd HHNE HP2 5 J8
The Rise AMSS HP7 113 G5
BLDK SG7 17 J2
BORE WD6 134 D1
EDGW HA8 134 F8
LCOL/BKTW AL2 85 H7
Rising Hill Cl NTHWD HA6 * 141 G1
Risingholme Cl BUSH WD23 132 F3
KTN/HRWW/WS HA3 143 J3
Risingholme Rd
KTN/HRWW/WS HA3 143 J4
Ritcroft Cl HHS/BOV HP3 82 F3
Ritcroft Dr HHS/BOV HP3 82 F3
Ritcroft St HHS/BOV HP3 82 F3
Ritz Ct POTB/CUF EN6 106 E5
Rivenhall End WGCE AL7 51 G7
River Av HOD EN11 72 F6
Riverbank HHW HP1 62 A6
Riverbanks Cl HARP AL5 47 G1
River Cl CHES/WCR EN8 110 E8
RSLP HA4 141 E8
River Ct HTCH/STOT SG5 157 P1
WARE SG12 * 53 J1
Riverdene EDGW HA8 135 G7
Riverfield La SBW CM21 183 Q6
Riverford Cl HARP AL5 46 F1
River Front EN EN1 125 H7
River Hl STALW/RED AL3 173 K7
River Md HTCH/STOT SG5 157 L3
River Meads WARE SG12 55 G8
Rivermill HLW CM20 2 C2
River Pk HHW HP1 4 A7
Riversend Rd HHS/BOV HP3 4 E9
Riversfield Rd EN EN1 125 J7
Rivershill HERT/WAT SG14 178 G6
Riverside BSF CM23 43 M2
BUNT SG9 159 J10
LCOL/BKTW AL2 104 C1
WLYN AL6 176 H12
Riverside Av BROX EN10 92 E4
Riverside Ct KGLGY WD4 100 F3
Riverside Ct CSHM HP5 * 97 G7
HLW CM20 183 N11
Riverside Dr
RKW/CH/CXG WD3 130 B4
Riverside Gdns BERK HP4 59 L8
ENC/FH EN2 125 G6
Riverside Ms BROX EN10 * 92 C5
WARE SG12 * 54 B4
Riverside Rd LTNN/LIM LU3 27 L4
OXHEY WD19 131 M2
STAL AL1 9 G8
Riversmead HOD EN11 72 E8
Riversmeet HERT/WAT SG14 52 F8
River St WARE SG12 54 C4
River Vw WGCE AL7 50 C3
River Wy HLW CM20 183 L12
LTNN/LIM LU3 27 J4
Rivett Cl BLDK SG7 149 L12
Robarts Cl PIN HA5 141 M7
Robbery Bottom La
WLYN AL6 177 M9
Robb Rd STAN HA7 143 L1
Robbs Cl HHW HP1 61 L8
Robe End HHW HP1 61 K8
Robert Av STAL AL1 85 G6
Robert Cl POTB/CUF EN6 106 C7
Roberts Cl CHES/WCR EN8 110 C4
Roberts Ct HTCHE/RSTV SG4 175 R3
Roberts La CFSP/GDCR SL9 128 E8
Robertson Cl BROX EN10 92 C8
Robertson Rd BERK HP4 80 B1
Roberts Rd MLHL NW7 136 C8
WATW WD18 13 G7
Roberts Wy HAT AL10 87 K1
Roberts Wood Dr
CFSP/GDCR SL9 128 D8
Robert Wallace Cl BSF CM23 166 B12
Robeson Wy BORE WD6 121 G5
Robina Cl NTHWD HA6 141 K4
Robin Cl MLHL NW7 135 J6
WARE SG12 73 G2
Robin Ct HARP AL5 * 46 F1
Robin Hl BERK HP4 80 A2
Robin Hood Dr BUSH WD23 118 D5
KTN/HRWW/WS HA3 143 K2
Robin Hood La HAT AL10 67 L7
Robin Hood Meadow
HHNE HP2 62 D5
Robin Hood Rd RBSF CM22 167 L4
Robin Md WGCE AL7 50 E4
Robin Pl GSTN WD25 * 101 M6
Robins Cl LCOL/BKTW AL2 104 C1
Robinsfield HHW HP1 4 A3
Robins Nest Hl HERT/BAY SG13 70 A8
Robinson Av CHESW EN7 108 F2
Robinson Cl BSF CM23 43 M4
ENC/FH EN2 125 G7
Robinson Crs BUSH WD23 133 G4
Robins Orch CFSP/GDCR SL9 138 C1
Robins Rd HHS/BOV HP3 5 M7
Robins Wy HAT AL10 87 K3
Robinswood LTNE LU2 28 C4
Robin Wy POTB/CUF EN6 108 C2
Robson Cl CFSP/GDCR SL9 128 C8
ENC/FH EN2 124 F6
Robsons Cl CHES/WCR EN8 110 A3
Rochester Av LTNE LU2 29 G5
Rochester Cl EN EN1 125 J5
Rochester Dr GSTN WD25 * 118 A1
PIN HA5 142 B7
Rochester Rd NTHWD HA6 141 K5
Rochester Wy
RKW/CH/CXG WD3 116 F8
ROY SG8 14 E5
Rochford Av WAB EN9 111 H8
Rochford Cl BROX EN10 92 C8
Rochford Dr LTNE LU2 29 J7
Rochford Rd BSF CM23 166 D12
Rockcliffe Av KGLGY WD4 100 F4
Rockfield Av WARE SG12 54 B2
Rockingham Cl LBUZ LU7 169 P6
Rockingham Ga BUSH WD23 133 G2
Rockingham Wy STVG SG1 10 F8
Rocklands Dr
KTN/HRWW/WS HA3 143 M4
Rockleigh HERT/WAT SG14 53 G7
Rockley Rd LTN LU1 40 E3
Rock Rd ROY SG8 14 D5
Rockways BAR EN5 135 K2
Rodeheath LTNW/LEA LU4 27 H6
Roden Cl HLWE CM17 76 D1
Rodgers Cl BORE WD6 134 B2
Rodings Rw BAR EN5 * 122 C8
Rodmell Slope
NFNCH/WDSPK N12 136 D8
Rodney Av STAL AL1 85 L4
Rodney Cl LTNW/LEA LU4 26 D6
Rodney Crs HOD EN11 72 E5
Rodney Gdns PIN HA5 141 M7
Rodwell Yd TRING HP23 57 L2
Roebuck Cl HERT/BAY SG13 53 L7
LTN LU1 40 E3
Roebuck Ct STVGE SG2 33 K8
Roebuck Ga STVGE SG2 33 K8
Roe Cl HTCH/STOT SG5 148 C8
Roedean Av PEND EN3 126 A5
Roedean Cl LTNE LU2 29 H6
PEND EN3 126 A5
Roe End La STALW/RED AL3 172 C5
Roefields Cl HHS/BOV HP3 81 L6
Roe Green Cl HAT AL10 87 J1
Roe Green La HAT AL10 67 K8
Roe Hill Cl HAT AL10 87 K1
Roehyde Wy HAT AL10 87 J3
Roestock Gdns STALE/WH AL4 87 J4
Roestock La STALE/WH AL4 87 H5
Rofant Rd NTHWD HA6 141 J1
Rogate Rd LTNE LU2 29 G4
Rogers Cl CHESW EN7 109 H1
Roger's La BUNT SG9 160 A4
Rogers Ruff NTHWD HA6 141 G3
Rogers Wk
NFNCH/WDSPK N12 136 F6
Rokewood Ms WARE SG12 54 B3
Roland St STAL AL1 9 M6
Rolfe Cl EBAR EN4 123 J8
Rolleston Cl WARE SG12 54 A2
Rollswood WGCE AL7 68 C2
Rollswood Rd WLYN AL6 176 G10
Rollys La BLDK SG7 149 P1
Roman Cl DEN/HRF UB9 139 L3
Roman Gdns DUN/HR/TOD LU5 25 M5
KGLGY WD4 100 F4
Roman La BLDK SG7 17 K1
Roman Rd BORE WD6 134 B2
Roman Ri SBW CM21 183 P7
Roman Rd
AMP/FLIT/BLC MK45 155 K2
HHW HP1 60 F4
LTNW/LEA LU4 27 J6
RAD WD7 119 L1
Romans End STALW/RED AL3 85 G4
Roman St HOD EN11 72 E6
Roman V HLWE CM17 183 N12
Roman Wk RAD WD7 * 119 K2
Roman Wy STALW/RED AL3 172 G3
STDN SG11 163 P10
WAB EN9 126 F1
WLYN AL6 177 J12
Romany Cl LWTH SG6 16 A3
Romany Ct HHNE HP2 83 G1
Romeland BORE WD6 134 B2
STALW/RED AL3 8 D6
WAB EN9 111 G7
Romeland Hl STALW/RED AL3 8 D6
Romilly Dr OXHEY WD19 132 C7
Ronart St
KTN/HRWW/WS HA3 143 K5
Rondini Av LTNN/LIM LU3 27 M7
Ronsons Wy STALE/WH AL4 65 K6
Rookery Dr LTNE LU2 28 C3
The Rookery STSD CM24 166 G5
Rookery Yd STVG SG1 10 B1
Rookes Cl LWTH SG6 16 F6
Rooks Cl WGCW AL8 50 B8
Rooks Hl RKW/CH/CXG WD3 116 A8
WGCW AL8 50 A8
Rooks Nest La ROY SG8 151 M6
Rook Tree Cl
HTCH/STOT SG5 * 148 E7
Rook Tree La HTCH/STOT SG5 148 D6
Rookwood Dr STVGE SG2 33 M8
Rosary Ct POTB/CUF EN6 106 F4
Rosary Gdns BUSH WD23 133 J3
Rose Acre STALW/RED AL3 173 P11
Roseacre Gdns WGCE AL7 51 G7
Roseacres SBW CM21 183 P6
Rosebank WAB EN9 111 J8
Rose Bank Cl
NFNCH/WDSPK N12 137 J8
Rosebarn La TRING HP23 168 H8
Roseberry Ct WAT WD17 117 L5
Rosebery BSF CM23 44 C3
Rosebery Av HARP AL5 46 D3
Rosebery Rd BUSH WD23 132 F4
RAYLNE/WEN HP22 168 D12
Rosebery Wy TRING HP23 169 M12
Rosebriar Wk WATN WD24 117 K2
Rose Cots ARL/CHE SG15 147 Q3
Rose Ct AMS HP6 113 J3
CHESW EN7 109 L1
DUN/WHIP LU6 37 H3
Rosecroft Ct NTHWD HA6 * 141 G1
Rosecroft Dr WAT WD17 117 J3
Rosecroft La WLYN AL6 177 N9
Rosecroft Wk PIN HA5 142 B7
Rosedale DUN/HR/TOD LU5 26 C4
WGCE AL7 50 D3
Rosedale Av CHESW EN7 109 K3
Rosedale Cl LCOL/BKTW AL2 102 C4
LTNN/LIM LU3 27 G2
STAN HA7 143 M1
Rosedale Wy CHESW EN7 109 L2
Rose Dr CSHM HP5 97 H6
Rose Gdns WATW WD18 12 D8
Roseheath HHW HP1 81 J1
Rosehill BERK HP4 79 M1
Rosehill Cl HOD EN11 72 D7
Rosehill Gdns ABLGY WD5 101 G6
Roselands Av HOD EN11 72 D5
Rose La STALE/WH AL4 48 A5
Rose Lawn BUSH WD23 133 G4
Rosemary Av ENC/FH EN2 125 H5
Rosemary Dr LCOL/BKTW AL2 85 L8
Rosemary La HNLW SG16 147 J6
Rose Md POTB/CUF EN6 107 G4
Rosemead RAYLNE/WEN HP22 56 C4
Rose Meadow STDN SG11 163 Q1
Rosemont Cl LWTH SG6 16 C3
Rosemoor Cl WGCE AL7 50 D8
Rosemount HLWW/ROY CM19 74 F8
Roseneath Wk EN EN1 125 J8
Rosens Wk EDGW HA8 134 F6
Rose V HOD EN11 72 E7
Rose Wk ROY SG8 14 D6
STALE/WH AL4 65 M8
The Rose Wk RAD WD7 119 M2
Roseway EDGW HA8 135 G7
Rose Wood Cl LTNE LU2 28 D7
Rosewood Ct HHW HP1 * 81 J1
Rosewood Dr ENC/FH EN2 124 E1
Roslyn Cl BROX EN10 92 C3
Roslyn Wy DUN/HR/TOD LU5 25 L4
Ross Av MLHL NW7 136 C8
Ross Cl KTN/HRWW/WS HA3 143 G2
LTN LU1 40 F3
Ross Ct STVGE SG2 11 M1
Ross Crs GSTN WD25 117 L1
Rossendale Cl ENC/FH EN2 124 F3
Rossetti Ldg ROY SG8 * 14 E5
Rossfold Rd LTNN/LIM LU3 27 H1
Rossington Av BORE WD6 120 C4
Rossington Cl EN EN1 125 M4
Rossiter Flds BAR EN5 136 C2

Rosslyn Av *EBAR* EN4 ....137 J2
Rosslyn Crs *HRW* HA1 ....143 K6
  LTNN/LIM LU3 ....28 E4
Rossmore Cl *PEND* EN3 ....28 E4
Rossway *LTN* LU1 ....40 F8
Ross Wy *NTHWD* HA6 ....131 K4
Rossway Dr *BUSH* WD23 ....133 G1
Rossway La *TRING* HP23 ....58 E5
Roswell Cl *CHES/WCR* EN8 ....110 C4
Rothamsted Av *HARP* AL5 ....46 D4
Rother Cl *GSTN* WD25 ....102 A8
Rother Fld *LTNE* LU2 ....29 H6
Rotherfield Rd *EN* EN1 ....126 B3
Rotherwood Cl *DUN/WHIP* LU6 ....25 J8
Rothesay Rd *LTN* LU1 ....6 C6
Rothschild Av
  RAYLNE/WEN HP22 ....168 C12
  HHW HP1 4
Roughdown Av *HHS/BOV* HP3 ....81 L5
Roughdown Rd *HHW* HP1 ....4 B8
Roughdown Villas Rd
  HHS/BOV HP3 ....81 L5
The Roughs *NTHWD* HA6 ....131 J6
Roughwood Cl *WAT* WD17 ....117 J4
Roughwood La *CSTG* HP8 ....128 C2
Roundabout La *WLYN* AL6 ....177 M9
Roundbush La *GSTN* WD25 ....119 G4
Round Coppice Rd *STSD* CM24 ....45 C1
Roundfield Av *HARP* AL5 ....47 H1
Roundhaye *STDN* SG11 ....163 P10
Roundhedge Wy
  ENC/FH EN2 ....124 D4
Roundhill Dr *ENC/FH* EN2 ....124 D4
Roundhills *WAB* EN9 ....111 J8
The Roundings
  HERT/BAY SG13 ....71 M4
Roundmoor Dr
  CHES/WCR EN8 ....110 C3
The Roundway *WATW* WD18 ....131 K4
Roundwood *KGLGY* WD4 ....100 C1
Roundwood Dr
  HTCHE/RSTV SG4 ....16 A1
  WLYN AL6 ....177 K9
Roundwood Dr *WGCW* AL8 ....50 A6
Roundwood Gdns *HARP* AL5 ....46 C5
Roundwood La *HARP* AL5 ....173 R6
Roundwood Pk *HARP* AL5 ....46 C7
Round Wood Rd *HARP* AL5 ....46 C7
Rounton Rd *WAB* EN9 ....111 J7
Rousebarn La
  RKW/CH/CXG WD3 ....116 F6
Rouse Ct *CFSP/GDCR* SL9 ....138 D7
Rowan Cl *HTCHE/RSTV* SG4 ....21 M1
  LCOL/BKTW AL2 ....102 E5
  LTN LU1 ....40 F2
  STALE/WH AL4 ....86 C2
Rowan Crs *LWTH* SG6 ....16 C3
  STVG SG1 ....33 H2
Rowan Dr *BROX* EN10 ....92 D6
Rowan Gv *HTCHE/RSTV* SG4 ....57 Q9
Rowans *WGCE* AL7 ....50 E4
The Rowans *BLDK* SG7 ....13 L7
  BROX EN10 ....92 C1
  CFSP/GDCR SL9 ....138 A5
  HHW HP1 ....4 A2
Rowantree Ms *ENC/FH* EN2 ....124 F6
Rowantree Rd *ENC/FH* EN2 ....124 F6
Rowan Wk *SBW* CM21 ....183 Q7
Rowan Wy *HARP* AL5 ....47 G5
Rowben Cl *TRDG/WHET* N20 ....136 F4
Rowborough Rd
  RAYLNE/WEN HP22 ....56 B6
Rowcroft *HHW* HP1 ....81 J3
Rowelfield *LTNE* LU2 ....29 G8
Rowen Wk *CSHM* HP5 ....96 F4
Rowington Ct *LTN* LU2 ....29 J7
Rowland Hill Ct *BUNT* SG9 ....159 J10
Rowland Rd *NTHWD* HA6 ....141 J2
Rowland Rd *STVG* SG1 ....10 F7
Rowlands Av *PIN* HA5 ....142 E1
Rowlands Cl *CHES/WCR* EN8 ....110 A4
Rowlandsfields
  CHES/WCR EN8 * 110 B4
Rowland Wy *LWTH* SG6 ....16 D3
Rowlatt Dr *STALW/RED* AL3 ....84 E4
Rowley Cl *OXHEY* WD19 ....13 L9
Rowley Green Rd *BAR* EN5 ....135 L1
Rowley's Rd *HERT/BAY* SG13 ....53 K6
Rowley Wk *HHNE* HP2 ....63 G5
Rowney La *BORE* WD6 ....121 H6
Rowney La *WARE* SG12 ....179 L6
Rowney Wd *SBW* CM21 ....183 M8
The Rows *CM20* 2 D5
Roxborough Rd *HRW* HA1 ....143 H7
Royal Av *CHES/WCR* EN8 ....110 C7
Royal Cl *HHS/BOV* HP3 5
Royal Dr *FBAR/BDGN* N11 ....137 L8
Royal Oak Cl *BUNT* SG9 ....158 H4
Royal Oak Gdns *BSF* CM23 ....43 L3
Royal Oak La *HTCH/STOT* SG5 ....156 F1
Royal Rd *STAL* AL1 ....85 M2
Royal Wk *DUN/WHIP* LU6 ....39 G2
Royce Cl *BROX* EN10 ....92 D3
  DUN/WHIP LU6 ....38 D2
Royce Gv *GSTN* WD25 ....101 K8
Roydon Cl *LTNW/LEA* LU4 ....26 E5
Roydon Ct *HHNE* HP2 ....63 G5
Roydon Rd *HLWW/ROY* CM19 ....74 C4
  WARE SG12 ....73 H1
Royle Cl *CFSP/GDCR* SL9 ....138 D3
Roy Rd *NTHWD* HA6 ....141 K2
Royse Gv *ROY* SG8 ....151 R1
Royston Cl *HERT/WAT* SG14 ....52 F7
Royston Gv *PIN* HA5 ....142 D1
Royston Park Rd *PIN* HA5 ....142 D1
Royston Rd *BLDK* SG7 ....149 L12
  ROY SG8 ....152 H2
  STAL AL1 ....85 M3
Rubin Pl *PEND* EN3 ....36 E3
Rucklers La *KGLGY* WD4 ....99 L2
Ruckles Cl *STVG* SG1 ....10 F4
Ruckles Wy *AMSS* HP7 ....113 G6
Rudham Rd *LWTH* SG6 ....17 G6
Rudolph Rd *BUSH* WD23 ....132 E2
Rudyard Cl *LTNW/LEA* LU4 ....27 H6
Rue De St Lawrence
  WAB EN9 ....111 G8
Rueley Dell Rd *LTNE* LU2 ....155 R11
Rufford Cl
  KTN/HRWW/WS HA3 ....143 L3
  WAT WD17 ....117 K3
Rugby Cl *HRW* HA1 ....143 J6
Rugby Wy *RKW/CH/CXG* WD3 ....130 F1
The Ruins *STALW/RED* AL3 ....173 R12
Rumballs Ct *BSF* CM23 ....43 J5
Rumballs Rd *HHS/BOV* HP3 ....82 A5
Rumbold Rd *HOD* EN11 ....73 G5
Rumsley *CHESW* EN7 ....109 L1

Runcie Cl *STALE/WH* AL4 ....65 L6
Runcorn Crs *HHNE* HP2 ....62 D6
Rundells *HLWS* CM18 ....95 L1
  LWTH SG6 ....17 H5
Runfold Av *LTNN/LEA* LU3 ....27 L4
Runham Av *LTNN/LEA* LU4 ....26 F5
Runham Rd *HHNE* HP2 ....5 H1
Runley Rd *LTN* LU1 ....40 D2
Runnalow *LWTH* SG6 ....16 F4
Runnymede Ct *LTNN/LIM* LU3 * 27 M3
Runrig Hl *AMS* HP6 ....113 J1
Runsley *WGCE* AL7 ....50 F4
The Runway *HAT* AL10 ....67 H6
Ruscombe Dr *LCOL/BKTW* AL2 ....84 F8
Rushall Gn *LTNE* LU2 ....29 H7
Rushby Md *HLWS* CM18 ....3 M8
Rushby Pl *LWTH* SG6 ....16 A4
Rushby Wk *LWTH* SG6 ....16 B3
Rush Cl *WARE* SG12 ....73 G1
Rushdene Av *STALW/RED* AL4 ....137 J3
Rushdene Rd *PIN* HA5 ....142 A8
Rushden Rd *BUNT* SG9 ....19 M1
Rush Dr *WAB* EN9 ....127 G2
Rushendon Furlong
  LBUZ LU7 ....169 Q4
Rushen Gn *HERT/BAY* SG13 ....72 A2
Rushes Md *HLWS* CM18 ....75 J7
Rushey Hl *ENC/FH* EN2 ....124 D8
Rushfield *POTB/CUF* EN6 ....106 B7
  SBW CM21 ....183 Q7
Rushfield Rd *WARE* SG12 ....54 D2
Rush Gn *WARE* SG12 ....180 G10
Rush La *RBSF* CM22 ....167 L5
Rushleigh Av *CHES/WCR* EN8 ....110 B4
Rushleigh Gn *BSF* CM23 ....43 K6
Rushmere La *CSHM* HP5 ....97 L2
Rushmoor Cl *PIN* HA5 ....141 M6
  RKW/CH/CXG WD3 ....130 B5
Rushmore Ct *WATW* WD18 * 131 H2
Rushout Av
  KTN/HRWW/WS HA3 ....143 M8
Rushton Av *WD25* 117 L1
Rushton Gv *HLWE* CM17 ....76 B5
Ruskin Av *WAB* EN9 ....111 J8
Ruskin Cl *CHESW* EN7 ....91 J8
Ruskin La *HTCHE/RSTV* SG4 ....20 A2
Rusland Park Rd *HRW* HA1 ....143 J6
Rusper Cl *STAN* HA7 ....134 A7
Rusper Gn *LTNE* LU2 ....29 H6
Russell Av *STALW/RED* AL3 ....8 A3
Russell Cl *AMS* HP6 ....113 J1
  DUN/WHIP LU6 ....172 A1
  NTHWD HA6 ....131 G8
  ROY SG8 ....145 P7
  STVG SG2 ....33 M7
Russell Ct *BAR* EN5 * 123 G3
  CSHM HP5 ....97 G3
Russell Crs *GSTN* WD25 ....117 H3
Russellcroft Rd *WGCW* AL8 ....50 A6
Russell Gdns *TRDG/WHET* N20 ....137 J3
Russell Gv *MLHL* NW7 ....135 J8
Russell La *TRDG/WHET* N20 ....137 K5
Russell Ms *LTN* LU1 * 6 D8
Russell Pl *HHS/BOV* HP3 ....81 M5
  HHW HP1 ....4 C8
Russell Ri *LTN* LU1 ....6 D8
Russell Rd *EN* EN1 ....125 K4
  NTHWD HA6 ....131 G6
  TRDG/WHET N20 ....137 J3
Russell's Dr *CHES/WCR* EN8 ....110 C4
Russell's Ride *CHES/WCR* EN8 ....110 B5
Russell St *LTN* LU1 ....6 D7
Russell Wy *OXHEY* WD19 ....131 M3
Russet Cl *CHESW* EN7 * 91 J8
Russet Dr *RAD* WD7 ....104 C3
  STALE/WH AL4 ....86 A3
The Russets *CFSP/GDCR* SL9 ....138 B4
Russett Hl *CFSP/GDCR* SL9 ....138 C5
Russett Wy *DUN/HR/TOD* LU5 ....26 B6
Russett Wd *WGCE* AL7 ....51 H8
Ruston Gdns *STHGT/OAK* N14 ....137 L2
Rutherford Cl *BORE* WD6 ....121 H3
  STVG SG1 ....32 E3
Ruthin Cl *LTN* LU1 ....6 E9
Ruthven Av *CHES/WCR* EN8 ....110 B7
Rutland Cts *LTNE* LU2 * 7 L5
Rutland Pl *BUSH* WD23 * 133 H4
Rutland Rd *HRW* HA1 ....143 G8
The Rutts *BUSH* WD23 ....133 H4
Ryall Cl *LCOL/BKTW* AL2 ....102 C3
Ryan Ct *OXHEY* WD19 * 132 C3
Ryan Wy *WATN* WD24 ....12 A5
Rydal Mt *POTB/CUF* EN6 * 106 C7
Rydal Wy *LTNN/LIM* LU3 ....27 M3
Ryder Av *HTCH/STOT* SG5 ....157 M2
Ryder Cl *BUSH* WD23 ....133 J2
  HERT/BAY SG13 ....53 M6
  HHS/BOV HP3 ....98 J2
Ryders Av *STALE/WH* AL4 ....8 C7
Ryder Seed Ms *STAL* AL1 * 8 E7
The Ryde *BRKMPK* AL9 ....68 A5
Rye Cl *HARP* AL5 ....46 E2
  STVG SG1 ....21 K6
Ryecroft *HAT* AL10 ....87 K2
  HLWW/ROY CM19 ....2 A7
  STVG SG1 ....10 E1
Ryecroft Cl *HHNE* HP2 ....83 G9
Ryecroft Crs *BAR* EN5 ....135 M1
Ryecroft Wy *LTNE* LU2 ....28 E6
Ryefeld Cl *HOD* EN11 ....72 F3
Ryefield *LTNN/LIM* LU3 ....154 G12
Ryefield Crs *PIN* HA5 ....141 L4
Ryefield Pde *NTHWD* HA6 * 141 L4
Rye Gdns *BLDK* SG7 ....149 M12
Rye Hill *HARP* AL5 ....46 F1
  LTNE LU2 ....29 H6
Rye Hill Rd *HLWS* CM18 ....95 H2
Ryelands *WGCE* AL7 ....68 D2
Rye Rd *HOD* EN11 ....72 F6
Ryes La *RBSF* CM22 ....184 H2
Rye St *BSF* CM23 ....43 J2
The Rye *DUN/WHIP* LU6 ....37 H2
Ryhope Rd *FBAR/BDGN* N11 ....137 M7
Rylands Heath *LTNE* LU2 ....28 A7
Ryley Cl *HNLW* SG16 ....147 K5
Rymill Cl *HHS/BOV* HP3 ....98 J2
Ryton Rd *LTN* LU1 ....6 A1

S

Saberton Cl *STALW/RED* AL3 ....63 K1
Sacombe Gn *LTNN/LIM* LU3 ....154 H12
Sacombe Green Rd
  WARE SG12 ....179 N5
Sacombe Pound *WARE* SG12 ....179 M7
Sacombe Rd *HERT/WAT* SG14 ....52 F7
  HHW HP1 ....61 K8
Sacombs Ash La *SBW* CM21 ....183 J2

Saddlers Cl *BAR* EN5 ....135 M1
  BLDK SG7 ....17 J1
  BORE WD6 * 135 H1
  BSF CM23 ....43 J5
Saddlers Pl *ROY* SG8 ....14 D6
Saddlescombe Wy
  NFNCH/WDSPK N12 ....136 B6
Sadleir Rd *STAL* AL1 ....85 J4
Sadler Cl *CHESW* EN7 ....91 G7
Sadlers Md *HLWS* CM18 ....3 M8
Sadlers Wy *HERT/WAT* SG14 ....52 E7
Sadlier Rd *STDN* SG11 ....163 P11
Saffron Cl *ARL/CHE* SG15 ....147 Q2
  HOD EN11 ....72 D6
  LTNE LU2 ....28 B3
Saffron Hl *LWTH* SG6 ....16 C3
Saffron La *HHW* HP1 ....81 L1
Saffron Mdw *STDN* SG11 ....163 Q11
Saffron Rd *DUN/WHIP* LU6 ....37 J3
Sainfoin End *HHNE* HP2 ....62 E6
St Agnells Ct *HHNE* HP2 ....62 E6
St Agnells La *HHNE* HP2 ....62 D5
St Albans Hwy
  HTCHE/RSTV SG4 ....31 K3
St Albans Hl *HHS/BOV* HP3 ....5 H8
St Albans La *ABLGY* WD5 ....83 K8
St Albans Link *STVG* SG1 ....21 K8
St Albans Rd *BAR* EN5 ....122 C5
  GSTN WD25 ....118 A1
  HHNE HP2 ....5 G5
  HTCHE/RSTV SG4 ....176 E9
  POTB/CUF EN6 ....105 J3
  STALW/RED AL3 ....64 A1
  WAT WD17 ....12 E2
  WATN WD24 ....117 M2
St Albans Rd East *HAT* AL10 ....68 A6
St Albans Rd West *HAT* AL10 ....67 H7
St Andrew Ms
  HERT/WAT SG14 * 53 G7
St Andrew's Av *HARP* AL5 ....46 D4
St Andrew's Cl *LTN* LU1 ....40 F8
  NFNCH/WDSPK N12 ....137 G7
St Andrews Ct *WAT* WD17 * 117 M5
St Andrews Dr *STVG* SG1 ....21 J7
St Andrews La
  DUN/HR/TOD LU5 ....26 A4
St Andrew's Meadow
  HLWS CM18 ....3 J8
St Andrew's Pl
  HTCHE/RSTV SG4 ....157 P7
St Andrew's Rd *EN* EN1 ....125 H7
  HHS/BOV HP3 ....82 A6
St Andrews Ter
  OXHEY WD19 * 132 A8
St Andrew St *HERT/WAT* SG14 ....53 G7
St Anne Rd *BAR* EN5 * 136 B1
St Anne's Cl *CHESW* EN7 ....109 K2
St Annes Dr *OXHEY* WD19 ....132 A7
St Anne's Pk *BROX* EN10 ....92 E2
St Annes Rd *DEN/HRF* UB9 ....140 A5
St Anne's Rd *HTCH/STOT* SG5 ....157 P5
St Annes Rd *LCOL/BKTW* AL2 ....104 B1
St Ann's Rd *HRW* HA1 ....143 J6
  LTN LU1 ....6 A9
St Anthonys Av *HHS/BOV* HP3 ....82 A4
St Audreys Cl *HAT* AL10 ....87 M3
St Audreys Gn *WGCE* AL7 ....50 D8
St Augusta Ct *STALW/RED* AL3 * 8 A3
St Augustine Av
  LTNN/LIM LU3 ....27 M6
St Augustine Cl
  HTCH/STOT SG5 ....157 P5
St Augustines Cl *BROX* EN10 ....92 D2
St Augustines Dr *BROX* EN10 ....92 D2
St Bernard's Cl *LTNN/LIM* LU3 ....28 A6
St Bernard's Rd *STALW/RED* AL3 ....8 F3
St Brelades Pl *STALE/WH* AL4 ....66 B6
St Catharine's Ct *BROX* EN10 ....92 D2
St Catherines Av *LTNN/LIM* LU3 ....27 M5
St Catherines Rd *RSLP* HA4 ....141 G7
St Christopher's Cl
  DUN/HR/TOD LU5 ....26 D1
St Christophers Ct
  RKW/CH/CXG WD3 * 115 H8
St Cross Cl *HOD* EN11 ....92 F1
St Cuthberts Gdns *PIN* HA5 * 142 D2
St Cuthberts Rd *HOD* EN11 ....73 G4
St David's Cl *HHS/BOV* HP3 ....83 H4
St David's Dr *BROX* EN10 ....92 D1
St Dunstan's Rd *WARE* SG12 ....182 B9
St Edmunds *BERK* HP4 ....80 A2
St Edmunds Av *RSLP* HA4 ....141 M6
St Edmunds Dr *STAN* HA7 ....143 L3
St Edmunds Wk *STALE/WH* AL4 ....86 A3
St Edmund's Wy *HLWE* CM17 ....76 A1
St Elmo Ct *HTCHE/RSTV* SG4 * 157 P8
St Ethelbert Av *LTNN/LIM* LU3 ....27 M5
St Etheldreda's Dr *HAT* AL10 ....68 A5
St Evroul Ct *WARE* SG12 ....54 B3
St Faith's Cl *ENC/FH* EN2 ....125 G5
St Faiths Cl *HTCHE/RSTV* SG4 ....157 P5
St Francis Cl *BUNT* SG9 ....159 K11
  OXHEY WD19 ....131 M4
  POTB/CUF EN6 ....107 G7
St Francis Dr *DEN/HRF* UB9 ....139 K8
St George's Dr *OXHEY* WD19 ....132 C6
St George's Rd *EN* EN1 ....125 K4
  HHS/BOV HP3 ....82 A6
  WATN WD24 ....117 M4
St George's Wy *STVG* SG1 ....10 D4
St Giles' Av *POTB/CUF* EN6 ....105 L7
St Giles Rd *HTCHE/RSTV* SG4 ....176 F7
St Helen's Cl *STALE/WH* AL4 ....48 B6
St Heliers Rd *STALE/WH* AL4 ....65 M5
St Ives Cl *LTNN/LIM* LU3 ....27 M6
  WLYN AL6 ....50 D2
St James Av *TRDG/WHET* N20 ....137 J6
St James Cl *DUN/HR/TOD* LU5 ....26 D5
  EBAR EN4 ....123 H7
St James Ct *HARP* AL5 ....46 F2
  HARP AL5 ....46 E2
St James Rd *LTNN/LIM* LU3 ....27 M6
St James's Rd *WATW* WD18 ....12 D1
St James's Rd *CHESW* EN7 ....91 G8
St James Wy *BSF* CM23 ....43 L7
St John Cl *LTN* LU1 ....6 A9
St Johns *STDN* SG11 ....163 Q10
St John's Av *FBAR/BDGN* N11 ....137 K8
St Johns Cl *LBUZ* LU7 ....24 A4
St John's Ct *POTB/CUF* EN6 ....107 G7
  TRDG/WHET N20 * 137 J3
St John's Ct *WLYN* AL6 ....177 J11
St John's Crs *STAL* AL1 ....85 M1
St John's Ct *HARP* AL5 ....47 G6
St John's Crs *STSD* CM24 ....166 C6
St John's La *STSD* CM24 ....166 C6
St Johns La *WARE* SG12 ....54 D7
St John's Rd *ARL/CHE* SG15 ....147 Q5

St Johns Rd *HARP* AL5 ....47 G6
St John's Rd *HHW* HP1 ....4 B6
  HRW HA1 ....143 H7
  HTCHE/RSTV SG4 ....157 P8
  STSD CM24 ....166 C6
  WAT WD17 ....12 F2
St John's Ter *ENC/FH* EN2 * 125 H3
St Johns Wk *HLWE* CM17 ....76 A1
St John's Well Ct *BERK* HP4 ....59 M8
St John's Well La *BERK* HP4 ....59 M8
St Joseph's Cl *LTNN/LIM* LU3 ....28 L5
St Joseph's Gn *WGCE* AL7 ....68 B2
St Joseph's Ct
  CHES/WCR EN8 ....110 C7
St Julian's Rd *STAL* AL1 ....8 E9
St Katharines Cl
  HTCH/STOT SG5 ....157 M2
St Katherine's Cl *BERK* HP4 ....59 K8
St Kilda Rd *LTNW/LEA* LU4 ....26 D5
St Kilda's Rd *HRW* HA1 ....143 J8
St Laurence Dr *BROX* EN10 ....92 C5
St Lawrence Cl *ABLGY* WD5 ....101 J4
  HHS/BOV HP3 ....98 E1
St Lawrence Dr *PIN* HA5 ....141 M7
St Lawrences Av *LTNN/LIM* LU3 ....28 A5
St Lawrence Wy
  LCOL/BKTW AL2 ....102 D4
St Leonards Cl *BUSH* WD23 ....13 L5
  HERT/WAT SG14 ....53 H5
St Leonard's Ct *STALE/WH* AL4 ....66 A4
St Leonards Crs *STALE/WH* AL4 ....66 A4
St Leonard's Rd *AMS* HP6 ....113 J1
St Leonard's Rd
  HERT/WAT SG14 ....53 H5
St Leonards Rd *WAB* EN9 ....93 H6
St Leonard's Wy
  DUN/WHIP LU6 ....37 J8
St Louis Cl *POTB/CUF* EN6 ....107 G7
St Luke's Av *ENC/FH* EN2 ....125 H4
St Luke's Cl *LTNW/LEA* LU4 ....27 J7
St Lukes Pl *STAL* AL1 * 85 M3
St Magnus Ct *HHS/BOV* HP3 ....82 F4
St Margaret Rd *LTNW/LEA* LU4 ....27 J7
St Margarets *LTNN/LIM* LU3 ....27 M5
  TRDG/WHET N20 ....137 G4
St Margaret's Cl *BERK* HP4 ....80 B2
St Margarets Cl *LTNN/LIM* LU3 ....154 F7
St Margarets Rd *EDGW* HA8 ....134 F8
  RSLP HA4 ....141 H8
  WARE SG12 ....54 C3
St Margarets Wy *HHNE* HP2 ....83 H2
St Mark's Cl *BAR* EN5 ....122 F7
St Marks Cl *STALE/WH* AL4 ....86 A4
St Martins Av *HHS/BOV* HP3 ....82 A6
St Martin's Cl *EN* EN1 ....125 M5
St Martins Cl *GTDUN* CM6 ....185 Q10
  HARP AL5 ....47 G1
  OXHEY WD19 ....132 A7
St Martins Rd *HOD* EN11 ....73 G8
St Martin's Rd *KNEB* SG3 ....177 N4
St Mary's Av *BERK* HP4 ....59 H7
  HTCH/STOT SG5 ....148 D7
St Mary's Cl *LTN* LU1 ....6 D9
  STVG SG1 ....21 J6
St Mary's Ct *DEN/HRF* UB9 ....139 M5
  HTCH/STOT SG5 ....156 F1
  LWTH SG6 ....16 E7
  STALW/RED AL3 ....173 Q12
St Marys Cl *STVGE* SG2 ....34 C7
  WATW WD18 * 13 G1
  WLYN AL6 ....177 J12
St Marys Ct *POTB/CUF* EN6 ....106 F6
St Marys Cl *WLYN* AL6 ....50 A1
St Mary's Dr *STSD* CM24 ....166 H7
St Marys Ga *DUN/WHIP* LU6 ....38 F1
St Mary's Glebe *LTNW/LEA* LU4 * 27
St Mary's La *HERT/WAT* SG14 ....70 D1
St Marys Pk *ROY* SG8 ....152 H2
St Mary's Ri *SHFD* SG17 ....146 D5
St Marys Ri *HTCHE/RSTV* SG4 ....30 B8
St Mary's Rd *CHES/WCR* EN8 ....110 A3
  LTN LU1 ....6 D9
  WAT WD17 * 13 G1
  WLYN AL6 ....50 A1
St Marys Ter *BORE* WD6 ....134 B2
St Marys Wk *WATW* WD18 * 13 G1
St Mary's Wk *STALE/WH* AL4 ....65 M6
St Mary's Wy *BLDK* SG7 ....13 J3
  CFSP/GDCR SL9 ....138 A3
  CSHM HP5 ....96 F6
St Matthews Cl *LTNE* LU2 ....7 G3
  OXHEY WD19 ....13 J9
St Michaels Av
  DUN/HR/TOD LU5 ....25 L5
St Michael's Av *HHS/BOV* HP3 ....82 A6
St Michaels Cl *HARP* AL5 ....47 H6
St Michael's Cl *HLWE* CM20 ....3 H1
  NFNCH/WDSPK N12 ....137 J8
St Michaels Cl
  RAYLNE/WEN HP22 ....56 A4
St Michaels Crs *LTNN/LIM* LU3 ....28 A6
  PIN HA5 ....142 C8
St Michaels Dr *GSTN* WD25 ....101 M7
St Michaels Mt
  HTCHE/RSTV SG4 ....157 Q5
St Michael's Rd *BROX* EN10 ....92 D7
St Michaels Rd
  HTCHE/RSTV SG4 ....157 R5
St Michael's St *STALW/RED* AL3 * 8 A4
St Michaels Wy
  POTB/CUF EN6 ....106 F4
St Mildreds Av *LTNN/LIM* LU3 ....27 M5
St Monicas Av *LTNN/LIM* LU3 ....27 M6
St Neots Cl *BORE* WD6 ....120 E4
St Nicholas Cl *AMSS* HP7 ....113 M5
  BORE WD6 ....134 B2
St Nicholas Fld *BSF* CM23 ....161 P9
St Nicholas Gn *HLWE* CM17 ....76 A4
St Nicholas Mt *HHW* HP1 ....81 K2
St Ninian's Ct
  TRDG/WHET N20 ....137 K6
St Olam's Cl *LTNN/LIM* LU3 ....27 M5
St Olives *HTCH/STOT* SG5 ....148 C7
St Onge Pde *EN* EN1 * 125 H7
St Paul's Cl *BORE* WD6 ....121 G1
St Paul's Gdns *LTN* LU1 ....41 M4
St Paul's Pl *STAL* AL1 ....9 G1
St Paul's Rd *HHNE* HP2 ....5 G1
  LTN LU1 ....41 J4
St Pauls Wy *WAB* EN9 * 111 H7
  WATN WD24 ....13 H2
St Peter's Av *ARL/CHE* SG15 ....147 Q2
St Peter's Cl *BAR* EN5 ....135 M1
  BUSH WD23 ....133 H4
St Peters Cl *HAT* AL10 ....67 J1
St Peter's Cl
  RKW/CH/CXG WD3 ....129 M5

STAL AL1 ....8 B9
St Peters Ct *CFSP/GDCR* SL9 * 138 C3
St Peters Hl *TRING* HP23 ....57 L1
St Peter's Rd *DUN/HR/TOD* LU5 ....39 C1
St Peters Rd *LTN* LU1 ....6 B5
St Peter's St *STAL* AL1 ....9 C5
St Peters Wy
  RKW/CH/CXG WD3 ....114 F8
St Ronans Ct *EBAR* EN4 ....123 H4
St Saviours Crs *LTN* LU1 ....6 D7
St Stephen's Av
  STALW/RED AL3 ....84 F5
St Stephen's Cl
  STALW/RED AL3 ....84 F5
St Stephen's Hl
  STALW/RED AL3 ....85 G4
St Stephens Rd *BAR* EN5 ....136 B5
St Stephen's Rd *PEND* EN3 ....126 B3
St Thomas' Dr *PIN* HA5 ....142 C5
St Thomas Pl *STALE/WH* AL4 ....48 B5
St Thomas's Cl *LTNE* LU2 ....28 E7
  WAB EN9 ....111 M7
St Thomas's Rd *LTNE* LU2 ....28 E7
St Ursula Gv *PIN* HA5 ....142 B7
St Vincent Gdns *LTNW/LEA* LU4 * 27 H6
St Vincents Cl *STALE/WH* AL4 ....85 L4
St Vincents Cots *WATW* WD18 * 12 C5
St Vincents La *MLHL* NW7 ....135 M7
St Vincent's Wy
  POTB/CUF EN6 ....107 G8
St Wilfrid's Ct *EBAR* EN4 * 137 J1
St Wilfrid's Rd *EBAR* EN4 ....137 H1
St Winifreds Av *LTNN/LIM* LU3 ....28 A5
Sakins Cft *HLWS* CM18 ....75 K8
Sale Pl *BLDK* SG7 ....149 K12
Salisbury Av *HARP* AL5 ....46 D3
  STAL AL1 ....85 M1
Salisbury Cl *AMSS* HP7 ....113 J5
  BSF CM23 ....43 M4
  HTCH/STOT SG5 ....148 B11
  POTB/CUF EN6 ....107 G6
Salisbury Crs *CHES/WCR* EN8 ....110 B6
Salisbury Gdns *WGCE* AL7 ....50 B8
Salisbury Hall Dr *HAT* AL10 ....67 H6
Salisbury Rd *BAR* EN5 ....122 C7
  BLDK SG7 ....149 J12
  HARP AL5 ....47 H2
  HOD EN11 ....73 G6
  HRW HA1 ....143 H7
  LTN LU1 ....6 D7
  PEND EN3 ....126 D3
  PIN HA5 ....141 L6
  STVG SG1 ....21 L7
  WATN WD24 ....117 M4
  WGCE AL7 * 50 D8
Salisbury Sq *HERT/WAT* SG14 * 53 H1
Sallowsprings *DUN/WHIP* LU6 ....38 D8
Sally Deards La *WLYN* AL6 ....176 H5
Salmon Cl *WGCE* AL7 ....50 E8
Salmond Cl *STAN* HA7 ....143 L1
Salmons Cl *WARE* SG12 ....54 B2
Saltdean Cl *LTNE* LU2 ....29 H6
Salters *BSF* CM23 ....43 J5
Salter's Cl *BERK* HP4 ....59 K7
Salters Cl *RKW/CH/CXG* WD3 ....130 C4
Salters Gdns *WAT* WD17 * 117 L5
Salters Wy *DUN/WHIP* LU6 ....25 K8
Saltfield Crs *LTNN/LEA* LU4 ....26 D5
Salusbury La *HTCH/STOT* SG5 ....156 E11
Salwey Crs *BROX* EN10 ....92 D2
Samian Ga *STALW/RED* AL3 ....84 D4
Sampson Av *BAR* EN5 ....136 B1
Samuel Cl *STAN* HA7 ....133 L5
Samuel Sq *STAL* AL1 * 8 E7
Sancroft Rd
  KTN/HRWW/WS HA3 ....143 K4
Sanctuary Cl *DEN/HRF* UB9 ....139 K8
Sandalls Spring *HHW* HP1 ....61 K8
Sandalwood Cl *LTNN/LIM* LU3 ....27 M2
Sanday Cl *HHS/BOV* HP3 ....82 F4
Sandbrook La *TRING* HP23 ....168 G3
Sandell Cl *LTNE* LU2 ....28 D7
Sandeman Gdns *WARE* SG12 ....54 C3
Sanderling Cl *WLYN* AL6 ....177 J12
Sanders Cl *LCOL/BKTW* AL2 ....104 B1
Sanders Ct *ENC/FH* EN2 * 124 F1
Sanders Rd *HHS/BOV* HP3 ....5 G9
Sandfield Rd *STAL* AL1 ....9 M5
Sandgate Rd *LTNW/LEA* LU4 ....27 H7
Sandhurst Av
  RYLN/HDSTN HA2 ....142 F8
Sandhurst Ct *HARP* AL5 ....47 H1
Sandifield *HAT* AL10 ....87 M3
Sandland Cl *DUN/WHIP* LU6 ....25 J8
Sandle Rd *BSF* CM23 ....44 A2
Sandon Cl *TRING* HP23 ....57 K1
Sandon Rd *CHES/WCR* EN8 ....110 A4
Sandover Cl *HTCHE/RSTV* SG4 ....157 R7
Sandown Rd *STVG* SG1 ....22 A8
  WATN WD24 ....118 A4
Sandpit La *STAL* AL1 ....9 H3
  STALE/WH AL4 ....66 M8
Sandpit Rd *WGCE* AL7 ....68 C1
Sandridgebury La
  STALW/RED AL3 ....65 J5
Sandridge Cl *EBAR* EN4 ....123 J3
  HRW HA1 ....143 J6
Sandridge Pk *STALW/RED* AL3 ....65 K5
Sandridge Rd *STAL* AL1 ....9 H2
Sandringham Av
  HLWW/ROY CM19 ....74 C5
Sandringham Cl *EN* EN1 ....125 J3
Sandringham Crs
  STALE/WH AL4 ....65 L6
Sandringham Dr
  DUN/HR/TOD LU5 ....26 C5
Sandringham Gdns *BSF* CM23 ....43 L4
Sandringham Rd
  POTB/CUF EN6 ....106 F4
  WATN WD24 ....117 M3
Sandringham Wy
  CHES/WCR EN8 ....110 A8
Sandwood Ms *CSHM* HP5 ....96 F4
Sandy Cl *HERT/WAT* SG14 ....52 F7
Sandycroft Rd *AMS* HP6 ....113 M5
Sandy Gv *HTCHE/RSTV* SG4 ....157 P7
Sandy La *BUSH* WD23 ....131 L6
  NTHWD HA6 ....131 L6
Sandy Ldg *PIN* HA5 * 142 E1
Sandy Lodge Ct *NTHWD* HA6 * 131 J4
Sandy Lodge La *NTHWD* HA6 ....131 J3
Sandy Lodge Rd
  RKW/CH/CXG WD3 ....130 F5
Sandy Lodge Wy *NTHWD* HA6 ....131 H4
Sandymount Av *STAN* HA7 ....134 A8
Sandy Ri *CFSP/GDCR* SL9 ....138 C3
Sanfoine *HTCHE/RSTV* SG4 ....20 A1
Sanfoin Rd *LTNW/LEA* LU4 ....26 B5
Santers La *POTB/CUF* EN6 ....106 C7
Santingfield North *LTN* LU1 ....6 A8

Santingfield South LTN LU1 40 F4
Sappers Cl SBW CM21 183 R7
Sargents STDN SG11 163 R12
Sarita Cl KTN/HRWW/WS HA3 143 H4
Sarnesfield Rd ENC/FH EN2 * 125 H8
Sarratt Av HHNE HP2 62 E5
Sarratt La RKW/CH/CXG WD3 115 M6
Sarum Pl HHNE HP2 62 C6
Sarum Rd LTNN/LIM LU3 27 J5
Satinwood Ct HHNE HP2 5 J6
Saturn Wy HHNE HP2 62 D7
Sauncey Av HARP AL5 46 F2
Sauncey Wd HARP AL5 47 H1
Sauncey Wood La HARP AL5 175 J12
Saunders Cl CHES/WCR EN8 110 A2
LWTH SG6 16 F2
Saunders End AMS HP6 96 A8
Savill Cl CHESW EN7 * 91 G7
Saville Cl SAFWS CB11 161 P5
Saville Rw PEND EN3 126 B6
Savoy Cl DEN/HRF UB9 140 B4
EDGW HA8 134 E8
Savoy Ms STAL AL1 84 F5
Savoy Pde EN EN1 * 125 J7
Savoy Wd HLWW/ROY CM19 94 E3
Sawbridgeworth Rd
RBSF CM22 184 B4
Sawells BROX EN10 92 D3
Sawpit La BSF CM23 161 R10
Sawtry Cl LTNN/LIM LU3 27 L3
Sawtry Wy BORE WD6 120 E4
Sawyers La POTB/CUF EN6 106 B8
Sawyers Wy HHNE HP2 5 K3
Saxon Av HTCH/STOT SG5 148 D5
Saxon Cl AMS HP6 113 H4
DUN/WHIP LU6 38 C1
HARP AL5 47 G1
LWTH SG6 148 D12
Saxon Ct BORE WD6 120 C5
Saxon Crs
AMP/FLIT/BLC MK45 155 J1
Saxon Rd LTNN/LIM LU3 27 M7
STALE/WH AL4 48 B6
WLYN AL6 49 M2
Saxon Wy BLDK SG7 149 M12
ROY SG8 15 K1
Saxtead Cl LTNE LU2 29 H8
Saxton Ms WAT WD17 * 117 L5
Sayers Gdns BERK HP4 59 L6
Sayer Wy KNEB SG3 177 M5
Sayesbury Av SBW CM21 183 P6
Sayesbury Rd SBW CM21 183 Q7
Sayes Gdns SBW CM21 183 R7
Saywell Rd LTNE LU2 7 M1
Sayward Cl CSHM HP5 97 H3
Scammell Wy WATW WD18 12 B9
Scarborough Av STVG SG1 32 E2
Scarlett Av RAYLNE/WEN HP22 56 C7
Scatterdells La KGLGY WD4 99 K4
Scatterdells Pk KGLGY WD4 * 99 L4
Scawsby Cl DUN/WHIP LU6 25 J8
Scaynes Link
NFNCH/WDSPK N12 136 E7
Scholars Cl BAR EN5 122 C8
Scholar's Hl WARE SG12 55 K1
Scholars Ms WGCW AL8 50 B5
Scholars Wk CFSP/GDCR SL9 138 C1
Scholars Wy AMS HP6 113 K4
School Cl BRKMPK AL9 69 K7
CSHM HP5 96 F2
STVGE SG2 11 L8
Schoolfields LWTH SG6 17 G4
School Gdns BERK HP4 60 F7
School La AMSS HP7 112 E5
BRKMPK AL9 69 K7
BUSH WD23 132 F4
CFSP/GDCR SL9 138 B4
CHONG CM5 77 H7
DUN/WHIP LU6 37 J3
DUN/WHIP LU6 171 P5
HAT AL10 67 M7
HERT/WAT SG14 178 G6
HLW CM20 3 G1
HTCH/STOT SG5 156 E10
HTCHE/RSTV SG4 18 A8
HTCHE/RSTV SG4 31 J3
LCOL/BKTW AL2 102 D8
LTNW/LEA LU4 27 H5
PIN HA5 * 142 C6
ROY SG8 153 J4
STVGE SG2 23 K6
STVGE SG2 34 C7
WLYN AL6 49 M1
WLYN AL6 51 J4
School Md ABLGY WD5 101 H6
School Pde DEN/HRF UB9 * 140 A4
School Rd POTB/CUF EN6 107 G4
School Rw HHW HP1 81 K3
School Wk LWTH SG6 16 F3
Schubert Rd BORE WD6 134 B2
Scot Gv PIN HA5 142 B2
Scotland Green Rd North
PEND EN3 126 B8
Scotscraig RAD WD7 119 K1
Scots Hl RKW/CH/CXG WD3 130 D2
Scots Hill Cl
RKW/CH/CXG WD3 130 D2
Scots Mill La
RKW/CH/CXG WD3 130 D2
Scott Av WARE SG12 72 F1
Scott Cl HOD EN11 73 G7
ROY SG8 14 E5
Scott Rd BSF CM23 43 L3
LTNN/LIM LU3 27 G2
STVGE SG2 11 L1
Scotts Cl WARE SG12 54 B5
Scotts Rd WARE SG12 54 B5
Scotts Vw WGCW AL8 50 A8
Scottswood Cl BUSH WD23 13 M1
Scottswood Rd BUSH WD23 13 M1
Scout Wy MLHL NW7 135 H7
Scriveners Cl HHNE HP2 5 H3
Scrubbits Sq RAD WD7 119 L1
Scrubbitts Park Rd RAD WD7 119 L1
Seabrook LTNW/LEA LU4 26 F6
Seabrook Rd KGLGY WD4 101 H2
Seacroft Gdns OXHEY WD19 132 B6
Seaford Cl LTNE LU2 29 G6
Seaford Rd EN EN1 125 J8
Seaforth Dr CHES/WCR EN8 110 B8
Seal Cl LTNW/LEA LU4 27 H6
Seaman Cl LCOL/BKTW AL2 85 H7
Seamons Cl DUN/WHIP LU6 39 H3
Searches La ABLGY WD5 102 A1
The Sears DUN/WHIP LU6 36 F4
Seaton Rd HHS/BOV HP3 5 G8
LCOL/BKTW AL2 104 B1
LTNW/LEA LU4 27 K6
Sebright Rd BAR EN5 122 B6
HHW HP1 4 A5
STALW/RED AL3 172 G4
Secker Crs
KTN/HRWW/WS HA3 143 G3
Second Av GSTN WD25 118 B1
HLW CM20 3 G7
HLWE CM17 75 M6
HLWS CM18 3 J7
LWTH SG6 17 G3
STSD CM24 167 K11
Sedbury Cl LTNN/LIM LU3 27 L3
Sedge Gn HLWW/ROY CM19 93 K1
WAB EN9 93 J2
Sedgwick Rd LTNW/LEA LU4 26 F2
Sedley Cl EN EN1 125 M4
Sedley Gv DEN/HRF UB9 140 A6
Seebohm Cl HTCH/STOT SG5 157 L4
The Seedbed Centre
HLWW/ROY CM19 74 E6
Seeleys HLWE CM17 76 A1
Sefton Av
KTN/HRWW/WS HA3 143 H3
MLHL NW7 135 H8
Sefton Cl STAL AL1 9 K3
Sefton Ct ENC/FH EN2 * 124 F6
WGCW AL8 67 M1
Sefton Rd STVG SG1 21 M8
Selbourne Rd LTNW/LEA LU4 27 K6
Selby Av STALW/RED AL3 8 E5
Selden Hl HHNE HP2 4 F5
Sele Mi HERT/WAT SG14 52 F7
Sele Rd HERT/WAT SG14 52 F7
Selina Cl LTNN/LIM LU3 27 G2
Sell Cl CHESW EN7 90 F7
Sells Rd WARE SG12 54 D3
Sellwood Dr BAR EN5 136 B1
Selsey Dr LTNE LU2 29 H4
Selvage La MLHL NW7 135 H8
Selway Cl PIN HA5 141 M6
Selwyn Av HAT AL10 87 H1
Selwyn Crs HAT AL10 67 J8
Selwyn Dr HAT AL10 67 J8
Sempill Rd HHNE HP2 5 H8
Senate Pl STVG SG1 21 M7
September Wy STAN HA7 143 M1
Sequoia Cl BUSH WD23 133 H4
Sequoia Pk PIN HA5 142 F1
Serby Av ROY SG8 14 D5
Sergehill La ABLGY WD5 83 L8
Serpentine Cl STVG SG1 22 A7
The Service Rd
POTB/CUF EN6 106 E6
Seven Acres NTHWD HA6 141 L1
Seventh Av STSD CM24 167 K11
Severalls Av CSHM HP5 97 G4
The Severalls LTNE LU2 28 F6
Severn Dr EN EN1 125 L4
Severnmead HHNE HP2 62 C7
Severnvale LCOL/BKTW AL2 * 104 D1
Severn Wy GSTN WD25 102 A8
STVG SG1 21 K6
Sewardstone Rd CHING E4 126 F8
WAB EN9 111 G8
Sewardstone St WAB EN9 111 G8
Sewardstone Wy WAB EN9 127 G2
Sewell Cl STALE/WH AL4 86 C2
Sewell Harris Cl HLW CM20 3 K3
Sewell La DUN/WHIP LU6 25 H7
Sewells WGCW AL8 50 C4
Sexton Cl CHESW EN7 90 F7
Seymour Av LTN LU1 7 H8
Seymour Cl PIN HA5 142 D3
Seymour Crs HHNE HP2 5 H2
Seymour Rd BERK HP4 59 J7
CSTG HP8 128 A7
LTN LU1 7 H9
STALW/RED AL3 65 J7
Seymours HLWW/ROY CM19 74 D8
Shackledell STVGE SG2 33 K7
Shacklegate La
HTCHE/RSTV SG4 175 R3
Shackleton Gdns BSF CM23 43 K3
Shackleton Spring STVGE SG2 11 J9
Shackleton Wy ABLGY WD5 * 101 L6
WGCE AL7 51 H7
Shady Bush Cl BUSH WD23 133 G3
Shady La WAT WD17 12 F2
Shaftenhoe End Rd ROY SG8 153 J4
Shaftesbury Av BAR EN5 123 G8
PEND EN3 126 B6
Shaftesbury Ct
RKW/CH/CXG WD3 * 131 G1
Shaftesbury Dr
HTCH/STOT SG5 148 A10
Shaftesbury Rd LTNW/LEA LU4 40 F1
WAT WD17 13 H4
Shaftesbury Wy ROY SG8 14 F8
Shaftsbury Wy KGLGY WD4 101 G1
Shakespeare ROY SG8 14 E5
Shakespeare Rd HARP AL5 46 F4
MLHL NW7 135 L7
Shakespeare St WATN WD24 117 M4
Shalcross Dr CHES/WCR EN8 110 D4
Shallcross Crs HAT AL10 87 K3
Shambrook Rd CHESW EN7 90 F7
Shamrock Wy STHGT/OAK N14 137 M4
Shangani Rd BSF CM23 43 M4
Shanklin Cl CHESW EN7 109 K3
LTNN/LIM LU3 27 L2
Shanklin Gdns OXHEY WD19 132 A7
Shannon Cl HNLW SG16 146 G7
Shantock Hall La
HHS/BOV HP3 98 C3
Shantock La HHS/BOV HP3 98 C4
Shantung Pl CSHM HP5 * 97 G7
Shapwick Cl FBAR/BDGN N11 137 K8
Sharmans Cl WLYN AL6 50 D1
Sharon Rd PEND EN3 126 C6
Sharose Ct STALW/RED AL3 172 G4
Sharpcroft HHNE HP2 62 B8
Sharpecroft HLWW/ROY CM19 2 D6
Sharpenhoe Rd LTNN/LIM LU3 154 F11
Sharpes La HHW HP1 80 F3
Sharples Gn LTNN/LIM LU3 27 M1
Sharps Wy HTCHE/RSTV SG4 157 Q5
Shawbridge HLWW/ROY CM19 75 G8
Shaw Cl BUSH WD23 133 J5
CHES/WCR EN8 110 A3
Shaw Rd PEND EN3 126 B5
The Shaws WGCE AL7 51 G8
The Shaw RBSF CM22 184 G6
The Shearers BSF CM23 43 H5
Sheares Hoppit WARE SG12 182 B7
Shearwater Cl STVGE SG2 34 B5
Sheepcot Dr GSTN WD25 102 A4
Sheepcote WGCE AL7 68 E2
Sheepcote Gdns
DEN/HRF UB9 139 L8
Sheepcote La BSF CM23 166 A2
STALE/WH AL4 48 C5
Sheepcote Rd HHNE HP2 5 K4
HRW HA1 143 K8
Sheepcot La GSTN WD25 101 L7
Sheepcroft Hl STVGE SG2 34 B6
Sheepfold La AMSS HP7 113 H5
Sheephouse Rd HHNE HP2 5 K6
Sheering Dr HLWE CM17 76 C2
Sheering Lower Rd
HLWE CM17 183 R10
Sheering Mill La SBW CM21 183 R7
Sheering Rd HLWE CM17 76 C1
Sheethanger La HHS/BOV HP3 81 L6
Shefford Rd SHFD SG17 146 E3
Shefton Ri NTHWD HA6 141 L2
Shelbourne Cl PIN HA5 142 D5
Sheldon Cl CHESW EN7 91 H8
HLWE CM17 76 C5
Shelford Rd BAR EN5 136 A2
Shelley Cl EDGW HA8 134 E7
HTCHE/RSTV SG4 20 A2
NTHWD HA6 131 K8
ROY SG8 14 E4
Shelley La DEN/HRF UB9 139 L2
Shelley Ms HHS/BOV HP3 * 4 F9
Shelley Rd CSHM HP5 96 F3
LTNW/LEA LU4 26 E7
Shelly Cl BORE WD6 120 E8
Shelton Wy LTNE LU2 28 E6
Shenfield Ct HLWS CM18 75 G8
Shenleybury RAD WD7 104 C4
Shenleybury Cots RAD WD7 104 C5
Shenley Hl RAD WD7 103 M8
Shenley La LCOL/BKTW AL2 85 M7
Shenley Rd BORE WD6 120 E7
HHNE HP2 62 F4
RAD WD7 120 B1
Shenstone Hl BERK HP4 60 C8
Shephall Gn STVGE SG2 33 M7
Shephall La STVGE SG2 33 K8
Shephall Vw STVG SG1 11 J4
Shephall Wy STVGE SG2 11 M7
Shepherd Cl ABLGY WD5 101 K4
ROY SG8 14 F8
Shepherd Rd LTNW/LEA LU4 26 C5
Shepherds Cl BSF CM23 43 J5
STAN HA7 133 L8
Shepherds Ct HERT/WAT SG14 53 G4
Shepherds Farm
RKW/CH/CXG WD3 129 L4
Shepherds Gn HHW HP1 81 J3
Shepherd's La
RKW/CH/CXG WD3 129 H2
Shepherds La STVG SG1 32 D3
Shepherds Md
HTCH/STOT SG5 157 N3
Shepherds Rd WATW WD18 12 B4
Shepherds Wk BUSH WD23 133 H5
Shepherds Wy BRKMPK AL9 107 G1
CSHM HP5 97 H7
HARP AL5 46 B1
RKW/CH/CXG WD3 129 M3
Shepley Ms PEND EN3 126 E4
Sheppard Cl EN EN1 125 M4
Sheppards HLWW/ROY CM19 74 D8
Sheppards Cl STALW/RED AL3 65 J7
Shepperton Cl BORE WD6 121 H5
Sheppey's La KGLGY WD4 101 J2
Sherards Orch
HLWW/ROY CM19 74 F7
Sheraton Cl BORE WD6 134 D1
Sheraton Ms WATW WD18 * 117 J8
Sherborne Av LTNE LU2 28 B3
PEND EN3 126 A6
Sherborne Pl NTHWD HA6 141 H1
Sherborne Wy
RKW/CH/CXG WD3 116 F8
Sherbourne Cl HHNE HP2 5 J5
Sherd Cl LTNN/LIM LU3 27 K2
Sheredes Dr HOD EN11 72 D8
Sherfield Av
RKW/CH/CXG WD3 130 B6
Sheridan Cl HHW HP1 4 B4
Sheridan Rd LTNN/LIM LU3 28 A7
OXHEY WD19 132 B3
Sheriden Cl DUN/WHIP LU6 25 M8
Sheriden Wk BROX EN10 92 C2
Sheriff Wy GSTN WD25 101 L7
Sheringham Av STVG SG1 20 F8
Sheringham Cl LTNE LU2 28 A2
Sherington Av PIN HA5 142 E2
Sherland Ct RAD WD7 * 119 L1
Shernbroke Rd WAB EN9 111 K8
Sherrardspark Rd WGCW AL8 50 A5
Sherrards Wy BAR EN5 136 E1
Shervington Gv
LTNN/LIM LU3 27 M6
Sherwood LWTH SG6 16 D1
Sherwood Av POTB/CUF EN6 106 C6
RSLP HA4 141 J8
STALE/WH AL4 65 M7
Sherwood Pl HHNE HP2 62 D6
Sherwood Rd LTNW/LEA LU4 27 L7
Sherwoods Ri HARP AL5 47 H5
Sherwoods Rd OXHEY WD19 132 C3
Sherwood St
TRDG/WHET N20 137 H6
Sherwood Ter
TRDG/WHET N20 137 H6
Shetland Cl BORE WD6 135 H2
Shillington Rd
HTCH/STOT SG5 146 A11
Shillitoe Av POTB/CUF EN6 106 B6
Shingle Cl LTNN/LIM LU3 27 L1
Shingle Ct WAB EN9 111 L7
Ship La LBUZ LU7 169 P6
Shire Cl BROX EN10 * 92 D8
Shire Ct STVG SG1 33 G2
Shire La CFSP/GDCR SL9 138 F1
CSTG HP8 128 F6
TRING HP23 57 J6
Shiremeade BORE WD6 134 D1
Shires Pk WGCE AL7 * 50 C5
The Shires GSTN WD25 101 M5
LTNE LU2 6 E2
ROY SG8 14 F7
Shirley Cl BROX EN10 92 D6
CHES/WCR EN8 110 A3
STVGE SG2 33 M1
Shirley Rd ABLGY WD5 101 K6
ENC/FH EN2 125 G7
LTN LU1 6 B4
STAL AL1 9 J7
Shooters Dr WAB EN9 93 J4
Shooters Rd ENC/FH EN2 124 E4
Shootersway BERK HP4 59 H8
TRING HP23 58 F7
Shootersway La BERK HP4 79 K2
Shootersway Pk BERK HP4 79 K1
Shoplands WGCW AL8 50 B4
Shoreham Cl STVG SG1 32 E1
Shortcroft BSF CM23 44 D1
Shortcroft Ct
AMP/FLIT/BLC MK45 154 H3
Shortgate
NFNCH/WDSPK N12 136 D7
Short Hale LBUZ LU7 169 P6
Shortlands Gn WGCE AL7 50 D8
Shortlands Pl BSF CM23 43 M1
Short La LCOL/BKTW AL2 102 C3
STVGE SG2 34 C5
Shortmead Dr
CHES/WCR EN8 110 C5
Shortway CSHM HP5 96 F3
Shothanger Wy HHS/BOV HP3 81 H7
Shottfield Cl STALE/WH AL4 66 A3
Shott La LWTH SG6 16 E3
The Shrubberies STAL AL1 * 8 E9
Shrubbery Gv ROY SG8 151 R1
The Shrubbery HHW HP1 81 J1
Shrub Hill Rd HHW HP1 81 K3
Shrubland Cl
TRDG/WHET N20 * 137 H5
Shrublands BRKMPK AL9 88 F8
Shrublands Av BERK HP4 79 L1
Shrublands Cl
TRDG/WHET N20 137 H4
Shrublands Rd BERK HP4 59 L8
The Shrublands
POTB/CUF EN6 106 C7
Shrubs Rd RKW/CH/CXG WD3 140 D1
Shugars Gn TRING HP23 169 M12
Shurland Av EBAR EN4 137 H2
Sibley Av HARP AL5 47 H6
Sibley Cl LTNE LU2 28 F6
Sibneys Gn HLWS CM18 95 J1
Sibthorpe Rd BRKMPK AL9 88 A6
Siccut Rd HTCHE/RSTV SG4 20 C5
Sicklefield Cl CHESW EN7 91 K8
Siddons Rd STVGE SG2 34 A3
Sidford Cl HHW HP1 81 K2
The Sidings BROX EN10 92 D4
HAT AL10 87 J1
HHNE HP2 5 G3
HNLW SG16 147 K6
Siding Wy LCOL/BKTW AL2 85 L8
Sidmouth Cl OXHEY WD19 131 M5
Sidney Rd RYLN/HDSTN HA2 143 G5
Sidney Ter BSF CM23 43 M3
The Sigers PIN HA5 141 M8
Signal Cl HNLW SG16 147 K6
Silam Rd STVG SG1 10 E5
Silecroft Rd LTNE LU2 7 L4
Silk Mill Rd OXHEY WD19 131 M3
STALW/RED AL3 63 M1
Silk Mill Wy TRING HP23 169 L12
Silverbirch Av HTCH/STOT SG5 148 D5
Silvercliffe Gdns EBAR EN4 123 J8
Silver Cl KTN/HRWW/WS HA3 143 H2
Silver Ct WGCE AL7 * 50 E6
Silverdale ENC/FH EN2 124 C8
Silverdale Rd BUSH WD23 13 M7
Silver Dell WATN WD24 117 K1
Silverfield BROX EN10 92 D4
Silver Hl BORE WD6 121 G2
Silver St BLDK SG7 149 P1
CHESW EN7 109 H4
EN EN1 125 H7
LTN LU1 6 F5
ROY SG8 145 M6
STSD CM24 166 F7
WAB EN9 111 G8
Silverthorn Dr HHS/BOV HP3 82 F6
Silver Trees LCOL/BKTW AL2 102 D4
Silverwood Cl NTHWD HA6 141 G3
Silvesters HLWW/ROY CM19 74 D7
Simmonds Ri HHNE HP2 4 F6
Simmons Cl
TRDG/WHET N20 137 J4
Simmons' Wy
TRDG/WHET N20 137 J5
Simon Dean HHS/BOV HP3 98 E1
Simpkins Dr
AMP/FLIT/BLC MK45 155 J1
Simplicity La HLWE CM17 76 B4
Simpson Cl LTNW/LEA LU4 27 H7
Simpson Dr BLDK SG7 17 K1
Sinclare Cl EN EN1 125 K5
Sinderby Cl BORE WD6 120 C5
Sinfield Cl STVG SG1 11 J4
Singleton Scarp
NFNCH/WDSPK N12 136 E8
Singlets La STALW/RED AL3 173 L7
Sir John Newsom Wy
WGCE AL7 68 C2
Sir Joseph's Wk HARP AL5 46 E5
Sir Peter's Wy BERK HP4 171 K2
Sirus Rd NTHWD HA6 131 L8
Sish Cl STVG SG1 10 D2
Sish La STVG SG1 10 C2
Siskin Cl BORE WD6 120 E8
BUSH WD23 13 M5
ROY SG8 14 F5
Sisson Cl STVGE SG2 34 A7
Sitwell Gv STAN HA7 133 K8
Six Acres HHS/BOV HP3 82 E5
Six Hills Rbt STVG SG1 10 C7
Six Hills Wy STVG SG1 10 A8
Sixth Av GSTN WD25 118 B1
LWTH SG6 17 G3
STSD CM24 167 L10
Skarnings Ct WAB EN9 111 L7
Skegness Rd STVG SG1 32 E1
Skegsbury La
HTCHE/RSTV SG4 175 K8
Skeins Wy SAFWS CB11 161 Q5
Skelton Cl LTNN/LIM LU3 154 H12
Sketty Rd EN EN1 125 K7
Skidmore Wy
RKW/CH/CXG WD3 130 C4
Skimpans Cl BRKMPK AL9 88 B6
Skimpot Rd LTNW/LEA LU4 26 E8
Skinners St BSF CM23 43 J5
Skipton Cl STVGE SG2 177 M1
Skua Cl LTNW/LEA LU4 26 E4
Skylark Cnr STVGE SG2 34 B6
Skylark Pl ROY SG8 14 F5
Skys Wood Rd STALE/WH AL4 65 M6
Slacksbury Hatch
HLWW/ROY CM19 2 B7
Slade Ct RAD WD7 119 L1
Slade Oak La DEN/HRF UB9 139 G8
Slades Cl ENC/FH EN2 124 E7
Slades Gdns ENC/FH EN2 124 E6
Slades Hl ENC/FH EN2 124 E7
Slades Ri ENC/FH EN2 124 E7
Slapton La DUN/WHIP LU6 36 C4
Slate Hall LTNN/LIM LU3 154 A9
Sleaford Gn OXHEY WD19 132 B6
Sleapcross Gdns
STALE/WH AL4 87 G3
Sleaps Hyde STVGE SG2 34 A8
Sleapshyde La STALE/WH AL4 87 G3
Sleddale HHNE HP2 62 C7
Sleets End HHW HP1 61 M8
Slicketts La DUN/WHIP LU6 37 K6
Slimmons Dr STALE/WH AL4 65 L6
Slipe La BROX EN10 92 D6
The Slipe LBUZ LU7 169 L2
Slip La KNEB SG3 176 H4
Slippers Hl HHNE HP2 82 B1
Sloan Ct STVG SG1 11 H2
Sloansway WGCE AL7 50 D4
Slowmans Cl LCOL/BKTW AL2 103 G2
The Slype STALE/WH AL4 175 L12
Small Acre HHW HP1 81 K2
Smallcroft WGCE AL7 50 F6
Smallford La STALE/WH AL4 86 F3
Smallwood Cl STALE/WH AL4 48 C6
Smarts Gn CHESW EN7 91 K8
Smeaton Cl WAB EN9 111 J7
Smeaton Rd PEND EN3 126 E3
Smithcombe Cl
AMP/FLIT/BLC MK45 155 J2
Smithfield HHNE HP2 62 B8
Smiths Ct EPP CM16 95 M7
Smith's End La ROY SG8 152 H4
Smiths La CHESW EN7 91 H8
Smith St WATW WD18 13 G6
The Smithy STDN SG11 164 H11
Smug Oak La LCOL/BKTW AL2 102 F4
Snailswell La HTCH/STOT SG5 147 N12
Snakes La EBAR EN4 123 M7
RBSF CM22 167 J3
Snaresbrook Dr STAN HA7 134 B7
Snatchup STALW/RED AL3 173 Q12
Snells La AMSS HP7 113 M6
Snells Md BUNT SG9 159 J10
Snells Wood Ct AMSS HP7 114 A6
The Snipe HTCHE/RSTV SG4 17 L8
Snowdonia Wy STVG SG1 21 L5
Snowdrop Cl BSF CM23 43 J3
Snowford Cl LTNN/LIM LU3 27 L2
Snowhill Cots CSHM HP5 79 K6
Soham Rd PEND EN3 126 D3
Solar Ct WATW WD18 * 12 A7
Solar Wy PEND EN3 126 D1
Solesbridge Cl
RKW/CH/CXG WD3 115 K7
Solesbridge La
RKW/CH/CXG WD3 115 K7
Sollershott East LWTH SG6 16 D5
Sollershott Hall LWTH SG6 * 16 D5
Sollershott West LWTH SG6 16 C5
Solomon's Hl
RKW/CH/CXG WD3 130 B3
Solway HHNE HP2 62 D8
Solway Rd North
LTNN/LIM LU3 27 L5
Solway Rd South
LTNN/LIM LU3 27 L6
Somaford Gv EBAR EN4 137 H2
Somerby Cl BROX EN10 92 E3
Somercoates Cl EBAR EN4 123 J7
Somerford Cl PIN HA5 141 L6
Someries Rd HARP AL5 47 G1
HHW HP1 61 K8
Somersby Cl LTN LU1 6 F9
Somerset Av LTNE LU2 7 L1
Somerset Rd BAR EN5 136 F1
HRW HA1 143 G8
PEND EN3 126 E4
Somersham WGCE AL7 51 H7
Somers Rd BRKMPK AL9 88 A6
Somers Sq BRKMPK AL9 88 A5
Somers Wy BUSH WD23 133 G3
Sommers Ct WARE SG12 * 54 C5
Sonia Cl OXHEY WD19 132 A3
Sonia Gdns
NFNCH/WDSPK N12 137 G7
The Sonnets HHW HP1 81 M8
Soothouse Spring
STALW/RED AL3 65 K6
Soper Ms PEND EN3 126 E4
Soper Sq HLWE CM17 76 A4
Sopers Rd POTB/CUF EN6 108 D3
Sopwell La STAL AL1 8 E7
Sorrel Cl LTNN/LIM LU3 27 L1
ROY SG8 15 G8
Sorrel Garth HTCHE/RSTV SG4 157 Q7
Sotheron Rd WAT WD17 13 G2
Souberie Av LWTH SG6 16 D4
Souldern St WATW WD18 12 D7
Southall Cl WARE SG12 54 B3
Southampton Gdns
LTNN/LIM LU3 154 D12
South Ap NTHWD HA6 131 H6
South Bank Rd BERK HP4 59 K7
Southbrook SBW CM21 183 Q8
Southbrook Dr
CHES/WCR EN8 110 B2
South Bucks Wy AMSS HP7 112 A4
CFSP/GDCR SL9 138 B2
Southbury Av EN EN1 125 L8
Southbury Rd EN EN1 125 K8
South Charlton Mead La
HOD EN11 73 G8
Southcliffe Dr CFSP/GDCR SL9 128 C8
South Cl BAR EN5 122 D7
BLDK SG7 17 K2
LCOL/BKTW AL2 84 F7
ROY SG8 14 C6
South Cottage Dr
RKW/CH/CXG WD3 129 K1
South Cottage Gdns
RKW/CH/CXG WD3 129 K1
South Dene MLHL NW7 135 H6
Southdown Ct HAT AL10 87 L3
Southdown Rd HARP AL5 46 F4
HAT AL10 87 L3
South Drift Wy LTN LU1 40 F3
South Dr POTB/CUF EN6 108 C4
STALE/WH AL4 86 B2
Southend Cl STVG SG1 10 B1
Southend La WAB EN9 111 M8
Southern Av HNLW SG16 147 K6
Southern Ri LTNE LU2 174 D10
Southern Ter HOD EN11 * 72 F4
Southern Wy DUN/WHIP LU6 171 Q5
HLWW/ROY CM19 74 E8
LWTH SG6 16 C1
Southernwood Cl HHNE HP2 5 M1
Southerton Wy RAD WD7 104 C7
Southfield BAR EN5 136 B2
STDN SG11 163 R6
WGCE AL7 68 B1
Southfield Av WATN WD24 118 A4
Southfield Pk
RYLN/HDSTN HA2 142 F6
Southfield Rd CHES/WCR EN8 110 C6
HOD EN11 72 E5
Southfields LWTH SG6 148 D12
STDN SG11 163 Q11
Southfields Rd DUN/WHIP LU6 39 H3
Southfield Wy STALE/WH AL4 66 B7
South Ga HLW CM20 2 E6
Southgate STVG SG1 10 D6
Southgate Rd POTB/CUF EN6 107 G7
South Hl NTHWD HA6 * 141 J3
South Hill Cl
HTCHE/RSTV SG4 * 157 Q7
South Hill Rd HHW HP1 4 D3
Southill La PIN HA5 141 L6
South Ley WGCE AL7 68 C2
South Lodge Crs ENC/FH EN2 124 B8
South Lodge Dr
STHGT/OAK N14 124 B8

Southmead Crs
CHES/WCR EN8 110 C4
Southmill Rd BSF CM23 44 A3
South Mt TRDG/WHET N20 * 137 G5
South Ordnance Rd
PEND EN3 126 E3
Southover
NFNCH/WDSPK N12 136 E7
South Pk CFSP/GDCR SL9 138 D7
South Park Av
RKW/CH/CXG WD3 129 K1
South Park Crs
CFSP/GDCR SL9 138 D7
South Park Dr
CFSP/GDCR SL9 138 C6
South Park Gdns BERK HP4 59 M8
South Park Vw
CFSP/GDCR SL9 138 D6
South Pl HLW CM20 75 L2
HTCH/STOT SG5 157 M5
South Riding LCOL/BKTW AL2 102 E4
South Rd AMS HP6 113 G2
BLDK SG7 17 K2
BSF CM23 44 A4
HLW CM20 75 L2
LTN LU1 6 F8
RKW/CH/CXG WD3 129 G1
STDN SG11 163 P11
Southsea Av WATW WD18 12 C5
Southsea Rd STVG SG1 32 F1
South Side CFSP/GDCR SL9 138 B5
South St BSF CM23 43 M3
HERT/WAT SG14 53 H7
WARE SG12 73 G1
South Vw LWTH SG6 16 D4
Southview Cl CHESW EN7 91 J8
South View Rd PIN HA5 141 M1
CFSP/GDCR SL9 138 B6
Southview Rd HARP AL5 47 G2
Southwark Cl STVG SG1 21 M8
South Wy CHING E4 126 F3
HAT AL10 87 L4
KGLGY WD4 101 H7
RYLN/HDSTN HA2 142 E6
Southway TRDG/WHET N20 136 E5
South Weald Dr WAB EN9 111 H7
Southwold Rd WATN WD24 118 A3
Southwood Rd
DUN/HR/TOD LU5 39 J3
Sovereign Ct HLWW/ROY CM19 74 F8
Sovereign Ms EBAR EN4 123 K7
Sovereign Pk HHNE HP2 * 62 F8
LTNW/LEA LU4 27 K8
STALE/WH AL4 86 B3
Sovereign Pl HRW HA1 143 K7
Sowerby Av LTNE LU2 29 G6
Sparhawke LWTH SG6 148 E12
Sparkbridge Rd HRW HA1 143 J6
Sparkford Gdns
FBAR/BDGN N11 137 L8
Sparrow Cl LTNW/LEA LU4 26 E5
Sparrow Dr STVGE SG2 34 A5
Sparrows Herne BUSH WD23 132 F3
Sparrow's La HLWE CM17 185 L12
Sparrows Wy BUSH WD23 * 133 G3
Sparrows Wick BUSH WD23 * 133 G4
Sparrowswick Ride
STALW/RED AL3 65 G5
Sparrow Wk GSTN WD25 117 L1
Spayne Cl LTNN/LIM LU3 27 M1
Spear Cl LTNN/LIM LU3 27 J3
Speedwell Cl HHW HP1 81 J3
LTNN/LIM LU3 27 L1
Speke Cl STVGE SG2 * 34 B4
Spellbrooke HTCH/STOT SG5 157 M5
Spellbrook La East
RBSF CM22 183 R1
Spellbrook La West
SBW CM21 183 P2
Spencer Av CHESW EN7 91 J8
Spencer Cl RBSF CM22 167 L2
STSD CM24 166 G7
Spencer Ga STAL AL1 9 H2
Spencer Pl STALE/WH AL4 66 A3
Spencer Rd FBAR/BDGN N11 137 M7
KTN/HRWW/WS HA3 143 J4
LTNN/LIM LU3 6 B1
Spencers Cft HLWS CM18 75 L7
Spencer St HERT/BAY SG13 53 J6
STALW/RED AL3 8 E5
Spencer Wk
RKW/CH/CXG WD3 130 A1
Spencer Wy HHW HP1 61 L7
LWTH SG6 16 D1
Spenser Cl ROY SG8 14 E4
Spenser Rd HARP AL5 47 G4
Sperberry Hl HTCHE/RSTV SG4 157 R11
Speyhawk Pl POTB/CUF EN6 106 F4
Spicersfield CHESW EN7 109 L1
Spicer St STALW/RED AL3 8 D6
Spindle Berry Cl WLYN AL6 * 177 N10
Spinney Crs DUN/WHIP LU6 38 D1
Spinney La WLYN AL6 177 K7
Spinney Pl AMSS HP7 * 113 G5
Spinney Rd LTNN/LIM LU3 27 H2
Spinneys Dr STALW/RED AL3 * 8 A9
Spinney St HERT/BAY SG13 53 L7
The Spinney BAR EN5 122 F6
BERK HP4 79 K2
BLDK SG7 17 J2
BROX EN10 92 D1
CSHM HP5 97 H3
GSTN WD25 119 G4
HARP AL5 46 C2
HERT/BAY SG13 53 K7
HLW CM20 3 M4
POTB/CUF EN6 107 H5
STAN HA7 134 C7
STSD CM24 166 G7
STVGE SG2 34 B2
WAT WD17 117 L5
WGCE AL7 50 C8
Spinning Wheel Md
HLWS CM18 75 L8
The Spire Green Centre
HLWW/ROY CM19 74 C6
The Spires HHNE HP2 4 F6
Spittlesea Rd LTNE LU2 174 A3
Spoondell DUN/WHIP LU6 38 D2
Spooners Dr LCOL/BKTW AL2 103 G1
Spratts La DUN/WHIP LU6 39 K8
Spreckley Cl HNLW SG16 147 K4
Spring Cl BAR EN5 136 B1
BORE WD6 120 E6
CSHM HP5 114 B2
DEN/HRF UB9 140 B3
Spring Court Rd ENC/FH EN2 124 E4
Spring Crofts BUSH WD23 132 E1
Spring Dr PIN HA5 141 L8
STVGE SG2 177 N1
Springett Pl AMS HP6 113 K3
Springfield BGSW SG18 144 C5
BUSH WD23 133 H4
Springfield Cl CSHM HP5 97 G7
NFNCH/WDSPK N12 136 F8
POTB/CUF EN6 107 H5
RKW/CH/CXG WD3 130 F1
STAN HA7 133 L6
Springfield Crs HARP AL5 46 E1
Spring Field Rd BERK HP4 59 K6
Springfield Rd
CHES/WCR EN8 110 C6
CSHM HP5 97 G6
DUN/WHIP LU6 38 B4
GSTN WD25 101 M7
HRW HA1 143 J8
LTNN/LIM LU3 28 A3
STAL AL1 9 M8
Springfields AMS HP6 113 G3
BROX EN10 92 D1
WAB EN9 111 J8
WGCW AL8 67 M1
Spring Garden La BERK HP4 59 H8
Spring Gdns GSTN WD25 118 A1
Spring Gln HAT AL10 87 K1
Springhall La SBW CM21 183 Q8
Springhall Rd SBW CM21 183 Q7
Springhead BLDK SG7 149 P1
Spring Hills HLW CM20 2 A3
Spring Lake STAN HA7 133 M7
Spring La BUNT SG9 158 A12
HHW HP1 81 L1
ROY SG8 14 A2
Springle La HERT/BAY SG13 72 D2
Spring Pl LTN LU1 6 E7
Spring Rd HARP AL5 173 Q5
LWTH SG6 16 C4
Springshott LWTH SG6 16 C4
The Springs BROX EN10 92 C7
HERT/BAY SG13 53 K6
Spring Valley Enterprise Centre
STALW/RED AL3 65 J6
Spring View Rd WARE SG12 54 A5
Spring Wk BROX EN10 92 A3
Spring Wy HHNE HP2 62 F8
Springwell Av
RKW/CH/CXG WD3 129 L5
Springwell Ct
RKW/CH/CXG WD3 * 129 L5
WARE SG12 * 73 G1
Springwell La DEN/HRF UB9 129 M8
RKW/CH/CXG WD3 129 L6
Springwood CHESW EN7 91 K8
Springwood Cl DEN/HRF UB9 140 B3
Springwood Crs EDGW HA8 135 G5
Springwood Wk
STALE/WH AL4 66 A7
Spruce Hl HLWS CM18 95 J1
Spruce Wy LCOL/BKTW AL2 102 F1
Spur Cl ABLGY WD5 101 H7
Spurcroft LTNN/LIM LU3 155 J12
Spur Rd EDGW HA8 134 C7
Spurrs Cl HTCHE/RSTV SG4 157 R6
The Spur CHES/WCR EN8 * 110 B2
STVG SG1 10 F6
Square St HLWE CM17 76 A4
The Square BROX EN10 92 C5
BUNT SG9 158 G4
DUN/WHIP LU6 38 F1
HHNE HP2 * 4 F3
MHAD SG10 181 R6
SBW CM21 183 Q7
STALW/RED AL3 173 P11
WATN WD24 117 M3
Squires Cl BSF CM23 43 J1
Squires Ride HHNE HP2 62 D4
Squirrel Cha HHW HP1 81 J1
Squirrels Cl BSF CM23 43 M1
NFNCH/WDSPK N12 137 G7
The Squirrels BUSH WD23 133 H2
HERT/BAY SG13 53 L7
PIN HA5 142 D5
Stablebridge Rd
RAYLNE/WEN HP22 56 D2
Stable Rd RAYLNE/WEN HP22 56 B6
Stables Ms BRKMPK AL9 * 107 H2
The Stables GSTN WD25 118 F2
Stable Yd LTN LU1 * 41 L8
Stackfield HLW CM20 75 M2
Stacklands WGCW AL8 67 M1
Staddles RBSF CM22 44 B8
Stadium Wy HLWW/ROY CM19 74 D4
Stafford Cl CHES/WCR EN8 109 M3
Stafford Dr BROX EN10 92 E2
Stafford Rd
KTN/HRWW/WS HA3 143 G2
Staffords HLWE CM17 76 C1
Stagg Hl EBAR EN4 123 H1
Stagg Green Av BRKMPK AL9 68 A6
Stag La BERK HP4 59 L8
RKW/CH/CXG WD3 129 G2
Stainer Rd BORE WD6 120 B5
Stainers BSF CM23 43 J4
Staines Sq DUN/WHIP LU6 39 G2
Stains Cl CHES/WCR EN8 110 C2
Stainton Rd PEND EN3 126 A5
Stake Piece Rd ROY SG8 14 D8
Stakers Ct HARP AL5 46 F4
Stamford Av ROY SG8 14 E6
Stamford Cl
KTN/HRWW/WS HA3 143 J2
POTB/CUF EN6 107 H6
Stamford Ct ROY SG8 14 E6
Stamford Rd WAT WD17 12 E1
Stanborough Av BORE WD6 120 E4
Stanborough Cl WGCW AL8 50 A8
Stanborough Gn WGCW AL8 68 A1
Stanborough La WGCW AL8 68 A1
Stanborough Ms WGCW AL8 68 B1
Stanborough Rd WGCW AL8 67 M2
Stanbridge Rd LBUZ LU7 24 B6
Stanbury Av WAT WD17 117 J3
Standale Gv RSLP HA4 141 G7
Standard Rd PEND EN3 126 C4
Standfield ABLGY WD5 101 J5
Standhill Cl HTCHE/RSTV SG4 157 P7
Standhill Rd
HTCHE/RSTV SG4 157 P7
Standingford
HLWW/ROY CM19 94 F2
Standon Ct STDN SG11 * 163 R12
Standon Hl STDN SG11 163 N11
Standon Rd STDN SG11 164 E10
Standring Ri HHS/BOV HP3 81 M5
HHW HP1 4 B8
Stane Cl BSF CM23 43 J5
Stane Fld LWTH SG6 16 F6
Stanelow Crs STDN SG11 163 P11
Stane St BLDK SG7 149 L12
Stanfields Ct HLW CM20 3 G5
Stanford Cl RSLP HA4 141 G8
Stanford Ct WAB EN9 111 L7
Stanford Rd FBAR/BDGN N11 137 K8
LTNE LU2 7 L1
Stangate Crs BORE WD6 135 J1
Stangate Gdns STAN HA7 133 M7
Stanhope Av
KTN/HRWW/WS HA3 143 H3
Stanhope Gdns MLHL NW7 135 K8
Stanhope Rd BAR EN5 136 B2
CHES/WCR EN8 110 C7
NFNCH/WDSPK N12 137 G8
STAL AL1 9 J6
Stanier Ri BERK HP4 59 K6
Stanley Av CSHM HP5 96 F5
LCOL/BKTW AL2 84 E7
Stanley Dr HAT AL10 87 M2
Stanley Gdns BORE WD6 120 C5
TRING HP23 57 K2
Stanley Hl AMSS HP7 113 J6
Stanley Hill Av AMSS HP7 113 H5
Stanley Rd EN EN1 125 J7
HERT/BAY SG13 53 J8
LTNN/LIM LU3 154 G8
NTHWD HA6 141 L3
STVGE SG2 33 M2
WAT WD17 13 H4
Stanley St LTN LU1 6 D7
Stanmore Cha STALE/WH AL4 86 B3
Stanmore Crs LTNN/LIM LU3 27 K5
Stanmore Hl STAN HA7 133 M7
Stanmore Rd STVG SG1 33 G2
WATN WD24 117 M5
Stanmount Rd
LCOL/BKTW AL2 * 84 E7
Stanstead Dr HOD EN11 72 F5
Stanstead Pl AMSS HP7 * 113 G5
Stanstead Rd HERT/BAY SG13 53 L6
HOD EN11 72 F5
WARE SG12 54 B8
Stansted Hl MHAD SG10 42 A8
Stansted Rd BSF CM23 44 A1
RBSF CM22 167 K5
Stanton Cl STALE/WH AL4 66 B6
Stanton Rd LTNW/LEA LU4 27 G7
Stanway Rd WAB EN9 111 L7
Staplefield Cl PIN HA5 142 C2
Stapleford WGCE AL7 51 G7
Stapleford Rd LTNE LU2 28 F5
Stapleton Cl POTB/CUF EN6 107 H5
Stapleton Rd BORE WD6 120 E4
Stapley Rd STALW/RED AL3 8 E4
Stapylton Rd BAR EN5 122 C7
Star Holme Ct WARE SG12 54 C4
Starkey Cl CHESW EN7 91 G7
Starlight Wy STALE/WH AL4 86 A4
Starling Cl PIN HA5 142 A5
Starling La POTB/CUF EN6 108 D2
Starling Pl GSTN WD25 * 102 A6
Star St WARE SG12 54 C4
Statham Cl LTNN/LIM LU3 154 H12
Station Ap BAR EN5 123 G8
CFSP/GDCR SL9 138 C7
CHES/WCR EN8 * 110 C8
FBAR/BDGN N11 137 M8
HARP AL5 46 F4
HTCHE/RSTV SG4 157 Q5
KNEB SG3 177 M4
NFNCH/WDSPK N12 136 F7
NTHWD HA6 141 J2
OXHEY WD19 132 B6
PIN HA5 142 C5
RAD WD7 119 L1
RKW/CH/CXG WD3 115 G8
WATW WD18 * 12 A5
Station Cl BRKMPK AL9 88 C8
POTB/CUF EN6 106 D5
Station Ct AMSS HP7 * 113 G4
Stationers Pl HHS/BOV HP3 82 C7
Station Footpath KGLGY WD4 100 F4
Station Ms POTB/CUF EN6 * 106 E5
Station Pde EBAR EN4 * 123 L8
KTN/HRWW/WS HA3 * 143 M4
Station Pl LWTH SG6 16 D3
Station Rd AMSS HP7 113 G5
ARL/CHE SG15 147 Q5
BAR EN5 136 F1
BERK HP4 60 B8
BLDK SG7 149 K12
BLDK SG7 149 R1
BORE WD6 120 E8
BRKMPK AL9 88 B7
BROX EN10 92 D2
BSF CM23 43 M2
BUNT SG9 159 J10
CFSP/GDCR SL9 138 C7
CHES/WCR EN8 110 E8
CSHM HP5 * 96 F5
DUN/HR/TOD LU5 39 H1
FBAR/BDGN N11 137 M8
HARP AL5 46 F4
HERT/WAT SG14 69 L2
HERT/WAT SG14 178 F6
HHW HP1 4 C7
HLWE CM17 76 A1
HNLW SG16 146 G7
HRW HA1 142 F7
KGLGY WD4 100 F4
KNEB SG3 177 M4
LBUZ LU7 24 B5
LBUZ LU7 169 Q4
LCOL/BKTW AL2 102 E5
LTN LU1 6 F4
LTNW/LEA LU4 27 J4
LWTH SG5 16 D3
MHAD SG10 181 Q8
POTB/CUF EN6 108 D3
RAD WD7 119 L1
RBSF CM22 167 L3
RKW/CH/CXG WD3 130 B3
ROY SG8 145 P9
RYLN/HDSTN HA2 142 F7
SBW CM21 183 R6
STALE/WH AL4 48 B4
STDN SG11 163 P10
STSD CM24 166 G7
TRING HP23 57 M1
TRING HP23 168 E5
WARE SG12 54 C4
WAT WD17 12 F1
WLYN AL6 50 C2
Station Wy LWTH SG6 16 C3
STAL AL1 9 J6
Staveley Rd DUN/WHIP LU6 38 F3
Steeplands BUSH WD23 132 F3
Steeple Vw BSF CM23 43 M1
Sten Cl PEND EN3 126 E3
Stephens Cl LTNE LU2 28 E6
Stephens Gdns LTNE LU2 28 E7
Stephenson Cl HOD EN11 73 H7
ROY SG8 14 C6
Stephenson Ms STVGE SG2 11 L6
Stephenson Wk
HTCH/STOT SG5 148 A11
Stephenson Wy BUSH WD23 13 K4
WATN WD24 118 B5
Stephenson Whf
HHS/BOV HP3 82 C6
Stephens Wy STALW/RED AL3 173 P12
Stephyns Chambers HHNE HP2 4 E5
Stepnells TRING HP23 169 L8
The Stepping Stones
LTNN/LIM LU3 * 27 J4
Sterling Av CHES/WCR EN8 110 B8
EDGW HA8 134 D7
Sterling Rd ENC/FH EN2 125 H5
Stevenage Crs BORE WD6 120 C5
Stevenage Ri HHNE HP2 62 D6
Stevenage Rd
HTCHE/RSTV SG4 157 P8
KNEB SG3 177 M2
STVG SG1 20 D7
STVGE SG2 34 D1
Stevens Cl PIN HA5 142 A7
POTB/CUF EN6 106 B7
Stevens Gn BUSH WD23 133 G4
Stevenson Cl BAR EN5 137 H2
Steward Cl CHES/WCR EN8 110 C4
Stewart Clark Ct
DUN/WHIP LU6 25 L8
Stewart Cl ABLGY WD5 101 L5
Stewart Rd HARP AL5 46 F3
The Stewarts BSF CM23 43 L2
Stewarts Wy BSF CM23 166 B3
Steynings Wy
NFNCH/WDSPK N12 136 E8
Stile Cft HLWS CM18 75 L7
Stilton Pth BORE WD6 120 E4
Stipers Cl DUN/WHIP LU6 39 J4
Stirling Cl HTCHE/RSTV SG4 * 20 A2
STVGE SG2 177 Q2
Stirling Rd
KTN/HRWW/WS HA3 143 K5
Stirling Wy ABLGY WD5 101 L6
BORE WD6 135 H2
WGCE AL7 51 J7
Stoat Cl HERT/BAY SG13 53 L7
Stobarts Cl KNEB SG3 177 M3
Stockbreach Cl HAT AL10 67 L7
Stockbreach Rd HAT AL10 67 L7
Stockbridge Cl CHESW EN7 91 J8
Stockens Dell KNEB SG3 177 M5
Stockens Gn KNEB SG3 177 M5
Stockers Farm Rd
RKW/CH/CXG WD3 130 A6
Stockfield Av HOD EN11 72 E5
Stockholm Wy LTNW/LEA LU4 27 J1
Stocking La ROY SG8 153 L12
Stockings La HERT/BAY SG13 70 B8
Stockingstone Rd LTNE LU2 28 C6
Stockingswater La PEND EN3 126 C7
Stockmen Fld BSF CM23 43 J4
Stockport Rd
RKW/CH/CXG WD3 129 G3
Stocks Mdw HHNE HP2 82 E1
Stocks Rd TRING HP23 170 C10
Stockton Cl BAR EN5 123 G8
Stockton Gdns MLHL NW7 135 H6
Stockwell Cl CHESW EN7 109 L2
Stockwell La CHESW EN7 109 M2
Stockwood Crs LTN LU1 6 E8
Stondon Rd SHFD SG17 146 E5
Stonecroft AMS HP6 112 A1
KNEB SG3 177 M4
Stonecroft Cl BAR EN5 121 M8
Stonecross STAL AL1 9 G3
Stonecross Rd HAT AL10 67 M6
Stone Gv STAN HA7 134 C7
Stonegrove Gdns EDGW HA8 134 C8
Stonehills WGCW AL8 50 B7
Stonelea Rd HHS/BOV HP3 5 K8
Stoneleigh SBW CM21 183 P6
Stoneleigh Av EN EN1 125 M4
Stoneleigh Cl CHES/WCR EN8 110 B7
LTNN/LIM LU3 27 M2
Stoneleigh Dr HOD EN11 72 F4
Stoneley LWTH SG6 148 D12
Stonemason Cl HARP AL5 46 E2
Stonemead WGCW AL8 50 B2
Stonesdale LTNW/LEA LU4 26 F5
Stoneways Cl LTNW/LEA LU4 27 G3
Stoney Cl BERK HP4 59 K7
Stoney Common STSD CM24 166 G8
Stoney Common Rd
STSD CM24 166 F8
Stoneycroft HHW HP1 81 L2
Stoney Cft TRING HP23 170 C12
Stoneycroft WGCE AL7 50 E6
Stoneyfield Dr STSD CM24 166 G8
Stoneyfields Gdns EDGW HA8 135 G7
Stoneyfields La EDGW HA8 135 G8
Stoneygate Rd LTNW/LEA LU4 27 H7
Stoney Gv CSHM HP5 97 H4
Stoney La CSHM HP5 78 D4
Stonnells Cl LWTH SG6 16 D1
Stony Cft STVG SG1 10 E3
Stonycroft Cl PEND EN3 126 C6
Stony Hills WARE SG12 179 L11
Stony La CSHM HP5 114 C3
LTNE LU2 29 M6
Stonyshotts WAB EN9 111 J7
Stopsley Wy LTNE LU2 28 E6
Storehouse La
HTCHE/RSTV SG4 157 P7
Storey St HHS/BOV HP3 82 B6
Stormont Rd HTCH/STOT SG5 157 P4
Stornoway HHS/BOV HP3 82 F4
Stortford Hall Pk BSF CM23 44 B1
Stortford Hall Rd BSF CM23 44 B1
Stortford Rd HOD EN11 72 F6
RBSF CM22 184 E5
SAFWS CB11 161 Q5
STDN SG11 163 R12
Stort Ldg BSF CM23 43 K1
Stort Mi HLW CM20 183 M11
Stort Rd BSF CM23 43 M3
Stort Valley Wy CHONG CM5 77 J8
EPP CM16 94 D6
HLWW/ROY CM19 73 K5
SBW CM21 183 P10
WAB EN9 93 M5
Stotfold Rd ARL/CHE SG15 147 Q1
HTCH/STOT SG5 148 B12
HTCHE/RSTV SG4 16 A8
Stowe Crs RSLP HA4 140 F8
The Stow HLW CM20 3 K3
Stox Md KTN/HRWW/WS HA3 143 H3
Strafford Cl POTB/CUF EN6 106 E6
Strafford Ct KNEB SG3 177 N4
Strafford Ga POTB/CUF EN6 106 E6
Strafford Rd BAR EN5 122 C7
The Straits WAB EN9 110 F6
Strandburgh Pl HHS/BOV HP3 82 F4
Strangers Wy LTNW/LEA LU4 27 G5
Strangeways WAT WD17 117 J2
Stratfield Dr BROX EN10 92 C1
Stratfield Rd BORE WD6 120 D7
Stratford Rd LTNW/LEA LU4 27 M8
WAT WD17 12 D1
Stratford Wy HHS/BOV HP3 81 M5
HHW HP1 4 B8
LCOL/BKTW AL2 102 D3
WAT WD17 12 B2
Strathearn Cots
TRDG/WHET N20 * 136 E6
Strathmore Av
HTCH/STOT SG5 157 N4
LTN LU1 41 J4
Strathmore Rd
HTCHE/RSTV SG4 175 Q3
Strathmore Wk LTN LU1 7 H8
Stratton Av ENC/FH EN2 125 H3
Stratton Gdns LTNE LU2 28 B5
Stratton Pl AMSS HP7 * 113 K5
Strawberry Crs
LCOL/BKTW AL2 85 M8
Strawberry Fld HAT AL10 87 L3
LTNN/LIM LU3 27 J2
Strawberry Flds WARE SG12 53 M3
Strawfields WGCE AL7 50 F6
Strawmead HAT AL10 67 M6
Straw Plait Wy ARL/CHE SG15 147 P5
Strayfield Rd ENC/FH EN2 124 E2
Streatley Rd LTNN/LIM LU3 154 C9
The Street BLDK SG7 19 G1
BSF CM23 161 P10
BUNT SG9 160 A11
KGLGY WD4 99 L5
RBSF CM22 45 G4
RBSF CM22 184 D9
STDN SG11 162 D10
STDN SG11 163 R6
Stretton Wy BORE WD6 120 C4
Stringers La STVGE SG2 34 C8
Stripling Wy WATW WD18 131 L2
Stroma Cl HHS/BOV HP3 83 G4
Stronnell Cl LTNE LU2 28 E6
Stronsay Cl HHS/BOV HP3 83 G4
Stuart Ct AMS HP6 * 113 H4
BORE WD6 134 B2
Stuart Dr HTCHE/RSTV SG4 157 R6
ROY SG8 14 E5
Stuart Pl LTN LU1 6 E6
Stuart Rd
AMP/FLIT/BLC MK45 155 J2
EBAR EN4 137 J3
KTN/HRWW/WS HA3 143 K5
WLYN AL6 49 M1
Stuarts Cl HHS/BOV HP3 5 G7
Stuart St DUN/WHIP LU6 25 L8
LTN LU1 6 E6
Stuart Wy CHESW EN7 109 M5
Stubbs Cl DUN/HR/TOD LU5 26 B4
Stubbs End Cl AMS HP6 113 J2
Stubbs Wd AMS HP6 113 J2
Stud Gn GSTN WD25 101 L6
Studham La BERK HP4 171 L5
The Studios BUSH WD23 132 E2
Studio Wy BORE WD6 121 G5
Studlands Ri ROY SG8 14 F7
Studley Rd LTNN/LIM LU3 6 D2
Sturgeon's Wy
HTCHE/RSTV SG4 157 R3
Sturla Cl HERT/WAT SG14 52 F6
Sturlas Wy CHES/WCR EN8 110 B7
Sturmer Cl STALE/WH AL4 86 A3
Sturrock Wy HTCHE/RSTV SG4 20 A3
Stylecroft Rd CSTG HP8 128 B5
Styles Cl LTNE LU2 29 G7
Such Cl LWTH SG6 16 F2
Sudbury Rd LTNW/LEA LU4 26 F3
Sudicamps Ct WAB EN9 111 L7
Suez Rd PEND EN3 126 C8
Suffolk Cl BORE WD6 135 H1
LCOL/BKTW AL2 86 A7
LTNW/LEA LU4 26 E6
Suffolk Rd DUN/HR/TOD LU5 39 K3
POTB/CUF EN6 106 C6
ROY SG8 14 F7
RYLN/HDSTN HA2 142 D8
Sugar La HHW HP1 80 F4
Sugden Ct DUN/WHIP LU6 38 E1
Sulgrave Crs TRING HP23 169 N12
Sullivan Crs DEN/HRF UB9 140 B4
Sullivan Wy BORE WD6 134 A2
Summer Dl WGCW AL8 50 B3
Summerfield HAT AL10 87 L3
Summerfield Cl
LCOL/BKTW AL2 86 A8
Summerfield Rd GSTN WD25 117 L1
LTN LU1 40 D1
Summer Gv BORE WD6 134 B2
Summer Hl BORE WD6 134 E1
Summerhill Ct STAL AL1 * 9 J3
Summerhouse La
DEN/HRF UB9 139 L2
GSTN WD25 119 G5
Summerhouse Wy
ABLGY WD5 101 K4
Summerleas Cl HHNE HP2 5 J2
Summerleys DUN/WHIP LU6 37 J5
Summer Pl WATW WD18 * 131 K2
Summersland Rd
STALE/WH AL4 66 A6
Summers Rd LTNE LU2 29 G8
Summer St LTN LU1 41 G7
Summers Wy
LCOL/BKTW AL2 * 104 C1
Summers Wd BORE WD6 * 120 F8
Summerswood La BORE WD6 121 J1
Summer Wk STALW/RED AL3 172 G4
Summit Rd POTB/CUF EN6 106 C4
Summit Wy STHGT/OAK N14 137 M5
Sumners Farm Cl
HLWW/ROY CM19 94 E2
Sumpter Yd STAL AL1 8 E6
Sunbower Av DUN/WHIP LU6 25 J6
Sunbury Av MLHL NW7 135 H8
Sunbury Ct BAR EN5 * 122 C8
Sunbury Gdns MLHL NW7 135 H8
Suncote Av DUN/WHIP LU6 25 J6
Suncote Cl DUN/WHIP LU6 25 J7
Sunderland Av STAL AL1 9 L3
Sunderland Gv GSTN WD25 101 K8
Sundew Rd HHW HP1 81 J4
Sundon Park Rd LTNN/LIM LU3 27 G1
Sundon Rd DUN/HR/TOD LU5 26 A4
DUN/HR/TOD LU5 154 A5
LTNN/LIM LU3 154 F8
Sundown Av DUN/HR/TOD LU5 39 H2
Sun Hl ROY SG8 14 D8
Sun La HARP AL5 46 E3
Sunmead Rd HHNE HP2 62 B8
Sunningdale BSF CM23 43 L3
LTNE LU2 28 D6
Sunningdale Cl STAN HA7 134 L2
Sunningdale Ldg EDGW HA8 * 134 D8
Sunningdale Ms WGCE AL7 * 50 D3
Sunny Bank LBUZ LU7 169 K2
Sunnybank Rd
POTB/CUF EN6 106 E7
Sunny Brook Cl
RAYLNE/WEN HP22 168 B11
Sunny Cft HLWS CM18 75 K8
Sunnydell LCOL/BKTW AL2 84 F8

Sunnyfield BRKMPK AL9 ...... 68 B5
 MLHL NW7 ...... 135 K7
Sunny HI BUNT SG9 ...... 159 J10
Sunnyhill Rd HHW HP1 ...... 4 B1
 RKW/CH/CXG WD3 ...... 139 H1
Sunnymead Orch BLDK SG7 ...... 150 A2
Sunnymede Av CSHM HP5 ...... 97 G2
The Sunny Rd PEND EN3 ...... 126 B5
Sunnyside STSD SG24 ...... 166 G2
 WAB EN9 ...... 93 K4
Sunnyside Rd CSHM HP5 ...... 96 K4
 HTCHE/RSTV SG4 ...... 157 Q7
Sunridge Av LTNE LU2 ...... 28 C7
Sunrise Crs HHS/BOV HP3 ...... 5 J8
Sunset Dr LTNE LU2 ...... 28 D6
Sunset Vw BAR EN5 ...... 122 C6
Sun St BLDK SG7 ...... 17 J1
 HTCH/STOT SG5 ...... 157 N7
 SBW CM21 ...... 183 R8
 WAB EN9 ...... 111 G7
Surrey PI TRING HP23 ...... 57 L2
Surrey Rd HRW HA1 ...... 143 G8
Surrey St LTN LU1 ...... 7 G8
Sursham CI STALW/RED AL3 ...... 172 C4
Sussex CI HOD EN11 ...... 72 E6
 LTNW/LEA LU4 ...... 26 D5
Sussex PI CFSP/GDCR SL9 ...... 138 C1
 LTNE LU2 ...... 29 H7
Sussex Ring
 NFNCH/WDSPK N12 ...... 136 E8
 WATN WD24 ...... 117 L4
Sussex Rd HRW HA1 ...... 143 G7
Sussex Wy EBAR EN4 ...... 137 M1
Sutcliffe CI BUSH WD23 ...... 119 G8
 STVG SG1 ...... 2 B3
Sutherland Av POTB/CUF EN6 ...... 108 B2
Sutherland CI BAR EN5 ...... 122 C4
Sutherland Ct WGCE AL7 ...... 50 D6
Sutherland Dr LTN LU1 ...... 6 D9
Sutherland Wy
 POTB/CUF EN6 ...... 108 B2
Sutton Acres RBSF CM22 ...... 184 D2
Sutton CI BROX EN10 ...... 92 C2
 PIN HA5 ...... 141 L7
 TRING HP23 ...... 169 M11
Sutton Ct WARE SG12 * 54 C5
Sutton Crs BAR EN5 ...... 136 B1
Sutton Gdns LTN LU1 ...... 40 B6
 LTNW/LIM LU3 ...... 27 H3
Sutton La BGSW SG18 ...... 144 B3
Sutton Rd STAL AL1 ...... 85 M3
 WAT WD17 ...... 13 G4
Swale CI STVG SG1 ...... 21 L6
Swallow CI BUSH WD23 ...... 132 F4
 LTNW/LEA LU4 ...... 26 E5
 RKW/CH/CXG WD3 ...... 130 A3
Swallow Ct WGCE AL7 * 50 D7
Swallowdale La HHNE HP2 ...... 62 E7
Swallow End WGCE AL7 ...... 50 D7
Swallowfields WGCE AL7 ...... 50 D7
Swallow Gdns HAT AL10 ...... 87 L2
Swallow La STAL AL1 ...... 85 M5
Swallow Oaks ABLGY WD5 ...... 101 K5
Swallow Pk HHNE HP2 ...... 62 F6
The Swallows WGCE AL7 ...... 50 D5
Swallowtail Wk BERK HP4 ...... 59 K6
Swan CI CSHM HP5 ...... 96 F1
 LBUZ LU7 ...... 36 E8
 RKW/CH/CXG WD3 ...... 130 A3
Swan Ct BSF CM23 ...... 43 M3
 HHNE HP2 ...... 8 E1
Swanells Wd DUN/WHIP LU6 ...... 171 P5
Swanfield Rd CHES/WCR EN8 ...... 110 C7
Swangley's La KNEB SG3 ...... 177 N4
Swanhill WGCE AL7 ...... 50 E4
Swanland Rd BRKMPK AL9 ...... 105 M7
 POTB/CUF EN6 ...... 105 M7
Swan La ROY SG8 ...... 145 M5
 TRDG/WHET N20 ...... 137 G6
Swanley Bar La
 POTB/CUF EN6 ...... 106 F2
Swanley Crs POTB/CUF EN6 ...... 106 F3
 LTNW/LEA LU4 ...... 26 E5
Swan Md HHS/BOV HP3 ...... 82 D7
 LTNW/LEA LU4 ...... 26 E5
Swann Rd RAYLNE/WEN HP22 ...... 56 A5
Swan & Pike Rd EN3 ...... 126 E4
Swans CI STALW/RED AL4 ...... 86 C3
Swan Rd CHES/WCR EN8 ...... 110 B8
Swansea Rd PEND EN3 ...... 126 A8
Swansons DUN/WHIP LU6 ...... 171 M8
Swanstand LWTH SG6 ...... 17 H5
Swanston Gra LTNW/LEA LU4 * 26 E5
Swanston Pth OXHEY WD19 ...... 132 A6
Swan St BLDK SG7 ...... 149 P1
Swan Wy PEND EN3 ...... 126 C3
Swasedale Rd LTNW/LIM LU3 ...... 27 K3
Sweet Briar BSF CM23 ...... 43 G1
 WGCE AL7 ...... 68 E1
Sweetbriar La HHW HP1 ...... 61 L7
Sweetmans Av PIN HA5 ...... 142 B5
Sweets Wy TRDG/WHET N20 ...... 137 H3
Sweyne HLWE CM17 ...... 76 A8
Sweyns Rd STVGE SG2 ...... 34 A1
Swift CI LWTH SG6 ...... 16 C1
 ROY SG8 ...... 14 E4
 WARE SG12 ...... 73 G2
Swiftfields WGCE AL7 ...... 50 D6
Swifts Green CI LTNE LU2 ...... 28 E1
Swifts Green Rd LTNE LU2 ...... 28 E1
Swinburne Av
 HTCH/STOT SG5 ...... 157 L4
Swinburne CI ROY SG8 ...... 14 E4
Swingate STVG SG1 ...... 10 C5
Swing Br LBUZ LU7 ...... 169 M4
Swing Gate La BERK HP4 ...... 80 B4
Swiss Av WATW WD18 ...... 13 J7
Swiss CI WATW WD18 ...... 117 J7
Sword CI BROX EN10 ...... 92 B2
Sworder CI LTNW/LIM LU3 ...... 154 F12
Sworders Yd BSF CM23 * 43 M2
Sycamore Ap
 RKW/CH/CXG WD3 ...... 131 G1
Sycamore Av HAT AL10 ...... 87 L1
Sycamore CI AMS HP6 ...... 113 H3
 BUSH WD23 ...... 13 M1
 CHESW EN7 ...... 109 K1
 EBAR EN4 ...... 137 H2
 EDGW HA8 ...... 135 G2
 GSTN WD25 ...... 117 M1
 HTCHE/RSTV SG4 ...... 154 C12
 LTNW/LIM LU3 ...... 154 C12
Sycamore Dene CSHM HP5 ...... 97 M2
Sycamore Dr LCOL/BKTW AL2 ...... 103 H1
 TRING HP23 ...... 169 G4
Sycamore Fld
 CM19 ...... 94 E1
Sycamore PI AMS HP6 * 113 H3
Sycamore RI BERK HP4 ...... 80 B2
Sycamore Rd AMS HP6 ...... 113 G3
 DUN/HR/TOD LU6 ...... 25 M3
 RKW/CH/CXG WD3 ...... 131 G1
The Sycamores BLDK SG7 ...... 149 J12

 BSF CM23 ...... 44 B3
 HHS/BOV HP3 ...... 81 K5
 RSLP HA4 ...... 103 M8
Sydney Chapman Wy
 BAR EN5 ...... 122 D6
Sydney Rd ENC/FH EN2 ...... 125 H3
 WAB EN9 ...... 12 A7
Sylam CI LTNN/LIM LU3 ...... 27 J2
Sylvandale WGCE AL7 ...... 51 G8
Sylvan CI HHNE HP2 ...... 82 E3
Sylvan Wy WGCE AL7 ...... 50 E4
Sylvesters HLWW/ROY CM19 ...... 74 D7
Sylvia Av PIN HA5 ...... 142 D1
Symonds Ct CHES/WCR EN8 ...... 110 B2
Symonds Green La STVG SG1 ...... 32 E2
Symonds Rd HTCH/STOT SG5 ...... 157 M5

T

Tabbs CI LWTH SG6 ...... 16 F1
Tacitus CI STVG SG1 ...... 34 A1
Tailors BSF CM23 ...... 43 H4
Takeley CI WAB EN9 ...... 111 H3
Talbot Av OXHEY WD19 ...... 132 C3
Talbot CI HHS/BOV HP3 * 5 G7
Talbot Rd HAT AL10 ...... 67 L5
 KTN/HRWW/WS HA3 ...... 143 K4
 LTNE LU2 ...... 7 J1
 RAYLNE/WEN HP22 ...... 168 C12
 RKW/CH/CXG WD3 ...... 130 C4
Talbot St HERT/BAY SG13 ...... 51 J7
 HTCH/STOT SG5 ...... 157 M5
Talbot Wy LWTH SG6 ...... 16 F1
Talisman St HTCHE/RSTV SG4 ...... 20 F8
Tallack CI KTN/HRWW/WS HA3 ...... 143 J1
Tallents Crs HARP AL5 ...... 47 H2
Tallis Wy BORE WD6 ...... 120 B5
Tall Oaks AMS HP6 ...... 113 H3
Tall Trees HTCHE/RSTV SG4 ...... 157 Q9
 ROY SG8 ...... 14 F7
Tamar CI STVG SG1 ...... 21 L6
Tamar Gn HHNE HP2 ...... 62 D5
Tamarisk CI STALW/RED AL3 ...... 65 H6
Tamarix Crs LCOL/BKTW AL2 ...... 85 L1
Tameton CI LTNE LU2 ...... 29 J7
Tamworth Rd HERT/BAY SG13 ...... 53 K6
Tancred Rd LTNE LU2 ...... 28 E5
Tanfield CI CHESW EN7 ...... 109 L1
Tanfield Gn LTNE LU2 ...... 29 J8
Tanglewood WLYN AL6 ...... 177 N10
Tanglewood CI STAN HA7 ...... 133 J5
Tankerfield PI STALW/RED AL3 ...... 8 B6
Tanners CI STALW/RED AL3 ...... 8 C5
Tanners Crs HERT/BAY SG13 ...... 71 G1
Tanners HI ABLGY WD5 ...... 101 K5
Tanners Wood La ABLGY WD5 ...... 101 J6
Tannery CI ROY SG8 ...... 14 D7
Tannery Drift ROY SG8 ...... 14 D7
The Tannery BUNT SG9 ...... 159 J10
Tannery Yd
 HTCHE/RSTV SG4 * 175 R3
Tansycroft WGCE AL7 ...... 51 F6
Tanworth CI NTHWD HA6 ...... 141 G1
Tanworth Gdns PIN HA5 ...... 141 M4
Tanyard La HTCHE/RSTV SG4 ...... 176 C6
Tanys Ct HLW CM20 ...... 3 L1
Tany's Dell HLW CM20 ...... 3 L1
Tapster St BAR EN5 ...... 122 D7
Taransey HHS/BOV HP3 ...... 5 H6
Tarnside Ct DUN/WHIP LU6 ...... 38 D8
Tarpan Wy BROX EN10 ...... 92 D8
Tarrant Dr HARP AL5 ...... 47 G6
Taskers Rw DUN/WHIP LU6 ...... 37 K5
Tassell Hall STALW/RED AL3 ...... 173 P11
Tate Gdns BUSH WD23 ...... 133 J3
Tate Rd CFSP/GDCR SL9 ...... 128 D8
Tates Wy STVG SG1 ...... 20 F7
Tatlers La STVGE SG2 ...... 34 B4
Tatsfield Av WAB EN9 ...... 93 H5
Tattersall Dr HHNE HP2 ...... 63 K8
Tattle HI HERT/WAT SG14 ...... 52 C3
Tatton St HLWE CM17 ...... 76 A4
Tauber CI BORE WD6 ...... 120 D8
Taunton Av LTNE LU2 ...... 7 M2
Taunton Dr ENC/FH EN2 ...... 124 E7
Taverners HHNE HP2 ...... 62 C8
Taverners Wy HOD EN11 ...... 72 E7
Tavistock Av STAL AL1 ...... 85 G5
Tavistock CI POTB/CUF EN6 ...... 107 H6
 STAL AL1 ...... 85 H5
Tavistock Crs LTN LU1 ...... 6 F7
Tavistock Pth STHGT/OAK N14 * 137 M2
Tavistock Rd WATN WD24 ...... 118 B5
Tavistock St DUN/WHIP LU6 ...... 25 L7
 LTN LU1 ...... 6 F8
Tawneys Rd HLWS CM18 ...... 75 K7
Taylifers HLWW/ROY CM19 ...... 94 C3
Taylor CI LTNE LU4 ...... 65 L6
Taylors Av HOD EN11 ...... 72 E7
Taylors End STSD CM24 ...... 167 N12
Taylor's La BAR EN5 ...... 122 D5
Taylors Md MLHL NW7 * 135 L4
Taylor's Rd HTCH/STOT SG5 ...... 148 D8
Taylor St LTN LU1 ...... 7 H3
Tayside Dr EDGW HA8 ...... 134 F6
Taywood CI STVGE SG2 ...... 33 M7
Teal CI PEND EN3 ...... 126 A7
Teal Dr NTHWD HA6 ...... 141 G2
Teal Wy HHS/BOV HP3 ...... 5 H6
Teasdale CI ROY SG8 ...... 14 D4
Teasel CI ROY SG8 ...... 14 D4
Teazle Md EPP CM16 ...... 95 M7
Tedder Av HNLW SG16 ...... 147 K4
Tedder Rd HHNE HP2 ...... 5 M1
 RAYLNE/WEN HP22 ...... 56 B7
Tees CI STVG SG1 ...... 21 K6
Teesdale HLW CM17 ...... 76 C2
 LTNW/LEA LU4 ...... 27 G4
Tee Side HERT/BAY SG13 ...... 53 M6
Telford CI STVGE SG2 ...... 11 L2
Telford CI WATN WD25 ...... 118 B3
Telford Rd LCOL/BKTW AL2 ...... 86 B5
Telford Wy LTN LU1 ...... 6 C1
Telscombe Wy LTNE LU2 ...... 29 L7
Temperance St STALW/RED AL3 ...... 8 B8
Templar Av LTNE LU2 ...... 28 C4
Templars Dr
 KTN/HRWW/WS HA3 * 143 H1
Templars La HTCHE/RSTV SG4 * 31 H7
Temple Av TRDG/WHET N20 ...... 137 H3
Temple Bank HLW CM20 ...... 183 M12
Temple CI CHESW EN7 ...... 109 L5
 HTCHE/RSTV SG4 ...... 157 M9
 LTNE LU2 * 28 C4
 WAT WD17 ...... 13 G3
Temple Ct BLDK SG7 * 17 K3

 POTB/CUF EN6 ...... 106 B5
Temple Flds HERT/WAT SG14 ...... 53 G4
Temple Gdns LWTH SG6 * 17 G1
 RKW/CH/CXG WD3 ...... 130 F6
Temple Gv ENC/FH EN2 ...... 124 F7
Temple La WARE SG12 ...... 179 N10
Temple Md HLWW/ROY CM19 ...... 73 M5
Temple Mead CI STAN HA7 ...... 143 M1
Templepan La
 RKW/CH/CXG WD3 ...... 116 C3
Temple Pde BAR EN5 * 137 H5
Temple Vw STALW/RED AL3 ...... 8 C2
Templewood WGCW AL8 ...... 50 B4
Tempsford WGCE AL7 ...... 51 H7
Tempsford CI ENC/FH EN2 ...... 125 G2
Tempsford Ct RYLN/HDSTN HA2 ...... 143 M4
Temsford CI RYLN/HDSTN HA2 ...... 143 M4
Tenby Av KTN/HRWW/WS HA3 ...... 143 M4
Tenby Dr LTNW/LEA LU4 ...... 27 K6
Tenby Rd PEND EN3 ...... 126 A7
Tendring Rd HLWS CM18 ...... 3 J9
The Tene BLDK SG7 ...... 17 K1
Tennand CI CHESW EN7 ...... 91 K8
Tennison Av BORE WD6 ...... 134 F1
Tenniswood Rd EN EN1 ...... 125 J2
Tennyson Av DUN/HR/TOD LU5 ...... 26 A3
 HTCHE/RSTV SG4 ...... 20 A3
 WAB EN9 ...... 111 J8
Tennyson CI ROY SG8 ...... 14 E4
Tennyson Rd HARP AL5 ...... 46 E2
 LCOL/BKTW AL2 ...... 84 E8
 LTN LU1 ...... 41 J4
 MLHL NW7 ...... 135 K8
 STSD CM24 ...... 167 L11
Tenth Av LTNW/LIM LU3 ...... 27 G2
 STSD CM24 ...... 167 L11
Tenzing Gv LTN LU1 ...... 6 C8
Tenzing Rd HHNE HP2 ...... 82 E3
Teresa Gdns CHES/WCR EN8 ...... 110 A8
Terminal Rd North
 STSD CM24 ...... 167 R10
Terminal Rd South
 RBSF CM22 ...... 167 R10
Terminus St HLW CM20 ...... 2 E5
Terrace Gdns WAT WD17 ...... 12 E1
The Terrace TRING HP23 ...... 57 L2
Terrilands PIN HA5 ...... 142 D5
Tethys Rd HHNE HP2 ...... 62 D7
Tewin CI STALE/WH AL4 ...... 46 A6
 WLYN AL6 ...... 177 Q12
Tewin Ct WGCE AL7 ...... 50 D6
Tewin HI WLYN AL6 ...... 49 J2
Tewin Rd HHNE HP2 ...... 83 G2
 WGCE AL7 ...... 50 D6
Tewkesbury Av PIN HA5 ...... 142 C1
Thackeray CI ROY SG8 ...... 14 E4
Thames CI LTNN/LIM LU3 ...... 27 M6
Thames Dr RSLP HA4 ...... 141 G8
Thamesdale LCOL/BKTW AL2 ...... 104 D1
Thames Rd LTNN/LIM LU3 ...... 27 M6
Thatcham Gdns
 TRDG/WHET N20 ...... 137 G3
Thatch CI LTNW/LEA LU4 ...... 26 C5
Thatchers End HTCHE/RSTV SG4 ...... 20 B1
The Thatchers BSF CM23 ...... 43 J5
Thaxted CI LTNE LU2 ...... 29 K7
Thaxted Wy WAB EN9 ...... 111 H3
Thaynesfield POTB/CUF EN6 ...... 107 H5
The Laurels LCOL/BKTW AL2 ...... 102 E2
Thelby CI LTNN/LIM LU3 ...... 27 K3
Thele Av WARE SG12 ...... 73 H1
Theleway CI HOD EN11 ...... 72 F4
Thellusson Wy
 RKW/CH/CXG WD3 ...... 129 K3
Thellusson Ct RAD WD7 ...... 119 L1
Theobald CI BORE WD6 ...... 120 D7
 RAD WD7 ...... 120 A2
Theobald's Rd POTB/CUF EN6 ...... 108 C4
Theobald St BORE WD6 ...... 120 D7
Theobalds Crs
 KTN/HRWW/WS HA3 ...... 143 H1
Theobald's CI POTB/CUF EN6 ...... 108 D4
Theobalds Gv
 CHES/WCR EN8 * 110 B6
Theobalds La CHES/WCR EN8 ...... 109 M6
Theobalds Park Rd
 ENC/FH EN2 ...... 124 F1
Theodora Wy PIN HA5 ...... 141 K5
Therfield Rd STALW/RED AL3 ...... 65 H5
Therfield Wk DUN/HR/TOD LU5 ...... 26 C3
Thetford Gdns LTNE LU2 ...... 28 B3
Theydon Ct WAB EN9 ...... 111 M7
Thieves La HERT/WAT SG14 ...... 52 D7
Third Av GSTN WD25 ...... 118 B1
 HLWW/ROY CM19 ...... 2 B9
 LTNN/LIM LU3 ...... 27 H7
 LWTH SG6 ...... 17 G2
 STSD CM24 ...... 167 K11
Thirlestone Rd LTNN/LEA LU4 ...... 24 H8
Thirlmere STVG SG1 ...... 22 A4
Thirlmere Dr STAL AL1 ...... 85 M4
Thirlmere Gdns NTHWD HA6 ...... 130 F8
Thirsk Rd BORE WD6 ...... 120 E4
Thirtieth St STSD CM24 ...... 167 P10
Thistle CI HHW HP1 ...... 81 J3
Thistlecroft HHW HP1 ...... 4 B5
Thistle Dr HAT AL10 ...... 67 K5
Thistle Gv WGCE AL7 ...... 69 G2
Thistle Rd LTN LU1 ...... 7 H3
The Thistles HHW HP1 ...... 81 M1
Thistley La HTCHE/RSTV SG4 ...... 157 P11
Thomas Rochford Wy
 CHES/WCR EN8 ...... 110 D1
Thomas Wy ROY SG8 ...... 14 E4
Thompsons CI CHESW EN7 ...... 109 K3
 HARP AL5 ...... 46 B2
Thompsons Meadow
 ROY SG8 ...... 145 M5
Thompson Wy
 RKW/CH/CXG WD3 ...... 129 L3
Thomson Rd
 KTN/HRWW/WS HA3 ...... 143 K4
Thorley HI BSF CM23 ...... 43 M4
Thorley La BSF CM23 ...... 43 M5
Thorley Park Rd BSF CM23 ...... 43 M5
Thorn Av BUSH WD23 ...... 133 G4
Thornbera CI BSF CM23 ...... 43 M5
Thornbera Gdns BSF CM23 ...... 43 M5
Thornbury DUN/HR/TOD LU5 ...... 26 A2
Thornbury Gdns BORE WD6 ...... 121 G4
Thornbury Rd HTCHE/RSTV SG4 ...... 20 B1
Thorncroft HHS/BOV HP3 ...... 82 F4
Thorndene Av
 TRDG/WHET N20 ...... 137 L4
Thorndyke Ct PIN HA5 ...... 142 D2
Thorne CI HHW HP1 ...... 4 B6

Thorne Wy RAYLNE/WEN HP22 ...... 56 E1
Thorneycroft CI LTNN/LIM LU3 ...... 27 M4
Thorneycroft Dr PEND EN3 ...... 126 E1
Thornfield BSF CM23 ...... 43 J3
Thorn Gv BSF CM23 ...... 44 B3
Thornhill AMSS HP7 ...... 112 C6
 DUN/HR/TOD LU5 ...... 26 B2
Thornhill Rd LTNW/LEA LU4 ...... 26 E2
 NTHWD HA6 ...... 131 G7
Thorn Rd DUN/HR/TOD LU5 ...... 25 M4
Thornton CI BORE WD6 ...... 121 G6
Thornton Gv PIN HA5 ...... 142 C1
Thornton Rd BAR EN5 ...... 122 C7
 POTB/CUF EN6 ...... 107 G4
Thornton St HERT/WAT SG14 ...... 53 H7
 STALW/RED AL3 ...... 8 C4
Thorn Tree Dr TRING HP23 ...... 57 K1
Thorn View Rd
 HHNE HP2 ...... 62 F6
Three Close La BERK HP4 ...... 80 C3
Three Closes HTCH/STOT SG5 ...... 156 E1
Three Corners HHS/BOV HP3 * 5 M7
Three Forests Wy EPP CM16 ...... 96 A2
 GTDUN CM6 ...... 185 R12
 HLWW/ROY CM19 ...... 73 K5
Three Forest Wy RBSF CM22 ...... 45 H4
Three Horseshoes Rd
 HLWW/ROY CM19 ...... 74 F7
Three Houses La
 HTCHE/RSTV SG4 ...... 176 C6
Three Meadows Ms
 KTN/HRWW/WS HA3 ...... 143 K3
Three Star Caravan Pk
 HNLW SG16 ...... 147 J6
Three Star Pk HNLW SG16 * 147 K6
Three Stiles STVGE SG2 ...... 35 J5
Three Valleys Wy BUSH WD23 ...... 13 K7
Tremhall Av RBSF CM22 ...... 44 F1
 STSD CM24 ...... 167 P12
Thresher CI BSF CM23 ...... 43 H4
 LTNE LU4 ...... 26 D4
Thricknells CI LTNN/LIM LU3 ...... 27 J2
Thrift Farm La BORE WD6 ...... 121 G6
Thriftfield HHNE HP2 ...... 62 B8
Thristers CI LWTH SG6 ...... 16 F5
Throcking La BUNT SG9 ...... 158 G8
Throcking Rd BUNT SG9 ...... 158 B9
Throstle PI GSTN WD25 * 102 A6
Thrums WATN WD24 ...... 117 M3
Thrush Av HAT AL10 ...... 67 K7
Thrush Gn RKW/CH/CXG WD3 ...... 130 A3
 RYLN/HDSTN HA2 ...... 142 C6
Thrush La POTB/CUF EN6 ...... 108 C2
Thumbswood WGCE AL7 ...... 68 C8
Thumpers HHNE HP2 ...... 62 C8
Thundercourt WARE SG12 ...... 54 B3
Thundridge CI WGCE AL7 ...... 50 F8
Thurgood Rd HOD EN11 ...... 72 E5
Thurlow CI LTNE LU2 ...... 29 J8
 STVG SG1 ...... 21 H8
Thurnall Av BLDK SG7 ...... 14 E8
Thurnall CI BLDK SG7 ...... 17 K1
Thurstans HLWW/ROY CM19 ...... 94 F2
Thyme CI LTNE LU2 ...... 28 C2
Tibbett CI DUN/WHIP LU6 ...... 39 G3
Tibbles CI GSTN WD25 ...... 118 C1
Tibbs Hill Rd ABLGY WD5 ...... 101 K4
Tiberius Rd LTNN/LIM LU3 ...... 27 K3
Tichborne RKW/CH/CXG WD3 ...... 129 H8
Tickenhall Dr HLWE CM17 ...... 76 B5
Tiger Moth Wy HAT AL10 ...... 67 H7
Tilbury Md HLWS CM18 ...... 3 M9
Tilecroft WGCW AL8 ...... 50 B4
Tilegate Rd CHONG CM5 ...... 77 H8
 HLWS CM18 ...... 75 K7
Tilehouse CI BORE WD6 ...... 120 D7
Tilehouse La DEN/HRF UB9 ...... 139 J3
Tilehouse St HTCH/STOT SG5 ...... 156 N6
Tilekiln CI CHESW EN7 ...... 109 K3
Tile Kiln CI HHS/BOV HP3 ...... 82 E3
Tile Kiln Crs HHS/BOV HP3 ...... 82 E3
Tile Kiln La HHS/BOV HP3 ...... 82 E3
Tilgate LTNE LU2 ...... 29 K7
Tillers Link STVGE SG2 ...... 33 L7
Tillingham Ct WAB EN9 ...... 111 L7
Tillingham Wy
 NFNCH/WDSPK N12 ...... 136 E7
Tillotson Rd
 KTN/HRWW/WS HA3 ...... 142 F2
Tilwicks Rd HLWS CM18 ...... 3 K9
Tilsworth Rd LBUZ LU7 ...... 24 A4
Tilsworth Wk STALE/WH AL4 ...... 66 A5
Timbercroft WGCE AL7 ...... 50 E4
Timber Orch HERT/WAT SG14 ...... 52 E3
Timberidge
 RKW/CH/CXG WD3 ...... 116 A8
Timbers CI HARP AL5 ...... 46 D3
Times CI HTCH/STOT SG5 ...... 157 M5
Timworth CI LTNE LU2 ...... 29 K8
Tingeys CI STALW/RED AL3 ...... 173 Q12
Tinkers La TRING HP23 ...... 58 E7
Tinsley CI LTN LU1 ...... 40 F4
Tintagel CI HHNE HP2 ...... 62 E5
 LTNN/LIM LU3 ...... 27 M5
Tintagel Dr STAN HA7 ...... 134 B4
Tintern CI HARP AL5 ...... 46 D3
 STVGE SG2 ...... 177 N2
Tinwell Ms BORE WD6 ...... 121 G4
Tippendell La LCOL/BKTW AL2 ...... 84 E7
Tippet Ct STVG SG1 ...... 10 D8
Tippett CI STVG SG1 * 10 D8
Tippetts CI ENC/FH EN2 ...... 125 J2
Tiptree Dr ENC/FH EN2 ...... 125 J4
Tiree CI HHS/BOV HP3 ...... 5 H6
Titan CI STALW/RED AL3 ...... 27 K8
Titan Rd HHNE HP2 ...... 7 D7
Titchfield Rd PEND EN3 ...... 126 C3
Titchmarsh CI ROY SG8 ...... 21 J8
Tithe Barn CI STAL AL1 ...... 85 L1
Tithe Barn Ct ABLGY WD5 ...... 101 J5
Tithe CI HTCHE/RSTV SG4 ...... 176 C6
Tithelands HLWW/ROY CM19 ...... 74 D7
Titian Av BUSH WD23 ...... 134 B1
Titmus CI STVG SG1 ...... 10 D3
Titmus Rd RAYLNE/WEN HP22 ...... 56 B6
Tiverton Ct HARP AL5 * 47 G4
Tiverton Rd POTB/CUF EN6 ...... 107 H3
Toddbrook HLWW/ROY CM19 ...... 8 B9
Toddington Rd LTNW/LEA LU4 ...... 26 C1
Toland CI LTNN/LIM LU3 ...... 27 G8
Tolcarne Dr PIN HA5 ...... 141 G6
Tollgate CI RKW/CH/CXG WD3 ...... 115 K8

Tollgate Rd CHES/WCR EN8 ...... 126 B1
 STALE/WH AL4 ...... 87 J6
Tollpit End HHW HP1 ...... 61 L7
Tollsworth Wy STDN SG11 ...... 163 N10
Tolmers Av POTB/CUF EN6 ...... 108 C3
Tolmers Gdns POTB/CUF EN6 ...... 108 C3
Tolmers Rd POTB/CUF EN6 ...... 108 C2
Tolpits CI WATW WD18 ...... 12 A8
Tolpits La WATW WD18 ...... 131 H5
Tomkins CI BORE WD6 ...... 120 C5
Tomlins CI ROY SG8 * 152 H4
Tomlinson Av LTNW/LEA LU4 ...... 26 D5
Tompkins CI
 RAYLNE/WEN HP22 ...... 56 D1
Toms Cft HHNE HP2 ...... 62 D8
Toms Fld HAT AL10 ...... 87 J1
Toms Hill CI TRING HP23 ...... 170 D12
Toms Hill Rd TRING HP23 ...... 170 D12
Tom's La KGLGY WD4 ...... 101 G2
Tooke CI PIN HA5 ...... 142 C3
Toorack Rd
 KTN/HRWW/WS HA3 ...... 143 H4
Tooveys Mill CI KGLGY WD4 ...... 100 E3
Topford Rd CFSP/GDCR SL9 ...... 138 B2
Top PK CFSP/GDCR SL9 ...... 138 A8
Topstreet Wy HARP AL5 ...... 47 G5
Tormay CI LBUZ LU7 ...... 36 B3
Torquay Crs STVG SG1 ...... 32 C5
Torquay Dr LTNW/LEA LU4 ...... 27 H5
Torrington Av
 NFNCH/WDSPK N12 ...... 137 J8
Torrington Dr POTB/CUF EN6 ...... 107 H6
Torrington Gv
 NFNCH/WDSPK N12 ...... 137 J8
Torrington Pk
 NFNCH/WDSPK N12 ...... 137 J7
Tortoiseshell Wy BERK HP4 ...... 59 M1
Torver Rd HRW HA1 ...... 143 J6
Torwood CI BERK HP4 ...... 79 K1
Tot La BSF CM23 ...... 166 F10
Totteridge Common
 TRDG/WHET N20 ...... 135 L5
Totteridge La
 TRDG/WHET N20 ...... 136 E5
Totteridge Rd PEND EN3 ...... 126 C1
Totteridge Village
 TRDG/WHET N20 ...... 136 C4
Totternhoe Rd DUN/WHIP LU6 ...... 37 H2
 DUN/WHIP LU6 ...... 38 C2
Totton Ms STALW/RED AL3 ...... 173 R12
Totts La STVGE SG2 ...... 35 G6
Toulmin Dr STALW/RED AL3 ...... 65 G6
Tovey Av HOD EN11 ...... 72 E5
Tovey CI LCOL/BKTW AL2 ...... 85 J5
 WAB EN9 ...... 93 J5
Tower CI BERK HP4 ...... 79 K2
 HTCHE/RSTV SG4 ...... 20 C6
Tower HI STALW/RED AL3 ...... 8 D8
 MHAD SG10 ...... 181 R7
Tower Rd HTCHE/RSTV SG4 ...... 176 C7
 LTNE LU2 ...... 7 K3
 WARE SG12 ...... 54 C3
Towers Rd PIN HA5 ...... 142 C3
The Towers STVG SG1 ...... 10 D6
Tower St HERT/WAT SG14 ...... 53 G5
Tower Vw BUSH WD23 ...... 133 J3
 HTCHE/RSTV SG4 ...... 175 P3
Tower Wy LTNE LU2 ...... 7 K3
Town Bridge Ct CSHM HP5 ...... 96 F6
Towne Rd ROY SG8 ...... 14 E8
Town Farm LBUZ LU7 ...... 169 L2
Town Farm CI ROY SG8 ...... 145 L4
Town Farm Crs STDN SG11 ...... 163 R11
Townfield CSHM HP5 ...... 96 F6
 RKW/CH/CXG WD3 ...... 130 A3
Town Field La CSTG HP8 ...... 128 A6
Town Flds HAT AL10 ...... 87 K1
Town Hall Ar BERK HP4 * 80 A1
Town La STVGE SG2 ...... 35 H6
Town Mead Rd WAB EN9 ...... 111 L8
Townsend HHNE HP2 ...... 62 B8
Townsend Av STAL AL1 ...... 9 G3
Townsend CI HARP AL5 ...... 46 B3
 HTCHE/RSTV SG4 ...... 157 Q11
 ROY SG8 ...... 152 H10
Townsend Dr STALW/RED AL3 ...... 8 F1
Townsend Farm Rd
 DUN/HR/TOD LU6 ...... 25 M6
Townsend La HARP AL5 ...... 46 B4
Townsend Rd CSHM HP5 ...... 96 F4
 HARP AL5 ...... 46 B3
Townsend Wy NTHWD HA6 ...... 141 G6
Townshend St HERT/BAY SG13 ...... 53 J7
Townside DUN/WHIP LU6 ...... 37 K6
Townsley CI LTN LU1 ...... 6 F8
Town Sq STVG SG1 ...... 10 C5
Tracyes Rd HLWS CM18 ...... 75 M7
Trafalgar CI STVG SG1 ...... 22 D3
Trafford CI RAD WD7 ...... 104 C6
 STVG SG1 ...... 21 J8
Traherne CI HTCHE/RSTV SG4 ...... 157 P9
Trajan Ga STVG SG1 ...... 22 B8
Trapp's Ct CSHM HP5 ...... 97 G7
Trapp's La CSHM HP5 ...... 97 G7
Trap Rd ROY SG8 ...... 145 N5
Trapstyle Rd WARE SG12 ...... 53 L3
Travellers CI BRKMPK AL9 ...... 88 A5
Travellers La HAT AL10 ...... 87 L2
Treacher's CI CSHM HP5 ...... 96 F5
Treacle La BUNT SG9 ...... 19 K6
Treacy CI BUSH WD23 ...... 133 J5
Trebellan Dr HHNE HP2 ...... 5 K1
Treehanger CI TRING HP23 ...... 57 M1
Treetops CI NTHWD HA6 ...... 131 H6
Trefoil CI LTNW/LEA LU4 ...... 26 D5
Trefusis Wk WAT WD17 ...... 117 J5
Tregelles Rd HOD EN11 ...... 72 E5
Tremaine Gv HHNE HP2 ...... 62 C6
Trenchard
 RAYLNE/WEN HP22 ...... 56 B7
Trenchard CI STAN HA7 ...... 143 M1
Trent CI RAD WD7 ...... 104 C6
 STVG SG1 ...... 21 J8
Trent Gdns STHGT/OAK N14 ...... 137 M2
Trent PK EBAR EN4 ...... 124 A6
Trent Rd LTNN/LIM LU3 ...... 27 M6
Trentwood Side ENC/FH EN2 ...... 124 D7
Tresco CI STVG SG1 ...... 32 C5
Trescott CI LTNE LU2 ...... 29 J8
Tretawn Gdns MLHL NW7 ...... 135 J2
Tretawn Pk MLHL NW7 ...... 135 J2
Trevalga Wy HHNE HP2 ...... 62 E5
Trevellance Wy GSTN WD25 ...... 102 A7
Trevelyan Wy BERK HP4 ...... 59 M1
Trevera Ct CHES/WCR EN8 ...... 110 C7
 HOD EN11 ...... 72 E5
Trevone Gdns PIN HA5 ...... 142 C8
Trevor CI EBAR EN4 ...... 137 H2

KTN/HRWW/WS HA3 ....143 K2
Trevor Rd HTCHE/RSTV SG4.. 157 Q5
Trevose Wy OXHEY WD19 ......132 A6
Trewenna Dr POTB/CUF EN6 ..107 H6
Triangle Pas EBAR EN4 *........123 C8
Trident Av HAT AL10 ....67 J7
Trident Dr DUN/WHIP LU6......
Trident Rd GSTN WD25.........105 K6
Triggs Wy LTNE LU2..............29 J6
Trigg Ter STVG SG1...............10 F2
Trimley Cl LTNW/LEA LU4.......26 F4
Trinder Rd BAR EN5...............136 A4
Tring Ford Rd TRING HP23.......169 L10
Tring HI TRING HP23..............57 G2
Tring Rd BERK HP4...............59 G6
   DUN/WHIP LU6..................170 E2
   RAYLNE/WEN HP22..............56 A8
   TRING HP23.....................168 B1
Trinity Cl BSF CM23..............43 M3
   NTHWD HA6.....................141 J7
Trinity Ct RKW/CH/CXG WD3 *..130 C5
Trinity Gv HERT/WAT SG14......53 G6
Trinity Hall Cl WATN WD24......13 H3
Trinity La CHES/WCR EN8........110 C6
Trinity Ms HHNE HP2.............83 H3
Trinity Pl STVG SG1...............10 C2
Trinity Rd HERT/BAY SG13.......72 A2
   HTCH/STOT SG5.................148 C6
   LTNN/LIM LU3...................4 E3
   STVG SG1........................10 B2
   WARE SG12......................54 C3
Trinity St BSF CM23...............43 M3
   ENC/FH EN2.....................2 E1
Trinity Wk HERT/BAY SG13......72 A2
Trinity Wy BSF CM23.............43 M3
Tripton Rd HLWS CM18..........3 H8
Tristan Ldg BLDK WD23 *........13 L6
Triton Wy HHNE HP2.............62 D8
Trojan Ct LTNW/LEA LU4 *.......27 K8
Troon Cl LTNE LU2................28 C3
Trooper Rd TRING HP23..........170 C12
Trotters Bottom BAR EN5........121 L3
Trotters Gap WARE SG12.........73 J1
Trotters Rd HLWS CM18.........18 C7
Trout Ri RKW/CH/CXG WD3......115 M7
Troutstream Wy
   RKW/CH/CXG WD3..............115 M8
Trouvere Pk HHW HP1............61 M8
Trowbridge Gdns LTNE LU2......28 C6
Trowley Bottom
   STALW/RED AL3..................173 K9
Trowley Hill Rd
   STALW/RED AL3..................173 K9
Trowley Ri ABLGY WD5............101 J5
Truemans Rd HTCH/STOT SG5...157 M4
Truesdale Dr DEN/HRF UB9.......140 A6
Trumper Rd STVG SG1.............33 K1
Trumpington Dr STAL AL1.........85 H5
Trundlers Wy BUSH WD23.........133 J4
Truro Ct AMS HP6 *...............113 H4
Truro Gdns LTNN/LIM LU3........27 M4
Trustees Wy DEN/HRF UB9.......139 K7
Trust Rd CHES/WCR EN8...........110 C8
Tubbs Cft WGCE AL7..............50 F8
Tucker's Rw BSF CM23............43 M3
Tucker St WD18..................13 G7
Tudor Av CHESW EN7.............118 B5
   WATN WD24....................118 B4
Tudor Cl AMP/FLIT/BLC MK45...155 J1
   CHESW EN7.....................109 M5
   HAT AL10........................87 J3
   PIN HA5.........................141 L7
   STVG SG1........................21 G8
   WARE SG12......................182 B9
Tudor Ct AMS HP6 *..............113 H4
   BORE WD6......................120 C6
   DUN/WHIP LU6..................25 L7
   HTCH/STOT SG5.................157 M7
   ROY SG8........................14 C1
Tudor Crs ENC/FH EN2............125 G5
Tudor Dr DUN/HR/TOD LU5.......26 C5
   WATN WD24....................118 B4
Tudor Manor Gdns
   GSTN WD25.....................102 B6
Tudor Orch BERK HP4 *...........59 J7
Tudor Pk AMS HP6................113 G3
Tudor Ri BROX EN10..............92 C3
Tudor Rd BAR EN5................122 E7
   KTN/HRWW/WS HA3............143 K1
   LTNW/LEA LU4 *................27 M7
   PIN HA5.........................142 A4
   STALW/RED AL3..................65 A3
   WLYN AL6.......................49 M2
Tudor Sq WARE SG12.............54 B4
Tudor Vls CHESW EN7 *...........109 J3
Tudor Wk WARE SG12.............54 B4
   WATN WD24....................118 B3
Tudor Wy HERT/WAT SG14.......52 E7
   RKW/CH/CXG WD3..............129 L4
   WAB EN9........................111 H7
Tudor Well Cl STAN HA7..........133 M8
Tuffnells Wy HARP AL5............46 A1
Tumbler Rd HLWS CM18.........3 L8
Tumbling Bay Weir
   WARE SG12 *...................54 D3
Tunfield Rd HOD EN11............71 F4
Tunners End CFSP/GDCR SL9....138 A3
Tunnel Wy LBUZ LU7..............169 H12
Tunnel Wood Cl WAT WD17.......117 K3
Tunnel Wood Rd WAT WD17......117 K3
Tunnmeade HLW CM20...........3 L3
Turf La HTCHE/RSTV SG4.........20 F5
Turkey St EN EN1.................125 L2
Turmore Dl WGCW AL8............50 A8
Turnberry Ct OXHEY WD19 *.....132 A6
Turnberry Dr LCOL/BKTW AL2...102 C4
Turner Cl DUN/HR/TOD LU5......26 B4
   STVG SG1........................21 G7
Turner Rd BUSH WD23............119 G8
Turners Cl HARP AL5..............47 G1
   HERT/WAT SG14.................52 A1
   TRDG/WHET N20................137 K6
Turners Crs BSF CM23.............43 J5
Turners HI CHES/WCR EN8........110 B4
Turners HI HHNE HP2.............5 H4
Turners Rd North LTNE LU2.......28 E7
Turners Rd South LTNE LU2.......7 K1
Turners Wk CSHM HP5............97 G4
Turners Wood Dr CSTG HP8......128 B6
Turneys Orch
   RKW/CH/CXG WD3..............129 H1
Turnford Pl BROX EN10 *.........92 C8
Turnford Vls BROX EN10 *........92 D8
Turnors HLW CM20................2 B2
Turnpike Cl DUN/WHIP LU6.......39 G3
Turnpike Dr LTNN/LIM LU3.......155 J12
Turnpike Gn HHNE HP2...........62 D6
Turnpike La HTCH/STOT SG5.....157 M2
The Turnstones GSTN WD25......118 C4
Turpin Cl BSF CM23...............126 E3
Turpins Cha WLYN AL6............177 M10

Turpins Cl HERT/WAT SG14.......52 D7
Turpin's Ride ROY SG8............14 E8
Turpins Ri WLYN AL6..............177 L10
Turpin's Ri STVGE SG2............33 J3
Turpin's Wy BLDK SG7............17 K2
Turvey Cl RAYLNE/WEN HP22....168 C12
Tussauds Cl
   RKW/CH/CXG WD3..............130 E1
Tuxford Cl BORE WD6 *...........120 C4
Tweed Cl BERK HP4...............59 M8
Tweenways CSHM HP5............97 H4
Twelve Acres WGCE AL7..........68 C1
Twentyfirst St STSD CM24........167 P11
Twickenham Gdns
   KTN/HRWW/WS HA3............143 J2
Twineham Gn
   NFNCH/WDSPK N12.............136 E7
Twin Foxes KNEB SG3.............177 N1
Twinwoods STVG SG1.............11 H6
The Twist TRING HP23............58 B3
Twitchell La
   RAYLNE/WEN HP22.............168 C12
The Twitchell BLDK SG7...........17 K1
Two Acres WGCE AL7.............68 C2
Two Beeches HHNE HP2 *........62 D6
Two Dells La CSHM HP5..........79 K6
Two Gates La CSHM HP5..........79 K6
Two Oaks Dr WLYN AL6...........177 Q11
Two Ponds La BERK HP4..........59 G7
Two Ridges Link LBUZ LU7........36 C3
   LBUZ LU7.......................170 B3
Two Waters Rd HHS/BOV HP3....4 A4
Twyford Bury La BSF CM23.......44 A5
Twyford Cl BSF CM23.............44 A4
Twyford Dr LTNE LU2.............29 H8
Twyford Gdns BSF CM23..........44 A4
Twyford Rd BSF CM23............44 A4
   STALE/WH AL4...................66 A6
Tyberry Rd PEND EN3............125 M7
Tye End STVGE SG2...............177 P1
Tye Green Rd RBSF CM22.........167 L6
Tye Green Village HLWS CM18 *..75 A8
Tyfield Cl CHES/WCR EN8.........110 A4
Tylers HARP AL5..................47 H4
Tylers Cswy HERT/BAY SG13.....90 A4
Tylersfield ABLGY WD5............101 K5
Tylers Hill Rd CSHM HP5.........97 K4
Tylers Md LTNE LU2...............28 C4
Tylers Rd HLWW/ROY CM19.....94 B2
Tylers Wd WLYN AL6..............177 Q11
Tylney Cft HLWW/ROY CM19.....94 F7
Tynedale LCOL/BKTW AL2........104 D1
Tynemouth Dr EN EN1...........125 L4
Typleden Cl HHNE HP2...........62 B8
Tysea Cl HLWS CM18.............75 K8
Tysea Rd HLWS CM18.............75 K8
Tysoe Av PEND EN3...............126 D2
Tythe Rd LTNW/LEA LU4..........27 G3
Tyttenhanger Gn
   STALE/WH AL4...................86 B5

U

Uckfield Rd PEND EN3............126 B3
Ufford Cl KTN/HRWW/WS HA3...142 F2
Ufford Rd
   KTN/HRWW/WS HA3............142 F2
Ullswater Cl STVG SG1............22 A7
Ullswater Rd DUN/WHIP LU6....38 F3
   HHS/BOV HP3...................83 G4
Ulverston Cl STAL AL1............9 K6
Ulverston Rd DUN/WHIP LU6....38 E3
Underacres Cl HHNE HP2.........82 E1
Underhill BAR EN5................136 E1
Underhill Ct BAR EN5 *...........136 E1
Underne Av STHGT/OAK N14....137 M5
Underwood Cl LTNN/LIM LU3....154 E12
Underwood Rd STVG SG1........21 G7
Union St BAR EN5.................122 C8
   DUN/WHIP LU6..................38 E1
   LTN LU1.........................6 C4
Union Ter BUNT SG9..............159 J10
Unity Rd PEND EN3...............126 A3
University Cl BUSH WD23.........118 D8
Unwin Cl LWTH SG6..............16 C5
Unwin Pl STVGE SG2..............34 A6
Unwin Rd STVGE SG2.............34 A6
Upcroft Av EDGW HA8............135 G8
Updale Cl POTB/CUF EN6.........106 C7
Uphill Dr MLHL NW7..............135 J3
Uphill Gv MLHL NW7..............135 J7
Uphill Rd MLHL NW7.............135 J7
Upland Av DUN/WHIP LU6.......25 M8
Upland Dr BRKMPK AL9..........69 H8
Upland Rd EPP CM16..............95 H7
Uplands LTNN/LIM LU3...........27 H1
   RKW/CH/CXG WD3..............130 D2
   STDN SG11......................163 R7
   STVGE SG2.....................34 B1
   WARE SG12......................54 B7
   WGCW AL8......................50 A3
Uplands Park Rd ENC/FH EN2....124 E6
Upland Wy EBAR EN4.............137 L4
The Uplands HARP AL5...........64 E1
   LCOL/BKTW AL2.................104 C1
Upper Ashlyns Rd BERK HP4.....79 M2
Upper Barn HHS/BOV HP3 *......5 L9
Upper Belmont Rd CSHM HP5...96 F2
Upper Bourne End La
   HHW HP1 *.....................80 F7
Upper Clabdens WARE SG12.....54 B5
Upper Culver Rd STAL AL1........9 H2
Upper Dagnall St
   STALW/RED AL3..................8 C5
Upperfield Rd WGCE AL7.........50 D8
Upper George St CSHM HP5......6 E5
   LTN LU1.........................6 E5
Upper Gladstone Rd
   CSHM HP5 *....................97 G4
Upper Gn WLYN AL6..............51 H1
Upper Green Rd WLYN AL6.......51 J2
Upper Hall Pk BERK HP4..........80 C3
Upper Heath Rd STAL AL1.......9 J1
Upper Hill Ri
   RKW/CH/CXG WD3..............129 M2
Upper Hitch OXHEY WD19.......132 C4
Upper Icknield Wy
   RAYLNE/WEN HP22.............56 B6
   TRING HP23.....................169 P9
Upper King St ROY SG8...........14 E7
Upper Lattimore Rd STAL AL1...9 H5
Upper Lea Valley Wk LTN LU1...174 A4
Upper Marlborough Rd
   STAL AL1........................9 G6
Upper Marsh La HOD EN11......72 E8
Upper Maylins LWTH SG6........17 G5

Upper Meadow CSHM HP5.......96 F4
Upper Mealines HLWS CM18.....75 L8
Upper Paddock Rd
   OXHEY WD19....................132 C2
Upper Park Rd
   FBAR/BDGN N11................137 M8
Upper Sales HHW HP1............81 K9
Upper Sean STVGE SG2...........11 K9
Upper Shot WGCE AL7............50 E4
Upper Stott CHESW EN7.........91 K8
Upper Station Rd RAD WD7......119 L1
Upperstone Cl
   CTH/STOT SG5..................148 D7
Upper Stonyfield
   HLWW/ROY CM19...............2 B6
Upper Tail OXHEY WD19..........132 C2
Upper Tilehouse St
   HTCH/STOT SG5.................157 M7
Upshire Rd WAB EN9..............111 K6
Upton Av STALW/RED AL3........8 A7
Upton Cl LCOL/BKTW AL2........85 H7
   LTNE LU2........................28 B3
Upton End Rd
   HTCH/STOT SG5.................146 B9
Upton Lodge Cl BUSH WD23.....133 C3
Upton Rd WATW WD18...........12 E5
Upway CFSP/GDCR SL9...........138 D3
Upwell Rd LTNE LU2..............28 F7
Uranus Rd HHNE HP2.............62 D8
Urban Rd BSF CM23..............44 B2
Uxbridge Rd
   RKW/CH/CXG WD3..............129 G7
Uxbridge Road (Harrow Weald)
   KTN/HRWW/WS HA3............143 G2
   STAN HA7.......................133 L8
Uxbridge Road (Hatch End)
   PIN HA5.........................142 C3
Uxbridge Road (Pinner)
   PIN HA5.........................142 B4
Uxbridge Road (Stanmore)
   STAN HA7.......................143 K1

V

Vache La CSTG HP8...............128 A5
Vache Ms CSTG HP8 *............128 B3
Vadis Cl LTNN/LIM LU3...........27 J2
Valance Rd SAFWS CB11.........161 N2
Vale Cl BORE WD6................134 F1
Vale Cl CFSP/GDCR SL9..........138 B3
   HARP AL5........................46 B1
Vale Ct STALE/WH AL4...........48 B6
Vale Cft PIN HA5.................142 C7
Vale Dr BAR EN5.................122 D8
Valence Dr CHESW EN7..........109 L2
Valence End DUN/WHIP LU6.....39 H3
Valencia Rd STAN HA7............134 A7
Valency Cl NTHWD HA6..........131 K7
Valentine Wy CSTG HP8..........128 B6
Valerian Wy STVGE SG2..........34 B1
Valerie Cl STAL AL1...............85 M2
Vale Ri CSHM HP5................97 F6
Vale Rd BERK HP4................59 G6
   CSHM HP5......................78 F6
Valeside HERT/WAT SG14........52 E8
The Vale CFSP/GDCR SL9........138 C3
Vallance Rd HARP AL5............47 G6
Vallans Cl WARE SG12............54 B5
Vallansgate STVGE SG2...........33 M8
Valley Av NFNCH/WDSPK N12...137 H7
Valley Cl BERK HP4...............171 L2
   DUN/WHIP LU6..................171 H9
   HERT/BAY SG13.................53 H8
   PIN HA5.........................141 M4
   WARE SG12......................53 M5
Valley Fields Crs ENC/FH EN2....124 E6
Valley Gn HHW HP1..............62 F4
The Valley Gn WGCW AL8........50 A6
Valley La STALW/RED AL3........172 G8
Valley Pk WATW WD18 *.........131 C3
Valley Ri GSTN WD25.............101 M7
   ROY SG8........................14 C7
   STALE/WH AL4...................47 K3
Valley Rd BERK HP4..............59 K7
   DUN/WHIP LU6..................171 P5
   HTCHE/RSTV SG4...............176 F8
   LWTH SG6.......................16 B2
   RKW/CH/CXG WD3..............129 L1
   STALW/RED AL3..................43 K8
   WGCW AL8......................49 M7
Valley Rd South
   HTCHE/RSTV SG4...............176 F9
Valleyside HHW HP1..............81 K2
The Valley HTCHE/RSTV SG4....175 Q2
Valley Vw BAR EN5...............136 C2
   CHESW EN7.....................109 G2
   CSHM HP5......................96 E3
Valley Wk RKW/CH/CXG WD3...131 G1
Valley Wy CFSP/GDCR SL9.......138 A3
   STVGE SG2.....................11 J8
Vanbrugh Dr
   DUN/HR/TOD LU5..............26 B4
Vancouver Rd BROX EN10........92 B7
Vanda Crs STAL AL1...............9 K7
Vantorts Cl SBW CM21...........183 Q5
Vantorts Rd SBW CM21..........183 Q8
Vardon Rd STVG SG1.............33 K1
Varna Cl LTNN/LIM LU3...........27 L6
Varney Cl CHESW EN7............109 L1
Varney Rd HHW HP1.............81 K2
Vaughan Md STALW/RED AL3...63 L1
Vaughan Rd HARP AL5............46 F4
   HTCH/STOT SG5.................148 C7
Vauxhall Rd HHNE HP2...........2 A2
   LTNE LU2........................41 M4
Vega Crs NTHWD HA6............131 K8
Vega Rd BUSH WD23.............133 G3
Velizy Av HLW CM20..............2 E4
Venables Ter STVG SG1 *.........33 J2
Venetia Rd LTNE LU2.............28 E5
Venice Av WATW WD18..........117 H3
Ventnor Av STAN HA7............143 M3
Ventnor Gdns LTNN/LIM LU3....27 K7
Ventura Pk LCOL/BKTW AL2.....103 K3
Venus Hi HHS/BOV HP3..........97 M1
Vera Ct OXHEY WD19.............132 B3
Ver-Colne Valley Wk
   HHS/BOV HP3...................98 B2
Ver-colne Valley Wk
   STALW/RED AL3..................8 A5
Ver-Colne Valley Wk
   WAT WD17......................13 H3
   WATN WD24....................118 C4
Verdure Cl GSTN WD25...........102 C6
Verey Rd DUN/HR/TOD LU5.....26 A7
Veritys HAT AL10.................67 L8

Verity Wy STVG SG1..............21 L8
Vermont Cl ENC/FH EN2.........124 F8
Verney Cl BERK HP4..............59 K8
Verney Ct
   TRING HP23.....................169 N12
Vernon Rd PEND EN3.............126 C2
   STAN HA7.......................143 L3
Vernon Dr DEN/HRF UB9.........140 A3
Vernon Pl DUN/HR/TOD LU5.....25 M8
Vernon Rd BUSH WD23...........13 L7
   LTN LU1.........................6 B4
Ver Rd STALW/RED AL3...........8 C5
   STALW/RED AL3..................46 A7
Verulam Cl WGCE AL7............50 D7
Verulam Gdns LTNN/LIM LU3....27 K3
Verulam Rd HTCH/STOT SG5....157 P5
   STALW/RED AL3..................8 B3
Verwood Dr EBAR EN4............123 K7
Verwood Rd
   RYLN/HDSTN HA2...............143 H12
Vespers Cl LTNW/LEA LU4........26 E7
Vesta Av STAL AL1...............85 L5
Vestry Cl LTN LU1................6 D2
Veysey Cl HHW HP1..............4 B6
Viaduct Rd WARE SG12...........54 C5
Viaduct Wy WGCE AL7...........50 D4
Vian Av EN EN1..................125 K1
Vicarage Cswy HERT/BAY SG13..71 M1
Vicarage Cl ARL/CHE SG15.......147 Q3
   HHW HP1 *.....................4 D6
   HTCH/STOT SG5.................146 B9
   POTB/CUF EN6..................106 C5
   POTB/CUF EN6..................107 K4
   STAL AL1........................85 G7
   STAN HA7.......................163 Q11
Vicarage Gdns BERK HP4.........60 G11
   STALW/RED AL3..................173 K6
   TRING HP23.....................169 L7
Vicarage La BSF CM23............52 P9
   HERT/WAT SG14.................52 F2
   HHS/BOV HP3...................80 F8
   KGLGY WD4.....................100 D3
   LBUZ LU7.......................169 R4
Vicarage Rd BERK HP4............60 G6
   BUNT SG9.......................159 J9
   DUN/HR/TOD LU5..............25 M4
   TRING HP23.....................58 B4
   TRING HP23.....................169 K7
   WARE SG12......................54 C4
   WATW WD18....................12 C9
Vicarage St LTN LU1..............7 H6
Vicarage Wy CFSP/GDCR SL9....138 B3
Vicarage Wd HLW CM20..........3 L4
Vicar's Cl EN EN1................125 J6
Vicerons Pl BSF CM23............43 K5
Victoria Cl EBAR EN4.............123 H8
   HRW HA1.......................143 K8
   RKW/CH/CXG WD3..............130 B3
Victoria Crs ROY SG8.............14 C6
Victoria Gv
   NFNCH/WDSPK N12.............137 H8
Victoria La BAR EN5..............122 D8
Victoria Rd BERK HP4.............80 A2
   BUSH WD23....................132 F4
   CHES/WCR EN8.................95 C5
   EBAR EN4......................123 H8
   HARP AL5.......................46 F4
   HTCH/STOT SG5.................157 M5
   MLHL NW7......................135 K8
   WAB EN9........................111 H8
   WATN WD24....................117 M4
Victoria St DUN/WHIP LU6.......25 L8
   LTN LU1.........................9 G6
   STAL AL1........................9 G6
Victor Rd RYLN/HDSTN HA2.....143 G5
Victor Smith Ct
   LCOL/BKTW AL2.................102 E5
Victors Wy BAR EN5..............122 D7
Victory Rd BERK HP4.............59 L8
View Cl HRW HA1................143 H6
View Rd POTB/CUF EN6..........107 K4
Vigors Cft HAT AL10..............87 K1
Village La HOD EN11.............73 H5
Village St HTCHE/RSTV SG4......32 D8
Village Wy AMSS HP7.............114 B6
   BLDK SG7.......................150 A2
Villa Rd LTNN/LIM LU3...........6 E3
Villiers Cl LTNW/LEA LU4.........27 H6
Villiers Crs STALE/WH AL4.......66 B7
Villiers Rd OXHEY WD19..........132 C2
Villiers St HERT/BAY SG13.......53 J7
Villiers-sur-Marne Av
   BSF CM23......................43 K5
Vincent Cl LWTH SG6.............17 G5
Vincent Ct BAR EN5..............122 E7
   CHES/WCR EN8.................110 C2
Vincent Rd LTNW/LEA LU4.......27 H5
Vincenzo Cl BRKMPK AL9........88 C3
Vine Cl WGCW AL8...............49 M7
Vine Gv HLW CM20..............182 H12
The Vineries EN EN1..............125 J7
Vineyards Rd POTB/CUF EN6....107 J4
The Vineyard WARE SG12........54 D3
Vinries Bank MLHL NW7..........135 M8
Vinters Av STVG SG1.............11 G5
Violet Av ENC/FH EN2............125 H4
Violet Wy RKW/CH/CXG WD3...116 A3
Virgil Dr BROX EN10..............92 D7
Virginia Cl LTNE LU2.............28 D6
Viscount Cl FBAR/BDGN N11....137 M8
   LTNN/LIM LU3...................27 L4
Vista Av PEND EN3...............126 A3
Vivian Cl OXHEY WD19...........131 L5
Vivian Gdns OXHEY WD19.......131 L4
Vixen Ct HAT AL10...............67 M6
Vixen Dr HERT/BAY SG13........53 L7
Vulcan Ga ENC/FH EN2...........124 E6
Vyse Cl BAR EN5.................122 A8

W

Wacketts CHESW EN7............109 L1
Waddesdon Cl LTNE LU2.........29 H7
Waddington Cl EN EN1...........125 J8
Waddington Rd STALW/RED AL3..8 A7
Waddling La STALE/WH AL4.....48 B4
Wadesmill Rd HERT/WAT SG14..53 H4
   WARE SG12.....................179 N12
The Wades HAT AL10.............87 L3
The Wade WGCE AL7.............68 D2
Wadham Rd ABLGY WD5.........101 K5
Wadhurst Av LTNN/LIM LU3.....28 A5
Wadley Cl HHNE HP2.............5 L4
Wadnall Wy KNEB SG3............177 M5
Waggoners Yd WARE SG12.......54 B3
Waggon Rd BAR EN5.............122 E1

Wagon Md RBSF CM22...........184 G6
Wagon Wy RKW/CH/CXG WD3..116 A3
Wagtail Cl EN EN1...............125 M5
Waight Cl HAT AL10..............67 J6
Wain Cl POTB/CUF EN6..........106 F3
Wainwright Cl BSF CM23.........43 J4
Wakefields Wk
   CHES/WCR EN8.................110 C5
Wakehams Hl PIN HA5............142 D5
Walcot Av LTNE LU2..............28 E7
Walcot Rd PEND EN3.............126 D6
Waldeck Rd LTN LU1.............6 C2
Waldegrave Pk HARP AL5........47 H4
Walden End WGCE AL7...........50 E5
Walden Pl WGCW AL8............50 B5
Walden Rd WGCW AL8...........50 A5
Waleran Cl STAN HA7............143 K1
Waleys Cl LTNN/LIM LU3.........27 J1
Walfield Av TRDG/WHET N20...136 F3
Walfords Cl HLWE CM17.........76 A2
Walgrave Rd DUN/HR/TOD LU5..28 E7
Walkden's BLDK SG7 *...........149 G1
Walkern Rd STVG SG1............33 H1
   STVGE SG2.....................34 E5
Walkers Cl HARP AL5.............47 G6
Walkers Ct HARP AL5 *...........47 G6
Walkers Rd HARP AL5............46 F6
Walkley Rd DUN/HR/TOD LU5...25 M5
The Walk POTB/CUF EN6.........106 C6
Wallace Dr DUN/WHIP LU6......37 J3
Wallace Ms DUN/WHIP LU6......37 J3
Wallace Wy HTCHE/RSTV SG4...157 Q2
The Walled Gdn WLYN AL6 *....50 C4
Waller Av LTNW/LEA LU4.........27 K6
Waller Dr NTHWD HA6...........141 J7
Waller's Cl ROY SG8..............153 P5
Wallers Wk HOD EN11...........72 F4
Wallingford Wk STAL AL1........85 H5
Wallington Cl RSLP HA4..........141 G8
Wallington Rd BLDK SG7.........17 L1
Walmar Cl EBAR EN4.............123 H5
Walnut Av BLDK SG7..............17 K3
Walnut Cl HTCH/STOT SG5.......148 D7
   HTCHE/RSTV SG4...............157 Q7
   LCOL/BKTW AL2.................102 F1
   LTNE LU2........................28 F6
   MHAD SG10.....................181 R7
   ROY SG8........................14 E7
Walnut Ct WGCE AL7.............68 C2
Walnut Dr BSF CM23.............43 K6
Walnut Gn BUSH WD23..........118 D6
Walnut Gv HHNE HP2.............5 G3
   WGCE AL7......................68 C2
Walnut Tree Av SBW CM21......183 Q5
Walnut Tree Cl
   CHES/WCR EN8.................110 B5
   HOD EN11......................72 E7
   STVGE SG2.....................11 J8
Walnut Tree Rd
   HTCH/STOT SG5.................156 F2
Walnut Tree Wk WARE SG12.....54 B3
Walnut Wk HERT/BAY SG13.....53 J7
Walnut Wy AMS HP6..............112 A1
   HTCH/STOT SG5.................157 N1
Walpole Cl PIN HA5..............142 E1
Walsham Cl STVGE SG2...........34 E5
Walsh Cl HTCH/STOT SG5........157 M6
Walshford Wy BORE WD6........120 C4
Walsingham Cl HAT AL10.........67 K7
   LTNE LU2........................28 F6
Walsingham Rd ENC/FH EN2....125 H8
Walsingham Wy
   LCOL/BKTW AL2.................104 A1
Walsworth Rd
   HTCHE/RSTV SG4...............157 Q6
Walters Cl CHESW EN7...........90 F7
Waltham Gdns PEND EN3........126 A2
Waltham Ga CHES/WCR EN8.....92 C8
Waltham Rd HTCHE/RSTV SG4...157 P7
   WAB EN9........................93 J8
Walton Cl HRW HA1..............143 H6
Walton Dr HRW HA1.............143 H6
Walton Gdns WAB EN9...........111 F5
Walton Rd BUSH WD23...........13 K5
   HOD EN11......................72 F5
   HRW HA1.......................143 H6
   WARE SG12......................54 B5
Walton St ENC/FH EN2...........125 H5
   STAL AL1........................9 H2
Walverns Cl OXHEY WD19.......132 A2
Wander Whf KGLGY WD4.........100 E5
Wandon Cl STVG SG1.............29 G5
Wannions Cl CSHM HP5..........97 L4
Wansbeck Cl STVG SG1...........21 L6
Wansford Pk BORE WD6..........121 H8
Warburton Cl
   KTN/HRWW/WS HA3............143 H1
Ward Cl CHESW EN7 *............109 L1
   STVG SG1........................54 A3
Warden Hill Cl LTNE LU2 *.......28 A1
Warden Hill Gdns LTNE LU2.....28 A1
Warden Hill Rd LTNE LU2........28 A1
Ward Hatch HLW CM20...........3 M1
Wardown Crs LTNE LU2...........28 E7
Ward Pl AMSS HP7 *.............112 F6
Wards La BORE WD6.............119 K6
Wareham's La
   HERT/WAT SG14.................53 G8
Warenford Wy BORE WD6........120 C3
Ware Park Rd HERT/WAT SG14...53 H5
Ware Rd HERT/BAY SG13.........53 J7
   HERT/WAT SG14.................53 J7
   HOD EN11......................72 E6
   WARE SG12......................182 A5
Wareside HHNE HP2..............62 E4
Wareside Cl WGCE AL7...........50 F8
Warham Rd
   KTN/HRWW/WS HA3............143 K4
Warlow Cl PEND EN3.............126 E3
Warmark Rd HHW HP1...........61 J8
Warminster Cl LTNE LU2.........29 K8
Warneford Av
   RAYLNE/WEN HP22.............56 B8
Warnford Pl OXHEY WD19.......13 L9
Warner Cl EBAR EN4.............123 J4
Warner Rd WARE SG12...........54 B5
Warners Av HOD EN11...........91 M8
Warners Cl STVGE SG2...........11 M8
Warners End Rd HHW HP1 *.....4 A1
Warngate
   POTB/CUF EN6..................106 A3
Warren Cl CHESW EN7............109 L5
Warren Dl WGCW AL8............50 B4
The Warren Dr LTNE LU2.........41 M8
Warrenfield Cl CHES/WCR EN8..109 L5
Warren Flds STAN HA7 *.........134 A7
Warrengate La
   POTB/CUF EN6..................106 A3
Warrengate Rd BRKMPK AL9....69 H5

Warren Gn *HAT* AL10.............67 M5
Warren Gv *BORE* WD6.............121 H8
Warren La *BLDK* SG7.............18 B2
   BUNT SG9.............23 N4
   STAN HA7.............133 L5
Warren Park Rd
   HERT/WAT SG14.............53 C6
Warren Pl *HERT/WAT* SG14 *.............53 H7
Warren Rd *BUSH* WD23.............133 G4
   LTN LU1.............40 D1
   STAL AL1.............85 G6
Warrensgreen La
   HTCHE/RSTV SG4.............22 B4
Warrens Shawe La *EDGW* HA8.............134 F5
Warren Ter *HERT/WAT* SG14.............53 H5
The Warren *CFSP/GDCR* SL9.............138 D2
   CSHM HP5.............96 C2
   HARP AL5.............46 E6
   KGLGY WD4.............100 D3
   RAD WD7.............103 L7
   ROY SG8.............14 E8
Warren Wy *WLYN* AL6.............50 C2
Warrington Rd *HRW* HA1.............143 J7
Warton Gn *LTNE* LU2.............29 J7
Warwick Av *EDGW* HA8.............108 B1
   POTB/CUF EN6.............108 B1
Warwick Cl *BUSH* WD23.............133 J3
   EBAR EN4.............137 H1
   HERT/BAY SG13.............71 G1
   POTB/CUF EN6.............108 B1
   RAYLNE/WEN HP22.............168 C12
Warwick Ct *LTNW/LEA* LU4 *.............6 A1
Warwick Dr *CHES/WCR* EN8.............110 D3
Warwick Ms
   RKW/CH/CXG WD3.............130 E2
Warwick Pde
   KTN/HRWW/WS HA3 *.............143 M4
Warwick Pl *BORE* WD6 *.............121 H7
Warwick Rd *BORE* WD6.............121 H7
   BSF CM23.............44 B3
   LBUZ LU7.............169 P6
   PEND EN3.............126 D3
   STAL AL1.............9 J3
   STVGE SG2.............11 M3
Warwick Rd East *LTNW/LEA* LU4 *.............6 A1
Warwick Rd West
   LTNW/LEA LU4.............27 M8
Warwick Wy
   RKW/CH/CXG WD3.............117 G8
Washbrook Cl
   AMP/FLIT/BLC MK45.............155 J4
Washington Av *HHNE* HP2.............62 C5
Wash La *POTB/CUF* EN6.............105 M7
The Wash *STDN* SG9.............161 K12
   HERT/WAT SG14.............53 H7
Watchlytes *WGCE* AL7.............51 G7
Watchmead *WGCE* AL7.............50 E7
The Watch
   NFNCH/WDSPK N12 *.............137 G7
Waterbeach *WGCE* AL7.............51 H7
Watercress Cl *CHESW* EN7.............91 H8
Watercress Rd *CHESW* EN7.............91 H8
Waterdale *HERT/BAY* SG13.............71 G1
Waterdell La *RKW/CH/CXG* WD3.............157 P11
Waterend La *STALE/WH* AL4.............49 G5
   STALW/RED AL3.............173 R12
Water End Rd *BERK* HP4.............60 D6
Waterfall Cl *HOD* EN11.............72 D6
Waterfield Rd *RKW/CH/CXG* WD3.............129 P2
   WGCE AL7.............50 F6
Waterfields Wy *BUSH* WD23.............13 K5
Waterford Common
   HERT/WAT SG14.............52 F7
The Waterfront *BORE* WD6 *.............130 C1
Water Gdns *STAN* HA7.............143 M1
The Watergate *OXHEY* WD19.............132 B5
Waterhouse Moor *HLWS* CM18.............3 H8
Waterhouse St *HHNE* HP2.............4 C2
Water La *BERK* HP4.............80 A1
   BSF CM23.............43 M1
   HHS/BOV HP3.............98 A3
   HLWW/ROY CM19.............94 C1
   HTCH/STOT SG5.............157 P4
   KGLGY WD4.............100 F3
   STSD CM24.............166 C7
   WAT WD17.............13 H6
Waterloo La *HTCH/STOT* SG5.............147 J11
Waterlow Rd *DUN/WHIP* LU6.............25 L8
Waterman *OXHEY* WD19.............131 M2
Watermark Wy
   HERT/BAY SG13.............53 K7
Water Meadow *CSHM* HP5.............96 F6
Watermeadow
   LCOL/BKTW AL2.............103 H2
Watermead Rd *LTNW/LIM* LU3.............27 N3
Watermill La *HERT/WAT* SG14.............53 H4
Water Rw *WARE* SG12 *.............54 B4
Waters Dr *RKW/CH/CXG* WD3.............130 C4
Waters End *HTCH/STOT* SG5.............148 C7
Waterside *CSHM* HP5.............97 G6
   DUN/WHIP LU6.............37 K5
   HARP AL5.............47 G2
   KGLGY WD4.............100 E3
   LCOL/BKTW AL2.............103 M8
   STSD CM24.............166 C7
   WGCE AL7.............50 E5
Waterside Ct *KGLGY* WD4.............100 E3
Waterside Ms *DEN/HRF* UB9 *.............139 L1
Waterslade La *LTNN/LIM* LU3.............27 M3
Watersmeet *HLWW/ROY* CM19.............94 F1
Watersplash Ct
   LCOL/BKTW AL2 *.............104 D1
Waterwick HI *SAFWS* CB11.............153 M7
Watery La *BSF* CM23.............165 Q4
   HAT AL10.............87 J1
   STALW/RED AL3.............173 N6
   TRING HP23.............35 P3
Watery Stones *SAFWS* CB11 *.............161 P5
Watford Field Rd *WATW* WD18 *.............13 H7
Watford Heath
   OXHEY WD19.............132 B3
Watford Heath Farm
   OXHEY WD19.............132 B3
Watford Int *WATN* WD24 *.............118 A3
Watford Rd *BORE* WD6.............134 A2
   KGLGY WD4.............100 C5
   LCOL/BKTW AL2.............84 B6
   NTHWD HA6.............141 K2
   RAD WD7.............119 J4
   RKW/CH/CXG WD3.............130 C2
   STAL AL1.............84 F5
Watford Wy (Barnet By-Pass)
   MLHL NW7.............135 J7
Watkin Ms *PEND* EN3.............126 A4
Watkins Ri *POTB/CUF* EN6.............106 C4
Watling Cl *HHNE* HP2.............62 C5
Watling Farm Cl *BORE* WD6.............134 A4

Watling Gdns *DUN/WHIP* LU6.............39 H3
Watling Knoll *RAD* WD7.............103 K7
Watling Pl *DUN/HR/TOD* LU5.............25 L6
Watling St *BORE* WD6.............120 A7
   DUN/WHIP LU6.............25 J6
   LCOL/BKTW AL2.............85 H7
   RAD WD7.............119 M4
   STAL AL1.............85 G6
Watlington Rd *HLWE* CM17.............76 B1
Watling Vw *STAL* AL1.............85 G6
Watson Av *STALW/RED* AL3.............65 K7
Watson Rd *STVG* SG1.............10 C3
Watson's Wk *STAL* AL1.............9 F3
Watton Rd *HERT/WAT* SG14.............178 E7
   KNEB SG3.............177 N4
   WARE SG12.............54 A3
Watts Cl *STDN* SG11.............164 H11
Wauluds Bank Dr
   LTNN/LIM LU3.............27 H1
Wauluf Cl *CHES/WCR* EN8.............110 C1
Waveney *HHNE* HP2.............62 D5
Waveney Rd *HARP* AL5.............47 J2
Waverley Cl *STVGE* SG2.............177 N1
Waverley Gdns *NTHWD* HA6.............141 L3
Waverley Rd *ENC/FH* EN2.............124 F8
   STALW/RED AL3.............85 J1
Waxwell La *PIN* HA5.............142 B5
Wayborne Gv *RSLP* HA4.............141 G8
Wayfarers Pk *BERK* HP4.............79 K1
Wayletts Dr *BSF* CM23.............44 B2
Wayre St *HLWE* CM17.............76 A1
Waysbrook *LWTH* SG6.............16 F5
Wayside *DUN/WHIP* LU6.............39 H4
   KGLGY WD4.............99 M4
   POTB/CUF EN6.............107 H6
   RAD WD7.............104 B7
Wayside Av *BUSH* WD23.............133 H2
The Wayside *HHS/BOV* HP3.............83 G3
Waymaker *LWTH* SG6.............16 E5
Waytemore Rd *BSF* CM23.............44 L3
Weald La *KTN/HRWW/WS* HA3.............143 H4
Weald Ri *KTN/HRWW/WS* HA3.............143 J2
Wealdwood Gdns *PIN* HA5.............142 F1
Weall Gn *GSTN* WD25.............101 M6
Weardale Gdns *ENC/FH* EN2.............125 H5
Weatherby *DUN/WHIP* LU6.............38 C1
Weatherby Rd *LTNW/LIM* LU3.............6 B9
Weavers Orch *ARL/CHE* SG15.............147 Q5
Weavers Rd *HERT/WAT* HP23.............71 J1
Weaver St *BSF* CM23.............43 J1
Weavers Wy *BLDK* SG7.............17 L1
Webb Cl *CSHM* HP5.............96 F4
   LWTH SG6.............16 B3
Webber Cl *BORE* WD6.............134 B2
Webb Ri *STVG* SG1.............2 A5
Webster Cl *WAB* EN9.............111 L7
Wedgewood Cl
   HTCHE/RSTV SG4.............20 A2
   NTHWD HA6 *.............141 G2
Wedgewood Ct *STVG* SG1.............22 A6
Wedgewood Dr *HLWE* CM17.............76 B6
Wedgewood Pk *STVG* SG1.............22 A7
Wedgewood Rd
   HTCHE/RSTV SG4.............157 R6
   LTNW/LEA LU4.............26 D5
Wedgewood Ga *STVG* SG1.............22 A7
Wedgewood Ga *STVG* SG1.............21 M7
Wedgewood Wy *STVG* SG1.............21 M7
Wedhey *HLW* CM20.............7 F4
Wedmore Rd
   HTCHE/RSTV SG4.............157 Q7
Wedon Wy *BLDK* SG7.............149 N9
Weedon HI *HNLW* SG16.............147 L4
Weedon Rd *AMS* HP6.............112 E2
Weighton Rd
   KTN/HRWW/WS HA3.............143 H3
Weirdale Av *TRDG/WHET* N20.............137 K5
Welbeck Cl *BORE* WD6.............120 C7
Welbeck Ri *HARP* AL5.............47 H2
Welbeck Rd *EBAR* EN4.............137 J1
   LTNE LU2.............29 J7
Welbury Av *LTNN/LIM* LU3.............28 A2
Welch HI *PIN* HA5 *.............142 A5
Welclose St *STALW/RED* AL3.............8 B6
Weldon Cl *LTNE* LU2.............29 K5
Weld Pl *FBAR/BDGN* N11 *.............137 M8
Welham Dr *BORE* WD6.............120 D5
   BRKMPK AL9.............88 A6
Welham Mnr *BRKMPK* AL9.............88 A6
Welkin Gn *HHNE* HP2.............83 G1
Wellacre Rd
   KTN/HRWW/WS HA3.............143 M8
Wellands *HAT* AL10.............67 H5
Well Ap *BAR* EN5.............136 A1
Wellbrook Ms *TRING* HP23 *.............57 M1
Wellbury Ter *HHNE* HP2.............83 G2
Wellcroft *LBUZ* LU7.............169 R4
Well Croft *HHW* HP1.............81 M1
Wellcroft Cl *WGCE* AL7.............68 C1
Wellcroft Rd *WGCE* AL7.............50 E8
Welldon Crs *HRW* HA1.............143 M7
Well End Rd *BORE* WD6.............121 G3
Wellen Ri *HHS/BOV* HP3.............5 F3
Weller Cl *AMS* HP6.............113 J3
Weller Rd *AMS* HP6.............113 J3
Welles Gv *CHESW* EN7.............109 G1
Wellesley *HLWW/ROY* CM19.............94 E2
Wellesley Crs *POTB/CUF* EN6.............106 C7
Wellesley Park Ms
   ENC/FH EN2.............124 F6
Wellesley Rd *HRW* HA1.............143 J1
Wellfield Av *LTNN/LIM* LU3.............27 G1
Wellfield Cl *HAT* AL10.............67 L6
Wellfield Rd *HAT* AL10.............67 L6
Well Garth *WGCE* AL7.............50 E7
Wellgate Rd *LTNW/LEA* LU4 *.............27 N7
Well Gn *HERT/WAT* SG14.............52 A1
Well Gv *TRDG/WHET* N20.............137 G6
Well Head Rd *DUN/WHIP* LU6.............38 D2
Wellhouse Cl *LTN* LU1.............40 E2
Wellhouse La *BAR* EN5.............122 A4
Wellingham Av
   HTCH/STOT SG5.............157 M4
Wellington Av *PIN* HA5.............142 D3
Wellington Dr *WGCE* AL7.............132 C6
Wellington Dr *WGCE* AL7.............51 G7
Wellington HI *LCOL/IC10* 127 M4
Wellington Pl *BROX* EN10 *.............92 A7
Wellington Rd
   KTN/HRWW/WS HA3.............143 J5
   LCOL/BKTW AL2.............86 B8
   PIN HA5.............142 B5
   STAL AL1.............85 M3
   STVGE SG2.............34 A1
   WAT WD17.............12 E1
Wellington St
   HERT/WAT SG14 *.............52 F6
   LTN LU1.............6 E6
Wellington Ter
   DUN/HR/TOD LU5.............39 G1
Well La *HLW* CM20.............74 D7

Wellonhead Br
   RAYLNE/WEN HP22.............56 D2
Well Rd *BAR* EN5.............136 A1
   POTB/CUF EN6.............107 J3
Well-Row Rd *HARP* AL5.............70 D7
Wells Cl *CHESW* EN7.............91 D7
   HARP AL5.............46 C1
   STALW/RED AL3.............8 C3
Wellsfield *BUSH* WD23.............13 L8
Wellside Cl *BAR* EN5.............122 A8
Wellstones *WAT* WD17.............12 F4
Wellswood Cl *HHNE* HP2.............82 F1
Wells Yd *WARE* SG12 *.............54 B4
Welsumer Wy
   CHES/WCR EN8.............110 B1
Weltmore Rd *LTNN/LIM* LU3.............27 N1
Welwyn By-Pass Rd *WLYN* AL6.............50 A2
Welwyn Ct *HHNE* HP2.............62 D6
Welwyn Hall Gdns *WLYN* AL6.............177 J12
Welwyn Rd *HERT/WAT* SG14.............177 M3
Wemborough Rd *STAN* HA7.............143 M5
Wendover Cl *HARP* AL5.............47 H4
   STALE/WH AL4.............66 A5
Wendover Hts
   RAYLNE/WEN HP22.............56 B8
Wendover Ldg *WLYN* AL6 *.............177 J12
Wendover Wy *BUSH* WD23.............133 J3
   LTNE LU2.............28 D6
Wengeo La *WARE* SG12.............53 M3
Wenham Pl *HAT* AL10.............67 L7
Wenlock Ct *LTNE* LU2.............6 F3
Wensley Cl *HAT* AL10.............47 H1
Wensleydale *HHNE* HP2.............62 C7
   LTNE LU2.............6 F1
Wensum Rd *STVG* SG1.............21 K6
Wensum Wy
   RKW/CH/CXG WD3.............130 B4
Wentbridge Pth *BORE* WD6.............120 C4
Wentworth Av *BORE* WD6.............134 D1
   LTNW/LEA LU4.............27 G4
Wentworth Cl *POTB/CUF* EN6.............106 C5
   WAT WD17.............117 K4
Wentworth Cots *STDN* SG11.............162 D11
Wentworth Dr *BSF* CM23.............43 K3
   PIN HA5.............141 L7
Wentworth Pl *CSHM* HP5 *.............97 C2
   STAN HA7.............143 M1
Wentworth Rd *BAR* EN5.............122 B6
   HERT/BAY SG13.............71 G2
Wentworth Wy *PIN* HA5.............142 A2
Wenwell Cl *RAYLNE/WEN* HP22.............56 C2
Wesley Cl *ARL/CHE* SG15.............147 Q5
   CHESW EN7.............109 G2
Wesley HI *CSHM* HP5.............96 C1
Wesley Rd *STALW/RED* AL3.............172 C4
Wessex Dr *PIN* HA5.............142 C2
West Acres *AMSS* HP7.............113 H6
Westall Cl *HERT/BAY* SG13.............53 C8
West Aly *HTCH/STOT* SG5.............157 M8
Westanley Av *AMSS* HP7.............113 H5
West Av *BLDK* SG7.............17 J1
   LCOL/BKTW AL2.............84 F7
West Bank *ENC/FH* EN2.............125 G7
Westbere Dr *STAN* HA7.............134 B6
Westbourne Ms *STAL* AL1.............8 B5
Westbourne Rd *LTNW/LEA* LU4.............6 A2
Westbrook Cl *HARP* AL5.............123 H7
   ROY SG8.............145 N9
Westbrook Crs *EBAR* EN4.............123 H7
West Burrowfield *WGCE* AL7.............68 A5
Westbury *CHES/WCR* EN8 *.............110 B4
Westbury Cl *DUN/HR/TOD* LU5.............25 M6
   HTCH/STOT SG5.............157 L5
Westbury Farm Cl
   HTCH/STOT SG5.............156 E10
Westbury Gdns *LTNE* LU2.............28 B6
Westbury Lodge Cl *PIN* HA5.............142 B5
Westbury Pl *LWTH* SG6.............16 C4
Westbury Ri *HLWE* CM17.............76 B6
Westbury Rd *NTHWD* HA6.............131 J7
   WATW WD18.............12 F7
Westbush Cl *HOD* EN11.............72 D6
West Chantry
   KTN/HRWW/WS HA3.............142 F3
West Cl *BAR* EN5.............135 M1
   EBAR EN4.............123 L4
   HOD EN11.............72 D6
   HTCHE/RSTV SG4.............157 R3
   STVG SG1.............11 L4
Westcombe Dr *BAR* EN5.............136 E1
West Common
   CFSP/GDCR SL9.............138 B7
   HARP AL5.............46 E6
West Common Cl *HARP* AL5.............46 E6
West Common Gv *HARP* AL5.............46 E6
West Common Wy *HARP* AL5.............46 E6
Westcott *WGCE* AL7.............51 H6
West Ct *ROY* SG8.............14 D7
Westcroft Cl *PEND* EN3.............126 A4
Westcroft Ct *BROX* EN10.............92 C1
Westdean La *CSHM* HP5.............96 A2
West Dene *HARP* AL5.............172 B9
Westdown Gdns
   DUN/WHIP LU6.............38 D2
West Dr *ARL/CHE* SG15.............147 Q5
   GSTN WD25.............117 M2
   HTCH/STOT SG5.............148 A10
   KTN/HRWW/WS HA3.............143 H1
West Drive Gdns
   KTN/HRWW/WS HA3.............143 H1
Westell Cl *BLDK* SG7.............17 L1
West End Av *PIN* HA5.............142 B6
West End Av *PIN* HA5.............142 B6
West End La *BAR* EN5.............122 B8
   BRKMPK AL9.............69 G8
   PIN HA5.............142 B6
West End Rd *BROX* EN10.............91 N5
   LBUZ LU7.............169 K2
Westerdale *HHNE* HP2.............14 F4
Western Av *HNLW* SG16.............147 K6
Western Cl *LWTH* SG6.............148 C12
Western Man *BSF* CM23.............136 F1
Western Pde *BAR* EN5.............136 E1
Western Rd *LTN* LU1.............6 C5
   TRING HP23.............57 K2
   WAB EN9.............93 J4
Western Ter *HOD* EN11 *.............72 F4
Western Wy *BAR* EN5.............136 E2
   DUN/HR/TOD LU5.............26 E3
   LWTH SG6.............148 C12
Westfield *AMS* HP6.............112 A1
   BRKMPK AL9.............88 A6
   HLWS CM18.............3 G8
   HLWS CM18.............3 G8
   WGCE AL7.............50 E6
Westfield Av *HARP* AL5.............46 E2
   WATN WD24.............118 B4
Westfield Cl *BSF* CM23.............43 J1

Westfield Ct *STALE/WH* AL4.............66 B7
   CHES/WCR EN8.............110 D5
   HTCH/STOT SG5.............157 M6
Westfield Dr *HARP* AL5.............46 F1
Westfield La *HTCH/STOT* SG5.............157 M6
Westfield Pk *PIN* HA5.............142 D2
Westfield Pl *HARP* AL5.............46 F1
Westfield Rd *BERK* HP4.............59 J7
   BSF CM23.............43 L1
   DUN/WHIP LU6.............25 K8
   HARP AL5.............46 F1
   HERT/WAT SG14.............53 C5
   HOD EN11.............72 D6
   LBUZ LU7.............169 P7
   MLHL NW7.............135 H6
West Ga *HLW* CM20.............2 D5
   STVG SG1.............10 D5
Westgate Ct *DUN/WHIP* LU6 *.............38 C1
West Hayes *RBSF* CM22.............184 C6
West HI *DUN/WHIP* LU6.............39 G4
   HTCH/STOT SG5.............157 M6
West Hill *HOD* EN11.............72 D5
West Hill Wy *TRDG/WHET* N20.............137 J4
Westholme *HTCH/STOT* SG5.............16 D1
West Hyde La *CFSP/GDCR* SL9.............138 D1
West La *HTCH/STOT* SG5.............146 F12
   HTCH/STOT SG5.............156 E11
Westlea Av *GSTN* WD25.............118 C3
Westlea Rd *BROX* EN10.............92 D5
Westlecote Gdns *LTNE* LU2.............28 B5
West Leith *TRING* HP23.............57 J4
Westly Wd *WGCE* AL7.............50 E6
West Md *WGCE* AL7.............68 F2
Westmeade Cl *CHESW* EN7.............109 M3
Westmill La *HTCH/STOT* SG5.............157 L3
Westmill Lawns
   HTCH/STOT SG5.............157 M4
Westmill Rd *HTCH/STOT* SG5.............157 L3
   WARE SG12.............53 M2
Westminster Ct *HARP* AL5 *.............47 G6
Westminster Gdns
   DUN/HR/TOD LU5.............26 A3
Westminster Ldg *STAL* AL1 *.............8 C9
West Moor *PEND* EN3.............126 B6
Westmoor *PEND* EN3.............126 B6
Westmorland Av
   LTNN/LIM LU3.............27 K4
Westmorland Rd *HRW* HA1.............142 F1
Weston Av *ROY* SG8.............21 J3
Weston Cl *POTB/CUF* EN6.............106 D6
Weston Dr *STAN* HA7.............143 K2
Weston Rd *ENC/FH* EN2.............125 H6
   STVG SG1.............33 J1
Weston Wy *DUN/WHIP* LU6.............38 C1
Westpole Av *EBAR* EN4.............123 M4
Westray *HHS/BOV* HP3.............83 G4
West Reach *STVGE* SG2.............33 K7
Westridge *CSHM* HP5.............96 C3
   HHW HP1.............81 K2
West Riding *LCOL/BKTW* AL2.............102 F5
   WLYN AL6.............177 R12
West Rd *BERK* HP4.............59 J5
   BSF CM23.............43 L3
   EBAR EN4.............137 L4
   HLW CM20.............7 L1
   STSD CM24.............166 C8
West Side *BROX* EN10.............92 C5
West Sq *HLW* CM20.............2 D5
West St *HERT/BAY* SG13.............53 C8
   LTNE LU2.............155 R12
   WARE SG12.............54 B4
   WAT WD17.............12 E1
West Towers *PIN* HA5.............141 L7
West Valley Rd *HHS/BOV* HP3.............82 A6
West Vw *CSHM* HP5.............97 H3
   HAT AL10.............67 L6
   LWTH SG6.............16 B5
Westview Ct *BORE* WD6.............134 B2
West View Gdns *BORE* WD6.............134 B2
Westview Ri *HHNE* HP2.............5 G1
West View Rd *STALW/RED* AL3.............8 A4
West Wk *EBAR* EN4.............137 L4
Westway *LTNE* LU2.............29 G5
West Wy *HARP* AL5.............46 F3
   PEND EN3.............126 F3
   PIN HA5.............142 B5
Westwick Cl *HHNE* HP2.............83 H3
Westwick Pl *GSTN* WD25.............102 A6
Westwick Rw *HHNE* HP2.............83 J1
Westwood Av
   HTCHE/RSTV SG4.............157 Q7
Westwood Dr *AMS* HP6.............114 B5
   POTB/CUF EN6.............106 A4
   RSLP HA4.............140 F8
Westwood Rd *AMS* HP6.............114 B5
Wetheral Dr *STAN* HA7.............143 M3
Wetherby Cl *STVG* SG1.............34 A1
Wetherby Rd *BORE* WD6.............120 C5
   ENC/FH EN2.............125 G2
Wetherfield *STSD* CM24.............166 F6
Wetherly Cl *HLWE* CM17.............76 B5
Wetherne Link *LTNW/LEA* LU4.............27 G4
Wexham Cl *LTNN/LIM* LU3.............27 J1
Weybourne Cl *HARP* AL5.............28 A2
Weybourne Dr *STAN* HA7.............143 H3
Wey La *CSHM* HP5.............96 F6
Weymouth Av *MLHL* NW7.............135 J3
Weymouth St *HHS/BOV* HP3.............82 A6
Weymouth Wk *STAN* HA7.............143 L1
Whaley Rd *POTB/CUF* EN6.............106 D7
Wharfedale *HHNE* HP2.............62 C7
   LTNW/LEA LU4.............6 B8
Wharf La *BERK* HP4.............59 J7
   RKW/CH/CXG WD3.............130 C3
Wharf Rd *BROX* EN10.............92 A3
   BSF CM23.............43 K3
   HHW HP1.............4 B7
Wharf Rw *RAYLNE/WEN* HP22 *.............56 K8
Wharley Hook *HLWS* CM18.............75 K8
Wheatbarn *WGCE* AL7.............50 E6
Wheat Cl *STALE/WH* AL4.............65 G4
Wheatcotes *KNEB* SG3.............177 N4
Wheatcroft *CHESW* EN7.............109 M2
Wheatfield *HAT* AL10.............67 M7
Wheatfield Av *HARP* AL5.............46 E8
Wheatfield Crs *ROY* SG8.............14 F5

Wheatfield Rd *HARP* AL5.............46 D8
   LTNW/LEA LU4.............26 C5
Wheatfields *HLWE* CM17.............183 P11
   PEND EN3.............126 C5
Wheathampstead Rd
   HARP AL5.............47 H5
Wheat HI *LWTH* SG6.............16 C2
Wheatlands *STVGE* SG2.............34 C3
Wheatley Cl *SBW* CM21.............183 N8
   WGCE AL7.............68 E1
Wheatley Dr *WGCE* AL7.............102 A8
Wheatley Rd *WGCE* AL7.............50 D8
Wheatleys *STALE/WH* AL4.............66 B7
Wheatley Wy *CFSP/GDCR* SL9.............138 C1
Wheatlock Rd
   STALW/RED AL3.............173 Q12
Wheatsheaf Dr *WARE* SG12.............53 M2
Wheatsheaf Rd *WARE* SG12.............182 B7
Wheelers *LWTH* SG6.............16 C2
Wheelers Dr *RSLP* HA4.............141 G8
Wheelers Gn *WAB* EN9.............93 K4
Wheelers La *HHNE* HP2.............5 J7
Wheelers Orch
   CFSP/GDCR SL9.............138 C1
Wheelright Cl *BUSH* WD23.............132 F2
Wheel Wright Cl
   HTCH/STOT SG5.............146 B8
Wheelwrights *BSF* CM23.............43 M5
Whempstead La *WARE* SG12.............179 K3
Whempstead Rd *STVGE* SG2.............35 K5
Whetstone Cl
   TRDG/WHET N20.............137 H5
   WLYN AL6.............50 D8
Whielden Hts *AMSS* HP7.............112 E7
Whielden La *AMSS* HP7.............112 D8
Whielden St *AMSS* HP7.............112 E7
Whieldon Grn *HLWE* CM17.............76 B6
Whinbush Wy *HTCH/STOT* SG5.............157 P5
Whinbush Rd *HTCH/STOT* SG5.............157 N5
Whippendell Rd *WATW* WD18.............12 A7
Whipperley Ring *LTN* LU1.............40 A6
Whipperley Wy *LTN* LU1.............6 B9
Whipsnade Rd *DUN/WHIP* LU6.............38 D2
Whisper Wd
   RKW/CH/CXG WD3.............115 M7
Whitby Rd *LTNN/LIM* LU3.............6 C5
Whitebarns La *BUNT* SG9.............160 C12
Whitebeam Cl *CHESW* EN7.............91 J8
Whitebeams *HAT* AL10.............87 L8
   LCOL/BKTW AL2.............102 F2
White Bear *STSD* CM24.............166 C5
Whitebroom Rd *HHW* HP1.............61 J8
Whitchurch Cl *LTNE* LU2.............29 H7
Whitchurch Gdns *LWTH* SG6.............16 E5
White Craig Cl *PIN* HA5.............132 E8
White Crs *RAYLNE/WEN* HP22.............56 B7
Whitecroft *STAL* AL1.............85 M5
Whitecroft Rd *LTNE* LU2.............7 K4
White Crofts *HTCH/STOT* SG5.............148 C6
Whitefield Av *LTNN/LIM* LU3.............27 G2
Whitefields Rd
   CHES/WCR EN8.............110 A2
Whitefriars Av
   KTN/HRWW/WS HA3.............143 J4
Whitefriars Dr
   KTN/HRWW/WS HA3.............143 J4
Whitegale Cl *HTCHE/RSTV* SG4.............157 Q7
White Gate Gdns
   KTN/HRWW/WS HA3.............143 J2
Whitegates
   RKW/CH/CXG WD3.............116 E8
Whitehall Av *WAB* EN9.............93 J4
Whitehall La *BSF* CM23.............166 B12
Whitehall Rd *BSF* CM23.............166 A12
Whitehands Cl *HOD* EN11.............72 D7
White Hart Cl *BUNT* SG9.............158 H9
White Hart Rd *HHNE* HP2.............5 M4
Whitehaven *CHESW* EN7.............109 J2
   LTNN/LIM LU3.............154 F12
Whitehaven Cl *CHESW* EN7.............109 J2
White Hedge Dr
   STALW/RED AL3.............8 C2
White Hern Ct
   CHES/WCR EN8.............110 A4
Whitehicks *LWTH* SG6.............148 E12
Whitehill Ct *BERK* HP4.............60 B8
Whitehill La *LBUZ* LU7.............169 P6
White Hill Rd
   AMP/FLIT/BLC MK45.............155 J2
Whitehill Rd *HTCHE/RSTV* SG4.............157 Q7
Whitehills Rd *HTCHE/RSTV* SG4.............157 Q8
White Horse La *KNEB* SG3.............177 P8
   LCOL/BKTW AL2.............86 B8
Whitehorse St *BLDK* SG7.............17 J1
Whitehorse Vw *HTCH/STOT* SG5.............154 F12
Whitehouse Av *BORE* WD6.............120 F8
White House Cl
   CFSP/GDCR SL9.............138 C2
Whitehouse Cl
   DUN/HR/TOD LU5.............25 M5
White House Dr *STAN* HA7.............134 A7
White House La *ABLGY* WD5.............83 M8
White House La *HTCH/STOT* SG5.............128 G5
Whitehouse Wy
   STHGT/OAK N14.............137 M5
Whitelands Av
   HTCH/STOT SG5.............157 P7
Whitelands Av
   RKW/CH/CXG WD3.............114 F7
White La *HTCHE/RSTV* SG4.............32 A3
Whiteleaf Rd *HHS/BOV* HP3.............4 D9
Whiteley Cl *WARE* SG12.............179 N2
Whiteley La *LWTH* SG6.............16 B5
Whiteley La *BUNT* SG9.............158 G2
White Lion Av *AMSS* HP7.............113 L5
White Lion Hill *HHS/BOV* HP3.............82 B6
White Lion Sq *HAT* AL10.............67 L7
White Lion Yd *CSHM* HP5.............97 C6
The White Ldg *BAR* EN5.............122 C6
White Orchards *STAN* HA7.............133 L8
   TRDG/WHET N20.............137 H5
White Post Fld *SBW* CM21.............183 P7
White Shack La
   RKW/CH/CXG WD3.............116 D3
Whitesmead Rd *STVG* SG1.............11 J2
Whitestone Wk *HHW* HP1.............61 J8
White Stubbs La *BROX* EN10.............91 K3
Whitethorn *WGCE* AL7.............50 E8
Whitethorn La *LWTH* SG6.............16 E6
Whitethorn Wy *LTN* LU1.............40 E5
Whitewaits *HLW* CM20.............3 H5

Whitewaybottom La
HTCHE/RSTV SG4 175 L5
LTNE LU2 175 K3
The White Wy *STVGE* SG2 34 A2
Whitewebbs La *ENC/FH* EN2 125 H1
Whitewebbs Pk
ENC/FH EN2 * 125 J1
Whitewebbs Rd *BERK* HP4 79 L1
Whitfield Wy
RKW/CH/CXG WD3 129 K4
Whit Hern Ct
CHES/WCR EN8 * 109 M4
Whitings Cl *HARP* AL5 47 H1
Whitings Rd *BAR* EN5 136 A1
Whiting Wy *ROY* SG8 15 K1
Whitiars Dr *KGLGY* WD4 100 D2
Whitley Cl *ABLGY* WD5 101 L6
Whitley Rd *HOD* EN11 72 F5
Whitmore Ct *FBAR/BDGN* N11 137 M8
Whitmores Wy *HHNE* HP2 82 F1
Whitney Dr *STVG* SG1 21 G8
Whittingham La *STVG* SG1 10 E1
Whittingstall Rd *HOD* EN11 72 F5
Whittington La *STVG* SG1 10 E1
Whittington Wy *BSF* CM23 43 L6
Whittle Cl *GSTN* WD25 101 K8
HNLW SG16 147 K5
Whittlesea Rd
KTN/HRWW/WS HA3 143 H5
Whittle Wy *STVG* SG1 33 H7
Whitwell Cl *LTNW/LIM* LU3 27 M1
Whitwell Rd *GSTN* WD25 118 B1
Whitworth Dr *PEND* EN3 126 E3
Whitworth Jones Av
HNLW SG16 147 L4
Whitworth Rd *STVG* SG1 21 M6
Whomerley Rd *STVG* SG1 10 F7
Whybrow Gdns *BERK* HP4 60 C7
Whydale Rd *ROY* SG8 14 F8
Whytingham Rd *TRING* HP23 58 A1
Wick Av *STALE/WH* AL4 48 B5
Wicken Flds *WARE* SG12 54 A2
Wickets End *RAD* WD7 104 C7
Wickfield *KNEB* SG3 * 177 N7
Wickfield Cl *KNEB* SG3 177 N7
Wickham Cl *DEN/HRF* UB9 140 B3
PEND EN3 125 M7
Wickham Rd
KTN/HRWW/WS HA3 143 H4
Wickhams Whf *WARE* SG12 * 54 C4
Wickham Wy *STDN* SG11 163 P10
Wick Hl *DUN/WHIP* LU6 172 B1
Wicklands Rd *WARE* SG12 182 B8
Wickmere Cl *LTN* LU2 28 A2
Wick Rd *TRING* HP23 58 A5
Wickstead Av *LTNW/LEA* LU4 27 J6
The Wick *HERT/WAT* SG14 52 F4
Widbury Gdns *WARE* SG12 54 D4
Widbury HI *WARE* SG12 54 E4
Widenham Cl *PIN* HA5 142 A7
Widewater Pl *DEN/HRF* UB9 * 140 A7
WARE SG12 182 B7
WCCE AL7 50 D7
Widford Ter *HHNE* HP2 62 E4
Widgeon Wy *GSTN* WD25 118 C2
Widmore Cl *BUSH* WD23 78 C8
Widmore Dr *HHNE* HP2 62 E8
Wieland Rd *NTHWD* HA6 141 L2
Wiggenhall Rd *WATW* WD18 12 F7
Wigginton Bottom
TRING HP23 58 B5
Wiggles La *TRING* HP23 169 K10
Wigmore La *LTNE* LU2 28 F6
Wigmore PI *LTN* LU2 29 J8
Wigmores North *WGCW* AL8 50 B6
Wigram Wy *STVGE* SG2 11 L2
Wilbury Cl *LWTH* SG6 16 A4
Wilbury Dr *DUN/HR/TOD* LU5 26 C7
Wilbury Hills Rd *LWTH* SG6 16 C1
Wilbury Rd *LWTH* SG6 16 A4
Wilbury Wy *HTCHE/RSTV* SG4 157 Q2
Wilcon Wy *GSTN* WD25 102 B8
Wilcot Av *OXHEY* WD19 132 C3
Wilcot Cl *OXHEY* WD19 132 C3
Wilcox Cl *BORE* WD6 121 G5
Wildacres *NTHWD* HA6 131 K7
Wild Cherry Dr *LTN* LU1 6 A4
The Wilderness *BERK* HP4 80 A1
Wildhill Rd *BRKMPK* AL9 88 D3
Wild Oaks Cl *NTHWD* HA6 141 K1
Wildwood *NTHWD* HA6 141 L1
Wildwood Av *LCOL/BKTW* AL2 102 D4
Wildwood La *STVG* SG1 10 F7
Wilford Cl *ENC/FH* EN2 * 125 H7
NTHWD HA6 141 L1
Wilga Rd *WLYN* AL6 176 H12
Wilkin's Green La *HAT* AL10 * 87 G1
Wilkins Green Ter
STALE/WH AL4 * 86 F2
Wilkins Av *WGCW* AL8 50 B8
Wilkinson Cl *CHESW* EN7 91 G8
Wilkinson Wy *HHS/BOV* HP3 82 D1
Willenhall Av *BAR* EN5 137 G2
Willenhall Rd *LTNW/LIM* LU3 27 L2
Willetts Ms *HOD* EN11 72 E6
William Carey Wy *HRW* HA1 143 M4
William Cl *HHS/BOV* HP3 82 B6
William Covell Cl
ENC/FH EN2 * 124 D1
William Dr *STAN* HA7 143 L1
William Moulder Ct *CSHM* HP5 96 F2
William Pl *STVGE* SG2 11 J3
Williamson Rd
RKW/CH/CXG WD3 129 L4
William St *BERK* HP4 80 B1
LTN LU2 13 K4
LTNE LU2 6 E2
STALW/RED AL3 172 C4
Williams Wy *RAD* WD7 119 M1
Willian Church Rd *LWTH* SG6 16 E7
Willian Rd *HTCHE/RSTV* SG4 157 R4
Willian Wy *LWTH* SG6 16 E5
Willinghall Cl *WAB* EN9 111 M6
Williton Rd *LTNE* LU2 28 F4
Willoughby Cl *BROX* EN10 92 D4
DUN/WHIP LU6 39 G2
Willoughby Rd *HARP* AL5 46 F7
Willoughby Wy
HTCHE/RSTV SG4 157 Q2
Willowbay Cl *BAR* EN5 136 B2
Willowby Cl *LCOL/BKTW* AL2 86 B8
Willow Cha *CSHM* HP5 96 F2
Willow Cl *BSF* CM23 43 L1
BUNT SG9 160 A9
CFSP/GDCR SL9 138 C4
CHESW EN7 91 J8
ROY SG8 151 R8
Willowcourt Av
KTN/HRWW/WS HA3 143 M7
Willow Crs *STAL* AL1 86 A2

Willow Dean *PIN* HA5 * 142 B4
Willow Dene *BUSH* WD23 133 J3
Willowdene *CHES/WCR* EN8 110 C1
HERT/WAT SG14 * 178 G6
Willow Dr *BAR* EN5 135 M8
Willow Dene *HHNE* HP2 * 142 B4
Willow Edge *KGLGY* WD4 100 C1
Willow End *NTHWD* HA6 141 L1
TRDG/WHET N20 136 H1
Willowfield *HLWS* CM18 75 H7
Willow Gv *WGCW* AL8 50 B4
Willow La *AMSS* HP7 113 K7
HTCH/STOT SG5 157 L7
WATW WD18 12 D8
Willowmead *HERT/WAT* SG14 52 E8
Willow Md *SBW* CM21 183 Q8
Willow Rd *ENE* EN1 125 J3
Willows Cl *PIN* HA5 142 A4
Willowside Wy *ROY* SG8 14 D5
Willows La *HHW* HP1 81 K6
Willows Link *STVGE* SG2 33 L8
Willow Springs *BSF* CM23 43 K1
The Willows *AMS* HP6 112 F1
BORE WD6 * 120 E5
DUN/WHIP LU6 37 H6
EBAR EN4 * 137 J2
HHNE HP2 62 F8
HTCHE/RSTV SG4 157 Q8
OXHEY WD19 131 M3
RKW/CH/CXG WD3 129 L5
STAL AL1 85 L6
STVGE SG2 177 N1
WARE SG12 72 F3
Willow Tree Wy
HTCH/STOT SG5 157 N3
Willow Vw *WARE* SG12 * 54 C5
Willow Wk *WLYN* AL6 177 J9
Willow Wy *HARP* AL5 47 G1
HAT AL10 87 K3
LCOL/BKTW AL2 102 E1
LTNN/LIM LU3 27 Q8
POTB/CUF EN6 106 F7
RKW/CH/CXG WD3 129 L6
STAL AL1 85 L6
Wilshere Dr
KTN/HRWW/WS HA3 143 J2
Wilson Cl *BSF* CM23 43 M4
STVG SG1 * 21 H8
Wilsons Cl *STVG* SG1 * 21 H8
Wilsons La *BLDK* SG7 149 N1
Wilstone Br *TRING* HP23 168 H8
Wilstone Rd *STALE/WH* AL4 66 A5
Wilton Cl *BSF* CM23 44 B2
Wilton Crs *HERT/BAY* SG13 71 G2
HTCH/STOT SG5 157 N4
Wilton Wy *HERT/BAY* SG13 71 G1
Wiltshire Cl *MLHL* NW7 * 135 L8
Wiltshire La *PIN* HA5 141 K5
Wiltshire Rd *STVGE* SG2 11 L3
Wimborne Cl *SBW* CM21 183 P7
Wimborne Gv *WAT* WD17 117 J3
Wimborne Rd *LTN* LU1 6 A4
Wimple Rd *LTNW/LEA* LU4 27 H6
Winch Cl *HTCHE/RSTV* SG4 * 176 F9
Winchdells *HHS/BOV* HP3 82 E5
Winchester Cl *AMSS* HP7 113 J5
BSF CM23 43 K5
STVG SG1 21 L7
Winchester Dr *PIN* HA5 142 B7
Winchester Gdns
LTNN/LIM LU3 154 E12
Winchester Wy
RKW/CH/CXG WD3 130 F1
Winchfield Cl *LTN* LU1 40 C5
Winchfield Wy
RKW/CH/CXG WD3 130 A3
Windermere Av *STAL* AL1 85 M4
Windermere Cl *DUN/WHIP* LU6 38 E2
HHS/BOV HP3 83 G3
RKW/CH/CXG WD3 129 H1
STVG SG1 21 L7
Windermere Crs *LTNN/LIM* LU3 27 K4
Windermere Hall *EDGW* HA8 * 134 D8
Windhill *BSF* CM23 43 J2
WGCE AL7 50 E6
Windhill Old Rd *BSF* CM23 43 J2
Winding Ms *MHAD* SG10 42 A5
Winding Shot *HHW* HP1 * 4 A1
Winding Shott *HERT/WAT* SG14 52 A1
Windmill Av *STALE/WH* AL4 66 A6
Windmill Dr
RKW/CH/CXG WD3 130 A2
Windmill Fld *WARE* SG12 54 B5
Windmill Flds *HLWE* CM17 76 D1
Windmill Gdns *ENC/FH* EN2 124 E6
ENC/FH EN2 * 124 F1
HTCHE/RSTV SG4 157 P6
KGLGY WD4 99 K6
Windmill La *BAR* EN5 135 K2
BUSH WD23 133 J4
CHES/WCR EN8 110 C4
HHNE HP2 5 K4
HTCHE/RSTV SG4 * 30 K7
LTN LU1 7 J7
STALW/RED AL3 173 J3
Windmill Rd *CFSP/GDCR* SL9 138 B2
HHNE HP2 5 J4
HTCHE/RSTV SG4 30 F7
KGLGY WD4 99 K6
STALW/RED AL3 84 C1
Windrush Cl *STVG* SG1 52 G5
Windsor Av *EDGW* HA8 134 C7
Windsor Cl *CHESW* EN7 109 L4
HHNE HP2 5 J6
HHS/BOV HP3 98 D3
NTHWD HA6 141 L4
STVGE SG2 177 D2
WLYN AL6 49 M2
Windsor Ct *AMS* HP6 * 113 H4
PIN HA5 * 142 B3
EBAR EN4 * 137 K2
HERT/WAT SG14 * 52 D6
Windsor Gdns *BSF* CM23 43 L8
Windsor Pde
AMP/FLIT/BLC MK45 * 155 J1

KTN/HRWW/WS HA3 143 G3
LBUZ LU7 169 N6
PEND EN3 126 E2
ROY SG8 * 151 R8
WATN WD24 118 A4
WLYN AL6 49 M2
Windsor St *LTN* LU1 6 E7
Windsor Wk *LTN* LU1 6 E7
Windsor Wy
RKW/CH/CXG WD3 129 L4
Windsor Wd *WAB* EN9 111 J7
Windward Cl *PEND* EN3 126 B1
Windy Ri *WARE* SG12 179 P2
Winfield St *DUN/WHIP* LU6 25 M8
Winford Dr *BROX* EN10 92 D4
Wingate Gdns *WLYN* AL6 * 176 H12
Wingate Rd *DUN/HR/TOD* LU5 26 C8
LTNW/LEA LU4 27 K7
Wingate Wy *STAL* AL1 * 9 M8
Wingfield Cl *WATW* WD18 * 131 H2
Wingrave Rd *TRING* HP23 168 H7
Winifred Pl
NFNCH/WDSPK N12 137 G8
Winifred Rd *HHS/BOV* HP3 82 B6
Winkers Cl *CFSP/GDCR* SL9 138 D3
Winkers La *CFSP/GDCR* SL9 138 D3
Winkfield Cl *LTNW/LEA* LU4 26 F8
Winnington Rd *PEND* EN3 126 A4
Winnipeg Wy *BROX* EN10 92 C7
Winscombe Wy *STAN* HA7 143 L8
Winsdon Rd *LTN* LU1 6 D7
Winslow Cl *LTNN/LIM* LU3 28 A5
PIN HA5 141 M8
Winston Churchill Wy
CHES/WCR EN8 110 A1
Winston Cl *HTCH/STOT* SG5 157 M6
KTN/HRWW/WS HA3 143 K1
Winston Ct
KTN/HRWW/WS HA3 142 F3
Winstone Cl *LTNN/LIM* LU3 96 F8
Winston Gdns *BERK* HP4 79 K1
Winstre Rd *BORE* WD6 120 E2
Wintercroft Rd *HOD* EN11 72 D7
Winters La *STVGE* SG2 22 F8
Winters Wy *WAB* EN9 111 L7
Winthorpe Gdns *BORE* WD6 120 D5
Winton Ap *RKW/CH/CXG* WD3 131 G1
Winton Cl *LTNE* LU2 28 B3
LWTH SG6 17 G1
Winton Crs *RKW/CH/CXG* WD3 130 F1
Winton Dr *CHES/WCR* EN8 110 C3
RKW/CH/CXG WD3 131 G1
Winton Rd *WARE* SG12 54 C5
The Wintons *BUSH* WD23 133 H4
Winton Ter *STAL* AL1 * 9 H8
Wisden Rd *STVG* SG1 21 K8
Wisdom Dr *HERT/BAY* SG13 53 J7
Wiseman Cl *LTNE* LU2 28 B2
Wisemans Gdns *SBW* CM21 183 N8
Wistaria Cl *LCOL/BKTW* AL2 85 M8
Wistlea Crs *STALE/WH* AL4 86 F4
Witchford *WCCE* AL7 51 H7
Withy Cl *LTNW/LEA* LU4 26 F4
Withy La *RSLP* HA4 141 G2
Withy Pl *LCOL/BKTW* AL2 102 F2
Witney Cl *PIN* HA5 142 D1
Witter Av *HTCH/STOT* SG5 157 N1
Wivelsfield *LTNE* LU2 37 J3
Wiveton Cl *LTNE* LU2 28 B3
Woburn Av *BAR* EN5 137 J2
Woburn Cl *BUSH* WD23 133 J2
STVGE SG2 177 Q2
Wodecroft Rd *LTNN/LIM* LU3 27 M1
Wolmer Cl *EDGW* HA8 134 E7
Wolmer Gdns *EDGW* HA8 134 E6
Wolsey Rd
KTN/HRWW/WS HA3 143 J5
Wolsey Av *CHESW* EN7 109 K3
Wolsey Rd *ENE* EN1 125 M6
HHNE HP2 5 H7
NTHWD HA6 131 H7
Wolstonbury
NFNCH/WDSPK N12 136 H8
Wolston Cl *LTN* LU1 6 B6
Wolverton Rd *STAN* HA7 143 M1
Wolvescroft *KNEB* SG3 * 177 N6
Wolves Mere *KNEB* SG3 177 N6
Wonnacott *PEND* EN3 126 B3
Woodacre Dr *WLYN* AL6 * 176 N9
Woodbank *RKW/CH/CXG* WD3 130 A4
Woodbank Av *CFSP/GDCR* SL9 138 A8
Woodbank Dr *CSTG* HP8 128 B3
Woodberry Av
RYLN/HDSTN HA2 143 G6
Woodbine Cl *HLWW/ROY* CM19 75 G7
Woodbine Gv *ENC/FH* EN2 125 H4
Woodbridge Cl *LTNW/LEA* LU4 27 J5
Woodbrook Gdns *WAB* EN9 111 J7
Woodbury HI *LTNE* LU2 28 C7
Woodbury Hill Pth *LTNE* LU2 28 C7
Wood Cl *DUN/WHIP* LU6 172 A1
HAT AL10 67 M8
Woodcock HI
RKW/CH/CXG WD3 130 C8
Woodcock Rd *LTN* LU1 40 B7
ROY SG8 14 F5
STVGE SG2 34 C4
Wood Common *HAT* AL10 67 M5
Woodcote Cl *LTNE* LU2 28 A1
Wood Crs *HHNE* HP2 5 G5
Woodcroft *HLWS* CM18 75 H7
Woodcroft Av *STAN* HA7 143 L3
WARE SG12 54 A3
Woodcroft Rd *CSHM* HP5 97 H2
Woodcutter Pl
LCOL/BKTW AL2 103 G1
Wood End Cl *LCOL/BKTW* AL2 103 G1
Wood End *HHNE* HP2 4 B2
Woodend Gdns *ENC/FH* EN2 124 C8
Wood End HI *HARP* AL5 46 E6
Wood End La *STALW/RED* AL3 172 H9
Wood End Rd *HARP* AL5 46 E6
Woodfall Av *BAR* EN5 136 D1
Woodfield Av *NTHWD* HA6 131 J7
Woodfield Cl *EN* EN1 125 J8
STSD CM24 166 F7
Woodfield Dr *EBAR* EN4 137 L4
Woodfield Gdns *HHS/BOV* HP3 83 G4
Woodfield Ga
DUN/HR/TOD LU5 39 G3
Woodfield Pk *AMS* HP6 112 F3
Woodfield Ri *BUSH* WD23 133 H3
Woodfield Rd *RAD* WD7 119 H3
STVG SG1 21 L8
WCCE AL7 50 D7
Woodfields *STSD* CM24 166 G2
WATW WD18 * 13 G6

Woodfield Ter *STSD* CM24 166 G7
Woodfield Wy *STALE/WH* AL4 66 A7
Woodford Ct *WCCE* AL9 111 L7
Woodford Crs *PIN* HA5 141 M4
Woodforde Cl *BLDK* SG7 149 Q1
Woodford Rd
DUN/HR/TOD LU5 26 C7
WAT WD17 12 A1
Woodgate *GSTN* WD25 101 M7
Woodgate Av *POTB/CUF* EN6 107 M7
Woodgate Crs *NTHWD* HA6 141 L1
Woodgate Ms *WAT* WD17 117 L5
Wood Green Cl *LTNE* LU2 28 F4
Woodgreen Rd *WAB* EN9 111 M7
Woodhall Cl *HERT/WAT* SG14 53 C5
Woodhall Ct *WCCE* AL7 50 C8
Woodhall Dr *PIN* HA5 142 B3
Woodhall Ga *PIN* HA5 142 B2
Woodhall La *HHNE* HP2 82 C1
OXHEY WD19 132 B6
RAD WD7 120 C1
WCCE AL7 68 C1
Woodham Wy *WARE* SG12 73 G1
Woodhill *HLWS* CM18 75 J8
Woodhill Av *CFSP/GDCR* SL9 138 D8
Woodhouse Eaves
NTHWD HA6 131 L8
Wood House La *BROX* EN10 91 K5
Woodhurst *LWTH* SG6 16 D1
Woodhurst Av *GSTN* WD25 101 L8
Woodhurst Dr *DEN/HRF* UB9 139 K7
Wooding Gv *HLWW/ROY* CM19 2 A4
Woodland Av *HHW* HP1 4 B4
Woodland Cl *HHW* HP1 4 B4
TRING HP23 57 K3
Woodland Ct *STALW/RED* AL3 * 65 K6
Woodland Dr *STALE/WH* AL4 86 A1
WAT WD17 12 C2
Woodland La
RKW/CH/CXG WD3 115 H7
Woodland Mt *HERT/BAY* SG13 53 K7
Woodland Pl *HHW* HP1 * 4 B4
Woodland Ri *DUN/WHIP* LU6 171 P2
WGCW AL8 50 A5
Woodland Rd
FBAR/BDGN N11 137 M8
HERT/BAY SG13 72 A2
RKW/CH/CXG WD3 129 K8
Woodlands *BRKMPK* AL9 106 F1
CFSP/GDCR SL9 138 D8
HARP AL5 46 C2
LCOL/BKTW AL2 103 G1
RAD WD7 103 L8
ROY SG8 14 F7
RYLN/HDSTN HA2 142 E6
Woodlands Av *BERK* HP4 80 B2
DUN/HR/TOD LU5 26 B2
Woodlands Cl *BORE* WD6 120 F8
CFSP/GDCR SL9 138 D8
TRING HP23 57 K3
Woodlands Dr *HOD* EN11 92 C1
KGLGY WD4 101 G2
STAN HA7 143 K1
Woodlands Meade
HTCHE/RSTV SG4 21 M1
The Woodlands *AMS* HP6 113 G5
STAN HA7 133 M8
STHGT/OAK N14 137 M4
Woodland Vw *CSHM* HP5 97 H7
Woodland Wy *ABLGY* WD5 101 K1
BLDK SG7 17 K3
CHESW EN7 108 F2
STVGE SG2 33 L8
STAN HA7 143 L1
Wood La *BSF* CM23 166 G11
BUNT SG9 160 C3
HHNE HP2 5 G6
STAN HA7 143 M6
Wood Lane End *HHNE* HP2 4 F7
Woodlea *LCOL/BKTW* AL2 84 F1
Woodlea Gv *NTHWD* HA6 141 G1
Woodley Ct *AMSS* HP7 113 H5
Woodley HI *HHS/BOV* HP3 5 H7
Woodman Rd *HHS/BOV* HP3 5 H7
Woodmans Yd *WAT* WD17 13 G4
Woodmere *LTNN/LIM* LU3 154 G12
Woodmere Av *WATN* WD24 118 A4
Woodmill Ms *HOD* EN11 72 F4
Woodpecker Cl *BSF* CM23 43 J3
BUSH WD23 133 G4
HAT AL10 * 87 K3
KTN/HRWW/WS HA3 143 L3
Woodredon Cl
HLWW/ROY CM19 * 73 M6
Wood Ride *EBAR* EN4 123 H5
Woodridge Cl *ENC/FH* EN2 * 124 C1
Woodridge Wy *NTHWD* HA6 141 G2
Woodridings Av *PIN* HA5 142 D3
Woodridings Cl *PIN* HA5 142 D2
Wood Ri *PIN* HA5 141 L7
Woods Av *HAT* AL10 * 87 L1
Woodshots Meadow
WATW WD18 131 H1
Woodside *BORE* WD6 120 D8
BSF CM23 44 D1
CHESW EN7 109 L5
DUN/WHIP LU6 37 J3
HERT/BAY SG13 72 A2
WATN WD24 117 J2
Woodside Av *AMS* HP6 113 H2
NFNCH/WDSPK N12 137 G6
Woodside Cl *CFSP/GDCR* SL9 138 C3
RSLP HA4 141 M6
STAN HA7 143 L1
Woodside Gdns
HTCH/STOT SG5 157 P6
Woodside Grange Rd
NFNCH/WDSPK N12 137 F7
Woodside Gv
NFNCH/WDSPK N12 137 G6
Woodside HI *CFSP/GDCR* SL9 138 C4
Woodside La *BRKMPK* AL9 88 D3
TRDG/WHET N20 136 H1
Woodside Pk
DUN/WHIP LU6 26 A6
Woodside Park Rd
NFNCH/WDSPK N12 137 F7
Woodside Rd *ABLGY* WD5 101 K1
AMS HP6 113 H5
LCOL/BKTW AL2 102 F7

LTN LU1 40 E8
NTHWD HA6 141 K1
WLYN AL6 50 D2
Woodside Wk *AMS* HP6 113 H5
Woods Pl *TRING* HP23 57 L2
The Woods *NTHWD* HA6 131 K8
RAD WD7 103 M8
Woodstock *KNEB* SG3 177 M6
Woodstock Cl *HERT/BAY* SG13 71 K1
Woodstock Rd *BROX* EN10 92 C1
BUSH WD23 133 J3
Woodstock Rd North *STAL* AL1 85 M1
Woodstock Rd South *STAL* AL1 85 M2
Wood St *BAR* EN5 122 A8
DUN/WHIP LU6 39 G1
LTN LU1 7 H8
Wood V *HAT* AL10 67 M8
Woodvale Pk *STAL* AL1 85 M2
Wood Vw *HHW* HP1 61 M8
POTB/CUF EN6 108 C1
Woodville Ct *WAT* WD17 12 C1
Woodville Court Ms
WAT WD17 * 12 C1
Woodville Pl *HERT/WAT* SG14 52 F5
Woodville Rd *BAR* EN5 122 F1
Woodward Gdns *STAN* HA7 143 K2
Woodwards *HLWW/ROY* CM19 75 G7
Woodway Crs *HRW* HA1 143 L8
Woodwicks *RKW/CH/CXG* WD3 128 A3
Woolams *STALW/RED* AL3 63 H8
Woolgrove Rd
HTCHE/RSTV SG4 157 Q4
Woollam Crs *STALW/RED* AL3 65 K6
Woollams *STALW/RED* AL3 63 L1
Woollard St *WAB* EN9 111 G8
Woollerton Cl
RAYLNE/WEN HP22 56 A8
Woolmans Cl *BROX* EN10 92 D4
Woolmer Cl *BORE* WD6 120 E4
Woolmerdine Ct *BUSH* WD23 13 G5
Woolmer Dr *HHNE* HP2 83 G2
Woolmers La *HERT/WAT* SG14 69 M3
Woolners Wy *STVG* SG1 2 A3
Woolpack Cl *DUN/WHIP* LU6 38 D1
Woolston Dr SG6 16 E5
Wootton Cl *LTNW/LIM* LU3 27 M2
Wootton Dr *HHNE* HP2 62 D5
Worboys Ct *ROY* SG8 145 M4
Worcester Crs *MLHL* NW7 135 J6
Worcester Rd *HARP* AL5 46 C7
Worcesters Av *ENE* EN1 125 K3
Wordsworth Cl *ROY* SG8 14 C4
Wordsworth Ct *HAT* AL10 67 L7
Wordsworth Gdns *BORE* WD6 134 L1
Wordsworth Rd *HARP* AL5 46 C2
LTNW/LEA LU4 26 E7
Works Rd *LWTH* SG6 16 F2
Worley Rd *STALW/RED* AL3 8 E4
Wormley Cl *HHW* HP1 4 A4
Wormley Lodge Cl *BROX* EN10 92 D5
Wormyngford Ct *WAB* EN9 111 L7
Worsdell Wy *HTCHE/RSTV* SG4 157 R6
Worsted La *ROY* SG9 159 Q10
Wortham La *ROY* SG8 14 F8
Wortham Wy *STVGE* SG2 33 L2
Worthington Rd
DUN/WHIP LU6 38 D1
The Wraglins *BSF* CM23 44 B4
Wrangley Ct *WAB* EN9 111 L7
Wratten Cl *HTCHE/RSTV* SG4 157 N7
Wratten Rd East
HTCH/STOT SG5 157 N7
Wratten Rd West
HTCH/STOT SG5 157 N7
Wrayfields *HTCH/STOT* SG5 148 F6
Wraysbury Cl *LTNW/LEA* LU4 26 E7
Wrenbrook Rd *BSF* CM23 43 M4
Wren Cl *HTCHE/RSTV* SG4 175 M8
LTNE LU2 29 G3
STVG SG2 * 33 L1
Wren Crs *BUSH* WD23 133 G4
Wren Dr *WAB* EN9 111 L8
Wrensfield *HHW* HP1 4 A4
The Wrens *HLWW/ROY* CM19 2 A4
Wren Wk *DUN/WHIP* LU6 37 J5
Wren Wd *WGCE* AL7 50 E6
Wrenwood Wy *PIN* HA5 141 M6
Wright Cl *LTNE* LU2 29 G3
Wright's Green La *RBSF* CM22 184 C2
Wrights Meadow *STVGE* SG2 34 C7
Wrights Orch *STVGE* SG2 34 C7
Wrotham Rd *BAR* EN5 122 C6
Wroxham Av *HHNE* HP2 5 L8
Wroxham Gdns *ENC/FH* EN2 124 E1
POTB/CUF EN6 106 B5
Wroxham Wy *HARP* AL5 47 G2
Wulfrath Wy *WARE* SG12 54 A2
Wulstan Pk *POTB/CUF* EN6 107 M7
Wulwards Cl *LTN* LU1 40 F7
Wyatt Cl *BUSH* WD23 133 J3
HTCH/STOT SG5 157 G5
Wyatt's Cl *RKW/CH/CXG* WD3 115 L7
Wyatt's Rd *RKW/CH/CXG* WD3 115 L7
Wyburn Av *BAR* EN5 122 D7
Wychdell *STVGE* SG2 177 Q1
Wych Elm *LTN* CM20 2 D4
Wych Elm La *WLYN* AL6 177 L6
Wych Elms *LCOL/BKTW* AL2 102 F2
Wycherley Crs *BAR* EN5 136 F2
Wychford Dr *SBW* CM21 183 N8
Wychwood Av *LTNE* LU2 28 C5
Wychwood Wy *NTHWD* HA6 141 K2
Wyckland Cl
HTCH/STOT SG5 * 148 C7
Wycliffe Cl *CHES/WCR* EN8 110 B3
LTNN/LIM LU3 28 C1
Wycombe Pl *STAL* AL1 * 65 M7
Wycombe Wy *LTNN/LIM* LU3 28 A1
STALE/WH AL4 65 M7
Wyddial Gn *WGCE* AL7 * 50 F7
Wye Cl *RSLP* HA4 141 M6
Wyedale *LCOL/BKTW* AL2 104 D1
The Wye *HHNE* HP2 62 F5
Wyevale Ct *NTHWD* HA6 141 L5
Wykeham Ri *TRDG/WHET* N20 136 C4
Wykeham Rd
KTN/HRWW/WS HA3 143 M6
Wyken Cl *LTNN/LIM* LU3 27 L2
Wykeridge Cl *CSHM* HP5 96 F1
Wylchin Cl *PIN* HA5 141 K6
Wyldwood Cl *HLWE* CM17 183 N11
Wyllyotts Pl *POTB/CUF* EN6 106 D6
Wylo Dr *BAR* EN5 135 K2
Wymondley Cl
HTCHE/RSTV SG4 157 Q7
Wymondley Rd
HTCHE/RSTV SG4 157 Q7
LWTH SG6 20 D1
Wynches Farm Dr
STALE/WH AL4 86 B1
Wynchgate
KTN/HRWW/WS HA3 143 J2
Wynchlands Crs *STALE/WH* AL4 86 D2

Wyndcroft CI *ENC/FH* EN2 ...... 124 F7
Wyndham Rd *EBAR* EN4 ...... 137 K4
LTNW/LEA LU4 ...... 27 G7
Wyndhams End *WGCE* AL7 ...... 68 D3
Wynlie Gdns *PIN* HA5 ...... 141 M4
Wynn CI *BLDK* SG7 ...... 149 L12
Wyre Gv *EDGW* HA8 ...... 134 F6
Wyrley Dell *LWTH* SG6 ...... 16 E6
Wyteleaf CI *RSLP* HA4 ...... 141 L8
Wyton *WGCE* AL7 ...... 51 H7
Wyvern CI *LTNW/LEA* LU4 ...... 27 J6

Y

Yardley *LWTH* SG6 ...... 16 F5
Yardley Av *LBUZ* LU7 ...... 169 N5
Yarmouth Rd *STVG* SG1 ...... 32 E2
WATN WD24 ...... 117 M4
Yarrowside *AMSS* HP7 ...... 113 M6
Yearling CI *WARE* SG12 ...... 54 D6
Ye Cnr *OXHEY* WD19 ...... 13 K9
Yeats CI *ROY* SG8 ...... 14 E4
Yeomanry Dr *BLDK* SG7 ...... 149 L12
Yeomans Acre *RSLP* HA4 ...... 141 L8
Yeomans Av *HARP* AL5 ...... 46 A2
Yeomans CI *BSF* CM23 ...... 43 K4
Yeomans Ct *HHNE* HP2 ...... 62 E4
Yeomans Dr *STVGE* SG2 ...... 34 C7
Yeomans Wy *PEND* EN3 * 125 M6
Yeovil Rd *LTNE* LU2 ...... 28 F7
Yew CI *CHESW* EN7 * 109 J1
Yew Gv *WGCE* AL7 ...... 51 G8
Yewlands *HOD* EN11 ...... 72 E8
SBW CM21 ...... 183 Q8
Yewlands Dr *HOD* EN11 ...... 72 E8
Yews Av *EN* EN1 ...... 125 M2
Yew St *DUN/HR/TOD* LU5 ...... 26 B2
Yew Tree CI *CSHM* HP5 ...... 97 L4
DUN/WHIP LU6 ...... 37 K4
Yewtree CI *LBUZ* LU7 ...... 169 Q4
RYLN/HDSTN HA2 ...... 142 F6
Yew Tree Ct *BORE* WD6 ...... 134 B2
Yew Tree Dr *HHS/BOV* HP3 ...... 98 F2
Yewtree End *LCOL/BKTW* AL2 ...... 102 F1
Yew Tree PI *BSF* CM23 ...... 43 M1
Yorke Ga *WAT* WD17 ...... 12 D1
Yorke Rd *RKW/CH/CXG* WD3 ...... 130 E2
Yorkes *HLWS* CM18 ...... 75 K7
York Rd *BAR* EN5 ...... 137 K4
CHES/WCR EN8 ...... 110 C8
HTCH/STOT SG5 ...... 157 N5
NTHWD HA6 ...... 141 L4
STAL AL1 ...... 9 H7
STVG SG1 ...... 21 K7
WATW WD18 ...... 13 H8
York St *LTNE* LU2 ...... 7 F1
York Ter *ENC/FH* EN2 ...... 125 G4
York Wy *GSTN* WD25 ...... 118 B2
HHNE HP2 ...... 5 L5
ROY SG8 ...... 14 C5
TRDG/WHET N20 ...... 137 K6
WLYN AL6 ...... 49 M2
Youngfield Rd *HHW* HP1 ...... 81 K1
Youngmans CI *ENC/FH* EN2 ...... 125 G5
Youngsbury La *WARE* SG12 ...... 180 B9
Youngs Ms *HERT/WAT* SG14 ...... 53 G7
Youngs Ri *WGCW* AL8 ...... 49 M7
Yukon Rd *BROX* EN10 ...... 92 C7
Yule CI *LCOL/BKTW* AL2 ...... 102 D4

Z

Zambesi Rd *BSF* CM23 ...... 43 M4

index - featured places

Abbeygate Business Centre
LTNE LU2 ...... 7 H4
Abbey Gateway
STALW/RED AL3 ...... 8 D6
Abbey Mead Industrial Park
WAB EN9 ...... 110 F8
Abbey Primary School
STAL AL1 ...... 8 D7
Abbey View Golf Club
STAL AL1 ...... 8 C8
Abbots Hill School
HHS/BOV HP3 ...... 82 F1
Abbots Langley Primary School
ABLGY WD5 ...... 101 J3
Abbotsweld Primary School
HLWS CM18 ...... 75 H7
Abbotswood Medical Centre
ABLGY WD5 ...... 101 L6
Aboyne Lodge Primary School
STALW/RED AL3 ...... 8 A4
Activity World
HAT AL10 ...... 67 M5
Adath Yisroel Cemetery
EN EN1 ...... 125 K5
Adeyfield School
HHNE HP2 ...... 5 M3
Airport Executive Industrial Park
LTNE LU2 ...... 174 B1
Akeman Business Park
TRING HP23 ...... 57 L2
Alban Arena Cinema
STAL AL1 ...... 8 C7
Alban Wood Primary School
GSTN WD25 ...... 101 M7
Albany School (Grant Maintained)
PEND EN3 ...... 126 B4
Albury Primary School
STDN SG11 ...... 164 G7
Aldbury Primary School
TRING HP23 ...... 170 C11
Aldenham Country Park
BORE WD6 ...... 133 M1
Aldenham Golf & Country Club
GSTN WD25 ...... 118 F4
Aldenham Preparatory School
BORE WD6 ...... 119 K6
Aldwickbury Park Golf Club
HARP AL5 ...... 47 J4
Aldwickbury School
HARP AL5 ...... 47 J5
Alexandra Business Centre
PEND EN3 ...... 126 B8
Algrey Trading Estate
HTCHE/RSTV SG4 ...... 157 Q4
Allied Business Centre
HARP AL5 ...... 47 G2
All Nations Christian College
WARE SG12 ...... 54 F6
All Saints CE Primary School
BSF CM23 ...... 44 B1
TRDG/WHET N20 ...... 137 H5
Allum Lane Cemetery
BORE WD6 ...... 134 C1
Almond Hill School
STVG SG1 ...... 33 H1
Almond Lane Cemetery
STVG SG1 ...... 33 J1
Alpha Business Park
BRKMPK AL9 ...... 88 A5
Alpha Preparatory School
HRW HA1 ...... 143 J7
Alsa Business Park
STSD CM24 ...... 166 H4
Amersham & Chiltern RFC
AMS HP6 ...... 112 E2
Amersham General Hospital
AMSS HP7 ...... 112 E7
Amersham Hill CC
AMS HP6 ...... 113 J4
The Amersham School
AMSS HP7 ...... 113 J6
Amersham Town FC
AMSS HP7 ...... 112 E5
Amersham & Wycombe College
AMSS HP7 ...... 113 K5
CSHM HP5 ...... 97 H1
Amwell View Special School
WARE SG12 ...... 72 F1
Andrews Lane J & I School
CHESW EN7 ...... 109 M2
Anglian Business Park
ROY SG8 ...... 14 C6
Anstey First School
BUNT SG9 ...... 160 A3
Apex Business Centre
DUN/HR/TOD LU5 ...... 26 A7
Applecroft JMI School
WGCW AL8 ...... 49 M7
Apsley Mills Retail Park
HHS/BOV HP3 ...... 82 C6
The Arcade
LWTH SG6 ...... 16 D3
Archgate Business Centre
NFNCH/WDSPK N12 ...... 137 G7
Ardeley Primary School
STVGE SG2 ...... 36 K6
Ardley Hill Lower School
DUN/WHIP LU6 ...... 39 G3
Ardmore House Hotel
STAL AL1 ...... 9 J3
Arianne Business Centre
DUN/HR/TOD LU5 ...... 25 M7
Arkley Golf Club
BAR EN5 ...... 135 K1

Arlesey FC
ARL/CHE SG15 ...... 147 Q6
Arndale Shopping Centre
LTN LU1 ...... 6 F5
Arnett Hills Primary School
RKW/CH/CXG WD3 ...... 129 L2
Arnold Middle School
AMP/FLIT/BLC MK45 ...... 155 K3
The Arthur Findlay College
STSD CM24 ...... 167 J8
Artsdepot
NFNCH/WDSPK N12 ...... 137 G8
The Arts Educational School
TRING HP23 ...... 57 M2
Ascot Business Centre
LTN LU1 ...... 6 D6
Ascot Industrial Estate
LWTH SG6 ...... 16 F2
Ashcroft High School
LTNE LU2 ...... 29 G7
Asheridge Road Industrial Estate
CSHM HP5 ...... 96 E3
Ashfield Junior School
BUSH WD23 ...... 132 F3
Ash Industrial Estate
HLWW/ROY CM19 ...... 74 D6
Ashley Business Centre
HTCH/STOT SG5 ...... 157 P5
Ashlyns School
BERK HP4 ...... 80 A3
Ashridge Estate (NT)
BERK HP4 ...... 170 E11
Ashridge Estate Visitor Centre
BERK HP4 ...... 170 E11
Ashridge Golf Club
BERK HP4 ...... 170 H10
Ashridge Management College
BERK HP4 ...... 171 J12
Ashton CE VA Middle School
DUN/WHIP LU6 ...... 25 M8
Ashton St Peters VA Lower School
DUN/HR/TOD LU5 ...... 26 A8
Ashtree Primary School
STVGE SG2 ...... 34 A5
Ash Valley Golf Club
MHAD HP2 ...... 181 R3
Ashville Trading Estate
BLDK SG7 ...... 149 K12
Asquith Court School
HARP AL5 ...... 46 D2
KTN/HRWW/WS HA3 ...... 143 M8
Asquith School
PEND EN3 ...... 126 A8
Astley Cooper School
HHNE HP2 ...... 62 E5
Aston Clinton School
AYLNE/WEN HP22 ...... 168 B12
Aston St Marys Primary School
STVGE SG2 ...... 34 C6
Aycliffe Drive Primary School
HHNE HP2 ...... 62 C6
Aylands School
PEND EN3 ...... 126 A2
Aylward First & Middle Schools
STAN HA7 ...... 134 B8
Baldock Cemetery
BLDK SG7 ...... 17 H1
Baldock Health Centre
BLDK SG7 ...... 17 K2
Baldock Industrial Estate
BLDK SG7 ...... 17 K2
Balloon Flights
AYLNE/WEN HP22 ...... 56 C1
Bamnister Stadium
KTN/HRWW/WS HA3 ...... 143 G1
Barbara Castle Health Centre
HLWW/ROY CM19 ...... 94 E1
Barclay School
STVG SG1 ...... 33 H1
Barkway CE First School
ROY SG8 ...... 152 E9
Barkway Park Golf Club
ROY SG8 ...... 152 G11
Barley VP First School
ROY SG8 ...... 153 J3
Barncroft JMI School
HHNE HP2 ...... 62 B5
Barnet College
BAR EN5 ...... 122 D8
EBAR EN4 ...... 137 K4
FBAR/BDGN N11 ...... 137 K6
NFNCH/WDSPK N12 ...... 137 G8
Barnet FC (Underhill)
BAR EN5 ...... 136 E1
Barnet General Hospital
BAR EN5 ...... 122 B8
Barnet Health Centre
BAR EN5 ...... 136 E1
Barnet Hill JMI School
BAR EN5 ...... 136 D1
Barnet Hospital Chest Clinic
BAR EN5 ...... 122 B8
Barnet Museum
BAR EN5 ...... 122 C8
Barnet Trading Estate
BAR EN5 ...... 122 D7
Barnfield College
LTN LU1 ...... 40 F1
LTNE LU2 ...... 28 F1
Barnfield College Technology Centre
LTNN/LIM LU3 ...... 27 M1

Barn Theatre
WGCW AL8 ...... 50 A7
Barnwell School
STVGE SG2 ...... 33 M7
Barratt Industrial Park
LTNE LU2 ...... 174 A3
Barrat Way Industrial Estate
RYLN/HDSTN HA2 ...... 143 H5
Barton Hills National Nature Reserve
AMP/FLIT/BLC MK45 ...... 155 K4
Barton Industrial Estate
AMP/FLIT/BLC MK45 ...... 154 G1
Barton Rovers FC
AMP/FLIT/BLC MK45 ...... 155 J3
Batchwood Golf Club
STALW/RED AL3 ...... 64 F7
Batchwood School
STALW/RED AL3 ...... 65 H7
Bayford Primary School
HERT/BAY SG13 ...... 70 D8
Bayhurst Wood Country Park
DEN/HRF UB9 ...... 140 D7
The Beacon School
AMS HP6 ...... 112 F1
Beales Hotel
HAT AL10 ...... 67 J7
Beaumont School
STALE/WH AL4 ...... 86 B1
The Bedford Arms Hotel
RKW/CH/CXG WD3 ...... 114 F4
Bedmond JMI School
ABLGY WD5 ...... 101 K2
Bedwell Community Centre
STVG SG1 ...... 11 H5
Bedwell Medical Centre
STVG SG1 ...... 11 H5
Bedwell Primary School
STVG SG1 ...... 11 J3
Beechfield JMI School
WATN WD24 ...... 117 J3
Beech Hill Community Primary School
LTNW/LEA LU4 ...... 6 A2
Beech Hyde Primary School
STALE/WH AL4 ...... 48 B6
Beechwood Park School
STALW/RED AL3 ...... 172 D8
Beechwood Primary School
LTNW/LEA LU4 ...... 27 J5
Beecroft Lower School
DUN/WHIP LU6 ...... 25 K8
Belcon Industrial Estate
HOD EN11 ...... 73 G7
Belgate JMI School
HHNE HP2 ...... 62 C8
Bell Lane Combined School
AMS HP6 ...... 113 M4
Belmont First School
KTN/HRWW/WS HA3 ...... 143 K4
Belmont (Mill Hill Preparatory School)
MLHL NW7 ...... 135 L6
Belswains Infant School
HHS/BOV HP3 ...... 82 B6
Bengeo Primary School
HERT/WAT SG14 ...... 53 G4
Benington Lordship
STVGE SG2 ...... 35 H3
Benington Primary School
STVGE SG2 ...... 35 H5
Bentfield Primary School
STSD CM24 ...... 166 F5
Bentley Wood Girls School
STAN HA7 ...... 133 K8
Berkeley Clinic
RKW/CH/CXG WD3 ...... 130 A4
Berkhamsted Castle (Remains)
BERK HP4 ...... 60 L8
Berkhamsted Collegiate Preparatory School
BERK HP4 ...... 79 M1
Berkhamsted Collegiate School (Castle Campus)
BERK HP4 ...... 80 A1
Berkhamsted FC
BERK HP4 ...... 59 M8
Berkhamsted Golf Club
BERK HP4 ...... 60 C6
Berkhamsted Health Centre
BERK HP4 ...... 59 L8
Berkhamsted School House
BERK HP4 ...... 80 A1
Berkhamsted Tennis Club
BERK HP4 ...... 60 A8
Bernards Heath Infant School
STAL AL1 ...... 9 J1
Bernards Heath Junior School
STALW/RED AL3 ...... 8 J7
Berrygrove Primary School
GSTN WD25 ...... 118 B1
Best Western Cumberland Hotel
HRW HA1 ...... 143 J7
Best Western Homestead Court Hotel
WGCE AL7 ...... 68 D7
Best Western Stansted Manor Hotel
BSF CM23 ...... 166 F12
Best Western the Roebuck Inn
STVGE SG2 ...... 33 K8
Best Western the Watermill Hotel
HHW HP1 ...... 81 G1

Best Western White House Hotel *WATW* WD18 ...... 12 E5
Beta Health Clinic
HHNE HP2 ...... 4 F2
Bigham's Park Farm
HHW HP1 ...... 61 J5
Birchanger CE Primary School
BSF CM23 ...... 166 F10
Birchanger Industrial Estate
BSF CM23 ...... 166 C11
Birchley Green Shopping Centre
HERT/WAT SG14 ...... 53 H7
Birchwood Avenue Primary School
HAT AL10 ...... 67 L6
Birchwood High School
BSF CM23 ...... 44 C1
Birchwood Industrial Area
BRKMPK AL9 ...... 68 A5
Birchwood Leisure Centre
HAT AL10 ...... 67 M6
Bishops Hatfield Girls School
HAT AL10 ...... 67 L8
Bishop's Park Health Centre
BSF CM23 ...... 43 M1
Bishops Stortford Business Centre
BSF CM23 ...... 44 A3
Bishops Stortford College
BSF CM23 ...... 43 L2
Bishop's Stortford Golf Club
BSF CM23 ...... 44 D2
The Bishops Stortford High School
BSF CM23 ...... 43 M5
Bishop's Stortford RFC
BSF CM23 ...... 165 R12
Bishops Wood Hospital
NTHWD HA6 ...... 140 F1
Bishop Wood School
TRING HP23 ...... 57 L2
Blue Gold Trading Estate
ARL/CHE SG15 ...... 147 Q4
The Bobsleigh Hotel
HHS/BOV HP3 ...... 80 F8
Bondor Business Centre
BLDK SG7 ...... 17 J2
Bonny Grove SPLD Base
CHESW EN7 ...... 109 L4
Borehamwood FC
BORE WD6 ...... 120 F6
Borehamwood Industrial Park
BORE WD6 ...... 121 H6
The Borough Industrial Estate
LTNN/LIM LU3 ...... 27 L6
Bosch Broadwater Park Business Estate
DEN/HRF UB9 ...... 139 L8
Botany Bay CC
ENC/FH EN2 ...... 124 B2
Boulevard 25 Retail Park
BORE WD6 ...... 120 E7
Bournehall J & I School
BUSH WD23 ...... 132 E1
Bovingdon Primary School
HHS/BOV HP3 ...... 98 F1
Bowmans Trading Estate
STVG SG1 ...... 32 F4
Boxmoor Golf Club
HHS/BOV HP3 ...... 81 J6
Boxmoor Primary School
HHW HP1 ...... 4 A4
Bramingham Business Park
LTNN/LIM LU3 ...... 27 M1
Bramingham Park Medical Centre
LTNN/LIM LU3 ...... 27 L1
Bramingham Park Study Centre
LTNN/LIM LU3 ...... 27 M1
Bramingham Primary School
LTNN/LIM LU3 ...... 154 H12
Brandles School
BLDK SG7 ...... 17 J2
Brays Grove School
HLWS CM18 ...... 75 M7
Breachwood Green JMI School
HTCHE/RSTV SG4 ...... 30 C8
Breakspear Crematorium
RSLP HA4 ...... 141 G7
Breakspeare School
ABLGY WD5 ...... 101 J5
Brewers Hill Middle School
DUN/WHIP LU6 ...... 25 J8
Brickendon Grange Golf Club
HERT/BAY SG13 ...... 90 F1
Bricket Wood Sports Centre
LCOL/BKTW AL2 ...... 102 F5
Brickfields Industrial Estate
HHNE HP2 ...... 62 F6
Bridgefate Business Centre
WGCE AL7 ...... 50 D6
Bridgewater Monument
BERK HP4 ...... 170 E10
Bridgewater School
BERK HP4 ...... 59 L7
Brimsdown Industrial Estate
PEND EN3 ...... 126 A6
Brimsdown Infant School
PEND EN3 ...... 126 B7
Britannia Business Centre
CHES/WCR EN8 ...... 110 D8
Britannia Business Park
CHES/WCR EN8 ...... 110 D8

Broadfield Infant School
HHNE HP2 ...... 5 K2
Broadfield Junior School
HHNE HP2 ...... 5 K3
Broadfields Primary School
EDGW HA8 ...... 134 E5
HLW CM20 ...... 3 H5
Broadmead School
LTN LU1 ...... 41 J4
Brockswood Primary School
HHNE HP2 ...... 63 G4
Bromet Primary School
OXHEY WD19 ...... 132 B3
Brookfield Retail Park
CHES/WCR EN8 ...... 110 B1
Brookland J & I School
CHES/WCR EN8 ...... 110 C2
Brookmans Park Golf Club
BRKMPK AL9 ...... 88 E7
Brookmans Park Primary School
BRKMPK AL9 ...... 88 C8
Brookmead School
LBUZ LU7 ...... 169 Q4
Brookside Business Centre
BSF CM23 ...... 43 M8
Broom Barns JMI School
STVG SG1 ...... 10 F6
Broomstick Industrial Estate
DUN/WHIP LU6 ...... 37 J5
Broxbourne Business Centre
CHES/WCR EN8 ...... 92 B8
Broxbourne Primary School
BROX EN10 ...... 92 E3
Broxbourne Sailing Club
WAB EN9 ...... 93 H2
The Broxbourne School
BROX EN10 ...... 92 C4
Broxbourne Sports Club
BROX EN10 ...... 92 D3
Broxbourne Wood National Nature Reserve
BROX EN10 ...... 91 H2
Brunswick Health Centre
FBAR/BDGN N11 ...... 137 L5
Brunswick Industrial Park
FBAR/BDGN N11 ...... 137 M7
Brunswick Park JMI School
STHGT/OAK N14 ...... 137 L4
Brushwood Junior School
CSHM HP5 ...... 97 J3
Bucks Chilterns University College
CSTG HP8 ...... 128 E5
The Bull Theatre
BAR EN5 ...... 122 D8
Buncefield Oil Refinery
HHNE HP2 ...... 63 H7
Burleigh Primary School
CHES/WCR EN8 ...... 110 B4
Burntmill Industrial Estate
HLW CM20 ...... 2 C1
Burnt Mill School
HLW CM20 ...... 3 H2
Bushey & Oxhey Infant School
OXHEY WD19 ...... 13 L9
Bushey Golf & Country Club
BUSH WD23 ...... 132 E2
Bushey Grove Leisure Centre *
BUSH WD23 ...... 118 D8
Bushey Hall Golf Club
BUSH WD23 ...... 13 M5
Bushey Hall School
BUSH WD23 ...... 132 D2
Bushey Hall Swimming Pool
BUSH WD23 ...... 132 D1
Bushey Health Centre
BUSH WD23 ...... 132 D2
Bushey Heath Primary School
BUSH WD23 ...... 133 H4
Bushey Jewish Cemetery
BUSH WD23 ...... 118 F7
Bushey Manor Junior School
BUSH WD23 ...... 132 D1
Bushey Meads School
BUSH WD23 ...... 133 G1
Bushey Museum & Art Gallery
BUSH WD23 ...... 132 E2
Bush Hall Hotel
BRKMPK AL9 ...... 68 B5
Bushmead Primary School
LTNE LU2 ...... 28 C4
Business Aviation Terminal
STSD CM24 ...... 167 K11
The Business Centre
LTNE LU2 ...... 7 J2
Business & Technology Centre
STVG SG1 ...... 32 F4
Byfleet Industrial Estate
WATW WD18 ...... 131 G4
Caddington Sports Club
LTN LU1 ...... 40 D6
Calcot Medical Centre
CFSP/GDCR SL9 ...... 138 B3
Camp Primary School
STAL AL1 ...... 85 M3
Camps Hill Community Primary School
STVGE SG2 ...... 11 M2
Campus West Cinema
WGCW AL8 ...... 50 B6
Campus West Leisure Centre
WGCW AL8 ...... 50 A6
Canary Club FC
HTCH/STOT SG5 ...... 157 N5
Cannon Lane First School
PIN HA5 ...... 142 B7

Canons Brook Golf Club *HLWW/ROY* CM19 ...74 E4
Capel Manor College *EN* EN1 ...125 M1
Capital Business Centre *WATN* WD24 ...118 B2
Cardiff Road Industrial Estate *WATW* WD18 ...12 F9
Cardinal Newman Catholic Secondary School *LTNN/LIM* LU3 ...155 J12
Carpenters Park Cemetery *OXHEY* WD19 ...132 D7
Carterhatch Infant School *EN* EN1 ...125 M5
Caryl Thomas Clinic *HRW* HA1 ...143 J6
Cassiobury J & I School *WAT* WD17 ...117 J5
Castle Hall Theatre & Civic Centre *HERT/WAT* SG14 ...53 G7
Castle Montessori School *BERK* HP4 ...80 B1
Cathedral & Abbey Church of St Alban *STAL* AL1 ...8 D6
Cattle Market *TRING* HP23 ...57 M1
The Causeway Business Centre *BSF* CM23 ...43 M2
The Cavendish School *HHW* HP1 ...4 B1
Cecil Park Clinic *PIN* HA5 ...142 C6
Cedars Manor School *KTN/HRWW/WS* HA3 ...143 G3
Central Primary School *WAT* WD17 ...13 H5
Chace Community School *EN* EN1 ...125 J5
Chadwell Springs Golf Club *WARE* SG12 ...54 A5
Chalfont Leisure Centre *CFSP/GDCR* SL9 ...138 A3
Chalfont St Peter FC *CFSP/GDCR* SL9 ...138 B2
Chalfont St Peter Infant School *CFSP/GDCR* SL9 ...138 A2
Chalfont St Peter Junior School *CFSP/GDCR* SL9 ...138 B2
The Chalfonts Community College *CFSP/GDCR* SL9 ...138 A2
Chalfonts & Gerrards Cross Health Clinic *CFSP/GDCR* SL9 ...138 B3
Challney High School for Boys & Community College *LTNW/LEA* LU4 ...27 G6
Challney High School for Girls *LTNW/LEA* LU4 ...27 G7
Chambersbury JMI School *HHS/BOV* HP3 ...82 F5
Chancellors School *BRKMPK* AL9 ...88 E7
Chantry J & I School *LTNW/LEA* LU4 ...26 D5
Chartridge Combined School *CSHM* HP5 ...96 A1
Chartridge Park Golf Club *CSHM* HP5 ...96 B2
Chase Farm Hospital *ENC/FH* EN2 ...124 E4
Chase Side Primary School *ENC/FH* EN2 ...125 G6
Chater Infant School *WATW* WD18 ...12 C6
Chater Junior School *WATW* WD18 ...12 D6
Chaulden Infant School *HHW* HP1 ...81 J3
Chaulden Junior School *HHW* HP1 ...81 K3
The Chauncy School *WARE* SG12 ...53 M3
Cheddington Combined School *LBUZ* LU7 ...169 L2
Chenies CC *RKW/CH/CXG* WD3 ...115 G5
Chenies Combined School *RKW/CH/CXG* WD3 ...114 E4
Chenies Manor House *RKW/CH/CXG* WD3 ...114 F4
Cherry Tree Primary School *WATN* WD24 ...117 L2
Chesfield Downs Golf Club *HTCHE/RSTV* SG4 ...21 H2
Chesham Bois CE Combined School *AMS* HP6 ...113 J1
Chesham Cemetery *CSHM* HP5 ...96 F4
Chesham Community Hospital *CSHM* HP5 ...97 G6
Chesham Health Centre *CSHM* HP5 ...96 F6
Chesham High School *CSHM* HP5 ...97 H4
Chesham Leisure Centre *CSHM* HP5 ...97 H5
Chesham & Ley Hill Golf Club *CSHM* HP5 ...98 A5
Chesham Park Community College *CSHM* HP5 ...96 A4
Chesham Preparatory School *CSHM* HP5 ...97 L1
Chesham United FC *CSHM* HP5 ...96 F1
Cheshunt Cemetery *CHESW* EN7 ...109 L3
Cheshunt Community Hospital *CHES/WCR* EN8 ...110 C5
Cheshunt FC *CHES/WCR* EN8 ...110 A4
Cheshunt Marriott Hotel *BROX* EN10 ...92 D8
Cheshunt Park Golf Club *CHESW* EN7 ...109 M1
Cheshunt School *CHESW* EN7 ...110 A4
Chesterfield Primary School *PEND* EN3 ...126 C3
Chestnut Lane First School *AMS* HP6 ...113 J2
Cheynes Infant School *LTNN/LIM* LU3 ...27 H1

Chicken Shed Theatre *STHGT/OAK* N14 ...137 L1
Chiltern FM *DUN/WHIP* LU6 ...25 L8
Chiltern Forest Golf Club *RAYLNE/WEN* HP22 ...56 D4
Chiltern Open Air Museum *CSTG* HP8 ...128 E5
Chiltern Park Industrial Estate *DUN/HR/TOD* LU5 ...26 B7
The Chiltern Pools *AMS* HP6 ...113 H4
The Chilterns Crematorium *AMSS* HP7 ...112 D7
Chishill Windmill *ROY* SG8 ...153 L3
Chorleywood Golf Club *RKW/CH/CXG* WD3 ...115 H8
Chorleywood Health Centre *RKW/CH/CXG* WD3 ...115 G8
Chorleywood Lawn Cemetery *RKW/CH/CXG* WD3 ...115 K7
Chorleywood Primary School *RKW/CH/CXG* WD3 ...129 G2
Chorleywood Road Cemetery *RKW/CH/CXG* WD3 ...130 B3
Christ Church CE Primary School *BAR* EN5 ...122 B6
Christ Church Primary School *RKW/CH/CXG* WD3 ...115 K8
Christ Church Primary School *WARE* SG12 ...54 C4
Christopher Place Shopping Centre *STALW/RED* AL3 ...8 E5
Church Farm Swimming Pool *EBAR* EN4 ...137 K4
Churchgate CE Primary School *HLWE* CM17 ...76 C2
Churchgate Shopping Centre *HTCH/STOT* SG5 ...157 N6
Church Hill Primary School *EBAR* EN4 ...137 K3
Church Langley Primary School *HLWE* CM17 ...76 A5
Church Street Industrial Estate *WARE* SG12 ...54 B3
Cineworld *BSF* CM23 ...43 M3
  EN EN1 ...125 L8
  HLW CM20 ...75 K1
  LTN LU1 ...6 E4
  STVG SG1 ...10 B6
Circle Business Centre *DUN/HR/TOD* LU5 ...25 L6
Civic Hall Cinema *HOD* EN11 ...72 D8
Civic Medical Centre *HRW* HA1 ...143 J7
Claggy Road Industrial Estate *HTCHE/RSTV* SG4 ...175 N7
Clarklands Industrial Estate *SBW* CM21 ...183 P4
Clavering Primary School *SAFWS* CB11 ...161 Q5
Clore Shalom School *RAD* WD7 ...104 C4
Coates Way JMI School *GSTN* WD25 ...102 C7
Cockernhoe Endowed Primary School *LTNE* LU2 ...29 K5
Cockfosters Sports Ground *EBAR* EN4 ...123 K7
Codicote Primary School *HTCHE/RSTV* SG4 ...176 E8
Coleman Business Centre *HTCHE/RSTV* SG4 ...175 N7
College Lake Wildlife Centre *TRING* HP23 ...169 N8
College of Osteopathy *BORE* WD6 ...120 F7
Collenswood School *STVGE* SG2 ...34 A5
Collett Special School *HHW* HP1 ...4 D1
The Collingwood Suite Conference Centre *WCCW* AL8 ...68 A1
Colnbrook School *OXHEY* WD19 ...132 A5
Colne Bridge Retail Park *WAT* WD17 ...13 K8
Colne Valley Retail Park *WAT* WD17 ...13 K7
Colney Fields Shopping Park *LCOL/BKTW* AL2 ...104 D2
Colney Heath JMI School *STALE/WH* AL4 ...87 G4
Colonial Business Park *WATN* WD24 ...118 A5
Comfort Hotel *ENC/FH* EN2 ...124 F6
Commonside School *HLWS* CM18 ...95 K1
Commonswood JMI School *WCCE* AL7 ...68 F2
Commonwealth College *LTN* LU1 ...6 E6
Community Care Centre *ENC/FH* EN2 ...125 H5
Community Leisure Centre *HLW* CM20 ...2 F6
Community Mental Health Centre *GSTN* WD25 ...102 A8
Corinium Industrial Estate *AMS* HP6 ...113 K4
Corn Exchange *HERT/WAT* SG14 ...53 H7
Corus Hotel *BORE* WD6 ...134 C3
Coteford Infant School *PIN* HA5 ...141 N7
Cotswold Business Park *LTN* LU1 ...40 B7
Cotton Brown Park *LWTH* SG6 ...17 H2
Countess Anne Primary School *HAT* AL10 ...67 M7
Courtland JMI School *MLHL* NW7 ...135 L3
Covered Market *STVG* SG1 ...10 D5
Cowley Hill Primary School *BORE* WD6 ...120 F5
CP House Business Centre *BUSH* WD23 ...118 D5
Crabtree Junior School *HARP* AL5 ...47 G4
Cranborne Industrial Estate *POTB/CUF* EN6 ...106 C4

Cranborne Primary School *POTB/CUF* EN6 ...106 C5
Cranbourne JMI School *HOD* EN11 ...72 F4
Crawley Green Infant School *LTNE* LU2 ...7 M4
Creswick Primary School *WCCE* AL7 ...68 B3
Crews Hill Golf Club *ENC/FH* EN2 ...108 D8
Cromer Road Primary School *BAR* EN5 ...122 F7
Cromwell Hotel *STVG* SG1 ...33 G1
Cromwell Medical Centre *CHESW* EN7 ...109 M4
Crown Business Estate *CSHM* HP5 ...97 G4
The Crown Hotel *AMSS* HP7 ...112 F6
Crown Prosecution Service *STAL* AL1 ...8 F1
Cuffley School *POTB/CUF* EN6 ...108 A7
Cunningham Hill J & I School *STAL* AL1 ...9 M9
Dacorum Athletics Track *HHNE* HP2 ...5 K6
Dacorum Education Support Centre *HHNE* HP2 ...82 E2
Dacre Education Support Centre *HHNE* HP2 ...82 E2
Dagnall County First School *BERK* HP4 ...171 J4
Dallow Junior School *LTN* LU1 ...6 C4
Dallow Primary School *LTN* LU1 ...6 C4
Dalroad Industrial Estate *LTN* LU1 ...6 A4
Dame Alice Owens School *POTB/CUF* EN6 ...106 C7
Danegrove Primary School *EBAR* EN4 ...137 J2
David Lloyd Sports Centre *EN* EN1 ...125 L6
Days Hotel *LTN* LU1 ...6 E6
  MLHL NW7 ...135 G5
Days Inn *BSF* CM23 ...44 E1
  POTB/CUF EN6 ...106 A8
De Bohun Primary School *STHGT/OAK* N14 ...137 M1
De Havilland Aircraft Heritage Centre & Mosquito Aircraft Museum *LCOL/BKTW* AL2 ...104 F3
De Havilland Primary School *HAT* AL10 ...87 L2
Delrow School *GSTN* WD25 ...119 G5
Denbigh High School *LTNN/LIM* LU3 ...28 A7
Denbigh Junior School *LTNN/LIM* LU3 ...27 M7
Denham Aerodrome *DEN/HRF* UB9 ...139 J7
Denham Golf Club *DEN/HRF* UB9 ...139 H8
Derwent Lower School *HNLW* SG16 ...147 K4
De Vere Theobalds Park Hotel *CHESW* EN7 ...109 L7
Dewhurst St Mary JMI School *CHES/WCR* EN8 ...109 M3
Diamond Industrial Centre *LWTH* SG6 ...17 G2
Divine Saviour RC Primary School *ABLGY* WD5 ...101 H6
Downfield Primary School *CHES/WCR* EN8 ...110 C5
Down Hall Country House Hotel *RBSF* CM22 ...184 G10
Downside Junior School *LTNW/LEA* LU4 ...27 J8
Downside Lower School *DUN/HR/TOD* LU5 ...39 J2
The Downs Primary School *HLW* CM20 ...2 F6
Dr Challoners Grammar School *AMS* HP6 ...113 G4
Dr Challoners High School *AMSS* HP7 ...113 M6
Driving School & Road Safety Centre *KTN/HRWW/WS* HA3 ...143 L5
Dukeminster Trading Estate *DUN/HR/TOD* LU5 ...26 A8
Duncombe School *HERT/WAT* SG14 ...53 G6
Dundale JM School *TRING* HP23 ...169 L12
Dundale Primary School *TRING* HP23 ...169 L12
Dunstable Cemetery *DUN/WHIP* LU6 ...38 E2
Dunstable College *DUN/HR/TOD* LU5 ...26 A8
Dunstable Downs Country Park *DUN/WHIP* LU6 ...38 D5
Dunstable Downs Golf Club *DUN/WHIP* LU6 ...38 D4
Dunstable FC *DUN/WHIP* LU6 ...25 K7
Dunstable Health Centre *DUN/WHIP* LU6 ...38 F1
Dunstable Icknield Lower School *DUN/WHIP* LU6 ...38 E1
Dunstable Leisure Centre *DUN/WHIP* LU6 ...25 M8
Dunstable Road Infant School *LTN* LU1 ...6 C4
Dunstable Town Bowls Club *DUN/WHIP* LU6 ...39 G2
Dunstable Town CC *DUN/WHIP* LU6 ...38 A2
Dunstablians RUFC *DUN/WHIP* LU6 ...25 J8
Dunton VC Lower School *BGSW* SG18 ...144 C4
Durants School *PEND* EN3 ...126 A5
East Barnet Health Centre *EBAR* EN4 ...137 H1

East Barnet School *EBAR* EN4 ...137 K2
Eastbrook Primary School *HHNE* HP2 ...62 D5
Eastbury Farm JMI School *NTHWD* HA6 ...131 K7
Eastcote CC *PIN* HA5 ...141 M7
Eastern Avenue Industrial Estate *DUN/HR/TOD* LU5 ...39 H1
Eastfield Primary School *PEND* EN3 ...126 B4
East Herts Golf Club *BUNT* SG9 ...163 M8
Eaton Bray Lower School *GSTN* WD25 ...37 J3
Edge Grove *GSTN* WD25 ...119 G3
Edgwarebury Cemetery *EDGW* HA8 ...134 E5
Edlesborough School *DUN/WHIP* LU6 ...37 J6
Edwinstree School *BUNT* SG9 ...158 H9
Egerton Rothesay Preparatory School *BERK* HP4 ...79 M1
Egerton Rothesay School *BERK* HP4 ...79 K1
Elangeni Junior School *AMS* HP6 ...113 J2
Eleanor Estate *CHES/WCR* EN8 ...110 D8
Ellern Mede School *TRDG/WHET* N20 ...136 B4
Elliswick Lawn Tennis Club *HARP* AL5 ...46 F3
Elmgrove Middle School *KTN/HRWW/WS* HA3 ...143 L6
The Elms Health Centre *POTB/CUF* EN6 ...107 G5
Elmtree Infant School *CSHM* HP5 ...96 F4
Elsenham Primary School *RBSF* CM22 ...167 M4
Elstree Aerodrome *BORE* WD6 ...119 K7
Elstree Golf & Country Club *BORE* WD6 ...120 B7
Elstree Studios *BORE* WD6 ...120 E7
Elstree Way Clinic *BORE* WD6 ...120 F6
Enfield Business Centre *PEND* EN3 ...126 A6
Enfield Chace Lower School *ENC/FH* EN2 ...125 J4
Enfield College *PEND* EN3 ...126 A7
Enfield County School *EN* EN1 ...125 H7
Enfield Crematorium *EN* EN1 ...125 M3
Enfield CC *EN* EN1 ...125 J8
Enfield Golf Club *ENC/FH* EN2 ...124 F8
Enfield Grammar School (Upper) *ENC/FH* EN2 ...125 H7
Epping Forest District Museum *WAB* EN9 ...111 G7
Epping House School *HERT/BAY* SG13 ...90 A3
Epping Upland CE Primary School *EPP* CM16 ...94 D7
Ermine Point Business Park *WARE* SG12 ...53 M1
Essendon Primary School *BRKMPK* AL9 ...69 K7
Everest Sports Club *CHES/WCR* EN8 ...109 M3
Eversley College *SBW* CM21 ...183 P7
Executive Park Industrial Estate *STAL* AL1 ...85 M2
Express by Holiday Inn *HHS/BOV* HP3 ...82 C7
  STALW/RED AL3 ...173 M7
  STSD CM24 ...167 R9
Fairbrook Medical Centre *BORE* WD6 ...120 F6
Fairfield Hospital *HTCH/STOT* SG5 ...148 A11
Fair Field Junior School *RAD* WD7 ...119 J2
Fairfields Primary School *CHESW* EN7 ...109 L1
Fairlands Primary School *STVG* SG1 ...10 D1
Fairview Industrial Estate *AMS* HP6 ...113 K4
Fairway Primary School *MLHL* NW7 ...135 H5
Falconer Special School *BUSH* WD23 ...132 D1
Family Leisure Centre *STVG* SG1 ...10 C5
Farley Junior School *LTN* LU1 ...6 D9
Farnham CE Primary School *BSF* CM23 ...165 R7
Fawbert & Barnard Infant School *SBW* CM21 ...183 Q7
Fawbert & Barnards (UNDL) Primary School *HLWE* CM17 ...76 A2
Fearnhill School *LWTH* SG6 ...16 A4
Fearnhill Sports Centre *LWTH* SG6 ...16 A4
Featherstone Wood Primary School *STVGE* SG2 ...34 A6
Ferrars J & I School *LTNW/LEA* LU4 ...26 F6
Fiddlebridge Industrial Centre *HAT* AL10 ...67 L7
Field Infant School *WATW* WD18 ...13 H7
Field Junior School *WATW* WD18 ...13 H7
Finchley Catholic High School *NFNCH/WDSPK* N12 ...137 G6
Finchley Industrial Centre *NFNCH/WDSPK* N12 ...137 G7
Firbank Industrial Estate *LTN* LU1 ...40 E1

Firs Hotel *HTCH/STOT* SG5 ...157 M5
First Garden City Heritage Museum *LWTH* SG6 ...16 E4
Fisher Industrial Estate *WATW* WD18 ...13 G8
Five Oaks Middle School *LTN* LU1 ...40 D1
Flamstead End Primary School *CHESW* EN7 ...109 L1
Flamstead JMI School *STALW/RED* AL3 ...173 K8
Fleetville Infant School *STAL* AL1 ...85 M2
Fleetville Junior School *STAL* AL1 ...9 M6
Florence Nightingale Health Centre *HLWE* CM17 ...76 A5
Flowers Industrial Estate *LTN* LU1 ...7 G5
Forres CP School *HOD* EN11 ...72 F4
Forty Hall *ENC/FH* EN2 ...125 K3
Forty Hill CE Primary School *ENC/FH* EN2 ...125 L4
The Forum Retail Park *STVG* SG1 ...10 C4
Forum Theatre *HAT* AL10 ...67 K3
Foulds School *BAR* EN5 ...122 B6
Four Swannes Primary School *CHES/WCR* EN8 ...110 C7
Foxdell Infant School *LTN* LU1 ...40 E1
Foxdell Junior School *LTN* LU1 ...40 C1
Francis Bacon School *STAL* AL1 ...85 M5
Francis Combe School *GSTN* WD25 ...102 A6
Freezywater St Georges CE Primary School *PEND* EN3 ...126 B2
Freman College *BUNT* SG9 ...158 H9
Friern Barnet School *FBAR/BDGN* N11 ...137 K8
Frithsden Vineyard *HHW* HP1 ...60 F5
Frithwood Primary School *NTHWD* HA6 ...141 K1
Frogmore Road Industrial Estate *HHS/BOV* HP3 ...5 G9
Furneux Pelham CE JMI School *BUNT* SG9 ...164 G1
Furze Field Leisure Centre *POTB/CUF* EN6 ...106 C5
Furzehill School *BORE* WD6 ...120 D7
Gaddesden Row CP School *HHNE* HP2 ...172 E10
Gade Valley JMI School *HHW* HP1 ...81 M1
Galaxy Leisure Centre *LTN* LU1 ...6 E4
Galleria Shopping Centre *HAT* AL10 ...67 K8
Garden Court Business Centre *WCCE* AL7 ...50 D7
Garden Fields JMI School *STALW/RED* AL3 ...65 H7
Garden of Rest Cemetery *CFSP/GDCR* SL9 ...138 D2
Gardens of the Rose (Royal National Rose) *LCOL/BKTW* AL2 ...84 D8
Garfield Primary School *FBAR/BDGN* N11 ...137 M8
Garston Clinic *WATN* WD24 ...117 M2
Garston JMI School *GSTN* WD25 ...118 B1
Garston Manor Special School *GSTN* WD25 ...102 A6
Garston Medical Centre *GSTN* WD25 ...118 A2
Gayhurst School *CFSP/GDCR* SL9 ...138 A6
Gazelda Industrial Estate *WAT* WD17 ...13 J7
George Spicer Primary School *EN* EN1 ...125 K7
George Street Primary School *HHNE* HP2 ...82 B1
Gerrards Cross Golf Club *CFSP/GDCR* SL9 ...138 D5
The Giles Infant School *STVG* SG1 ...21 K8
Glenwood School *DUN/WHIP* LU6 ...39 J4
Go Bowling *DUN/HR/TOD* LU5 ...25 M8
Goffs Oak JMI School *CHESW* EN7 ...108 F2
Goffs School *CHESW* EN7 ...109 L3
Goldfield Infant School *TRING* HP23 ...57 K2
Golds Nurseries Business Park *RBSF* CM22 ...167 L2
Goodwyn School *MLHL* NW7 ...135 G2
Gooseberry Hill Health Centre *LTNN/LIM* LU3 ...27 M2
Gordon Craig Theatre *STVG* SG1 ...10 B5
Gorhambury (Remains) *STALW/RED* AL3 ...83 M1
Gosling Ski & Board Centre *WGCW* AL8 ...68 A2
Gosling Sports Park *WGCW* AL8 ...68 A1
Gothic Mede Lower School *ARL/CHE* SG15 ...147 Q4
Grange Junior School *LWTH* SG6 ...148 D11
Grange Paddocks Pool & Gym *BSF* CM23 ...166 B12
Grange Park Primary School *WCHMH* N21 ...124 E8
Grangewood School *PIN* HA5 ...141 L7
Grasvenor Avenue Infant School *BAR* EN5 ...136 E2
Graveley Primary School *HTCHE/RSTV* SG4 ...20 F5
Great Gaddesden JMI School *HHW* HP1 ...61 M10

Great Hadham Golf & Country
Club
MHAD SG10 .... 42 D5
Greatham Road Industrial
Estate *BUSH* WD23 .... 13 L5
Great Wood Country Park
POTB/CUF EN6 .... 89 L8
Grebe House Wildlife Centre &
Gardens
STALW/RED AL3 .... 8 A6
Green End Business Centre
RKW/CH/CXG WD3 ..... 115 L3
Greenfield Primary School
OXHEY WD19 .... 132 A8
Greenhill College
HRW HA1 .... 143 K7
The Greenhouse Health Centre
LTN LU1 .... 6 D4
Green Lane Industrial Estate
LWTH SG6 .... 16 F2
Green Lanes Primary School
HAT AL10 .... 67 K4
The Green Man Hotel
HLWE CM17 .... 76 B1
Greenside Special School
STVGE SG2 .... 33 L7
Greenway First School
BERK HP4 .... 79 K1
Greenwood Park Leisure Centre
LCOL/BKTW AL2 .... 84 F7
Greneway Middle School
ROY SG8 .... 14 F6
Griffin Golf Club
LTN LU1 .... 40 B3
Grimsdyke First & Middle
School
PIN HA5 .... 142 D1
Grims Dyke Golf Club
PIN HA5 .... 132 E8
Grim's Dyke Hotel
KTN/HRWW/WS HA3 .... 133 G7
Grovehill Medical Centre
HHNE HP2 .... 62 D6
The Grove Hotel
RKW/CH/CXG WD3 ..... 117 G3
The Grove Infant School
HARP AL5 .... 47 H5
The Grove Junior School
HARP AL5 .... 47 H5
Grovelands Business Centre
HHNE HP2 .... 63 G8
Grove Road Primary School
TRING HP23 .... 169 M12
Grove Theatre
DUN/WHIP LU6 .... 25 M8
Grundy Park Leisure Centre
CHES/WCR EN8 .... 110 C4
The Gryphon Industrial Park
STALW/RED AL3 .... 65 K6
Guardian Industrial Estate
LTN LU1 .... 6 B4
Guilden Morden Cemetery
ROY SG8 .... 145 N4
Guilden Morden CE Primary
School
ROY SG8 .... 145 M4
Gunnels Wood Industrial
Estate
STVG SG1 .... 10 C9
Gunpowder Park
WAB EN9 .... 127 G2
Haberdasher Askes Pre
Preparatory School
LCOL/BKTW AL2 .... 102 F2
The Haberdashers Askes
School
BORE WD6 .... 119 M7
Haberdashers RUFC
BORE WD6 .... 120 D6
Hadley Wood Golf Club
EBAR EN4 .... 123 J5
Hadley Wood Primary School
EBAR EN4 .... 123 G4
Hadrian Lower School
DUN/HR/TOD LU5 .... 26 C7
Haileybury College
HERT/BAY SG13 .... 72 B3
Haileybury College Track
HERT/BAY SG13 .... 72 B3
Hailey Hall Special School
HERT/BAY SG13 .... 72 D3
The Hall Pre Preparatory
School
NTHWD HA6 .... 141 H1
Halton Camp
RAYLNE/WEN HP22 .... 56 C6
Halton Combined School
RAYLNE/WEN HP22 .... 56 B6
Halyard High School
LTNW/LEA LU4 .... 26 D6
The Hammond JMI School
HHNE HP2 .... 62 D6
Haperbury Hospital
RAD WD7 .... 104 A5
Happy Valley Industrial
Estate
KGLCY WD4 .... 100 F2
The Harefield Academy
DEN/HRF UB9 .... 140 B3
Harefield CC
DEN/HRF UB9 .... 140 A4
Harefield Health Centre
DEN/HRF UB9 .... 140 A3
Harefield Hospital
DEN/HRF UB9 .... 140 A3
Harefield Infant School
DEN/HRF UB9 .... 139 M4
Harefield Junior School
DEN/HRF UB9 .... 140 A3
Harefield Road Industrial
Estate
RKW/CH/CXG WD3 ..... 130 C7
Haresfoot School
BERK HP4 .... 79 M4
Haresfoot Senior School
BERK HP4 .... 60 E7
Hare Street Primary School
HLWW/ROY CM19 .... 2 C7
Harewood Down Golf Club
CSTG HP8 .... 113 M8
Harkness Industrial Estate
BORE WD6 .... 120 E8
The Harlequin Shopping
Centre
WAT WD17 .... 13 G3
Harlington Upper School
DUN/HR/TOD LU5 .... 154 A2
Harlowbury Primary School
HLWE CM17 .... 76 B1
Harlow Business Park
HLWW/ROY CM19 .... 74 C5
Harlow College
HLW CM20 .... 2 E7

Harlow College Recreation
Centre *HLW* CM20 .... 3 G5
Harlow Museum
(Passmores House)
HLWS CM18 .... 2 D9
Harlow RFC
HLW CM20 .... 2 B2
Harlow Town FC
HLWW/ROY CM19 .... 74 C4
Harlyn Primary School
PIN HA5 .... 141 M5
Harpenden Common Golf Club
HARP AL5 .... 46 F7
Harpenden Golf Club
HARP AL5 .... 46 D8
Harpenden Health Centre
HARP AL5 .... 46 E3
Harpenden Hospital
HARP AL5 .... 46 E1
Harpenden House Hotel
HARP AL5 .... 46 F5
Harpenden Memorial Hospital
HARP AL5 .... 46 F3
Harpenden RUFC
HARP AL5 .... 46 C7
Harpenden Sports Centre
HARP AL5 .... 46 E5
Harpenden Swimming Pool
HARP AL5 .... 46 E4
Harrow Arts Centre
PIN HA5 .... 142 E2
Harrow Cemetery
HRW HA1 .... 143 H8
Harrow College
KTN/HRWW/WS HA3 .... 143 J1
Harrow Crown Courts
HRW HA1 .... 143 H5
Harrow Heritage Museum
RYLN/HDSTN HA2 .... 143 G5
Harrow High School
HRW HA1 .... 143 L8
Harrow Leisure Centre
KTN/HRWW/WS HA3 .... 143 K5
Harrow RFC
STAN HA7 .... 133 M6
Harrow Weald Cemetery
KTN/HRWW/WS HA3 .... 143 J1
Hartham Pool
HERT/WAT SG14 .... 53 H6
Hart Hill Primary School
LTNE LU2 .... 7 J3
Hartsbourne Primary School
BUSH WD23 .... 133 H5
Hartsfield Primary School
BLDK SG7 .... 17 K1
Hartspring Industrial Park
BUSH WD23 .... 118 E6
Hartspring Sports Centre
BUSH WD23 .... 118 E6
Harvey Centre
HLW CM20 .... 2 E6
Harvey Road Primary School
RKW/CH/CXG WD3 ..... 130 E2
Harwood Hill JMI School
WGCW AL8 .... 50 C3
Harwood Park Crematorium
STVGE SG2 .... 177 Q3
Haslemere Business Centre
EN EN1 .... 125 M8
Haslemere Industrial Estate
BSF CM23 .... 44 A5
HLWW/ROY CM19 .... 74 E6
WGCE AL7 .... 50 C8
Haste Hill Golf Club
NTHWD HA6 .... 141 J4
Hastingswood Business Centre
HLWE CM17 .... 76 A7
Hatch End High School
KTN/HRWW/WS HA3 .... 142 F2
Hatch End Swimming Pool
PIN HA5 .... 142 E2
Hatfield Business Park
HAT AL10 .... 67 J8
Hatfield Forest National
Nature Reserve
RBSF CM22 .... 45 K4
Hatfield Forest (NT)
RBSF CM22 .... 45 L4
Hatfield Heath Primary School
RBSF CM22 .... 184 G6
Hatfield House, Park & Gardens
BRKMPK AL9 .... 68 B8
Hatfield House Tennis Club
BRKMPK AL9 .... 68 B8
Hatfield Leisure Centre
HAT AL10 .... 87 M2
Hatfield London Country Club
BRKMPK AL9 .... 89 K1
Hatfield Road Cemetery
STAL AL1 .... 9 L6
Hatfield Swim Centre
HAT AL10 .... 67 L7
Hawridge & Cholesbury CE
Comb School
CSHM HP5 .... 78 C3
Hawthorn Park Lower
School
DUN/HR/TOD LU5 .... 26 B3
Haydon School
PIN HA5 .... 141 K5
Haywood Grove School
HHNE HP2 .... 62 E6
Heathcote School
STVGE SG2 .... 33 L7
Heatherton House School
AMS HP6 .... 113 G2
Heathfield Lower School
LTN LU1 .... 40 C5
Heathlands Special School
STALW/RED AL3 .... 65 J7
Heath Lane Cemetery
HHW HP1 .... 4 D4
Heath Mount Pre Preparatory
School
HERT/WAT SG14 .... 179 K7
Hemel Hempstead (Camelot)
RFC HHW HP1 .... 81 K4
Hemel Hempstead General
Hospital
HHNE HP2 .... 5 G4
Hemel Hempstead RLFC
HHNE HP2 .... 62 D7
Hemel Hempstead School
HHW HP1 .... 4 D5
Hemel Hempstead Silver Blades
Ice Rink
HHNE HP2 .... 5 L5
Hemel Hempstead Sports Centre
HHW HP1 .... 4 D6
Hemel Hempstead Town CC
HHW HP1 .... 4 E7
Hemel Hempstead United FC
HHNE HP2 .... 82 F2

Hemel Ski Centre
HHNE HP2 .... 5 K6
Henlow Airfield
SHFD SG17 .... 147 J3
Henlow Industrial Estate
HNLW SG16 .... 147 K6
Heritage Close Shopping Centre
STALW/RED AL3 .... 8 D6
Heritage House Special School
CSHM HP5 .... 97 H4
Heron Trading Estate
LTNN/LIM LU3 .... 27 G2
Hertford C&CC Site
HERT/BAY SG13 .... 71 K1
Hertford Cemetery
HERT/WAT SG14 .... 52 F6
Hertford County Hospital
HERT/WAT SG14 .... 52 F7
Hertford Heath Primary School
HERT/BAY SG13 .... 71 M7
Hertford Museum
HERT/WAT SG14 .... 53 H7
Hertford Regional College
BROX EN10 .... 92 D7
WARE SG12 .... 54 B5
Hertford Regional College
(Northgate Centre)
BSF CM23 .... 43 M1
Hertford St Andrew Primary
School
HERT/WAT SG14 .... 52 D6
Hertfordshire Business Centre
LCOL/BKTW AL2 .... 86 B8
Hertfordshire Country Club
WGCE AL7 .... 68 A2
Hertfordshire & Essex
Community Hospital
BSF CM23 .... 44 C3
Hertfordshire & Essex High School
BSF CM23 .... 44 B2
Herts County Agricultural
Showground
STALW/RED AL3 .... 173 N8
Hertsmere Jewish Primary
School
RAD WD7 .... 120 A4
Hertswood School & Sports
Centre
BORE WD6 .... 121 G5
Hester House
HLW CM20 .... 2 C3
Hexton Primary School
HTCH/STOT SG5 .... 155 N4
High Beech CE Primary School
LOU IG10 .... 127 L4
High Beeches Primary School
HARP AL5 .... 47 H5
High Beech Golf Club
LOU IG10 .... 127 M3
Highbridge Retail Park
WAB EN9 .... 110 F8
Highbury Infant School
HTCHE/RSTV SG4 .... 157 P7
Highfield School
LWTH SG6 .... 16 B6
Highgate Montessori School
BAR EN5 .... 122 C7
Highover JMI School
HTCHE/RSTV SG4 .... 16 A4
High Street Business Park
CHES/WCR EN8 .... 110 C6
Hightown Recreation Centre
LTNE LU2 .... 6 F3
Highwayman Hotel
DUN/WHIP LU6 .... 39 H3
Highwood Primary School
BUSH WD23 .... 118 C5
High Wych Primary School
SBW CM21 .... 183 M4
Hillborough Infant School
LTN LU1 .... 6 A6
Hillcrest Special School
DUN/HR/TOD LU5 .... 26 C8
Hille Business Centre
WATN WD24 .... 117 M5
Hill Farm Industrial Estate
GSTN WD25 .... 101 K7
Hill Fort
LBUZ LU7 .... 170 C3
STALE/WH AL4 .... 48 D6
Hillgrove Business Park
WAB EN9 .... 93 G4
Hillhouse CE VC Primary
School
WAB EN9 .... 111 K7
Hillingdon Borough FC
RSLP HA4 .... 140 F7
Hillmead JMI School
BSF CM23 .... 166 E12
Hillmead Primary School
BSF CM23 .... 43 J2
Hill Shott Infant School
LWTH SG6 .... 16 E3
Hillside Infant School
NTHWD HA6 .... 141 L2
Hitchin Boys School
HTCH/STOT SG5 .... 157 N5
The Hitchin Business Centre
HTCHE/RSTV SG4 .... 157 Q1
Hitchin Cemetery
HTCHE/RSTV SG4 .... 157 P7
Hitchin CC
HTCH/STOT SG5 .... 157 L6
Hitchin Girls School
HTCHE/RSTV SG4 .... 157 P6
Hitchin Road Industrial &
Business Centre
ARL/CHE SG15 .... 147 P6
Hitchin Swimming Pool
HTCH/STOT SG5 .... 157 N5
HM Prison
HHS/BOV HP3 .... 80 D8
Hobbs Hill Wood Primary
School
HHS/BOV HP3 .... 82 H4
Hobletts Manor Junior School
HHNE HP2 .... 82 K1
Hockerill Anglo European
College
BSF CM23 .... 44 A2
Hockerill Sports Club
BSF CM23 .... 44 B4
Hoddesdon Health Centre
HOD EN11 .... 72 E6
Hoddesdon Industrial Estate
HOD EN11 .... 73 G6
Hoddesdon Lawn Tennis Club
HOD EN11 .... 72 D7

Holdbrook Primary School
CHES/WCR EN8 .... 110 D8
Holiday Inn
BORE WD6 .... 121 J7
STALW/RED AL3 .... 173 J5
Holland House School
EDGW HA8 .... 134 E7
Hollies Way Industrial Estate
POTB/CUF EN6 .... 106 F3
Hollybush Primary School
HERT/WAT SG14 .... 52 E7
Holly Industrial Park
WATN WD24 .... 118 A5
Holly Park JMI School
FBAR/BDGN N11 .... 137 L8
Holly Street Trading Estate
LTN LU1 .... 6 F7
Hollywood Bowl
STVG SG1 .... 10 A6
Holmshill School
BORE WD6 .... 121 G6
Holtsmere End Junior School
HHNE HP2 .... 62 F5
Holwell J & I School
WGCE AL7 .... 50 C8
Holy Cross Catholic Primary
School
HLWS CM18 .... 75 L7
Holy Rood Catholic Primary
School
WAT WD17 .... 117 H2
Holy Trinity CE Primary School
NTHWD HA6 .... 141 G1
Holy Trinity Primary School
CHES/WCR EN8 .... 110 B6
Holywell School
WATW WD18 .... 131 K2
Home Farm Industrial Estate
WARE SG12 .... 55 K8
Home Park Industrial Estate
KGLCY WD4 .... 100 F5
Homerswood J & I School
WGCW AL8 .... 50 B3
The Homeopathic Health
Centre
MLHL NW7 .... 135 M2
Honilands Primary School
EN EN1 .... 125 M2
Hormead Primary School
BUNT SG9 .... 159 R9
Horseshoe Business Park
LCOL/BKTW AL2 .... 102 F4
Hotel Ibis
LTNE LU2 .... 174 A2
STVG SG1 .... 10 C4
Hotel St Lawrence
LTN LU1 .... 6 F5
Hot Shots Ten Pin Bowling
HHNE HP2 .... 5 L5
Houghton Regis Health Centre
DUN/HR/TOD LU5 .... 25 M4
Houghton Regis Lower School
DUN/HR/TOD LU5 .... 25 L5
Houghton Regis Medical Centre
DUN/HR/TOD LU5 .... 26 A4
Houghton Regis Trading Centre
DUN/HR/TOD LU5 .... 25 M5
House on the Hill Museum
Adventure
STSD CM24 .... 166 H6
Howard Business Park
WAB EN9 .... 111 H8
The Howard Centre
WGCW AL8 .... 50 B7
Howard Industrial Estate
CSHM HP5 .... 97 G3
Howe Dell Primary School
HAT AL10 .... 67 M8
Howe Green House School
RBSF CM22 .... 44 D7
How Wood Primary School
LCOL/BKTW AL2 .... 103 G1
HSBC Group Management
Training College
LCOL/BKTW AL2 .... 103 G5
Hunsdon Primary School
WARE SG12 .... 182 B8
Hurst Drive Primary School
CHES/WCR EN8 .... 110 A8
Hyatt Trading Estate
STVG SG1 .... 32 E4
Hyde Heath Infant School
AMS HP6 .... 96 A8
Ickleford Primary School
HTCH/STOT SG5 .... 157 N1
Icknield First School
ROY SG8 .... 14 F6
Icknield High School
LTNN/LIM LU3 .... 28 A4
Icknield Infant School
LWTH SG6 .... 16 B3
Icknield Primary School
LTNN/LIM LU3 .... 27 M4
Icknield Way Industrial
Estate
TR!NG HP23 .... 57 J1
Immanuel College
BUSH WD23 .... 133 J3
Innellan House School
PIN HA5 .... 142 C5
Innkeeper's Lodge
BORE WD6 .... 121 G6
LCOL/BKTW AL2 .... 104 C1
Innova Business Park
PEND EN3 .... 126 D2
International University
BUSH WD23 .... 118 D8
Ivinghoe Business Centre
DUN/HR/TOD LU5 .... 25 M6
Jerounds Junior School
HLWW/ROY CM19 .... 74 F8
John Colet School
RAYLNE/WEN HP22 .... 56 A8
John Dony Field Centre
LTNE LU2 .... 28 C3
John F Kennedy RC School
HHW HP1 .... 81 K1
John Henry Newman RC School
STVG SG1 .... 20 F8
John Penrose School
DEN/HRF UB9 .... 140 A4
John Penrose Sports Centre
DEN/HRF UB9 .... 140 A4
The John Warner School
HOD EN11 .... 72 F4
Jubilee Centre
STALW/RED AL3 .... 8 F4
Jubilee Trading Estate
LWTH SG6 .... 17 G2
The Junior School
BSF CM23 .... 43 K2
Jupiter Drive JMI School
HHNE HP2 .... 62 D8

Katherines Primary School
HLWW/ROY CM19 .... 74 D7
Keats House Health Centre
HLWS CM18 .... 75 K8
Kenilworth Primary School
BORE WD6 .... 121 H7
Kensworth Lower School
DUN/WHIP LU6 .... 172 B1
Keys Meadow Primary School
PEND EN3 .... 126 D2
Khalsa College London
HRW HA1 .... 143 K8
Killigrew Infant School
LCOL/BKTW AL2 .... 84 F7
Kimpton JMI School
HTCHE/RSTV SG4 .... 175 N8
Kinetic Business Centre
BORE WD6 .... 120 D7
King Harold School
WAB EN9 .... 111 J7
Kingsbury Watermill Museum
& Waffle House
STALW/RED AL3 .... 8 A4
Kings College Sports Ground
RSLP HA4 .... 141 J8
Kingscote Pre Preparatory
School
CFSP/GDCR SL9 .... 138 C5
Kingshill Primary School
WARE SG12 .... 54 B2
Kingshott School
HTCHE/RSTV SG4 .... 157 R8
Kings Houghton Middle School
DUN/HR/TOD LU5 .... 26 B2
Kings Langley Primary School
KGLGY WD4 .... 100 D2
Kings Langley School
KGLGY WD4 .... 100 C3
Kingsmead School
EN EN1 .... 125 L7
Kingsmoor Primary School
HLWW/ROY CM19 .... 95 G1
Kingsmoor Recreation Centre
HLWW/ROY CM19 .... 94 F1
The Kings Oak Private
Hospital
ENC/FH EN2 .... 124 E4
Kings Park Industrial Estate
KGLGY WD4 .... 100 F3
The Kings School
HARP AL5 .... 46 D1
Kingsway Industrial Estate
LTN LU1 .... 40 E1
Kingsway Infant School
GSTN WD25 .... 101 L8
Kingsway Junior School
GSTN WD25 .... 101 L8
Knebworth Golf Club
KNEB SG3 .... 177 M3
Knebworth House, Gardens &
Country Park
KNEB SG3 .... 176 H3
Knebworth Physiotherapy
Clinic
STVGE SG2 .... 177 Q2
Knightsfield School
WCCW AL8 .... 50 A2
Knights Templar School
BLDK SG7 .... 17 J1
Knutsford School
WATN WD24 .... 118 B4
Ladbrooke Primary School
POTB/CUF EN6 .... 106 F6
Lady Zia Werner School
LTNE LU2 .... 28 F6
Laharna Trading Estate
WATN WD24 .... 118 A4
Laings Sports Ground
BAR EN5 .... 121 J8
Lakeside Special School
WGCW AL8 .... 67 M1
Lancaster Road Industrial
Estate
EBAR EN4 .... 137 H1
Lancot Lower School
DUN/WHIP LU6 .... 38 C1
Langley Terrace Industrial
Park
LTN LU1 .... 7 G8
Lannock Primary School
LWTH SG6 .... 17 G5
Lark Rise Lower School
DUN/WHIP LU6 .... 38 F3
Larwood School
STVG SG1 .... 11 G1
Latton Bush Business Centre
HLWS CM18 .... 75 K8
Laurence Haines School
WATW WD18 .... 12 D9
Lavender Primary School
ENC/FH EN2 .... 125 H4
Lawrence Industrial Estate
DUN/WHIP LU6 .... 25 K7
Layston First School
BUNT SG9 .... 159 K9
Leagrave Health Centre
LTNW/LEA LU4 .... 27 G5
Leagrave J & I School
LTNW/LEA LU4 .... 27 G5
Leah Manning Centre
HLW CM20 .... 2 F3
Lea Industrial Estate
HARP AL5 .... 47 G1
Lealands High School
LTNN/LIM LU3 .... 27 G1
Lea Manor High School
LTNN/LIM LU3 .... 27 K1
Lea Manor Recreation Centre
LTNN/LIM LU3 .... 27 J1
The Lea Primary School
HARP AL5 .... 46 E1
Lea Road Industrial Park
CHES/WCR EN8 .... 110 E8
Leaside Business Centre
PEND EN3 .... 126 D6
Lea Valley High School
EN EN1 .... 126 A1
Leavesden Green JMI School
GSTN WD25 .... 101 L8
Leavesden Hospital
ABLGY WD5 .... 101 L5
Lee Valley Campsite
CHE E4 .... 126 F6
Lee Valley Caravan Park
HOD EN11 .... 93 G1
Lee Valley Park
WAB EN9 .... 110 F2
Lee Valley Park Farms
WAB EN9 .... 111 G2
Letchmore Infant School
STVG SG1 .... 33 H2
Letchworth Business Centre
LWTH SG6 .... 17 G3

Letchworth Garden City FC
LWTH SG6 .... 17 G4
Letchworth Golf Club
LWTH SG6 .... 16 D7
Letchworth Icknield Cemetery
LWTH SG6 .... 16 A5
Letchworth Museum & Art Gallery
LWTH SG6 .... 16 D4
Letchworth Swimming Pool
LWTH SG6 .... 16 E2
The Leventhorpe School
SBW CM21 .... 183 Q5
Leverstock Green JMI School
HHNE HP2 .... 83 H3
Leverstock Green Lawn Tennis Club
HHS/BOV HP3 .... 82 F4
The Leverton Infant School
WAB EN9 .... 111 K8
The Leverton Junior School
WAB EN9 .... 111 K8
Lewsey Farm Clinic
LTNW/LEA LU4 .... 26 D5
Ley Hill CC
CSHM HP5 .... 98 A5
Ley Hill School
CSHM HP5 .... 97 M4
Ley Park Primary School
BROX EN10 .... 92 D4
Leys Primary School
STVG SG1 .... 21 L7
The Library Theatre
LTN LU1 .... 6 E5
Lime Walk JMI School
HHNE HP2 .... 5 K6
Links Business Centre
BSF CM23 .... 43 C2
Lismarrine Industrial Park
BORE WD6 .... 133 M2
Lister Hospital
STVG SG1 .... 20 F7
Lister House Surgery
HAT AL10 .... 67 L7
Lister Medical Centre
HLWW/ROY CM19 .... 75 G8
Little Chalfont Golf Club
AMS HP6 .... 114 C4
Little Chalfont Primary School
AMS HP6 .... 114 C5
Little Gaddesden CE Primary School
BERK HP4 .... 171 J9
Little Green Junior School
RKW/CH/CXG WD3 .... 116 E7
Little Hadham Primary School
STDN SG11 .... 165 J11
Little Hallingbury CE Primary School
RBSF CM22 .... 184 C1
Little Hay Golf Complex
HHS/BOV HP3 .... 81 G6
Little Heath Primary School
POTB/CUF EN6 .... 107 G4
Little Munden CE Primary School
WARE SG12 .... 179 N1
Little Parndon Primary School
HLW CM20 .... 2 B4
Little Reddings Primary School
BUSH WD23 .... 132 F1
Little St Helens School
NTHWD HA6 .... 141 J1
Little Spring Primary School
CSHM HP5 .... 96 F2
The Little Theatre
DUN/WHIP LU6 .... 39 G1
Liverpool Road Health Centre
LTN LU1 .... 6 D5
Livingstone Primary School
EBAR EN4 .... 123 H7
Lochinver House School
POTB/CUF EN6 .... 106 F4
Lockers Park School
HHW HP1 .... 4 C2
Lodge Clinic
LTN LU1 .... 6 F6
Lodge Farm Primary School
STVGE SG2 .... 34 A2
Lodge Sun Sports Club
WAT WD17 .... 117 J5
London Academy
EDGW HA8 .... 134 D7
London Colney JMI School
LCOL/BKTW AL2 .... 86 B7
London Colney Nature Reserve
LCOL/BKTW AL2 .... 104 C2
London School of Theology
NTHWD HA6 .... 141 H1
Longdean School
HHS/BOV HP3 .... 82 D7
Longfield Primary School
RYLN/HDSTN HA2 .... 142 E8
Long Island Hotel
RKW/CH/CXG WD3 .... 130 B3
Longlands Primary School
BROX EN10 .... 92 C7
Long Marston JMI School
TRING HP23 .... 168 C1
Longmeadow Primary School
STVGE SG2 .... 33 M8
Longwood School
BUSH WD23 .... 13 M5
Lonsdale School
STVG SG1 .... 11 H1
Lordship Farm School
LWTH SG6 .... 16 E6
Loreto College
STAL AL1 .... 9 H5
Lowewood Museum
HOD EN11 .... 72 E8
Lowfield Sports Ground
HOD EN11 .... 72 D7
Luton Airport
LTNE LU2 .... 174 B2
Luton Church Cemetery
LTNE LU2 .... 7 K6
Luton Co-operative Sports Club
LTNE LU2 .... 28 D7
Luton & Dunstable Education Centre
LTNW/LEA LU4 .... 26 C1
Luton Hoo Hotel
LTN LU1 .... 41 L7
Luton Retail Park
LTN LU1 .... 7 K8
Luton RUFC
LTNE LU2 .... 41 G6
Luton Sixth Form College
LTNE LU2 .... 28 D7

Luton Town FC (Kenilworth Road)
LTNW/LEA LU4 .... 6 A3
Lyndhurst Middle School
BORE WD6 .... 120 D5
Lyonsdown School
BAR EN5 .... 137 G1
Madison Bowl
NTHWD HA6 .... 141 J2
Madrassa Islamic School
LTN LU1 .... 6 B2
Maidenhall Junior School
LTNW/LEA LU4 .... 27 L7
Maltings Arts Theatre
STAL AL1 .... 8 F6
The Maltings Industrial Estate
SBW CM21 .... 183 R7
WARE SG12 .... 73 H1
The Maltings Shopping Centre
STAL AL1 .... 8 E6
Maltmans Green School
CFSP/GDCR SL9 .... 138 A5
Malvern Way Infant School
RKW/CH/CXG WD3 .... 131 G1
Mandeville Health Centre
STAL AL1 .... 85 H5
Mandeville Primary School
SBW CM21 .... 183 P6
STAL AL1 .... 85 H5
Manland Primary School
HARP AL5 .... 46 F2
Manor Fields Primary School
BSF CM23 .... 43 K4
Manor Lodge School
RAD WD7 .... 105 G4
Manor of Groves Golf Club
SBW CM21 .... 183 K7
Manor of Groves Hotel
SBW CM21 .... 183 K7
Manor Place Industrial Estate
BORE WD6 .... 121 G7
Manshead CE School
LTN LU1 .... 39 K4
Manuden Primary School
BSF CM23 .... 166 C4
Maple Cross Industrial Estate
RKW/CH/CXG WD3 .... 129 J7
Maple Cross JMI School
RKW/CH/CXG WD3 .... 129 H8
Maple Primary School
STAL AL1 .... 9 G4
Maple River Industrial Estate
HLW CM20 .... 183 M11
Margaret Wix JMI School
STALW/RED AL3 .... 65 G6
Mark Hall Community School & Sports College
HLWE CM17 .... 76 A2
Mark Hall Cycle Museum
HLW CM20 .... 3 M1
Markyate Village School
STALW/RED AL3 .... 172 F3
Marlborough First & Middle School
HRW HA1 .... 143 J6
Marlborough School
STAL AL1 .... 85 G5
Marlin Montessori School
BERK HP4 .... 79 M1
Marlowes Health Centre
HHNE HP2 .... 4 E2
Marlowes Shopping Centre
HHNE HP2 .... 4 F4
Marquis Business Centre
BLDK SG7 .... 149 L12
Marriott Hanbury Manor Hotel & Country Club
WARE SG12 .... 180 A12
Marriotts School
STVGE SG2 .... 11 K3
Marshgate Trading Estate
HERT/BAY SG13 .... 53 J6
Marsworth CE Infant School
TRING HP23 .... 169 L1
Martindale JMI School
HHW HP1 .... 81 K1
Martinfield Business Centre
WGCE AL7 .... 50 D6
Martins Wood Primary School
STVG SG1 .... 21 M8
Mary Exton Primary School
HTCHE/RSTV SG4 .... 20 A2
Marymead Industrial Estate
STVGE SG2 .... 177 P1
Mathilda Marks Kennedy Primary School
MLHL NW7 .... 135 H8
Maunds Wood CP School
HLWS CM18 .... 95 H1
Mayfield Infant School
CHES/WCR EN8 .... 110 C1
Mayfield School
PIN HA5 .... 142 C5
The Mead Business Centre
HERT/BAY SG13 .... 53 J6
Mead Industrial Park
HLW CM20 .... 75 K1
Meadow Wood School
BUSH WD23 .... 133 G1
The Mead School
HLWS CM18 .... 75 J7
The Meads Primary School
LTNN/LIM LU3 .... 27 K3
Meppershall Lower School
SHFD SG17 .... 146 D4
Mercers College
WARE SG12 .... 54 A4
Merchant Taylors School
NTHWD HA6 .... 131 J4
The Meridian School
ROY SG8 .... 15 G5
Merry Hill Infant School
BUSH WD23 .... 132 F3
Merryhills Clinic
ENC/FH EN2 .... 124 D7
Merryhills Primary School
ENC/FH EN2 .... 124 D8
Meryfield Primary School
BORE WD6 .... 120 D5
Metropolis Centre
BORE WD6 .... 120 D5
Metropolitan Police Bushey Sports Ground
BUSH WD23 .... 118 E7
Micklem JMI School
HHW HP1 .... 81 K1
Middlesex University
EBAR EN4 .... 137 L2
STHGT/OAK N14 .... 124 A8
Middlesex University (Trent Park Campus)
EBAR EN4 .... 124 A6

Middleton Special School
.... 54 B6
Mid Herts Golf Club
STALE/WH AL4 .... 48 B1
Millbrook School
CHES/WCR EN8 .... 110 C3
Millfield First School
BUNT SG9 .... 159 J10
Mill Green Golf Club
WGCE AL7 .... 68 D4
Mill Hill County High School
MLHL NW7 .... 135 J5
The Mill Hill CC
MLHL NW7 .... 136 A6
Mill Hill Golf Club
MLHL NW7 .... 135 J5
Mill Hill School
MLHL NW7 .... 135 M7
Mill Mead J & I School
HERT/WAT SG14 .... 53 G7
Mill River Trading Estate
PEND EN3 .... 126 C8
Mill Studio Business Centre
WARE SG12 .... 54 C4
Mill Vale Middle School
DUN/HR/TOD LU5 .... 26 C7
Monken Hadley CE Primary School
BAR EN5 .... 122 E5
Monkfrith Primary School
EBAR EN4 .... 137 L3
Monksmead School
BORE WD6 .... 121 G7
Monks Walk School
WGCW AL8 .... 50 A2
Monkswood Retail Park
STVG SG1 .... 10 E8
Monro Industrial Estate
CHES/WCR EN8 .... 110 C8
Montessori School
RBSF CM22 .... 167 R10
Moorlands School
LTNW/LEA LU4 .... 27 G6
Moor Park Golf Club
RKW/CH/CXG WD3 .... 130 F6
Moor Park Industrial Estate
WATW WD18 .... 131 G3
Moreton Park Industrial Estate
LTNE LU2 .... 28 E7
Morgans JMI School
HERT/BAY SG13 .... 71 H1
Moss Bury JMI School
STVG SG1 .... 33 L2
Mountfitchet Castle Experience
STSD CM24 .... 166 H7
The Mountfitchet High School
STSD CM24 .... 166 H9
Mount Grace School
POTB/CUF EN6 .... 106 F4
Mount Pleasant Golf Club
HNLW SG16 .... 146 H6
Mount Pleasant Lane J & I School
LCOL/BKTW AL2 .... 102 C5
Mount School
MLHL NW7 .... 135 M4
Mount Vernon Hospital
NTHWD HA6 .... 130 F8
Mowat Industrial Estate
WATN WD24 .... 118 A4
MS Business Centre
PIN HA5 .... 142 B5
MSF Whitehall College
BSF CM23 .... 166 A12
Museum of Domestic Design & Architecture
EBAR EN4 .... 137 L1
Nascot Wood Infant School
WAT WD17 .... 117 L4
Nash Mills Primary School
HHS/BOV HP3 .... 82 D7
Natural Art Gallery & Science Pictures
HTCH/STOT SG5 .... 157 N7
The Natural History Museum at Tring
TRING HP23 .... 57 L2
Nazeing CP School
WAB EN9 .... 93 J5
Nazeing Glass Industrial Estate
BROX EN10 .... 93 G3
Nazeing Golf Club
WAB EN9 .... 94 A6
Nazeing Park School
WAB EN9 .... 94 A4
Newberries Primary School
RAD WD7 .... 120 A1
New Cemetery
BSF CM23 .... 43 L3
New Elgiva Theatre
CSHM HP5 .... 96 F5
New England Industrial Estate
HOD EN11 .... 73 G6
New River Trading Estate
CHES/WCR EN8 .... 92 B8
New Southgate Cemetery
FBAR/BDGN N11 .... 137 M6
New Southgate Crematorium
FBAR/BDGN N11 .... 137 M6
Newtown School
CSHM HP5 .... 97 G3
New Town Trading Estate
LTN LU1 .... 7 G9
Nicholas Breakspear RC School
STALE/WH AL4 .... 86 C3
Noam Primary School
NFNCH/WDSPK N12 .... 136 F8
Nobel School
STVGE SG2 .... 34 A2
Norbury First & Middle School
HRW HA1 .... 143 J7
Norman Booth Leisure Centre
HLWE CM17 .... 76 B2
Northaw Primary School
POTB/CUF EN6 .... 107 L3
Northchurch CC
BERK HP4 .... 59 H6
Northfields Infant School
LWTH SG6 .... 148 D12
The Northfields Technology College
DUN/HR/TOD LU5 .... 25 L6
Northgate Business Centre
EN EN1 .... 125 M7
Northgate Primary School
BSF CM23 .... 166 A12
North Hertfordshire College
LWTH SG6 .... 16 D3
STVG SG1 .... 10 D7

Optima Business Park
HOD EN11 .... 73 G6
Orchard House Industrial Estate
CSHM HP5 .... 97 G6
Orchard Primary School
WATN WD24 .... 117 K2
Orchard School
AMP/FLIT/BLC MK45 .... 155 J4
Oughtonhead Common Nature Reserve
HTCH/STOT SG5 .... 157 K4
Oughton Primary School
HTCH/STOT SG5 .... 157 L4
Our Lady of Lourdes RC Primary School
FBAR/BDGN N11 .... 137 M8
Our Ladys Catholic Primary School
AMS HP6 .... 112 F1
Our Ladys RC Primary School
HTCH/STOT SG5 .... 157 N3
WGCE AL7 .... 68 C1
Oxen Industrial Estate
LTNE LU2 .... 7 J2
Oxhey Park Golf Centre
OXHEY WD19 .... 132 B4
Oxhey Wood Primary School
OXHEY WD19 .... 132 A7
Paines Lane Cemetery
PIN HA5 .... 142 C5
Palace Gardens Shopping Centre
ENC/FH EN2 .... 125 H7
Palace Theatre
WAT WD17 .... 12 F4
Panshanger Aerodrome
WGCE AL7 .... 51 J7
Panshanger Golf & Squash Complex
WGCE AL7 .... 51 G5
Panshanger JMI School
WGCE AL7 .... 50 E6
Paradise Swimming Pools
MLHL NW7 .... 135 J8
Paradise Wildlife Park
BROX EN10 .... 91 K3
Paramount Industrial Estate
WATN WD24 .... 118 A4
Park Avenue Clinic
WAT WD17 .... 12 D2
Park Avenue Industrial Estate
LTNN/LIM LU3 .... 26 F2
Park Farm Industrial Estate
BUNT SG9 .... 158 H8
Parkfield Medical Centre
POTB/CUF EN6 .... 106 F6
Parkgate Infant School
WATN WD24 .... 118 A3
Parkgate Junior School
WATN WD24 .... 118 A3
Park Industrial Estate
LCOL/BKTW AL2 .... 103 J1
Parkside Primary School
BORE WD6 .... 120 D4
Park Street CE Primary School
LCOL/BKTW AL2 .... 103 H1
Parmiters School
GSTN WD25 .... 102 A5
Parndon Wood
HLWS CM18 .... 95 H3
Parndon Wood Cemetery
HLWW/ROY CM19 .... 95 G3
Parndon Wood Crematorium
HLWW/ROY CM19 .... 95 G3
Parsonage Farm Industrial Estate
STSD CM24 .... 166 H10
Passmores School & Technology College
HLWS CM18 .... 75 H7
Pear Tree Mead Primary School
HLWS CM18 .... 75 L8
Peartree Spring Junior School
STVG SG1 .... 11 K9
Peckworth Industrial Estate
HNLW SG16 .... 147 J5
Peerglow Industrial Estate
WATW WD18 .... 130 F3
Pendley Manor Hotel
TRING HP23 .... 58 C1
Peterborough & St Margaret's School
STAN HA7 .... 133 J6
Peterswood Infant School
HLWS CM18 .... 95 H1
Phoenix Business Centre
CSHM HP5 .... 96 F4
Phoenix Industrial Estate
HRW HA1 .... 143 K6
Pinehill Hospital
HTCHE/RSTV SG4 .... 157 Q6
Pinewood Special School
WARE SG12 .... 54 B6
Pin Green Industrial Estate
STVG SG1 .... 21 M7
Pinner Hill Golf Club
PIN HA5 .... 141 M1
Pinner Medical Centre
PIN HA5 .... 142 C6
Pinner Park Primary School
PIN HA5 .... 142 F5
Pinner View Medical Centre
HRW HA1 .... 143 G7
Pinner Wood School
PIN HA5 .... 142 A3
Pirton Cross
HTCH/STOT SG5 .... 157 J6
Pirton Hill Infant School
LTNW/LEA LU4 .... 26 F3
Pirton Primary School
HTCH/STOT SG5 .... 156 E1
Pitstone Green Business Park
LBUZ LU7 .... 169 P7
Pitstone Green Windmill (NT)
LBUZ LU7 .... 169 R5
Pixies Hill Primary School
HHW HP1 .... 81 K5
Pixmore Junior School
LWTH SG6 .... 16 E4
Playhouse Theatre
HLW CM20 .... 2 E6
Plaza Business Centre
PEND EN3 .... 126 D6
Ponders End Industrial Estate
PEND EN3 .... 126 D8
Ponsbourne Park Hotel
HERT/BAY SG13 .... 90 C5
Ponsbourne St Marys Primary School
HERT/BAY SG13 .... 90 C5

North Hertfordshire College (Hitchin Centre)
HTCHE/RSTV SG4 .... 157 R5
North Hertfordshire College (Stevenage Centre)
STVG SG1 .... 10 D7
North Hertfordshire College for the Arts
HTCHE/RSTV SG4 .... 16 A8
North Hertfordshire Leisure Centre
LWTH SG6 .... 17 G3
North Hertfordshire Secondary Centre
LWTH SG6 .... 16 B6
North Herts Music School
HTCHE/RSTV SG4 .... 157 Q6
The North London Hospice
NFNCH/WDSPK N12 .... 136 F6
North Luton Industrial Estate
LTNW/LEA LU4 .... 26 F2
North Middlesex Golf Club
NFNCH/WDSPK N12 .... 137 H6
North Mymms CC
BRKMPK AL9 .... 87 L8
North Orbital Trading Estate
STAL AL1 .... 85 L6
Northside Primary School
NFNCH/WDSPK N12 .... 137 G8
North Watford Cemetery
GSTN WD25 .... 117 L1
North Watford Health Clinic
GSTN WD25 .... 102 B8
Northway School
MLHL NW7 .... 135 H5
North & West Essex Adult Community College
HLW CM20 .... 2 D3
Northwood Cemetery
NTHWD HA6 .... 141 K4
Northwood College
NTHWD HA6 .... 141 H2
Northwood FC
NTHWD HA6 .... 141 K4
Northwood Golf Club
NTHWD HA6 .... 141 H2
Northwood & Pinner Community Hospital
NTHWD HA6 .... 141 L3
Northwood Preparatory School
RKW/CH/CXG WD3 .... 131 G5
Northwood School
NTHWD HA6 .... 141 M3
Northwood Sports Centre
NTHWD HA6 .... 141 M3
Norton Road Primary School
LTNN/LIM LU3 .... 27 K5
Norton St Nicholas Primary School
LWTH SG6 .... 148 G12
Novotel
STVG SG1 .... 33 G3
Nower Hill High School
PIN HA5 .... 142 E6
Nuffield Hospital
ENC/FH EN2 .... 124 E6
Nup End Industrial Estate
KNEB SG3 .... 176 H5
Oakfield Business Corner
LWTH SG6 .... 16 G2
Oakland CP School
EBAR EN4 .... 137 K2
Oaklands College
BORE WD6 .... 121 G6
HARP AL5 .... 46 F4
HAT AL10 .... 67 L8
STAL AL1 .... 9 H5
STALE/WH AL4 .... 86 C1
WGCW AL8 .... 50 B6
Oaklands JMI School
WLYN AL6 .... 177 L10
Oakleigh School
TRDG/WHET N20 .... 137 J6
Oakmere Primary School
POTB/CUF EN6 .... 107 H6
The Oaks Industrial Estate
HLW CM20 .... 75 K2
Oak View Primary School
HAT AL10 .... 87 M1
Oakwood Estate
HLW CM20 .... 75 L1
Oakwood JMI School
STALE/WH AL4 .... 86 A1
Oasis Academy
PEND EN3 .... 126 D3
Oasis Academy Enfield
PEND EN3 .... 126 D2
Odeon Cinema
BAR EN5 .... 136 E1
CFSP/GDCR SL9 .... 138 C7
HAT AL10 .... 67 K7
HHNE HP2 .... 5 K5
Odhams Industrial Estate
WATN WD24 .... 118 A4
Odhams Trading Estate
WATN WD24 .... 117 L2
Officers Lawn Tennis Club
RAYLNE/WEN HP22 .... 56 A4
Offley Cross
HTCH/STOT SG5 .... 157 K8
Offley Endowed Primary School
HTCH/STOT SG5 .... 156 E10
Old Airfield Industrial Estate
TRING HP23 .... 168 H4
Old Boys School
STDN SG11 .... 163 R6
Old Fold Manor Golf Club
BAR EN5 .... 122 C5
Old Harlow Health Centre
HLWE CM17 .... 76 A1
Old Lyonian Sports Ground
RYLN/HDSTN HA2 .... 143 G8
Old Merchant Taylors Sports Club
RKW/CH/CXG WD3 .... 116 F8
Old Millinians Sports Ground
RYLN/HDSTN HA2 .... 142 F7
Old Oak Close Industrial Estate
ARL/CHE SG15 .... 147 Q1
Old Owens Sports Ground
TRDG/WHET N20 .... 137 H2
Old Palace Lodge
DUN/HR/TOD LU5 .... 39 G1
Old Verulamians RFC
LCOL/BKTW AL2 .... 86 A7
Onslow St Audreys School
HAT AL10 .... 67 M8

Ponsbourne Tunnel
  HERT/BAY SG13 ....90 D6
Pope Paul RC Primary School
  POTB/CUF EN6 ....106 D7
Porters Park Golf Club
  RAD WD7 ....104 A8
Portland Industrial Estate
  ARL/CHE SG15 ....147 P7
Potten End First School
  BERK HP4 ....60 F7
Potterells Medical Centre
  BRKMPK AL9 ....88 B7
Potters Bar CC
  POTB/CUF EN6 ....106 F6
Potters Bar FC
  POTB/CUF EN6 ....106 F6
Potters Bar Golf Club
  POTB/CUF EN6 ....106 E5
Potter Street Primary School
  HLWE CM17 ....75 M7
Prae Wood Primary School
  STALW/RED AL3 ....84 E3
Premier Inn
  BORE WD6 ....121 H7
  DUN/HR/TOD LU5 ....26 E1
  LTN LU1 ....7 J8
  STVG SG1 ....10 A8
Presdales School
  WARE SG12 ....54 E5
Preston Primary School
  HTCHE/RSTV SG4 ....31 H3
Priestmead Middle School
  KTN/HRWW/WS HA3 ....143 M5
Prince of Wales Primary
  School
  PEND EN3 ....126 D3
Princess Alexandra Hospital
  HLW CM20 ....2 C5
The Princess Helena College
  HTCHE/RSTV SG4 ....31 J3
Priors Wood JMI School
  WARE SG12 ....54 E2
Priory Cinema
  ROY SG8 ....14 E7
Priory Middle School
  DUN/HR LU6 ....39 G1
Priory School
  HTCH/STOT SG5 ....157 N3
The Priory
  HTCH/STOT SG5 ....157 N7
Prospect Industrial Estate
  CSHM HP5 ....97 G6
Puller Memorial CE (VA)
  Primary School
  STDN SG11 ....180 C7
Pump House Theatre
  WAT WD17 ....13 J7
Purford Green Infant School
  HLWS CM18 ....75 L7
Purford Green Junior School
  HLWS CM18 ....3 M9
Purwell Primary School
  HTCHE/RSTV SG4 ....20 A1
Putteridge High School
  LTNE LU2 ....29 G4
Putteridge J & I School
  LTNE LU2 ....29 G4
Putteridge Recreation Centre
  LTNE LU2 ....29 G4
Pygtile School
  AMP/FLIT/BLC MK45 ....154 E7
Quadrant Shopping Centre
  DUN/WHIP LU6 ....25 M8
Quality Hotel
  HRW HA1 ....143 H8
  STAL AL1 ....85 K4
Queen Elizabeth II Hospital
  WGCE AL7 ....68 E3
Queen Elizabeth Leisure
  Centre
  BAR EN5 ....122 D8
Queen Elizabeths Boys
  School
  BAR EN5 ....122 B7
Queen Elizabeths Girls School
  BAR EN5 ....122 D8
Queen Elizabeth Stadium
  EN EN1 ....125 K6
Queen Mother Theatre
  HTCH/STOT SG5 ....157 P6
Queensbury School
  DUN/WHIP LU6 ....38 E3
Queensgate Centre
  HLW CM20 ....75 J1
Queens School
  BUSH WD23 ....118 D7
Queensway Business
  Centre
  PEND EN3 ....126 A8
Queensway Health Centre
  HAT AL10 ....67 M7
Queenswell J & I School
  TRDG/WHET N20 ....137 H5
Queenswood School
  BRKMPK AL9 ....107 H2
Queen Victoria Memorial
  Hospital
  WLYN AL6 ....49 L1
Rabia Boys School
  LTNW/LEA LU4 ....27 L8
Rabia Girls School
  LTNW/LEA LU4 ....27 L8
Radburn Primary School
  LWTH SG6 ....17 G4
Radlett CC
  RAD WD7 ....119 M3
Radlett Lodge School
  RAD WD7 ....104 A6
Radlett Preparatory School
  RAD WD7 ....120 A4
RAF Edlesborough
  STDN SG11 ....163 Q10
Ramada Hotel
  GSTN WD25 ....119 G7
  HAT AL10 ....67 J8
  STALW/RED AL3 ....63 J2
Ramridge Primary School
  LTNE LU2 ....28 F7
Ramsey Manor Lower School
  AMP/FLIT/BLC MK45 ....155 K3
Rathbone School
  LTN LU1 ....6 E4
Ravensburgh Castle
  HTCH/STOT SG5 ....155 M5
Ravenscroft School
  TRDG/WHET N20 ....136 D3
Raynham Road Industrial
  Estate
  BSF CM23 ....44 B1

Redbournbury Mill
  STALW/RED AL3 ....64 B3
Redbourn Golf Club
  STALW/RED AL3 ....173 R8
Redbourn Industrial Centre
  STALW/RED AL3 ....173 R12
Redbourn Infant School
  STALW/RED AL3 ....173 Q11
Redbourn Recreation Centre
  STALW/RED AL3 ....173 Q10
Redcoats Farmhouse Hotel
  HTCHE/RSTV SG4 ....20 B7
Reddiford School
  PIN HA5 ....142 C6
Reddings Primary School
  HHS/BOV HP3 ....5 L7
Red Rose Trading Estate
  EBAR EN4 ....137 H1
Reed First School
  ROY SG8 ....152 A8
Reedings Junior School
  SBW CM21 ....183 Q6
Rhodes Farm Clinic
  MLHL NW7 ....136 A7
Richard Hale School
  HERT/BAY SG13 ....53 H8
Richard Whittington Primary
  School
  BSF CM23 ....43 L5
Richmond Hill Special School
  LTNE LU2 ....28 C7
Rickmansworth Park Primary
  School
  RKW/CH/CXG WD3 ....130 C3
Rickmansworth PNEU School
  RKW/CH/CXG WD3 ....130 A2
Rickmansworth Public Golf
  Club
  RKW/CH/CXG WD3 ....130 D5
Rickmansworth School
  RKW/CH/CXG WD3 ....130 D2
Rickmansworth Sports Club
  RKW/CH/CXG WD3 ....130 C2
Ridlins Wood Athletics Track
  STVGE SG2 ....34 A7
River Lee Country Park
  WAB EN9 ....92 F6
River Park Industrial Estate
  BERK HP4 ....59 L8
Riverside Business Park
  STSD CM24 ....166 G7
Riverside Industrial Estate
  HARP AL5 ....47 C1
  LCOL/BKTW AL2 ....104 C1
Riverside Shopping Centre
  HHW HP1 ....4 E5
Roaring Meg Retail Park
  STVG SG1 ....10 E5
Robertswood Combined
  School
  CFSP/GDCR SL9 ....138 D2
Roebuck Hotel
  WARE SG12 ....54 A3
Roebuck Primary School
  STVGE SG2 ....33 K7
Roebuck Retail Park
  STVG SG1 ....33 J7
Roecroft Lower School
  HTCH/STOT SG5 ....148 E7
Roger Bannister Sports
  Ground
  KTN/HRWW/WS HA3 ....143 G1
Roman Theatre of
  Verulamium
  STALW/RED AL3 ....84 E2
Roman Way First School
  ROY SG8 ....14 D4
Rosary Priory High School
  BUSH WD23 ....133 J2
The Rose & Crown Hotel
  TRING HP23 ....57 M2
Rosedale Clinic
  CHESW EN7 ....109 L2
Roseland JMI School
  HOD EN11 ....72 D4
Rosh Pinah Primary School
  EDGW HA8 ....134 F5
Rossgate JMI School
  HHW HP1 ....61 L8
Rothesay Road Cemetery
  LTN LU1 ....6 C6
Round Diamond Primary
  School
  STVG SG1 ....21 M6
Roundwood Park School
  HARP AL5 ....46 C3
Roundwood Primary School
  HARP AL5 ....46 C3
Rowans Primary School
  WGCE AL7 ....50 E4
Rowley Lane Maccabi Sports
  Ground
  BORE WD6 ....135 J2
Royal Chace Hotel
  ENC/FH EN2 ....124 D4
Royal Gunpowder Mills
  WAB EN9 ....110 F6
Royal Masonic School for Girls
  RKW/CH/CXG WD3 ....130 B3
Royal National Orthopaedic
  Hospital
  STAN HA7 ....133 M4
Royal Veterinary College
  BRKMPK AL9 ....106 B2
Roydonbury Industrial Estate
  HLWW/ROY CM19 ....74 D5
Roydon CP School
  HLWW/ROY CM19 ....73 M5
Royston Cemetery
  ROY SG8 ....14 E6
Royston & District Hospital
  MHAD SG10 ....182 F3
Royston Golf Club
  ROY SG8 ....14 D7
Royston Health Centre
  ROY SG8 ....14 E7
Royston Museum
  ROY SG8 ....14 D7
Royston Swimming Pool
  ROY SG8 ....14 D7
Royston Town FC
  ROY SG8 ....14 F6
Rudolf Steiner School
  KGLGY WD4 ....100 C3
Ruislip Woods National
  Nature Reserve
  NTHWD HA6 ....141 G5
Russell Clinic
  STALW/RED AL3 ....8 E5
The Russell School
  RKW/CH/CXG WD3 ....114 F8
Russet House School
  EN EN1 ....125 M5

The Ryde Primary School
  BRKMPK AL9 ....68 A5
Rye House Stadium
  HOD EN11 ....73 H5
Rye Meads RSPB Reserve
  HOD EN11 ....73 H4
Rye Park Industrial Estate
  HOD EN11 ....73 J5
Sacred Heart Language
  College
  KTN/HRWW/WS HA3 ....143 J4
Sacred Heart Primary School
  LTNE LU2 ....28 E6
Sacred Heart RC JMI School
  TRDG/WHET N20 ....137 J5
Sacred Heart RC Primary
  School
  OXHEY WD19 ....132 D2
  WARE SG12 ....54 A4
Safari Cinema & Bingo
  HRW HA1 ....143 K7
Saffron Green Primary School
  BORE WD6 ....121 H8
St Adrians RC Primary School
  STAL AL1 ....85 K7
St Alban & St Stephen Infant
  School
  STAL AL1 ....9 K7
St Alban & St Stephen RC JM
  School
  STAL AL1 ....9 L6
St Albans City FC
  STAL AL1 ....9 J4
St Albans City Hospital
  STALW/RED AL3 ....8 D2
St Albans Girls School
  STALW/RED AL3 ....65 J6
St Albans High School for Girls
  STAL AL1 ....9 G3
St Albans Lawn Tennis Club
  STALE/WH AL4 ....66 A8
St Albans Museum
  STAL AL1 ....9 G4
St Albans Musical Museum
  LCOL/BKTW AL2 ....102 F2
St Albans Music School
  STALW/RED AL3 ....65 H7
St Albans Organ Museum
  STAL AL1 ....85 M3
St Albans Primary School
  HLW CM20 ....3 J2
St Albans Principal Health
  Centre
  STAL AL1 ....9 G5
St Albans Retail Park
  STAL AL1 ....85 H4
St Albans School
  STALW/RED AL3 ....8 D6
St Albert the Great RC
  Primary School
  HHNE HP2 ....82 A7
St Andrews CE JMI School
  TRDG/WHET N20 ....136 D5
St Andrews CE Primary School
  EN EN1 ....125 H6
  HTCHE/RSTV SG4 ....157 Q6
  MHAD SG10 ....181 R7
St Andrews Primary School
  WARE SG12 ....73 H1
St Andrews School
  RYLN/HDSTN HA2 ....142 F7
St Annes Catholic High School
  for Girls
  ENC/FH EN2 ....125 H8
St Ann's Shopping Centre
  HRW HA1 ....143 J8
St Anthonys RC Primary
  School
  WATW WD18 ....131 J1
St Augustines RC Primary
  School
  HOD EN11 ....72 F8
St Bartholomews CE School
  TRING HP23 ....58 B4
St Bernadette RC Primary
  School
  LCOL/BKTW AL2 ....104 B1
St Catherine of Sienna RC
  Primary
  GSTN WD25 ....102 B6
St Catherines Hoddesdon CE
  Primary School
  HOD EN11 ....72 F7
St Catherines Primary School
  WARE SG12 ....53 M3
St Catherines RC School
  BAR EN5 ....122 D8
St Christopher School
  LWTH SG6 ....16 D6
St Christophers Lower School
  DUN/HR/TOD LU5 ....26 D7
St Clement Danes School
  RKW/CH/CXG WD3 ....115 H6
St Clements Junior School
  CHES/WCR EN8 ....110 C1
St Columbas Preparatory
  School
  STALW/RED AL3 ....8 B9
St Cross RC Primary School
  HOD EN11 ....92 E1
St Cuthbert Mayne RC Primary
  School
  HHW HP1 ....81 M1
St Dominic RC Primary
  School
  HARP AL5 ....46 D7
St Edmunds College & St Hugh's
  Preparatory School
  STDN SG11 ....163 L12
St Elizabeths Centre
  MHAD SG10 ....182 F3
St Francis College
  LWTH SG6 ....16 C4
St Georges CE Infant School
  AMSS HP7 ....113 J4
St Georges Industrial Estate
  AMSS HP7 ....113 K4
St Georges RC Primary School
  ENC/FH EN2 ....125 H6
St Georges School
  DUN/HR/TOD LU5 ....39 G1
St Georges School Technology
  College
  HARP AL5 ....46 D7
St Georges Shopping Centre
  & Cinema
  HRW HA1 ....143 H8
St Giles Primary School
  POTB/CUF EN6 ....105 L6
St Helens Primary School
  STALE/WH AL4 ....48 B5
St Helens School
  NTHWD HA6 ....141 J1

St Hildas School
  BUSH WD23 ....132 F3
  HARP AL5 ....46 D3
St Ignatius College
  ENC/FH EN2 ....125 L3
St Ippollitts Cemetery
  HTCHE/RSTV SG4 ....157 R11
St Ippolyts Primary School
  HTCHE/RSTV SG4 ....157 R10
St James CE Primary School
  HLWS CM18 ....95 H1
  PEND EN3 ....126 A6
St Joan of Arc RC School
  RKW/CH/CXG WD3 ....130 C3
St John Fisher RC First &
  Middle School
  PIN HA5 ....142 E2
St John Fisher RC Primary
  School
  STALE/WH AL4 ....66 A7
St Johns CE J & I (Mixed)
  WGCW AL8 ....49 K8
St Johns CE Primary School
  ENC/FH EN2 ....124 F2
  FBAR/BDGN N11 ....137 K7
  TRDG/WHET N20 ....137 K7
  WLYN AL6 ....50 D3
St Johns Church of England
  School
  STAN HA7 ....133 L7
St Johns Infant School
  RAD WD7 ....119 K1
St Johns Preparatory School
  POTB/CUF EN6 ....107 J8
St Johns RC Primary School
  BLDK SG7 ....17 K2
  RKW/CH/CXG WD3 ....129 M4
St Johns School
  NTHWD HA6 ....141 M1
St Johns Senior School
  ENC/FH EN2 ....124 E5
St John the Baptist Primary
  School
  WARE SG12 ....54 E8
St Josephs CE Combined
  School
  CFSP/GDCR SL9 ....138 B7
St Josephs Infant School
  LTNN/LIM LU3 ....27 L1
St Josephs in the Park
  HERT/WAT SG14 ....70 E1
St Joseph's Primary School
  HERT/WAT SG14 ....52 E8
St Joseph's RC College
  MLHL NW7 ....135 K7
St Josephs RC First & Middle
  School
  KTN/HRWW/WS HA3 ....143 L4
St Josephs RC JMI School
  CHES/WCR EN8 ....110 C2
St Josephs RC Primary School
  BSF CM23 ....43 K2
  OXHEY WD19 ....131 M6
St Lawrence CE School
  WAB EN9 ....111 K7
St Lukes Catholic Primary
  School
  HLWW/ROY CM19 ....75 G7
St Lukes Special School
  STALW/RED AL3 ....173 Q11
St Margaret Clitherow RC
  Primary School
  STVGE SG2 ....33 K7
St Margaret of Scotland
  Infant School
  LTN LU1 ....40 F4
St Margaret of Scotland
  Junior School
  LTN LU1 ....40 F4
St Margarets School
  BUSH WD23 ....132 E3
St Marks West Essex Catholic
  School
  HLWS CM18 ....3 G8
St Marthas Junior School
  BAR EN5 ....122 C6
St Marthas Senior School
  EBAR EN4 ....122 C6
St Martin de Porres Primary
  School
  LTNW/LEA LU4 ....26 E5
St Martins School
  MLHL NW7 ....135 J8
St Marys Abbey
  MLHL NW7 ....135 J7
St Marys Catholic School
  BSF CM23 ....43 L2
St Marys CE Combined
  School
  AMSS HP7 ....112 F5
St Mary's Cemetery
  AMSS HP7 ....112 F6
St Marys CE Primary School
  EBAR EN4 ....137 J2
  RBSF CM22 ....185 M3
  STSD CM24 ....166 C6
St Marys First School
  BERK HP4 ....59 J7
St Marys High School
  CHESW EN7 ....109 M4
St Marys Junior School
  BLDK SG7 ....17 J3
  WARE SG12 ....54 B2
St Marys Lower School
  HTCH/STOT SG5 ....148 E7
  LTN LU1 ....39 K3
St Marys Primary School
  BRKMPK AL9 ....87 M3
St Marys RC Primary School
  PEND EN3 ....126 B8
  ROY SG8 ....14 E6
St Marys School
  CFSP/GDCR SL9 ....138 C2
St Matthews Infant School
  LTNE LU2 ....7 G2
St Meryl JMI School
  OXHEY WD19 ....132 C5
St Michaels Catholic Grammar
  School
  NFNCH/WDSPK N12 ....136 F1
St Michaels CE Primary School
  BSF CM23 ....43 L2
  ENC/FH EN2 ....125 L3
St Michaels CE VA Primary
  School
  STALW/RED AL3 ....8 A3
St Michael's Manor Hotel
  STALW/RED AL3 ....8 B5
St Michaels Primary School
  KNEB SG3 ....177 N7
St Michaels RC School
  GSTN WD25 ....102 A6

St Nicholas Health Centre
  STVG SG1 ....21 K7
St Nicholas Primary School
  HARP AL5 ....46 E4
St Nicholas Recreation Centre
  STVG SG1 ....21 M6
St Nicholas School
  BORE WD6 ....134 C2
  HLWE CM17 ....76 D2
St Pauls CE Primary School
  KGLGY WD4 ....100 F8
  FBAR/BDGN N11 ....137 L8
  MLHL NW7 ....135 M7
St Pauls Primary School
  KGLGY WD4 ....99 L5
St Pauls RC Primary School
  CHESW EN7 ....109 M1
St Pauls Walden Primary
  School
  HTCHE/RSTV SG4 ....175 P2
St Peters JMI School
  STAL AL1 ....9 G8
St Peters Primary School
  RKW/CH/CXG WD3 ....129 M4
St Philip Howard Catholic
  Primary School
  HAT AL10 ....67 M8
St Roses RC Infant School
  HHW HP1 ....81 L4
St Teresa RC First &
  Middle School
  KTN/HRWW/WS HA3 ....143 G3
St Teresa's RC Primary School
  BORE WD6 ....120 F6
St Thomas More RC Primary
  School
  BERK HP4 ....79 L1
  LWTH SG6 ....16 B5
St Thomas of Canterbury RC
  Primary School
  STDN SG11 ....163 N10
St Vincent de Paul RC JMI
  School
  STVG SG1 ....11 J3
St Vincents Hospital
  PIN HA5 ....141 J5
St Vincents Lower School
  DUN/HR/TOD LU5 ....26 A4
St Vincents RC Primary School
  MLHL NW7 ....135 M7
Salcombe Preparatory School
  (Infants)
  STHGT/OAK N14 ....137 M2
Salcombe Preparatory School
  (Juniors)
  STHGT/OAK N14 ....137 M3
Salisbury Infant School
  HAT AL10 ....67 M6
Salisbury Lawn Tennis Club
  STAL AL1 ....85 M1
Salvatorian College
  KTN/HRWW/WS HA3 ....143 H4
Samuel Lucas Primary School
  HTCH/STOT SG5 ....157 M6
Sandon JMI School
  BUNT SG9 ....150 H12
Sandown Road Industrial
  Estate
  WATN WD24 ....118 A3
Sandridge Gate Business
  Centre
  STALE/WH AL4 ....65 K6
Sandridge School
  STALE/WH AL4 ....66 D3
Sandridge Youth Club & Sports
  Centre
  STALW/RED AL3 ....65 M4
Sandringham School
  STALE/WH AL4 ....65 M6
Sandy Lodge Golf Club
  NTHWD HA6 ....131 H5
Saracen Industrial Area
  HHNE HP2 ....62 F8
Sarbir Industrial Park
  HLW CM20 ....183 N12
Sarratt School
  RKW/CH/CXG WD3 ....115 L2
Sauncey Wood Primary
  School
  HARP AL5 ....47 H1
Sawbridge Health Clinic
  SBW CM21 ....183 Q7
Saxeway Business Centre
  CSHM HP5 ....96 C2
Sceptre School
  LTNW/LEA LU4 ....26 F3
Scott's Grotto
  WARE SG12 ....54 B5
Sebright School
  STALW/RED AL3 ....172 F5
The Sele School
  HERT/WAT SG14 ....52 D7
Shaftesbury High School
  KTN/HRWW/WS HA3 ....142 F3
Shaftesbury Industrial Centre
  LWTH SG6 ....16 F2
Shakespeare Industrial Estate
  WATN WD24 ....117 L4
Shaw's Corner (NT)
  WLYN AL6 ....176 A11
Sheepcot Medical Centre
  GSTN WD25 ....102 A8
Sheering CE Primary School
  RBSF CM22 ....184 D8
Shefford Business Park
  SHFD SG17 ....146 H2
Shendish Manor Golf Club
  HHS/BOV HP3 ....82 B3
Shenley Primary School
  RAD WD7 ....104 D8
Shenval Industrial Estate
  HLW CM20 ....75 L1
Shephalbury Park Primary
  School
  STVGE SG2 ....33 M8
Shepherd Primary School
  RKW/CH/CXG WD3 ....129 L4
Sheredes School
  HOD EN11 ....72 D8
Sherrardswood School
  WLYN AL6 ....177 K12
Shillington Lower School
  HTCH/STOT SG5 ....146 A7
Shire Horse Centre
  CSTG HP8 ....128 E6
The Shire London
  BAR EN5 ....122 A4
Silkmead Farm Industrial
  Estate BUNT SG9 ....159 P6
Silk Mill House Museum
  STALW/RED AL3 ....173 Q12
Simon Balle School
  HERT/BAY SG13 ....53 J8

Sir Frederic Osborn School
WGCE AL7 .... 50 F6
Sir James Altham Swimming
Pool
OXHEY WD19 .... 132 C8
Sir John Lawes School
HARP AL5 .... 47 G2
Sir John Newsom School
WGCE AL7 .... 68 C1
Sir Thomas Lipton Memorial
Hospital
STHGT/OAK N14 .... 137 M3
Skidmore Clinic
RKW/CH/CXG WD3 .... 130 C4
Skyswood JMI School
STALE/WH AL4 .... 66 A7
Sleep Inn Baldock
BLDK SG7 .... 148 H7
Slip End Lower School
LTN LU1 .... 40 F8
Smug Oak Green Business
Centre
LCOL/BKTW AL2 .... 102 F3
Snap Theatre
BSF CM23 .... 43 M2
Someries Castle
LTNE LU2 .... 174 C4
Someries J & I School
LTNE LU2 .... 29 G6
Sopwell House Hotel Country
Club & Spa
STAL AL1 .... 85 K6
South Bedfordshire Golf Club
LTNE LU2 .... 155 K11
Southbury Primary School
PEND EN3 .... 125 M8
Southdown Industrial Estate
HARP AL5 .... 47 G5
Southfield Infant School
LTNW/LEA LU4 .... 26 D5
Southgate Compton CC
EBAR EN4 .... 123 K8
Southgate Health Centre
STVG SG1 .... 10 C6
Southgate School
EBAR EN4 .... 137 M1
South Herts Golf Club
TRDG/WHET N20 .... 136 E4
South Hill JMI School
HHW HP1 .... 4 D4
South Luton High School
LTN LU1 .... 41 K4
Southmill Trading Centre
BSF CM23 .... 44 A3
Sovereign Business Centre
PEND EN3 .... 126 D7
Spellbrook Primary School
BSF CM23 .... 183 R2
Sphere Industrial Estate
STAL AL1 .... 9 M7
The Spinney Infant School
HLW CM20 .... 3 M4
The Spinney Junior School
HLW CM20 .... 3 M4
The Spires Shopping Centre
BAR EN5 .... 122 C7
Springmead JMI School
WCCE AL7 .... 51 G6
Stadium Industrial Estate
LTNW/LEA LU4 .... 26 F7
Stags School
STALW/RED AL3 .... 65 J6
Stanborough Primary School
GSTN WD25 .... 118 A1
Stanborough School
GSTN WD25 .... 117 M1
WGCW AL8 .... 67 M1
Stanbridge Lower School
LBUZ LU7 .... 24 B4
Standon Business Park
STDN SG11 .... 163 Q12
Standon Health Centre
STDN SG11 .... 163 Q11
Stanley Hill Cemetery
AMSS HP7 .... 113 J6
Stanmore College
STAN HA7 .... 143 M1
Stanmore Golf Club
STAN HA7 .... 143 M2
Stanmore Road Health Centre
STVG SG1 .... 33 G2
Stansted Airport
STSD CM24 .... 167 Q10
Stansted Airport Terminal
Building
STSD CM24 .... 167 R9
Stansted Clinic
STSD CM24 .... 166 G6
Stansted Mountfitchet
Windmill
STSD CM24 .... 166 F7
Stapleford Primary School
HERT/WAT SG14 .... 179 J10
Staple Tye Shopping Centre
HLWS CM18 .... 75 H8
Steeple Morden CE Primary
School
ROY SG8 .... 145 N7
Stevenage Arts & Leisure
Centre
STVG SG1 .... 10 C5
Stevenage Borough FC
STVGE SG2 .... 33 J7
Stevenage Business Park
STVG SG1 .... 22 A7
Stevenage CC
STVG SG1 .... 10 C3
Stevenage Golf Centre
STVGE SG2 .... 34 C8
Stevenage Leisure Park
STVG SG1 .... 10 A6
Stevenage Museum
STVG SG1 .... 10 E5
Stevenage Register Office
STVG SG1 .... 10 C6
Stevenage St Nicholas CE
Primary School
STVG SG1 .... 11 G4
Stevenage Swimming Centre
STVG SG1 .... 10 D4
Stewards School
HLWS CM18 .... 95 G1
Stirling Industrial Centre
BORE WD6 .... 135 H1
Stirling Retail Park
BORE WD6 .... 135 H2
Stocks Golf & Country Club
TRING HP23 .... 170 C10
Stockwell Lodge Medical
Centre *CHESW EN7* 109 L1
Stockwood Craft Museum &
Gardens
LTN LU1 .... 41 H5

Stockwood Park Athletic
Track
LTN LU1 .... 41 H6
Stockwood Park Country Park
LTN LU1 .... 41 H6
Stockwood Park Golf Club
LTN LU1 .... 41 H5
Stondon Lower School
HNLW SG16 .... 146 G6
Stondon Museum & Garden
Centre
HNLW SG16 .... 146 H6
Stonehill Primary School
LWTH SG6 .... 148 C12
Stony Dean Special School
AMSS HP7 .... 113 K5
Stopsley High School
LTNE LU2 .... 28 D5
Stopsley Primary School
LTNE LU2 .... 28 E5
Stopsley Sports Centre &
Sports Ground
LTNE LU2 .... 28 E4
Stormont School
POTB/CUF EN6 .... 107 G5
Stortford Hall Industrial Park
BSF CM23 .... 44 B2
Stort Valley Industrial Estate
BSF CM23 .... 166 D11
Stotfold Cemetery
HTCH/STOT SG5 .... 148 F6
Stotfold Health Centre
HTCH/STOT SG5 .... 148 C7
Strathmore Infant School
HTCH/STOT SG5 .... 157 N3
Streetfield Middle School
DUN/HR/TOD LU5 .... 39 J3
Stroud Wood Business Centre
LCOL/BKTW AL2 .... 103 J1
Studham Lower School
DUN/WHIP LU6 .... 171 P5
Studlands Rise First School
ROY SG8 .... 14 F8
Suffolks Primary School
EN EN1 .... 125 M6
Summercroft Junior School
BSF CM23 .... 44 C1
Summerswood Primary School
BORE WD6 .... 120 F8
Sumners Community
Recreation Centre
HLWW/ROY CM19 .... 94 E1
Sunderland Estate
KGLGY WD4 .... 100 F3
Sundon Business Park
LTNN/LIM LU3 .... 26 F1
Sundon Hills Country Park
LTNN/LIM LU3 .... 154 C7
Sundon Industrial Estate
LTNN/LIM LU3 .... 26 F1
Sundon Lower School
LTNN/LIM LU3 .... 154 B9
Sundon Medical Centre
LTNN/LIM LU3 .... 27 G2
Sundon Park Junior School
LTNN/LIM LU3 .... 27 G1
Sun Hotel
HTCH/STOT SG5 .... 157 N7
Sunshine House School
NTHWD HA6 .... 141 H1
Surrey Street Primary School
LTN LU1 .... 7 G8
Susi Earnshaw Theatre School
BAR EN5 .... 122 D7
Swallow Dell Primary School
WGCE AL7 .... 50 E8
Swing Gate First School
BERK HP4 .... 80 B2
The Symonds Green Health
Centre
STVG SG1 .... 32 E2
Tabard RFC
RAD WD7 .... 119 M3
TA Centre
HRW HA1 .... 143 K7
Tanners Wood Primary
School
ABLGY WD5 .... 101 J6
Tannery Drift First School
ROY SG8 .... 14 D7
Tanys Dell Primary School
HLW CM20 .... 75 L2
Taylor Trading Estate
HERT/BAY SG13 .... 53 M6
Telmere Industrial Estate
LTN LU1 .... 7 G8
Templewood Primary School
WGCW AL8 .... 50 A5
Tennyson Road Primary School
LTN LU1 .... 6 E9
Tewin Bury Farm Hotel
WLYN AL6 .... 51 G4
Tewin Cowper Primary School
WLYN AL6 .... 51 J3
Tewin Road Business Centre
WGCE AL7 .... 50 C6
Tewin Water School
WLYN AL6 .... 50 E3
Thames Industrial Estate
DUN/WHIP LU6 .... 39 G1
The Elms Football & Tennis
Club
STAN HA7 .... 133 M8
Theobald Business Centre
HTCHE/RSTV SG4 .... 157 P2
Theobalds Park C&CC Site
CHESW EN8 .... 109 L8
Therfield First School
ROY SG8 .... 151 M6
Therfield Heath Nature
Reserve
ROY SG8 .... 151 N1
Thistle Hotel
LCOL/BKTW AL2 .... 102 D1
Thomas Alleyne School
STVG SG1 .... 33 G1
The Thomas Coram Middle
School
BERK HP4 .... 80 B3
Thomas Harding Junior
School
CSHM HP5 .... 96 F6
The Thomas Rivers Medical
Centre
SBW CM21 .... 183 N8
Thomas Whitehead CE School
DUN/HR/TOD LU5 .... 25 M4
Thorley Hill Primary School
BSF CM23 .... 43 M5
Thorn Grove Primary School
BSF CM23 .... 44 B3
Thornhill Lower School
DUN/HR/TOD LU5 .... 26 B2

Thorpe House School
CFSP/GDCR SL9 .... 138 C6
Thundridge Business Park
WARE SG12 .... 180 B10
Thundridge CE Primary School
WARE SG12 .... 180 B10
Tilehouse Combined School
DEN/HRF UB9 .... 139 J8
Tilsworth Golf Centre
LBUZ LU7 .... 24 F3
Timbers Clinic
KTN/HRWW/WS HA3 ... 143 H1
Tithe Farm Lower School
DUN/HR/TOD LU5 .... 25 M3
Tonwell St Marys Primary
School
WARE SG12 .... 179 N10
Torrington Clinic
NFNCH/WDSPK N12 ..... 137 G8
Torrington Park Health Centre
NFNCH/WDSPK N12 ..... 137 G7
Totteridge CC
TRDG/WHET N20 .... 136 E5
Totternhoe FC
DUN/WHIP LU6 .... 38 A2
Totternhoe Lower School
DUN/WHIP LU6 .... 37 M2
Totternhoe Quarry Nature
Reserve
DUN/WHIP LU6 .... 37 M1
Townsend CE School
STALW/RED AL3 .... 65 G5
Townsend Industrial Estate
DUN/HR/TOD LU5 .... 25 M5
Trafalgar Trading Estate
PEND EN3 .... 126 D8
Travellers Lane Industrial
Estate
HAT AL10 .... 87 M4
Travelodge
BLDK SG7 .... 148 F4
CHES/WCR EN8 .... 110 A3
HAT AL10 .... 67 K7
HHNE HP2 .... 4 F5
HLW CM20 .... 75 H2
WATW WD18 .... 12 F5
Tree Cathedral (NT)
DUN/WHIP LU6 .... 38 D8
Trent CE Primary School
EBAR EN4 .... 123 K8
Trent Country Park
EBAR EN4 .... 123 L6
Trent Park Cemetery
EBAR EN4 .... 123 L7
Trent Park Golf Club
STHGT/OAK N14 .... 124 A8
Tricor Business Park
CHES/WCR EN8 .... 110 C8
Tricor Trading Estate
CHES/WCR EN8 .... 110 C8
Trident Industrial Estate
HOD EN11 .... 73 G6
Tring Business Centre
TRING HP23 .... 57 J1
Tring Cemetery
TRING HP23 .... 57 J2
Tring Health Centre
TRING HP23 .... 57 M1
Tring Reservoirs National
Nature Reserve
TRING HP23 .... 169 K9
Tring School
TRING HP23 .... 57 M1
Tring Sports Centre
TRING HP23 .... 57 M1
Trotts Hill Primary School
STVG SG1 .... 21 K8
Troy Industrial Estate
HRW HA1 .... 143 K7
Trust Industrial Estate
HTCHE/RSTV SG4 .... 157 Q7
Tudor Enterprise Park
KTN/HRWW/WS HA3 ... 143 H5
Tudor Lodge Hotel
PIN HA5 .... 141 M8
Tudor Primary School
HHNE HP2 .... 5 H6
Turnford School
CHES/WCR EN8 .... 110 C2
The Two Brewers Hotel
KGLGY WD4 .... 99 L5
Two Waters JMI School
HHS/BOV HP3 .... 82 B7
Twyford Business Centre
BSF CM23 .... 44 A4
Underhill Infant School
BAR EN5 .... 136 C1
University of Bedfordshire
LTN LU1 .... 7 G6
LTNE LU2 .... 29 H3
University of Hertfordshire
HAT AL10 .... 67 L7
HERT/BAY SG13 .... 70 F4
STAL AL1 .... 9 J8
University of Hertfordshire
(College Lane Campus)
HAT AL10 .... 67 H8
University of Hertfordshire
(de Havilland Campus)
HAT AL10 .... 67 H8
University of Hertfordshire
Faculty of Law
STAL AL1 .... 9 G4
University of Hertfordshire
(Fielder Centre)
HAT AL10 .... 67 H5
University of London
ENC/FH EN2 .... 125 L2
Upper Clapton RFC
EPP CM16 .... 95 M6
Upshire Primary School
WAB EN9 .... 111 M7
The Vale Cemetery
LTNE LU2 .... 28 F3
The Vale Crematorium
LTNE LU2 .... 28 F3
Vale Industrial Estate
WATW WD18 .... 131 G4
Vaughan First & Middle
School
RYLN/HDSTN HA2 .... 143 G8
Verulam Golf Club
STAL AL1 .... 85 K4
Verulam Industrial Estate
STAL AL1 .... 9 J9
Verulamium Museum
STALW/RED AL3 .... 8 A5
Verulam School
STAL AL1 .... 9 M4
Vicarage Road Cemetery
WATW WD18 .... 12 D6
Victoria CE First School
BERK HP4 .... 80 A1

Victoria Square Business Area
STAL AL1 .... 9 J7
Vita et Pax School
STHGT/OAK N14 .... 137 M1
Vue Cinema
GSTN WD25 .... 102 A7
HRW HA1 .... 143 J8
Walkern Primary School
STVG SG2 .... 34 F1
Waltham Abbey Gatehouse,
Bridge & Entrance
to Cloisters
WAB EN9 .... 111 G7
Waltham Abbey Marriott
Hotel
WAB EN9 .... 111 K8
Waltham Abbey Swimming
Pool
WAB EN9 .... 127 H1
Waltham Holy Cross Infant
School
WAB EN9 .... 111 H7
Warden Hill Infant School
LTNN/LIM LU3 .... 28 A2
Warden Hill Junior School
LTNN/LIM LU3 .... 28 A2
Wardown House
(Luton Museum & Gallery)
LTNN/LIM LU3 .... 28 B6
Wardown Swimming & Leisure
Centre
LTNN/LIM LU3 .... 28 B7
Ware Cemetery
WARE SG12 .... 53 M2
Wareside Primary School
WARE SG12 .... 55 J2
Warren Dell Primary School
OXHEY WD19 .... 132 A6
Warrenwood Industrial Estate
HERT/WAT SG14 .... 178 H11
Watchlytes School
WGCE AL7 .... 50 F7
Water Gardens Shopping
Centre
HLW CM20 .... 2 E6
Water Lane Primary School
HLWW/ROY CM19 .... 94 E1
Watermill Business Centre
PEND EN3 .... 126 D6
Watermill Industrial Estate
BUNT SG9 .... 159 J11
Waterside Combined School
CSHM HP5 .... 97 H7
Waterside Industrial Estate
HOD EN11 .... 73 H8
Waterside School
BSF CM23 .... 166 A6
Watersmeet Centre
RKW/CH/CXG WD3 .... 130 C3
Waterways Business Centre
PEND EN3 .... 126 D4
Waterways Heritage Museum
RKW/CH/CXG WD3 .... 130 C4
Watford Arches Retail Park
WAT WD17 .... 13 J8
Watford Business Centre
WAT WD17 .... 12 C3
Watford FC & Saracens RFC
(Vicarage Road Stadium)
WATW WD18 .... 12 E7
Watford General Hospital
WATW WD18 .... 12 E8
Watford Grammar School
for Boys
WATW WD18 .... 12 A5
Watford Grammar School
for Girls
WATW WD18 .... 13 C7
Watford Museum
WAT WD17 .... 13 H7
Watford Sports & Leisure
Centre *GSTN WD25* 102 A7
Watling Lower School
DUN/WHIP LU6 .... 38 F2
Watling View Special School
STAL AL1 .... 85 H6
Watton-at-Stone Primary
School
HERT/WAT SG14 .... 178 F6
Waulud Primary School
LTNN/LIM LU3 .... 27 J2
Waverley Industrial Estate
HRW HA1 .... 143 H5
Waverley School
PEND EN3 .... 126 A8
Weald Middle School
KTN/HRWW/WS HA3 ... 143 K2
Weatherfield Special School
DUN/WHIP LU6 .... 25 J8
Wedgewood Gate Industrial
Estate
STVG SG1 .... 21 M7
Welwyn Garden City CC
WGCW AL8 .... 50 B3
Welwyn Garden City Football &
Social Club
WGCE AL7 .... 50 A8
Welwyn Garden City Golf Club
WGCW AL8 .... 49 M7
Welwyn RFC
WGCW AL8 .... 50 A8
Welwyn Roman Baths
WLYN AL6 .... 50 B1
Welwyn St Marys Primary
School
WLYN AL6 .... 49 M1
Welwyn Tennis Club
WLYN AL6 .... 49 M1
Welwyn Viaduct
WGCW AL8 .... 50 C3
Wenlock Junior School
LTNE LU2 .... 7 M4
The Wenta Business Centre
WATN WD24 .... 118 B3
Westbrook Hay Preparatory
School
HHW HP1 .... 81 H5
Westbury Primary School
LWTH SG6 .... 16 C4
Western House Hospital
WARE SG12 .... 54 B3
West Essex Golf Club
CHING E4 .... 127 J8
Westfield Cemetery
HARP AL5 .... 46 E1
Westfield Community Primary
School
HOD EN11 .... 72 D6
Westfield Community
Technology College
WATW WD18 .... 12 A1
Westfield First School
BERK HP4 .... 59 K8

Westgate Centre
STVG SG1 .... 10 C4
Westgate Shopping Centre
STVG SG1 .... 10 D4
West Herts Business Centre
BORE WD6 .... 120 F7
West Herts Cemetery
GSTN WD25 .... 102 A5
West Herts College
(Cassio Campus)
WAT WD17 .... 117 L4
West Herts College
(Dacorum Campus)
HHNE HP2 .... 4 E1
West Herts College
(Leggatts Campus)
WATN WD24 .... 117 L2
West Herts College
(Watford Campus)
WAT WD17 .... 12 C2
West Herts Crematorium
GSTN WD25 .... 102 A5
West Herts Golf Club
RKW/CH/CXG WD3 .... 117 H7
West Lodge Middle School
PIN HA5 .... 142 B6
West Lodge Park Hotel
EBAR EN4 .... 123 K4
Westminster Lodge Athletic
Track
STALW/RED AL3 .... 8 B8
Westminster Lodge Leisure
Centre & Pool
STAL AL1 .... 8 D9
Weston Primary School
HTCHE/RSTV SG4 .... 18 A8
Weston Road Cemetery
STVG SG1 .... 21 J5
Westwood School
BUSH WD23 .... 133 H5
Wheatcroft School
HERT/BAY SG13 .... 53 L6
Wheatfields Junior School
STALE/WH AL4 .... 65 M6
Whelpley Hill Park
CSHM HP5 .... 80 B8
Whipperley Infant School
LTN LU1 .... 40 E3
Whipsnade Park Golf Club
BERK HP4 .... 171 L4
Whipsnade Wild Animal
Park
DUN/WHIP LU6 .... 171 M2
Whitefield Junior School
LTNN/LIM LU3 .... 27 J1
Whitefriars First & Middle
School
KTN/HRWW/WS HA3 ... 143 J4
Whitefriars Trading Estate
KTN/HRWW/WS HA3 ... 143 H4
Whitehall Estate
HLWW/ROY CM19 .... 74 C6
Whiteheath Infant School
RSLP HA4 .... 140 F8
Whiteheath Junior School
RSLP HA4 .... 141 G8
White Hill Community Centre
CSHM HP5 .... 97 G5
Whitehill Golf Club
WARE SG12 .... 179 Q3
Whitehill Junior School
HTCHE/RSTV SG4 .... 157 Q8
White Lion
BERK HP4 .... 171 K2
White Lion Retail Park
DUN/HR/TOD LU5 .... 26 A8
Whiterose Trading Estate
EBAR EN4 .... 137 J3
The Whitewebbs Museum of
Transport & Industry
ENC/FH EN2 .... 124 F1
Whitewebbs Park Golf Club
ENC/FH EN2 .... 125 H3
Whitings Hill Primary School
BAR EN5 .... 136 A1
Whittal Industrial Estate
STVG SG1 .... 10 A5
Widewater Business Centre
DEN/HRF UB9 .... 140 A7
Widford J & I School
WARE SG12 .... 182 B5
Wigmore Primary School
LTNE LU2 .... 29 J7
Wilbury Junior School
LWTH SG6 .... 16 C3
William Austin Infant School
LTNN/LIM LU3 .... 28 A5
William Austin Junior
School
LTNN/LIM LU3 .... 28 A5
William Penn Leisure Centre
RKW/CH/CXG WD3 .... 129 K4
William Ransom JMI School
HTCHE/RSTV SG4 .... 157 R6
Willowfield Lower School
LTN LU1 .... 40 D5
Willowgate Trading Estate
LTNN/LIM LU3 .... 26 F1
Wilshere Dacre Junior
School
HTCH/STOT SG5 .... 157 N5
Wilstone Reservoir Nature
Reserve
TRING HP23 .... 168 H10
Windermere JMI Primary
School
STAL AL1 .... 85 M4
Windhill Primary School
BSF CM23 .... 43 L4
Windmill Trading Estate
LTN LU1 .... 7 K6
Windsor Industrial Estate
HERT/BAY SG13 .... 53 M5
Wisteria House Clinic
WLYN AL6 .... 176 H11
Wodson Park Sport &
Recreation Centre
WARE SG12 .... 54 B1
Wolsey Business Park
WATN WD24 .... 131 H3
Woodcock Hill Cemetery
RKW/CH/CXG WD3 .... 130 B7
Wood End School
BERK HP4 .... 46 B3
Woodfield Special School
HHS/BOV HP3 .... 83 G4
Wood Green Animal Shelter
ROY SG8 .... 153 Q2
Woodhall School
OXHEY WD19 .... 132 C7
Woodlands First & Middle
School
KTN/HRWW/WS HA3 ... 143 C2

Woodlands Primary School
BORE WD6 .... **120** E5
Woodlands Secondary School
LTNN/LIM LU3 .... **27** K2
Woodridge Primary School
NFNCH/WDSPK N12 .... **136** E6
Woodside Clinic
DUN/HR/TOD LU5 .... **39** H1
Woodside Farm & Wildfowl
Park
STALW/RED AL3 .... **172** H1
Woodside Industrial Estate
DUN/HR/TOD LU5 .... **26** B6

Woodside Industrial Park
LWTH SG6 .... **16** F2
Woodside Junior School
AMS HP6 .... **113** J4
Woodside Park Golf Club
NFNCH/WDSPK N12 .... **136** E7
Woodside Park Industrial
Estate
DUN/HR/TOD LU5 .... **26** A6
Woodside Park International
School
FBAR/BDGN N11 .... **137** K8
NFNCH/WDSPK N12 .... **136** F7

Woodside Primary School
CHESW EN7 .... **109** G3
Woodside Stadium
GSTN WD25 .... **102** A7
Woodwell Cemetery
HHNE HP2 .... **83** H1
Woolenwick Junior School
STVG SG1 .... **32** F3
Woolgrove School
LWTH SG6 .... **17** H4
Worcesters Primary
School
ENC/FH EN2 .... **125** K4

Wormley Primary School
BROX EN10 .... **92** C5
The Wroxham School
POTB/CUF EN6 .... **106** A5
The Wyllyotts Centre
Cinema
POTB/CUF EN6 .... **106** D6
Wymondley Primary School
HTCHE/RSTV SG4 .... **20** C5
Yavneh College
BORE WD6 .... **120** F8
Ye Olde Fighting Cocks Inn
STALW/RED AL3 .... **8** C7

Yorke Mead Primary School
RKW/CH/CXG WD3 .... **130** E1
York House School
RKW/CH/CXG WD3 .... **116** D6

Acknowledgements

Schools address data provided by Education Direct.

Petrol station information supplied by Johnsons.

Garden centre information provided by:

Garden Centre Association — Britains best garden centres

Wyevale Garden Centres

The statement on the front cover of this atlas is sourced, selected and quoted
from a reader comment and feedback form received in 2004

SPEED READING

Speed camera locations

Speed camera locations provided in association with RoadPilot Ltd

RoadPilot is the developer of one of the largest and most accurate databases of speed camera locations in the UK and Europe. It has provided the speed camera information in this atlas. RoadPilot is the UK's pioneer and market leader in GPS (Global Positioning System) road safety technologies.

microGo (pictured right) is RoadPilot's latest in-car speed camera location system. It improves road safety by alerting you to the location of accident black spots,

fixed and mobile camera sites. RoadPilot's microGo does not jam police lasers and is therefore completely legal.

RoadPilot's database of fixed camera locations has been compiled with the full co-operation of regional police forces and the Safety Camera Partnerships.

For more information on RoadPilot's GPS road safety products, please visit **www.roadpilot.com** or telephone 0870 240 1701

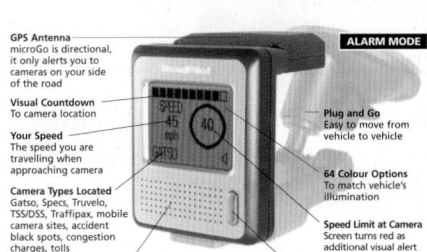

RoadPilot

GPS Antenna
microGo is directional, it only alerts you to cameras on your side of the road

Visual Countdown
To camera location

Your Speed
The speed you are travelling when approaching camera

Camera Types Located
Gatso, Specs, Truvelo, TSS/DSS, Traffipax, mobile camera sites, accident black spots, congestion charges, tolls

Voice Warnings
Only if you are exceeding the speed limit at the camera

ALARM MODE

Plug and Go
Easy to move from vehicle to vehicle

64 Colour Options
To match vehicle's illumination

Speed Limit at Camera
Screen turns red as additional visual alert

Single Button Operation
For easy access to speed display, camera warning, rescue me location, trip computer, congestion charge, max speed alarm, date and time

AA **Street by Street** QUESTIONNAIRE

Dear Atlas User
Your comments, opinions and recommendations are very important to us.
So please help us to improve our street atlases by taking a few minutes to complete this simple questionnaire.

You do not need a stamp (unless posted outside the UK). If you do not want to remove this page from your street atlas, then photocopy it or write your answers on a plain sheet of paper.

Send to: Marketing Assistant, AA Publishing, 14th Floor Fanum House,
        Freepost SCE 4598, Basingstoke RG21 4GY

ABOUT THE ATLAS...

Please state which city / town / county street atlas you bought:
_____
_____

Where did you buy the atlas? (City, Town, County)
_____

For what purpose? (please tick all applicable)

To use in your own local area ☐   **To use on business or at work** ☐

Visiting a strange place ☐   **In the car** ☐   **On foot** ☐

Other (please state)
_____

Have you ever used any street atlases other than AA Street by Street?

Yes ☐   **No** ☐

If so, which ones?
_____

Is there any aspect of our street atlases that could be improved?
(Please continue on a separate sheet if necessary)
_____
_____
_____
_____

MX116x

continued overleaf

Please list the features you found most useful:

_____

_____

_____

Please list the features you found least useful:

_____

_____

_____

LOCAL KNOWLEDGE...

Local knowledge is invaluable. Whilst every attempt has been made to make the information contained in this atlas as accurate as possible, should you notice any inaccuracies, please detail them below (if necessary, use a blank piece of paper) or e-mail us at _streetbystreet@theAA.com_

_____

_____

_____

_____

ABOUT YOU...

Name (Mr/Mrs/Ms) _____

Address _____

Postcode

Daytime tel no _____

E-mail address _____

Which age group are you in?

Under 25 ☐   25-34 ☐   35-44 ☐   45-54 ☐   55-64 ☐   65+ ☐

Are you an AA member?   Yes ☐   No ☐

Do you have Internet access?   Yes ☐   No ☐

_____

_____

Thank you for taking the time to complete this questionnaire. Please send it to us as soon as possible, and remember, you do not need a stamp (unless posted outside the UK).

We may use information we hold about you to telephone or email you about other products and services offered by the AA, we do NOT disclose this information to third parties.

Please tick here if you do not wish to hear about products and services from the AA. ☐

MX116x